# SCHULZ
## AND PEANUTS

# BOOKS BY DAVID MICHAELIS

*Schulz and Peanuts: A Biography*

*N. C. Wyeth: A Biography*

*Boy, Girl, Boy, Girl*

*The Best of Friends*

*Mushroom* (coauthor)

"A classic American story. . . . Michaelis tells this story brightly and engagingly. . . . The smartest thing he has done is to pepper his pages with [ ] strips from . . . ." —Charles McGrath, *The New York Times Book Review*

"Exhaustive, fascinating. . . . Michaelis convincingly argues that [ ] flected mid-century America." —*People* (four-star [ ])

"A dynamic character study and a penetrating literary analysis. . . . Michaelis makes wonderful use of the [comic] strips, reproducing scores to emphasize points of connection between Schulz's life and work." —*Newsweek*

"Sensitive and satisfying. . . . David Michaelis shows us how generic postwar anxiety and personal grief combined to create the most popular comic strip ever written. . . . Fascinating." —*The Washington Post Book World*

"Commanding. . . . Michaelis has done a masterly job of assembling the often puzzling and even contradictory pieces of Schulz's life into a convincing whole. His book . . . makes a strong argument that, like Charlie Brown, Charles Schulz deserves that highest of encomiums: a good man."
—*The San Francisco Chronicle Book Review* (cover review)

"Fascinating. . . . Perceptive and compelling. . . . Michaelis presents the fullest picture we have yet of the cartoonist's life and personality. . . . This book finally introduces Charles Schulz to us all."
—Bill Watterson, *The Wall Street Journal*

"Fascinating. . . . Rich, appreciative, closely researched. . . . As Mr. Michaelis's biography brilliantly shows, Schulz sometimes used *Peanuts* to allegorize and make sense of his secret life." —Nicholson Baker, *The New York Observer*

"Vivid. . . . Illuminating. . . . *Schulz and Peanuts* is as meticulous in its evocation of a sensitive soul's temperament as any first-rate cartoon by 'Sparky' himself."
—*Entertainment Weekly*

"*Schulz and Peanuts* tells the story of the cartoonist from first strip to last, capturing Schulz in all his bitter, melancholic, midwestern glory, and clearing away the decades of merchandise and clutter that surround him to show the original vision: one man's expression of longing and fear."
—Rich Cohen, *The Los Angeles Times Book Review*

"Insightful. . . . Michaelis's wonderful book shows how the events and relationships in *Peanuts* are, almost unfailingly, events and relationships distilled from Schulz's life."               —*Sports Illustrated*

"Exceptional. . . . Affectionate yet critical. . . . David Michaelis is a perceptive cultural observer with great powers of interpretation. . . . *Schulz and Peanuts* takes us inside the mind of a fundamentally solitary man whose simple-looking comic strip became a visual reflection, interpretation of and guide to the times."               —*The Boston Globe*

"Charles Schulz's cartoons have a profound depth and resonance that touched the soul of modern America. . . . With great research and sensitivity, Michaelis takes us on a wondrous journey through the worlds of Charlie Brown and Charles Schulz."               —Walter Isaacson

"A landmark biography. . . . The most significant work written about one of the century's undisputed pop culture giants. . . . The most exhaustive biography ever of an American cartoonist."               —*The Los Angeles Times*

"A deftly written, intellectually exhilarating biography."
               —Jonathan Franzen, *The Guardian* (London)

"One of my great regrets is that I missed my chance to meet 'Sparky' Schulz in person. David Michaelis now has given me that opportunity, thanks to his insightful rendering of the life of this American treasure." —Walter Cronkite

"Like all true biographers, Michaelis refuses to buy into Schulz's version of his own life, and the resulting portrait goes far beyond the conventional notion that Schulz was the grown-up version of Charlie Brown."
               —Laura Miller, Salon.com

"Admiring. . . . Honest. . . . Definitive. . . . Michaelis does such a remarkable job of teasing out of his research and interviews with friends and family the actual personality of this contradictory and complex genius that it is amazing he never met Schulz. . . . A fine example of the art of biography at its most compelling."               —*The Richmond Times-Dispatch*

"An excellent biography."               —Garrison Keillor, *The Chicago Tribune*

"Impressive. . . . *Schulz and Peanuts* offers great detail on Schulz's metamorphosis into a complex and multifaceted individual. . . . In the end, the Charles M. Schulz of *Schulz and Peanuts* no longer seems the enigma we once imagined."
               —*The Christian Science Monitor*

# SCHULZ

## AND PEANUTS

## A BIOGRAPHY

# DAVID MICHAELIS

HARPER PERENNIAL

NEW YORK • LONDON • TORONTO • SYDNEY • NEW DELHI • AUCKLAND

HARPER ● PERENNIAL

All cartoon strips: PEANUTS © United Feature Syndicate, Inc. PEANUTS is a registered trademark of United Feature Syndicate, Inc. All rights reserved.

Except as noted below, all images are courtesy of the Charles M. Schulz Museum and Research Center, Santa Rosa, California (CMSMRC): INSERT 1: Page 6, top: Minnesota Historical Society, St. Paul, MN. Page 7: courtesy of Lester Greenig. Page 9, bottom: courtesy of Elmer Hagemeyer. Pages 12, top; 13, top; 14, all: courtesy of Art Instruction, Inc. Page 12, bottom: courtesy of Betty Bissonette. Page 13, bottom right: courtesy of Jim Sasseville. Page 16: PEANUTS © United Feature Syndicate, Inc. PEANUTS is a registered trademark of United Feature Syndicate, Inc. All rights reserved. Permission granted by United Media. INSERT 2: Page 1, bottom: courtesy of Charlene Neal. Page 2, top: courtesy of Lester Greenig; bottom: courtesy of Louanne and Philip Van Pelt. Page 3, top: courtesy of Louanne and Philip Van Pelt. Page 3, middle and bottom: photograph by Jim Hansen; LOOK Magazine Collection, Library of Congress, Prints & Photographs Division; courtesy of Mrs. Doris Henderson. Page 6, top: courtesy of Louanne and Philip Van Pelt; middle: photograph by and courtesy of John LeBaron. Page 7, top: photograph by Tom Vano, CMSMRC; bottom: photograph by Douglas Jones; LOOK Magazine Collection, Library of Congress, Prints & Photographs Division. Page 8, top: courtesy of Joyce Doty; bottom: Mike Roberts Color Productions, Berkeley, CA 94710, courtesy of Jean F. Schulz. Page 9, bottom: photograph by Tom Vano, CMSMRC. Page 10, top [Holograph photo] and bottom: courtesy of Tracey O'Hearen. Page 11, top: courtesy of Jean F. Schulz; bottom: photograph by Jerry Muegle, CMSMRC. Page 12: photograph by Jean Schulz, CMSMRC. Page 13: photograph by Brian Lanker, CMSMRC. Page 15: photograph by and courtesy of Holger Kiefel. Page 16: photograph by and courtesy of Holger Kiefel.

A hardcover edition of this book was published in 2007 by HarperCollins Publishers.

FIRST HARPER PERENNIAL EDITION PUBLISHED 2008.

*Designed by William Ruoto*

Library of Congress Cataloging-in-Publication Data is available upon request.

ISBN 978-0-06-093799-7

08 09 10 11 12 NMSG/RRD 10 9 8 7 6 5 4 3 2 1

TO JAMIE AND HENRY AND DIANA

# CONTENTS

## PART FOUR: PUSHING WEST

## PART FIVE: ZENITH

## PART SIX: EMPIRE OF ONE

# PREFACE

WHEN CHARLES SCHULZ DIED, he left behind fifty years of clues about his life embedded in his cartoons. For a man thought to be reserved, he gave an astonishing number of interviews, in which he spoke in revealing detail and sometimes with surprising candor. As an adult, he made a habit of asking pointed, often personal questions of whomever crossed his path, and he sought a nuanced understanding of life's mysteries wherever he went. Yet he showed not the faintest interest in comprehending himself and the implications of his work. He insisted that his comic strip speak for and about him.

Like many artists, Schulz maintained that he could be known only through his creation. In the quiet of his studio in the northern California town of Santa Rosa, he ransacked his most private memories and personal quirks, encoding them daily in four (later, three) carefully crafted panels of comic art. "A cartoon," he had been taught by a correspondence course in the 1940s, "is really a picture demonstrating one thought in the guise of another." Every chance he got, he offered his readers a key: "If somebody reads my strip every day, they'll know me for sure—they'll know exactly what I am."

Those who really did know him understood that he was "hard to know, hard to understand," and, as at least one friend recognized: "He didn't want to get too close to anybody." Another friend familiar with his ways said, "He liked to think of himself as a simple man, but he was not simple—he was enigmatic and complex." He bore about him an air of mystery, a need for privacy. The word most often used to describe him, after "shy" and "humble," was "complicated."

Part of Schulz's mystique was his total self-sufficiency. For nearly fifty years, according to his legend, he had been "the only human being ever to write, pencil, ink, or letter the *Peanuts* comic strip." He had drawn every single one of the 17,897 strips—all without assistants. Even more important, he had never taken ideas from others; every installment of *Peanuts* was his and his alone, illuminating the world, while allowing—indeed, empowering—the cartoonist to remain walled off from it. In order to do what he had done, he had to be alone, solely in charge of his modest but complete universe. A more gregarious, more balanced person could not have created the long-suffering but unsinkable Charlie Brown; crabby, often venomous Lucy; philosophical Linus; tomboyish Peppermint Patty; single-minded Schroeder; and grandiose, self-involved Snoopy. "A normal person couldn't do it," he had himself contended.

And yet, again and again, he told them that he was "just an ordinary fellow," "just an ordinary midwesterner," little changed from the "nothing young man" who had grown up in St. Paul, the only son of a corner barber and a kindly, loving mother. His ambition, he often said, was "to be as well-liked as my father." Even when he became the highest-paid cartoonist in the world, and with every other measure of success in his field—and even some that had never been thought of before him—he would say, "Have I had enormous success? Do you think so?" Always he came back to being the barber's son, the boy on the corner of Selby and Snelling.

To his millions of fans, the creator of *Peanuts* appeared as a friendly neighborhood presence—he himself joked that he looked like a druggist. The word *Schulz* derives from a German occupational name meaning "village mayor," and he had indeed made himself the overseer of what Walter Cronkite aptly called "a cartoon village," global in its reach. He was presented to his public as "a warm, comfortable, familiar and easy-to-love friend of the world." People everywhere felt that they had grown up with him, been healed by him in childhood, comforted in adolescence, and soothed in adulthood. Complete strangers considered him family. Yet at the height of his fame, Schulz was asked, "Do you feel available for all the world to see?" only to answer self-contradictorily, "Yes, but I don't let them see me."

"It is almost as if Charles Schulz died with a secret locked inside him," suggested one newspaper columnist.

He had let his public know just so much, even about *Peanuts*. Except for acknowledging that Snoopy had been modeled on Spike, the wildly independent dog of his own childhood, he deliberately left unanswered any questions about whether Charlie Brown and Lucy, in their respective anxieties and viciousness, had real-life models, and would deny any parallels between his characters' relationships with each other and his own relationships in the present, occasionally alluding to personal disappointments and embarrassments that had befallen him in days past, or simply outflanking all analogical inquiry by claiming that all of it was him: "These are all my lives," he said.

"If you're going to create cartoon characters you can create them only from your own personality. You really can't create too much by observing other people. There's just not that much to observe"—a startling statement from one who was endlessly observing and who had a great eye.

Cartooning can be intensely personal and expressive. Schulz needed to know that he was reaching the reader with his own voice—almost as if his medium were radio—for he wanted his audience to identify not with him but with his temperament. As time went on, and *Peanuts'* mass appeal expanded from its first vogue among hip, college-educated circles to being all things to all people, he less and less trusted the reader to recognize how much of himself was being obliquely expressed through the week's panels. Whereas he initially saw the value in people imagining that he was Charlie Brown, by 1972 he was answering the standard, ten-times-a-week question "Is Charlie Brown really your alter ego?" by saying, with a chuckle, "Not really, although it makes a good story."

Ten years later, the novelist Laurie Colwin inquired whether someone who had followed the strip from the outset "could actually write a biographical portrait of you?" Schulz answered in his mildest voice: "I think so. You'd have to be pretty bright, I suppose."

One essayist had greeted the news of his retirement with yet another answer: "We can't think of any American more deserving of a Rosebud-style search for biographical meaning. But Schulz, always a master of [four]-frame narrative, has already put the pieces together for us."

Indeed, he had: in 1941, Orson Welles's *Citizen Kane* had come to the Park Theatre in St. Paul, and an electrified Sparky Schulz immediately recognized its greatness. Over the years, it would become a personal fascination, his favorite movie.

He absorbed the story again and again, perhaps as many as forty times: that of a powerful and private man, an only child, taken in boyhood from his estranged parents—thrust from his home in an isolated shack on the snowy prairie, sped by locomotive to the center of American life, where, raised by a banker, he rises to kingly but isolated eminence in his unfinishable castle, Xanadu. Like Welles's hero, Charles Foster Kane, who "got everything he wanted, and then lost it," Charles Monroe Schulz would succeed on a scale beyond the grandest of his childhood dreams, and yet he would struggle to love and be loved.

All his life he felt alone, spending most of his adult half-century yearning to be taken care of, to be understood. Why? If his mother had loved him so well as a boy, where had it begun, this painful sense that the thing he needed most had been taken from him?

When called on to discuss his life, he never began at the beginning, never with his birth, on November 26, 1922, or his early years, but always with his mother's death on March 1, 1943, his own departure for the war, and the merciless speed of it all: in that week, Dena Halverson Schulz had died on a Monday, she was buried Friday, and by Saturday the army had taken him away.

The story always started with a lonesome young man, no more than a boy, being carried away on a train through the snow.

# PART ONE

# NORTHWEST

*When he was little, Gatsby got a sled for*
*Christmas, and he called it "Rosebud"!*

CHARLES M. SCHULZ, *PEANUTS*

# CHAPTER 1

# SPARKY

*We'll probably never see each other again.*
—DENA HALVERSON SCHULZ

THE GREAT TROOP TRAIN, a quarter-mile of olive green carriages, rolled out of the depot and into the storm. Nearly a foot of snow had fallen on the Northwest through the day, and now, in the short winter afternoon, the blizzard veiled the domed heights of the State Capitol in St. Paul and the pyramid-capped Foshay Tower, tallest building in Minneapolis. Snow curtained the Twin Cities from one another, blurring everyday distances. Only the railroad and streetcar tracks cut clear black lines into the mounting white cover.

In the Pullman, Sparky kept to himself. No one yet knew him. At roll call he had come after "Schaust" and before "Sciortino," but except for his place in the company roster he seemed to have no connection to the men and, as one of his seatmates was to recall, "no interest in joining in any conversation," not even about the weather. The snowflakes swirling at the Pullman windows only contributed to his impression that he had been thrown among "wild people."

To his fellow recruits he presented himself as nondescript: simple, bland, unassuming—just another face in the crowd. With his regular looks, he passed for ordinary so easily that most people believed him when he insisted, as he did so often in later years, that he was a "nothing," a "nobody," an "uncomplicated man with ordinary interests," although anyone who could attract attention to himself by being so sensitive and insecure had to be complicated.

Don Schaust, then seated alongside Schulz in the Pullman, later recalled that, as they rumbled across the Twin Cities, his seatmate remained silent, "very quiet, very low . . . deep in his own misery," and how he had asked himself, "What's the matter with this guy?"

No matter what the others said or did, Sparky sat watching the snow sweep up to and pull away from the window, giving no sign that he had just come through the worst days of his life.

HE WOULD NEVER DISCUSS the actual kind of cancer that had struck his mother. Throughout his life, friends, business associates, and most of his relatives believed that Dena Schulz had been the victim of colorectal cancer. In fact, the primary site of his mother's illness was the cervix, and she had been seriously ill since 1938. As early as his sophomore year in high school, Sparky had come home to a bedridden mother.

Some evenings she had been too ill to put food on the table; some nights he had been awakened by her cries of pain. But no one spoke directly about her affliction; only Sparky's father and his mother's trusted sister Marion knew its source, and they would not identify it as cancer in Sparky's presence until after it had reached its fourth and final stage—in November 1942, the same month he was drafted.

On February 28, 1943, with a day pass from Fort Snelling, Sparky returned from his army barracks to his mother's bedside, mounting the stairs to the second-floor apartment at the corner of Selby and North Snelling Avenues to which the Schulzes had moved so that his father, at work in his barbershop on Selby, and the druggist in his pharmacy around the corner, could race upstairs to administer morphine during the worst of Dena's agonies.

That evening, before reporting back to barracks, Sparky went into his mother's bedroom. She was turned away from him in her bed against the wall, opposite the windows that overlooked the street. He said he guessed it was time to go.

"Yes," she said, "I suppose we should say good-bye."

She turned her gaze as best she could. "Well," she said, "good-bye, Sparky. We'll probably never see each other again."

Later he said, "I'll never get over that scene as long as I live," and indeed he could not, down to his own dying day. It was certainly the worst night of his life, the night of "my greatest tragedy"—which he repeatedly put into the terms of his passionate sense of unfulfillment that his mother "never had the opportunity to see me get anything published."

He saw her always from a distance, and as the years went by, with each stoical retelling, the moment became more and more iconic. It was safely frozen in time—as puzzling a farewell in its quiet, coolheaded resolve as the lines spoken by the mother as she prepares to lose her son in *Citizen Kane*: "I've got his trunk all packed. I've had it packed for a week now." Frequently, often publicly, Sparky laid out the terrible resigned pathos of what his mother had said to him that night. Only as he got older and experienced parenthood himself would he "understand the pain and fear she must have had, thinking about what was to become of me."

THE BLIZZARD HAD BROUGHT everything to a halt. But the train drummed on across St. Paul, and landmarks familiar even in the snow slipped past his window, alerting him that his own neighborhood was approaching. Then there it was for all to see.

Mud-brown, two-storied brick buildings huddled along his snowbound street. From where the Great Northern Railway overpass crossed North Snelling he could see down to the Selby intersection two blocks to the south, where since Monday he had sleepwalked through funeral arrangements with his father in his family's rented walk-up. Even before this week of calamities, he had considered this part of St. Paul the setting of "my most influential section of life as a child."

Above the buildings to his right, a Greek-pedimented entrance marked the huge elementary school he had attended. He could see Dayton Avenue, a sidestreet among whose small, somber dwellings Carl and Dena had lived in 1921, during the first year of their marriage, and, next door, the roof under which his father had sheltered the family during the Great Depression, some of the lonelier years of Sparky's childhood, and the scanty back-yard where the kooky puppy Spike, living in his own world, had gobbled up some glass. There, on the corner of Selby and Snelling, was their street-car stop, whence came, among his earliest memories, the image of himself getting aboard with his mother, a small boy on a stiff cane seat, off to the department stores. . . .

The trip downtown was easy; the streetcar free and airy, full of light. On the return trip, the car became crowded. Saturday was the big shop-ping day in St. Paul; package-burdened passengers flocked in to fill every seat. When the next woman or girl appeared, it was standard procedure for a young man, even a small boy accompanying his mother, to get up for her. Sparky observed this courtesy, although it meant that he had to strug-gle to keep by Dena's side: first one new passenger, then another, displaced him as the car swayed this way and that, and with each additional surge of homeward-bound shoppers at the major intersections, they were pushed farther and farther apart. Finally, he lost sight of her altogether and from that moment on was locked in his terror, imagining as clearly as if it had already happened that when the streetcar glided up its double rails to their corner she would forget him and step off by herself, leaving the trolley to carry him away, trapped and alone.

In later years, he would ridicule the idea that his mother would have forgotten or overlooked him: "She would never have done that." She was not, by nature, absentminded. Indeed, the record shows that Dena was an attentive, even fussy, caregiver to her only child. But no matter what hap-pened to Charles Schulz for the rest of his life—even when he married and started a family and became known as a cartoonist, then was lionized as a figure of national wisdom, a philosopher-king beloved by millions, a "seer" revered to the point of idolatry, his standing measured in four decades of unremitting worldwide recognition as one of the most beloved artists on earth—he felt unseen. He never stopped believing that he had been forsaken and would be left behind, that *nobody cared.*

In his work, indifference would be the dominant response to love. When his characters attempt to love, they are met not just by rejection but by ongoing cold, even brutal, indifference, manifested either as insensitivity or as deeply fatalistic acceptance.

As a boy, he had been loved by his mother, or so he insisted. But Dena Halverson Schulz had a remote quality: she could be distant, cool, elusive, mocking, and a little scornful, and she was foxy by nature, with a sense of humor that her son remembered as sly. Something had very early entered Sparky's bond with her that made him fear that when he turned around she would not be there.

And now of course that is exactly what had happened, leaving him to stare, unguided, unsupported, out of a troop train window: she had left him to soldier on by himself.

Until he went into the army, he had spent just two nights in his life apart from his mother (on a three-day golf tournament, when he was eighteen) and had suffered intense homesickness. He had never imagined traveling anywhere without her. He had never seen the ocean, much less been to sea. He had never stayed in a hotel or eaten a meal in a nice restaurant. He was a stranger to the world.

Since graduating from Central High School two years earlier, he had lived a boy's life, sheltered from hardship and hard times by his parents. His father backed him and did his banking for him, though there was not much to sock away; employment after high school had amounted to nothing more than delivering groceries. He had never outgrown his childish nickname, Sparky, or his awkwardness with girls. He knew nothing about the arts of love and had never had a sweetheart—only distant crushes and movie dreams, and no more than soda dates with the daughters of family friends. His mother was the only female who mattered.

And now she would never come back, would never know him as he grew older; and here he was, a "sad sack" indeed, a boy among men dressed in khaki, many of whom, perhaps he among them, would not come back or grow older either, for they were roaring through the bitter cold toward some unknown place where they would be given rifles and taught to kill.

"I wonder how I ever survived," he said later.

He had always solved his problems by going off by himself and drawing. Turning his hand loose with India ink and a crow-quill pen cured most things. In his duffel, he had brought along a specially made sketchbook and some pencils. For the time being, he could doodle or sketch his own cameos of army life; he still entertained the idea that the army might be able to make official use of him as an artist. But he could no longer comfort himself with ambition. His oldest desire, to draw a newspaper comic strip, which had sprung from the part of him that was determined to show that he was different and better than his relatives, had now curdled, along with everything else. For even if he survived combat and came home with arms and wrists and hands and fingers, the time was now gone forever when he could have proved to his mother that he was something after all.

All he could do now was become a soldier. Gathering speed, the train seemed to sweep what was left of St. Paul up to the window and then snatch it away. Selby and Snelling, the intersection of his life, flashed by, vanishing into the snow.

# CHAPTER 2

# RELATIVES

*Just because you're related to people doesn't mean you have to like them!*
—*PEANUTS*

BARBERS STARTING OUT IN the Midwest customarily put their names on their businesses, but Carl Schulz did not announce himself when he opened his shop at the intersection of Selby and Snelling Avenues. This was the spring of 1918, a year after the United States declared Germany its enemy, and the newly mobilized Commission of Public Safety had sent undercover agents into every German saloon and shop in St. Paul. An unfamiliar place called "Carl's" or "Schulz's" would have been as likely to invite a mob through its front door as a paying customer. Even well-established members of the city's Summit Avenue elite—the prosperous makers of railroads, beer, meat, and farm machinery—were taking on Anglo-Saxon externals in the hope of saving their children "from the odium attached to a German name."

Carl had been born in Stendhal, in Saxony-Anhalt, in northcentral Germany, in April 1897, the only one among four siblings not born in the United States. Raised on the family farm in Turtle Lake, Wisconsin, he attended the German grammar school. Neither of his parents ever learned to speak English, and he, Carl Fred Schulz, as he signed himself, was proud of his German heritage—at least until America entered the war against Germany.

After 1918, Carl Schulz showed no trace of German inflection in his midwestern accent. He considered himself American—American enough, at any rate, that applying for formal citizenship seemed superfluous. He waited until the age of thirty-seven to become a naturalized citizen of the United States. Whenever called upon to speak German, he disavowed command of the language that his parents had never stopped speaking. He rarely identified Germany as his birthplace. A barber who worked the chair beside Carl's for over ten years said, "He never told me he was born in Germany. He never told me a thing about it." When a niece needled him about masking his ethnicity, Carl would say, "Why do you always bring it up?" She shot back: "Because you always try to forget it."

Carl made every effort through hard work, good grooming, and cheerful countenance to be a model American. He gave his shop the most wholesome, American name he could think of—the Family Barber Shop—and posted his motto behind his barber's chair: IT PAYS TO LOOK WELL, as American a principle as could be found.

THE INTERSECTION WAS KNOWN as a go-getters' corner. The surrounding streets were dirt, but here two streetcar lines crossed, carrying passengers to and from downtown St. Paul and distant Minneapolis. It was an ideal location. When the Armistice was signed and the troops came home, discarding their campaign hats and Sam Browne belts, the corner caught them all. As the 1920s roared, a "New York fever" flared among Carl's friends, but he was not drawn east. He had faith in his corner and had also found a partner and true friend, Eric Oscar Bernard Carlson, a handsome, unassuming Swede, who had come to America in 1913 and whom he had met at barber college in Minneapolis.

With postwar business booming in the Twin Cities and Eric Carlson his trusted partner in the Family Barber Shop, Carl fanned out into several additional enterprises. Records are scant, but if Carl's customers' memories and family anecdote can be relied on, he was proprietor of as many as three barbershops at once. Through "some miracle of ambition," as Charles Schulz later saw it, Carl's operations would also include at least one and perhaps two filling stations, with no fewer than a dozen men on the payroll.

But he was "working too hard, trying to do too much, and he had some kind of a breakdown," a local pastor recalled. "As far as I remember, [it was] the only time he talked about a health problem." Carl worried that he had an ulcer. For a year, from 1919 to 1920, he ate nothing but Cream of Wheat at every meal. "He gave up the other shops," the Reverend Frederick Shackleton recalled, "and decided just to have the one barbershop with two or three chairs and not be a big entrepreneur. He was in favor of a quiet, settled life."

According to the family story, Carl had always been too ambitious to settle down, too busy for romance. He had left his parents' farm in 1916 and spent a summer pitching hay on his uncle's place in Nebraska, saving for barber college. Years later, Charles Schulz drew a strip in which a son makes a special trip to his father's barbershop to ask if his dad knows "anything about love." When the reply proves unhelpful, he makes his father's excuses for him: "No, I understand. You were pretty busy there in barber school."

Carl's ulcer forced him to make a slower start on the day. He took his breakfast every morning at the LaBelle Home Pastry Shop on Selby, just down the street from work, where they served plain hot cereal the way he liked it and the waitress who catered to his special needs had a lovely face and a sweet way of ducking her chin that made her beautiful eyes look big and round and watchful.

Dena Bertina Halverson had a pretty smile that could slide through a coquettish pout into a firm, maternal line of serious concern. The fourth child of nine, she mothered her younger siblings, and when she learned that this shaky young entrepreneur was ordering hot cereal to ease his pain, her depth of solicitude touched his heart. Though Carl did not know it and would not realize the truth until the day she died, Dena Halverson was a full four years older than he. When they met, Dena told him she was twenty-five; in fact, she was twenty-seven—old for a bride in those years.

On May 2, 1920, Carl Schulz and Dena Halverson were married by a Lutheran minister in Minneapolis, with Dena's younger brother Silas and her older married sister, Ida, for witnesses. Two years later, the Schulzes moved from predominantly Roman Catholic St. Paul to Lutheran Minneapolis. Dena was pregnant and may have wanted to be closer to her family, or perhaps she felt that Minneapolis would put her a step up—her Norwegian clan distrusted Catholics—but there is no record of her motives. Her family was dispersed around her in a scatter of nearby apartments a block away from Elliot Park, a once-elegant neighborhood of ornamental brick buildings darkened by soot and divided into meager accommodations for working people.

The Schulzes rented a five-room flat at 919 Chicago Avenue South, with Dena's widowed mother, Sophia, living just three doors away. Harris Halverson, a taxi driver, and his wife, Lottie Mae, occupied the apartment directly above Carl and Dena's, and were a social fixture at the Schulzes' every Friday night, where the young couples played a card game called Five Hundred. Any further visitors to the Schulz household were almost always other members of Dena's family.

With so many of her relatives around, one might imagine that the birth of Dena's first child would have been jubilant news in family correspondence. We know that Dena gave birth on a Sunday, and we may infer from the birth certificate that she delivered at home. Yet if her mother or any of Dena's many sisters or sisters-in-law took note of the time of day, or whether or not a doctor was summoned, or how the baby looked, the information has not survived. We have to rely on Carl, the fussy, routinized German, for details. "Dear Folks," he scribbled on a postcard to Dena's Uncle Lars and Aunt Gusta at the Borgen farm in Spring Valley, "I spose you will be surprised to hear we had a 9 lb Boy Nov. 26 . . ."

Carl and Dena named their son Charles Monroe—the middle name in honor of Dena's brother, who now worked the second chair in the Family Barber Shop. But both names became vestigial from the moment they were bestowed, unused by parents, relatives, and friends. A day or two after Charles was born, another of Dena's brothers visited her bedside, most likely the thirty-two-year-old bachelor, Oscar, the oldest male in the family, a railroad brakeman. On seeing his new nephew, this Halverson sibling is supposed to have turned, not to his sister but to Carl, who loved the comics, and said, "By golly, we're going to call him 'Spark Plug.' "

Four months earlier, in the last week of July 1922, millions of readers from Maine to California watched the cartoonist Billy DeBeck build a new kind of suspense into the comics as he ran a horse race through the black-and-white panels of *Barney Google*. Set in the shady worlds of the racetrack, pool hall, and fight ring, DeBeck's strip followed the misadventures of a henpecked gambler with eyes popping out of his head and "a wife three times his size." The feature had been flagging since its debut in June 1919. Then, on July 17, 1922, a chance encounter on the sidewalk outside the Pastime Jockey Club saddled Barney with an also-ran racehorse ominously named Spark Plug. DeBeck had planned to milk this unlikely entrant for no more than a week's worth of comedy. But when Barney entered the two-year-old in the Abadaba Handicap—and "Sparky" actually won the $50,000 purse—his new sidekick turned *Barney Google* into a sensation.

Readers took to heart the homely racehorse whose sad eyes were patterned by two inked ovals and who stood cloaked withers-to-hooves in a buttoned yellow blanket. Toys, merchandise, and popular songs followed, as, overnight, Spark Plug became a household presence as recognized and marketable in the new consumer culture of the 1920s as the Arrow Collar Man.

No one would remember what Dena Schulz's visiting brother had seen in the baby's face that reminded him of a woeful horse. To journalists and devotees, the name of a perennial loser with a homely face and a mild manner seemed tailor-made to prefigure the patterns of the cartoonist's life and work. In years to come, the nickname—streamlined into "Sparky" by his cousin Shirley—would be glossed, treasured, all but gilded as a true relic: the earliest evidence of his destiny. It would seem wonderful, mystical even, that he had been dubbed Sparky in the cradle, as if the comics had been Charles Schulz's birthright. The timing, moreover, would be smoothed down to the point of a miracle—Schulz, in one telling, being swaddled in the nationally electric name no more than ten minutes after he appeared on earth.

But the proper name on his birth certificate foretold as much as the too-apt-to-be-true nickname. "Charles" would be the name he answered to at school and in the army—wherever officialdom was concerned. It was also used by acquaintances, strangers, and, later, modified to "Charlie," by people who wanted to get too close too soon. Schulz could always tell at once, from the name by which someone greeted him, whether or not that person knew him—and, more important, knew him as he wanted to be known. "Charles," with its stodgy, drawn-out syllable, fell on his ear as an alien phoniness reinforcing his life's most constant theme: that people didn't know him, didn't understand who he was. But when someone approached him with "Sparky"—the sound smacked of midwestern gumption and pluck, of innocence combined with aggressiveness—he had to decide how much of himself he would reveal.

AS SPARKY TURNED FIVE in November 1927, the family moved back across the Mississippi to a quiet neighborhood in St. Paul. Photographs of his parents outside the bungalow at 1680 James Avenue show a handsome, well-dressed couple. In these images, as in other photographs of their earliest days together, neither Carl nor Dena seems to give money a thought. They are always well turned out. Dena's Norwegian clan referred to them as "Dena and her man." One Halverson niece recalled, "They were crazy about each other. Schulz would always help her with her coat."

Carl's courteous gestures and meticulous appearance—he kept the crease in his trousers pinched razor-sharp—set him apart. "He didn't look like he was from the working class," recalled his nephew Carl F. Fuelling. "His shoes were always shined. He wore good suits and white shirts and a necktie. His hair was combed straight back from a high forehead. He was always smiling and he had a little stomach"—a proud sign, in Germany, of bourgeois wealth and comfort. His manner, too, was infused with a rosy, well-tended German pride. Carl patted his belly when he was pleased, and enjoyed picking out tunes on his Echo mouth organ, though the songs he knew were American prairie numbers such as Thurland Chattaway's "Redwing."

Dena called her husband "Schulz"—she did not like the name Carl. "Well, Schulz and I have to go now," she would say to her sisters. "The Schulzes were classy people, but they weren't phony," said Dena's niece, Patricia Swanson. "They were good-hearted, tenderhearted. They respected each other."

Dena may have respected Carl, but she gave his family the impression that she felt she was better than they were. It was one of her unarticulated characteristics—the vanity that led her to conceal her true age was another—and it had a significant effect on Charles Schulz's life and personality. For all her natural tendency to dote and be kind, she could hold herself proud and scornful.

Her sense of superiority is not easily explained. Dena had no social credentials from which to condescend and no sense of herself as elevated in mind or spirit. Dena Bertina Halverson was a farm girl, born to Norwegian parents in Pierce County, Wisconsin. Dena's father, Torjus Halverson, had been brought from Norway as a small child in 1866. His family had no money and lived with relatives in Martell, a farming township in Wisconsin. According to family lore, the Halversons had to render soup from the bark of trees to survive their first winter. Dena's questions in life were of the everyday kind; her education had ended in the early grades of grammar school; she was neither religiously observant nor pious. And though perhaps better-looking than the Schulzes—certainly more dashing—the Halverson men and women of her generation were no more prosperous than Carl or his brother's and sisters' families, and none of them had married above what people still called "their station."

The Halversons were exactly like hundreds of thousands of other second-generation Nordic immigrants in the Old Northwest in the 1920s, moving off the family farm and into the working class of the great industrial cities. Unlike the region's German Americans, who carried institutions with them, the Norse farmers came unprepared and "brought nothing new," wrote Sinclair Lewis in 1923. Norwegians accepted no more of America than they had to. Physical evidence of German culture could be found on the lintels and pediments of libraries and athletic unions, music clubs and shops, and businesses in the center city before 1918. The Norwegians, meanwhile, having "permitted their traditions to be snatched away," as Lewis noted, produced a single secular institution from which to launch themselves into American life: the family farm.

The Borgen farm in Spring Valley, Wisconsin, embraced 120 acres; produced chickens, eggs, and milk; and was Dena's family's one great claim to solvency and rootedness. Lars Borgen, born in Norway in 1863, had bought it for $5,500 in 1905. His wife, Augusta, kept the place manicured, her topiary trimmed into globular forms, and her kitchen brightened by plants perched on stands. Over the door, a .22-caliber rifle hung on nails.

Dena's aloofness toward her German in-laws grew out of clannishness. If the Halversons were a cut above the Schulzes, it was in the scale and strength of the family circle and in the special identity that the Halversons took from their circle's extra-tight "doubleness." When Dena's mother, Anna Sophia Borgen, married Tom Halverson, Sophia's brother Lars had married Tom's sister Augusta. The ten surviving Borgen children—six more died at birth or from childhood illnesses—were therefore cousins twice over to Dena and her eight siblings.

Dena's branch of the clan, the Halversons, had another reason for redoubling their attachment to the Borgens. Dena's father, Tom, had proved ill-suited to farming in America. Family tradition tells of his inability to slaughter animals—even decapitating a chicken was too much for him. He bought a mill and made skis the old Norwegian way. Eventually, he left the mill behind, too, and removed himself to Portland, Oregon, where he worked in a shipyard before being killed by the influenza epidemic of 1918.

Increasingly nomadic and rootless, Dena and her brothers and sisters shared with their double cousins a stubborn distrust of the new and the modern. Even in the urbanizing world of the 1920s, their hearts remained rooted in their land: a rolling farm dotted with firs, saturated with summer sunshine, beset by winter cold and ice, and replenished by dry, sweet autumn air at "thrashing time." It wasn't Norway, perhaps, but it was their own kind of Wisconsin.

Dena's pride was also grounded in the standing she had achieved inside the clan. She loved her sisters and brothers and kinfolk, but even more she loved being the hub in the double-belted family wheel. "In a large family there will invariably be one person to whom the others will turn when they're in trouble, and my mother was that one. They always looked to Dena when they needed help," Sparky said later. She took charge of younger siblings and cousins, stray nieces and nephews. She gave the children their family nicknames. "Dena was sort of like my mother's mother," said one niece. "She was more a mom than a sister."

In the city, she kept a pot of coffee on the stove alongside something she had baked. The Schulzes had no telephone (few families in the neighborhood did), so drop-ins came "out of the sky."* Members of the clan "would always come home to Dena when they were in trouble," Sparky recalled later. She was a maven for family news and gossip, carrying on whole conversations with sisters in Norwegian to exclude husbands or children from family secrets.

Carl, an admired outsider in Dena's family, was uneasy with his own relatives. He had entered marriage as a man alone. In 1916, his parents, Karl and Emma, and his younger brother Fred moved to a farm in Decatur, Indiana, from which Karl sent the occasional scrawl in German. No love was lost between Carl and his older sister, who, at seventeen, had gotten pregnant by a hired hand from a nearby farm in Polk County, Wisconsin. Elsie had married Alvin Frentzel in December 1911, only to be deserted by him twelve days later. Karl and Emma Schulz raised Elsie's daughter, Esther, as their own, but the shame of the whole wretched business gave birth to a family fiction. Not until she was twelve did Esther learn that her "older sister," Elsie, was actually her mother.

The adult lives of Carl and his siblings were marked by debilitating, undiagnosed forms of depression. In 1921, Elsie Schulz remarried—a farmer, Otto Fuelling—in Decatur, where she raised five children, born at three-year intervals. Her anguish and aggression would later be understood in the family as what is now termed bipolar disorder, but when her children were young, they knew only that Elsie was "agitated and moving around, and busy, busy, busy. She wouldn't let us sit down," recalled Carl F. Fuelling. "I always had to be busy. And she became angry. She was always kind of angry, and she struck out physically all the time. We had a rough childhood." For that matter, Fuelling added, "I never saw any of my family lovey-dovey with each other, or touch each other, or even call each other nice names. It was kind of a Schulz thing: we were all kind of cold."

Carl Schulz's younger sister Alma, a saleswoman at Dayton's department store, also lived on the east side of St. Paul, with her husband, William Wegwerth, a wholesale grocery salesman. Unlike Carl, William didn't own a car; he had a truck for business but claimed to be reluctant to use it

---

*"Relatives are like mail-order catalogs." Snoopy observed. "They come out of nowhere."

to pay a social call. The only one who readily traveled the relatively short distance between the two households was Carl—and by himself, without Dena.

With Carl's family, Dena was polite but absent. As time went on, the Wegwerths' only child, Bill, born in 1931, would come to realize that chronic, debilitating illness, more than pride, had contributed to her sense of detachment.

SUNDAY MORNINGS, EVEN WHEN the thermometer could not tremble above ten degrees above zero—warm enough for his father to start the Ford— Sparky's mother bundled him into his Sunday best, and he crowded between his well-dressed parents in a miniature version of his father's winter coat, as they rumbled away from the safety of the house in the city to visit relatives in Wisconsin. On his lap, the lemon pie his mother had gotten up early to bake warmed his thighs; once more her sisters would have to say that Dena had made the best, flakiest, finest piecrust of all the Halverson women.

Carl drove them out along the state route into open country—a semi-wilderness of wooded hills, black fir groves, and snow-covered meadows gathering around smudgy farmhouses, the outbuildings scattered like matchsticks over the clean white landscape. The Borgen farm was marked by a solitary mailbox on a post where the road came to an end at Martell in Spring Valley. Sparky recalled that he never "could figure out who the people were, and I just hated going there. I was always uncomfortable and was so glad when we left."

Understandably, the sheer numbers of his mother's relatives bewildered the young Sparky Schulz. The cast of rustic characters that stretched into the extended Halverson clan's further reaches numbered in the dozens. Altogether, the two original mixed pairings of Halverson-Borgen brothers and sisters had produced twenty-five children in Dena's generation, nineteen of whom survived into adulthood. To complicate matters, the Norwegian families of Spring Valley bore the same, sometimes complexly related, Scandinavian patronymics, and, anyway, they tended to intermarry. One spring day in 1928, no fewer than twenty-six Borgens, Swansons, Halversons, Hansons, and Bredahls spilled out of the farmhouse to have their picture taken before Aunt Gusta's well-kept hedges.

In the photograph—taken on Easter Sunday, to judge by the clothing and the light—Dena appears front and center, not reinforced by husband and son but anchoring a body of her kinfolk. Carl, his amiable German face shadowed by a fedora, stands three rows behind his wife, among hardened, handsome Norwegian women—tough cookies, all. Sparky Schulz, five years old, stands scowling in front of his mother, but not touching her. Although Dena's cousin Lillian Hanson holds her son Richard to her front—and Raymond Swanson does the same with his little brother Stanley, known as "Smiler"—Dena has positioned herself behind Sparky with folded arms, leaving him on his own in the hodgepodge of relatives. And he alone among fourteen males in the group observes the rule that hats are not worn by gentlemen having their photograph taken. Having doffed his cap for the picture, he holds it in both hands and squints, his well-barbered blond hair shining under the sun, his fancy new overcoat standing out among his relatives' mended clothes.

Sparky's discomfort among his mother's people makes all too much sense: out here on the farm, where she was mother to them all, was he still her favorite?

He was equally disoriented by the coarse and brutal country. "I always regarded myself as a city boy," he explained. "I grew up on the sidewalks, not in the country." Between the town boy and the farmboy of the 1920s and '30s there stretched a wide gulf. Farmboys witnessed birth, copulation, and death as a matter of course, as part of the raw world, which skimped on the education, medical care, and hot and cold running water that city slickers took for granted. National radio broadcasting had begun to collapse the distance, but for a lone city boy among rural cousins and frightening farm animals, there was a world of difference between town and country.

From the moment bespectacled, Sunday-best Sparky climbed out of his father's flivver, he felt menaced. Two huge, barking collies greeted the fender of the Schulzes' Ford as they pulled up in front of the farmhouse. The adult Schulz would recall how he dreaded having to dismount amid these charging, teeth-baring beasts, how they instilled a lasting fear: "I've always had a fondness for dogs, although I've always been a little afraid of them," he wrote, emphasizing that he remained permanently "leery about dogs who come charging up to me barking loudly."

While the adults visited around the kitchen table, sometimes lapsing into Norwegian, sometimes laughing over things Sparky did not under-stand, he would sink into frustrated isolation, stubbornly refusing to join his peers. "You couldn't get him to go out of the house," one cousin explained. "You'd have to beg him to do anything." "He never ran outside and did boy stuff," another recalled.

To judge by the family photograph album, Dena fussed excessively over her only child. Whenever a camera came out for an occasion, Dena invariably dolled Sparky up in a Buster Brown suit with detach-able starched collar, cuffs, waistcoat, and sturdy leather lace-up shoes. On casual occasions, she outfitted him in a newsboy cap, with a stylish striped cardigan and razor-creased short pants, or a beanie with knickers and argyle knee socks—normal getups for boys of his generation, but whose crisp newness would not have gone unnoticed. Around the peaked lapels of a winter coat made of thick, well-cut wool with padded shoulders and generous flap pockets, a fancy white scarf draped without purpose. In one photograph, taken at about age six, he sits on the grass of a St. Paul park, in velvet suit and Eton collar, earnestly posed under a lacquered Oriental parasol.

He *was* a model boy—if the model is a mother's boy. Unlike the comic strip hero Buster Brown, Sparky rarely, if ever, got into trouble, taking no physical risks. He could not have worried his mother if he tried. Up to the age of eight, he preferred girls as playmates, tricycles to two-wheelers, and cartoons to western movies. "He was very well-behaved and very neat," Carl said later. "When he'd go to bed at night, his little ten-cent cars and all his papers—everything had to be in their place." He kept his own room clean and helped Dena around the house. "I was pretty good at sweeping and dusting," he explained, recalling a day when "two ladies came to visit my mother and as they were leaving I heard them talking about me. One of them said, 'He's such a nice boy, isn't he?' And I thought, 'Oh, boy, is that all I'll be all my life?' "

In a 1951 strip he pictured a boy like himself reflecting (before such a thought carried extra baggage), "I bet I'd make a pretty good housewife."

On the farm, he was far too neat. His mother had made him too pre-sentable to join in the rural rough-and-tumble of tag and hide-and-seek. Dena, moreover, insisted that he wear his overcoat and Sunday muffler if he went outdoors. More than dressed for the weather, he appeared decorated. His cousins' knickers and open shirts and sweater-vests displayed a world of wear and tear, of grass stains and grease smudges and farm chores. Sparky's clothes were spotless.

Lost between the adults at the kitchen table and the children doing odd jobs in the barnyard—between the longing to venture forth and the fear of what would become of him if he did—he felt naked to a world of threat. "Children," he would later say, "aren't allowed to cover up. Their faults are right out there for everyone to see. They can be criticized for them and pushed around, and tugged here and there by their parents and other kids that they are forced to be with."

Believing that his mother had left him open to his relatives' harsh scrutiny and that his cousins could see right into his weaknesses, he shrank from their cracks and countercracks. The lack of maternal reinforcement baffled him, almost to the point of tears, and he hated it. Of course, he could not cry or say how deeply he resented this lack of commitment—resented being so dependent on his mother; hated her for bringing him here to this frozen wasteland and leaving him to make friends with these country kids; hated being, always, the only boy who wore spectacles.

"Only four years old, and already I need glasses," Charlie Brown would lament.

Growing into boyhood, he found the nerve one Sunday to venture out of his mother's eyeshot and drifted around the barnyard by himself, only to be bombarded with corncobs by a male cousin, several years his senior, and another farmboy—an unprovoked meanness that he never forgot or forgave. Something like eight years later, on a Sunday visit in his teens, he took advantage of a backyard game of catch to hurl the baseball as hard as he could at his tormentor: "I was a good ball player by then and I got a little bit of revenge because I could throw the ball so hard he couldn't handle it." Schulz was sixty-six when he told this story. "Anyway, I got a little bit of revenge out of that."

OUT IN WISCONSIN, IN the reconstituted settings of his mother's upbringing, he learned to be fearful of the poverty from which she had sprung, and into which he felt his own family might fall back without the sober, steady presence of his hardworking father. "In our circle of relatives and friends," Sparky recalled, "my dad was thought to be very successful—probably the most successful one. He was the only one who really did something with his life."

"I wonder what would happen to us if Dad lost his barber shop," Charlie Brown would ask many years later.

"We'd probably starve to death," his sister would reply.

The frail and contingent nature of the capacity to survive became a steady undercurrent of Schulz's work: the idea of starving to death figured into as many as twenty of his mature narratives. "They're just about to starve to death," Charlie Brown says to his grandmother in explaining one of the episodes in his own "human interest" comic strip, "when she comes up with a baked-bean hot dish!" But, he goes on, "The little kid wonders where the beans came from . . . then he notices something! His Bean-Bag is missing!"

Freezing to death, a not unreasonable fear for a boy growing up in a state that experiences the coldest morning temperatures in the Lower Forty-eight, would offer no fewer than fifteen motifs, and survival itself thirty. "So long, have a good day . . . Survive!" cries an older sister, as her little brother bundles off to school on an ordinary winter morning. For Sparky on the way to school, thirty degrees below zero, with a whip-like wind making it feel another twenty degrees colder, was an "ordinary" temperature.

On the farm, white summer heat was no less numbing. He felt especially stung one midsummer when inserted into the rural slum inhabited by some Borgen cousins who had settled into a dilapidated shanty upslope of the main farmhouse. This branch of the Borgens was dirt-poor, "almost like hillbillies," Schulz later observed. When he and his parents arrived, cousins who ran the tavern in nearby Martell had to bring oversheets and pillowcases, or else Sparky would have had to sleep on mildewed mattress ticking stuffed with straw. "Talk about bare living," Schulz later recalled. "I just hated being there," although he nevertheless worried what his judgment made him sound like. "I wasn't snobbish or anything, but I just wasn't used to this kind of really down-to-earth, poor living."

These pitiable people didn't seem to belong to him, or he to them. They were part of a meager life that seemed, he later wrote, "almost to have happened to someone else." He was different—the only child, coming from the city, with hidden talents; the only sensitive boy among oafish rustics—and he felt the difference keenly.

Sometimes children will take up the little gentleman in their group as a mascot—the "lively one"—his cleverness and originality ultimately conceded the attention and loyalty they deserve. But in Sparky's extended family, it would be years before he could be seen and appreciated for his talents. No one, least of all his mother, seemed to understand. He himself could not come out with it and say that he was different and should be treated differently. He was very firmly meant to keep such thoughts and feelings to himself. And in his sulky anger at going unnoticed, except as a target for corncobs, he kept boiling behind a cool facade a vast resentment against these loutish country cousins to whom he was humiliatingly kin.

His city-dwelling relatives on his father's side came in for slightly less contempt, but he held it against them that they were uneducated. Meanwhile, on visits among the farm folk, he removed himself to the corner. His parents made no comment and allowed him to withdraw from the family scene with a stubby pencil and a scrap of paper. Drawing diminished him, however, among the Borgen and Swanson males. His female cousins would sometimes show interest, asking for a likeness—the kiss of death; drawing made him girlish, signifying that the city boy had opted out of manly competition. His cousin David Swanson recalled that in the outdoor world of Wisconsin in the 1920s and '30s, men hunted and fished and, at most, assembled some kind of collection (usually an arsenal of slightly earlier vintage than the guns they hunted with). Sparky didn't seem to care. "He would stay inside, drawing funny pictures."

HIS NORWEGIAN RELATIVES FACED adversity with a grim humor. Life was hard, went the clan's credo, and no one outside the family could understand so well, or tease you out of your gloom so pointedly, as someone within the circle of blood. The Halversons met hardship with drollery, orneriness, restraint. They did not indulge in German sentimentality or "in the cheering luxury of tears," as F. Scott Fitzgerald said of Minnesota's Scandinavians.

They traded in a special brand of bleak amusement, a mordant comic sensibility that acknowledged that life in all its forms was a little bizarre.

The Halversons had a particular way of showing affection, especially to those who had disappointed them. They loved, or at least accepted, one another with scorn and joshing and ridicule. They delighted in needling banter. Above all, they never gave up on each other; the very power of family forgiveness rested upon their morose, withering mockery.

Throughout a long winter evening of visiting, talking, and drinking, a Swanson cousin might tease his Halverson host by threatening to overstay his welcome. Better still if the visitor had a broken leg or immobilizing illness. In their final exchange, the guest would say, "What if I'm never able to get out of this chair?"

"I'll sell the house."

Charles Schulz later contrasted his parents' family traditions. His father's side showed him that nothing whatsoever would get done if one were not orderly and clean, regular as clockwork. Schulzes needed to be in control, eager to think up clever solutions to life's flow of problems. "That's using your head!" was the greatest compliment his father could bestow. The Halversons, however, needed to let go. "My mother's side of the family [was] where the humor seemed to be. But that side of the family [was] more erratic, even though they did laugh a lot and seemed to have creative senses of humor, but I don't think they were able to find any place in which they could channel it."

They sidestepped demons—or at least made their choice of them—by drinking. When Prohibition clamped down, Sparky's Norwegian uncles prepared their own raisin wine in cellar jugs. As a boy, he would stand mesmerized, nose to the glass, watching the raisins rise and fall on the awakening currents of fermentation. Later, he was to reflect that the uncles got along well with each other and with his parents "as long as they didn't drink."

"Sometimes I think they all had too much to drink. I don't think my mother and dad ever drank that much, but I knew some of the other relatives did. A few of my uncles had trouble drinking—drinking was always a problem among people like that. But my dad—that's where he stood out, because he just seemed to be a little more ambitious." The striving entrepreneur who had soothed his troubled stomach with a year of Cream of Wheat was not likely to subject himself to the angers and hangovers of the safety-valve boozer.

When the Norwegian uncles drank, they would sit in their sleeveless undershirts, passing from the droll and talkative to the needling and loud, thence to the argumentative and bullying, until finally, fully inebriated, they would tumble outside and come to blows, snarling like dogs as they wrestled in the snowbanks. The next day they would disavow any knowledge of or responsibility for what had happened the previous night. Sparky learned to fear his uncles in this state and kept away from them on mornings when they appeared in their slept-in clothes, eyes lowered, hair coarse and tufty, as if what had really happened overnight was that they had become old.

Humor restored the balance, the saving grace of a world where darkness lurked behind each door. The Halversons behaved brainlessly, living from moment to moment, sometimes like wild men, slumped and silent one minute, boiling up like geysers the next, seconds later rolling and clawing in the snow, living literally and metaphorically the Scandinavian tradition of the sauna. The Halverson women kept what control they could of their dissipated husbands and crazy sons, whose work and homes, endlessly broken into by drink, spiraled down toward the menial and the ramshackle.

Baking was a steadying source of pride in the Borgen-Halverson circle, the women jockeying to see who could make the best of everything. To break bread with the Borgens at their long wooden table entailed being stuffed by Dena's sisters with pies and cookies and variations on Norwegian sweet rolls, *boller,* or more substantially, *skolebrod,* with a yellow "egg" in the middle, spread with sugar frosting and sprinkled with coconut. The lifelong abhorrence of the dry, stringy texture of coconut on baked goods, which Charles Schulz repeatedly vented in his comic strip, first made itself felt at these Sunday extravaganzas. "I always hated staying in these people's places for lunch," recalled Sparky. In Hudson, his mother's aunt Amanda Swanson would make the Schulzes a special Sunday dinner featuring sauerkraut and spareribs, Carl's favorite dishes. To Sparky, always a picky eater, these were "strange foods." He lived in fear that the formidable Aunt Gusta would force him to eat traditional dishes—foul, fishy Norwegian *lutefisk* and *lefse.*

Great-aunt Gusta was, by all accounts, as strong-willed a woman as any Sparky later encountered in the stories and drawings of James Thurber—a counterpoint, certainly, to her brother Tom Halverson, Sparky's grandfather, whose farm had foundered on his inability to lop the heads off chickens, man in charge though he might be. Into her nineties, Gusta, also called "Ma," rose at four every morning, pulled great lengths of long, fine, white hair into a bun, set her jaw against the cold, and went out and milked the cows. Her dry, bony hands were hard as gravel.

Her gangling, sticklike sons helped her keep the place going. Leonard, the younger, and the better dresser, was the more sensible and popular of the two. Eddie, the older and more eccentric, looked like a vagabond; cows had stepped on his bare feet so often that his pulped toes had finally set like pretzels. Neither son would every marry.

If the matriarchal farm tended to unsex and weaken the younger Borgen men, liberation from the land had left the Halverson men of the modern generation no road maps for life. Two of Sparky's uncles, Monroe and Silas, died early, mainly from drink. His cousins Russell and Reuben Helgeson and Raymond and Merrill Swanson would also drift into alcoholism. His uncle Oscar, the railroad brakeman, was at his post when his train accidentally ran over a man; the stricken Oscar swallowed carbolic acid. Dena's father had been an alcoholic, and his disease may have played a role in the central fact of Halverson family history: the failure of Tom Halverson's farm, the loss of the land, and the dispersal of Dena and her brothers and sisters to their fates in the new industrial cities.

To the end of his life Charles Schulz could count on his fingers the number of times he had drunk alcohol. His mother's family implanted a permanent fear that he, a creature of habit, might end up destroyed by bad ways, as had been so many of his kin. He insisted, therefore, on being totally in control of mind and body. Even one glass of wine was too much. He must never lose self-mastery.

And yet, he believed, his mother's family had given him the greater part of his identity as a second-generation American: "I always regarded myself really as being Norwegian and not German."

When they returned to the safety of the city each Sunday afternoon—the ordeal of visiting done with, at least for now—the streets of St. Paul were eerily emptied by the Sabbath and the cold. Under a waning light, they drove past dismal sidewalks and bungalows, where nothing moved in the frosty air, and gigantic, creaking gutter icicles grew yet more grotesque as the dusk closed in.

After a day with her family, his mother indulged in the Halverson habit of sucking air through her teeth to draw in the word *ya*. Inhaling the affirmative was her clan's way of declaring and accepting that life was hard but more or less worthwhile. As Carl pulled the car smartly to the side of the house, Dena would draw back her lips, sharply taking into her lungs all that was sad and lost to her. Then, after a long exhalation, she would brighten as she murmured a pet phrase from an old song: "Home again, Finnegan!"

# CHAPTER 3

# THE ART OF BARBERING

*Don't get a big head.*
—CARL F. SCHULZ

FROM HIS MOTHER'S NORWEGIAN clan he learned grim humor and impulse; from his German father, hard work and public relations.

The corner barbershop was the Gibraltar of Carl's life and, to the end of his days, commanded his stout devotion. No matter how the city expanded, no matter where the great mass of consumers went next, he would always say, "If you give your customers fair treatment, friendly service, and good merchandise, they will remain your customers."

In more than forty-five years on the corner, Carl never took a real vacation. He worked, he slept, he read the newspaper, ritually perusing the comic pages with Sparky. Infrequent fishing expeditions to Mille Lacs, a hundred miles to the north, afforded him his sole getaway. Six days a week, from eight in the morning until the regulation six o'clock closing time, he cut hair.

On his feet a minimum ten hours a day, Carl held himself erect, smiling, ready to serve. Having locked his chair in place when a customer departed, he would come immediately to attention, seat the new arrival, unlock the chair, and pump it to an appropriate height. Then—in one deft motion, like the matador with his cape—he would swirl the haircloth in a wide swing so that it fell gently around the customer without touching his skin. Next came the white neck-strip, unfolded before the Adam's apple, overlapped and clipped at the nape, the setup completed by tucking a small towel into the collar and turning it down over the haircloth. Carl would wash his hands with soap and water and dry them. Only then would barber and patron, framed by the first panel of the mirror that ran the length of the shop, meet with an equally ritualized response:

"So—what'll it be?"

Barbering had become highly regulated when Carl entered the field before World War I, and Minnesota's laws for the licensing of barbers, passed in 1897, had become models for the rest of the country. He was a classic member of that new generation of barbers who brought courtesy, dignity, hygiene, sobriety, and efficiency to a trade known for loud profanity, liquor breath, and unsanitary practices. In his shop, recalled one customer, "Everything was always immaculate." Off-color stories were not welcome from the customers' bench; pinups and lewd calendars had no place on the walls. Strangers might ask the barber for a joke or even a fish story, but straight-spined Carl Schulz did not traffic in low humor; nor did he swear, offer opinions, or speak his piece on the pennant race. Low talk—barnyard smut—was just the kind of thing he had been striving to get away from by fulfilling his ambitions. He would tolerate good-humored blather from his regulars but never crudity. His one personal indulgence was a cigar, which he smoked by inches throughout the day, but never while serving a customer.

The Family Barber Shop of later years was a bright white box, spruce and gleaming, lined with spotless mirrors and outfitted with louvered blinds on the front window, linoleum checkerboard floor tiles, and a stainless steel coatrack overlooking metal-armed customers' chairs. The shop of Charles Schulz's boyhood had offered a tidy but manlier aspect, with wooden floor-planking, beadboard trim, green paper window shades, lightbulbs suspended in porcelain fixtures, and, to the left as you walked in the front door, a stiff-backed customers' bench as well as an assortment of hard-seated chairs, including one handcrafted wooden rocker.

To the right stood the barbers' thrones, three in a row, hefted hydraulically from their enameled bases, with white enamel arm tips and upholstered oxblood leather arms, seats, chairbacks, and adjustable neck- and footrests. Carl ruled over the first chair; his associate manned the second; a "Saturday man" came in to help on the third; at the rear, a black handyman named Floyd ran a shoeshine concession.

Carl operated his chair noiselessly, pumping it up with gentle skill.

Standing tall, his shoes polished, his white smock clean and pressed, he cut a regal figure, recalled one nephew. "He always looked like a silver dollar," said a niece. Whenever he stropped his razor Carl would smile and say, in his soft, deep voice, "It takes an expert." He was a true craftsman, setting store by the correct instruments: plain shears and a comb, properly sterilized. Carl did not trust the popular new tooth-notched thinning shears and did not permit his associates to use them. Nor did he have confidence in the fancy finger rests on French-made shears, preferring always the plainer German design. He preferred the traditional lather brush and mug to the electric latherizer, and rejected the double-edged safety razor, putting his faith in the open cutthroat blade. With a straight razor, he could shave a man in fewer than fourteen strokes. He never hurried one patron to make way for the next; he knew how to combat foot fatigue by standing in comfortable shoes a shoulders' width apart, distributing his weight evenly from heel to toe. If asked how he managed to stay on his feet all day, he would cheerfully demonstrate this master-barber's skill. In later years, he displayed this quietly effective technique to one of Sparky's dates, and a snapshot survives from the 1940s in which Sparky, presenting himself to the camera, has adopted, as if it were his own natural stance, the posture with which Carl greeted the customers who were the organizing principle of his world.

As a boy, Sparky took special interest in his father's workmanship. He loved to sit on the bench, waiting for the close of the business day. The shop was a place of craft and routine, of tersely told incidents—far more of a community center in those days of few telephones and the walking city. Here, too, were interesting things to look at: three sequentially paneled mirrors in which appeared the tilted heads, foreshortened throats, and draped torsos of men and boys. The lettering on the front window also held special appeal: the reversed words FAMILY BARBER SHOP suspended on the glass in block letters through which one could see the corner's doings on ice-cold Minnesota days. Stepping inside the shop's front door, eyelashes white with sleet, regulars would murmur their hellos through clouds of condensed breath. Outside, fixed to the front of the brown brick building, the barber pole—a rising spiral of blue, red, and white—energized the blank frozen spaces of the midwestern winter street.

Sparky liked best the sensations of approaching the warm shop at the end of a frigid day, as his father was at work on the last customer. "Almost all of us, if not all of us, have the desire to be somebody," Charles Schulz would later say. "This doesn't mean that you necessarily want to be rich and famous or anything like that, but you want to be somebody." In the Family Barber Shop, he was gratified to see how important a man his father was. Barbers maintained a modestly high status in prewar Minnesota—the licensing examinations Carl was required to pass would have challenged a medical student; moreover, he was boss in his own shop, and this marked his son as something more than ordinary lower middle class. Furthermore, when Sparky walked through the door, Carl would pause at his work to give his son a big smile and a hello, and then turn back to his customer, letting Sparky have the run of the latest *Saturday Evening Post*. "He also never objected," Sparky recalled, "if I rang the NO SALE key on the cash register and removed a nickel for a candy bar."

This favored standing in his father's clean, wholesome establishment gave Sparky his place in the world, charging him with the dignity of one of the neighborhood's institutions and making him a recognized person around the Selby-Snelling intersection. People at the bank (with its pen and inkwell always waiting on the table in the middle) knew Sparky Schulz. They knew him at Sheady's drugstore and across the street at Weber's Restaurant, where the waitresses called out "Hey, Sparky!" But more important than the warm welcomes of the neighborhood was the notice that Carl himself gave to Sparky's comings and goings. No matter how busy Carl was—even if the shop was full of customers—he always stopped to greet his boy coming through the door.

Sparky, in turn, was proud of his father. Once in childhood he had given his teddy bear a haircut. In later years, Charles Schulz made a point of saying that although most people did not consider barbering an important occupation, he deemed his father's life's work an honorable profession.

Carl had mastered a modest but demanding trade by making the most of himself. Even more significant to Sparky, his father had earned a respected place in the community. People said that Carl Schulz should have been a state senator. And, indeed, in his particular calling Carl's political accomplishments would prove to be substantial. From 1928, he served in local and state chapters of the Associated Master Barbers and Beauticians and held high offices in the national organization. At the state level, he contributed to several pieces of legislation that elevated the craft in Minnesota by establishing better hours and prices, sanitary regulations, and legislation governing barber schools. When Carl exercised political muscle as a local leader, the national organization noted that "things got better all over."

Sparky recalled thinking as a boy: "I hope I will be as well-liked as my father." But what did being liked mean to Carl? It meant good business—a lesson not lost on Sparky, as Carl annually expanded his circle of friends and associates on citywide master-barbers' picnics in Wildwood Park, to which Sparky—but not Dena—accompanied his smiling, pomaded, shirt-sleeved dad. *It pays to look well.* It paid to win friends.

The working precepts of Carl's business, standardized in the trade's official text, *The Art and Science of Barbering*, framed the resolves of Sparky's boyhood. In time, without his noticing it, they established the professional tactics of Charles Schulz's entire career:

1. *Maintain a good posture.*
2. *Wear an easy cheerful countenance.*
3. *Constantly practice friendliness.*
4. *Speak distinctly.*
5. *Don't be overly inclined to give advice.*
6. *Don't be didactic.*
7. *Be a good listener. A good listener asks leading questions.*
8. *Be essentially informal.*
9. *One's success in any avenue of life depends a great deal upon his selling ability.*
10. *Don't take yourself too seriously.*

After seeing the last customer out the door, Carl would relight his cigar, pull the front shades, and close up shop. Then he and Sparky would walk to the far corner of Snelling and take the streetcar home, its icy windows steamed by interior warmth in the winter months. Years later, Carl could still recall how Sparky, at three or four, would draw with his finger on the panel of night-blackened glass—"a picture of something that maybe he'd seen that day."

IN 1927, WHEN SPARKY was four, Carl moved the family from Minneapolis to a rented two-story stucco bungalow in St. Paul, a mile and a half south of the barbershop. The house at 1680 James Avenue faced the open air and snow-covered fields of Mattocks Park, where Sparky attended kindergarten at the Mattocks School. A year later, the Schulzes moved around the corner to 473 Macalester Avenue.

Until junior high school, all Charles Schulz's schools were literally within a stone's throw of his front door. On any given day, his mother was seldom more than a block from wherever he might be. Like the mothers he would later place offstage in his comic strip, she kept Sparky always in the corner of her eye, calling him from neighbors' sandboxes whenever "she just wanted to know where I was."

As his cousins recalled her, Dena was kind and gentle, always smiling. In the memories of his childhood friends, she appears distant, reserved, forbidding—a "rather stern-faced lady in dark clothes." Sparky and his neighborhood companions did not naturally gravitate to the Schulz household. Richard Hackney, who lived nearby at 1674 James Avenue, could not "remember ever playing at his house. . . . Playing didn't seem to come into it."

Sherman Plepler lived around the corner on Randolph Avenue, attended the Mattocks School and became Sparky's closest boyhood friend. He, too, was an only child. "Shermy" played the violin, and on warm afternoons his lessons could be heard all over the neighborhood, as could his mother's voice. Mary Beck Plepler, Romanian by birth, was a fine pianist. Sherman's father, Albert, a refugee from czarist Russia, had survived the pogroms in Kiev and had become foreman at the family-run Victory Printing Company in St. Paul. Beethoven was Mary Plepler's favorite composer, and Sparky liked to come over and listen to her play— his first exposure to a cultured Jewish household in which classical music was naturally in the air. "He used to spend a lot of time in my home,"

Shermy would recall. "He always seemed more relaxed and happier there. My mother was an extrovert, interested in people—the complete opposite of his mother."

When Shermy knocked at 473 Macalester, Dena would come to the door. "She'd say, 'Sparky, Shermy's here.' Then we'd go out. That was my relationship with his parents. She never said, 'Come in.' I must have been in Sparky's backyard pitching and batting a thousand times, by the *hour*. But I can count on one hand the number of times I was in his home. They always stopped me at the door."

Dena likewise discouraged her woman neighbors from visiting. Outside the extended Norwegian clan, she had little or no social life; Dena and Carl together had made friends with only one or two couples from his circle of barbershop associates and trade association acquaintances. Even relatives recalled that Dena was "hard to visit with." She did not ask other women for their recipes, nor did she share her crochet designs or family photos—sure signs in that time and place of a determination to hold the world at arm's length. "They were quite a private family," recalled his cousin Shirley Gish VonderHaar.

Later, Sherman Plepler would maintain that Dena, for all her distance and reserve, was not actually unfriendly. It was just that Sparky's friends did not know where they stood with his mother and, according to Plepler, neither did Sparky. Cool to the world, warm at home, cheerful one minute, aloof the next, Dena did not trust people to like her.

"I look back with great sadness," Sparky said later, "upon something which in those days puzzled me a good deal. Our school had a little monthly contest wherein the class that had the most parents attend one of the evening PTA meetings would be rewarded with cake and ice cream. I recall that our class won at least two or three times, but I always felt puzzled and I suppose somewhat guilty, because I knew that my mother had not attended any of these afternoon PTA sessions. I am afraid my mother simply did not feel she was sophisticated enough to mingle with the other parents. This, of course, would have been completely untrue, for, although my mother went no further than the third grade, she certainly knew how to talk with other people. Perhaps she felt that she did not have the right type of clothes. I do not know. . . . It would have been wonderful if someone could have explained to my mother that she need not have felt inadequate."

The truth is, Dena cut quite a figure. That she was pretty and feminine and proud of her well-pressed clothes and patent-leather shoes stands out among the memories of the girls and young women who admired her. She was "a *beautiful* lady," and "her home was spotless, and when she went out she was like a walking China doll." In photographs taken in the 1920s, we can see her making a noticeable effort to keep up with changing styles, dressing fashionably when calling on family members, in a new, not thrift-shop fur coat with shawl collar, an assortment of cloche hats, and a long string of pearls—if anything, overdressed for an afternoon with the PTA.

Where the other ladies outgunned her was in vocabulary. Sparky was right: she could "talk with other people." But only a minute of such talk brought it home to Dena Schulz that those other ladies knew how to talk the talk. They subscribed to the better magazines; they read abridged articles in *Reader's Digest*; they knew the names and buzzwords of the moment. Dena was tied not by her apron strings but by her tongue.

Intimidated by books and wholly uninterested in magazines, she spelled phonetically: Wednesday was "Wensday." She didn't consider her thoughts important enough to be set down in letters or diaries; a postcard dashed off to the folks on the farm covered everything that she had to say. By all accounts intelligent, she nevertheless had not been taught to become anything more than what she already was: a good wife and the trusted sister in the family.

Modesty and vanity mingled to guard her home life. On the one hand, she did not consider herself the equal of women in the PTA; on the other, she thought herself better than her in-laws, dressed like a woman with airs, and lied about her age. Sparky, in turn, was protective of his mother. To make her look good—or at least better than she appeared to herself—he was a good boy, on good behavior. He wore what she wanted him to wear, with a frown but without complaint. At a neighbor's request, and at his mother's enthusiastic bidding, Sparky modeled knickers at the Emporium department store in St. Paul and from the dollar he earned, immediately spent twenty cents on a ceramic frog for his mother.

HIS PARENTS GAVE HIM a small blackboard with the alphabet printed on a paper roll at the top. Pulling a piece of white chalk across the dark surface, he drew, by his own count, hundreds of pictures. "For years, that blackboard was my friend." But pictures alone did not occupy him. As he drew, he studied the shapes and sequences of the block letters on top, and by kindergarten he knew his ABCs.

A heavily varnished, child-sized rolltop desk, about two feet tall— another present from his parents—occupied a special place in the corner of the living rooms of the houses of his first years, and in later life he identified the blackboard and the rolltop as the "most valuable and important possessions of my childhood."

Charles Schulz's earliest-remembered composition, with its juxtaposition of extremes and temperatures, could serve as a coat of arms for the two sides of his family. At kindergarten, his teacher handed out big crayons and sheets of white butcher paper and told the children to put down whatever came into their minds. Sparky first drew a man shoveling against a Minnesota snowstorm; then, out of one of the waist-high snowbanks, he grew its counterpoint: a tall, green palm tree.

One source for this surreal contrast was his Halverson uncle and namesake, Monroe, called Monte. Newly married, having adopted a suddenly orphaned nephew, Monte had resettled from the frozen Twin Cities in the curiously named subtropical town of Needles in the southwest California desert. When one of his letters included the tiny snapshot of a tree that Dena passed around, Sparky seized on this image of the good life far away in the sun—this "palm" tree.

His teacher took notice. He forgot her name but remembered her as the first person to recognize his ability.

"Some day, Charles," she said, "you're going to be an artist."

# CHAPTER 4

# EAST COMES WEST

*In the beginning there was Cold and Heat. . . . Here, in this yawning void, flanked by light and dark, lay the origin of all life, in the encounter between ice and fire.*

— TOR ÅGE BRINGSVÆRD,

"NORSE MYTHOLOGY"

"IT SEEMS BEYOND THE comprehension of people that someone can be born to draw comic strips," he would say a little indignantly, "but I think I was. My ambition from earliest memory was to produce a daily comic strip."

Challenging an understandable skepticism, he always insisted that he had known he would be a cartoonist "way back into his childhood, as long as [he] could remember." What was hard for people to believe, however, was not the age at which he claimed to have defined his life's work but the certainty of his conviction and the solitary, inward nature of his dream.

For the rest of his life, six remained the age of self-discovery for Charles Schulz. It was also the year during which his extended family, following the lead of his cousin Shirley Russ, began calling him "Sparky," dropping "Charles" forever. Six, too, is the age at which Schulz would later cast Charlie Brown's first awakening to life's disappointments—in one instance, a loss of pride so extreme that even to Charlie Brown it seems unnatural to sustain such damage "when he's only six years old."

And this sudden insight did, in fact, overtake Schulz at the age of six. For if Sparky opened his eyes to ambition sometime in 1928 or '29—to the fanatical (his word) part of himself that would not rest until he had claimed his true home in the comics—then however long his dream had percolated among the dotted blue, yellow, and red inks of the funny pages on cold Sunday mornings at home in St. Paul, Minnesota, his awareness of

his special talent came to him in the desolate sun-bleached vistas of Needles, California, a railroad town huddled into an oasis under the gaze of its
two namesake peaks dominating the skyline at the far end of the Mojave
Desert.

At the age of six, Charles Schulz underwent a dazing displacement,
compounded by deprivation. He was taken away from the square mile of
St. Paul that he knew as home, and the change forced him—for the first
time but not the last—to discover himself.

BY 1929, CARL'S PARTNER, Eric Carlson, had married, started a family, and
decided that he wanted to try small-town living. He rented a house in
Breckenridge, on the North Dakota border just south of Fargo, and left his
partnership in the Family Barber Shop on Selby with the understanding
that if he didn't like life on the Plains, he would return within a year. But
soon after settling in, he was overcome by a high fever and died at the age
of thirty-six.

The death of his partner and friend shook Carl and may have contributed to his willingness to upend his business, but it does not explain
what would take this steady, well-ordered barber to a scruffy town in a
faraway wilderness. Sixty years later, puzzling over the decision, Charles
Schulz could recall only that he had never been told "what family problems caused us to make the move."

And indeed three blows had fallen on the Halverson clan in the early
months of 1929. First, Dena's older sister Ida Halverson Roberts died of
tuberculosis at forty-one. Then Ida's husband, Charles, a St. Paul police
officer, was shot dead in a gun battle. Meanwhile, Howard, their son, was
diagnosed with tuberculosis; the doctor advised Monte Halverson, who
had adopted his orphaned nephew, to move the boy to a hotter, drier
climate.

By March, Monte, twenty-six, his wife, Frances, twenty, and Howard, had set out for a new life in California, aiming to settle in the Long
Beach area. But with the Mojave still ahead of them, and because he saw
at once the advantages to Howard's health of living in a place whose climate "cures many ills and produces none," as the local newspaper billed it,
Monte pulled off U.S. Route 66 into the oasis around Needles.

Founded in 1883 at the junction of two railroads, Needles in its heyday had been known as the "Gateway to the Great Empire [of] Southern California." The Needles of 1929 was still more boom than bust. The railroad was the town's lifeline. Consolidated into the Santa Fe Railway, the tracks of the old Atchison, Topeka, and Santa Fe coast lines came from the east, jumped the Colorado River on a cantilever bridge, snaked into Needles, and then went west out of town on the old Southern Pacific tracks, following the rising basin of the Mojave. Through Needles, according to the town slogan, "The East Comes West and the West Goes East."

Monte Halverson opened a barbershop at 125 Front Street, and was soon writing enthusiastic accounts of oasis life to his mother and the Halversons in Minnesota—Dena and her sister Ella and brother Silas and their young families. He offered Carl a share in the new shop, sending snapshots of a front-parlor establishment in a prosperous townscape lush with surrounding flowers, shrubs, and lawns shaded by regal Washingtonia palms.

But Carl had set his sights on Sacramento. The part of him that would pursue ever-higher office in his calling, from city on to national organizations, must have seen golden opportunities in establishing himself in another state capital. For, as Sparky understood it, his father planned to move his family and business to Needles and work in Uncle Monte's shop only long enough to qualify for his California license. Then the Schulzes would settle permanently in the fertile northern valley.

Carl sold the Family Barber Shop's equipment for $100, and in the summer of 1929, at the age of thirty-two, strapped a tent and tent poles to the running board of the family's '28 Ford, into which he, Dena, and Sparky squeezed their belongings and Sparky's dog, a Boston bull terrier named Snooky. Dena's sister Ella, her husband Albert Russ, a dark-eyed, swarthily handsome and magnetic French Canadian known as Frenchy, and their eight-year-old daughter, Shirley, fell in behind in a second Model T, and the caravan set out on its uncertain journey across America.

The trip took two weeks. Gravel and corduroy planked roads meant days of creaking along with rare bursts of a top speed of forty miles per hour. Evenings, the travelers cooked meals over a portable gas stove and camped out, pitching the big oil-treated tent at the roadside or in a campground. This was the era of motoring when Americans first took to the highways to see the country. On rare nights, the Schulzes and Russes stopped in what were called tourist cabins—little more than boxy wooden shelters offering a door and a window and a share in the latrine behind. Sparky would recall wondering what it would be like to stay in a real hotel room. "Hotels were absolutely out," he later explained. "There wasn't such a thing as staying in a hotel."

As they reached the crest of the temperate valley of the Great River, Frenchy hoisted Sparky onto a picnic table. Far in the distance, what at first looked like clouds shaped majestically up into an impression that so awed the boy that he never forgot the sight: "I suppose they were the Rockies."

ACROSS THE CONTINENTAL DIVIDE, the cars rumbled through the Arizona desert. Here, they came upon tortured stones and fantastic vistas, preternaturally clear under the scorching desert light. Just inside the eastern California border, where mountain time yields to Pacific time, the bleached hues of the vast arid landscape changed. Down below the playa, 481 feet above sea level, in a shallow bowl on the west bank of the Colorado, the miles of uneven sepia and mustard tints suddenly turned a bright kelly green. Water dropping into the river valley from ancient underground reservoirs burst into an oasis. Travelers approached through a lane of tamarind and pepper trees.

They paraded into Needles on a hot summer night, motoring to the stucco bungalow on Collins Street where Monte lived with Frances and Howard. Sparky's grandmother Sophia had also arrived by then and taken up residence with Monte in exchange for laundering the barbershop linens. The searing desert breeze rippled steam towels and haircloths on the clothesline behind the bungalow, while Monte and Silas languished over their beer in sleeveless undershirts at a round table. "And that," Sparky later said, emphasizing his sense of unsavoriness and anticlimax, "was my entrance to Needles, California."

Heat hovered over the rooms like a solid presence, baking the plaster until it cracked. To lie in bed was to roast. At midnight, the temperature could be as high as 112 degrees, and never descended below the high 90s before spiking again at sunrise. Opening the windows did nothing but bring into the room the odors of some greasy dish cooking on a neighbor's stove. The only relief was afforded by small electric fans, which stirred the heat-drawn odors from room to room. The air at daybreak was far too tor-rid for morning dew to condense on any surface. Hung-out laundry did not so much dry overnight as become flammable by morning.

By day, sun broiled the vast playa above the town—120 degrees in the shade of a cottonwood tree was normal for Needles in summer. Most winter nights, the translucent air turned the dry gullies into such iceboxes that he could hear rocks cracking in the cold. In May and September, the old wooden tinderbox of a schoolhouse was frequently shut to protect the children from heatstroke. Such little rain as fell came briefly and violently, blasting flash floods out of nowhere.

Needles, Sparky decided, was "a miserable place."

Carl moved the family into a scruffy three-room bungalow at the corner of Palm Way and Bazoobuth Street, which set him back $28 a month. Ella and her family took one room until Frenchy got a job as a garage mechanic and the Russes moved to the end of Palm Way.

The Schulzes' bungalow had originally been a company cottage, built by the railroad in 1901 and rented cheaply as an enticement for employees to put up with the inhuman heat. The Minnesotans found the walls and ceilings and baseboards so badly caked with desert dust and insects dead and living that they had to use a garden hose to make the place habitable. The Santa Fe Railroad, a block from their front door, was now a permanent neighbor, and the rush and roar of long-distance trains and the stench of toilets draining onto the tracks was in their ears and nostrils every hour of the day and night.

His parents had stranded him in a place of hazardous extremes. That August, a few days after the Schulzes arrived, the local newspaper announced: SIX-FOOT RATTLER KILLED BY MAN AT THE NEEDLES DAIRY. Not long afterward, in one of the Halverson family bungalows, the adults heard Sparky screaming and, dashing to help, found him being pursued by his eight-year-old cousin Shirley Russ brandishing a live sidewinder, a small rattlesnake that moves with a lateral looping motion.

In the realignment of family life in Needles, Shirley, a tomboy and her family's only child after her baby sister Peggy died of spinal meningitis, was one of the two cousins who became Sparky's honorary siblings. Howard Roberts, dark and handsome at sixteen, fitted the bill of an idolized older brother to be imitated in every possible way. Sparky studied his gestures and mannerisms, especially the way the older boy kept his hands inside the pockets of his big checkered football sweater as he strode to school. "Naturally I walked around with my hands in my pockets just like that," Schulz recalled. "Howard was what we might call today 'cool.' "

Shirley Russ—Dena had nicknamed her Dodi—was the only other child on Palm Way near Sparky's age. The two strays became constant companions, playing jacks and checkers and climbing a tree in the Russes' yard, or skipping down to the Santa Fe terminal to join the idlers waiting for the next train. Occasionally, their bored persistence was rewarded by the unannounced appearance of a special railway car, such as that attached to Santa Fe train number 19 bound for Los Angeles, which on October 1, 1930, whisked through Needles the great champion of the comics, William Randolph Hearst himself, and his attendants and hangers-on. Another train chugged in one evening with the big-wheeled tricycle Carl and Dena had ordered from Montgomery Ward for Sparky's seventh birthday.

If Sparky was timid and shy, the snake-charming Shirley was brave and outgoing. In Needles, goes the family story, Sparky delivered the popular *Liberty* magazine to neighbors, but, lacking the nerve to ask for payment, sent Shirley around to pick up the nickel. When each cousin had earned a dime, they bought booklets entitled *How to Draw*. "He could draw right away," Shirley later recalled. "He had a knack for it."

THE NEW D STREET School was still under construction when Sparky and Dena and Sophia started up the hill to register Sparky on September 16, 1929.

He began second grade in the baking heat of the old wooden primary school, a three-story Victorian structure surrounded by barren, gritty lots. Townspeople called it the "Castle on the Hill"—its dark pitched roof and gabled windows could be seen a mile away. Protected from the savage if infrequent flooding of the Colorado River, the old building was not, however, immune to earthquakes, and the town had decided to build a new, one-story structure into which the D Street School would move that November.

Sparky entered the classroom of Miss Johanna T. Gruys, a twenty-year-old teacher from New Mexico, who placed crayons and paper before her pupils and asked for a drawing on the first day. Whereupon Sparky, who, on his journey across the continent, had been fascinated to discover that a car could not cross a range by going straight up and over it, sketched the family Ford winding its way around a mountainside.

He was smart in school, although he would recall feeling ill at ease, with himself as well as with others: "I never was very friendly. I never had any friends." He felt a singular passion for a little girl named Marie Holland, the brown-haired daughter of a railroad engineer, who became the first of many distant princesses onto whom Charles Schulz projected a deep connection. "She was very cute," he would say almost seventy years later, recalling the way that Marie's light brown hair flew off her shoulders when she skipped or ran. But more than her beauty, what made Marie exceptional in Sparky's eyes was her intelligence. Few words passed between them, but that was the point: with her, there was no need for talk.

Three months into the school year, their status as intellectual equals became official when the December 6, 1929, *Needles Nugget* announced that out of approximately thirty-one pupils in the second grade, Charles Schulz was one of two to make the honor roll; he would ever after remember Marie Holland as his fellow achiever. In his memory, he and she were paraded up to the high school for a formal ceremony during which they sat on a bench, feeling small and uncomfortable, with the eyes of the older students on them. Records, however, list Rosie Herrera as Charles Schulz's companion honoree, and it was her name, not Marie Holland's, that appeared beside Sparky's in the newspaper. But Sparky had projected his deepest romantic yearnings on Marie Holland, and nothing would change not just his first romantic feelings but his first transforming fantasies.

One evening, he and Marie encountered each another outside his house on Palm Way. Dusk had streaked the desert sky a vibrant blue and pink. They ran to the corner and back; he later recalled a wild sense of drawing close, of being whole and complete, instead of feeling, as he so often did, lost and alone. He had no memory of their ever seeing each other again. In adult life, he once tried to look her up through the Needles Chamber of Commerce, and throughout his life, on the rare occasions that Charles Schulz crossed paths with someone who had lived in or visited their desert town between the wars, his first words would always be, "Did you know a Marie Holland in Needles?"

In 1989, a few years after learning of her death, he wrote off his memories of her—and those of his younger self. Hiding behind a fluttery laugh, he said, "Undoubtedly, she had no recollection of me anyway."

On December 20, the D Street School began its seven days of Christmas vacation. By keeping the break short, classes could be ended earlier that spring, before the heat descended. Meanwhile, the school held a Christmas pageant to round out the first semester. Sparky lined up onstage with thirteen other children from various grades, holding letters that spelled out M-E-R-R-Y C-H-R-I-S-T-M-A-S. Each child had been rehearsed to step forward in turn and sing out a sentence to illuminate his or her letter. Sparky, with the "A," knew his piece by heart: *'A' stands for all of us—all of us! 'A' stands for all-of-us!*

The first couple of performers started hoarse and frightened, swallowing their lines behind the large letters. As the spotlight moved down the row, Sparky could tell that somewhere between the first "R"s and the "H," stage fright had become contagious. Hearing each letter become more strangulated than the last, the teacher scurried out from the wings to urge the succeeding placardeers to sing louder.

At his penultimate place in line, Sparky vowed to be bold. "I kept thinking, 'Boy, when they get to me, I'm going to speak up. I'm not going to be like that.'" Sixty years later, he could still recall his surprise and hurt when he indeed spoke up, projecting his voice loud and clear to the back of the audience. But instead of hearing applause, he was shocked to be answered by a cackle. "It kind of hurt my feelings because, after all, I'm doing it right. Those other dumb kids, they didn't speak it loud enough."

At home after the performance, Sparky asked his mother why someone had laughed at him. And while there may well have been an element of amused admiration in her response, especially as Sparky was discernibly young and small for his class, Dena could not resist twitting her delicate son with his own aggressiveness. "Well," she said, "you *did* sing yours kind of loud and fast."

★  ★  ★

TRUTH IS SEARED INTO simplicity in the desert, as it is frozen clear on the highest peaks or lifted from fog far out at sea. In the isolated Needles of 1930, people often came face-to-face with themselves and their loved ones for the first time. Even with railroad traffic, Needles was an islanded desert community—a "little sandy town," Sparky called it. Almost no one owned a car or had anywhere to go, and practically every adult among its 3,144 people was employed by the railroad. "You couldn't run to the next town for entertainment," recalled one of the young women who worked, as did Sparky's aunt Ella, as a Harvey Girl in the famed restaurant chain's Santa Fe depot outlet. "People were thrown together for everything. People did a lot of things together and became very close."

The Halverson clan tightened to the snapping point. The four families picnicked on the Colorado River, gathered in each other's parched back-yards to gulp down sweating bottles of beer, drove up into the desert on summer evenings to feel the breeze over the playa before descending again into the oven. On Sundays, they crowded into a car or two to strike out on daylong excursions across the baked country. One such jaunt saw several of the uncles burying a large quantity of bootleg whiskey in the desert floor.

On another Sunday outing—to Las Vegas, a hundred miles to the north—two cars got lost by following a corduroy planked road into the desert until, sometime after noon, it brought them to a filling station in an otherwise total wasteland. A small grocery and café were attached to the pump shed where the travelers filled their gasoline tanks. With the kind of spontaneity that characterized the Halversons, they sat down in the café for a laugh and some illegal refreshment. The uncles gulped beer—a lot of it—and several hours later, as Sparky recalled it, "Si and Monroe were feel-ing pretty good. They were not staggering drunk, but they had certainly had too much to drink."

They were, happily, the only customers in this last-chance café. Mon-roe told the man who ran the place that he was a barber, and the next thing anyone knew, the man was sitting down and Monroe was giving him a shampoo, lathering his head with a bottle of beer. Meanwhile, Sparky's mother and Aunt Ella had gone off, perhaps at least nominally to look for the ladies' room, and perhaps, a little giddy from beer, in search of spur-of-the-moment fun. In any event, somewhere in the back of the café, they came across a shipping case loaded with bottles of vanilla extract, and while one sister kept watch, the other sneaked the whole case into the back of one of the cars.

Theft was not among Dena's usual weaknesses, but without her law-abiding husband to keep her in check—Carl seems not to have been along that day—she apparently felt free enough, with her younger sister as an eager accomplice, to engage in a foxy caper.

On that "strange day," as Sparky later characterized it, he was well aware of his mother's misconduct. But neither then nor later did he hold her accountable. He registered only the facts of the matter: Dena and Ella tipsily stole a case of vanilla extract. "What they were going to do with all these bottles of vanilla, I don't know. I suppose they used vanilla extract in their cooking." He took no account of the extract's alcohol content. That his mother and the grown-ups in charge of him were inebriated to the point of risking the law or an ugly accident on those appalling roads—if not already drunk enough to want to keep tippling, in private and for free, a cooking product with 35 percent ethyl alcohol—seems not to have occurred to him.

Darkness had descended on the desert by the time they pulled out of the café, whose proprietors were still unaware of the missing extract bottles. Not long after moving off across the barrens, the cars stopped so that someone could go to the bathroom. Everybody got out, and within seconds Monroe and Silas were at each other's throats, wrestling in the glare of the headlights, rolling around on the grit and sand. As the fight thrashed on, Dena and Ella tiptoed behind one of the cars through the back shadow of the headlights to sample their private stock. No sooner had they uncapped the bottles and put them to their lips than they discovered that all they had done was carry off a case of empties. So disappointed were the sisters, as Sparky recalled that moment, that "they proceeded to do something that gave me great delight."

While his pie-eyed uncles carried on in the road, his mother and his aunt, in their nice print dresses, moved into the headlights' arc at the edge of darkness. The Halverson clan had evolved an almost voluptuous embrace of defeat, but now Dena trumped idiot frustration by dramatizing it. She and her sister pitched the empty bottles one by one out into the desert. Since they had a full two dozen dead soldiers to bury, now and then one of these would shatter on a rock in the dark, and Sparky found a curious pleasure in waiting, ear cocked, for the satisfying sound of glass bursting against stone as his mother winged empties into the night.

IN THE SUMMER OF 1931, the Schulzes pulled up stakes and moved back to Minnesota. This time, no caravans lined up to bear cousins into the wilderness; no shared hardships or beery reunions supervened to bring them all closer. The Schulzes simply went home, perhaps pointedly leaving no explanation in the family record for their parting of the ways with the stick-together Halverson clan.

Charles Schulz described his family's two years in Needles as "a miserable life." Pressed to tell the family tale for the benefit of his own children, Sparky presented his life in the desert as a kind of martyrdom to drunken uncles and insect-infested bungalows, with the occasional freak of nature, such as on the winter morning in 1930 when a snowstorm blanketed the desert inches deep around the palm trees on the edge of town—Sparky's first drawing as a kindergartner in Minnesota come to life.

If his parents entertained enduring feelings about this interlude, Sparky was not privy to them. He said little about how they had weathered desert life: "I suppose there were some happy times." Dena and Carl's tenth wedding anniversary had come and gone on May 2, 1930, but whether they included that day among the happy times in Needles, and whether the move to the Southwest with Dena's clan had been constricting or liberating, not even their son could tell.

Carl is notably absent from the wild and desolate scenes in Sparky's memory. The desert seems to have neither usurped nor strengthened his father's reason, though it magnified his personality just as crisply as it did Dena's: even in the crushing heat, Carl felt no need, if we go by the photographs, to discard his coat, his collar, or his calm good sense. It would seem that he itched only to leave California behind and get home to work in the astringent Old Northwest.

As an adult, Charles Schulz remained unwilling to read his parents beyond a certain point, never holding them to account for that unfathomable odyssey. Of his own forlornness in the scorched and shut-in town, he provided only hints. His piercing powers of observation were reserved for his art. Needles and the fearful deracination it represented in his family's life took on its truest proportions in his comic strip. He left it to an outcast—his most isolated character, Spike, a gaunt, desert-hardened dog who lives abandoned in a wasteland outside that clearly unlonged-for community—to bring into focus the desert's peculiar immediacy and remoteness, its simultaneous double power to magnify the truth and shimmeringly to distance the viewer from harsh reality.

It always seemed strange to Sparky that, from the moment his relatives landed in the hot, dry climate that was intended to cure his tubercular cousin, no one ever mentioned the disease or took satisfaction in what appeared to be Howard's full recovery. Sparky himself never once saw Howard cough unduly or show any symptoms of consumption. Yet more strange for a boy with infected lungs, Howard was elected "yell leader" of the sophomore class at Needles High School in September 1929 and was also cast—from a "good number who turned out for tryouts," as the local paper reported—in a school play that was all about talking, Lawrence Grattan's *The Gossipy Sex.*

The contradictions of his mother's clan in the Southwest, like their defeats and disappointments in life along the Northwest frontier, remained a mystery that Charles Schulz never probed.

Dena prepared her son for the defeat that, she took for granted, an indifferent world would impose on his ambitions. When Sparky spoke up for himself, she put him in his place. (His coming through in the clutch at the Christmas play is an outstanding example of the family dynamic, but yet more telling is her deflating response to it.) Whenever he displayed aggressiveness, vitality, independence, spontaneity—those qualities that, in other words, brought out his enterprising male spirit—Dena undercut him, perhaps recognizing the very traits that, compounded with alcohol, had taken her brothers away from her mother. She may have wanted, first and foremost, to protect Sparky, lest those qualities destroy him, too. Or she may have been thinking of their small family of three. For if not nipped in the bud, the same free spirit, combined in Sparky's case with his father's quiet but unyielding ambition, could someday, she might logically have reasoned, carry her only son away from her and Carl into that larger world that she never tried to understand.

"Why is it that as soon as a person states his ambition, everyone tries to discourage him?" one of Schulz's strip characters would ask.

"Because you're stupid, that's why!" replies a sibling.

# PART TWO

# SON OF GOD

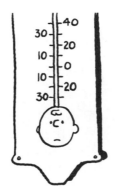

*The truth was that Jay Gatsby of West Egg,*
*Long Island, sprang from his Platonic conception*
*of himself. He was a son of God . . .*

F. SCOTT FITZGERALD, *THE GREAT GATSBY*

# CHAPTER 5

# DISGUISED

*My ordinary appearance was a perfect disguise.*
—CHARLES M. SCHULZ

HIS FATHER REPLANTED THEM in St. Paul, this time for keeps. "Security," Sparky wrote years later, "is having a home town."

In September 1931, after a summer of squeezing in among another set of Dena's relatives in Oak Park Heights alongside the St. Croix River, the Schulzes resumed city life. Carl reclaimed the lease on the Family Barber Shop at $75 per month, and was lucky to regain his place on the corner. The nation's hard times meant that hundreds of thousands of Minnesotans were out of work; St. Paul was not the same freewheeling town they had left in the summer of 1929.

Clannish St. Paul, a river city fringed by "shacks and chateaux," had turned suspicious in the 1930s. Denounced in editorials across the country as a "hotbed of crime," a "haven for criminals," the "poison spot of the nation," the "Saintly City" was turning firmly inward. Power resided in the churches and their ethnically defined congregations, with Roman Catholics holding sway over Lutherans in the city hierarchy.

High on the crest of Summit Hill, the Roman Catholic Cathedral of St. Paul climbed into the wide midwestern sky. Taller than the St. Paul architect Cass Gilbert's white marble-domed State Capitol, more extravagant than the red-stone Romanesque mansions built by nineteenth-century industrialists on the adjacent bluff overlooking the Mississippi, the three-thousand-seat church reached higher than any other building in the city. Its command of St. Paul's most prominent hill gave it an omnipotent and untouchable quality, exciting an already spooked working class into bigoted zealotry. Extremists among the city's Lutherans, including at least one aunt on Dena's side of the family, suspected the Roman Catholic prelates of storing an arsenal in the cathedral's catacombs, preparing for a seizure of power.

★  ★  ★

THE MAYFAIR APARTMENTS, A very un-British mass of flat-topped brown brick, stood on a corner where busy Snelling Avenue crossed Dayton, a quiet side street a block from the barbershop. A second-floor flat rented for only a dollar more per week than had the Palm Way bungalow in Needles, and Sparky had less than a hundred yards to walk to his formidable new school diagonally across Dayton Avenue.

The Sparky who entered fifth grade at the Richards Gordon Elementary School wore horn-rimmed glasses, knickers buckled at the knee, and an aviator's cap cinched tightly beneath his chin (all the other boys wore their earflaps loose). This odd simulacrum of a World War I flying ace had completed third grade in Needles the previous spring, but Mary Larkin, principal of Richards Gordon, pronouncing Charles Schulz exceptionally bright and fully prepared for Miss Kelly's B-5 class, skipped him over the fourth grade. It would be a fateful decision.

Once again he was called forward among his peers, only to be cast as the runt. By being promoted in standing, he had been demoted in stature. Some of his male classmates now had as much as six inches on him and fifth-grade girls towered over his head.

What would return most sharply when he looked back at Richards Gordon was a sense of being trapped where he was not appreciated. Size mattered in middle school. By seventh grade, it was not only classmates who dwarfed Sparky, it was the system itself. Seventh-grade boys were called upon to join the ranks of the school's leaders, the boys summoned at intervals from Miss Lynn's A-7 classroom to the principal's office for induction into the prestige and power of school safety patrol. The class stilled, all learning halted, as the chosen boy left the room. When he strutted back, made newly potent, all eyes registered his air of triumph and a "striking leather belt with an attached shoulder strap and a silver badge."

As the class applauded, the chosen boy underwent a moment of transformation that Schulz would never forget. "When I got called to the office, I was a nobody," reflects Charlie Brown. "Now, I'm a man with a badge!"

But Sparky himself was neither big enough nor forceful enough to qualify for safety patrol. He lived with his small body as with a handicap. Girls, deemed too weak for the job, were never chosen either; in school they were second-class citizens. So Sparky's smaller size not only devalued him as a boy, it made him, essentially, a girl.

His sole triumph was in penmanship, and even this he shared (again) with a girl. His hand was gifted with a smoothness and continuity that made him a natural for the gently inclined letters and symmetrical loops of the Palmer Method, introduced by A. N. Palmer in 1894 so that businessmen might combine the speed of cursive with the legibility of printing. Sparky was right-handed—another bit of good fortune, since the Palmer Method, which had become the most popular uniform style of penmanship taught in American schools, required left-handed pupils to switch hands. One day an important announcement came down from the principal's office to Miss Kelly's class. Charles Schulz and Lois Martin were to be honored with the Palmer Method pin and certificate. Lois, who sat at the desk beside Sparky's, would recall how their classmates snickered as the two were marched off to become the fifth grade's prissy Palmer exemplars.

ONCE HE TOOK PEN in hand, Charles Schulz was a standout. "All the way through school I could draw better [than] or as well as anyone in the class except for perhaps one or two others." For seventh-graders at Richards Gordon, art class alternated with music ("I used to just hate the days that we had music"); but even in art, drawing with pen and ink was deemed too advanced for the majority, and Sparky rarely got a chance to make letters in any medium more challenging than poster paints.

Nevertheless, drawing assignments did come his way, however infrequent and often trite. In January 1934, seventh-graders were told to render something they had seen over Christmas. Every student depicted a scene of children ice-skating on a frozen pond. Just as routinely, everybody drew a hole in the ice by placing a black spot of ink on the white paper. "It was traditional in Minnesota," Schulz reflected later, "that if you drew somebody skating on a pond you always drew a hole in the ice." And alongside the hole, the pupils just as routinely drew a sign dominating the pondscape with its warning: DANGER.

Sparky had never really examined a hole in the ice. His father's fishing trips to Mille Lacs were limited to spring or summer. But they had studied the comics together, and he knew that, with a single curved line and finessed shading, he could pull the viewer's eye not toward a spot of black ink on a page but into a ragged hole hacked into frozen water ten inches thick. Years later, he would remember his teacher's astonishment as she stood behind him, marveling that "Charles," alone among his classmates, had taught himself to evoke ice not as a glittering surface but as a solid mass.

In seventh grade, he found another opportunity to shine when Miss Lynn, setting the class to draw editorial cartoons for social studies, praised his contribution, but for some reason—perhaps, he later thought, intending to submit the class's work to a newspaper—handed the drawing to another pupil for the lines to be inked in more darkly. Insulted to the core at her insensitive, misconceived improvement, he still did not let on. "What a dumb thing to do," he said later, adding, "Sometimes teachers aren't very smart." And yet, "I didn't dare say anything." He might be boiling mad, but kept his anger undercover, an early but clear example of a lifetime inclination to conceal hurt and the harsher emotions that follow upon it, the better to brood upon them. He explained his inability to express frustration and anger in terms of a view of life that he came to call "removal of the lids":

> We are all pretty much what we are going to be early in our lives. Our personalities and characteristics are established, usually by the time we are five or six years old, but the lids are on. We are like boiling pots on a stove, and when we are small, the adults keep the lids on. As children, we cannot express ourselves the way we would like to, but as we grow older, the lids pop off, and the characteristics come out . . .

With his parents' help, he kept a lid on his intelligence. Meanwhile, he found safety in his plain, determinedly ordinary surroundings, relaxing into that part of himself that was authentically mild and cool, and concealing

Sparky so well behind the bland cover of Charles as to be certain that were he to cross paths with a schoolmate or teacher at some unexpected spot on the streets of St. Paul he would go unrecognized. How, he reasoned, could anyone find identifying details in so featureless a face? Charles Schulz later connected this fantasy—of total vengeful invisibility among people who should have been dazzled by his extraordinariness—with memories of shopping excursions with his mother.

He never recalled any actual moment in which a specific schoolmate or teacher had brushed past without taking notice, remembering only his surprise that anyone *could* recognize this "bland, stupid-looking kid." He liked to think that his face looked blank to the point of having no identity at all, and he was convinced that his "ordinary appearance was a perfect disguise."

He did not say why he needed a disguise, or what it was that appearing "ordinary" prevented people from seeing about him. A woman friend who in 1967 accompanied him on shopping excursions around San Francisco at the height of his early fame observed that "Sparky was a genius at becoming invisible." Above all, the disguise of ordinariness allowed him to test whether anyone saw him truly. Who would make the effort to brush away his crude self-belittlement to reveal the golden presence within?

He himself would assert only that there was "something wrong with somebody who has thoughts like that." He called it a "weird kind of thinking" and revealed that "it was this weird kind of thinking that prompted Charlie Brown's round, ordinary face"—a misleading description, of course; for it would take ongoing genius, more than "weird thinking," to anchor that enormous head in a real world.

Time and again, the authority figures of his childhood recognized Sparky as exceptional. His school principals singled him out from among dozens of children for rapid advancement and honors. Adults around him discerned his intellectual gifts. "His mind," according to one teacher, "was working every minute." He himself knew that he was "bright and conscientious during that period," but he did not feel valued.

"Dumb" was a word that Schulz used frequently when describing the authorities of his childhood. From relatives to gym teachers, no one was smart enough to see him for the boy he knew himself to be. Art teachers were "always pretty nice," but they frustrated him by "bringing the whole class down to the lowest denominator" with senseless projects that "just drove me out of my mind." His frustrations were "the teacher's fault." But, outside school, someone else was failing to pay attention as well.

Dena hardly seemed to notice when he failed arithmetic in seventh grade, a setback that shocked *him*. Up to that point, his marks had been excellent. A girl in his class sneaked a look at his final grade, reporting to another girl: "Hah! Charles got an E." To the jolt of his sudden, inexplicable fall was added the sting of their jeering. In eighth grade, he flunked algebra, Latin, and English, and still "no one said anything" at home. Neither of his parents went to talk to his teacher. He did not know why and put it out of his mind as soon as possible.

Sherman Plepler would later say of Sparky and his parents, "To me, it was a strange relationship. They were not very concerned about how he did in school. They never questioned why he was failing." Years later, asked how his parents felt about his report cards, Sparky could only allow himself to reply, "I never really knew. They never said anything to me. They were very nice people. They never got mad at me, and they never punished me for getting bad grades."

"He's a very understanding person," says Charlie Brown, when the school principal asks him what he thinks his father will say about the trouble he is in. "He won't condemn me . . . I don't think he'll say much . . . Mom is the same way."

His father chalked up the poor marks to a lack of curiosity, a rather conspicuous trait of his own. "If Sparky was interested in knowing something, he'd know it," said Carl. "Why, when he was ten or eleven, he could draw every president right out of the air without copying, and in order, too. And it would look just like them. That's how good he knew his presidents." Years later, asked about Sparky's failing grades by a writer for *The Saturday Evening Post*, Carl replied, "What do you mean? I always thought he did pretty well."

The school system that had pushed Sparky ahead as a smart kid now held him back as a dunce. He repeated eighth grade, and then, in the fall of 1936, moved up to Maria Sanford Junior High School, which stood three stories high on the west side of Cambridge Street between St. Paul's two great avenues, Summit and Grand—a long brick fortress, built in 1927, behind whose crenellated roofline and arched stone entryways all ninth-graders enrolled until Central High became a four-year school in 1943.

To Sparky, Maria Sanford felt "like a jail." Every moment of the day was regimented. Students attended classes on the platoon system: a bell rang, and everyone lined up quickly in the halls, a huge phonograph horn blaring march music as squads tramped from class to class. During rainstorms, he noticed that in the classroom, "with the lights on, and the rain and darkness outside, there [was] a sort of a medieval atmosphere." He characterized his teachers as "strict and harsh" and himself as "dumb and immature"; he certainly adapted to his new surroundings by failing "everything in sight." Yet, to his everlasting disgust, "Not one teacher *ever* called me to her desk and said, 'What seems to be the problem, Charles?' "

He was determined to believe that his teachers, like his relatives, were not smart enough to single him out as someone special; yet this obtuseness diminished them much less than it injured his pride. It also displaced the responsibility for discerning his uniqueness—and the hurtful consequences of failing to do so—from Carl, and especially from Dena. Again and again, he withdrew behind the appearance of humility into a hurt silence. One English assignment required him to write about Shakespeare, and it occurred to him that he could make some drawings to accompany the theme—but he held back, telling himself that it "wouldn't be fair, because the other kids in the class can't draw. So why should I take advantage of something I can do that they can't?"

In class the next day, he was dumbfounded to learn that another student—a boy not known to have artistic flair—had gone right ahead and illustrated his project, producing ten pictures in watercolor, which earned the teacher's highest praise. Somehow this other boy had not thought it wrong "to take advantage" of his abilities or indeed to awaken them where they had been unsuspected. Only Sparky seemed to believe that using an exceptional talent "was a rather egotistical thing to do."

After class, the teacher took Sparky aside. "Charles," she said, "why didn't *you* do something like that?"

Deeply surprised that she knew his secret, he stood sunk in embarrassment. Not merely did he give her no explanation, but, frightened to find his recognition fantasies coming true, he fell back onto playing dumb on a truly strategic basis: from then on, he rarely volunteered an answer in class and was stubbornly reluctant when called upon.

THE FAMILY BARBER SHOP was a safe place in uncertain times. With Carl back on the corner, Sparky could reclaim his special standing in the neighborhood. As the only son of a solvent businessman, he knew himself to be the exception among boys around Selby and Snelling. In the lean years of Charles Schulz's boyhood, out-of-work fathers were commonplace; serious pursuit of a job meant going wherever a man could find work that paid, even if to cities whose distance dictated long absences from home. "You didn't ask a guy where his father was," recalled Schulz's Minneapolis contemporary, the writer Samuel Hynes. "He might be crazy, or in jail, or dead."

Even during the great drought of 1934, when Carl's customers' scalps were sometimes crusted with the grainy dust that blew endlessly into the city—topsoil from the distant, plowed-under, and dried-out prairie—Carl managed to keep the family comparatively secure. On Friday evenings, he pulled the front shades, taking customers from the bench until as late as eight or nine. Saturdays he sometimes worked straight through till ten at night. From each twenty-five-cent haircut, he took home, by Sparky's recollection, a nickel. In fact, Carl had a greater share in the earnings at the Family Barber Shop than Sparky knew. As was customary, Carl, as boss, took the lion's share of every dollar produced by the work of his associate barbers; by the 1940s, his portion would reach as much as 65 percent.

Sparky gave no thought to money. "I never felt that I wanted for anything." His father gave him ice skates, hockey sticks, and a baseball glove, and he paid $4 a week over six weeks for a boy's bicycle. Sparky never thought of himself as being either poor or rich. When most of his cousins' families could not afford a car, the Schulzes drove a secondhand 1934 Ford; they sat down to three meals a day. Doctors and dentists lived in nicer houses farther out of town, he knew, but his parents lived with dignity, and he was proud of them. He had no awareness that the pancakes served at supper actually represented strict economy on his mother's part. Even when the Depression showed in Carl's earnings, forcing the family to move to a smaller apartment on the noisier Snelling Avenue side of the Mayfair, Sparky did not feel deprived.

But as Sparky grew older, Carl deflated his son's sense of specialness. In the Family Barber Shop's pecking order, customers came first. Throughout the Depression years, if a regular came in while Sparky was in his father's chair, Sparky had to step down so that Carl could turn his full charm and attention on the paying presence, apparently indifferent to—indeed, it seemed to Sparky, unaware of—the ridiculous state in which he had left his son. When the customer vacated the chair, Carl would always finish the job, but by then, having been relegated to wait stiffly on the bench with "half a haircut," Sparky felt half-butchered.

One of Carl's associates in the 1930s, Lloyd Neumann, judged Sparky to be a potentially very presentable kid but also noticed that his father gave him awkward haircuts. "He used to cut his hair so funny that he never was good-looking." Carl seemed to be letting the boy know that he had better not think too well of himself, had better not let his special status as the barber's son literally go to his head—and just as literally cut him down to size.

Sparky later recalled that his father never once struck him. Carl seldom became openly angry, though he did not hesitate to deflate Sparky's grander feelings and impulses: "Put a lid on it" or "Sometimes it's good not to talk too much—people put you down as bragging" or, simply but tellingly, "Don't get a big head."

Carl equated achievement with egotistical display. He did not want people thinking him extravagant in anything except perhaps self-effacement, and this cast of mind he passed on to his son. "I've always had the fear of being ostentatious—of people thinking that these things have gone to my head," Charles Schulz said later. "I didn't want to be accused of thinking I was better than I really was." All his adult life he tried to keep his head from being turned by his achievement.

The same code that made him put caution and humility above vitality and self-confidence applied equally to art. When asked why he did not want to be called an artist, he would explain with an image from trench warfare, "I don't want to stick my head up too high."

It was always the head that was threatened by bigness. In this, the Schulzes were representative of a culture in which it was impertinent to express one's uniqueness and talent. The plain people of Minnesota dreaded self-aggrandizement. "It was part of being a Minnesotan," recalled a friend of Sparky's. "You didn't think well of yourself, and if you did, you didn't show it." You didn't show it because the Minnesota of Sparky's childhood was a tall-poppy culture that struck the heads off its brightest flowers. Lutheranism, which teaches harsh self-discipline, tends to be defined by the idea of the tall poppy. The term originates from Roman tradition and mingles coincidentally with the history of barbering, which recalls the introduction of the razor to ancient Romans by the first of the Tarquin kings, the last of whom, Tarquinius Superbus (534–510 BC), asked his father how he should rule the recently conquered city of Gabii. The old king rose and silently led his son through the garden, lopping the heads off the tallest poppies.

Sparky's father, meanwhile, lopped the hair off his son's head, and later, one of Sparky's strip characters would cry to a friend whose own father was responding to the rising cost of haircuts by planning to cut his son's hair himself at home, "I hope he cuts your ears off!"

Carl had no use for what went on inside a head. "Customers usually do not wish to delve into a knotty problem" went the wisdom of the trade. Barbers should "choose a subject about which it is easy to make a few passing remarks. Most customers would rather relax and talk in a lighter vein than to [sic] become involved in a philosophical discussion." Carl considered thinking itself an extravagance—even a danger. "If you read too many books," he cautioned, "your head will fall off."

The warning sank in. "When I try to read books on subjects like psychology," Charles Schulz declared, "the words just pass right through as though I had a glass head." In later life, he met and compared notes with Umberto Eco, but came to their meeting already "sure that . . . I'm in over my head"—just as he liked to say that he had "got in over my head" by skipping the fourth grade, a grimly vigilant self-deprecation that he would summarize at the very end of his life in words that extended far beyond his unwillingness to be seen as an artist: "You don't want to feel too good about yourself, and you don't want to put your head up too high, because then you could be shot down."

One day Charles Schulz would create a character with a big head.

He would, moreover, place that big head on a child's body, where it was unthreatening. And he would delineate the character as a determined, strong-willed, yet almost willfully ineffectual boy who would make himself known to the world as a loser but who would dream of becoming, among other things, president of the United States, a five-star general, and a "big-time operator." One or two of the boy's companions would encourage him in his "big" thinking, only to turn right around and laugh in his face when he admitted to the full grandeur of his ambitions. His own father told him that he might be able to run for president someday but probably wouldn't get the father's vote.

INTELLIGENCE WAS NOT PRIZED in boys in the Minnesota of Schulz's upbringing; it was punished by bigger boys and scorned by desirable girls. "You're so intelligent, and I'm so tired of it all," a girl snaps at a bespectacled, bookish boy—first in the rough sketch for a cartoon gag that an older Sparky Schulz would try on *The Saturday Evening Post* and then recast for his first comic feature, *Li'l Folks*.

Learning was not honored at home. And not just learning, plain intellectual activity—even the kind that went in those days with bridge, Mah-Jongg, *Gone With the Wind* as a book, and Sunday-supplement science. "There was no driving pursuit of education in our family," he later wrote. There were few, if any, books in the Schulz house. "I don't recall my dad ever reading a book." His mother came from a family whose first American generation had owned only one book, even if it read that one rigorously: the Holy Bible.

Sparky taught himself to read for pleasure. His fondness for books reached back to the little blue readers that had thrilled him in first grade. In school, he had also discovered Mary Mapes Dodge's classic, *Hans Brinker: or, The Silver Skates* and decided at the benchmark age of six that he read "pretty well"—so well that he grew impatient with classmates who could not read as fast as he. Yet he never showed impatience with his parents. If he were going to improve his mind, he would have to find his way to books on his own. Week after week, he clipped newspaper coupons and redeemed them at Sheady's drugstore until he had amassed every volume of a cheap encyclopedia.

He also taught himself basic social skills. Conversation was not practiced at home. When any of Dena's relatives dropped in, they would cluster around the kitchen table, the men overdressed for the city, the women fragrant with talcum. The visit would proceed by speculative nods over folded arms. No one spoke about himself. A man's car or truck would be the most personal subject about which he could be asked to talk. The supreme test of a car was whether you could drive it up a hill in what the relatives called "high." "Schulz, could you make it up the hill in high?" the men would ask, and Carl would nod and say, yes, the Ford could make it up any kind of a hill without having to shift into second gear—the '34 Ford had eight cylinders. And everyone would fold his arms and nod.

Pulled into this bobble-headed group, Sparky would open his ears, dismayed. "Sometimes the conversations were very dull. I could never figure out why the conversations weren't more animated." His cousin Shirley Gish VonderHaar, had the same impression of Sparky's family. Visiting the Schulzes, she said, "It was hard to build up a close relationship. When you got together with them, if you didn't do the talking, then no one would talk. They would just sit there with their arms folded."

Shirley's mother, Josie Bredahl Gish, was Dena's first cousin; both were reserved almost to the point of paralysis. "It was hard for them to express themselves," said Shirley. "If you tried to kiss my mother on the cheek, she'd turn away from you. She didn't mean to, she just didn't know how to respond."

Returning from a family reunion, one of Schulz's strip characters lamented, "What a disappointment! None of us spoke the same language! We were all strangers."

Charles Schulz was gripped by the lifelong fear of being a bore. In years to come he would often say, "I am always afraid when I'm around other people that I'm going to say things so drab and dull, I'll bore the whole crowd." But it was *he* who had been bored; his uneducated relatives bored him, just as his parents' semiliteracy frightened him.

Charles Schulz saw himself as bland, even as "blank," but it was not he who was featureless, it was the world he grew up in—flat, impoverished in language, stricken by silences, stripped to essentials, or less. "Speech is civilization itself," wrote Thomas Mann. "The word, even the most con-tradictious word, preserves contact—it is silence which isolates."

When Sparky's family sat down to visit with out-of-town relatives, they were sealed off. The radio, which became part of the Schulz household in the 1930s, broke that silence, offering overheard conversation, a common culture. Radio trained Sparky's ear for spoken dialogue and the individual-ized note of one person talking to another. His shyness, too, was gratified by radio, as was his family's. People so withdrawn found it satisfying to have contact with human beings they were never going to meet. One night, when Carl and Dena had taken Sparky to the movies, they had a brief dis-cussion, then turned to Sparky: "Which would you rather do, see the rest of the movie, or go home and listen to *Amos 'n' Andy?*" For all that he adored the movies and their immense glamour, Sparky voted for the more intimate world created by Freeman F. Gosden and Charles J. Correll.

Six nights a week, at seven o'clock, the Schulzes tuned in along with some forty million Americans—about a third of the nation paused while preparing supper—to hear the continuing story of Amos Jones and Andy Brown, black farmhands from rural Georgia who had come to Chicago's South Side as part of the Great Migration of African Americans. Compared at the time to blackface minstrel shows and accused in later years of racial ste-reotyping, *Amos 'n' Andy* partook of both elements, but it also offered some-thing new in American entertainment—a realistic comic strip of the air.

The secret of the show's success was that Gosden and Correll had cre-ated characters, not gags. Taking two of the most popular elements from newspaper comics, they merged, for the first time in the broadcast medium, recurring characters with continuous story lines. Amos and Andy became real people, bendable but not breakable—beloved by the audience in ways that no minstrel entertainers had ever been. People everywhere, black and white, recognized someone they knew in Amos Jones or Andy Brown. Attending to their daily lives and struggles, keeping time by a steady tempo of brief epiphanies and small incidents, each tiny audience huddled around its radio set cumulatively felt the sheer ongoing vitality of life.

WHEN FAMILY OR FRIENDS visited at the Mayfair Apartments, Sparky was allowed to remain aloof at his drawing—although Carl, who regularly put himself out to drive over to South Minneapolis so that Ellen and Charlotte Carlson, widow and daughter of his former partner, could join such special occasions as birthdays and Sunday suppers, sharply remonstrated with him. Charlotte Carlson always remembered Sparky sitting by himself in the corner when they arrived, his nose practically touching his scrap of drawing paper, even as "people were trying to get him to enter more into the conversation and into the group. His mother was always protective of him. 'Let him alone!' she would say."

Other cousins remembered young Sparky doodling randomly anywhere and at any time—in the backyard while visiting, in a corner by himself when everyone else was playing, even on more formal occasions such as family wedding receptions: "always drawing something with a pencil." Indeed, he carried a sharpened pencil everywhere he went. But he never acted the artist; he just scribbled away as if he were incapable of doing anything else. A dozen times a day, he pulled out his pencil, made a fast doodle, and put the pencil back. His cousin Donald Gish, up in Little Falls, Minnesota, recalled pulling on his first pair of long pants—hand-me-downs from Cousin Sparky in St. Paul—and discovering a hole in the right-side pocket.

The Norwegian clan forced upon him rivals against whom he had to prove himself. The family would remember Reuben Helgeson for his popularity and mechanical talent. "Everybody liked Reuben." One Sunday when Sparky was ten, on a family outing to the Helgesons in Wisconsin, Reuben had become the supreme object of everyone's attention by making a drawing of a man sitting on a log. Sparky and his parents—and what had seemed like his mother's entire extended clan—had gathered around. Everyone had spoken well of the drawing, an unusual occurrence among his unappreciative relatives. Anything notable enough to halt general conversation and gather the room's interest was in great danger of becoming the object of sarcasm or pointed silence. Then it had been Sparky's turn to admire his cousin's drawing. "That's nice," he had said, while concealing the more fundamental assessment: *What's so great about that? It's good, but it's not that good. I could do that.*

Before that day, Sparky would not have thought to subject his own scribblings to the mockery of a family gathering. "It never occurred to me that I could draw these things. I didn't really know at the time the joy of drawing or what you really could do with it."

Similarly—on another family outing, this time to the Swansons in Hudson, Wisconsin—his older cousin Raymond showed Sparky the cover of the loose-leaf binder issued to him at school, on which he had drawn a bronco rider. Neither Raymond nor Sparky could conceal their excitement over the nearly subversive act of defacing school property. "Why hadn't I ever thought of drawing something on the cover of a loose-leaf binder? All of a sudden it occurred to me I could do that."

So much of what followed in later years can be ascribed to these moments of suddenly assertive self-belief: he could draw—and draw better than his unwitting rivals. Armed with Cousin Raymond's idea and Disney's prestige, he won his first popularity at Richards Gordon School by putting such characters as Mickey Mouse and the Three Little Pigs on his classmates' binders. The demand both pleased and unnerved him—the drawings were his but not his—and he would later compare his classmates to autograph seekers. But by admitting that he wanted the special status that cartooning could bring (and which he felt to be somehow already his), he became conscious not only of his desire but of his will.

THE UNSPOKEN TRUTH WAS that he was smarter than his parents. Carl and Dena trusted in material goods, handmade objects, craftsmanship—things well done. Carl was a stolid mixture of the conventional and the independent. "My philosophy," he would say, "is that the whole thing in life is doing what you like to do." What Carl liked to do was work. He believed that native intelligence should be used to earn a living and get ahead. Who had time to sit around listening to the radio? Even the Sunday ritual of following the strips with Sparky could be cumbersome. "I was awful glad when he got old enough to read the comics himself," Carl would say in later years. "It made things easier."

When Carl set out to be naturalized in 1935, at the age of thirty-seven, he called on his twelve-year-old to help prepare for the citizenship test. In 1940, when elected secretary-treasurer of the state organization of Associated Master Barbers and Beauticians, he struggled with the job; ill-equipped to handle paperwork, he enlisted Sparky to render the barely decipherable scrawled notes that he brought home from meetings into standard English and legible Palmer script. "I usually grumbled," Sparky recalled, "but I always did it." He never took credit for this assistance, but in his work, Charles Schulz would record the anguish of a barber's son guiltily stricken by his father's struggles. Charlie Brown remembers how hard his father worked to give the family a respectable life and how it felt to see tears running down his father's cheeks when he read letters in the newspaper attacking barbers for raising the price of a haircut—until, frantic with the memories, he grabs Schroeder's shirt with both hands and screams, "YOU DON'T KNOW WHAT IT'S LIKE!!"

Sparky protectively explained away his parents' limitations by emphasizing how early their schooling had been cut off or how Carl had overcome his deficiencies through the redemptive power of work. He liked to tell how his father, with only the beginnings of a grammar-school education, had made the grade as an independent entrepreneur. "That took a lot of ambition," Charles Schulz would say. "And it was simply the lack of education that kept him from going even farther"—as far, even, he liked to think, as the State Senate.

But more than lack of education, the real deficiency lay in a lack of curiosity. As adults, his parents had quit learning—quit asking—altogether. Carl was self-made but not self-educated. Even during the Depression, he could give Sparky a new toy or piece of sports equipment, but it did not occur to him to see that his son had music in his life. "Sparky stated many times that he wished that he had been taught an instrument," recalled his violin-playing friend Sherman Plepler.

Schulz later described Charlie Brown as a "very decent, caring little boy" whose trouble in life came from the fact that "he is surrounded by people who don't have any idea what's going on." Neither Carl nor Dena was confident enough to investigate the cultural world or to feel comfortable with what Carl called "good reading stuff." His grandmother's thinking was shot through with superstition and the Old World certainty that luck angers the gods. Sophia Halverson shied from any piece of good fortune, certain that misfortune must follow: "If you're too happy today, something bad will happen to you tomorrow"; indeed, "If you laugh at the dinner table, you'll cry before bed."

He challenged his Norse grandmother with the language of the new country, playing a game in which he was the teacher, she the pupil—grandson, after all, outranking grandmother as a native in the adopted country. Standing at his childhood blackboard, he would subject his unschooled elder to elementary spelling tests, slapping Sophia with a failing grade when she rendered "know" as "no."

And yet, in the first panel of the strip above, was it a marvelous misspelling—or unconscious malice on Schulz's part—to render "vale" as "veil"?

Sparky had the upper hand in following sports and at the movies, too. As the Minneapolis golfer Patty Berg rose to prominence as a young amateur in the 1930s, Sophia followed her victories in the newspapers, although, Sparky remembered, "She had to ask me which was the better score, a high one or a low one." On the nights when Carl and Dena went out, Sophia would take Sparky to the Park Theatre, around the corner on Selby. The program would begin with a comedy short, then Movietone News would run a newsreel that closed with the words "The End," at which point Sparky was always afraid that his grandmother would think that the whole show was over and get up to leave. Each time, he would turn to her and whisper, "That just means the newsreel is over, Gramma. The real show is still coming."

"Yes, I know," Sophia always answered with commendable restraint.

No matter how often they performed this routine, Sparky never trusted the old Norwegian woman to have mastered the usages of the American movie house. "It took me about forty years to realize that Gramma was a lot smarter than I thought she was."

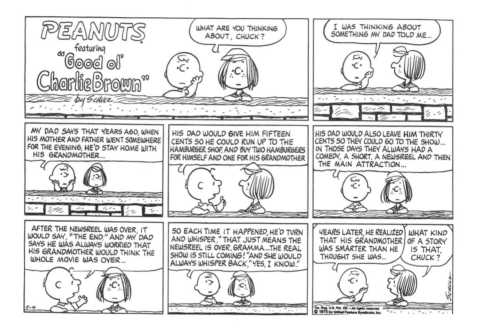

The relative Sparky identified with was his mother's youngest sister, Marion. She knew how to talk. A sensitive conversationalist with children and adults alike, she could exchange views on almost any topic. She herself had gotten no further than sixth grade, but was not intimidated by intelligence in others and married a man with an IQ of 182. In the Halverson clan, it was well known that the kindly Marion was "death" on one institution: "There was nobody more against the Catholic Church than Marion," who routinely referred to the Sovereign Pontiff as "the Poop." But of all the relatives, Marion was also the most interested in books. "She had a great mind, was always reading," recalled her daughter-in-law. "When she read Rachel Carson's *Silent Spring*, she talked about nothing else." In 1952 she joined the Great Books and Great Ideas programs started by the Columbia professor Mortimer Adler; visiting with other subscribers for discussions in one another's homes, she was the one who energized the group. Not surprisingly, she was also the relative who accepted and, most of all, understood Sparky. "Marion was never condemning," he said; she was a bright spot in a dim world that did not believe in him. More than anyone else in the Halverson tribe, Marion reassured him that he was both lovable and deserving of love.

ON HIS ELEVENTH BIRTHDAY, when Dena took him clothes shopping, he found *How to Draw Cartoons*, by that master of the single-frame serial, Clare Briggs, who had died not long before. This was a more sophisticated manual than the dime-store handbook he had bought in Needles, the essentials of the craft being illustrated by examples from Briggs's long-running motto series, including *When a Feller Needs a Friend*, nostalgically depicting small-town incidents in which good-hearted boys find themselves subjected to life's painful moments of embarrassment, humiliation, frustration, and downright fear. The scenarios are standard—one boy mocked for using his little sister's sled, another humiliated when his mother and a saleslady openly discuss trying on new underwear in the aisle of a department store—but the undercurrent of real sadness in each vignette arises from the unspoken absence of fathers and reinforcing older males.

Schulz studied the text, copying Briggs's examples, which drew on the leading cartoonists of the 1920s and '30s. He sized up pen lines: Thomas A. ("Tad") Dorgan's tight crosshatch; Winsor McCay's fantastic vanishing points; Harold Webster's hairline figures; the loose, freehanded loops and stitches with which Percy Crosby chronicled *Skippy*, like a wooden spool paying out black thread; Frank King's simple, mirror-vivid unfolding of everyday life, as well as his exuberant experiments in fantasy and parody, which rendered the home folks of *Gasoline Alley* in the dynamic excesses of modernism, German expressionism, woodcut, and surrealism, idioms to which his consumers were for the most part unexposed, and therefore more reactive.

"From that point on," Sparky said, "I was totally fascinated by the style[s] of drawing that different people had."

He became in his own eyes a formal student of this compelling skill, and as soon as the family returned to St. Paul, he biked to the public library and pulled down from its stained-maple shelves any book with a pen-and-ink cartoon in it.

# CHAPTER 6

# ORDINARY JOES

*In the Thirties and Forties when I was growing up, the cartoonist occupied a place in the cultural hierarchy not far below that of the movie star and the inventor.*

—JOHN UPDIKE

THE COMICS WERE AMERICA'S first transcontinental medium of entertainment, preceded only by the serial novel, the illustrated magazine, and the printed popular song. In 1902, William Randolph Hearst, the flamboyant thirty-three-year-old owner of the *New York Morning Journal*, himself a bit of a cartoon—big man, small voice—hit on the ingenious idea of increasing net revenues by selling other newspaper owners the right to reproduce his comic strips in a hundred other cities simultaneously.

This mass-market appeal, to become known as syndication, made comics a national institution and the Sunday comics a fought-over fixture in family life. Syndicates—agencies determined to supply every city, town, and village newspaper in the United States and Canada with comic features, articles, and photographs—redefined the identity of local sheets. As *The New Yorker*'s press critic Robert Benchley lamented in 1932, the most popular newspaper in any given city was no longer the one that offered the best balance of national news and local features, but "the one which carries the syndicated comic strip—*The Gumps*."

With a market as vast as even one-half of the nation to satisfy, syndicated comics had to be all things to all people. Strips diversified. Early readers had recognized idiosyncratic types—Frederick Burr Opper's well-meaning idiot, *Happy Hooligan*; Rube Goldberg's foolish innocent, *Boob McNutt*; Rudolph Dirks's rowdy rascals, *The Katzenjammer Kids*; George McManus's diamond-in-the-rough ex-bricklayer, Jiggs, and his *Social Register* wannabe Maggie. However, the '20s and '30s readership identified with entire types of comic—domestic strips like *The Gumps, Gasoline*

*Alley*, and *Blondie*; "married" strips such as *Bringing Up Father, Mr. and Mrs.*, and *The Timid Soul*; "girl" strips like *Ella Cinders, Fritzi Ritz, Winnie Winkle*, and *Betty*; adventure strips like *Terry and the Pirates, Joe Palooka*, and *Mickey Finn*; and "hillbilly" strips such as *Li'l Abner* and *Snuffy Smith*. As syndicates competed, they rarely tried out new characters, instead playing it safe by duplicating a rival's success in a new genre such as science fiction with a space opera of their own. Thus, *Buck Rogers* begat *Flash Gordon* . . .

By the mid-1930s, Sunday comics sections had ballooned from the standard eight pages of the 1920s to sixteen pages, and sometimes thirty-two. Seven major syndicates and two hundred cartoonists divided among them (mostly fifty-fifty) the greater part of the profits from an $8-million-a-year industry. If $10,000 had been a huge salary for a star cartoonist before syndication took firm hold in 1912, then by 1916 the consistency and demands of production—313 daily strips and fifty-two Sunday pages each year—made $150,000 ($1.8 million now) realistic take-home pay for a syndicated comic strip artist who, above all, was expected to please everybody everywhere all the time.

The power of syndication derived from the simultaneity and range with which the individual cartoonist could broadcast an idea. Such glamour as resided in the business lay in the major cartoonists' image as regular guys, Cinderella spokesmen for the common man, who happened to be earning salaries greater than that of the president of the United States. As Babe Ruth said of a similar disparity with Herbert Hoover in 1931, "I had a better year."

Readers believed that the men behind the strips were ordinary Joes blessed with perseverance and humor—basement tinkerers in gags and laughs. Henry Conway Fisher, the medium's first millionaire, creator of *Mutt and Jeff*, was always "Bud" Fisher. Tailoring the talent to mirror the tastes of a young, striving audience, the plain-sense practical managers at the syndicates all but ordered their cartoonists to stay down on the farm: "Only by retaining this commonness amidst great wealth, like Jiggs in *Bringing Up Father*, can they avoid the occupational diseases of the comic-strip business." According to United Feature Syndicate, the worst pitfalls for a citified cartoonist were "big-headedness, boredom, brain-fag, [and] the bottle."

Syndication had liberated the profession from the bullpen at the back of a metropolitan daily newsroom, where city editors literally fenced their ink-stained wretches to pen the day's batch before they got too drunk to meet a deadline. Now the truly successful cartoonist could work anywhere he liked; if in two months he was able to produce a year's releases, "he can take a trip around the world, go to Florida for the winter, or travel far into the woods on a hunting trip," as one 1926 manual advertised the good life to those entertaining such ambitions. But lest such aspirants vanish up the Amazon like so many Teddy Roosevelts, they were put on abrupt warning by United Feature Syndicate's managing editor, William Lass: "No comic artist can afford to sever his umbilical cord to the belly of the common people."

And it was in the mind of those "common" readers that the most masterful cartoonists created the medium's grand illusion: without actually knowing very much at all about any comic's characters, each reader felt a deep sense of intimate contact. The best-drawn members of the cast served as vivid projections against which the most casual onlooker could burn bits and pieces of himself and those around him. Comic types contracted into manageable space the characteristics of relatives, friends, neighbors, and bosses, exposing to their readerships their own appetites and weaknesses, and made it safe to laugh them off. Even those who did not read the comics somehow absorbed the names, personalities, and traits of comic strip heroes. "Jiggs and Mutt-and-Jeff and Skinnay and the Gumps have entered into our existence as definitely as Roosevelt and more deeply than Pickwick," wrote one critic in the 1920s.

Comics were rooted in character and its flaws, the most beloved of their inhabitants being the ones most recognizably deficient. The very name of Caspar Milquetoast, the radically timid soul whom Harold Webster introduced in 1925, entered a language of universal types. To call someone a "Milquetoast" was as identifying as to say he was a Scrooge or a Lothario, a Pollyanna or a Hamlet.

The daily reader's relationship to a cherished character proved unique in the thinking world of playgoers and novel readers. The aficionado of a strip saw his favorites not as actors limited to a fictive world that shut down when the morning edition wrapped the garbage but as ongoing partners in his own experience. And, unlike the presiding figures of some classic read long ago, here were presences fresh every day with the season's fads and phrases on their lips.

The comics that evoked personal identification were driven by compulsions and crusades: Wimpy's finagling of burgers, Batman's unending mission to rid the world of evil. Even the stock melodrama of Orphan Annie's plucky self-reliance in the face of endless danger made an exemplar of being true to oneself; e. e. cummings would explain the unexplainable—Krazy Kat's immortal love for Ignatz Mouse—by saying, "Krazy is herself."

Comics had no need to put character to some final, conclusive test; even seemingly self-contained episodes in adventure strips need have no substantial outcome. Like radio serials in the '30s and television soap operas in the '60s and '70s, comic strips opened onto worlds that could not be *allowed* to come to a full stop—the compulsive quality of its "endless art" possessed something of the time suspension found in hypnosis. But a work of art, Aristotle prescribes, must have a beginning, a middle, and an end. Comics and their creators cheated time. Only *Gasoline Alley* let its characters grow up. The childhood of Orphan Annie was prolonged decade after decade. Every boy in the comics was more or less a Peter Pan—from Mickey Dugan, Richard Outcault's *Yellow Kid* ur-brat, to the endearing scamp Skippy, by way of Ernie Bushmiller's pug-nosed Sluggo. Any character could be prolonged indefinitely, a younger cartoonist hired to take up where a retiring master left off.

The charm of a strip as artfully drawn as *Krazy Kat* was that it would never resolve itself. The essential action—a cat loves a mouse who rejects the cat who is loved by a dog who, always a bit too late, polices the mouse, as each day the mouse tries to test the cat's love (or his own power) by bouncing a brick off the cat's head—could, and if possible would, go on forever. George Herriman initiated a kind of immortality by creating a world of highly repetitive forms, which, through daily, weekly, and annual patterning, made the familiar infinite. Considered abstractly, this ought to have been a bore; comic strips with their serial and cyclical patterns ought to have grown stale. But each day came a new twist, and like all really artful change-ringing, the endless escape into novelty within a deliberately restricted form generated its own compelling force. Character, expressed through issues repeatedly left unresolved, each day invited readers to renew their interest: how would Ignatz Mouse attempt to knock Krazy Kat out of her happy fantasy *this time*?

The strip's artistic supremacy was rooted in a powerful continuity of draftsmanship. The readership didn't so much know about the characters as it experienced the artistry with which Herriman drew the dead-end desert landscapes against which Krazy's passion for Ignatz was endlessly renewed. It was an optical, not an intellectual, world into which the reader had entered, a world in which night was interchangeable with day, and love always found itself overridden by malice whose very misery was thereupon transmuted—with a ZIP! and a POW! and a flock of hovering hearts—to loopy joy.

Many readers, puzzled by Herriman's lyrical wordplay, ethereal fancies, and androgynous heroine, plain did not understand *Krazy Kat* and complained to the Hearst newspapers, whose editors forwarded the complaints to the boss, who remained steadfast. Herriman had been the *San Francisco Examiner*'s first circulation-building cartoonist. No matter how many readers didn't get him, Hearst ran Herriman in all his Sunday arts sections and inserted a four-minute animated cartoon short of *Krazy* into his International Film Service newsreels. Several full-length adaptations reached the screen, and in 1922, John Alden Carpenter staged a *Krazy Kat* ballet at Town Hall in New York.

Many forms of entertainment invented in America have first been stereotyped and dismissed (often accurately) as crude, only to win popular recognition after the first immense, untouchable record breaker has appeared: Henry Ford for the automobile, Chaplin for the movies, Babe Ruth for baseball, Charles Lindbergh for aviation, Louis Armstrong for jazz. Yet the comics still lacked a single towering force who could fuse commerce with art.

Critics anointed Herriman the only great artist in his field, but no matter how original and aesthetically pleasing, Herriman could not become the Sultan of the Strips. Even at the height of its popularity, *Krazy Kat* never ran in more than 40 newspapers; by the end of the '30s, Chic Young's *Blondie* was appearing in as many as 850. Well paid as Herriman was, his weekly earnings amounted to less than half the $1,600 earned by *The Gumps*' Sidney Smith. Timid and solitary, Herriman did not want to be an industry powerhouse. A lifetime contract with Hearst sheltered him from marketplace concerns and a fickle public. However intriguing to intellectuals, his feature never became a franchise.

But what would happen when a cartoonist combined the commercial pull of a *Buster Brown* and the artistry of a Herriman? And then went further by speaking not just to the young and the newly arrived but to all people? The comics awaited, as critic Gilbert Seldes put it in 1924, "a universal genius."

FOR A SCHOOLBOY IN St. Paul, wasting time on the comics sections was considered, at best, a guilty pleasure. Studying the comics was crackbrained and probably self-destructive, and *drawing* cartoons was all but degenerate. "Having the ambition to do a comic strip was such a far-out ambition that at that time," Sparky recalled, "it was considered almost like going to the moon." If he told any of his mother's contemporaries that he was going to be a syndicated cartoonist, the answer was, "That's nice. Tell me about it later. I'm running errands."

"Nobody knew how even to talk about it."

If comics were for children, immigrants, laborers, and uneducated dimwits, as the backbone of the country believed, then people like Carl and Dena Schulz and their neighbors would naturally have wanted to wash their hands of them as soon as possible.

At home, Sparky drew on soft, yellowing paper removed a page at a time, with his mother's permission, from an unused scrapbook. Pricey artstore supplies did not fall within the family's Depression budget; he would have to wait until he was earning $9 a week as a grocery clerk to work with Bristol board and Higgins India ink and Craftint doubletone. Meanwhile he experimented on his father's limited supply of laundry cardboards (Carl sent out only white shirts); although the backings offered a tantalizingly slick cream surface for his pen line, immediately beneath lay a pulpy layer of cardboard into which India ink tended to spread.

He drew by imitating the features in the St. Paul and Minneapolis newspapers, learning to draw with his eyes, relishing the stark contrast in the colorless pages of the daily newspaper—the beautiful, wintry world of black and white. As he ran his eye over each of the features, his gaze would follow the crisp pen strokes and ultrasharp silhouetted figures that leaped from Lyman Young's brand-new adventure strip, *Tim Tyler's Luck*.

He liked Young's realistic settings, which offered precisely drawn panoramas and deep perspectives along the decks of ships at sea. He admired the way Young's shadow treatment of an African lion or a black panther made every flank of the beast sinister with power. He copied Young's simplified forms, learning with his hand how cartoonists obtain their effects.

His favorite feature was the adventure strip *Buck Rogers in the 25th Century A.D.* Created by John Dille, a syndicate editor, and drawn by Lt. Richard Calkins, U.S. Army, and a team of consulting scientists, *Buck Rogers* had just made the jump from the daily editions to the Sunday supplements. The big color format showed Sparky how lovingly Calkins drew the warm and familiar details of everyday life to heighten the eerie otherness of a cold universe in which Asian warlords have conquered America.

He made a thorough investigation of Walt Disney's characters and tried to copy the craftsmanship and finish of Elzie Crisler Segar's *Thimble Theatre*, featuring Popeye. In 1934, the eleven-year-old Sparky bought what is alleged to be the very first comic book—*Famous Funnies*, a ten-cent anthology of reprints from the syndicated strips. Four years later, he shifted allegiance overnight to a new caped hero whose name was not yet well enough known to be featured on the cover of *Action Comics #1*—Superman.

Here was an extraordinary being who masked his superiority to ordinary mortals behind a mild manner, a regular face, horn-rimmed glasses, and a name that sounded as sissified as "Charles." But no matter how shy and clumsy Superman tried to be as "Clark," no matter how many humiliations he endured under the cover of a journalistic Milquetoast, his true potency had to make itself felt. Superman was a castaway from another world, Krypton. His plain, ordinary adoptive parents were kindhearted custodians who knew how to plant crops, fatten animals, and wait for rain, but not how to guide a boy who could leap tall buildings in a single bound. Yet it was with their upright, modest dignity that Superman survived life as Clark Kent.

In 1936 Carl moved the family from Mayfair Apartments to a small rented bungalow down the block, at 1602 Dayton Avenue, where Sparky learned to share a bedroom with his grandmother when Sophia Halverson, as she periodically did, returned from household stints with each of her children in California to move in with the Schulzes. She snored. Night after night when he was in eighth grade, Sparky was kept awake by his grandmother's snoring. Dena tried to make it up to the boy by relaxing the household's strict rule against using the dining room table for drawing. But before he could open his ink bottle, he had to fold and carefully lay away the well-starched tablecloth and fancy coverlet that Dena herself had crocheted, and then put down newspaper.

Here his neatness came in handy. Cartooning was a fastidious medium, the trickiest part coming just before a drawing got finished. As the thick black ink glistened on a sheet of cotton rag paper bought at Scott's five-and-dime on Snelling Avenue, the work had to be completed without brushing the still-wet lines with his sleeve or dropping a fresh blot onto a dry detail.

Having dutifully put away the table arrangements, he would bend over the paper, tense, almost sick with excitement, as his pen followed the arched back of the panther threatening Tim Tyler last Sunday. Sometimes he drifted just far enough outside the forms of the cartoonist he was imitating to find himself watching in surprise as his pen point twisted a mouth or curved an eyebrow in a way that seemed somehow distinctively his. But design, proportions, pacing still belonged to the masters, and his drawings still lacked the professionalism that he was ever more aware of pursuing. The worst of it was that, when he was done, he never quite knew what to do with these crude, disenfranchised derivatives.

EACH YEAR WHEN ONE of the professional ice shows came to St. Paul, students in ninth grade at Maria Sanford Junior High School could compete for free tickets by creating posters to advertise it; each, almost without exception, reproduced standard male or female skaters twirling on the ice. Sparky, now expert at drawing Popeye, who had never resorted to skates in his official adventures, set out to put the Sailor Man himself on ice. This, he thought, was catchy—more interesting, at any rate, than the poster that Stanley Loeffler, the rather businesslike boy seated next to him, had drawn of a polar bear coming out of an igloo. "What in the world," Sparky said to himself, "does that have to do with an ice show?" His own poster sparkled with show-business flair. His clean lettering, "much superior to all the others," gave him further confidence, and several of his classmates were enthusiastic, telling him that he was the sure winner. But the judges put aside run-of-the-mill skating activities and rewarded the unsettling originality of Stanley Loeffler's bear.

"It was a good lesson," Schulz later said, "one of the most important lessons of my life."

Reflecting on the impulse that had made him draw Popeye on his classmates' school notebooks, he realized how much he had wanted to win affection. "People," he realized, "simply like cartoons." Cartooning was a way of engaging people's attention, generating pleasure without dangerous emotional overtones. But it was not Sparky to whom they responded when he handed over a Popeye—their excitement was at the entry into their mundane private context of the famous character who had compelled his pen. In the transaction between cartoonist and audience, the artist was required to remain invisible, overlaid by his own efforts, and this essential condition—that he erase himself as an actual part of striving to prove his worth—matched everything Sparky had learned about loving and being loved. "My mother was proud of my drawing," he said, "but she didn't know what to do with it." Neither did anyone else. Of all the drawings and doodles that he made and distributed at Halverson clan gatherings, no single one was preserved.

If Dena took pride in Sparky—and those who knew her say she did—she must also have been afraid of his strange, singular dream, afraid for him. An overly sensitive boy who thought himself special was bound to be brought back to earth with a shock. Above all else, it was Sparky's sense of being exceptional that unsettled her. *She* didn't expect the world to treat her with tenderness or imagination; why should things turn out differently for her son?

Dena had never been encouraged to contemplate going beyond the roles she had been prepared for in third grade. She could indulge Sparky's drawing and admire his handiwork with a pen; it was fine for diversion or, at most, a hobby, but nothing in her experience made drawing more than an odd, trivial pastime. To entertain serious ambition and, what was more, awaken real ability, ran counter to Dena's experience as a Halverson. Her family combined toughness with aversion to risk. Sparky's upbringing had been crowded with sturdy, good-humored people who prided themselves on being able to take all that life dished out, but who at the same time never went any further than they had to.

Charles Schulz's parents, Carl Frederick Schulz and Dena Bertina Halverson, Minneapolis, Minnesota, May 1920.

Charles Monroe Schulz, 1924.

Howard Roberts, a cousin, holds the football for Sparky, St. Paul, Minnesota, 1925.

Carl Schulz maintained a public presence that his son admired. "All I want," said Sparky in later years, "is for people to like me, like they did my father."

Dena Schulz, 1920s. "Perhaps she felt that she did not have the right type of clothes. . . . It would have been wonderful if someone could have explained to my mother that she need not have felt inadequate."

C. F. SCHULZ, Prop.

# THE FAMILY BARBER SHOP

1574 Selby Ave.,
at SNELLING

"IT PAYS TO LOOK WELL"

We Wish YOU

A Happy and Prosperous New Year

4 6

The striking fact of his appearance was his neatness. "It wasn't hard to keep him clean like with some kids," said his father. "He never horsed around much."

The boy in spotless clothes grew up to create a character who became known all over the world for doing nothing but being dirty.

Sparky and his first dog, Snooky, posed here with a backyard snowman, Minneapolis, Minnesota, circa 1926.

Sparky with his uncle Silas and newborn cousin, Gaylon "Corky" Halverson. Needles, California, September 1929.

Sparky (*third row, left*) in the seventh grade at Richards Gordon Elementary School, St. Paul, Minnesota, 1933. "All through grade school I was the smallest kid in the class."

Suppertime, 1930s. The Schulz family dog, Spike, served as a model for Snoopy.

Spike, with Dena and Carl. "He was a wild creature," Schulz later wrote. "I don't believe he was ever completely tamed. He had a vocabulary of understanding approximately fifty words, and he loved to ride in the car."

Before and after the war: With his parents, 1942, approaching draft age . . . and in 1945, as staff sergeant and squad leader, with Virginia Howley, his wartime sweetheart, and Carl.

Intersection of Selby (*center*) and Snelling (*right*), in St. Paul, Minnesota, circa 1932. The barber pole for Carl's shop is visible, in shadow, under the corner streetlamp. The Schulzes' second-floor apartment, where they moved in the summer of 1942, is at 170 North Snelling (entrance to right of striped awning). Sparky's bedroom window is at right, above the vacant storefront; Carl and Dena's, at left.

Sparky's maternal grandmother, Sophia Halverson (*left*) and his beloved aunt Marion (*right*), both became offstage presences in *Peanuts*. Peppermint Patty was patterned after the looks and personality of his warmhearted tomboy cousin, Patty Swanson (*center*).

Dena.

With his first comrades-in-arms, Marvin Tack and Larry Payne, at Camp Campbell, Kentucky, 1943.

With Virginia Howley, 1944, St. Paul, Minnesota. "I never really did what we call 'fall in love' until I was in the army, and I had a nurse that I liked a lot."

Elmer Hagemeyer, leader of the mortar squad (1st Platoon, Company B), was ten years older than Schulz. "He became very much like an older brother to me," recalled Sparky.

On furlough at the Starlight Roof and Zodiac Room atop St. Louis's Chase Hotel, May 1944. *Left to right:* Sgt. Schulz, Margaret and S/Sgt. Elmer Hagemeyer, T/Sgt. Robert Knoten (platoon leader of Company B), Ileen Knoten, and an unidentified couple.

During basic training, Schulz illustrated Elmer Hagemeyer's letters home with drawings of army life.

"I must have been one of the last people in the world that others would have thought could ever have become the squad leader of a light machine gun squad. But I did become one, and I was proud of that."

"Chateau of the
'Bad Neighbor'!"

Normandy, February 1945. In a pencil drawing from Sparky's army sketchbook: the open-sided shed where Schulz's squad bivouacked at the Château de Malvoisine.

August 1945. The returning veteran posed for an article in the *St. Paul Daily News*: "SOLDIER HOME ON VISIT—Has Comic Strip Plans."

The Art Instruction building, adjoining the Bureau of Engraving, a vast printing enterprise under the same ownership, filled half a city block in downtown Minneapolis.

Sparky coached the company's ladies' softball team, the Bureaucats. Donna Mae Johnson (*front row, third from left*), on whom Schulz based the Little Red-Haired Girl, played second base. "I couldn't play softball at all," Donna recalled. "But I kept going and kept making a fool of myself all summer because he was the coach."

Correcting home-study lessons in the Educational Department at Art Instruction, 1952. Every day at four o'clock, Sparky whistled the "Grand March" from *Aïda*, joined midstanza in relays by Frieda Rich and Frank Wing (*back row, second and third from left*), Linus Maurer (*back row, third from right*), Charlie Brown (*second row, right*), and others around the room.

Schulz's colleagues observed that the essential physical characteristics of the *Peanuts* gang originated in Frieda Rich. "The way she stood, sat, and moved—and the relative size of the head and the body," reflected Hal Lamson. Here Frieda is photographed at a wedding in the 1950s.

Frieda alongside a desk at Art Instruction, in a pencil sketch by Jim Sasseville.

"They were all ambitious," said Schulz of his fellow instructors. "Each of them had his or her desire, whether it was to be a fashion artist, or a cartoonist, or a painter."

Charlie F. Brown.

George Letness.

Jim Sasseville.

David Ratner.

Judy Halverson.

"DOG?... WHY, NO....
WHAT MAKES YOU THINK
I'VE SEEN YOUR DOG?"

On June 8, 1947, the *Minneapolis Star Tribune* began publishing *Sparky's Li'l Folks*. Schulz soon moved the weekly feature to the *St. Paul Pioneer Press* and *Dispatch*, where it ran all but unnoticed on the women's page until the paper let it go in January 1950. By then, he jokingly called himself the "world's most unknown cartoonist."

## Charles Schulz...

Born in Minneapolis 27 years ago. Art Instruction correspondence course and night sketching classes at Minneapolis School of Art. Saw action as light-machine-gun squad leader in France and Germany during World War II. After war, became successful Saturday Evening Post contributor, instructor at Art Instruction, Inc., and cartoonist for St. Paul Pioneer Press, where Peanuts was created. His Post cartoons have been reprinted in the U. S. and many foreign countries.

## UNITED FEATURES

**PEANUTS** *by SCHULZ*

WATCH
OUT
FOR
CHILDREN

The GREATEST little Sensation
Since TOM THUMB!

The first advertisement for *Peanuts*, which debuted October 2, 1950.

Her clan might respect Sparky's skill and admire his ambition (even if they never said so), but in their world, drawing was not man's work, nothing to put food on the table. Irving and Amanda Swanson, who ran a dry-cleaning business out of the basement of their house in Hudson, Wisconsin, did not think much of Sparky's prospects: "That kid isn't going to be worth five cents when he grows up," said Irving. "All he wants to do is scribble." Up in Little Falls, Minnesota, Josie and Vern Gish discounted Sparky's frenetic pastime. "With all the doodling he did," said his cousin Shirley Gish VonderHaar, "a lot of people didn't have a lot of faith in him, our family included." Only Aunt Marion had said, "You just wait and see. Someday he's going to make it."

As was the case with his hero George Herriman, Schulz used cartooning to take "a sort of revenge on the world." A friend with whom Sparky would later share memories of "his 'dumb relatives' who didn't see things in him" recalled that "except Marion, whom he adored, he was scornful of his relatives. He would say that he wanted to *show* those people."

Surprisingly, it was his grandmother who placed confidence, as his mother could not, in that part of him that wanted to make itself felt as different. The more he hung back, the more Sophia Halverson urged him forward. "You've got to show some gumption, got to go out and do things." She appeared in Charles Schulz's life story as the flinty, warmhearted matriarch who accommodated Sparky's passion for hockey by standing, broom in hand, before an imaginary goal under the basement stairs as he shot tennis balls at her. "I like to think she made a lot of great saves," he always said. Her greatest save was the boy himself.

For lack of a written record, little can be known for sure of Dena's qualms about her son's future. We do know that her own hopes and fears had been shaped above all by her father's inability to reestablish himself in America before the First World War. "One day Dad actually did disappear . . . we never knew where he went," recalls Snoopy on the doghouse roof. "Now our family is scattered all over. . . . Spike's in Needles . . . Belle's in Kansas City . . . I don't know where any of the others are . . ." The Halversons were a family in decline, Dena's brothers struggling—in some cases having already conclusively failed—to find their places among a new, more competitive working class. "Why should her son be any different?" asked one relative. A cousin who knew Dena and Sparky during this formative period recalled Dena's contracted expectations: "I don't think she thought he would amount to very much."

Most of all, Sparky would remember his mother's frustration—she who had tried to be the great resource for her relatives—at having nothing to offer on this central preoccupation. Neither Dena nor Carl "discouraged me in the least," he would recall, "but they were always a little dismayed that they didn't know how to help me."

Even as Dena worried for him, she must have believed somewhere in the back of her mind that he could do it. One Monday evening in February 1934, when Dena noticed an announcement in the newspaper—an exhibition of comic strip art, opening at the St. Paul Public Library—she made sure that, as soon as Carl had closed up shop the next day, the whole family attended the show.

Framed comic strips thronged a spacious room on the library's third floor: Percy Crosby's *Skippy*, Ham Fisher's *Joe Palooka*, Milt Gross's *Dave's Delicatessen* and *Count Screwloose*, Rudolph Dirks's *Katzenjammer Kids* as drawn by Harold Knerr. Sparky had never before seen original work by the professionals. He knew comics only as newspaper features, not as raw extensions of the artist's hand. But here hung several hundred lengths of layered illustration board stroked in dense ink more purely black and warmly alive than the engraving process allowed for. Here, so much more vital than he had ever imagined, were actual pen lines. Sparky could walk right up to Roy Crane's panels in a Sunday page for *Wash Tubbs* and see where the ink had dried to a gloss that still picked up light.

Outside the panels, cryptic instructions had been penciled in the margin; sky blue arrows aimed to catch an editor's eye. Inside the panels, there were unexpected traces of effort: accidental blots, glue stains and tape bits, strips of paper pasted to correct mistakes in lettering, unerased letters, registration marks, residues of white gouache, pentimenti reversing all kinds of slips and false starts—a whole unseen world of reasoning and revision had passed over the drawing board before mechanical reproduction reduced and tightened the lines. Here, too, shone the effortless effects of freehand brushwork, delicate lettering, translucent watercolor washes—all the backstage craft of comic strip showmanship. Here, institutionalized as adult masterworks, towered the sources of what had been for Sparky child's play, but which hard study had taught him was even harder work.

Beneath the surface details, behind the beauty of pen technique and the fascinating implications of paste-overs and other previously unseen fixes, lay a mystery of which he felt he was somehow already possessed. Comics could say the things that people were only dimly aware of feeling. But they were drawn as "funny pictures," presented in sequences timed for laughter. In every cartoon lurked something private and unknowable, yet linked to qualities so clear and direct that people everywhere could laugh at their own expense.

It was funny, Sparky thought, to see a character get hit on the head, and not just because, in the canon of the comics, nothing was funnier than a player discomfiting his prey. There was magic in this violence: Popeye could be flattened, his head orbited by sharp-pointed stars, half-moons, and miniature Saturns, but in the next panel, he was his indestructibly assertive self again. You could not be hurt in the comics. Cartoon people lived outside of time. Instead of misery and suffering, cartoon hurt induced pleasure in the form of an Olympian release of anger or its comic counterpoint, unlimited love.

Having peered at every panel in the exhibition, Sparky went home, eager to test himself against his predecessors. He pulled out the strips he had been drawing and saw in an instant how his pen lines lay limp on the page, how far he still had to go. His panels were "not even *close* to being as good as what these professionals were doing." Right then and there, he tore them up. "I knew that I had to start over again."

# CHAPTER 7

# SPIKE AND THE GANG

*"Who drew the picture?"*
*"I did—I don't like to be alone."*
—PERCY CROSBY,

SKIPPY

BY 1937, AS ST. PAUL began to pull out of the worst of hard times, the Schulzes had moved back to Macalester Avenue, a tree-shrouded neighborhood of working families living in neat frame houses on forty-foot-wide lots, each with a garage on the side and a scrap of lawn in back.

Sparky's old house—the one he had lived in at age six, before moving to Needles—was at the center of an inviting, two-block network of boys and alleys. But during his first six months back on Macalester, he avoided making friends, preferring to shift for himself. Out in the neighborhood, he had no clear idea how to talk to the kids he saw playing on the streets. This disconnection was puzzling even to him: "I don't know what it was, but [I] certainly was not happy and carefree."

He liked to think that he was good at playing alone, and although he would later acknowledge having felt lonesome and incomplete, he saw no reason to be unhappy. His parents loved him, he reasoned, and nothing bad had ever happened to them or to him.

As before, he kept to himself, doodling indoors or playing backyard games. On icy winter evenings, his father would glaze the small yard behind the house with fresh coats of water from the garden hose so that the next afternoon Sparky could pull on his skates and play hockey. It took six months for Sparky to feel a part of the neighborhood. He made his first social breakthrough on home ice—in the larger sense, therefore, on his own terms, which set a pattern for his life: "Some kid came over once and saw my skating rink in the backyard. And we played hockey, and he was surprised that I could beat him."

He chose for companions strays like himself, the only child or only boy in a family: Sherman Plepler at 1607 Randolph Avenue; Arthur Whitlock, a fellow loner, at 1611 Randolph; Thomas Hewson, the youngest kid in the neighborhood, at 1619 Randolph; Stewart Wright, even quieter than Sparky and also interested in drawing, at 1602 James Avenue. Jimmy Clark, smaller than the rest of them but a good ballplayer, lived a little farther away; Gordon Watson, the strongest among them, was about a mile away; Richard Hannegan, the group's extrovert, lived on James Avenue, a block from Sparky, and was known as "the boss of the neighborhood." But it was Sparky who, that first spring in his new territory, organized the boys into a baseball team.

He dubbed them the "Tetie Whops"—no one can remember why—and put aside his drawing to pitch or catch every game they played. From the mound, or behind home plate, he commanded his team from baseball's two most powerful positions. He relished being, as he put it, "in on all the plays." He "liked people to do things his way," one of the gang recalled.

Sparky may have been slight, and although he did not like contact sports, he was aggressive; boys challenging him in a pickup hockey game were often surprised at his will to win. He played hard—so hard that one of his shots on goal gave Shermy Plepler a concussion. Another day, in a touch-football game on James Avenue, while covering little Tommy Hewson on a pass play, he trod on the younger boy's heel, dropping him to the pavement, and would never forget seeing Tommy "getting up with his wrist twisted at an impossible angle," just as Shermy, his forehead bloodied by Sparky's shot, would "never forget how scared Sparky was as he helped me home for medical aid."

He was surprised by his own strength and influence. Most mothers' boys are not even part of a gang, much less a competitor in the group; boys subject to an infatuation like cartooning drift off into another world. Gordon Watson, the gang's clutch hitter, recalled that after baseball games the boys would sometimes sit around the Schulzes' basement. "We'd talk about the game and what we should have done, and why we lost it or won it. And Sparky would just sit in the corner. He didn't pay any attention to us—he was over there drawing. He was *always* drawing when we were around."

Sparky had it both ways; at the same time that he was becoming an artist and a dreamer, he was becoming an influential, highly visible member of a team. "I lived two lives," he later explained. "In school, I was a nothing. Around my own neighborhood, in my own real life, I was something."

BY THE SECOND WINTER on Macalester, boys were coming regularly to Sparky's rink, their skates hanging by laces tied like scarves around their necks. Three or four to a team filled the ice. For pads, they strapped old issues of *Collier's* magazine to their shins with rubber inner tubes. Sparky devised the goalie's padding: rolled-up newspapers inside a gunnysack for his legs; a baseball catcher's gear for his face and chest. But, as one of Schulz's characters later said, "One patch of ice doth not a winter make."

His boyhood dream was to skate on "a perfect sheet of ice." A neighborhood parochial school boasted a real rink, and on more than one cold afternoon, the Tetie Whops changed into their skates in the basement of one of the gang, then hobbled down four blocks of alleys and boosted each other over the fence. The watchman at Nativity of Our Lord Catholic School looked the other way as they sneaked onto the ice—clean ice, with real boards, real hockey goals. When someone scored, the boys could hear the puck hit the netting, and they would fling their arms in the air. They played through dusk and by moonlight; Sparky would ever after include among his fondest childhood memories the freedom and exhilaration of skating on moonlit ice.

All his life, in public and private, he would speak of being bullied on St. Paul's streets and in playgrounds. In his memory, whole blocks existed in which the Macalester and Randolph boys never dared venture because "there were bigger and uglier kids that lived around there." He considered his neighborhood to have been "medium-tough," yet a school friend, Jack "Pudge" Geduldig, who lived on Stanford Avenue, five blocks away, judged that "there was no such thing as 'rough neighborhoods' in St. Paul, except down at the levee."

With a bitterness that actually increased as he grew older, Sparky insisted that it had been "almost impossible to go to the playground and enjoy yourself without some older, bigger kid coming and spoiling it." His childhood had been tainted by "kids that push you down and knock you

over and won't let you swing on the swings that you want to swing on."
As often as not, he spoke of these bullies in the present tense.

Schulz's closest friend in the neighborhood, Sherman Plepler, who
became a high school teacher and therefore an eyewitness to playground
cruelty, understood why his friend felt threatened: Sparky was small, and
even as a teenager he was the kind of kid whose lunch money was likely to
be stolen by some roughneck.

But neither Plepler nor Gordon Watson nor Tom Hewson nor Dick
Hannegan could recall any instance when Sparky himself was picked on. As
grown men remembering games more than sixty years earlier, the boys in
Sparky's gang could describe specific plays—whole sequences of action—
in which Sparky's aggressive style inflicted accidental injury on others. But
no memory survives of Sparky's being baited or pushed around or knocked
down by a particular bully on a particular playground. The lack of specific-
ity is telling; people angered by an injustice recall precisely what injury was
done, as did Schulz when he cited another enemy, however unintentional,
of childhood security: "Adults forget what a real struggle it is out on that
playground when you're pushed out there and you're on your own and
you have to fit in. You have to maybe find a friend who's a little bit bigger
than you are to protect you, or you have to do all sorts of little things to
survive on that playground. Well, the adults don't worry about that. So a
child gets pushed down: 'Well, it's good for you and it'll teach you to be a
man.' What's a skinned knee? It doesn't mean anything."

Until Sparky found a place among the boys in his neighborhood, he
was all but alone. The gang offered protection. Neighborhood sports were
the one place where he could let off steam. More than at school or with
parents or relatives, a gang of good kids, flanked by a dog who bared his
teeth at the right moment, was the place in which a brotherless boy could
take refuge.

To what degree he sustained physical abuse on the playground remains undeterminable; late in life, he conceded, "Maybe a lot of it was [my] own imagination." What his companions could corroborate was the barber's son's real grounds for feeling unprotected.

In St. Paul, with his father fortressed in the barbershop, Sparky was hesitant to go to his mother over playground harassment. "Mothers," he once said, "I don't think they have any idea what male children go through."

But the fact was, Carl would not have had much idea either about what Sparky was going through because he had never spent much time on a playing field—he worked too hard, or so the story went. But he had time to flood the backyard for Sparky's hockey rink, and to cut and trim the grass and plant soup cans in the lawn each spring so that Sparky could practice putting. He kept his son supplied with all manner of sporting goods (Sparky later remembered himself as the only kid in his neighborhood gang with a catcher's mitt) and drove him and two friends to play eighteen holes at the Keller Golf Course, north of the city, but he himself would not play.

Why wasn't Carl interested in playing, or watching Sparky play, the games themselves?

On the rare Saturday that Carl left the barbershop early enough to drive up to northern Minnesota for an overnight family fishing expedition, Sparky would hopefully bring along his catcher's mitt and fielder's glove, liking to practice his pitches and throw hard. During one of those lakeside interludes in early adolescence he discovered something about the father he had always deemed invincible: "My dad wasn't a good enough ballplayer. He was afraid to have me pitch to him."

And so another man found himself drafted to substitute for Carl—a former associate at the Family Barber Shop. Albert Roman Desterhoff and his wife, Clara, often went fishing with the Schulzes. The Desterhoffs were childless. In 1937 Al was forty-eight, a veteran of the First World War. Unafraid of getting hurt in a game of catch, Al could handle Sparky's fastest pitches and liked to pull on the spare mitt and toss the ball by the lake. To Sparky, Al Desterhoff was "one of these rare men who could play catch with a teenager and make you feel like [he was] really enjoying it."

Sparky felt his father's absence most keenly during the summer of

1937, which was, nevertheless, as he always said, "one of the outstanding summers of my life"—the "summer that I shall always remember," made memorable by a man named Harry Schwabel. Harry, as everyone called him, was athletics director at the Edgecumbe playground on the border of Sparky's neighborhood. That summer he organized a four-team baseball league in which Sparky played every Tuesday and Thursday.

He could hardly wait for game days. Now that he had been elected team manager, he could never sleep Mondays or Wednesdays, and he carried the equipment the twelve blocks to Edgecumbe, arriving before anyone, at eight-thirty in the morning, half an hour before game time. The field was flanked by the railroad tracks behind Mill Road; Great Northern Railway locomotives lumbered past, hooting through the underpasses at Lexington Parkway and St. Clair Avenue, as Sparky sat on the bench, calculating batting averages. On the field, he still pitched or caught; indeed, one afternoon he pitched a no-hitter. In the season's series, his team won the championship.

He would have no memory—no picture exists in the family album—of either parent attending his games that summer. But he never forgot Harry Schwabel. That same memorable summer, the neighborhood boys gathered in the evenings after supper for softball at Mattocks Park, one boy's father joining in. The other players envied that boy because his father hit and fielded well and was a good sport. "Not that we were at all critical of our own fathers," Sparky hastened to gloss the memory, "for we were well aware of the difficulties of the Depression, and knew how hard they worked, but still, the envy was there."

The advantages passed along by his solvent father made it hard for Sparky to ask the old man to take time off work just to play ball. Carl's generosity came with obligations: "I'd give anything to be playing football right now," Charlie Brown says on his tricycle. When Patty asks why he doesn't, he explains, "My dad said he paid twenty-five dollars for this tri-cycle. . . . I feel obligated to ride it."

Sparky saw only dedication in his father's six-day-a-week, year-round grind. But it was more complicated than that: his father's life was con-stricted by fear, and getting smacked by a fastball was not the only thing Carl was afraid of. Sparky later recognized something pathological in his father's distress at having to abandon, even for a day, the daily routines of the shop. "He used his work, the barbershop, as a reason never to travel or do anything. He never went anywhere by himself, either. Even when he went fishing there had to be someone else along." Given the perspec-tive of many years and thinking over certain things his father had said, Charles Schulz identified his father's anxiety as agoraphobia—the fear of open places.

The barbershop was Carl's rock, and he clung to it. Even when there was money for a real vacation, he refused to go farther than the lakes north of the city. The expedition to Needles had been more than enough. Per-haps western space had permanently overloaded Carl. So long as contact with his customers kept him hedged against his fears, he was content, if not eager, to put work first, even if this meant spending less time with wife and son. Carl Schulz, citizen of St. Paul, needed to be anchored to his cor-ner, fortified by a daily dose of barbershop routine.

DOGS WERE ANOTHER OF Carl's comforts, and he had a knack for making light comedy of them—and with them, occasionally playing to Sparky's first dog, Snooky, by appearing gruff even while happily spoiling him. But Carl and Sparky's sorrow over losing Snooky to the fender of a taxicab had long since yielded to the giddy reign of Snooky's successor.

Spike had come to the Schulzes as a puppy, all skin and bones, the gift of a friend. He was a "hound mixture," white with black spots, more pointer than beagle, and quickly revealed himself to be one of a kind: he knew how to ring a doorbell, and without being trained—simply by observing daily life at home—had learned to wait for the evening newspaper, bring potatoes up from the cellar, or put a paw on an arm of Carl's easy chair, signaling that it was time to go for the Sunday papers.

From the start, Spike was the family clown, with Carl as his straight man: waiting behind the front door in the afternoon for his master to come home, and, at the first hint of his approach, heading for where Sparky, all prepared, would swing open the back door to make possible a trajectory ending in a dramatic snatch of the evening newspaper from under Carl's arm at the garage, thence reversing into a rocket loop back to the living room, to wait for Carl to settle down after supper with the newspaper and a cigar. The moment the first cigar ash rustled into the standing ashtray beside Carl's easy chair, recalled a visitor, Spike would "be there and he'd lick that ash."

Spike had an array of quirks. He slept in a wicker clothes basket in the hallway, preferably under a blanket. He disdained to drink from a dog's dish, preferring—in fact, demanding—cold running water from the tap at the bathroom sink, putting one paw on the sink and standing there until someone came in and turned the faucet for him.

Loving to eat, he ate almost anything. Once, when Sparky was playing with a rubber ball attached to a wooden paddle, the elastic band broke, whereupon Spike chased down the ball, grabbed it in his teeth, and swallowed it, only to throw it back up that night after eating too much spaghetti. Another time, he leaped to the edge of Carl's dresser top, grabbed a roll of bills, and chewed the master barber's profits to shreds. One day, Sparky saw quite clearly that Spike had somehow gotten a double-edged razor blade into his mouth. As a puppy, he had once eaten small shards of broken glass. But, like a character in the comics, the dog was indestructible, slavering up pins from Dena's sewing basket and tacks and screws off the basement floor; he bared his teeth at anyone on the block he didn't like.

Indeed, Spike would be remembered by the Schulzes' neighbors, for all Sparky's protests to the contrary, as the meanest dog on the block. At his most playful, he would wait during the neighborhood boys' winter street games to plunge out snarling when one fell down, to snatch the stocking cap off the boy's head. Sherman Plepler recalled the constant fear of being bitten and Sparky's hilarity at the other boys' fear of his dog. "Spike would scare me to death, and Sparky thought this quite funny."

Spike's bad manners delighted Sparky: "How many times do I have to tell you?! Just the paper . . . Not the whole paperboy!!" the master of a Spike-like dog chuckles indulgently in Schulz's first comic feature, *Li'l Folks*. But his dog's extreme behavior was also one more thing that set Sparky apart. Charlie Brown would introduce his family to his "pencil pal" by writing about his father, a barber; his mother, a housewife; and his dog, who was "kind of crazy." According to one of Sparky's cousins, Spike carried his peculiarities to the point that he was deemed to be capable of illicit overtures. Dena once revealed to Carl's sister Elsie that on brutally hot summer days on Macalester Avenue she would sometimes strip down to her slip and underwear while scrubbing the kitchen floor. At this vision of Dena, unclothed, down on her hands and knees, Elsie exclaimed, "With that dog around?"

Charlie Brown's refrain could have been Sparky's: "Why can't I have a normal dog like everyone else?"

ALONE WITH PEN, INK, and paper at the dining room table, Sparky carried on a conversation with himself. Whenever he loaded a nib with India ink, he felt a nervous intensity growing within him—an odd, almost unbearable sensation of being at once supercharged and steady as a rock. And from this tension would force its way an idea so pure and clear and elastic that it was as if a balloon had been released to rise slowly through his concentration. Then, as his pen line pulled the idea onto and across the white paper, this soaring alertness mounted, pushing to the point of extremest tension—then burst, as if the pen point itself had split the balloon, and he would find himself alone at the dining room table, laughing with joy at the strange pressure and release.

That first winter back in the house on Macalester, he sent a pen-and-ink drawing to the syndicated comic feature *Believe It or Not!* To render Spike as a subject worthy of Ripley's daily offering of odd facts and conversation-piece marvels, Sparky drew him in profile as a trained sporting dog (the better to contrast with his actual habits), sitting on his haunches, alert as a hunter. Robert Ripley, a high school dropout from Santa Rosa, California, who had sold his first cartoon at age fourteen, accepted the submission and gave it good play.

On February 22, 1937, Spike appeared beneath drawings of a seventy-five-year-old "petrified apple" and alongside the champion cigar smoker of Tampa, Florida. Stern in his field pose, Spike went unnamed. The caption reported that C. F. Schulz of St. Paul owned a "hunting dog that eats pins, tacks, screws and razor blades." The byline read, "Drawn by Sparky."

So he had made it into print, like his host, at fourteen. And perhaps the most marvelous fact of all was that, when millions of readers turned to the comics pages that Monday morning, the global reach of William Randolph Hearst's King Features Syndicate ensured that the name "Sparky" was on display in as many as three hundred newspapers in twenty-three countries around the world.

Another four months would creep by on Macalester Avenue before he graduated from junior high.

# CHAPTER 8

# CLASS OF ONE

*Sparky never was one to go around relying on other people.*
—CARL F. SCHULZ

HIS MOTHER OCCUPIED THE central place in his heart. The intensity of that bond would remain alive to the day he died; she was a presence in everything he did; her looks and most distinctive qualities reappeared in the women of his life and in his art. Yet in Charles Schulz's memories, the flesh-and-blood Dena is a mist—not a woman you would depend on; not the solid anchor of Halverson family legend. Everything about her in his recollections is restrained. He cannot bring himself to evoke her as a personality, and he keeps the details of her face, her body, her tastes, even her smile, as vague as those of the object of Charlie Brown's frustrated longing, the Little Red-Haired Girl. He describes his mother only in terms of her voice, gentle and low, a disembodied whisper—the first sound he heard every morning before school: *Sparky, it's time to get up.*

IN 1937 ST. PAUL'S Central High School was a highly regarded three-year institution known for its devoted faculty, its large, energetic student body, and an atmosphere of enterprise and purpose. Its austere brick citadel loomed over terraced lawns at the end of Lexington Parkway. The school, the oldest of its kind in Minnesota, was a brisk walk or a ten-cent streetcar ride from the Schulzes' house. Sparky entered, as every student did, in the tenth grade, to take his place in a class of some 550 students. There, in a single semester, he failed three subjects, while somehow squeaking by in German. As before, no parent-teacher conference took place; neither parent seemed to notice that he was in trouble, but at report card time, the physics teacher, Mr. Eastman, summoned students one by one from the laboratory benches to his desk to review their marks.

Eastman typified Central's hardy lifelong teachers. He maintained a professorial appearance, wearing three-piece tweed suits and old-fashioned wire-rimmed spectacles, registering students' progress in a grade book otherwise kept under lock and key—from which he looked up to fix his gaze on Sparky. "What seems to be the trouble?"

Sparky said he didn't know. "I think maybe this is out of my line."

"Oh?" said Eastman, his red pencil poised. "What's your line?"

"I guess cartooning."

Eastman snorted. Uncertain whether he was being put on, he gave Sparky a firm, searching look, but saw him to be in earnest and brought his red pencil down.

Not satisfied simply to record an E, the failing grade at Central, he dug his pencil point into the surface of Schulz's report card, pressing harder and harder, until the scarlet "E" was deeply embedded in the paper—deep enough, Sparky realized, "so it couldn't be altered." He would never know whether or not his mention of cartooning (which might also indicate an expertise at lettering) had combined with his apparently casual performance to induce the sense that he was capable of forgery. In Sparky's opinion, Eastman had summed him up on the basis of a one-sentence exchange as being of defective character, and that was insult enough.

He reacted by retreating yet further under cover, camouflaging himself once again as a "stupid," "silly" kid, but signaling from his concealment a desperate longing to be pursued. The following semester, Sparky repeated the subjects he had failed, and this time earned passing marks in everything but physics. Again, curiously, neither of his parents said anything about the improvement or took stock of his schooling in any way.

In later life, Charles Schulz would puzzle over his father and mother's passivity toward his academic trouble and vaguely excuse them, as he had earlier: "They didn't have the background to understand it." But Carl Schulz was not a simpleton. Even if he did not know the best way to help an intelligent, talented, athletic boy, he certainly knew that his son was clever enough to get good grades when he wanted to. Smart boys did not fail three subjects in one semester at an above-average Minnesota high school unless something was drastically wrong.

ON NOVEMBER 4, 1940, Dena presented herself at Dr. Gustaf Edlund's examination room, knowing only that sharp pains in the innermost parts of her lower anatomy were keeping her up nights. Sometimes the pain was so strong it made her cry out.

Dr. Edlund's notations, rounded off over months and turning into years, show that a malignant lesion must have established itself in her cervix as early as the previous March, the onset dating at least as far back as March 1938—Sparky's first spring in high school. By now, however, the neoplasm had spread. A new method for early diagnosis of cells taken from the cervix, the "Pap" test developed by the pathologist George Papanicolaou, had begun to be used in 1940, but for Dena it was already too late.

Cancer of the cervix starts on the uterine side of the cervical canal, where the lower end of the uterus meets the apex of the vagina, the affected cells metastasizing gradually. If undetected, a lesion can linger in the lining of the cervix for several years. The cancer advances to its second stage when the growth has progressed to malignancy, invading the muscles of the cervix and the grainy upper walls of the vagina. At the third stage, the tumor can grow large enough to block the tubes connecting the kidneys to the bladder, and indeed choke off the bowel. In the fourth and final stage, the tumor spreads throughout the pelvis, invading the rectum, lymph nodes, and lower vagina. Of all cancers, it is one of the most cruel, degrading, malodorous, and lethal.

Gustaf Edlund kept from Dena everything but what she knew already, namely, that she was sick. He did not tell her that her life was in danger or that her disease had no cure. Only "cancer quacks" sounded the alarm, demanding payment in advance for useless procedures, promising cures to the poor and the ignorant. Dr. Edlund, a reputable physician practicing family medicine at 120 North Snelling, two blocks from the Family Barber Shop, and attending staff meetings at nearby Midway Hospital, could offer little more than mild palliatives for her pain. Possibly, he discussed the diagnosis in general terms with Carl, but whatever Carl knew he kept to himself. Dena was told to stay in bed and rest.

TO OUTWARD APPEARANCE, NOTHING was amiss. Carl met the crisis in his usual steadfast way: he went right on cutting hair. Endurance was, after all, as much the responsibility of patients and families as that of doctors. From Sparky was kept the essential fact: he was told nothing about the disease or its location; merely that his mother was not feeling well this morning. On

Dena's good days, Spike was allowed to jump up and curl himself next to her feet on the bed. When she had strength to sit up, she kept busy with her needle, mending, crocheting. Theirs was not a religious household; in the early stages of Dena's illness, none of the Schulzes turned to the Lutheran church, or even to the Bible, for comfort or hope.

By day, Dena was like the still center of a hurricane. "She was sick," recalled a nephew who visited, "but she would smile and talk and I had no idea that it was that serious—maybe just a temporary illness. She was always very pleasant and pretty much happy when I would be in there by her."

Bill Wegwerth, Carl's sister Alma's seven-year-old son, had been taking accordion lessons and was therefore enlisted for recitals at Dena's bedside. The Wegwerths and Carl and Sparky would gather around Dena's bed, and Bill would squeeze out a few numbers: "My Bonnie Lies Over the Ocean" and "Over the Waves," a favorite oompa-pa piece.

Propped up against her clean linen, Dena would smile and look happy, "and then we'd get out of there," Bill recalled. "It really was a sickroom." The grown-ups would stay and visit a little longer, while Bill and Sparky would slip out to the kitchen, and Bill would get Sparky to draw for him in the scrapbook he would bring over. Bill's age dates the bedside recitals to 1938. This would mean that during Sparky's sophomore and junior years in high school, he came home most days to a household in which his mother was confined to bed. In adult years, Bill Wegwerth could not recall seeing Dena in the kitchen or anywhere else in the house. "I only remember her as being bedridden."

Some nights, Sparky was awakened by a cry of pain from the privacy of his parents' bedroom. The following morning, mother and son greeted each other as if nothing had broken the night silence. In 1940, mothers did not talk to sons about their cervixes; sons did not question mothers about unexplained agonies in the dark hours. Illness was a vulgarly morbid subject, unfit for family conversation. He later remembered how quiet and dark the house became during these months.

None of Dena's visitors were told the nature of her illness, even relatives with serious "female" conditions of their own. Dena's cousin Josie Bredahl Gish suffered from excessive menstrual flow and came every few weeks from Little Falls to St. Paul for an aggressive course of radiation treatment. Her children often accompanied her, staying over with the Schulzes. The Gishes could see that Dena was frail, indeed somehow stricken, but knew only that she was "sick with different things—[the doctors] never could put their finger on it. It was this, it was that." Twelve-year-old Shirley Gish VonderHaar noticed, "It was hard on Sparky."

For one thing, he was not getting enough to eat. Dena did not have the strength to market or to cook. Shirley would later recall that she and her family—most unexpectedly, dealing with kitchen-proud Dena—"went away from that house hungry." When Sparky returned the visit, the Gishes noted his surprise at the abundance of their table in Little Falls. "He couldn't believe all the food we had. It was different from home."

"Security is knowing there's some more pie left," he later wrote. In the same vein he added, "Security is hearing your mother in the kitchen when you come home from school."

HE DRIFTED THROUGH CENTRAL HIGH, a short, thin boy—"so thin," one teacher remarked, "he had to hold up his pants with suspenders *and* a belt." Punctual, rarely absent, he clocked in for first period, then marked time until the last bell clanged and he was free to get back to his neighborhood "where things were better." "My life was waiting for school to end and to get home with the other guys."

His daily ordeal began as soon as he mounted the wide, triple-tiered steps to the school's front entry, a stone arch set beneath crenellated battlements in the castle tower. Before classes at Central, the most visible students gathered in cliques by the trophy cases outside the principal's office in the front hall. To be a "front-haller" at Central, a school of more than two thousand students, was to have been somehow recognized for one's prowess, whether as an athlete, as a smooth talker, as a slick ballroom dancer, or simply as a member of one of the ubiquitous student clubs—even the stamp club gave one standing. Most boys joined, at the very least, one of the school's three intramural YMCA-style athletic clubs. Sparky joined none.

He sought to belong nowhere in Central's highly developed social hierarchy. His interests coincided with any number of organizations—the arts club, Thumb Tacks; the bowling club; the radio workshop. He did not need to wait to be asked to join, and the clubs' importance was beyond question. "It was a big school," a classmate recalled, "and if you weren't in a club, you were just sort of wandering around by yourself."

Sparky—still "Charles" to students and teachers alike—was not just a "back-haller." He was lost. "No one knew him except the guys on the golf team," said his teammate Pudge Geduldig. He might have capitalized on the prestige afforded by his rank on a varsity team, even the comparatively unglamorous golf squad, but not many knew that for the 1940 Minutemen, runners-up for the city championship, Sparky was not only a letterman but also the number two golfer in a school of nearly a thousand boys. Yet he could not bring himself to claim the varsity letter that was his to wear—the big red "C" he had envied for two years on upperclassmen's sweaters. By some administrative error, his letter was held up until after he graduated; he did not seek to expedite it.

All his life, Charles Schulz measured himself by the way other people viewed him, not by what he set out to be. He was ambitious, in the Dale Carnegie sense typical of his generation, but he did not care as much about influencing other people as he did about controlling his own fluctuating sense of self-worth. "It was my own fault," he would later say of his misery at Central. "I was extremely immature. All I was interested in were art and golf."

His contemporaries scarcely existed for him, except as reminders of his self-imposed exile. In the fall of his junior year, a faculty advisor finally urged him to join the art club. Between forty and fifty students belonged to Thumb Tacks, which met after hours to make posters for school groups, to draw elaborate layouts for the school yearbook, and to prepare group exhibitions of student artwork. Sparky was more than qualified: he was probably the only nationally published artist trying out for the club.

At the appointed hour, he took himself to the brightly lit classroom in which Thumb Tacks met, only to hesitate at the doorway. Except for one other short fellow, Sparky was smaller than most male Thumb Tacks (many of whom seemed to hover over six feet), though he looked and dressed no differently than anyone else in the clean-cut, well-groomed art crowd. But the room was vast, the voices were loud, and everyone seemed so sure of himself. Losing his nerve, Sparky turned on his heel and fled. Afterward, the faculty advisor asked why he had run away from peers who shared his passion for drawing and design. "They're brutes," he blurted out.

As a senior he consented to join the Thumb Tacks and the yearbook staff—at least he appeared in their official yearbook photographs. In reality, he spent as little time as possible in these circles and would always deny having belonged to any club in high school, just as he would insist on portraying himself as the wounded party in most of his high school dealings. It was the other kids, he insisted, who had excluded him.

"I wasn't actually hated," he would say of his years at Central High. "Nobody cared that much." For good or ill, he hadn't let them.

And to them, it was he who seemed not to care. It was "Charles" who did not bother to make a favorable impression, to remember names, or even just to lighten up and try to be friendly. It would take decades for him to see that his timidity—the shyness behind which he operated as he yearned, and even sometimes aimed, for approval—was "a form of egotism." Far advanced into international success, he could finally say, "I suppose I'm the worst kind of egotist, the kind who pretends to be humble."

He played the part of the wallflower whose shyness draws the attention the subject feels he deserves. In the rough sketch for a gag cartoon of the '40s, he depicted this exact type: a round-headed girl in her overcoat calls over her shoulder from the doorway to a social gathering where the other teenagers, in letter sweaters and pleated skirts, are paired off and holding hands: "I said, 'I hate to break up the party, but I have to be going!' " Twenty years later, pulling on his coat, Charlie Brown himself would call from the doorway: "Well, I hate to spoil all the fun, but I have to be going."

At Central, he made his boyish avoidance of others look—at least in his own eyes—like others' rejection of him. For the rest of his school days, he would hide out, covering up by means of this reversal. In the meantime, he thought of himself as a thwarted innocent, a lonely, misunderstood, good-hearted kid who wanted only to earn a little recognition for the things at which he was somehow masterful. He seems never to have admitted how seriously he took himself, how ambitious and competitive he really was, and how entitled to receive special attention for his unique gifts and extreme sensitivity—and how all of this contributed to both the development of his talent and drive and, under pressure, his romantic, wound-and-bow, energizing sense of injury.

To cite one example out of many, he recalled the day when he made "the terrible mistake" of showing his silver-haired English teacher Gertrude Borden a 1936 comic book–style adaptation of *A Tale of Two Cities*, which Miss Borden, a no-nonsense native Minnesotan who had been teaching English at Central High for almost two decades, treated "with absolute scorn." This convinced Schulz, when he looked back on the incident years later, that his teacher had "made a terrible mistake, because she missed the opportunity of having a conversation with me. Here was her chance to help me, but she didn't. . . . This is just another incident that I've held against teachers."

But a sense of the implications and possibilities of the popular culture was still a rare and very high culture phenomenon; Miss Borden, fighting the battles of classic literature, would have been remarkable had she been able to see the artistic interest of a comic book.

AT HOME IN THE evening, he rewarded himself with solitude, shutting himself into his room to draw. Cartooning gave him something that nothing else could: proof of his power.

He solved the problem of his stature at school by drawing powerful little people at home, creating a character named Little Julius, who served, perhaps without his intending it, as his double—a "little Caesar," a figure of power who just happened to be an ordinary guy.

One night in January of his senior year, his mother came into his room. "Look here in the newspaper. It says, 'Do you like to draw?' "—and she showed Sparky an advertisement for mail-order art lessons.

*Draw Me!* said a pouting girl, fashionably adorned.

The school in question boasted of opening doors to "big money" for cartoonists who completed its course: up to $5,000 a year—more than five times the median national family income. The advertisement urged Sparky to find out if he had "money-making art talent." The course cost an incredible $170 ($2,000 in today's money)—70 percent higher than a year's tuition at the University of Minnesota. But an applicant who copied the side view of the pouting girl and sent it in would be eligible to win a free course. He had *nothing to lose, everything to gain.*

As it turned out, his skills were insufficient to win a free course. As many as five other applicants in 1940 were judged to have more "valuable art talent" than Charles Schulz. Sparky's five-inch-high ink replication of the pouting girl failed to show "real ability" but had enough "merit," apparently, for the school to send a recruiter from the business department to the Schulzes' door.

It was a biting winter night; almost sixty years later, Sparky could still remember the salesman "coming up on the cold, storm-doored porch" of 473 Macalester. Once inside, he fanned out twelve pale blue, perfect-bound booklets embodying Divisions 1 through 12 of the Modern Illustrating and Cartooning course, and let the Schulzes handle these voluminously illustrated texts. He brought out samples of the artists' paraphernalia furnished at no extra charge to each student. The T square, the personalized Federal Schools pencils, the dusty art-gum eraser, the gleaming compass—all seemed to confer importance on the entire family.

The recruiter reminded the Schulzes of the *wasted hours* that could be turned into *golden opportunities*, and of the *personal criticism* that Sparky would be receiving from *professional artists*, and of how this *individual instruction* could be turned into *paying results*. "Cartoonists make big money," the school declared. By *capitalizing on their humorous ideas*, cartoonists like Frank King and Sidney Smith made $100,000 a year. "YOU may have ideas that are equally good," clamored the school's business office; or again: "Every laugh means money for the man who creates it." Surely a man of Carl Schulz's business acumen, a figure of significance in community affairs—surely *he* could see the practical wisdom of making a relatively small investment in talent so valuable?

"The road to bigger things is open to you if you will but take the first step," murmured the brochure. "The statement from the financial head of the school is an agreement upon which you can rely."

But how would Carl foot the bill? Could he, who brought home a little more than half of every fifty-cent haircut, afford the school's exorbitant fee of $170 when Carl's idea of a great extravagance never went higher than a new $9 fishing reel? Had Dena suggested, say, a new four-piece bedroom suite, at $49.50, it would clearly have been out of the question. At that rate, if Sparky must get an art education, why not apply for one of the less expensive night courses offered by an art school in the Twin Cities?

"I was afraid to go to art school," he would say in later years. "I just knew that I'd be out of place, [that] I couldn't see myself sitting in a room where everyone else in the room could draw much better than I; and this way I was protected by drawing at home and simply mailing my drawings in and having them criticized."

He would go at his own speed: *Each student is really a class of one and can go just as fast or as slow as they* [sic] *desire.* More than anything, it was the step-by-step demonstrations of cartooning and pen technique that impressed Sparky. Carl liked the emphasis on practical applications of a student's abilities. He did not intend to stop Sparky from trying to be a comic strip artist—"not that I could have anyway"—but he particularly liked the sound of an art course that offered training in the "Business End of Illustrating and Cartooning," reflecting later, "I figured in the back of my mind that if he never got a strip, there were always other branches of drawing—like in advertising or in clothes designing." In the end, Sparky recalled, the salesman "sold us."

On February 19, 1940, his father enrolled him as a home-study student in the Federal School of Illustrating and Cartooning. As it turned out, Carl had trouble keeping up with the $10 monthly payments, and all too soon dunning letters from the school's business office bombarded Macalester Avenue. Their progressively more drastic tone worried Sparky, but when he actually voiced these fears to his father, Carl told him not to be too concerned—they would manage. Sparky later learned that his father had simply become accustomed to owing money.

STARTING IN MARCH OF his senior year—the same month by which his mother's tumor must have turned malignant—he put aside his schoolwork to complete his first assignments. In Division 1, the student had to prepare pencil studies in shading, perspective, and action. By following Bart Pen Practice No. 4403, he had to demonstrate proficiency in pen lines in three tones. He then bundled his drawings into an envelope, took the packet to the post office, and held his breath until a letter came back across the river containing the instructor's criticism.

Records of his studies do not survive. In memory, Charles Schulz saw himself awaiting the arrival of each successive division, then poring over its fresh blue booklet. In Division 2, he treasured the samples of Charles Dana Gibson's pen technique and followed along as the master built up facial features stroke by stroke. In Division 3, he studied the muscle action of hands and feet in as much depth as Carl's barber-college course in anatomy.

With Division 5 came the drawing of children, featuring Clare Briggs's advice on using the familiar people and scenes of one's own boyhood for the "Boy Subject," Fontaine Fox of *Toonerville Folks* discussing the special demands made by a humorous single-panel cartoon appearing simultaneously in dozens of different markets, and Bart's seminar on the art of lettering, going back to Greek and Roman inscriptions.

"If that course did nothing else," Schulz would say, "it taught me to value good drawing in comics and good pen work." He began to see that ink had qualities not unlike paint—how it could be transparent or opaque, built up or stripped down. And he learned how different qualities of lines drawn in various tones and thicknesses could evoke different feelings.

HIS FATHER NOTICED THAT Sparky "never seemed to take to girls," and wondered if "maybe his size was the reason."

Size was indeed one obstacle. In his sophomore year, some oaf in his class tagged him "the shorty of Central."

Literally the "ninety-seven-pound weakling" of Charles Atlas's body-building advertisements, which so successfully fed on the uncertainties of those who sought self-improvement from the back of comic books, Sparky stood no taller than five feet, six inches, and no matter how much he grew or filled out, the school's chestbeaters considered him fair game. "I was regarded by many as kind of sissified, which I resented because I really was not a sissy."

With girls, timidity was the problem. His female classmates found him marked by an extreme reserve. The words applied by girls who knew him at Central—"proper and retiring," "bashful," "innately shy," a "brain"—describe a boy who was "not a lot of fun," as one front-haller remembered him. A popular girl in his class described Sparky as "this wimpy little kid," adding, "We liked him, but he just didn't have much to offer."

He "wasn't unusual in the fact that he didn't ask anybody out," said a classmate. "There were some that dated, but there were a lot of people that didn't date." What was unusual was his inability to initiate any conversation at all. Even tossing out the simplest hello in the hallways was agony. "He just couldn't put himself forward," says his classmate Patricia Wysocky. "It was just not his nature to push himself into any crowd and say, 'Hi, I'm Charlie.' That wasn't him at all."

The prettier the girl, the more petrified he became. On a family visit to the Swansons in Hudson, Wisconsin, when he was seventeen, he spent a good deal of time just standing at the window of his cousins' house to watch a cute blonde walk past the lilac bushes lining the sidewalk. Jane Gilbertson was a friend of his cousin Dorothy, and Sparky wanted very much to know her, but he remained paralyzed. "He never did go out with her," said his cousin Lorraine. "He'd stand in the window and watch her go by on St. Croix. He'd say, 'Oh, I'd like to meet her.' Very quiet, so no one else would hear it."

In one sense, he was satisfied with being unseen, for he had an almost magical belief that, sooner or later, he had to be discovered. The question was, by whom? Who would come along and see that his was, as Charlie Brown would later say of himself, a "personality that will probably inspire a heroic symphony"?

Studied disappearance is a powerful technique for asserting presence, especially for a boy who thinks himself ugly. He was sharply critical of his looks, especially his nose, which he considered large—though, in truth, it was regular in size and shape, descending in a straight line to end in a rounded button. For all that, he compared himself with pointed disfavor to other boys in his neighborhood: "I had some friends who were nice-looking young people, and I always felt handicapped by that, and felt that nobody would ever care about anybody who looked like me." One of his favorite moments in the movies was the famous climax of Chaplin's tale of blind love, *City Lights,* when the flower girl regains her sight and for the first time sees her hero for who he really is—and yet, through the turmoil of her emotions, still loves the Tramp. This scene would keep its poignancy for Sparky all his life.

He had an eye for a cute girl whom he saw mornings on the Selby Lake streetcar he took to school: a skinny little brunette, with large, warm, dark brown eyes. "He knew her name and wanted to get better acquainted," a golf-team friend recalled, "but he didn't have the guts." He kept Lyala—pronounced *Lila*—Bischoff under daily surveillance for two years, never mustering the courage to speak to her. Thirty-five years later, in his fifties, when he could have introduced himself, Schulz asked his old teammate Pudge Geduldig to look her up during a visit to the Twin Cities and pose a couple of questions: Did she remember him from the streetcar? Had she *seen* him?

By all accounts, girls wanted to like him. Ann Kennedy could have been speaking for many classmates when she told him, "You're terrible quiet . . . but you're smart."

Other statements recorded in fountain pen in Schulz's copy of the 1940 yearbook reveal a boy whose female contemporaries wanted to appreciate him but were thwarted. The sullen, heavily defended Charles Schulz they knew was a superior draftsman and an outstanding student in the commercial law class that Central then offered. He himself may have been uncertain about what he had to give the world, but male and female classmates alike esteemed his talents. Time and again, the classmates who signed his yearbook—girls as often as boys—thanked him for some special quality of help, making clear their gratitude for Sparky's having taught them and their appreciation of his growing expertise. "Maybe if I keep at it long enough, I'll be as good as you," wrote Helen Burt, an aspiring artist. In his mechanical drawing class he shared a desk with Marcia Correll, whose real popularity and prettiness did not mean that she knew how to use a protractor. "He explained to me how to use it," she recalled, "and guided me through the class and I ended up getting an 'A.' " But when she tried to talk to Sparky outside of class, he clammed up.

Sherman Plepler had been the first companion with whom Sparky found pleasure in the give-and-take of friendship. Both felt themselves loners, and when they went places together as teenagers—Saturday matinees or ball games or ice shows—they always arrived early. ("Security is getting to the theater before the box office opens.") With time to kill, they would observe people and compare notes, finding humor in routine situations and plain long talks. In *Peanuts*, the character Shermy would be the first friend with whom Charlie Brown would have "a real adult conversation."

Earning pocket money as a caddy at St. Paul's Highland Park Golf Course, Sparky found among his fellows a second type of friend—a comrade in competition. Jim Cummings also lived around the corner, at 1657 Randolph Avenue. He was about as tall as Sparky, with fine features and fair hair. The other caddies noticed that they were also temperamentally alike: quiet and introverted—neither dated in high school—but joyfully competitive with one another. "They respected each other," recalled another of the group; "he was the guy Schulz liked the best."

In school, he established a third kind of friendship—with the only male classmate whom he could talk to about drawing: Charles Brown.

A CLASSMATE WHO KNEW them both as seniors would remember the two Charleses as inseparable at lunchtime.

Charles Brown was a moonfaced boy, short and stocky, with brown hair—sufficiently fascinated by Sparky's drawing to spend much of the school day encouraging other students to have a look at the latest cartoons, thus drawing Sparky into situations, especially with girls, from which he would otherwise have fled. Charles Brown, for example, had a friend, Doris Marriott, and Doris in her turn had a friend, Patricia Hanratty. In good weather, the four sat down to bag lunches on the school's front steps.

Sparky had a hard time knowing what to say, remaining mute as the others struck up a conversation. "And then his friend would say something to him and he'd loosen up," Patricia recalled. "He would never say the first word, but he was very, very pleasant when he started talking. Once he was in the conversation he was perfectly normal and relaxed. I'm sure that without his friend, Charlie [Schulz] would never have come up the steps and sat down with us."

Broad balustrades enclosed the front terrace. On fine windless days Charles Brown would prod Sparky to open his book bag and spread the latest correspondence-course cartoons on the balustrade. "Charles Brown was the one who always said, 'Show them this,' " said Patricia. "Charles Schulz would never bring out his cartoons. Charles Brown was the one who did that for him."

One day the cartoon characters were children—Sparky's Division Five studies. "Show her those," urged Charles Brown, and Sparky handed around the loose sheets of drawing paper. Years later, Patricia simply remembered, "It impressed me that he could sketch like that, but it didn't strike me that the cartoons were outstanding."

THE ONE BRIGHT SPOT at Central High was Minette Paro's classroom. Miss Paro, an independent-minded New Englander with a degree from the Pratt Institute of Art in Brooklyn, had been teaching at Central since 1923. Her students of the late 1930s remembered her as "the most caring and nurturing teacher one could have." Her gift was for encouragement, especially toward the shy and the insecure; one such pupil recalled that Miss Paro "did so much to try to build us up and make us feel important and talented." Sparky called her kind, considerate, the one teacher he liked, and even he conceded that the course in advanced illustration that he took from her in spring 1940 yielded him his only triumph at Central.

Miss Paro handed each student a twelve-by-eighteen-inch sheet of drawing paper: "Draw anything you can think of—in sets of three, on one side of the paper." Sparky, she recalled, "couldn't wait for me to stop talking."

Without a moment of uncertainty, he swooped into the assignment, swiftly and deftly summoning radiant lightbulbs and belching smokestacks, each sketch perfectly matched to its two mates. Stylized catchers' mitts, barbers' poles, artists' palettes, and cheerleaders' megaphones leapt from his pencil point. He abstracted dozens of everyday objects into cartoon icons: smiling suns, fuming cigars, beaming flashlights, spinning tops, burning fuses, sparkling diamonds. He seized on big themes and made them his own: the telephone, the American flag, the swastika, the almighty dollar. From his pen emerged a cornucopia of skeleton keys, lightning bolts, milking stools, umbrellas, carrots, dentures, blue ribbons, hand clippers, wristwatches, fingerprints, footprints, baby carriages, ball caps, ink bottles, gravestones, traffic lights, flowerpots, baseball bats, thunderclouds, golf bags, paintbrushes, steering wheels, doorknobs, framed portraits, wedges of layer cake, lengths of chain, constellations of stars, flights of ghosts.

He chose subjects that no one else had thought of drawing or would think of drawing: halos, scimitars, pediments, anchors, targets, staples, springs, skulls, combs, boots, stools, gloves. Three cloud-wracked moons appeared, and a trio of men with long noses. He drew a set of question marks—and one brand-name product, Wheaties, plus recognizable pictographs of people and places such as the United States of America, Adolf Hitler, the North Star State of Minnesota, and one name standing unchallenged among the taken-for-granted furniture of everyday life:

*CHARLES SCHULZ*
*CHARLES SCHULZ*
*CHARLES SCHULZ*

Nor was this just any practice signature. In youth, we all experiment by penning our names as signatory extensions of ourselves. But did anyone else in the class grant him or herself permission to let his or her name stand as boldly as the Breakfast of Champions among the massive skyline presences of American life?

Some other students struggled merely to bring off three drawings of even one object. Charles Schulz filled his entire sheet in less than five minutes. "His mind," said Minette Paro, "was working faster than his fingers." His drawings, stylized as cartoons, pulsed with professionalism. To catch so many things so fast and so economically seemed to reveal an extraordinary confidence in his powers, and it was this force and independence of thinking that bowled Miss Paro over. She held up Charles's spectacular array of triplicates as an example to the rest of the class.

★   ★   ★

BY SPARKY'S SENIOR YEAR Dena was fighting for her life. Sparky was told nothing of the progress of the disease, but could not have helped noticing her decline. Little wonder that at school he buried himself in a passivity indistinguishable from stupidity, while he was learning at home that ignorance was his strongest armor—for such time as Dena had left. His father wanted, of course, not to frighten him, or Dena. But, perhaps without meaning to, Carl, in step with Dr. Edlund, ended up insulting Sparky's intelligence even as he excited his fears.

In any case, Sparky knew enough to be apprehensive. On the very far side of the cancer's triumph, Linus Van Pelt would lie sleeplessly worrying in his dark bunk at summer camp, progressing from the predictable fear of snakes crawling into his cabin to a sudden, unexpected elaboration of panic: "What if my mother and dad move away while I'm gone, *and don't tell me?*"

Throughout his years at Central, the sense of doom bearing down would prevail over nearly every aspect of his experience, becoming a watershed in the formation of his character. When his father tried to sum up Sparky's life during high school, the Sparky he remembered was well-behaved, conscientious, self-controlled: no outbursts, no raised voices, no harsh words, no disturbance of any kind. He comported himself not so much as a teenager but as a perfect little adult, or as what children call "a little old man," a figure who takes refuge from a threatening world in a simulacrum of adulthood. The one feeling that he admitted to struggling with during the years of his mother's dying was frustration. But lest she be further burdened, he kept that, and more, to himself. He later said of those years, "It took me a long time to become a human being."

As a teenager, he had come to sense that he could not trust what he was, or was not, being told at home: "Adults seem to keep things hidden from you—things that they think you shouldn't hear about, which is nonsense," he later said. His parents' tiptoeing kept him a child, straining his relations with peers and deepening his desolation at school.

That last spring at Central, his champion Minette Paro, as faculty advisor to the yearbook, invited her star pupil to submit to the *Cehisean* a series of drawings about school activities. Flattered to be singled out, Sparky quickly executed several views of student life that, so far as memory went, seemed to please Miss Paro, and he understandably anticipated their publication. Come the last week of school, the newly published yearbook popped, hot off the press, all over the hallways, and Sparky thumbed through the glossy pages, first eagerly and then with mounting dismay, for, no escaping it, the drawings had not been published.

Years later, a reporter put it to Schulz: "Did you ask the teacher what happened to them?" and Schulz replied, "No, I wouldn't have had the nerve."

But it was fraternity—collegiality—that was lacking, not courage. Though not a team player by nature, Sparky was on the *Cehisean* staff, listed as one of the "efficient helpers" to the art editor, Richard Ruhme. He may not have trusted himself to strike up a private conversation with that smoother, better-connected classmate, and he may have run afoul of other "Cehisean Heads" such as the photography editor, Stanley Loeffler, of whose prizewinning polar bear Sparky had been so dismissive, or the boys' sports editor, David Morris, who had dubbed him "the shorty of Central."

Finding it impossible to brush the chips off his shoulder and team up with his artistically minded peers, Sparky had put his faith in Miss Paro's patronage. But was it precisely this that may have given his yearbook colleagues a sense that he expected preferential treatment? Could they have come to conclude that the mostly absent Schulz thought himself their superior, not least because he had already published a drawing in a worldwide syndicated comic feature?

In the decades to come he never tired of bringing this up, always calling it his first major rejection. It was certainly his first major intellectual grudge. As the years went by and high school yearbook editors came to him by the hundreds from all over America for permission to publish likenesses of his characters, he imbued this procession with fairy-tale vindicatory power, as each approved drawing in a new annual heaped before him "a stack tall enough to reach the ceiling," a beanstalk capable of delivering—his word— revenge.

But revenge on whom? Who is the villain of this piece? Miss Paro? Richard Ruhme? The whole yearbook staff?

As with the bullies on the playgrounds of his childhood, he never identified his antagonist. And in this case he never learned what had happened to his drawings. "To this day," he wrote in 1975, "I do not know why they were rejected." The story had no resolution; his stubbornly held resentment had no ending. He would never try to come to terms with his own part in it, or ever fully uncover the forces that had blocked him. And so, arrested, bitter, he spent a startling amount of time over nearly sixty years polishing a cameo of boyish helplessness and frustration.

That he should entertain hard feelings was not unreasonable. Graphically, the *Cehisean* of his high school years was the equal of a college publication today—an attractive place for any aspiring artist to publish. Sparky's collection of yearbooks, dating back to 1937, show that he had paid close attention to the annual since his first year. The quality of its drawings is uniformly high; nearly professional talent shows up on every page, always in service to its class and school. The yearbook was not looking for a star turn—no one boy's individualist bravura performance, pen flying across the page, dashing off identical sets of threes. Each year the *Cehisean* was dominated by a single visual motif; whether Art Deco (1937) or Indian folkways (1938), the yearbook staff subordinated its collective talent to a common style and theme.

Colonial silhouettes were the motif for the Minuteman Class of 1940; Richard Ruhme's bell-ringing town crier served as frontispiece. Whether or not Sparky was aware of the controlling idiom (if he wasn't, he must have been even more remote from his fellows than it seemed), he submitted scenes of contemporary student life in a style of his own, including one drawing of a boy studying in the library. His work, exceptional as it may have been, fell perhaps not on any lack of merit, but simply because it failed to connect with the overall design. Perhaps it simply got lost between the conflicting wishes of the faculty advisor and the student editors. In the end, however, school politics had little to do with Schulz's explicit refusal to confront the truth—namely, that if anyone was responsible for this particular "rejection," it was himself.

From "earliest memory," Charles Schulz felt sure that, despite the indifference of everyone around him, he had been "born to draw comic strips." But now, in the final days of his formal education, the stunning unconcern of his peers united with the horror and senselessness of his mother's suffering to challenge his one great dream, the only solace that Sparky had allowed himself.

The Central High School yearbook proved to have been the last chance for Dena Schulz to see her son's work in print. Her unmentionable disease was the wellspring of anger and sadness and frustration that fed Schulz's undying disappointment. What kept itself fiercely alive for more than five decades was the shock of realization in June 1940 that, once his part in the yearbook had come to nothing, he had little time left to show his mother that he was something.

# CHAPTER 9

# ALONE

*I don't think she thought he would amount to very much.*
—SHIRLEY GISH VONDERHAAR

JUST AS LIFE WAS supposed to be starting, it seemed to be ending. "The two years following high school were extremely difficult," Schulz wrote later, "for this was the time that my mother was suffering so much with her illness."

On June 14, as France was falling to the Germans, and the Wehrmacht prepared to march down the Champs Élysées, Sparky paraded in the Class of 1940's triumphal procession at commencement exercises in St. Paul's City Auditorium. His diploma entitled him to enroll with more than fourteen thousand other students at the University of Minnesota the following fall. Most of his friends were already planning to attend "the U," where tuition cost $100 a year, but for Sparky there was no question of his becoming a college man. "It was obvious I wasn't smart enough."

Sherman Plepler would later recall that during the spring of his senior year Sparky told him that he had met with a counselor at school who had advised him to forget about college and to think instead about a vocation. But Schulz's last high school report card shows a boy who excelled in college-level courses like Commercial Law and Advanced Illustration. Thirteen out of sixteen grades recorded in four courses over the final four marking periods of senior year are A or better, with three A's in Commercial Law and two in Economics. In two art courses, he received Central's rarest grade, the almost unheard-of double-A for excellence. His lowest grade was a B. He himself was well aware that his marks "show," as he later put it, "that I was not as dumb as everyone has said I was," although he could not resist also contending that his final display of brightness was only because he had had a light schedule during his last half-semester.

Simply by graduating, Sparky had surpassed his parents. He was acutely conscious of belonging to "the first generation to be able to complete high school." As if to affirm solidarity with Carl and Dena, he ever after down-played his lively intellect and stressed the absence of college from his own education, always insisting that he would have flunked out "in the first quarter." Repeatedly, he contended that he "wouldn't have made it" and expressed thankfulness for having had parents "who didn't force me to go to the University of Minnesota," and who tolerated his choosing instead to pursue a "strange profession, one which they didn't understand, one which no one else around us understood." He would always say of his parents, "They let me be what I wanted to be."

They wanted him to cartoon. Carl and Dena may not have under-stood the life of the feature cartoonist, but they did know that they would not lose Sparky to it as they would have lost him to college. They simply loaned him to his room every night—a silent, straining presence behind a closed door. Many years later, and by that time a dedicated reader of his-tory, divinity, and biography, he was asked to pick a time and a place in history that more than any other he would wish to visit. One might have expected him to wish to travel back to biblical times, or to the log-cabin years of his hero Lincoln. Instead, he chose to recapture a cabin-snug, prai-rie period in his own life—the years just after high school, when he was living with his parents in St. Paul.

College would have been far more disruptive to this fragile little world. Cartooning meant that boyhood and parenthood could go on uninter-rupted at 473 Macalester: a continuity crucial in the face of Dena's misery and—grim new development—the fraying of Carl and Dena's marriage.

MORE AND MORE, HE served as a buffer between his parents.

"You know," Dena said one day, "I'm getting so I don't trust anybody anymore. I don't believe anybody. The only person that I believe is Sparky. I believe everything he says."

"Don't you believe *me*?" said Carl.

"No, Schulz," said Dena. "No, I don't even believe you."

Over the previous decade, Dena and Carl had been seen by friends and relatives as a happy if not especially demonstrative couple. But now a separateness was making itself apparent between the two, and Sparky felt it. Increasingly, he noticed a new restless quality in his father, as another personality, testy and hard-nosed, broke through Carl's accommodating surface.

On Sunday evenings Dena and Carl regularly attended Dish Night at the Park Theatre so that Dena could collect, one piece at a time, the full set of giveaways. But then, in sudden revolt against this enforced patterning, Carl turned frosty and, claiming he could no longer afford twenty cents for the tickets, refused to be suckered any further by the gimmick.

He might as well have taken a hammer to the preciously accumulated dinnerware. "It was a bad sign," Sparky realized, "and a real mystery to me." His father's revolt meant that Sparky replaced Carl as Dena's date on her big night out, and his late-teenage Sunday evenings came thus to be given over to escorting his dressed-up mother to the movies, sharing a single bag of hot buttered popcorn through the newsreel, the picture, and the associate feature (such as Laurel and Hardy in *Block-Heads* or a Disney cartoon short)—all until this elaborate setup culminated in the ritual of claiming the payoff: a new bone-white dish, cup, or saucer pulled by the ushers from huge excelsior-filled wooden crates under the marquee.

To Sparky's envy, his mother took special interest in his friend Jim Cummings, who would stop in from around the corner to pick him up for the streetcar ride to Highland Park. Athletically built and by all accounts a good-looking young man with "a warmth and a friendliness about him," he was bonded to Sparky by a substitute sibling rivalry; they even had reciprocal nicknames for each other: "Dub" and "Pro," which played on the poorest and best strokes in golf. "You could feel how competitive Cummings was and how competitive Schulz felt toward him," recalled a fellow golfer at Highland Park.

Dena was oddly free and easy with Sparky's comrade in competition. She might sit Jim down in the kitchen with a wedge of her lemon pie, or compliment him on how fine he looked today and how nicely polished his shoes were, or ask how he had liked last week's double feature at the Park, in all of which, she relegated Sparky to a childlike marginality (with jealous feelings to match) while maneuvering Jim into a precocious manhood. Norwegian women of Dena's generation liked their men virile. We can't know for sure what drew her attention to Jim, but, according to one of Dena's nieces, she treated him the way Halverson women had been taught to treat men: feeding them, praising them, making them feel like kings of the castle.

What we do know is that Sparky thought he had to work hard to get a woman's attention, and that his conviction that he was ugly kept him for years even from trying. When he was asked late in life what he would like to be could he be completely different, he replied, "I'd like to have been better-looking." It would be years before he realized that the women who noticed him were those to whom he revealed himself.

STAMPED AS HIS PARENTS' son, the Charles Schulz who started into the life of work in 1940 was more generally a product of a boyhood between the world wars, a time when the good male American was supposedly two things: aggressive yet innocent.

That first summer after high school, Sparky caddied, earning enough to buy a secondhand typewriter, which, by "pounding all night" on it, he mastered. Completing a supplementary business course offered by Federal Schools, he learned how to write a proper commercial letter and promptly inquired of Mr. Walt Disney at Burbank, California, about a job. Back came a printed application form. This he filled out, carefully following the instructions for submitting a sample of his work—a cartoon of a Disney character fixing a clock by shoveling the works back inside. All too soon afterward, he received a pedantic form letter "regretting" that he was unqualified.

Next he applied to Gilberton Publications, a textbook company in New York City. That year, 1941, Albert Lewis Kanter, one of the company's traveling sales representatives, had hit on the idea of turning masterworks of world literature into comic books—*Classics Illustrated*, initially *Classic Comics*. Sparky offered his services as artist for their version of his favorite novel, P. C. Wren's tale of the Foreign Legion, *Beau Geste*. He got no reply.

It pained his parents not to be able to know how to help him. Grabbing at straws, Carl asked his salesman brother-in-law in East St. Paul, William Wegwerth, if he knew anybody whom Sparky could see or talk to. Carl took to buttonholing customers; one day at the barbershop a young man who was "trying to do some writing" said he would be interested in seeing what Carl's son was "trying to do." So Sparky gathered up his latest drawings and presented himself at the other young hopeful's bachelor-style rooming house. "We sat there all evening, and he talked nonstop about his writing and his ambitions. It was a total waste. He didn't know anything about comic strips or anything like that. . . . I was forever being falsely recommended during that time, or so it seemed."

He would see those first years out of high school as one of the hardest times in his life. Set on being a comic strip artist, he "had no way of knowing how to do it." Even the more accessible market for gag cartoons in national magazines was a "struggle . . . because I had no one, really, to show me how to do it."

In a narrow alcove in the attic on Macalester, he worked long, solitary hours at night, his makeshift drawing board divided between the panels of a comic strip about the Foreign Legion, which he had researched at the St. Paul Public Library, and his rough sketches for magazine cartoons about golf and Ping-Pong and pinball. One of his first attempts showed a pinball player who has just started a new round only to watch in frozen amazement as the silver ball rockets out through the end of the machine.

Every morning as Carl left for work, he would take Sparky's latest parcel of sketches, neatly addressed to *Collier's* or *The Saturday Evening Post*, to mail at the post office near the barbershop.

The gag cartoon was the ideal form for a young man who needed to prove in a hurry to his mother that his ambitions were reasonable and visibly capable of fulfillment. An aspiring playwright or novelist would have needed an entire summer, or more, to have a chance of showing his stuff. As an aspiring cartoonist, Sparky could feed the morning mail with rough sketches, proving day in, day out, that he could produce. Every single day he had "something in the mail working for him," and this was demonstrably not stuff that everyone could do.

Faithfully he sent off the sketches, and the following week, back they would come in their self-addressed, stamped envelopes, never a penciled "OK," just a lengthening quilt of form rejection slips. Nearly forty years later, Charles Schulz could "still recall vividly the sinking feeling on reading the brief note that told me my submission was not worthy." And not one note, but so many.

"He'd throw [his rejected submissions] in the incinerator," Carl recalled, "and start all over."

Not a discouraging word was spoken in the house, although Sparky was surrounded by pessimism and worried silence. His father simply wanted to clear out of Sparky's way long enough for the boy to get ahead. As in so many immigrant families, the parents underestimated what they had to give a child growing up in the new culture; whatever Carl had to contribute might only obstruct Sparky's chances. "All I was hoping," Carl would recall a quarter-century later, trying to recapitulate the future as seen from 1941, "was that he'd get settled and have a house."

His mother feared for Sparky as he roughed out ideas and typed up gag lines—ten to a batch—for cartoons he hoped would appeal to national magazines. Dena saw that he was aspiring to the wrong line of work for a prude. With war in Europe and men everywhere in uniform, it was no longer a matter of artistic sensibility but an issue of manhood, and she tried to wean Sparky away from his delicacy. One day she suggested that perhaps his gags weren't "smutty" enough.

She may have been right. The magazine cartoons of 1941 were full of innuendo, far more so than was allowed in newspaper comics, which catered to a broader and therefore more easily offendable audience. In a typical *Collier's* cartoon of this period, a sexy young housemaid, dark-haired and leggy, runs out onto a suburban sidewalk, her brief black skirt and white apron flying, to greet her Romeo with open arms. In the background, we see half a dozen other women outside their houses waiting for the same man. At the curb, a mild-mannered milkman turns to a passing postman: "I often wonder what the fellow on this route before me was like."

This was the period in which Sparky was delivering groceries once or twice a week to a beautiful dark-haired lady in her early twenties. "She always answered the door in a sheer dressing gown," he recalled. "After paying me what she owed, she always gave me a nickel"—the only customer who tipped him. But if these professional experiences inspired a humorous take on sex, Sparky put no suggestion of it into his work. Always the hyperconscious observer, ever the shy boy whom puberty almost seemed to have passed by, he could not cast himself, even in fun, as the object of housewifely lust. "My problem," he said, "was that I couldn't have drawn a 'smutty' cartoon if I had tried."

Years later, he guessed at the origin of what had become an enduring cast of temperament. His father had never told milkman jokes or used vulgar language, although now and then he could unleash a "damn" or a "hell," but Sparky could not manage even those mild vices. "I don't know what made me that way. Maybe there's some kind of a fatal flaw or something. I don't know what it is, but that's just the way I am. It was just the way we lived." And then he realized what the "fatal flaw" had been: "Maybe I'm competitive, that's all. You have to be." Sparky certainly had to. The thought of sinking back into the uneducated wasteland from which his parents had uneasily risen was a Schulz family anxiety: "I wasn't going to be dragged down."

By then he had completed the second part of the Federal Schools business course—in business etiquette. "I was very earnest in learning more about how to do things right. I wanted to know how to eat properly, how to speak properly, how to write properly." In refining his habits, he set himself apart from his relatives and from his generation. Not swearing was a way of distinguishing himself from the mass of other young men in the 1940s over whom he was certain that he possessed deep but still barely tangible advantages—and of identifying himself as cultivated, smart, on the rise.

BUT WAS HE SOMETHING—or nothing? This was the question that his mother's illness set before him with unnatural urgency, and that he found he could not answer for himself. He needed the world to understand him—to appreciate those special qualities that marked him—but he did not know where to go to elicit such recognition. Staying put in St. Paul exaggerated his sense of distance from the real world where he felt his place to be. Again and again, Sparky complained that he knew nobody who knew anything about drawing cartoons.

Around the corner on Randolph Avenue, Sherman Plepler's father and mother took an interest in Sparky's work after high school. The cultivated, musical Pleplers knew he was completing the Federal Schools correspondence course and admired his perseverance, noting that he "pursued art work diligently, *believing* in it." Albert Plepler would later bluntly characterize Sparky's reaction to the teaching methods and instructors at the Federal Schools as "defiance," recalling that he had been "opposed to the conventional, accepted, and approved at the time."

But defiance did not mean dynamism. Sparky's decision to remain at 473 Macalester Avenue made even Minneapolis, fifteen miles upstream, seem far away—not so much an energizing sense of Sparky against the world as a debilitating feeling that the world did not care enough even to resist him. He waited until Frank Wing had officially graduated him from Federal Schools, Inc.—on December 1, 1941—before driving his father's Ford over to ask his instructor for advice.

Frank Wing was a distinguished man in a dark cutaway, with rounded shoulders and small, dark eyes lying flat behind wire-rim spectacles that glittered as he shook his head over Sparky's latest sketches. A pen-and-ink perfectionist, Wing believed in literal drawing: an artist who wanted to embark upon the gleeful distortions of the cartoon form must first learn to render the true human figure. His brow would darken as he looked over Sparky's work ("He couldn't really tell me what was wrong with it") and once more urged Sparky to draw from life and to consider the *whole* subject he was drawing—posture, the way the neck met the shoulders, the shape of the hands and feet, the hang of the clothing.

Sparky countered: "Well, look at Popeye. Elzie Segar doesn't draw real people."

Wing liked *Popeye* but could not explain why Segar's drawing worked on its own terms. The old newspaper-trained artist could only express his contempt for the crudity of drawing in the new cartoons with which Schulz felt so deep an affinity. "He never could explain to me why Popeye was good. And that always puzzled me. He couldn't tell me what marvelous quality was there . . . or why the supposedly crude drawings in Popeye were actually wonderful."

Wing was literal, but not literal enough to see how his medium was being changed by the throbbing vitality of an original like Popeye. Segar had created a character whom people loved, not because he was a salty old sailor man with anchors tattooed on his arms, but because Popeye summed up in a single quality what an American man had to be to survive the 1930s: a fighter. Almost a decade before bullets bounced off Superman's chest, Segar capitalized on the comics' simplest convention—the very thing for which pain stars and swirling planets and ideographs like SOCK! had been invented: immunity to suffering, a fresh start in every strip. Popeye was indestructible; no weapon could overpower his "muskles," no villain could defeat his cranky defiance. "I yam what I yam" identified a national archetype, a gunslinger whose "guns" were forearms the size of torpedoes.

As the Federal Schools' publication, *The Illustrator*, was later to concede, Sparky Schulz "was very discouraged by his teachers."

THE FIRST WINTER AFTER high school, Dena Schulz saw another advertisement and encouraged Sparky to enroll in the night course offered by a local comic strip artist, Leonard F. Kleis, whose three-panel strip in the *St. Paul Pioneer Press*, *Virgil*, depicted a scrappy little boy with a big head and button eyes. The class met on Tuesday evenings in a downtown St. Paul extension of the University of Minnesota.

The first night, Kleis set out to gauge the abilities of his ten students by having them copy several strip characters, including Dagwood and Blondie, which he had reproduced on large sheets of paper tacked to the wall. Sparky was finished while the others had barely begun, impressing Kleis, like Miss Paro before him, with his speed and fluency. Thereafter, Kleis took Sparky seriously, and Sparky in his turn began to look forward to Tuesday evenings. Kleis's night class was "really exactly what I wanted to do and when I was the most happy."

Having established himself as the pupil best prepared for a career in cartooning, he turned his attention to a petite, round-faced girl seated two chairs away. Naomi Cohn had a delicately modeled mouth, a witty way with words, and thick brown hair parted on the side and worn to her shoulders. She was, he later said, the "prettiest little girl I had ever seen. And I wanted so much to talk to her." But he had a rival, "some idiot little kid who kept drawing Bugs Bunny and saying that it was his character," and who not only had the audacity to press his attentions, but even asked her name—"and I'd get so mad at this kid because he had the nerve to talk to her, and I didn't."

Kleis gave him an opening by directing each student to conceive and draw a comic strip; he was so enthusiastic when he saw the neatly and professionally lettered Foreign Legion narrative that Schulz had been evolving that he passed the boards from hand to hand among all the pupils. But it was Naomi Cohn who took a special interest. Her large brown eyes widened. "Oh, that's so neat!"

Sparky would never forget the words, or the feelings that flooded through him at that moment, not just of being gratified and flattered but of being worthy of the attention, and perhaps even the affection, of a pretty girl. For all that, he slipped away at the end of class without daring to speak a word to someone who so obviously appreciated his work.

IN 1941 SPARKY LISTED himself in the *St. Paul City Directory* as "artist." He worked meantime as a grocery clerk but could never remember the price of anything on the shelves and was too awkward to make himself useful to customers. Given a chance to deliver the groceries instead, he was forever being scared off by barking dogs and was relieved to learn one Saturday afternoon that he was fired. He then threw himself into a second job as a delivery boy, this time running packages downtown for a printing company, all the while sizing up office buildings on St. Paul's narrow streets as settings for the action of a new adventure comic strip that he had set out to develop at night, along the lines of Roy Crane's *Wash Tubbs* and *Captain Easy*.

His drawing was improving, he could tell; the lights and shadows that he caught at their contrasting moments throughout the day on the grid-like office facades gave his work a new starkness and clarity. He learned to silhouette figures and landscapes that he had previously been compelled to light stiffly from in front.

Sometimes, he lingered on the southwest corner of Fourth and Minnesota streets, peering through vast, colonnaded ground-floor picture windows at the *St. Paul Dispatch* and *Pioneer Press* plant, whose "famous twelve-hour service" of morning, evening, and Sunday editions kept a small city of presses continually at work; or he waited for the moment when the black torrent of newsprint gave way to the rainbow of Sunday comics tumbling across the metal rollers, a sight that always made him wonder if he "would ever see my own comics on those presses." His favorite book that year was a memoir of Jazz Age newspapering, *My Last Million Readers*, which held special appeal since its author, Emile Gauvreau had been an aspiring cartoonist who became an editor at Hearst's *New York Mirror*, and Sparky dreamed of someday working at a city-room desk.

Further upstream, the graphic arts industry of Minneapolis, which had been a powerhouse in the 1920s, was reawakening. Perhaps four hundred firms sought employees in all aspects of printing and publishing, and one day Sparky answered a classified ad for a "junior artist" in a direct-mail advertising company. At Gile Letter Service, he filled out an application that called for sample drawings, including one of a radio tower. He well knew the awesome KSTP six-hundred-footer that dominated the skyline between the Twin Cities, and he pulled up and sketched it on his drive back to St. Paul, returning the next day to submit his illustration directly to Mr. Gile himself. His memory of the boss's reaction has the transformative quality of a fairy tale: "Lo and behold, I got hired. And I was quite proud."

The next morning, assured of his destiny, he rose and left the house at six to catch the Minneapolis streetcar. But instead of artwork to ratify a sense of his powers, he was assigned to sweeping out the offices and given stacks of paper to bundle together, one sheet at a time. But still he did not mind, because he was supervised by a "wonderful lady, in her forties, with reddish hair, a little bit on the stout side," who took personal charge and made him feel that she had seen at once that he was special. But after about a week of unvaried sweeping and bundling, he said to her, "When is it that, perhaps, I will get to do some kind of art work?"

She sighed, tutted, and rolled her eyes, saying, "He did it again!" The boss was forever misleading young men into the belief that he would help them become the artists they longed to be when all he required was a delivery boy. All the same, Sparky needed a job, and, liking the office's sympathetic den mother, he stayed on into the summer, spending $1.29 of his first $14 paycheck on a collection of magazine cartoons. When the other young man in the office, "not an artist but actually a bona fide delivery boy," noticed Schulz completely absorbed in *Collier's Collects Its Wits*, he "couldn't believe that anybody would waste two dollars and fifty cents [*sic*] on a book of cartoons. It was beyond his comprehension."

By fall, when six months' notionally artistic employment had yielded one assignment to draw minuscule decorations on a mimeographed promotional sheet, Sparky quit, disillusioned. But his next job, as an office boy at Northwest Printing and Binding, was much the same, until he noticed something powerful among the people who worked at the hardest jobs in the plant:

> At noon, they would all gather down at the end of this room, and they would play pinochle, and eat their lunch. And you could hear them laughing, and having a wonderful time. When one o'clock came, they'd go back to working again. These were the people that held everything together. It wasn't the boss and the other partners. It was these workers, with their common sense, who just seemed somehow to know what is right and what is wrong. I think it's what we call the great middle class. There are the radicals on both sides, left and right; and the people that do strange things. But there are still the people with the common sense that hold everything together.

One night he drew a sketch of the man who worked the big paper-cutting machine; when he actually nerved himself to present it to its subject, no honor could have been greater. "Oh, he was so pleased with it, and all the people that worked with him in the place came and looked at it. And for the next hour, I got lots of attention and that made me feel good."

He quit the job after his boss berated him for taking two days off to play in a golf tournament, but not before making one of the essential discoveries of his career. He had identified the kind of people who made up his most natural audience—and glimpsed at first hand the essential transaction that would bind him to them.

At his next job in a direct-mail advertising company, the Associated Letter Service in downtown St. Paul, two young women, Marie Lick and her friend June, sometimes sat at a table in the same small workroom, addressing labels for the bundles that Sparky had tied. Working on his feet with four other young men, he wrapped tabloid-sized bales of advertising material from eight in the morning to four-thirty in the afternoon—and for the first few days, thought he was going to lose his mind. But he and the other young men "soon developed pride in our speed and dexterity in tying up bundles," and in that pride, he discovered that he could turn aside to laugh and joke with Marie and June, finding it possible to have fun with young women while they yet took him seriously. More surprising still, he was the only one of the young men who exercised such charm. "And I thought, 'Why is this? I've always been kind of shy, and stupid, and yet here I am—and they liked me.' I discovered the wonderful feeling for the first time in my life of being liked."

IN THE SPRING OF 1942, Dena had rallied. Recovery seemed possible. "You know how cancer patients seem to get much, much better?" said Dena's niece, Patricia Swanson, Marion's daughter. "We thought she was going to live. She started to clean up, to wear nice clothes again. She was happy. She started having her sister Marion over. Everything was going to be OK." She started to live once more.

One morning in the first weeks of May, with her hair freshly curled, she put on a nice dress—yellow with a floral pattern. She ironed her apron and put that on, too, but just as she was walking from bedroom to bathroom, she started bleeding—"from the female parts," recalled Pat Swanson—the most common symptom of cervical cancer.

Dr. Edlund sent her into Midway Hospital, an old-style three-story brick institution with narrow hallways and small rooms. It had been four years since the onset of the disease; cancer had invaded the uterine wall, dictating a hysterectomy. Afterward, she was bedridden again but still hopeful. "She thought she would beat it," said Patty Swanson. Then in the summer agony struck again, now low in her pelvis, and the nights at 473 Macalester were once more broken by sudden outcries.

Carl turned for help to John F. Sheady, the druggist around the corner from the Family Barber Shop. It happened that a walk-up apartment fell vacant on the second floor of the two-story corner building that housed the barbershop on Selby, the Sheady drugstore on Snelling, and O'Gara's bar. Hearing of this just as he saw Dena slide back from the false hopes of spring, Carl moved his family into No. 2, 170 North Snelling, so that he could be close to Dena and Dena close to the druggist. If she was having an attack, Carl and Mr. Sheady could hurry upstairs to supply comfort and—by now, alas, probably more important—morphine.

It was summer when the Schulzes settled into the two-bedroom apartment, joined on camp cots in the living room by Dena's sister Marion and her daughter Patty, then twelve, who had come to help take care of Dena. They had no air-conditioning; on a hot night the open windows let in the hissing of brakes as the Snelling Avenue streetcar puffed to a stop below Dena's sickroom. Until eleven o'clock every sultry night, the neon sign from Lux Liquors filled Dena's room with its tatty glow: a neon whiskey bottle pulsed from red through orange to yellow to green over the walls of the apartment.

In later years, when close friends recalled Sparky's responses to the final stages of his mother's disease, always emphasizing how hard it had been for him to get over this racking ordeal and its pathetic end, they spoke as if offering the latest evidence of his well-known oversensitivity. "You don't take the death of a loved one as hard as he did," went the opinion of at least one of his Minnesota friends. But no one who spoke of Sparky and Dena on these terms had been aware of the basic nature of her disease, much less in the stark human terms of its complications.

Each day during this time, Sparky returned from his latest job at another direct-mail company to the demoralizing reek of the whole apartment and of his mother's room in particular. All his life he had labored under the sense that adults were hiding things—"things that they think you shouldn't hear about"—and here it was again, evidence that he was deemed too sensitive or too unprepared to register his mother's appalling extremity. But nothing could mask the sharp tang of the sickroom. Air it out as often as they tried, the apartment would start to stink again, as if the walls themselves had gone soft with rot.

Yet no one spoke of it. Only in his imagination could he confront "the terror and the agony she must have gone through, dying that long, lingering death." For Sparky, the most harrowing part of his mother's torment was that no one told her that her disease was incurable. She remained in the dark until the bitter end.

ONE NIGHT, SPARKY VISITED in her room and found himself cornered by the point-blank question "Why can't they help me? Can't they do anything?" And of course, he had no idea what to say. He had no words because he had been given none. Together, they stood excluded from the adult world and its greatest secret. "I felt so bad about it," he would say.

This was the first time that he realized how she was being deceived "for her own good." His father and Dr. Edlund and Aunt Marion—all, in their sincere but uncomprehending ways, were shutting her out, treating her as if she was not aware and deadly afraid of what she must undergo, and it made Sparky mad. "In my anger, I went out in the kitchen, where my dad was standing with my aunt Marion."

In the record he left of his reactions in this time he would acknowledge being furious at this one moment:

"Why don't they do something?" he demanded. "What is wrong?"

Aunt Marion turned to him and said, "Sparky, your mother has cancer."

It was the first time he had heard the word applied to her.

Soon afterward, riding the streetcar home from his job, his gaze rested on one of the car cards up among the advertisements: COME UNTO ME, ALL YE THAT LABOR AND ARE HEAVY LADEN, AND I WILL GIVE YOU REST.

"What a marvelous statement," he recalled thinking.

WITHIN DAYS OF HIS twentieth birthday, November 26, 1942, Sparky received his draft notice, with orders to report to the induction center at Fort Snelling, across the Mississippi. He was furloughed home for Christmas. Dena's misery was now so extreme that she could no longer receive visitors. Spike was no longer allowed to lie on her bed and offer comfort, and even Sparky hesitated in the doorway. His cousin Patty remembered him looking in at his mother, dying before his eyes. Neither would again press the point of what she was suffering from, or whether she could be saved. He remembered Dena saying only one thing about the future: "If we ever have another dog, I think we should name him Snoopy."

*Snupi* is a Norwegian term of endearment; a mother might so call her young child. Whether that was in Dena's thinking is not known, but the prospect of a dog named Snoopy had, for the moment at least, the quality of extending their life together into a future that it seemed they were no longer likely to have.

Around Christmas, Carl asked the minister of a nearby Lutheran church to visit his dying wife. The Schulzes were not members of that parish, but Carl was sure that such a call would lift Dena's spirits, and they made arrangements; however, the minister failed to keep the appointment. So Carl turned to a customer, the Reverend George A. Edes, a personable man with a strong smile, pastor of the Merriam Park Church of God a few blocks to the west, who came, and came at once.

During the holiday, a young woman exactly Sparky's age appeared at the apartment with Mr. Edes, who had suggested that perhaps Dena would be relieved in her suffering if she could hear a little music. And so Bernetta Nelson, with her bright yellow hair and sunny disposition, stood singing a cappella in the little room above the streetcar intersection, as the neon whiskey bottle cast its glow over the edge of Dena's pillow.

Throughout January and February 1943, Dena was in and out of Midway Hospital. The turning point—the moment to which Sparky would return again and again—came on Sunday, February 28.

That morning a twelve-panel color page in the comics section had shown Joe Palooka going into the army, and how his mother had to teach Mrs. Highsnute about sugar and gasoline rationing. In the evening, Sparky went into his mother's bedroom. He had to report to Fort Snelling in an hour.

She was turned away from him in her bed against the wall, opposite the windows that overlooked the street. He said he guessed it was time to say good night.

"Yes," she said, "I suppose we should say good-bye."

She turned her gaze as best she could—it was a struggle to move at all. "Well," she said. "Good-bye, Sparky. We'll probably never see each other again."

The next day, Monday, March 1, Dena took another turn for the worse, and Carl went to get Sparky from the barracks at Fort Snelling.

Sparky was called to the big dayroom. By then his father was slumped down in the telephone booth, through whose glass Sparky could see him talking wearily, and then, all at once, choking up and beginning to cry. In a minute, he had pulled himself together, squared his shoulders into the barber's good posture, and swung the door open.

They faced one another across the dayroom. Their eyes met; Carl nodded once, then lifted his shoulders helplessly, his face falling. Neither husband nor son had been with her when she died in her bed at 3:32 P.M. By the time Sparky and Carl got home, the men from the funeral home had taken her away.

Dena Bertina Halverson Schulz had turned fifty on February 7, having lied about her age, even to her husband. Her gravestone would be marked not with her actual birth year, 1893, but with the year that she had always claimed as her own, 1895; in the days following her funeral, tongues wagged around the Selby-Snelling intersection about how shocked Carl had been to learn his wife's true age.

Roselawn, a new cemetery on the northern edge of St. Paul, had one geographical oddity. Its northern border ran east to west a few hundred feet above Dena's grave along the forty-fifth parallel of north latitude, placing Roselawn notionally halfway between the equator and the North Pole. Dena had given her only child an upbringing marked by extremes of heat and cold; now she rested an equal distance between the two.

. . . And then he was aboard the great troop train, roaring south through the snowy night, surrounded by men heading with him to war— unable once again to speak. His whole life as he had known it was cut short. Like the victim of a stroke, he would have to learn his every word all over again.

# GI INTERLUDE:
## 1943 – 1945

*. . . With my own hands then*
*I decked for the grave, and the dead I buried;*
*A half-year brought me this to bear,*
*And no one came to comfort me.*
*Then bound I was, and taken in war . . .*
　　—THE POETIC EDDA, *GUTHRUNARKVITHA I*

IT WAS THE NEXT morning. He did not know where he was, or where the U.S. Army was taking him, or what was going to happen next—only that his mother had been right: they had never seen each other again.

The recruits detrained into mist and acrid coal smoke. They were loaded onto trucks, hauled past MPs guarding a big camp entrance, and delivered to a drill field, where they fell out and formed up for roll call, thence trooping to a supply room to draw string-tied government-issue mattresses and bedding, which they lugged down treeless streets of vacant barracks and mess halls set on cinder-block foundations. All around them sprawled freshly seeded drill fields, tar paper hutments, and parade grounds: the newly built Camp Campbell.

The raw base straddled the state line, one foot in western Kentucky, the other in northern Tennessee. Campbell was a division post, designed to garrison and train as many as twenty-four thousand soldiers simultaneously—the elements of two full army divisions. Sparky's new quarters, like every other white clapboard barracks on the post, looked like a misplaced schoolhouse.

"The first few days—maybe a week or so—I was totally alone," he recalled. "I didn't know a soul." Disoriented, numb with bereavement, he had perhaps more to keep to himself than the ordinary sad sack, and that first night in the barracks he made sure no one could hear him when he wept himself to sleep. It was one thing to be green in "this man's army," another thing to be known right off as a crybaby.

The first time he heard a machine gun on the firing range he was stunned into complete immobility. Never in his life had he handled so much as an air rifle, but training would reveal him to be a steady marksman. On the range, he distinguished himself as one of the company's better shots, scoring 100 out of a possible 150 with the revolver, and 43 of 51 with the machine gun.

He learned to strip and reassemble the infantry's standard weapon, the semiautomatic M1 Garand rifle, but the first time he was given a light machine gun to dismantle, he thought, "I'll never learn how to do this."

Respectful of rank, he was nevertheless unused to addressing anyone his own age as "Sir." He felt deeply uneasy being under anyone's thumb, but the sense of duty and honor, an army's chief defenses against chaos, were his, too; and when Sparky saw others go AWOL from Campbell only to get brought back by the MPs, he could appreciate the impulse to get out from under—while knowing himself to be no hell-raiser. "I was always one to follow orders and do what I was supposed to do."

Habitually neat and organized, acutely observant, disinclined to speak, Schulz was bound to survive—indeed, to a modest but surprising degree to prosper—in an institution whose golden rule was "Keep your eyes open and your mouth shut." But at the start, everything about army life only added to his distress: sleeping in freezing-cold, overcrowded barracks on bunks two feet apart; standing in chow lines; being pounded directly and indirectly by an everyday language shot through, as he later said, by the "worst vulgarities imaginable." For a picky eater in civilian life, sensitive to profanity (even words like "stink" or "fink" sounded ugly to his ears), it was bad enough to have to choke down strange, coarse dishes like creamed chipped beef on burnt toast, but in the foulmouthed mess hall Sparky had further to force himself to stomach "shit on a shingle" or even "creamed foreskins."

As never before, he was living in an all-male world. When the GIs were shown educational films on the dangers of venereal disease, Schulz was appalled that women were viewed as little more than risky receptacles for lust. "It seemed wrong to me but it didn't seem to occur to anybody else." Susceptible as the next man to the pinups that papered the barracks, he nevertheless remained immune to tough talk about dames and to the bragging that seemed to infect everybody before liberty in Nashville or Memphis. He had come into the army a virgin and would remain celibate, his code of conduct uncorrupted by the surrounding culture of gross bravado.

Low man in the ranks, he knew where he stood in the army's hierarchy. And though he had been "tossed in with people from all over the country," the majority of men in Bravo Company of the Eighth Armored Infantry Battalion were midwesterners like him. Even so, he found it difficult to establish himself in the pecking order of a rifle company in which "some of the men are smarter than you, some are dumber, some are bigger and stronger, and there are all sorts of different kinds of personalities."

One morning at reveille, he made a friend: "I looked across the barracks, and there was a blond kid, and he kind of smiled at me, and we said good morning, and we became acquainted. His name was Marvin Tack, and he was from a small town in Minnesota, and he was a very strong Lutheran boy—a very decent kid."

During the ten-minute breaks in training sessions, Schulz and Tack would sit together and talk about their lives as they imagined them in the future—Schulz in cartooning, Tack in the ministry. In due course they joined up with another Minnesotan from their barracks, Larry Payne, "kind of a spoiled, overweight kid" from Minneapolis, as Schulz remembered him, and the three buddies would go together, as if in a detail, to the recreation hall at the PX, or to the evening movie. By June, however, Tack and Payne had been reassigned to barracks at the far end of camp. Eventually both were sent overseas and Schulz lost track of them, but he would always say that the bond formed among the three Minnesotans, rooted in common values and a shared moral code, had helped get him through infantry training.

Cold snaps followed upon heatwaves into May. "I have never seen a country that could get so hot and so cold in so short a time," he wrote to his cousins in Little Falls, Minnesota. As the training progressed, he was inoculated to the ripping passage of gunfire, here calibrated to tear the empty air, but which in a few months would be looking for him. He crawled under barbed wire hung with bloody animal entrails and flattened himself to the dirt as tracer ammo burned four feet over his head. At a distant corner of the post, he learned to fight literally hand to hand through a replica German village flying the swastika. When Pvt. Schulz at last proposed himself for sign painting to Bravo Company's master sergeant, Lawrence "Mac" McMahan, he presented his artist's credentials as a graduate of the Federal Schools, noting his proficiency in lettering.

McMahan looked him over narrowly. "What we need in this outfit," he said, "are riflemen, not artists."

IT WAS ELMER ROY HAGEMEYER who initiated him into army brotherhood.

Elmer came from a family of St. Louis policemen and had served three years on the force with his father and a younger brother before being drafted. His patrolman's laconic authority, combined with a deadpan wit and a big, friendly smile, had quickly made him a corporal; First Platoon called him "Sheriff." Speaking his measured phrases in an accent known in St. Louis as "Southside Dutch," Elmer at thirty-one was among the oldest in the company—ten years older than Sparky.

They met that first spring, when Schulz, facing a tour of guard duty, came down with diarrhea. The army wasn't about to release a private to sick call for a mere case of "the GIs"—a dose of paregoric was the most he could hope for. But Cpl. Hagemeyer took pity and used his influence with the first sergeant to find him a replacement. Hagemeyer would later say of himself and Schulz, "I big-brothered him."

Every trainee had to make adjustments to army life, but Elmer could see that Sparky was not letting go of home and homesickness without a fight. "He would clam up, and you could tell by the look on his face that he was lonely and depressed." This, compounded in Sparky's case by the desolation of Dena's death, was a classic problem for the army in the Second World War, when hundreds of thousands of conscripts could not adapt to regulations and had to be passed over for infantry training. The army termed these men "mother's sons." Asked decades later what Schulz had been like in his first months at Camp Campbell, Elmer remarked, "He was a mother's boy. He depended on his mother a lot. He needed somebody to help him and make him feel more secure, and I felt I was capable of doing that."

On furlough, Elmer asked Sparky home to St. Louis, where his wife, Margaret, had moved back into her parents' house for the duration. Sparky gratefully settled into a guest cot in the attic, and Margaret Hagemeyer took a shine to him. The three stepped out for evenings at the swanky Starlight Roof and Zodiac Room atop St. Louis's Chase Hotel, where Elmer introduced him to a newly popular rum concoction, the daiquiri, which Sparky barely touched, and Margaret tried to teach him to dance. Margaret and Sparky "got along terrifically," Elmer remarked decades later, "and I guess that was maybe where he really realized that you could have a good relation with a woman."

Elmer's companionship and Margaret's affection lifted his spirits. Back on the post Sparky wrote a cheerful note thanking his Gish cousins for a box of cookies and caramels: "You couldn't have sent a thing any better except maybe Hedy Lamarr."

Twenty-two years later, revisiting his experience as a lonesome draftee at Camp Campbell, Schulz would recapitulate his transformation from grieving "mother's son" to confident soldier and give to Charlie Brown the role played in real life by Elmer Roy Hagemeyer; consciously or not assigning the name Roy to the lonesome camper whose new friend helps him "break those old apron strings," and clamping on both their heads something much closer to the GI overseas cap of the Second World War than anything sported by civilian campers of the 1960s:

Sparky's army letters would occasionally include a sardonic drawing making light of some incident at Campbell—the loss of his first buddies, Tack and Payne, for example, being now sufficiently in the past to be spun into a comic scene of himself in fatigues, foolish tears leaking into his hands as he slumps on the edge of the bottom bunk. These teases, tossed off with a few flicks of the fountain pen, nevertheless exuded a truthful and charming freehand simplicity.

By contrast, labored pencil portraits of army life darkened the pages of his sketchbook. A restless determination showed, too, in barracks scenes titled "No Reveille on Sunday morning," "Pin-up Collection," "A Corner in S/Sgt Knoten's Room." The sketchbook's overall title, *As We Were*, and its attempts at wartime gag cartoons on the alternating pages, evidenced a comprehensive vision and purpose. But he had only to compare his own half-formed, unmuddied GIs to Bill Mauldin's grimly authentic frontline foot soldiers, Willie and Joe, in the American soldier's newspaper, *Stars and Stripes*, to recognize his own shortcomings as a war cartoonist.

Yet as he drew for a family audience in the so much less public and permanent medium of personal correspondence, his hand loosened. These simple miniatures, though not intended as finished work, capture the droll humor of the time as well as or better than the standard grin-and-bear-it pictorial humor of *Stars and Stripes* or *Yank*. A style is beginning to emerge from Pvt. Schulz's dot-eyed, circle-faced, squiggle-nosed GIs, their not infrequent disappointments and frustration manifesting in two parenthetic lines bracketing the eyes. Yet Schulz later maintained that none of his wartime efforts had been good enough for publication, even though the *St. Paul Pioneer Press* of January 9, 1944, ran five of Sparky's barracks sketches and one of his gag cartoons on a full page of the Sunday rotogravure section.

BY JUNE 1943, HE had put on twenty-five pounds—all muscle, hard from exercise.

He had begun basic training at odds with the army and, more significantly, with what Elmer saw as "a small idea about himself." By Sparky's own account, he had gone through "the ordinary infantryman sufferings . . . the wrenching away from home ties, being forced to do things where there was no return at all." But here he was, thirteen weeks later, all the way up from buck private to private first class—an old hand: "A whole bunch of new, extremely unfortunate, and slightly on the bewildered side men are coming in tomorrow," he noted on June 7. "I feel sorry for them. These ball[s] and chains get pretty heavy at times."

Promoted to corporal in the fall of 1943, Schulz was selected to become one of the "GI schoolteachers" who would train the youngest and smartest of the new transfers. Once again, Sparky's brightness and dedication set him apart, and in this case may have helped keep him alive. Selected to remain at Camp Campbell, he fell behind the typical trajectory for civilian draftees his age—those born in 1922 or 1923—whose units by early 1944 were being shipped to England, destined for the horrors of Omaha Beach and St. Lô, the Hedgerows and Hürtgen Forest, Bastogne and the Bulge. Held back for the training cadre, Schulz would follow the comparatively safer path of American males born in 1924, 1925, and 1926. "He became a leader without actually intending to," recalled one of the new men. "It was kind of thrust on him by his intelligence and his capability with weapons."

On February 11, 1944, Sparky was promoted to buck sergeant. After years of feeling underestimated, he registered surprise and pleasure at this display of official confidence. In a cartoon self-portrait drawn for Margaret Hagemeyer, an arrow disclosed the improbable identity behind the sarge's stripes: "Schulz (Believe it or not)."

His exceptional marksmanship, yet further evidence of his hand-and-eye coordination, made it natural for him to be designated assistant leader of the First Platoon's machine-gun squad. (Bravo Company contained three rifle platoons, each split into five twelve-man squads—headquarters, mortar, machine-gun, and two of plain riflemen.) He found himself under Staff Sgt. Glover Herren, a hardheaded Tennessean who so mercilessly rode the "know-it-all eighteen-year-old brats" that he was soon reassigned, leaving Sgt. Schulz to take over as one of the platoon's five squad leaders.

Until now, Sparky had never thought of himself as top dog of any outfit, even when he had been the de facto or elected leader—a standing that, even though he had earned it both with his neighborhood bunch and as manager of the Edgecumbe Park baseball team, had never led his family or him to take pride in the strengths or accomplishments that had gotten him there. Home and school alike had taught him to discount, even to conceal, this very real part of his potential. But in the army he had earned the right literally to wear his pride on his sleeve. Further promotion to staff sergeant in September 1944 put a rocker under his buck sergeant's stripes, and for the first time in his life he felt entitled to be "very proud."

Schulz's assistant squad leader, Sgt. Jon J. Hopkins, a college-educated high school English teacher from Chicago, who surpassed him in formal attainments, was "kind of jealous of us," recalled Elmer Hagemeyer. "Hopkins could not understand how Schulz and I got to be squad leaders because he had much more education than we did."

Schulz had brought his models of primacy not from school but from home. He was not the textbook leader who goes out front, but the sage to whom people turn. His mother had been a steady counselor among the awkward squads of the Halverson clan, his father a duty-bound staff sergeant motivating S1 and S2 assistants and an orderly for shoeshining at his barbershop "headquarters," and it came naturally for Staff Sgt. Schulz to deal out sympathy and discipline in equal measure when discontented young trainees brought him their troubles.

If the men relished Schulz's sense of humor, they appreciated even more his dedication to the squad. When he received an anxious letter from Pfc. Frank Dieffenwierth's mother, he very typically went without the opening scenes of the evening movie in order to reply, giving Minnie

Dieffenwierth his word that he would do his best to take care of her boy. The men valued the respect he showed each of them personally, "which could not always have been easy," said one. "We were a motley crew."

His squad comprised eleven other young men barely out of their teens, most drafted immediately after high school. Schulz felt closer to these dogfaces than he had to any group of male contemporaries that he had previously known. "I admired many of them because they were decent fellows," he said later, emphasizing how flattered—and grateful—he felt to be "accepted by some of these men as their friend." They thought of him as "our Sergeant Schulz" or as "our Company artist," and he won an easy popularity, as he had in grade school, by transferring his cartoons onto the personal property and effects of others. Elmer Hagemeyer's letters home to Margaret were not the only ones adorned with Sparky's vignettes of army life. One man claimed that Schulz covered the departing squad's barracks walls with "round-headed characters."

Letting go, he was surprised to feel an almost sacred joy at being part of something bigger than himself. Serving Bravo Company as an information noncom, he worked with his commissioned opposite numbers at division and battalion level to give weekly briefings on national and world events, complete with maps and pointer. He prepared by reading *Time*, "astounded at what a person could learn" from a weekly newsmagazine. As a leader, Schulz discovered that he could do more than he had ever thought possible. His stamina increased on hikes and runs to the point of "being able to run forever." Even given such minor chores as laundry, bunk making, and sewing, he found satisfaction as he mastered tasks that at home had been done for him. He spent less and less time with his sketchbook.

He subscribed to the *Infantry Journal*; studied all phases of the combined use of tanks, infantry, and artillery; and informed himself on tactics, boning up on the enemy's pre-blitzkrieg principles of combat as plotted in *Infantry Attacks*, a 1937 textbook by none other than Erwin Rommel, the legendary Desert Fox and general field marshal. He read up so diligently on everything from weaponry to arm and hand signals that one of the squad's favorite joshes became "Put away that manual, Schulz!"

Finding freedom in the single-mindedness of soldiering, he no longer lingered over "his plans for afterward," remembered Donald McClane.

"He had made up his mind to be a squad leader. It was some kind of statement that he could do it."

"He matured," observed one of his men, Everett V. Little, Jr., and did so by cutting himself a deeper niche. It was the turning point of his life in the army: "I finally wanted to be a good soldier, and I worked hard at it."

IN THE FALL OF 1944, the men began to worry that the Twentieth Armored Division was going to sit out the war "rooted in this Kentucky mud." Then came the cold, and with it, hard ground and their overseas orders. On battle footing at last, the Twentieth streamlined itself into a fighting unit of ten thousand men, packing all equipment into crates and Cosmoline for a winter crossing of the North Atlantic.

Under gray skies and bare trees, Staff Sgt. Schulz and his fellow noncoms lined up for the camp photographer. Looking every inch the team player, with his trouser legs bloused and his blue-corded overseas cap set low in front, high in back, and cocked at a rakish tilt, Sparky presented the most confident face he had ever shown a camera. He had gone into the army thinking himself worthless, faceless even; he had expected to be lost among men. But he had found himself among brothers-in-arms.

His last furlough was at home in St. Paul, and for the first time, he came home to romance. He paid court to a young woman he had met on his own. Virginia Howley was a pretty brunette, training in a St. Paul nursing school. How they first met we do not know; in later life Schulz kept the details under wraps, although he would concede five decades later that he had, indeed, fallen in love for the first time when he was in the army and that his sweetheart had been Roman Catholic and a nurse.

Virginia gave Sparky a studio portrait of herself in starched hospital whites to carry in his barracks bag. She had a broad, beautiful smile, and he always remembered the way it lit up her big brown eyes, especially the "one eye that was just slightly tilted." Before Sparky shipped overseas they posed together on Virginia's front steps. She is wearing saddle shoes, bobby sox, a short black skirt that shows off her long, slender legs, a wool sweater, and a gold locket on a chain, and has curled her lustrous dark hair into a wave.

Wet-combed, under a regulation cut, Sparky sits uncomfortably beside her in his dress uniform, elbows on knees, fingers bunched together, a smile drying on his face. After the first snap, he dares—or is encouraged—to slip his arm around her shoulder. And so Virginia and Sparky clearly present themselves in that fleeting afternoon light as a wartime couple: the slim, smiling soldier boy on leave, proudly showing off his stripes and his girl. One snapshot reveals both to be wearing shining gold bands on their ring fingers, but whether this sunny moment on the front steps had been an occasion to exchange promises, or what the rings express about their feelings for each other and the future, has not come down to us.

While at home, Sparky tried to accustom himself to thinking of his mother in the past tense, bracing himself for changes inside of "our now more or less family," as he sought to describe what remained from the earthquake that had shaken the life out of Apartment No. 2, 170 North Snelling Avenue. There, in the very rooms where Carl and Mr. Sheady had tried to contain Dena's suffering, Sparky found a new, robust female figure very much on the scene.

Annabelle Victoria Anderson had been born to a Norwegian father and a Swedish mother forty-seven years before; stout verging on plump, and never married, she lived in her own house at 1163 Edgerton Street, in the heart of a new Swedish neighborhood between Geranium and Rose avenues, where the more ambitious residents of St. Paul's old Swede Hollow ghetto had migrated. A sweet-tempered, independent soul, she had worked as a professional photographer and as a finisher at the Golling Studio, which specialized in portraying family groups, weddings, and the St. Paul Central High School classes of Sparky's era. With the war, she had moved to a defense job with Northwest Airlines at St. Paul's airfield.

Since just before Pearl Harbor, she had somehow gotten into the habit of dolling herself up for Tuesday evening "Ladies Nites" at the newly opened Prom Ballroom, "the Northwest's most beautiful rendezvous." There, in the racy, sofa-lined art deco lobby, or at the edge of the twelve-thousand-square-foot solid maple dance floor where so many Minnesotans met during the war years, Annabelle would "stand and wait for somebody to ask her to dance," a friend recalled. "And [yet] many, many times she came home alone on the streetcar." But one night, Carl Schulz approached her.

Soon they were visiting one another's homes, Carl, a lonesome widower, in spite of the attentions of Marion and Dena's mother, talked constantly of his dead wife. Well-wishing friends had begun to advise him that he could be happy again if only he remarried, but he insisted that Sparky still came first, and though he quickly drew close to Annabelle and began to relish the prospect of a new life with her, he made it plain that he could not marry until his son had returned from the war and was himself married and settled.

For Sparky, Annabelle's presence during this last furlough only underlined his mother's irrevocable absence. In a letter to Annabelle, he directly expressed his gratitude to her for the "fine things" that she was doing for his father, and told her how comforting it was to hear from Aunt Marion that she was "always very good to Grandma." But only someone so close as Sherman Plepler would hear the heart's truth: that Sparky was "absolutely crushed" to see his mother replaced in his father's affections. Seeing Carl settling into the routines of another woman's house, he could not help but feel what was left of his security caving in. Annabelle's twenty-five-year-old niece, Justine Anderson, lived across Edgerton Street: "I saw Sparky sitting on Annabelle's steps with his head in his hands, and he looked . . . very, very sad. The thing that stands out in my mind is hearing the elders—the grown-ups—say how heartbroken Sparky was; that he was grieving terribly about his mother."

Upon his return to Camp Campbell, Annabelle went out of her way to be good to Sparky, sending not only regular letters and batches of home-made cookies—which could only have begged comparison with Dena's superb baking—but also something that Sparky could not have expected from either of his parents: a book. On his twenty-second birthday, November 26, 1944, Annabelle mailed him his favorite angel food cake. "You certainly couldn't have sent anything any better," he responded, going on to thank her for some birthday cash that "went for a steak a foot long this evening." At the letter's end, one of his by now characteristically round-headed staff sergeants, this one clearly famished, is taking knife and fork to a massive sirloin.

It had been, he reported, a quiet birthday. With a week of muddy maneuvers behind him, he treated himself to a clean uniform and an afternoon at *Meet Me in St. Louis*, a "really enjoyable picture all done up in Technicolor with lots of music." He reiterated his thanks: "Thoughtfulness & Angel-food cake make a fine birthday present." For the next six months Annabelle's remarkable confections and snapshots from home—one artist to another—reached him whenever his unit took mail call. "You certainly have been wonderful to me."

It was furthermore handy to have a professional photographer back home. When Virginia failed to write or send fresh pictures as often as Sparky would have liked, we find him counting on Annabelle: "I could really use a few Virginia snapshots to bring back those ol' proverbial memories of better days," he blurted, adding more breezily, "Yeah man."

Among his buddies in the barracks, he always referred to Virginia under the more sober designation of "Miss Howley," a form that suggests the formality of the time but which even his comrades ribbed him about, as if Schulz thought he was some kind of knight errant questing to honor his lady love.

HE HAD NEVER BEFORE seen the ocean when, in Boston Harbor on February 5, 1945, the outfit boarded a luxury liner that had been remade into the U.S. Army Transport *Brazil*.

The crossing took thirteen days, their convoy zigzagging through wind-driven winter seas to avoid U-boats. They landed at Le Havre on February 18. The next morning, a cold, gray drizzle exposed "a city flattened." The coastal defenses of Hitler's Atlantic Wall lay in ruins. Sea-weary, the soldiers staggered down the wet gangplank, pushed forward by the weight of overstuffed duffels, rifles, gas masks, and bedrolls. As orientation noncom, Schulz had also to carry a long tube of maps, convinced that the additional weight would off-balance him into the icy harbor.

Safely disembarked, the division proceeded to its staging area, Schulz and his squad being billeted in a château twenty miles east of Rouen, capital of medieval Normandy. Supplies would take weeks to catch up, and so First Platoon spent the rest of February and all of March at the Château de Malvoisine—the Castle of the Bad Neighbor Woman. That evening, the helmeted GIs reached the crossroad hamlet of Croisy on the Andelle, a trout stream on whose grassy banks they found their storybook stronghold, conical towers crowning all five corners and a turreted gate lodge with a slate roof.

Posting two men at the ancient entry, First Platoon distributed its squads throughout the château's spacious stone-floored rooms. Schulz's men drew the airless, hay-covered attic the first night, and then were transferred to the open-sided shed that ran the length of the castle's high outer wall. Under timbers and a tiled roof, the air was frigid, the dirt hard, nor did the morning offer more to eat than a frozen hunk of local but days-old brown bread. The February wind cut through their field jackets. All Sparky felt necessary to tell a friend about those first nights was "I never want to be cold and hungry again." But in this temporary postponement of war, in the lands where Charlemagne's feeble successor, Charles the Simple, had assimilated the invading Norsemen with land and holy baptism a thousand years before, Staff Sgt. Schulz unrolled his sleeping bag and made himself at home.

WAR HAD CHANGED TIME, alternating tedious, uncomfortable eternity with sudden merciless terror. As Staff Sgt. J. D. Salinger observed in his 1945 story "A Boy in France," wartime was "crazy time, nobody's time." "We're here for life," Schulz thought in the idle hours left after half-days of calisthenics and hikes. One such afternoon he came across a man in his squad, the rural Floridian Frank Dieffenwierth, outside the château, sketching the vine-covered castle wall and gate lodge. He looked over Dieffenwierth's shoulder and gave him a lesson in perspective; later on they went out to draw the surrounding countryside.

He hardened himself to a habit of not thinking about the past—now too distant and unreal to contemplate—or the future. The present was endlessly patched together out of an open-ended sequence of moments advancing toward the test of battle. "Honestly, Frank," he later confided to Dieffenwierth, "I didn't think it was ever going to end." He learned to steady himself with the details of the platoon's training around the château. Mail arrived to break the monotony. Now that he was overseas, his father sent a box of candy bars once a week and tried to get off a letter every day. "All the letters read about the same," Sparky later recalled: the St. Paul weather, then Carl had to take Spike out for a walk, and abruptly the letter would end. "But," insisted his son, "I appreciated it so much."

ON EASTER SUNDAY, APRIL 1, the platoon moved out in two columns of ten-ton fighting vehicles dubbed *Salty Baldy, Sidownbud, Snowballs N All, Big Surprise, Stardust,* and (Schulz's own) *Sparky.* Protected by half an inch of armor plating in front and a quarter of an inch on the back and sides, Sparky and his eleven men motored to war in an open-topped workhorse just two feet longer and one foot wider than a six-passenger luxury town car.

Putting the flat northern rim of France behind them, the convoy crossed into Belgium, bivouacked in an orchard near Charleroi, then rolled eastward through the Netherlands panhandle, crossing the German border at Übach-Palenberg, north of Aachen, where they pitched camp and spent the next eight days fine-tuning their equipment. On April 11, attached now as infantry support to the Ninth Tank Battalion, they pushed deeper into the Reich, bypassing Bonn, where some resting armored soldiers recognized the division and taunted, "Well, the Twentieth finally got over here. The war must be about won now." By nightfall—a dark night with low clouds—they reached the Rhine.

The Nazis had destroyed forty-five of the bridges spanning Germany's chief waterway, the Americans only being able to take the Remagen bridge on March 7, breaching what amounted in the German mind to a sacred moat. According to German folklore, if an enemy ever crossed the "wide and winding" Rhine, the doom of Germany would follow. Disappointed at how little they could see of the fabled river, the Liberators rolled across the Rhine on the General Hodges Bridge at Bad Godesberg, whose barge pontoons the Nazis were still trying to blow up with floating mines. Crossing to the river's hilly east bank, Schulz's men felt as if they had finally arrived in enemy country. The steep, winding road, which climbed through dark pine forests, did not just connect with the E-5 autobahn, it was their pathway into the enemy heartland.

The convoy cut diagonally southeastward. The Germany that Karl and Emma Schulz's grandson ground through at the bow of a U.S. Army half-track was a depopulated ruin. Driving toward Munich, he passed through or by Rothenburg, Feuchtwangen, Nördlingen, Donauwörth, Affing, Rossbach, and Dachau, a route that the postwar German tourist industry would attempt to sanitize as the "Romantische Strasse," but which in April 1945 offered anything but romance. All that month, Schulz and his squad tracked through mounds of shattered stone, hills of bricks, villages reduced to rubble, here and there a wall standing—"Everything was bombed out, crushed, every building shot up; bullet holes were every place"—the men hunting deer and wild pig to supplement rations and scouting constantly for "souvenirs."

There was no eye contact with the enemy until, on April 29, the convoy, pushing in single file down a narrow road from the north, approached Rossbach, steadily trading the lead among platoons for alertness' sake. As the advance tanks and half-tracks entered the village, white flags flew from every window, but the lead vehicle was barely halfway through when a pocket of German resistance opened fire. Bullets struck half-track *Sparky*, punching holes in a bazooka. In accordance with operational ground rules, the Americans burned the village down. Schulz would ever after recall a "hysterical woman standing in her front yard while her house was on fire and all the cows were walking around."

Later that day, the convoy reached Dachau, with the mission of capturing bridges spanning the unfordably deep and broad Amper River, final obstacle in the Allied path to the Bavarian capital; but as the task force reached the autobahn bridge—one of two still standing—German engineers blew it up. The First Platoon dug in for the night.

At daybreak on April 30, the task force swung northeastward along the river to seize the first bridge at Dachau, but four divisions were simultaneously pressing toward Munich—the Twentieth Armored Liberators, the Third, the Forty-Fifth Thunderbirds, and the Forty-Second Rainbow—and a spectacular traffic jam had tied them up.

Barreling toward the Amper, the First Platoon, farthest forward, had advanced nearly to the end of the road. Behind Schulz's half-track, parallel to the column of stalled fighting machines, lay a moat and fence, behind which loomed a guard tower and neat rows of wooden camp buildings— the Dachau concentration camp. Various squads and tanks from the Forty-Second Rainbow, Twentieth Armored, and Ninth Tank Battalion had burst the main gates open at dawn the day before, but Schulz's platoon was ordered to move on and leave the camp to the supporting infantry. In all of Bravo Company, the Third Platoon was nearest to the camp entrance, but, as Pfc. Arthur C. Lynch would write, "We youngsters [in the Third Platoon] had no idea of the history that was taking place to our left. We never did go across the moat and go into the camp."

Pressing on toward the Amper, the convoy's troops were surprised to have "simply run across [the camp] by accident on our way to Munich," and many would not grasp the scope of Hitler's Final Solution until later. One man recorded Dachau in his field diary as the place "where we found the Cognac cellar." When asked what impact the discovery of the death camp and its horrors had on him, Schulz would answer, "I didn't see that much of it." On that last Monday of April 1945, only a few men from the First Platoon ventured into the camp. "It was a terrible sight," said one. "I never want to see anything like that again." Others discovered a photographer taking pictures of the horrors inside the camp and paid him fifty cents each to have copies sent to their home addresses in the States. Schulz would recall four emaciated survivors stumbling along the stalled column, stopping now and then to hug the side of the American tanks.

The next day, news reached the convoy that Hitler was dead in the Berlin Führerbunker—later to be revealed a suicide. Just hours afterward, it faced weapon-to-weapon resistance for the first time, when it came under rifle fire from a concealed position across a field outside Munich. Someone in Schulz's half-track spotted the nest and returned fire, but missed; Schulz himself had jumped to the heavy machine gun, wheeled it around, and pulled the trigger, which "just went click." In his excitement, he had forgotten that a .50-caliber had to be engaged not once but twice, and the brief delay gave the two Germans in the foxhole time enough to rush out and surrender.

Now events were racing along—Berlin fell on May 2, the German commands surrendering later that day in Italy and capitulating two days after that in the Netherlands, Denmark, and northwest Germany. On May 4, as the convoy ground toward Salzburg, which had been part of the Reich since 1938, Schulz's section of the task force halted in a small Bavarian village to give first aid to a wounded German soldier who had been left behind when his unit pulled out. Scouting alone at the edge of the village, Sparky stumbled onto a Wehrmacht artillery emplacement whose stairs descended into a dugout painted entirely black. Like every other man in his company, he was determined to bring home a trophy— Lugers or bolt-action Mausers were the prize keepsakes—and thought he might find some such here. But when he reached for a concussion grenade to roll into the dugout and wipe out any diehards, a little white dog appeared and trotted down the steps. Schulz could bring himself neither to harm the dog nor to follow it into enemy quarters, and returned to the half-track empty-handed.

By the time the convoy forded the Salzach River to enter what had been Austria on the afternoon of May 4, men in various squads of Bravo Company had recorded in their diaries uncovering "all types of German weapons" in a Nazi ordnance depot. "Got plenty of pistols and souvenirs here," noted one GI. On May 5, scavenging through a Wehrmacht quartermaster depot in Salzburg, Sparky came upon a cache of weapons from which he could at last claim a trophy. At that very moment, however, an officer strode in and began to rake Schulz, senior enlisted man though he was, for being off-limits. As it turned out, Sparky and he knew each other, having worked together during Sparky's tenure as Bravo Company information officer, which won him unofficial permission to take a pistol.

Over centuries of war, conquerors brandishing plundered firearms have been a menace, above all to themselves, and the final days of the Second World War in Europe were no different for the Twentieth Armored Liberators. "Everyone seemed to have acquired pistols . . . of every make and caliber," a man in Schulz's company later wrote. Another remembered May 5, 1945—only three days shy of VE Day, and in no serious contact with the enemy—as among the scariest he spent overseas. In the Eighth Armored Battalion's Bravo Company alone, no fewer than four men managed to shoot either comrades or themselves.

On that dangerous day, Sparky sized up his souvenir pistol as he and a squad mate, Pvt. William Stearns, were passing time on the porch of a house. Across the street the medic from another platoon was talking to a sergeant. The Geneva Accords of 1929 had mandated that medics' headgear—in the U.S. Army, a green steel helmet—be boldly painted on all four sides with a red cross inside a white circle. The aid man's insignia was so conspicuous that in Western European theaters of combat, where the Germans for the most part respected their status, medics still grimly joked among themselves that the army was asking them to go into battle with targets on their foreheads; in the Pacific, the Japanese, who had never signed the accords, actually did treat this simple design "as a bull's-eye."

That triumphant day in Hitler's own country, Sparky put aside everything he had learned about handling a weapon. Without checking to see whether a live round remained in the chamber of his newly acquired Luger, he drew a bead on the medic's red cross. "I aimed very carefully at that helmet and pulled the trigger very slowly," he later stated, adding that he did not hear the report "but felt the pistol recoil." The bullet, to his horror, "grazed the medic's cheek" but luckily did no serious harm.

But this did not free Schulz from an unending burden of guilt; if anything, it intensified it. He had held a man's life in his hands—a comrade's—and could easily have killed him without purpose or meaning. In years to come he reflected that everything "might have changed if that bullet had hit a few inches away." One of his strip characters, forced to leave home because of nothing more than a momentary lapse in the line of duty, would mutter, "Make one mistake, and you pay for it the rest of your life!"

In a 1952 gag, Charlie Brown aims a new toy pistol at Shermy with a sudden cry of "BANG!" only to peer down with real surprise and regret: "Gee, I'm sorry . . . it went off!" Twelve years later, Linus, in a more philosophical mode, addresses the larger and more general question of accountability, that classical separator of men from boys: "Why do I do stupid things? Why don't I think? What's the matter with me? Where's my sense of responsibility? . . . Then I ask myself, am I really responsible? Is it really my fault when I do something wrong? Must I answer for my mistakes? . . . Who is responsible? Who is accountable?" In no fewer than five future strips, Linus would conclude, "Five hundred years from now, who'll know the difference?"

HAVING LOST 46 MEN killed in action and 134 wounded, the Twentieth Armored considered itself the luckiest division in Europe.* Of the 250 men that Bravo Company had brought to France, 249 were coming home; one man had been fatally burned while cleaning his clothes with gasoline.

But the war was not over for Staff Sgt. Schulz. In the Pacific, VE Day—May 8, 1945—meant only that reinforcements were on the way. More than 170,596 American lives had been laid down in storming the island chains that constituted imperial Japan's outer defenses. Subduing the fanatical home islands was expected to cost the Allies a million and a quarter more men. Senior enlisted men like Schulz, without enough combat "points" from European action, were slated to serve in the amphibious assault against the Empire's fortified core, the Tokyo plain of eastern Honshu. "Operation Coronet," scheduled for Y-Day, March 1, 1946, would throw twenty-eight combat divisions—including the Twentieth Armored—against one million Japanese defenders, besides unreckonable multitudes of self-immolating civilians, prepared to trade and take lives for every inch of their homeland. General George C. Marshall, Army Chief of Staff, expected a First World War type of bloodbath that would see as many as a thousand Americans dying every hour before the beachhead could be consolidated.

In Germany, Schulz knew full well that his unit was lined up to storm the world's most suicidally intransigent nation. It was, he later said, "one of the most dreaded things." Neither he nor his men "could conceive of getting on another troopship and going clear across the Pacific. It was beyond our imagination."

Before leaving Germany, he was put in for a decoration. The Combat Infantryman Badge (CIB), a silver-bordered bar overlying an oak wreath on which a 1795 Springfield Arsenal musket sits against a field of blue

---

*The Third Armored Division, by contrast, had lost 1,810 dead and 6,963 wounded.

enamel, was a new honor, awarded to World War II soldiers for satisfactory performance of duty while engaged in active ground combat. Known as "the fighter badge," it would come to have a special unspoken meaning among men back from the line; it was the only decoration they would wear. It meant that Sparky had proved himself. Half a century later, when asked to identify his most treasured possession, Charles Schulz did not speak of the cars he enjoyed driving or the books he loved to read or even the tools of his trade; no memento of his childhood or youth had ended up mattering to him half so much as did the CIB. For the rest of his life a singular note of pride entered his voice when he spoke, very simply, of his wartime service: "I was a foot soldier."

ON JULY 1, SPARKY predicted to Annabelle that he would be home on a thirty-day rest and recuperation furlough in August. "I can hardly wait," he wrote. "All the little things that we used to take for granted & considered commonplace will now be unbelievable wondrous luxuries; movies, sundaes, hamburgers, Coca-Colas . . . wow!"

His father had been keeping Sparky posted daily on an operation that Annabelle had to undergo, and Sparky replied with sincere concern about her "ordeal at the hospital," writing to her sympathetically: "I don't care for hospitals. We had far too much to do with them, & it would suit me fine if I never see another one"; then, shifting direction: "Now of course the (ahem) nurses' home is a different story! However, I haven't heard from Virginia for almost two months, & can't figure it out. It's going to make a mighty dull furlough for me if she's not there when I arrive."

On July 27, Sparky sailed for home on an overcrowded troopship, tying up in New York harbor eleven days later, Tuesday, August 7, 1945. Newsboys greeted the troops on the gangplank, bawling, "EXTRA! EXTRA! Read all about it!" The United States had exploded an "atomic bomb"

over the city of Hiroshima, killing, as was later established, almost eighty thousand Japanese. As the world held its breath waiting for Japan's unconditional surrender, Sparky took two nights of liberty in New York City, then traveled to St. Paul, arriving at the Union Depot just as word came through that Nagasaki had been struck. He shouldered his barracks bag and rode the streetcar home to Selby and Snelling.

On the corner, the brown-brick storefronts looked the same as ever. Walking into the Family Barber Shop, he set down his duffel. Carl was working on a customer. "Well," Sparky announced, "that's it"—he had done his bit; he was home. But his father stayed with the customer, did not come forward. "No one gave me a hug," Sparky later recalled. "We didn't have any party. . . . That was it." Carl went right on cutting hair. "He couldn't stop."

AS SO OFTEN BEFORE the war, the moment that should have belonged to the son belonged to the customers.

After VJ Day, the scene repeated itself on Main Streets all over the country, as GIs came home on thirty-day furloughs, expecting the brass bands and parades galore that had greeted their fathers after the Armistice of November 1918, only to discover a "strange embarrassment" as they were met by more or less subtle forms of reserve. The "World War" of 1914–1918 had been going to end war, but a war ended by a potentially world-ending weapon was closing on an uncertain note, and, as *Time* reported, August 1945 was a "pageantry-less" moment in American towns and whistlestops.

Schulz called his homecoming "kind of a letdown." On reflection, he would go further: "That was robbery. I didn't get to be in a parade . . . or anything like that. But I felt very good about myself those days, [and] I came home with a good feeling of self-worth."

In August 1945, he had reason to be jubilant over his accomplishment. The hypersensitive boy too small to earn a Sam Browne belt on the school safety patrol had worked his way up through the ranks and come home decorated, with three stripes and a rocker on his arm. Sparky had been "a young guy who nobody ever thought would amount to much"; he had gone in "with a bunch of men," as he told it, "and I became a man."

He grew to his full height, a hairbreadth under six feet (much taller above the national average then than now), gained weight (mostly muscle), and carried himself with his shoulders back and his head held high. A new glow of confidence shines through snapshots taken at Annabelle's house on Edgerton Road during his furlough: Sparky and Virginia Howley, accompanied by Carl, have come over to visit Annabelle as a couple. Sparky—living in his uniform rather than merely posing in it—holds the now womanly Virginia close. No longer does he crouch stiffly alongside her or appear uncertain what to do with his hands; standing tall and at ease, he beams his delight in firmly wrapping an arm around Virginia's slim waist, while she, resplendent in a white summer dress, leans into Sparky on one side and sweetly and casually hooks arms with Carl on the other.

Another picture taken that summer day is suffused with an almost languid sense of closeness and togetherness—something new in the annals of Schulz family photography. Prewar snapshots in which Sparky poses with his parents show Dena holding herself proud but reserved beside her son, literally putting inches between Sparky and herself. The same went for pictures with his grandmother Sophia or his Norwegian aunts—no touching. Now, seated on the back steps at 1163 Edgerton, it is as if he has been freed from a lifelong restraint. Buxom, motherly Annabelle curves along Sparky's left flank—close enough, surely, for him to feel her warmth through the thin summer dress, while Virginia reclines cozily on the step below, her shoulders squeezed between Sparky's khaki knees, her smiling face brushing against his right sleeve, as his arm drapes casually over her shoulder.

He had never looked freer to be himself. In those first days at home, "I felt like somebody." More comfortable with his masculinity than ever before, he could now take stock of his powers. "By golly, if that isn't a man, I don't know what is." Elmer Hagemeyer had noticed the change: "By the time he got out of the army he was a bigger, better, stronger person than when he went in." Sparky himself would call this "the high point in my life as far as having confidence."

It did not last. "Those first few months I was home were probably the best months of feeling good about myself I've had in my whole life," he repeated over the years. For a fittingly Charlie Brown effect, he would add, "It lasted about twelve minutes. And then I was back to being my regular self."

"But," he would repeat, adding one more piece to the puzzle, "I felt good about myself then; I was ambitious, very ambitious."

Ambition—the renewal of the dream—was the stabilizing force between the fluctuations of boyhood and manhood. The army and the war had dug a trench that would ever after divide him: on the one side, the vulnerable, hypersensitive boy whom only war could have remade; on the other, the strong, glad man he had briefly been but could be again. For many years, he would straddle this line, staking claims on one side or the other.

The American newspaper, which would serve as the scaffolding on which the dream—and the reality—of Charles Schulz would be raised, claimed him just as quickly. That same August, from among millions of returning veterans, he somehow caught the eye of a newspaper editor and got his definitely unusual ambitions written up.

"SOLDIER HOME ON VISIT—Has Comic Strip Plans," announced the *St. Paul Daily News.*

Here, too, was the first whiff of the ordinary man as "philosopher": "Schulz saw enough of battle, murder, and sudden death to make his philosophy a really functional thing," states the article, hinting that the war has bestowed on this prematurely wise twenty-two-year-old midwesterner an all-embracing Lincolnian vision: "I saw 'em go down, from raw private to high ranking officer. . . . I just had to begin to believe that all men are equal and that the best as well as the worst can happen to any of them."

The article is illustrated by two Schulz cartoons, one lampooning the comforts of an officer's bivouac gear, the other, "Displaced Personnel, V-E Plus 3," spoofing the confusion in Germany at the moment of victory, as a U.S. Army corporal frantically seeks to process a lost soldier who can only mumble, "Me, Rooskie."

The accompanying photograph shows the handsome, decorated veteran holding a sketch pad. On the fourth finger of his left hand he still wears the ring that appears in snapshots taken on Virginia Howley's front steps in 1944.

Eager to revive the courtship in full, Sparky took it as a good sign that Virginia was wearing white the day they visited at Annabelle's. He had developed a theory that such apparel on a date meant that a girl cared for him because "she could only wear the dress once, [and] she wouldn't waste a dry cleaning job on someone she didn't like. It always made me feel kind of good if my date wore white."

They picked up where they had left off in 1944. But their evenings together now seemed almost too full of possibilities. Dutifully, he learned to dance—to lead—and they went out every night, feeling all but certain, as he later recalled, "that we might be in love." The trouble was that, for all his newfound masculinity, he was somehow unable to give up being the bashful boy of his earlier crushes. "I didn't know how to be a good boyfriend," he said later, "and I still didn't know how to show her a good time." He tried giving Virginia a wristwatch, but somehow the present failed to have the hoped-for effect.

At some point that August, Sparky came to the conclusion that Virginia "didn't care much about me anymore." She had, in any case, developed at least one other serious interest, and when Sparky refused to compete for her, the romance cooled. In this, too, the pattern for his life was being set.

ON SUNDAY AFTERNOON, SEPTEMBER 16, 1945—two weeks after Japan's formal surrender—Staff Sgt. Charles Schulz boarded a troop train at the St. Paul Union Depot, this time bound for Camp McCoy, Wisconsin.

It was a replay of his first traumatic leave-taking, and it hit him hard— to the point of taking it out on Annabelle, the maternal figure in "our now more or less family," to whom he wrote from Camp McCoy four days later to apologize "for the crabby way I acted to you the night before I left." Crabby indeed; he had let her know, in so many words, that he did not want her coming with his father to see him off at the depot. "I was so completely disgusted & discouraged with everything for having to leave home again that I could hardly stand it, and I didn't want you or Bus or Marion, or Virginia, or anyone around in case I sort of broke up. I don't think I have ever felt so lonesome before in my life."

Later that fall, he was transferred to Camp Cooke, halfway down the California coast. This sudden return to military life exaggerated his fears that the army might never let him out; but the atom bombs brought Japan to surrender, forever changing the course of his life and of all those scheduled for Operation Coronet. Although not officially discharged until January 1946, Schulz and his squad were back home in time for Thanksgiving.

Once again, instead of parading down North Snelling Avenue, he tiptoed back into civilian life, taking note of the latest-model cars, how women's skirts were celebrating the end of fabric shortages with a plunge to the ankle, the new hairstyles—he would have to get the hang of things all over again. The comics, he was glad to see, were more plentiful than ever, despite wartime newsprint shortages and the death of George Herriman in 1944. Comic strips, John Gunther noted in 1945, had been "one of the chief centripetal forces" pulling the United States together through the war. Chic Young's *Blondie* had become the champion, now appearing in an unheard-of thousand daily and Sunday newspapers around the world, netting Young an annual income of $300,000 (at least $1.8 million today), when median family income in 1946 was about $2,000.

There were other unreal survivors of the world before the war. Poor Spike was still alive, by now eleven years old—but Carl had overfed him while Sparky was overseas. "You can see how fat our dog is," Carl wrote to a relative on the back of a snapshot whose border he inked with the new nickname: "Fat Stuff." Spike looks like a balloon with legs.

They were his last legs. That winter, the veterinarian advised putting him down. Sparky took Spike for one more hobbled walk, then Carl helped him into the car and drove away. "That was the last I saw of him."

# PART THREE

# MIDDLE WEST

*Isn't that astounding: that a businessman
like that should have become fond of me,
a nothing young man from St. Paul?*

C.M.S.

# CHAPTER 10

# BREAKING THE ICE

*I didn't know if I'd fit anywhere, but it didn't matter. I wanted to be a cartoonist, period.*

—C.M.S.

SPRING CAME EARLY THE first year after the war, jonquils defying the March chill.

He lived with his father in the five-room apartment over the barbershop. With postwar housing scarce, Carl economized by renting out two rooms to a nurse and a waitress whose husbands were still in the Pacific. The women washed their clothes in the kitchen sink with pails of hot water from the stove. Sparky shared Carl's bedroom and took meals with his father at Weber's Restaurant across Selby.

In February a fire had started in the basement, cause unknown, and swept through the building, sending Carl and Sparky scrambling onto the roof of O'Gara's bar in the middle of the night. Fire hoses swamped the Family Barber Shop, collapsing its floor and wiping out Sparky's collection of Big Little Books, the small, blocky volumes of text and cartoons that cost a dime and retold adventures of Dick Tracy, Tarzan, and other newsprint and pulp demigods of the 1930s—another loss that seemed to certify the irretrievability of life before the war. Icicles hung from the smoke-smeared walls, but Carl got the shop back open within a month.

By the end of February, Sparky had drawn sample pages of three comic book stories—a war episode involving GIs on a half-track, a fantasy with "cute little fanciful" characters he called Brownies, and a jungle adventure—all of which he bundled off to a comics publisher in New York, only to receive word that the publisher did not buy from freelancers. Undaunted, he repackaged his samples for William Randolph Hearst's King Features Syndicate in New York City, and mailed one more application with sketches to Walt Disney Studios in Hollywood. While waiting to hear from the coasts, he made the rounds in Minneapolis and St. Paul.

He took advantage of the GI Bill to present himself at the Minneapolis School of Art, the academy attached to the august Minneapolis Institute of Arts. He signed up for life drawing but had no intention of becoming an art bum, daubing paint on canvas at taxpayers' expense until he had somehow gotten a foothold in cartooning. An emboldened Charles Schulz took his samples and "headed out into the cold cruel world to see who wanted to be lucky enough to employ me."

His alma mater in art, Federal Schools, Inc., of Minneapolis—now called Art Instruction—supplied vocational guidance to graduates. Sparky answered job listings in advertising and industrial arts departments, but with nothing to show beyond sample comic panels, he had to agree with his interviewers that he would rather be a cartoonist than have a hand in any of the processes of commercial art.

Five nights each week Sparky came home empty-handed to draw sample comics. He still was not sure how to find his own style of drawing. Sometimes, having scattered some quick-handed cartoons of army life across a letter to his friend Dieffenwierth, he would preempt criticism with the urgent scribble: "SEE? NO TALENT WHATSOEVER!!" Yet, it was in these very cartoons, when Schulz reduced his line to its simplest, that a style began to form. When his hand was free, he naturally drew little vignettes dominated by round-headed figures, choosing as his theme moments that seemed to catch everyday ordeals. His most casual doodle came off the pen fresh, witty, true to experience; by comparison, his laborious pencil sketches of posed models were pat and unoriginal.

In his twice-a-week night class at the Minneapolis School of Art, where he was supposed to become "thoroughly acquainted with the human figure as a means of artistic expression," he told himself that he "wasn't especially good at it," and since formal study only revealed how far he had to go as a mainstream artist and would not help him clarify his singular talent, he decided that life drawing was a waste of time. The following semester, he enrolled in another night class but never again showed up at the studio, and the young woman who marked attendance would years later recall telling herself, "He'll never amount to anything."

Every morning before setting out to look for work, he stopped in at his father's shop to check the mail. Carl, who rose first, made a habit of taking the morning letters from their apartment house with him to work, forcing Sparky "to rush into the place interrupting a shave or a shampoo to inquire if there are any letters for me from Hearst or Disney." Under the customers' eyes, Carl would ask how things were coming. Sparky took his exit line from what a *Life* article had said about Frank King's earnings from *Gasoline Alley*: "Wait 'til I make a thousand dollars a week!" And the men under the haircloths and hot towels would wave him out into the cold, chuckling at the impossibility.

IN THE MIDDLE OF March 1946, Art Instruction's vocational department sent him to the Catechetical Guild Educational Society, a publisher of Roman Catholic teaching aids in downtown St. Paul, where he turned over his sample panels to the art director and prepared for the usual dismissal. To his surprise, the unsmiling man behind the desk looked up and met his eye. "I think I may have something for you," said Roman Baltes. "I like your lettering."

Baltes, a thirty-eight-year-old cartoonist raised in Sleepy Eye, Minnesota, had gone west to work at Walt Disney Studios before returning to St. Paul to edit a Catholic comic magazine, the "Timeless— Truthful—Telling" *Topix*, a forty-eight-page monthly that featured Prince-Valiant–like narratives of saints and martyrs drawn in a conventional style by a staff of three. Baltes needed a pen-and-ink man who could successively letter the dialogue balloons left blank in the English-language, Spanish, and French editions each month. He hired Schulz at a dollar and a half per hour.

Sparky admitted to Dieffenwierth that *Topix* was "devoted to religious stories which of course really doesn't suit me at all." He added, "Catholics! They dog me. I can't get away from 'em." But Baltes had also offered the possibility of publishing a page of Schulz's original cartoons as a regular feature, and that "was number one! The first rung on the ladder. Nothing too important, but a start."

"What I am trying to do," he went on, "is just get enough stuff printed to get a good collection to show that I have left the amateur bracket when I go see those New York syndicate wolves."

Sparky's letters to Dieffenwierth over this period have a charm and bite that reveal his devotion to his craft as well as the absolute nature of his ambition. When, for example, he heard that his old squad mate had moved to New York City, the cultural capital on which Schulz had pinned his highest hopes for syndication, he cast his friend as a rival. But on learning that the artistically inclined Dieffenwierth had put aside drawing to study voice, he replied, "In a way, I am glad. It cuts down on competition. Which brings us to the inevitable subject of myself. I have been putting in some long days, Frank."

Reading these letters later, Schulz was struck by the "fanatical ambition" of his earlier self. "In those letters, I was so goal-oriented. I knew what I wanted . . ." One note to his friend's "big time New York address" made it clear how well he knew that the slightest falling-off of commitment would leave him stuck in the "amateur bracket." But the army had given him a new make on the larger terrain, for on the page his voice and manner—sardonic, droll, sometimes sarcastic and cutting—were the idiom and posture of millions of men his age who had passed through the system and survived the war. His harsher thoughts broke through this seen-it-all generational tone as acidly humorous asides. When he wrote to Dieffenwierth, he was thinking and talking like a GI.

VETERANS COMING HOME TO any midland city found the principal Christian denominations clearly marked: the Episcopalian parish church evoked Anglican tradition in its lavish half-timbering; the Catholic cathedral's domed basilica proclaimed its place in a universal order; Lutheranism showed its stolid presence in brick churches quietly displaying modest, useful banners announcing bingo and bake sales, their pinnacled bell towers culminating in tall Gothic spires; the Methodist and Presbyterian churches, the one built of stone, the other of wood, thrust tall white steeples over opposite corners of a well-tended thoroughfare, invariably Church Street.

The Church of God had no defining style or architectural tradition. It barely announced itself, except as a plain statement of opposition to what it quietly deemed the excesses of sectarian Christianity. "Why should there be so many different churches?" its challenging pioneer, Daniel Sidney Warner, had asked himself and some thirty other Christians in the village of Beaver Dam, Indiana, in 1881. "Why must we divide ourselves into Baptists, Methodists, Lutherans, and all the others? Why can we not live together as brothers and sisters in one great church family under God?"

From its beginnings in Indiana and Michigan, the Church of God resisted being identified as a religious denomination. Calling itself a "movement," it placed no restrictions on membership, embracing all Christian believers. Membership arose from and rested on a believer's love of Jesus Christ and faith in His Kingdom; there was no call to prove one's piety or social credentials or wealth. Sparky's father had begun attending services at the Merriam Park Church of God after Dena's death. Born, raised, and married in the Lutheran Church, Carl saw himself as "just average religious." He associated Lutheranism with narrowness and pomposity, and both he and Sparky held a deep grudge against it on account of the Lutheran minister's failure to keep his appointment at Dena's deathbed. By contrast, George Edes, the pastor at the Merriam Park Church of God, conducted a funeral service for Dena that Carl and Sparky never forgot for its simplicity and dignity.

Sparky started accompanying his father on Sundays. He had never been baptized, never formally accepted the doctrines of Christianity. Yet stepping into the earnest, warmly personal embrace of the Church of God, he felt spiritually at home for the first time in his life. He appreciated the church's inclusive spirit. That he did not have to prove that he belonged made him feel closer to his fellow worshippers and to God. He liked the small size of the congregation—about sixty-five people, mainly young couples squeezed into the plain white clapboard building on North Prior. Almost all the men were veterans. Fred Shackleton, a client of Carl's who was the church's new pastor, was Sparky's age; the two young men liked each other, playing golf together. Sparky enjoyed frequent visits with Fred and his wife, Doris. Shackleton recalled, "We talked a lot about being a Christian."

They also discussed the war, although Shackleton had received a minister's deferment. The more Sparky thought about it, the more he saw God's hand in his survival, believing that God had shepherded him through the twin catastrophes of his mother's death and the greatest shedding of blood in history. "I started going to church just out of a feeling of gratitude that I had survived all of that. I felt that God protected me and helped me and gave me the strength to survive because I could have gone off in all sorts of wrong directions."

It deepened into a conviction: God had spared him; God had pulled him through. As Sparky got to know the other young veterans and their wives at the Church of God, he felt a deep sense of connection and understanding, and for that, too, he was grateful. Among these other parishioners, his thoughtfulness and reserve and, above all, his apartness, made a strong impression. The women of the church in particular noticed that he seemed alone in the world.

"I won't talk about it, but I was very lonely after the war," Sparky later said. "I know what it feels like to spend a whole weekend all by yourself and no one wants you at all. . . . The church gave me a place to go."

One day Fred Shackleton urged Sparky to open himself to Jesus Christ—"He was not at that point committed to Christ, but he was warm"—and suggested they kneel together and pray. And so they did, getting down on their knees in the quiet of the office. Shackleton bowed his head, but before another word could be spoken, Sparky said, "I'm just not ready for this," and got up.

THAT SUMMER, STILL LOOKING for the first crack through which to enter the world of syndicated cartooning, he paid a visit to Frank Wing at Art Instruction, Inc. The school's headquarters filled half a city block in downtown Minneapolis, rising three stories to a flat warehouse roof from both sides of the corner at South Fourth Street and Fifth Avenue South, like a generous helping of American pie.

Sparky asked his former teacher's advice about the GI combat strip that he had begun to develop. Wing discouraged him, predicting little "chance for that kind of cartoon at a time when people [are] fed up with wars," but urged him to consider taking over for a vacationing instructor in the Educational Department. And so Sparky reported for work, tall and lean in his army khakis on July 11, 1946.

The job entailed reviewing and grading a home student's completed practice lesson, and indicating improvements by making overlay sketches on tissue or in red or blue pencil directly on the composition. Then the instructor explained his corrections into a Dictaphone, sometimes offering a paragraph or two of additional pointers before turning the cylinder over to the second-floor typing pool, from which a stenographer would bring a transcript up for signature. The mail room, the school's "traffic center," would send the corrected work back third-class to the student, the instructor's letter going first-class.

Instruction by mail—"distance learning," it was optimistically called—appealed to the same mass audience as that for which syndicated newspaper comics had been invented. From 1946 on, tens of thousands of new pupils signed up each year at home-study schools in commercial art. "Manila envelopes poured in like mad," sighed one of Schulz's former colleagues. On any given day, the bulk of these exercises came from students just starting out in the first or second division. Correcting twenty to thirty sets of Division 2 lessons was a good day's work. "Speed-grading was essential," recalled one instructor.

As they faced the mind-dulling daily repetition of as many as two dozen renditions of the same Fat Man Looking Up, the same Normal Man Looking Around, the same Water Tower in Two-Point Perspective, instructors were encouraged to use an intricate alphanumeric system of prewritten, preparagraphed sentences. If, for example, a student's line was shaky or indistinct or too heavy, the instructor would simply consult the booklet of codes and dictate to his machine accordingly—A-6 (shaky line), A-7 (indistinct line), A-8 (overinked line)—whereupon the stenographers would insert the appropriate boilerplate "so it looked like you wrote everything," recalled a veteran of the process. As one instructor put it, "They had a paragraph for every damn situation you could think of." Still another marveled, "They had alternate form paragraphs in case two neighbors were students, so they wouldn't get the same letter."

Art Instruction promised students the personal attention of an instructor, its promotional materials emphasizing "the INDIVIDUAL instruction that makes our art education so valuable." Its salesmen reminded potential students that their instructors were all artists in their own right. "The thoroughness, care and individual quality of their criticism and grading of your drawings will amaze you." But unbeknown to the students, instructors rarely responded on an individual basis until they were correcting lessons in the later divisions, which most students never reached.

Considered a strikingly efficient and forward-looking technique by the school's executives, Art Instruction's canned battery of art criticism made some of the instructors queasy. "At first it bothered me. It seemed dishonest," recalled one. "I think I was a bit appalled at first by the form letters that they wrote," said another. "But in the long run I could see no other way." For his part, Sparky saw nothing phony in the alphanumeric system, and eventually rewrote and updated some of the standard paragraphs. Yet however many overinked Fat Men Looking Up (G–8) and ill-proportioned laughing mouths (C–4) commanded his attention, he could not believe his luck. His dream of someday having a desk at a newspaper seemed, in a way, to have come true. In his eyes Art Instruction, Inc., was a "wonderful place to get started because the atmosphere was not unlike that of a newspaper office."

Walter J. Wilwerding, a specialist in wildlife painting, was the department supervisor when Schulz first arrived. He presided at the rear in a kind of managing editor's office, from which he would step out into the big room, a nattily dressed man with dark, piercing eyes, thinning gray hair, and a pencil mustache, to start the workday with a chanted mantra about his ulcer: "No pancakes, no syrup, no coffee." The younger instructors would faithfully trade the ominous refrain back and forth with the chief until everyone was laughing.

Before leaving at the end of the day, Wilwerding would stroll to the tall windows overlooking South Fourth Street and peer up into the sky. "Mare's-tails, Frank," he would intone prophetically, and Wing, working like a watchmaker to finish a lesson and already irritated by a day of Wilwerding's pointless interruptions, would bend still lower to his task. More than the other paternalistic sages at Art Instruction, Wing was a reminder to Sparky of how far he had come—both from the sensitive, suffering home-study student and from the "damned pest" into which he had made himself in Wing's eyes when he appeared for private consultations as a graduate.

Punching out at five, Sparky hopped the streetcar for the Catechetical Guild in downtown St. Paul to pick up a new layout that Roman Baltes had telephoned about that afternoon and needed overnight. He finally sat down at a folding card table wedged into the apartment's kitchen, where he would work until every balloon in the latest *Topix* spread was filled, leaving the finished pages outside Baltes's door bright and early on his way to work the next morning.

In August 1946, hired by Art Instruction at $32 a week as a permanent full-time instructor, he invested his first paycheck in a professional drawing board, installing it in the room where his mother had died, which he proudly called his studio. On two of this sanctuary's walls he pinned drawings and cartoons by his new friends at Art Instruction. Through fall and winter he worked his day job and night jobs, crisscrossing the Twin Cities by streetcar, relishing the new speed and control he felt in his pen lines. In September, Baltes rewarded his efficiency, reliability, and thoroughness by having him draw the climactic panels of *Is This Tomorrow?*—a dire prophecy of a Communist takeover tricked out as a "public service comic book."

Baltes also made good on his promise to publish Sparky's one-page monthly feature. The premier installment of *Just Keep Laughing* appeared in February 1947, the first of its color panels depicting a professor, distinctly modeled on Frank Wing—receding hairline, pince-nez such as Wing had worn earlier, archaic cutaway—meeting "the new instructor in ancient history," a living hieroglyph called Miss Folsom, whose pharaonic profile broods in ironic contrast with a highly modern chair and desk patterned after those in the updated Educational Department.

Schulz credited *Grin and Bear It,* a single panel by sports cartoonist George Lichty, as the feature's formal exemplar. Percy Crosby's inspiration can also be seen in the loosely drawn little boy and girl sitting on the curb in front of a Skippy-size fence, and Disney's influence shows in the plucky little bugs driven into a "new large economy size" cereal box by the infuriating housing shortage. But the panel on the lower right defines Schulz's pen style, themes, and humor—even its transmutation of autobiographical fact: a yellow-haired boy, the very image of Sparky at eight, gives his aproned mother a proper vase on her birthday, as a Spike-like dog cocks an ear, and the boy says, "Happy Birthday, Mom, and if you don't like it, the man said I could exchange it for a hockey puck!"

The momentous publication—"my first appearance in print as a comic artist," he was to call it—coincided with the birthday of the lost mother briefly resurrected in his color panel. On February 7, 1947, Dena Schulz would have been fifty-four.

ONE WEDNESDAY EVENING, PIERCED by a shivering loneliness, Sparky wandered over to the Merriam Park Church of God, his first visit to a church on any day but Sunday. As he climbed the steps, he noticed that the sign announcing the evening prayer service needed painting.

There was another difference that night. Sparky's pastor and friend, Frederick Shackleton, had moved on to another congregation; the new man, Marvin Forbes, was older (fifty-six), shorter, stocky, with the burly physique of a high school wrestler, thinning light-brown hair over a high forehead, and pale blue eyes. His one real suit was so spectacularly rumpled that a Merriam Park celebrant would say, "He always looked like he'd just woken up."

Coming after George Edes and Fred Shackleton, both of whom had been well-dressed, personable, and educated, Marvin Forbes was a change indeed. He had attended neither college nor seminary, but he possessed a raw, unpolished charm. He preached without notes or text and was natural on his feet, a formidable speaker. When Brother Forbes spoke out, Sparky's skin prickled and he could feel the hair on his head down to its roots. In one of the gag cartoons Schulz drew for the Church of God's *Youth* magazine, an enthusiastic teenager bursts out after service, "I wish ol' King Herod had been here, Brother Forbes. You would have had him all shook up!" Schulz would later concede that Forbes made grammatical errors "now and then" in his sermons. "He murdered the English language," said another parishioner. "His pronunciation was terrible; you'd lose your train of thought listening to him," added another. But, Sparky recalled, no one minded: "There was so much heart in his preaching."

When Schulz introduced himself to Forbes after his first Wednesday evening prayer service, he offered to touch up the faded lettering on the sign out front, and from that night on was looking for ways to help out around the church. He regularly attended each week's full round of devotions, including both Sunday morning worship and vespers, often sitting at the back with Ruth Forbes and the couple's three children. Before long, he was regularly sharing a root beer with Marvin and Ruth at their all-purpose kitchen table in the small, remodeled Sunday school rooms that were all the church could afford to offer as a parsonage—domestic arrangements later remembered as "tough living" by members of the congregation, especially for a family with a nine-year-old boy and two younger girls.

But, Ruth still noticed, "He was alone and you just could imagine he was lonely; and I think he found some fellowship with us that helped him take care of that. He loved family." Ruth also recalled Sparky regretting one evening that he had been an only child and adding that he "hoped that some day he would have a large family."

He looked up to Marvin Forbes as to a tutor, especially in these early stages of his spiritual awakening, when he sought the Bible as a guide to life. Sparky underlined scriptural passages, and Brother Forbes discussed those passages with his protégé over root beers. Visit by visit, Sparky borrowed, read, and returned at his next call, book after book by such Church of God thinkers as H. M. Riggle, F. G. Smith, and Charles E. Brown, this last of whom worked on his readers to see the two sides of faith—"visible and invisible"—into which sectarian Protestantism had divided the body of Christ's church and the fleshly and spiritual impulses of believers.

Sparky attended adult Sunday school taught by Mary Ramsperger, to whom he also drew close. "He kind of adopted the family," recalled her daughter, named Mary as well. "He needed a family and he thought a great deal of my mother." Through the elder Mary he came to know her son, Harold, two years Sparky's senior, and his wife Elaine, newlyweds living in a little apartment above the elder Mrs. Ramsperger, one block from St. Paul's Como Lake. The Ramspergers were a musical family: Harold, a tenor who worked in the paint department of the Great Northern Railway, was the congregation's musical leader; Elaine studied voice and sang in church. At home their rooms were forever awash in symphonies from 78-rpm records. Sparky had never met anyone with whom he felt more at ease. Harold was like a true brother: Sparky could talk to him about anything, even Krazy Kat, and feel completely understood.

His life—just a year earlier, weekdays of patchy social encounters and weekends that stretched out devoid of all human contact—was now packed with youth group activities. A typical week offered Wednesday-night and Sunday-night prayer meetings attended by the most dedicated church members, Sparky always coming to both. The youth group would get together to socialize at the house of one of the married couples after the Sunday-evening service, usually Dolores and Bill Edes's place in South Minneapolis. The main service of the week took place at eleven on Sunday morning, preceded by Sunday school. Throughout the long Minnesota winters, the men of the youth group met to play hockey. One of the group's traditions every New Year's Eve was a Watch Night service, in which they would come together to observe the passing of the year with prayers, testimony, music, and hymns. Then, in caps and mufflers and high spirits, they would go off to a rink and skate through the thrilling icy night.

His new friends at the Church of God visited the apartment on North

Snelling. Carl and Sparky, no longer having to share a bedroom (the war-time wives had moved on), slept in the side-by-side rooms overlooking Lux Liquors, and served take-out food when they had guests. Stout, sweet-tempered Annabelle Anderson still looked after Carl, but he held to his vow not to remarry until Sparky was married, and so Sparky was allowed to keep Annabelle at arm's length—even, at times, to hold her at a scorn-ful distance, nevertheless showing the open side of his heart when a caring woman like Mary Ramsperger cooked for him and his father. He formed the habit, which would last for years, of casting as a maternal figure which-ever good soul set before him such comforting foods as his mother had once made. All he wanted in life seemed to waft from Mary Ramsperger's warm, soft-crusted apple pie with vanilla ice cream slowly and delectably soaking through the pastry.

His aunt Marion remained Dena's strongest surrogate. "She was kind of a rock for him," said one relative. The extended family often styled Marion as Sparky's "second mother," and their love was reciprocal. For years into the future, Marion's daughter Patty would insist that her mother loved Sparky more than she loved her: "She always babied him," just as Sparky played up to this and "always talked to her with a soft voice."

WHATEVER SPARKY'S ACTION-STORY dreams, when Roman Baltes published another installment of *Just Keep Laughing* in April 1947, its creator was so pleased with the brush technique in the four serial panels that he devoted his evenings to developing the idea of a comic serial, also in four panels, which would show recurring child characters in ongoing settings and sit-uations. But now, instead of including parents and teachers as he had in the earlier parts of *Just Keep Laughing*, he eliminated grown-ups entirely. "I began to experiment with drawing little, tiny kids." But this was no straight line of destiny: "I must confess that, at the time, I had only a meager interest in drawing little kids. I drew them because they were what sold."

One day Schulz took a batch of these cartoons to the *Minneapolis Star Tribune*. The editor liked them, bought them, and published the first block of four as a panel entitled *Sparky's Li'l Folks* on Sunday, June 8, 1947, fol-lowing up with another the next week, then offered to publish the feature "off and on during the summer." But Sparky balked at this arrangement: to appear only as time and space permitted "was not too satisfying to someone as impatient and dedicated as I," and he took his work across the river to the *St. Paul Pioneer Press* and the *Dispatch*.

The managing editor, Vernon E. "Doug" Fairbanks, could not promise space in the daily comics page but liked the feature and asked Schulz to bring it in once a week. And so, on June 22, the third installment of *Li'l Folks*—"By Sparky"—debuted, without a word of introduction, in the upper left corner of the *Pioneer Press*'s News About Women department, shoehorned in above the report that "Miss Virginia Radabaugh Names Wedding Attendants."

The postwar wedding pages were in some ways an ideal dress window for a cartoon featuring multiple match-offs of nicely dressed boys and girls deeply engaged on a new front of the war between the sexes. In the first installment, a boy with two pairs of boxing gloves says to the prim girl on the sofa: "Oh, rats, you never want to do anything." Elsewhere on the page, a girl at her bedroom window breaks it to her suitor, halfway up the ladder: "Mom says I can't elope with you tonight. I've got too much homework to do." Another little girl rebukes the boy at her side: "I don't see why you have to carry all those marbles in one pocket."

Week after week, the girls grew increasingly frustrated with the boys. A doll-carrying young lady considerately explains from her doorway to a cap-in-hand caller: "It's not that I don't like you . . . I just can't stand the sight of you." Another girl, bow in hair, baseball bat in fist, dictates the script to another anxiously courteous visitor: "Aren't you glad to see me?"

The war had broken up families, dividing the experience of men and women. Schulz's vaudeville sense of humor, honed by radio, slipped naturally toward this theme. It was relations between the sexes that gave a hard edge, forged in another kind of war, even to a newsy letter to Fred and Doris Shackleton: "By the way, I'm thinking of writing a couple epic poems. See what you think of the titles. 'He grabbed her by the collar because he liked to hear her holler.' 'He grabbed her by the gullet, as he shot her with a bullet.' "

In *Li'l Folks*, the frustrations of the vulnerable master sex and the effortless superiority of its opposite number would intensify as the feature developed: A bruised boy laid out flat on the sidewalk mumbles to his pal, ". . . And the next thing I knew, she hit me over the head with her mad-money!" A teeth-gritting girl pounds her victim while his friend pleads,

"But he's a boy, and boys are bigger than girls. They're stronger, an' got more muscles an' . . ." Another boy, also about to be slugged, prefigures Linus Van Pelt by blurting, "Don't hit me! Just say something sarcastic!"

TO BE A CARTOONIST is to speak, not only to draw. Comics *say* things. The words must come from somewhere, and when Schulz told his fellow Minnesotan Cpl. Donald Schaust at Camp Campbell that he aimed to be a cartoonist, he further confessed that he was not so much concerned with his ability to draw funny pictures as he was worried about whether he "would be able to put words in the characters' mouths."

Where did the voices of *Li'l Folks'* ceaselessly opposed girls and boys come from? In Schulz's childhood, the girl cousins he played with had done all the talking. Then came the terrifying beauties who left him voiceless: Jane Gilbertson, whose blond presence had outshone the lilac bushes in his cousins' yard in Hudson, Wisconsin; skinny little Lyala Bischoff on the Selby Lake streetcar; Naomi Cohn, that other petite brunette, the evening star of the cartooning class. "I can't help it," Charlie Brown would explain, ". . . pretty faces make me nervous." The talkative *and* pretty Virginia Howley had had no peacetime successor.

Now came Judy Halverson (whose Swedish ancestors bore no relation to his mother's people). Of all the Educational Department's young eligibles, he chose to ask out Art Instruction's veritable belle of the ball. But, for all her strong qualities—she was trim and, again, brunette, clearheaded, candid, hardworking, an excellent draftswoman—it was her touch of self-doubt that made her particularly appealing. Sparky and she were fewer than three months apart in age; but he was that rarity among twenty-five-year-olds in the late 1940s: a man with access to a car, his father's old Ford—so their dating could be independent but casual. They could go places without necessarily going steady, which was the way they both wanted it—on picnics and to a lakeshore restaurant at Lake Minnetonka.

Occasionally they played tennis. She let him teach her golf and take her to a ball game; he consented to visit her relatives at their cabin at Balsam Lake. And no matter where they were or what they were doing, Judy's lovely, throaty voice carried the conversation.

It wasn't supposed to get serious, but after a time he was enraptured. Without ever coming right out with it—he made no formal proposal—he let Judy know that he wanted to marry her. Judy made it equally clear that she didn't want to get married; she wanted to be an artist. He maintained that that was fine, that each could have a studio. But not even on those terms would she accept.

During this period, observers of Sparky's relations with women in general and with Judy Halverson in particular recalled that marriage was uppermost in his thoughts. "He wanted to get married," recalled another instructor, Paul Olsen, "so, immediately after he was going with a girl, he scared them off with too much responsibility"—or as his friend and colleague David Ratner put it, "He scared a lot of girls. He was too serious, too soon. With Judy he pushed marriage too hard. He just scared her." But Ratner also contended that Sparky's reasons for moving so directly toward his goal were typical of a certain kind of young man in that time and place: "He was very moral. The idea of having sex outside of marriage was anathema to him. At the same time, he was probably a very sexual person."

There are also people—and Schulz certainly was one—who have to be refused in order to fall deeply in love. Then they can maintain the supplicant's role in which they are most comfortable. In being turned down, or turned aside, by Judy Halverson, Sparky became at once more devoted and suddenly resentful. He mooned briefly over the rejection, then, back at Art Instruction, brooded at his desk and dropped bitter comments. "She was the one that rejected him," reflected a colleague, "and I think a lot of his attitude was, 'Well. She'll be sorry.' "

At his drawing board, however, he found a more lighthearted if not kinder, approach. As he would do with other injuries in his life, he treasured the hurt that Judy had inflicted by putting her into a cartoon.

WITH LI'L FOLKS launched in St. Paul, he made his first trip to Chicago to try out the syndicates that summer of 1947, bearing a package of some fifteen samples, which outlined the story of a tomboy named Judy who does not speak. Comic panels made an awkward package for a young man whose profoundest instinct in public was to blend in. Unlike the rough sketches for gags, which fitted onto an ordinary sheet of drawing paper, the sample panels for a comic strip were drawn on long, rectangular, multiply boards whose size and shape never failed to invite comment, even from complete strangers.

These samples featured an unnamed boy who did all the talking for the powerfully silent Judy. Each punch line began with the boy saying, "Judy says . . ." It was the first time he had activated his innate humor by inverting the natural order as he knew it. For in real life, of course, Judy Halverson had done the talking for Sparky, except to speak the words he most wanted to hear.

Boarding the eight A.M. Burlington *Zephyr* at Union Depot, samples wrapped between loose pieces of cardboard, he managed to go the next 350 miles without exchanging a word with anyone. Well-barbered, dressed in his one good suit, he breakfasted alone in the dining car. As the *Zephyr* sped him away from St. Paul, past the lazy towns and little cities along the banks of the Mississippi—Red Wing, Winona, La Crosse, Prairie du Chien—the river and sky grew wider at his right elbow. Here was the great corridor of commerce, beyond which the cornstalked countryside stretched flat across the land, interrupted now and then by sandlot ball fields, swimming holes, redbrick schoolhouses, and proud college avenues of vaulted elms.

To the passing eye of a young cartoonist halfway through the twentieth century, each midland township with its grassy hundred-acre tracts of well-spaced houses, each of these with its morning newspaper folded and waiting on the front porch, must have seemed hungry to absorb all the inked panels and brushwork he could deliver. Years later, Schulz would evoke the simple certainty of those early mornings when "Minnesota and my dreams of becoming a cartoonist united."

The *Zephyr* streaked south toward Iowa and the spires of Dubuque, where the dining-car steward announced lunch. Then came Galena, Illinois, hometown of Ulysses S. Grant, where the train veered away from the upper Mississippi basin and sped east toward Lake Michigan. Arriving in Chicago at three in the afternoon, Sparky sought lodging, conscious as he signed the guest register that for the first time he was checking into a hotel by himself. He rose at sunup the next morning, ready to make the rounds.

Without an appointment—he did not know he was supposed to have one—he found his way to the Tribune Tower and presented himself at the Chicago Tribune–New York News Syndicate, purveyors of such warhorses of the comics page as *Gasoline Alley, Terry and the Pirates, Dick Tracy,* and *The Gumps,* but could advance no further than the receptionist. However,

on North La Salle Street, he managed to get shown in to the editor of
Publishers Syndicate, source of the Gallup Poll and "serious" comics like
*Mary Worth.*

Pale, grim-faced Harold H. Anderson neither stood nor greeted his
visitor but indifferently stated his own name and then fell silent, waiting
for samples. Sparky felt confident about the work and made a strong presentation. Anderson scarcely listened. Having snatched up the bundle and
set the samples on his big desk like an uncut deck of cards, he lifted a board
or two at random, peeking in at a panel, then gathered up the whole batch
and shoved it back. "Not professional enough."

Schulz never forgot the slight. For years afterward, as their paths crossed
and recrossed in their tiny profession, Schulz built a case against Anderson.
"You idiot," he recalled thinking at the time. "You don't even ask where
I'm from! Did I have a nice trip down? All the niceties of life." He himself
later dedicated hours of his time to fledgling cartoonists, often taking them
to lunch and empathizing with their most personal concerns.

To a marketing eye like Anderson's, Schulz's pen line could not possibly carry the ongoing drive of a daily strip over the years. Schulz's fresh,
clean-cut draftsmanship, to say nothing of children with flattened-out,
noddy heads and bodies smaller than midgets', could not have been further
from the heavily shaded realism and solemn story lines of problem-solving
strips like *Rex Morgan, M.D.* and *Judge Parker,* which Publishers Syndicate
was now betting would be the postwar trend. As further features like *Steve
Roper* proliferated, the less space there would be for a bunch of wisen-
heimer kids saying things that made fun of the very pablum that these
didactic soap operas were dishing out.

Schulz's panels, hybrids of the gag cartoon and the comic strip, bewildered syndicate editors like Anderson, who prided themselves on their
responsiveness, through "research know-how," to changing tastes in existing comics. Was his Judy, for example, a little girl in a panel cartoon or a
character in a comic strip, and why couldn't she talk without the help of
the boy in the feature? Why, for that matter, did Schulz's *Li'l Folks* talk like
grown-ups, when anyone could see that they were barely out of the cradle,
albeit a very strange cradle?

Not every editor's eye in Chicago was sightless. At the Chicago Sun-
Times Syndicate, Schulz received encouragement from Walt Ditzen, a

comic strip artist who drew a syndicated strip about football (*Fan Fare*). He was impressed with the quality of Schulz's pen line. After perusing the first sample panels of *Judy Says*, he exclaimed, "I certainly cannot say no to this. We'll have to take it in to the president."

Ditzen escorted Sparky into the office and introduced him: "Harry," as Schulz recalled it, "I just want you to see the work here of this young man. I think he's really good."

Harry Baker looked at the work. "Well," he said. And then, abruptly: "No."

Undaunted, Sparky packed up his samples and, for all his disappointment, boarded the return train still full of excitement, still full of the day's enterprise. He would ever after recall the feeling of going home with his first rejections to start all over again: "I was never discouraged. I always knew that I was getting closer and closer."

IN HIS FIRST DAYS at Art Instruction he had panicked a little, "coming in totally cold to this room that had about fifteen people in it." But these first trips away from the Cities moved him to overcome his paralyzing self-consciousness. Breaking the ice was still hardest, and Sparky used the trains to and from Chicago to develop the natural touch with a new acquaintance. He would be forever curious about such junctions in people's lives, later asking one colleague, "When did you learn the art of conversation?"—as if everyone had on some special day "learned" to talk with others. The morning *Zephyr*, its passengers reading newspapers and readying themselves for the big city, let him rest on his old ways—he could ride the seven hours to Chicago in silence.

Forcing himself to be personable, he sometimes took a seat in the club car, where he would have to talk. One day he sat down opposite a pretty girl with a popular new novel that he himself had already read. For once, he had an icebreaker at hand and could ask what she thought of the book. She liked it very much. Now it was his turn to carry the conversation, and he could think of nothing to say. He let a moment pass. Then another moment slipped away, and then another, and finally silence reasserted itself, whereupon, in plain panic, he got up and fled.

He came to see that the better part of his shyness was really vanity, or self-centeredness. "Shyness is an illusion," he would say, late in life. "If you get out and do something and talk to people, you don't have to be shy. Shyness is the overtly self-conscious thinking that you are the only person in the world; that how you look and what you do is of any importance."

In his new friendships he could be self-absorbed to the point of solipsism. With Judy Halverson, he was often thinking of himself. On a visit to her relatives at the Balsam Lake cabin, he and Judy were walking in a fenced pasture on the place, when, hearing the sound of hooves, they looked up to see heifers charging. Without a thought for his date, Sparky made for the fences—the city boy, not realizing that cows are merely nearsighted and curious, scrambled onto the fence and picked his way over barbed wire, leaving Judy to fend for herself. Another time, they left work together to play tennis, and Sparky drove them over to St. Paul, stopping briefly at his apartment on North Snelling to change into tennis clothes while Judy waited in the car. Across the avenue she saw a bakery. Typically, for thoughtfulness was one of her qualities, she raced over to buy some freshly baked cookies, a treat she gave to Sparky as soon as he got back in. Starting the engine and putting the car in gear, he popped one in his mouth only to step on the brake, lean out the window, and hawk up a big, disgusted "Ptooey!" as he spat the uneaten mouthful into the gutter. Without apology, without acknowledging Judy's surprise, he announced that he *hated* coconut.

In a few years, the whole sequence of events appeared in Schulz's panels: Violet treats Charlie Brown to a "very special mud pie," which she gives him with a polite, ladylike "pardon my fingers." Violet has sprinkled the pie with coconut, and Charlie Brown reacts just as Sparky did to Judy's gift—only the sound of revulsion is different ("Phooey," not "Ptooey"), and Charlie Brown is able, as Sparky was not, to apologize for bad manners.

The most striking parallel, however, between the real-life working out of the relationship between Judy Halverson and Charles Schulz and its controlled comic strip depiction as that between Violet and Charlie Brown is not just that Violet does not love Charlie Brown, but that Charlie Brown, jilted, deprived, strikes back at Violet with the flip side of his powerful sentiments: when he complains that nobody loves him, Violet and her sidekick, Patty, try to buck him up by saying that it's not true; *they* love him. To which he replies with the brutal tactlessness of misery, "Yes, but nobody important loves me."

★  ★  ★

NO SOONER HAD *LI'L FOLKS* begun appearing regularly in St. Paul than a special delivery arrived from Los Angeles that put Sparky truly on the spot: nothing more—or less—than a form letter inviting Charles Schulz to the Walt Disney Studios for a standard one-month tryout. The studio on Hyperion Avenue taught the art and science of animation to young as-yet-unknowns like Walt Kelly, Hank Ketcham, Bill Peet, and Gus Arriola, and was known to aspiring cartoonists of Schulz's generation as the "Mouse Factory" or the "University of Walt Disney."

Stimulated by his growing ambition—and an equally powerful naïveté—Sparky was tempted to follow in the footsteps of his first editor, Roman Baltes, who had worked on the revolutionary animated feature *Snow White and the Seven Dwarfs*. But going to Hollywood would mean giving up *Li'l Folks*. A tryout was only a tryout, but *Li'l Folks* was a real feature—it just happened not to be on the daily comics page or in the Sunday comics supplement. Still, it was training Sparky to develop ideas, to draw on a regular schedule, and to meet deadlines. With ever-increasing confidence, he could see that his work was "getting better all the time." By the fall of 1947, he even had hopes of publishing the panels in book form.

At the same time, the *St. Paul Pioneer Press* had put nothing in writing; Sparky had no contract. Accounts would vary as to how much he was paid—the editors afterward claimed that Schulz had drawn *Li'l Folks* for free; Sparky recalled pocketing $10 a week, nearly a third of the full-time pay of a skilled laborer.

Money, in any case, was the least of his concerns. He was unmarried, living with his father—Carl paid the rent—and his expenses were relatively small. His Art Instruction salary, combined with freelance earnings from *Topix*, covered books, records, concert tickets, and occasional trips to Chicago to canvass the syndicates. Beyond that, his most expensive wish was for a complete set of golf clubs to replace the ones kicking around since high school.

Carl advised against the Disney tryout and recalled telling Sparky: "What you have now, you have. But if you go to Disney, they'll have it." Later, when an interviewer made almost the same point ("If you had gone to Walt Disney, you would have been just one more person there in his empire"), Schulz revealed more of himself than he had perhaps intended when he shot back, "No, I would have taken over the whole operation."

The gag cartooning game, which offered the other alternative path to a would-be syndicated cartoonist, had brought him only rejections. Sparky had begun to doubt whether he had what it took to sustain himself though the "brutal business" of what his contemporary Ketcham, then freelancing in New York, called "trying to be funny for money." Gag cartoonists could not afford to be sensitive. "If you want to make a decent living at it," advised the professionals at Art Instruction, "be smart instead of temperamental." Each evening, as Sparky came home to pick up his mail at the Family Barber Shop, he braced himself for "the bitter blow of opening the envelope and seeing a note that said, 'Sorry, nothing this week.' " For a sensitive young man, the great advantage of comic strips and syndication was that once the cartoonist had sold his strip to the syndicate, it was the syndicate's job to sell to the editors.

His highest target continued to be *The Saturday Evening Post*. Too much the perfectionist to risk Harold Ross's *New Yorker*, known in the trade as "every gag cartoonist's Everest," he had begun to develop and submit to the *Post* one of the staples of gag cartooning, the "kid cartoon." As a midwestern freelancer, far from the traditional Wednesday "look day," when cartoonists thronged editors' desks in New York City with brief but intense showings of their rough sketches, Schulz had no idea how the home offices reacted to his submissions until the *Post*'s cartoon editor, a habitual, Irish curmudgeon, John Bailey, flagged one bunch with a few words of encouragement and a layering of practical advice.

At Art Instruction, Schulz learned to trust colleagues to help develop his sense of audience, slipping a draft before a receptive friend and waiting for the laugh. "I'd come back from lunch and there would be a cartoon sitting on my desk—a pencil sketch—that Sparky had drawn," recalled Pat Blaise Telfer. "He would watch my reaction and if he saw my shoulders shaking he knew it was a good one, and he would ink it in." Sometimes, two colleagues passing by would see the cartoon waiting on someone else's desk, bend down together to read it, and find themselves swept up by laughter.

One of the younger instructors from the Minneapolis School of Art, Larry Dominic, who drew horses, told Sparky that he liked the way his kids crouched. Frank Wing responded to the way they walked: "You should draw more of those little kids, Sparky. They are pretty good." Walter Wilwerding looked over one attempt and said, "You're having fun, aren't you?" Years later, Sparky would remember such remarks as the "little things that people say that keep you going."

At Disney's new studio in Burbank, he would have to start on the bottom rung, as a $22.50-per-week "in-betweener," pumping out hundreds of the maddeningly similar drawings that moved Disney's animated characters from action to manic action. Sparky had no interest in such chores, yet in 1947, Disney Studios was still the place for a promising cartoonist. In an agony of doubt, he consulted the revered Marvin Forbes, who took him for a pastoral walk-and-talk along the banks of the Upper Mississippi. Schulz later credited Forbes with urging him to put aside fear of further rejection and go on submitting to *The Saturday Evening Post* as he drew his weekly feature and worked at Art Instruction.

From the riverbank, he could not but see that St. Paul and Minneapolis were no longer the same cities he had known even a year earlier. Since coming home from the war, a solitary young survivor from a vanished past, he had found new worlds in his old hometown, perhaps most real among them that of the spirit. The evidence was all around and within him. He no longer felt alone.

And he had friends: his newfound circle at Art Instruction made music, literature, and discussion of modernist painting part of his everyday life. He still teed off with his old pals the golfers, fellow caddies and teammates at Central High—though no longer on Sundays, for now he went to his group at the Church of God. And, finally, kept separate and discrete from each group, there were the girls he dated and the girls he dreamed of dating.

In this neatly compartmentalized world—the setting for the happiest part of his life, he always maintained—he spent the next five years. Art Instruction, Inc., in particular, turned out to be much more than a job. "That was the start," he could say, "of a whole new life."

CHAPTER 11

# HEADS AND
# BODIES

*The secret of drawing a convincing head is to aim at form.*
—C.M.S., AT ART INSTRUCTION, INC., 1948

IN THE AFTERNOONS, Charlie Brown, the Educational Department's good-hearted joker, assisted by Hedy Angelikis, the most popular of the younger women, would preside over an informal period known as Fun and Games. Charlie Brown (not the same Charles Brown whom Sparky knew in high school) had majored in art at the University of Minnesota, and now, at twenty-one, to quote from his own third-person account, was spending his free time "searching for himself by getting lost in bars, dating, reading, college parties, music, drawing, movies, and dreams."

Born Charles Francis Brown in Minneapolis, he was universally known in the department as Charlie Brown, or Good ol' Charlie Brown. As "the instigator" of Fun and Games, he would lead off by drawing a face and then folding the paper over to draw the beginning of a neck for the next person. Then, openly or furtively, depending on Walter Wilwerding's mood, this "head" would be handed on to the next instructor, with a whispered "Needs a body," or, if he had started with a torso, "Needs a head." The resulting combinations, passed around for everyone to see, were so original or dreamlike, or even so sinister, that thrilled, nervous laughter would sweep the room.

The Educational Department provided Sparky with the closest thing to the college life he had forgone. It was "a room full of very talented people—a great place for me to grow up after World War Two."

Reaching his desk each morning at eight, he found that, as usual, Claude Botts, a fifteen-year veteran of the department, had set the stage by doling out identical stacks of manila envelopes on each instructor's desktop, whose contents the recipients would scan for especially laughable—and sharable—versions of the usual student blunders.

Even quiet Sparky would occasionally entertain the room with the latest truly classic howler. Here, for instance, instead of the thumbnail sketch asked for in a Division 2 assignment, was a detailed rendering of the student's own thumb; instead of the matchstick figures for which a cartooning instructor had asked, another student had glued actual matchsticks to a sheet of paper. Yet a third, new to artists' materials, was baffled to find "two pieces of paper stuck together there"—a two-ply Bristol board. Still another took at face value the instruction to paint a particular lesson "on" the drawing board provided in each student's kit and had mailed back the "finished" board, to remain on display throughout Schulz's teaching years.

Sparky loved the mornings when the studio light fell soft and even across the adjoining desks and each instructor made an entrance to his or her accustomed place. He saw the Educational Department as a "terrific setting for a play"—the older faculty, for instance, whom everyone would remember as "characters," such as Louise Cassidy at the front desk by the window, a lively, well-dressed spinster in her late sixties who kept her hair blond, cut in bangs, and pulled into Danish-pastry-like buns on the sides of her head; she drove a coupé from the '30s and inspired one of the younger instructors to pattern a comic strip after her called *Auntie Climax*.

In contrast to the old guard, as represented by Wing and Wilwerding, Schulz's group of young instructors were the new regime, bound by friendships, romances, and even marriages—painters and illustrators and graphic designers, their lives and ambitions disrupted by slump and war, now breaking open their obstructed paths. They were smart and amusing, neither sophisticates nor bumpkins; ambitious about art, competitive at games, droll and wry in humor, teasing and challenging in friendship, who banded together at coffee break and again at lunchtime, often huddling into a bridge game at one of the desks. "We had a lot in common," a participant recalled, "the same attitude toward everything."

The core of the younger group included Judy Halverson and Patricia Blaise, the pretty pair of former Minneapolis School of Art honor students who were both talented painters and University of Minnesota alumnae and were almost like sisters; the beautiful figure artist Ellen Murray; and the highly animated Canadian transplant Frieda Rich. But the group was kept exclusive by the art school men, David Ratner, George Letness, Paul Olsen, Jim Sasseville, and Bill Ryan, lately cronies in the academy studios, which most of them had attended on the GI Bill. Dedicated painters, they loved to draw, gathering in the garret rooms that Louise Cassidy rented to Jim Sasseville in her house on Third Street, where they would drink beer, wolf down Louise's asparagus omelets, and sketch one another on four-inch-by-seven-inch scratch paper. Back at their desks, they would challenge each other to tests of speed and powers of observation, whether rendering likenesses in the mode of formal portraits or, more casually but no less professionally, in caricatures, cartoons, and doodles.

They were known as the "Bureau's drawers" (Art Instruction shared the building with its parent graphic arts colossus, the Bureau of Engraving). Naturally, in such a competitive group, one unquestionable "top drawer" had to establish himself; this proved to be the reserved, smart, handsome George Letness, whom David Ratner had dubbed "the hottest artist in our class," by universal consent the best draftsman and oil painter at the academy. He had arrived at the desk adjoining Schulz's in 1949, displacing Sparky as the shyest man in the room. Both were simultaneously reticent and competitive, displayed comparable senses of humor, and eventually became the "two best friends" among the younger instructors. Four years Sparky's junior and of doubly Scandinavian descent, Letness noticed that although Schulz was, like him, reserved and hampered by the Scandinavian impulse to deflate oneself before another could do it for him, his neighbor had "a lot of self-confidence. He was pretty sure of himself."

Good-natured, outgoing David Ratner, with deep brow and kindly brown eyes, had many admirers in the second-floor stenographic pool. At Minneapolis Central High, he had been the Class of 1941's "one real artist—not the artist-type that we knew about from the movies, but a good guy who could paint," recalled his classmate Samuel Hynes. Art-savvy from a postwar year at the Grande Chaumière in Paris, Ratner was still everybody's favorite guy and a serious, respected painter.

Jim Sasseville, witty, literary, a lover of poetry and comic strips, with long-lashed dark eyes and a full head of dark hair, was universally considered the most inventive draftsman in the younger set—by none more outspokenly than Sparky, who envied Sasseville his facility in drawing beautiful girls and adventure-strip characters. They became friends immediately, linked by their love of *Krazy Kat* and *Wash Tubbs* and *Captain Easy*.

In the beginning, Sparky stood apart from the art academy crowd. "There was always something a little uncomfortable with him," reflected David Ratner. "He was much more competitive than he seemed to be," said Paul Olsen. "He gave the impression, with his cartoons, that he was a loser. But [Sparky] was kind of aggressive in some ways, and he was a winner." "I think he knew what he had," suggested Hal Lamson. "Some of that humble approach wasn't totally honest. I think he knew he had something good. He knew where he wanted to go with it, too . . . which gave him a real advantage over a lot of us. Here we were painters who were trying to be cartoonists. We didn't have that vision about ourselves."

To George Letness, it seemed that everyone in the academy clique "had a cartoon in the bottom drawer that was [his or her] passport to immortality." Cartooning was seen as a form worth mastering in itself while also offering a more commercially rational path to fame and fortune than did the trend-haunted world of high art; but figure drawing and painting in oils remained the great pursuits. The academy men and women would go back together to their alma mater for weekly figure-study sessions, hiring models to sit for them in the nude, and though invited, Sparky nonetheless did not attend. "He knew himself better than anyone, and drawing a nude just wasn't what he wanted to do," said David Ratner. If Sparky felt awkward about the model's nakedness, as several of the clique suspected, he said nothing about it.

Schulz felt that he was "the only one that was really working on a comic strip." Several others "were trying," including Charlie Brown and one of their young sidekicks, Linus Maurer, but "basically," as he was to repeat over the years, "I was the really fanatical one along those lines." It was this, more than anything, that set him apart.

Designated "artist-instructors" by the school, the faculty were encour-

HEADS AND BODIES 185

aged, once they had dealt with their daily load, to work at their desks on their own projects, thereby setting an example to the invisible student body. Schulz filled every such free moment and sheet of paper with penciled roughs for gag cartoons, using the Art Instruction mail room's well-designed envelopes and abundant cardboards and modern "mailing systems" to send out batches of ten. Wilwerding reminisced to Sparky that as a beginning artist he never let himself "be caught without something in the mail." Sparky, enterprising, disciplined, "unbelievably determined"— ever the company's purest product—put the tip into action, pausing only to pass along this latest lesson in the American language of hustle to his old buddy Dieffenwierth: "That's the secret, Frank. Always have an iron in the fire. Always have another angle ready to go. . . . I'm expecting you to throw yourself wholeheartedly into this art business now. Remember, if you can't outplay them, you have to outwork them."

For the forty-one months between February 1947 and June 1950, Schulz tried never to let a week go by without having a submission "working" for him at *The Saturday Evening Post*, *This Week*, or *Collier's*. "This way," he told himself and others, "you are never without hope"—a formulation typical of the change that had come over him as an instructor. For it was his department's atmosphere of playfulness mingled with decorum, camaraderie shot through with competition, and discipline offset by an almost childlike spirit of improvisation that freed him from his longstanding sense of being thwarted by the world.

ONE SPRING DAY IN 1948, Sparky dipped his pen and drew the fresh idea that gripped him straight out as a finished cartoon: a little boy sits reading at the end of an impossibly long chaise longue, his legs stretching still farther onto a supremely redundant ottoman. Thinking of the gag cartoons he had loved before the war—"the little kids with the great big heads," as he summarized them—Sparky hypertrophied the head, shortened the arms, and knew immediately that he was on the right track.

He sent off the cartoon fully inked to *The Saturday Evening Post* without waiting for the go-ahead from the magazine's cartoon editor, John Bailey. A few days later, Bailey wrote: "Check Tuesday for spot drawing of boy on lounge," which Sparky first took to mean that he should check his mail on Tuesday for the rejected drawing. But that night over supper, he suddenly said to his father, "You know, I think I'm wrong. I think this means they're going to send me a check on Tuesday," and indeed this interpretation proved right: $40 (a week's income for a median family)— "my first major sale." When the drawing itself was published, just a few weeks later, his colleagues circled his desk. Ordinarily, the whole process of getting a cartoon into the venerable *Post* took months. Yet here their boy was, all at once, the hero of the hour, and under a mature byline, too. In the St. Paul paper he was still "Sparky." Here, coming into the purview of the whole respectability of the country, was *Charles Schulz*.

WHEN HE HAD BEGUN drawing weekly installments of *Li'l Folks* in June 1947, the boys and girls in his panels stood three heads tall—normal scale for the presentation of children in a cartoon. Over the next twelve months, as the heads themselves gradually dilated, the torsos and limbs contracted, and by the end of 1948 the proportions and modeling of forms had substantially changed. Boys and girls now stood two and a half heads high overall, the girls as big and strong as the boys. None of the children was pretty, let alone cute. The sharp, clean pen lines establishing their bodies and clothing were increasingly economical and understated, the heads ever more round. Yet even without necks or shoulders or any delineation of joints at the knees or elbows or wrists, as 1949 began each child still looked relatively normal in size and scale.

But by June of that year, the heads of Schulz's kids had swelled, each being almost three-quarters as far across as the torso in width alone—the mouth, in some renderings, as wide as the waist. Crown to toe, the figures now stood just two heads high, the head equal in height to the entire aggregate of torso and legs, the arms too short for fingertips to reach higher than the ears. Another cartoon character soon to make his debut, Hank Ketcham's Dennis the Menace, though speaking like a child and drawn at the more normal proportion of three heads tall, looked, in Ketcham's words, "like a midget." But, over time, "as in the real world," Ketcham explained, "once you get to know these funny-looking folks, you enjoy them and no longer consider them grotesque."

Schulz's *Li'l Folks*—normal-looking kids at the start of their run— provided the body types that would help him create a radically original comic strip in 1950. But what precipitated this metamorphosis? Did particular conditions in his life between 1947 and 1949 account for these changes?

FRIEDA MAE RICH JOINED the Art Instruction faculty in 1948. She was a dwarf, born with a condition that limited her adult height to four feet. Witty, charming, morally courageous, she wore her dark, curly hair with great satisfaction and prided herself on her singing voice—at Art Instruction's Christmas parties, she would blacken her main upper incisors, don an overlong flannel nightgown, and sing and mince her way through "All I Want for Christmas Is My Two Front Teeth" to Charlie Brown's piano accompaniment. Many remembered the quickness and depth of her wonderful laugh. By all accounts, Frieda was intelligent, considered herself a good conversationalist, and took pride in being a member of countless social groups and civic organizations.

She was twenty-seven, and had never let her size stop her. When as a teenager in Winnipeg she realized that her parents and siblings would only go on overprotecting and even babying her, she left home to pursue an art career in Minneapolis. Graduating from the Minneapolis School of Art, she had become a skilled commercial artist. At Art Instruction, she taught freehand drawing and layout just across the aisle from Schulz. They became friends, visiting frequently desk to desk; she adored Sparky and admired his work. "She just worshipped Charles Schulz," said George Letness.

When Frieda put her elbows on Sparky's desktop, she did not have to lean over. Hal Lamson, who sat in front of her, recalled how "she'd be resting on her elbows, the way the *Peanuts* characters rest their elbows on the stone wall while they talk." When she sat at her desk chair, her feet would plank outward in front of her, never touching the ground. "Her legs would be straight out, just the way Schroeder would be when he played the piano."

What Schulz felt about Frieda's condition we do not know, but he often puzzled over his own characters' dwarflike proportions and sometimes demonstrated how their contracted limbs put certain basic skills beyond them: "Charlie Brown can't ride a tricycle. His arms and legs are too short. There are a lot of things Charlie Brown can't do. He can't get his arms up over his head." Schulz found that the ratio structure of the daily comic strip panel itself prohibited drawing his people as an ensemble: "Their heads are so big I can't group them all together." He called attention to the fact that "in my strip I cannot ever show a child pouring water over another child's head, because their arms are too short to reach around their large heads." In one strip, as Lucy and Linus shelter under a large umbrella, she asks whether it's still raining, but when Linus holds out his hand, he still can't tell: "My arms are too short!"

In the friendly atmosphere and frumpy decorum of the Educational Department, where Frieda Rich was beloved, Wilwerding treated her as if she were a Dickens character, sallying out of his office on the far side of her desk to make affectionate double-punning jest of her by drawing the attention of the room at large to the "poor little Rich girl."

Later Frieda's colleagues referred to her as a midget, or "a little midget girl," or "the little cripple gal," or even "a bossy, sassy little thing." One of the women who worked with her at Art Instruction said of her naturally curly dark hair: "She was glad she had it because she didn't have much else." David Ratner contended that none of her friends in the Educational Department ever kidded her about her size or the fact that she was Jewish, but there certainly were occasions when Frieda's dwarfism made her an object of mockery among the young instructors.

Every six weeks, a small group gathered to play hearts at the home of Jim Sasseville's friend Jack Bittner in Minneapolis. "They would always tease her, because she couldn't reach the cards," remembered Jack's sister Barbara. "When they would deal the cards out, she'd always have to reach up on the table and they would tease her because her arms were so short. But she took the teasing well and she had a good sense of humor and she was a lot of fun."

Frieda outbid small-mindedness in others by enlarging her own personality. She was proud to be Jewish. She did not consider herself a dwarf—dwarfs were, in her words, "characters in legends from the bearded old forests"; she was a four-foot-tall woman. No matter how much the others mocked her, she maintained her dignity. She spoke her mind about anti-Semitism or any other subject that offended her sense of justice. "She was very short in stature but tall in spirit," a colleague would recall, and this essential character, more than such secondary extremities as "naturally curly hair," helped to mold the identity of Schulz's characters.

Charlie Brown handles without self-pity insults that would push real children to the breaking point. Pigpen routinely sails through slights that would reduce real children to tears. Schulz's characters reminded people of the never-ceasing struggle to confront one's vulnerabilities with dignity. Humanity was created to be strong; yet, to be strong and still to fail is one of the universally identifying human experiences. Charlie Brown never quits, and that unyielding quality had been prefigured in Frieda Rich, the "poor little Rich girl" who was able to take as humor and with humor what would otherwise have produced bitter rage.

Among Sparky's colleagues, Hal Lamson and others recognized that "the physical characteristics of the *Peanuts* gang were lifted right from her body. The way she stood, sat, and moved—and the relative size of the head and the body"—passed directly into the strip.

Frieda had one magic quality that reached deep into *Peanuts*: she was an adult in a child-shaped body. In Norse mythology, dwarfs, present at the creation, representing order and reason, had magic powers to fashion a god's or hero's life-partner weapon: Thor's hammer, Siegfried's blade. Frieda, present at the creation of *Peanuts*, helped to forge Schulz's greatest instrument: his characters' union of constrained size with irreducible strength.

CHAPTER 12

# FAITH

*Kids finally sold. So I just kept on drawing kids.*
—C.M.S.

HIS PASSAGE TO BELIEF was completed that summer of 1948.

Sparky was baptized in Lake Phalen, on the northern fringe of St. Paul, in the middle of July, wading in up to his chest, barefoot and in street clothes. Under the gaze of the congregation onshore, Brother Marvin Forbes uttered the sacrament of baptism, placed a hand on Sparky's head, and pushed him under, joining him to the company of Christ's redeemed believers.

His friends at Art Instruction did not at first know of all this. As so often with the big postwar changes in Schulz's life, he first confided the good news to Frank Dieffenwierth, recalling how he had heard from another squad mate "soon after we all got home and were all busy getting reconverted," who wrote to say that while he believed that God might exist, he doubted whether any religion or set of beliefs could offer proof of God in the universe and thus considered himself an agnostic. "That, I am glad to say, is not what I have turned out to be," reported Sparky on July 17. "I wasn't a steady churchgoer when you knew me, but I did believe in God. My lack of formal religion was due merely to not knowing better. Now, however, I am right where I belong. I am a firm believer in Jesus Christ."

Strikingly, he went on to break the news of another conversion: "It will probably come as a pleasant surprise to you that I hereby revoke all my past views on art. From here on in I am a full-fledged modernist. I didn't know what I was talking about before. In fact I represented the very type of person that I now so deeply despise. I used to tell you that I couldn't see anything in this 'painting without drawing' business, but since then I have learned that the abstractionists, impressionists, etc., can draw better than the conservatives. Well, I'll be!"

". . . I have not only turned modernist in art, but am now a lover of classical music. Boy, what a change. They'll never know me in the next war."

The earlier Sparky had been "impatient with art," and considered himself "one of the staunchest opponents of classical music." To the amazement of Dieffenwierth and his other army buddy, Donald McClane, he knew nothing beyond the Tin Pan Alley canon until he saw a movie about the life of George Gershwin. At their urging, he also tried the waltzes of Johann Strauss. In 1946, he spent the last of his army separation pay on a recording that "opened up a whole new world for me"—Beethoven's Second Symphony.

In his first two years back in civilian life he bought more than fifty record albums—Berlioz, Haydn, Mendelssohn, Mozart, and his favorite, the great German Romantic articulator of frustration, Brahms. He spent a "minor fortune" on a huge Zenith "combination" radio-phonograph with the new long-playing record attachment built into the console. Sparky remade Dena's old room with "walls of records"—more than some of his brothers and sisters in Christ had ever before seen in a private home.

This individual development coincided with a national trend. Classical music was attracting so many new aficionados that by 1955 some 35 million people would attend musical performances—more than twice that year's ticket buyers to major league baseball games. Long-playing records added to the increasing momentum. "This is really something," Sparky exclaimed in January 1949, "an entire symphony on one record!" By June that year he had collected all of Beethoven's symphonies on LP except the Third, while taking in a performance of *Die Fledermaus*, the much-anticipated centerpiece of Old Vienna Night at the St. Paul Auditorium.

He got together on weekend evenings with his new friends at Art Instruction to listen to classical recordings and play unorthodox games of hearts. At work in the afternoons, they tested one another's command of the genre. Someone would whistle a theme, pass it midstanza to his neighbor, and then wait for those at the next row of desks to pick up the line, proceeding around the room in relays until the final note died away. The musically self-educated George Letness took a good-naturedly rivalrous pleasure in trying to baffle Sparky.

But the self-abnegating side of Sparky belittled his capacity for informed hearing. Like his father, he had the ability to whistle entire musical themes from memory, and two different boys in Schulz cartoons of this period would boast of their ability to whistle the entire score of *Die Fledermaus*.

His tastes expanded. He joined the Book of the Month Club in 1948, and massive novels and works of history and biography soon overflowed his two small bookcases. On the streetcar in the morning, he read *War and Peace* and *The Great Gatsby* to prepare for the day at Art Instruction. At the same time, he studied the Bible "constantly" and kept up his end of theological discussions with Brother Forbes.

EVERY JUNE, MEMBERS OF the Church of God movement gathered under a great white tent at its headquarters town of Anderson, Indiana, for a vast, old-fashioned camp meeting. Sparky attended in 1949, and found all his commitments confirmed.

His initial hesitations, washed away in the waters of Phalen Lake, now passed into ecstasy amid passionate hymn raising and familial warmth in the summery Indiana night. "One of the great memories of my life is standing next to my friend Harold Ramsperger in camp meeting singing 'Blessed Assurance.' " Years later, the actress Geraldine Page's evocation of the powerful old evangelical hymn in *The Trip to Bountiful* flooded him with emotion in a northern California movie theater. "I started trembling. It was everything I could do to keep from breaking down."

His baptism imparted a new sense of wholeness. His work improved; he was conscious of a purpose and, as never before, of a sense of identity. For the first time since his mother's death, his days were suffused with meaning. Here was the real start of the new life toward which he had been struggling since his return from the war. Why hadn't he seen it before?

"There is no doubt in my mind that the Church of God is it," he wrote to his old pastor, Fred Shackleton, who with his wife and young son had hosted Sparky in Anderson. "So firmly convinced am I of this that I have been instrumental in having [a] series of articles run in the St. Paul paper . . ."

Fresh back from Indiana, he had bought half-page advertisements in the *Pioneer Press*, presenting the primary doctrines of the Church of God stated by Charles E. Brown, editor in chief of the church's official newspaper, the *Gospel Trumpet*—yet a third "Charles Brown" appearing in Charles Schulz's life. "He was quite zealous," recalled Frederick Shackleton. "He wanted to make a commitment, he wanted to do something. . . . He wanted to count."

Inspired by this example, his youth group Bible class at the Merriam Park church decided that each of them should take some sort of public stand for Christ. Henceforth, they convened outdoor testimony meetings, gathering among the street people at corners of the seedy blocks around the Seventh Street Union Gospel Mission in downtown St. Paul, where the plainly dressed but well-groomed little group would flip a coin to see who would speak first.

The tongue-tied young soldier had found it virtually impossible to so much as strike up an acquaintance with a Macalaster Avenue neighbor in the fields of France. His retiring mother had been awed into silence by the respectable ladies of the PTA. Now a vibrant convert was triumphantly testifying his love of Jesus Christ to the harsh indifference of skid row. "It was rather difficult for me, yet I felt driven to stand up . . . and say something. So, with the streetcars going by, I stepped out on the sidewalk and managed some way to make my statement for the Lord."

HE WOULD DESCRIBE IT as a social problem, indeed sometimes as his "only" problem: "I had trouble balancing my life after the war. I now had three elements to balance and they didn't balance because the people simply didn't mix, and that was difficult."

He laid out the three concentric circles in his postwar life as follows: The first ring consisted of his old neighborhood pals and rivals at games, including Jim Cummings and Pudge Geduldig—the "golf kids," as he once called them, who "were foreign completely to church and art and cartooning." Then came his "bright" friends at Art Instruction, who in turn were set against the "decent" and "very nice people" in the youth group at the Church of God. "That put me in three different social groups, and they didn't overlap. They didn't meet."

He tried several times to weave friends from each strand together, proudly inviting his old friend Sherman Plepler to play violin at a Church of God service ("It was surprising to me to find out how religious he was," said Plepler. "He had never discussed it") or bringing over a date from Art Instruction. He even thought to bring his church group over for Sunday service at a girlfriend's Lutheran church to play volleyball afterward in the basement gymnasium. "But it never really worked. It was an impossible mix."

With his churchgoing friends, Sparky could be lighthearted and funny; he "had a chuckle for everything," recalled Ruth Forbes. "You didn't know if he was sad or not. And he didn't want to talk about illnesses or being sick. One day we were talking about something and I asked him . . . 'If you were [sick], would you tell me?' He said, 'Nope.' " His lifelong sense of aloneness and incompleteness made itself felt in each group, often when he least expected it. At camp meeting in Anderson, Indiana—as joyful an occasion as he had experienced in years—he stayed with Fred and Doris Shackleton, whose small son Martin charmed and entertained him. Perhaps this glimpse of a happy child so well cared for by his parents was what did it, but in the midst of his intense pleasure at being among a small, loving family, Sparky suddenly lost his way: "I was having a wonderful time. Then, on the third day, I felt terribly lonely."

With his Art Instruction friends he could be censorious, casting a cold glance from behind the mild chuckle. One evening, George Letness spilled beer on himself at a party and received a scornful look that as much as said, *You deserve that for drinking beer.* Sparky never gathered for cocktails after work across the street with the other instructors, where the tone of conversation would be quite different from when Sparky *was* around—"more raucous and personal," recalled Hal Lamson.

As a suitor, he was vulnerable, sometimes going so far as to confess to his dates that he was depressed, but more often simply presenting himself as defeated in advance; melancholy acceptance was far the easier alternative to revealing how actually hurt and angry he was. Those closest to him understood that he was still bereaved, still lost and alone. At all events, he was more conscious of the abyss—and more aware that that was where his comic ideas came from—than he dared show.

Sex grappled with his acutely ingrained sense of what was fitting, more significantly part of the problem than he cared to admit. "He had a real passion for the ladies, and that was in conflict with his highly moral Christian passions," said David Ratner. Only later in life would Schulz acknowledge that his inhibitions about finding a girlfriend in his congregation "caused me a lot of trouble: Say, if I liked a certain girl for instance, maybe she was with the correspondence school, but then I didn't have any girlfriends in the church group. There were no girls that fascinated me in church. A lot of the people were already married. I never had any girlfriends in the church. . . . So nothing worked, nothing connected. That made it very awkward."

Pretty, petite Naomi Cohn, the "cute little girl" Sparky had been unable to speak to in night-class cartooning before the war, had looped back into his life through a mutual friend at Art Instruction. In the intervening years, she had attended the Minneapolis School of Art, adopted a beret as her signature headgear, and was now a copy artist at the telephone company. By all accounts Sparky had a deep crush on Naomi, who was to many a charming creature—"a very sexy, passionate young woman," one colleague recalled—with a truly original sense of humor. Sparky took her on a date, of which years later he would say only that, up close, he had found a flaw in his princess: he did not like the elementary, exclamatory way she talked, still using such expressions as "Oh, it's so neat!" But to the end of his life he would keep snapshots of her from the 1940s in his desk drawer, and in 1998 an acutely perceptive and empathic dark-haired girl called Naomi, who wears a beret, became the last new character to enter the strip. She appears, of course, in the middle of an otherwise unacknowledged illness:

Among his male contemporaries at Art Instruction he stood apart—a teetotaler, a practicing Christian, and, with each step upward, a professional cartoonist. According to Hal Lamson, Sparky became the unspoken leader in the group that played pool during lunch hour at a nearby hall. When Lamson or Sasseville or Ratner told a joke, the other men would first gauge Schulz's reaction before laughing themselves. The first time Lamson cracked an off-color witticism, the silence—and the stern look he got from Sparky—stayed with him for the next fifty years. Lamson had grown up on a farm; trading jokes was the natural thing to do when a group of men gathered around a pool table. Sparky was too soberly principled for this kind of male bonding. The childhood world from which he sought escape was a world of drunken jokesters. He did not like—or trust—conversation that took refuge from serious considerations in barnyard ribaldry.

He was a leader in his church youth group, too. By the time the youth Bible class held its third testimony meeting at the Union Gospel Mission, Sparky had been elected president. Accepting the call, he nevertheless found it no easy commitment to carry out his responsibilities, chief among them testifying on behalf of the group to the men of the Union. "I found myself that night standing on the sidewalk preaching, without having any real ability for this sort of thing," he recalled. In the middle of his address, he happened to glance to his left, and there, on the curb, stood two of his golfing buddies, staring at him in complete surprise. "They did not even know that I attended church," much less rallied unbelievers on street corners, "and they were astounded to discover me, and I was astounded that they would discover that I was standing there."

His hypersensitivity only made matters worse. Even at the best of times he had a genius for being uncomfortable with others, and as David Ratner would recall, "Some people were very uncomfortable with him because he was uncomfortable with himself." Getting on well and being an intimate friend are, after all, different matters; had he been able even to trade off-color jokes, he would have had a different world to operate in. Again and again at Art Instruction, his reserve and inhibition kept him from connecting with fellow instructors, like Patricia Blaise Telfer: "We knew him but we didn't know him underneath his skin, as we knew some others, like Charlie Brown; we felt we knew Charlie Brown's whole body because he was so open."

What his colleagues at Art Instruction did perceive was the strength of Sparky's faith: "There was a certainty about it: *This is the way it is.*" To Paul Olsen, an atheist, Sparky seemed "very fundamentalist." George Letness, a lapsed Roman Catholic, sensed a deep piety in Schulz, and avoided the subject altogether. Charlie Brown engaged Schulz in debates about papal infallibility, the confessional, birth control, and the Bible's depiction of alcohol, trying to convince him that the New Testament sanctioned moderate drinking, and Sparky arguing that the wine that Jesus wrought for the wedding at Cana of Galilee had not been fermented.

Like Sparky, Charlie Brown attended parties with the other young instructors, and he also had in common with his friend a desire to be liked: "I never could handle rejection." But Schulz had harnessed himself to disciplines and forms, to work and to "holy living"—above all, to a controlled, orderly life. Charlie Brown thrived on disorder, on imprudent living—invited to three parties on the same evening, trying to make it to all of them, "and in a way," he later wrote, "never making any of them." Of Charlie Brown in this period, Schulz, at his most diplomatic, would later say, "He was a very bright young man with a lot of enthusiasm for life. I began to tease him about his love for parties, and I used to say, 'Here comes Good Ol' Charlie Brown, now we can have a good time.' "

"Alcohol did not enter Sparky's life," Brown recalled. "It was 'against his religion' as we said in those days. He did not participate in our gang's cocktail hours, but I sure did. At this time I was collecting friends like a child collects autographs; not unlike the words Charlie Schulz put in Charlie Brown's mouth, 'I need all the friends I can get.' "

At the core of Schulz's social problem lay a similar longing. Like Charlie Francis Brown, Sparky yearned to be liked—by everybody. In a later time, by which his central character had become one of the principal imaginary citizens of the United States, Schulz, cornered into summing him up, would say, "Well, Charlie Brown has this terrible quality where he's not satisfied to be liked by just a few people or to be fairly well liked. He wants to be well liked by everyone." Or even just by someone:

Sparky still wanted to be as well liked as his father had been among his many constituent customers, and he set this wish among his highest ambitions. But he also acknowledged that this wish, which would forever keep Charlie Brown "striving after something which really can't be obtained," had destabilized his early manhood. Behind it stood the question of his life: *Will I be—was I ever—truly loved?*

The one unifier—the one place in his life after the war where he could combine all the parts of his character into a powerful, coherent whole—was strip cartooning.

IN JULY 1948, SPARKY found two letters waiting for him at the Family Barber Shop. King Features in New York rejected his *Li'l Folks* submission, explaining that they had just started another feature with kids. "Oh, well," Sparky recalled thinking. "That's the way it goes. Another rejection." But Ernest Lynn, the keenly farsighted features director of Newspaper Enterprise Association (NEA)—the E. W. Scripps–owned syndicate for Roy Crane's *Wash Tubbs* and J. R. Williams's *Out Our Way*, two of Sparky's favorites—praised Sparky's work and invited him to headquarters in Ohio with an eye toward a one-year Sunday contract.

The syndicate flew him to Cleveland on a Sunday—his first airplane ride. As he passed over the grid of green pastures, marveling at the broadsheet immensity and neatness of the heartland, he was no less impressed by the fact that his fare had been paid for. The next day NEA made its offer, and Sparky returned to Minnesota a syndicated cartoonist, striding back into the Educational Department to his colleagues' applause. His initial struggle over, he thought he had reached the pinnacle of professional recognition. The syndicate sent him a contract; he signed it, and mailed Cleveland enough panels to launch the feature and keep it going for six weeks. They also took his photograph for the sales booklet that would be presented to managing editors throughout the country when the salesmen hit the road with *Li'l Folks* in their marketing portfolios.

Then the gods took it all back. Without explanation—only later would the story be told that Ernest Lynn had been unable to persuade his sales department that a large market existed for such work—NEA broke the contract and returned the six unpublished panels, cutting Schulz a $100 check as severance pay. "I got as close as a person can possibly get without getting it," he told Dieffenwierth. "Now I'm right back where I started, drawing for the St. Paul paper once a week, and selling to the *Post* whenever I can think of anything funny. I'm working on some other angles, however," he added, "so will make it yet. That's the secret, Frank. Always have an iron in the fire. Always have another angle ready to go."

He took this as the driving principle of his life's work. "I am quite sure that . . . I would have sold something eventually," he later wrote. "With me, it was not a matter of how I became a cartoonist, but a matter of when." This was also Charlie Brown's principle; but he went ever-onward without his "when" arriving. For his creator, now, the determination to try again, the refusal to give in, were about to pay off in ways of which the spunkiest baseball manager—or a Cleveland syndicate's sales department—could not have dreamt.

ONE EVENING IN 1949, Sparky gathered with his friends after a concert at the house of one of the young instructors. Introduced to a stranger, he braced for the usual slap of shyness to shut his mouth. But just as the introduction was about to leave them in silence, the other asked Sparky what he did for a living. For the first time in his life he not only felt unambiguously entitled to say "I am a cartoonist" but was thrilled to be able to reach over to their host's coffee table for the latest *Saturday Evening Post*: "Incidentally, this is some of my work right here," and, what was more, he could point out not one but *two* cartoons in this particular issue. "It made me feel great."

All the same, he still had to be funny again the next morning—and the morning after that—and he wondered how he would keep the jokes going out and the checks coming in if he did not have a regular market for his work.

In June 1949, Harold L. Phillips, an editor of the *Gospel Trumpet*, was seriously considering a weekly panel cartoon. Before the war, church publications had almost never used cartoons, but cartoon panels and cartoon techniques, used by the army for presenting necessary information vividly and concisely to millions of GIs, were finding an increasingly wider place in the postwar consumer culture. Schulz took the train to Anderson to meet with Steele C. Smith, president of the Gospel Trumpet Company. "I would have been very happy to have accepted some sort of job," he later wrote.

"He had made a decision to serve Christ," Fred Shackleton recalled. "He had this talent. He wanted his life to be significant. Perhaps this was a way."

Why not move to Anderson? After all, in St. Paul he felt completely invisible. That July, he jokingly called himself the "world's most unknown cartoonist." *Li'l Folks* ran week after week without ever gaining him a single reaction from any of the paper's editors—except that they reduced its panel from a width of three columns to two—nor any word from readers. Unbeknown to Schulz, other Twin Cities cartoonists closely followed the feature, considering it, one recalled, a "very clever strip," but none had written to its creator. Schulz was so tentative about his place in the newspaper's pecking order, remembered the city editor, that he made a point of arriving at the city room to turn in his originals when no one was there.

Sparky summoned the nerve to ask "Doug" Fairbanks, the managing editor (who handled all features, including those for the Sunday paper), for more space, or at least that the feature be restored to its original three columns. He was turned down, but still went on to suggest that the feature be buffed up with spot colors from time to time. Fairbanks, tightly budgeted, had to refuse: such window dressing was not important to the

Ridder family, whose newspaper chain published the *Pioneer Press*. Well, replied Sparky, how about running it on the same page with rest of the comics? Another no.

"Then maybe I should stop drawing it."

"Let's drop it," agreed Fairbanks.

After that, Sparky set his sights firmly on Steele Smith and the Gospel Trumpet Company. "If he had offered me a job with their publications, I would have moved to Anderson, Indiana. To me, it would have been like a pilgrimage."

But Smith and Phillips were puzzled about how to employ Schulz; they "couldn't figure out where just such a strange talent would fit," as Sparky remembered it. Only later, when he was an established and popular cartoonist, would his church's youth magazine show an interest. Even when Schulz's single-panel cartoons, *Young Pillars*, began to appear every other week in *Youth* (a tall young man stands up in church: "I appreciate being nominated as president of our youth group, but I am afraid that I must decline on the grounds that I am too stupid!"), Harold Phillips was initially "very concerned" about how church leaders would react. So the response from Anderson—yet another no—was doubly disappointing. Still, by the end of 1949, Charles M. Schulz was listed in the *St. Paul City Directory* not, as he previously had been, as an "artist" or "laborer," but as a "cartoonist."

Early in 1950, as he knuckled down to approach the syndicates in New York, it dawned on him that his style was so simple he would have to give the editors something more. Instead of drawing a single-panel cartoon with a single gag line, he drew two gag-line cartoons, one above the other. "I figured I'll be smart, I'll give the editor two cartoons for the price of one, and this will be a good sales gimmick. I was looking for an angle. I figured if I'm going to break into this business, I've got to do something which is a little bit different."

# CHAPTER 13

# REDHEADS

*. . . A girl with reddish hair and a golden skin had remained for me the inaccessible ideal.*

—PROUST

IT WAS AWKWARD ENOUGH to be forever balancing among three sets of friends, but now he had met a girl who didn't fit with any of them—a soft-skinned, rosy-cheeked Swede, pretty and petite, with red hair, bright blue eyes, and a radiant smile: "I just thought she was wonderful." Her name was Donna Mae Johnson, and she worked down in Accounting.

As he came into the office each morning, he now made a habit of stopping on the second floor to dash off a cartoon that filled up the entire appointments leaf for that day of her desk calendar, as if taking a lover's possession of all her hours. But in the Educational Department, "None of us knew anything about her," recalled Patricia Blaise Telfer. Not even George Letness, at the adjoining desk, knew of the courtship. When she came up to visit one afternoon, Sparky chatted with her for ten minutes but seemed "so ill at ease and kind of embarrassed," said Letness, "I thought he'd introduce me, but it was as if I didn't exist and she didn't exist. She left and I didn't say anything to him."

In February 1950 he asked her on a date. Her family lived at 3245 Longfellow Avenue in Minneapolis, where Erick Johnson, a Swedish-born upholsterer, ran his business out of the house. When Sparky came calling, Donna's father embarrassed her by subjecting the lean, lightweight, twenty-seven-year-old cartoonist to the same interrogation he had given every boy she had brought home in high school: "Play football?"

Donna's mother thought Sparky a nice young man: "If my mother didn't like a guy, she told me right out." Indeed, Mabel Johnson advised Donna against marrying one suitor solely on the grounds that the boy's parents were divorced and disqualified another because he was Roman

Catholic, but when she learned that Sparky's favorite boyhood dish was Scandinavian pancakes, she warmly plied him with stacks of that delicacy.

When her path crossed Sparky's, Donna was twenty-one, with at least three steady admirers—chief among them Alan Wold, two months her senior, who had dated her since 1948 and known her for too many years before that to count as a new boyfriend: they had grown up together, been in the same classes since eighth grade, and attended the same church. Their parents knew each other. Al's father, Leonard E. Wold, a carpenter, built bodies for Greyhound buses; his mother, Nellie, was a housewife. Al's family lived in the same Longfellow neighborhood, a stone's throw from Holy Trinity Lutheran Church, the nearly half-century-old congregation in which the Johnsons worshipped and Donna sang in the choir and met weekly with her friends in the Sewing Club. Already joined by so many ties, the two seemed made for one another. "People mistook us for brother and sister," she would recall. They were even same-shade redheads.

Not only between the two families but among friends and neighbors at Holy Trinity there hung the unspoken assumption that Al and Donna would be married at the old brick church and then take their place among the Young Married group at choir rehearsal, lunch box auctions, song-fests, toboggan parties, wiener roasts, and picnics; however, Al appeared to be in no hurry to propose. A navy veteran, he was working in the parts department at International Harvester, studying to take his firefighter's test. Whenever a new beau came into Donna's life, Al, so far from dropping out, simply required corresponding dates: for every stroll Donna went on with Sparky, she must take an equally long walk with Al.

Al was already the constant, anchoring her to the domestic life she dreamed of. Sparky, the romantic interloper, the St. Paulite, was nearly seven years older than the young Minneapolitans. Sensitive, serious, intense, often turned out in a pale gray shirt with a jazzy black zigzag around the waist, Sparky was a man apart from Donna's other suitors, not courting Donna alone but wooing her family—"the only one of my boy-friends who was nice" to her younger sister, Margaret. When Donna was sick and stayed home from work, Sparky sent her roses. With his father's Ford and one or two *Saturday Evening Post* fees each month, he could take her places, show her things, hold the car door as she alighted.

After their first date—at the Ice Capades—he gave her a miniature-piano music box that played "The Skater's Waltz." Their second, in March, consisted of a steak dinner and a visit to *Intruder in the Dust*, a Hollywood adaptation of William Faulkner's bestseller. St. Patrick's Day brought a box of candy and a drawing of Donna, her hair brushed in with a wash of red watercolor. But it had been on their third date the previous evening that she had been introduced to Carl, who confided that he was waiting for Sparky to marry before he himself married again, and, surely not coincidentally, that Sparky had turned out his empty pockets and told her how he wished for a diamond ring to put on her finger right then and there.

All of this had exactly the effect on Al Wold that Donna hoped for. On days she dated Sparky, she tabulated Al's reactions on what was left of her desk calendar, recording on March 6 (the steak-and-movie evening) that Al had called twice and had twice come over to her house. On March 23, when Sparky took her to a hockey game, "Al called 8, 9, 10. Mad at me!" On April 11, she had to compete for space on her desk calendar with a sketch of herself in her duckbill baseball cap and doughy-fingered fielder's glove to register one more call from Al. Years later, she confided to a friend of Sparky's, "I knew quite soon in the relationship that it was Al that I wanted," and yet, "I really loved Sparky too at the same time." In another, more public, accounting of the romance, she spoke of "a terrible decision to have to make, because I really loved both Al and Sparky," demanding of herself in her diary of May 8, 1950: "How will you ever decide?"

By this point, Sparky had taken her to see *The Red Shoes* at the World Theater in downtown St. Paul, the Cities' grandest, most elegant movie palace, where they settled into burgundy-upholstered seats as the old gilt-and-gesso Schubert Playhouse's velvet curtain parted on tragic romance. Hans Christian Andersen's fairy tale seemed almost to have been filmed for them—Moira Shearer, the undecided redhead to top all undecided redheads, dancing her character, the ballerina Victoria Page, who reels "dangerously between two loves"; yet even when she chooses the rising composer, played by Marius Goring, he still cannot prevent his rival from luring her back to her true and first love, dancing. For Sparky, as for a whole generation of aspiring artists and moviemakers, *The Red Shoes* daringly evoked a world devoted to art. Michael Powell and Emeric Pressburger's lush Technicolor masterpiece was so richly saturated with tone and tint that the ballerina's flaming hair and her composer-lover's pale blue eyes—the one feature so similar to Donna's, the other to Sparky's—seared their way unsettlingly into the hearts and minds of millions.

Donna's judgment, originally "weighted a little in Al's favor," continued to teeter. When on that third date Sparky had wished a ring onto her finger, she had thought how that "would sure put me on the spot." But by May, it was she who was in a hurry, more than once suggesting on those lengthening walks with Sparky through the unfolding spring that they elope—to Iowa, the traditional getaway for Minnesotan lovebirds.

To Donna, elopement made real sense. On the one hand, if Al's inaction finally defaulted her into the arms of the more romantic Sparky, she would be cheated of a marriage in the Lutheran high style: "If I had planned a wedding with Sparky I didn't think anyone would come. We had a whole churchful of friends expecting Al and me to marry"—after all, Holy Trinity stood virtually in Al's backyard. On the other hand, if word of her intention to slip away with Sparky reached Al before the fact, this would surely force him to stand up and fight for her. But it was Sparky who talked her out of running off, more than once insisting, "We can't do that. Your folks would be so disappointed."

Trying hard, as always, to harmonize the "good man" he was and the "roughneck" he wished to be, he would later say, "That's what I get for being a nice guy." Perhaps he really was unsure how to carry the romance to its next level, later, indeed, revealing to his cousin Patty that he had given Donna a Bible as a date present: "How's that for corny?" he said. "Well, what should you have done?" asked Patty. "I should have taken her to bed," he replied.

WHILE DONNA PUZZLED OVER her choices, Sparky awaited another verdict. Having developed his two-for-the-price-of-one gimmick earlier that spring, he dispatched fifteen two-tiered panels to United Feature Syndicate in New York City—work that he considered his best to date. "I knew this was going to come close."

A month dragged by, then another week, and another. Surely such silence could only mean the cartoons had been lost in the mail—he dashed off a description to New York. But unbeknown to Sparky, United Feature Syndicate, marketers of such cultural landmarks as *Li'l Abner*, *Nancy*, and Eleanor Roosevelt's daily column, "My Day," received an average of twenty new strip ideas each week, of which perhaps one might be tried out in any given year, making odds of a thousand to one against any submission. But such calculations did not, in fact, reckon the whole story, for, in the spring of 1950, syndicated comics were increasingly ripe for the challenge of a comic strip artist with an original eye.

Newspaper circulation had reached its zenith, but with the coming of television and the new consumer society, all that was about to change. Between 1946 and 1966, one in every four morning dailies expired. For the moment, however, with television still in its formative stages—a mere three million American families owned a TV in 1950—nearly one hundred million Americans, one-half to two-thirds of the nation, still read the comics every day. Within five years, television would glare into thirty-two million homes, and by 1959, the average family would spread the attention of one member or more over six hours a day to "the one-eyed monster," as that generation's nervous intellectuals would dub it—a command of interest never before matched or sustained by any form of show business.

The most vibrant strips—*Li'l Abner, Blondie, Gasoline Alley, Dick Tracy, Nancy*—had all debuted before the war. Comics created by GI artists for the black-and-white starkness of wartime found peace too complex. Meantime, postwar newcomers tended to be cautious, "following paths worn as deep as the wheel ruts of Pompeii," as William Lass had put it in *The Saturday Review* just two years before, citing the displacement of the syndicate editor by salesmen as the prime force in the booming postwar marketplace.

"Comic art needs and awaits a young man with fresh ideas, a new approach to humor and delight in humanity, a new character with a story to tell." And, Lass had added with even more striking prescience, "I will cheerfully predict that he will be another man of the people . . . not college-educated . . . a delightfully ordinary Joe blessed with humor or keen perception."

WITH NOTHING RESOLVED, EITHER with Donna or with the syndicate, Sparky began experimenting at his office desk with a three-panel feature whose action was sparked by the briefest of incidents.

Before the war, such ensemble kids' strips as Gene Byrnes's *Reg'lar Fellers* featured some distinctly unsavory gang inhabiting a dingy neighborhood, whose diet of daily adventure offered nothing more thought-provoking than cutting school and dreaming up what mischief they could next get into. Sparky knew *Reg'lar Fellers* and its imitators, including Augustus "Ad" Carter's *Just Kids*, from Big Little Books and the volumes of comic reprints he had bought a decade before. By the spring of 1950, only months after *Reg'lar Fellers* had ceased publication, he sensed that the time had come "to break away from the old kids' strips . . . where the kids are just . . . bouncing around the neighborhood, jumping over fire hydrants while they're talking, and doing sort of meaningless stuff. I just knew that it was possible to go beyond that."

In exploring his own distinctly different brand of "very slight incidents," he nevertheless took a staple setup from the traditional kids' strip—one urchin trying to mooch food from another—and gave it a twist: an angry little girl asks a smiling boy for a bite of his ice cream cone, but no sooner tastes it than she spits it right back out, indignantly asking what kind of ice cream that could be. "I didn't say it was ice cream," he replies. "It's mashed potato."

Schulz later said, "Nobody had ever done this type of humor before in comic strips. I think I was the first one to use the real minimum gag." If the traditional comic strip neighborhood rabble of the 1920s and '30s had revolved around the harsh prankishness of urban working-class boys, forever drawing on that wellspring of child savagery, Hogan's Alley in *The Yellow Kid*, then Schulz's new midcentury strip unfolded from his own life's lesson, practically instilled by his Norwegian cousinhood, that "little kids can be very nasty to each other."

He was so excited by these developments as to brush Norwegian self-policing aside and tell George Letness, "I think I've got something. I'm on to something really new."

From the adjoining desk, Letness looked on in amazement as Schulz included in his batch of submissions a strip so primitive and simple as almost to confound understanding: the same angry little girl who cadged her disillusioning mouthful of potato is sloshing through a downpour, muttering, "Rain, rain, rain, rain . . ." The boy comes beaming toward her from the opposite direction, this time holding a surely welcome umbrella. Then, in the unseen space between the second and third panels, the girl has commandeered the umbrella and continues on her way wreathed in smiles, while the boy, left exposed to the elements, slogs on nonetheless, reduced by some law of conservation to muttering in his turn, "Rain, rain, rain, rain . . ."

"This guy doesn't have a chance," Letness would reflect—thinking more of artist than of subject. But the terrible zero-sum logic of the strip, already visible in the umbrella sequence, dictated that the more often Schulz's "little folks" lost, the more "that guy" was going to win.

SPARKY HAD FINISHED SIX of these new minimal strips when a letter finally arrived from New York. The syndicate was interested in the two-tier panel feature, and James L. Freeman, editorial director of United Feature, invited him to headquarters. "Well, if I'm going to New York," he thought, as he told the tale in later years, "I should show them some of the other things that I've been doing, just to show them how versatile I am."

On Sunday, June 11, he left by rail, samples of the new feature packaged under his arm, and checked into the massive 1,100-room Roosevelt Hotel at Madison and Forty-fifth, where his door opened onto a corridor so long as to seem a trick of perspective. Here he was, at last, among the titanic cityscapes of Winsor McCay—in the metropolis where George Herriman had gone to work in 1910 as a young staff artist for Hearst's *Evening Journal*. Sparky had spent some days in Manhattan at the end of the war, but "something about being there with the intent to sell a comic strip made it all the more wonderful." He loved New York "immediately."

Early the next morning, well before any editor would be available, he set off for the syndicate's offices in the Daily News Building at 220 East Forty-second Street. It was drizzling when he entered the thirty-six-story, vertically striped skyscraper whose parapet, setbacks, and lobby rotunda displaying a vast globe were suggestive of Superman's *Daily Planet* tower. Up on the eleventh floor, no one was stirring at UFS except the switchboard operator, who offered to hold Sparky's samples at her desk while he went back out into the rain for breakfast. Upon his return on the stroke of ten, he was ushered into Freeman's office, where he was astounded to learn that while he had been cooling his heels at breakfast, the syndicate executives had arrived, opened his samples, and passed them around as if they were nothing more than a packet of pumpkin seeds.

Jim Freeman, the quiet, gentle-voiced editorial director, was the first to speak, commending Schulz on the two-tiered panel's "charm, its characters, its style of humor." However much the market was flooded with panels, these new strip samples had all of the best standard panel's engaging quality and something more: "We think we'd rather have a strip, if you think you could draw a strip."

Vice president and general manager Laurence Rutman spoke for the syndicate when he asked, "Could you create some definite characters?"

And Sparky replied yes and yes. The initial interview over, he returned to his hotel to await final word. The executives withdrew behind closed doors. Rutman, who had been "badly fooled" in the past, already believed in Schulz. The work, he contended, was unique and beautifully executed— worth the gamble. Freeman was also in favor of giving the strip a chance, but much of top management did not believe that Schulz's "brief incidents" and disc-headed kids had sales potential, and for a day Jim Freeman called in salesmen and at least one other cartoonist to consult over the samples.

Harry Gilburt, director of sales, had been at the syndicate only four years, but was steeped in newspapers, going back to his days on the *Milwaukee Journal* and at the Bell Syndicate, where he, a graduate of New York's City College, had started as a shipping clerk. Gilburt had already established himself as one of the best salesmen in the business and would later take credit for casting the deciding vote, but the record shows that he was pessimistic about Schulz's sales potential, and his uncertainty persuaded others that some gimmick would be needed to sell the strip. So, as Sparky was to recall, "like syndicate people do, they began to fiddle around with it."

Gilburt divided the panels horizontally, proposing to broaden the feature's appeal with a "little kid strip at the top and a teen-age strip at the bottom." Anxious to please, Sparky went along with this busy notion, although when he returned to his drawing board and roughed out the idea, he saw at once that the double tier, practical for a single-panel feature, would only be disorienting over a four-panel strip. Freeman agreed with him, and the syndicate quickly abandoned the piggybacked teenage feature, with Freeman concluding, "We'll just have the kid thing."

Harry Gilburt nonetheless sought to assert the authority of his judgment one more time before Schulz returned to the drawing board: "I would suggest that you don't try to make the strips too subtle."

"Well, if you're expecting another Nancy and Sluggo, you're not going to get it," replied Sparky. For though he could appreciate Ernie Bushmiller's deadpan whimsy—and would later regret his smart-aleck tone with the sales director—he remained firm in his resolve to rise above the plodding, gag-a-day sensibility of United Feature Syndicate's most popular kid strip.

The salesmen's first field reports confirmed Gilburt's initial pessimism. In Chicago, for example, where Gilburt had expected interest from the *Daily News*, the managing editor turned them down flat. So the executives in New York made another judgment of long-lasting effect—on the art of Schulz's comic strip, on his relations with the syndicate, and ultimately on the future of the whole genre of newspaper comic strips. The new strip would sell better if it were reduced in size and presented to newspaper editors as a "space-saver."

Instead of the conventional feature, which ran across four columns (about seven and a half inches) and whose panels occupied two and one-eighth inches from top to bottom, Schulz's strip would be reduced to fit across only three columns, losing two inches across and a full inch vertically in the process. His small, nearly square panels—the size of "four air-mail stamps," he would later say—could appear in any of three layouts: horizontally, vertically in one column, or stacked two on two. These "nuggets of humor" could be used, the salesmen emphasized, to "solve tough make-up problems" and "enrich any page of your newspaper . . . front, editorial, classified, or regular comic pages." Best of all, the strip's "clever, subtle humor" and "universally appealing characters" would use less space to bring more readers back to more parts of the paper each day—every publisher's dream.

This peeved Sparky. To justify the reduction to him, the syndicate executives insisted that a paper shortage had increased editors' usual reluctance to take on new strips and that promoting the new format as a space-saver would increase sales. "We have to do *something* to help get a feature into a paper," they insisted.

Meanwhile, *Editor & Publisher*, the industry's trade magazine, was assuring editors that newsprint was in good supply, and Sparky suspected that the executives were lying to him to cover up their lack of confidence in the strip; for the rest of his life he would resent this, not as a clumsy rationalization but as a conscious breach of faith. He became particularly indignant when, having from the outset been assigned a substandard space to frame his work, he noticed three years later that UFS allowed Al Capp and Bob Lubbers to launch a new strip, *Long Sam*, in panels not only larger than standard but flagrantly larger.

Every day on every comics page, every cartoonist had to fight for his share of attention, but Sparky's would also be the smallest feature presented on the page—if his panels even turned up among the other comics and hadn't been spot-dropped into the classifieds to solve a makeup problem. Some cartoonists tried to grab the reader's eye by squaring their panels in thick black borders; others made dramatic use of solid black backgrounds. As Sparky set himself through draft after experimental draft to make the most of his shrunken panels, it came to him that the less he drew, the more he caught the eye. He would "fight back by using white space," for "on a page jammed with comic strips, a small feature with lots of white space attracted attention."

This tighter style forced itself upon him overnight; having already taken *Li'l Folks*'s unbordered cameos and distilled the situations down to the slightest of incidents, he found himself simplifying his figures, too. Against the rounded forms of his *Pioneer Press* characters, the children of the new strip appeared to be two-dimensional cutouts. Later, when he tried to work out how the sacrifice of space had affected the development of his art, he reflected, "I could have done more with some of the drawing, but maybe it would have spoiled it—maybe it wouldn't have helped it at all."

Squeezed by administrative fiat away from busily drawn people, the new personalities only became more definite, more intensely themselves, their statements starker. For the more they developed complex powers and appetites while staying faithful to their cut-out, shadow–play simplicity, the easier it would be for Schulz to declare the hard things he was set on saying.

As they took shape on his drawing board, these still-to-be-named figures would at first seem overly simple, even to those whose names he would borrow for them. When Sparky returned to Art Instruction he showed the first "definite" character to his friend Charlie Francis Brown, who later recalled his friend's quiet confidence when he came over to Brown's desk to announce, "I have a new idea but it involves using your name."

Sure, Brown remembered replying, but he did "want to see what I'm going to look like." Whereupon Schulz laid before him a drawing of the little balloon-headed boy on whom he had begun to focus the strip. Charlie Brown studied the figure for a moment, then asked, "Couldn't you make him look a little more like Steve Canyon? Or Superman? He looks so simple, don't you think?"

With his huge, weightless sphere of a head, Charlie Brown looked like an Alka-Seltzer advertisement, but his utterances stood out all the more for the flatness of his form, which somehow underlined the flatness of his speech. If Charlie Brown's head had had mass and weight, it would have been distressing; Schulz lightened his characters by counterposing their simplicity of line against the enduring substance of what they had to say.

As Schulz began drawing it in 1950, the depiction of Charlie Brown and his gang would be continuous in idiom with the way they phrased their thoughts in "very brief incidents" told with an almost aggressive economy. Yet the more he found a harmony between pen line and story line, the more resistance he encountered from old-fashioned syndicate executives who wanted only to package unchallenging, risk-free characters, as familiar and likable as one's own children. The former UFS executive William Lass had typified the old-timer's point of view when he argued in 1948, "You do not willingly laugh at the jokes of disagreeable people, or take much interest in the daily lives of strangers; but you roar when your own little boy merely says 'peanuts.' "

THE NEXT THING WAS to name the strip. Everyone liked the title of Schulz's *Pioneer Press* feature, and so, partly for considerations that would soon become paramount, the new strip was tweaked into *Li'l Folk*. On Wednesday, June 14, Larry Rutman offered the standard five-year contract: the syndicate would own the copyright on the characters and split profits fifty-fifty.

Sparky appeared before a notary public, signed the agreement in a confident, clear hand, then boarded a westbound train, treating himself to a victory steak in the dining car. Returning to St. Paul "with great hope for the future," he went straight to Donna, arriving at her house at ten-forty in the evening, and put her immediately to the test: he announced his news, presented her with a keepsake from the hotel jewelry shop—a rhinestone-encrusted gold compact, with lipstick, powder, and vial of perfume—and then, as he later recalled, "I suppose I said we should get married or something." But all she could say was, "I don't want to marry anybody. I just wish everybody would leave me alone."

He left her with another present, a soft, whiskered white cat toy, which he instructed her to keep to herself until she was ready to marry him, and then to place it on his desk at work as a secret signal.

Over the next three catless weeks, Sparky went all out, inviting her on dates—a picnic, a movie—and one morning even drove up to the Johnsons' in a brand-new car. For more than thirty years, the Schulzes had been a Ford family (Lutherans drove Fords, Catholics Chevrolets). On the strength of his contract, he bought the 1950 two-door Tudor sedan, priced at $1,750—the first new car that anyone in Sparky's family had ever owned. He loved it at once and ever after recalled his elation and wonderment each time he pocketed the key—a pride of ownership such as he never quite felt toward any other automobile.

His father's Fords had come only in black. The Tudor's steel body, however, could be enameled with any one of ten "baked-on" colors, and Sparky picked a green so deep and lustrous that his rapturous attempts to catch its exact shade in conversation with his friends at Art Instruction led them to mockingly insist on calling it chartreuse. To the finally syndicated romantic, this was assuredly the green of fresh starts—a car "with a future built-in," an emerald to sweep a red-haired girl off her feet.

That sunny Saturday, June 24, Donna's mother watched Sparky hold open the car door and drive Donna off, not to return until well after nightfall. No sooner was Donna safely home than Mabel Johnson confessed that she thought the two of them had run off to Iowa and gotten married. On the contrary, it was Donna who was now stalling for time. On the first of July, Al Wold proposed, and Donna realized that she would have to make up her mind once and for all. She nonetheless continued to test her feelings for Sparky "up to the last minute."

That Sunday evening, word came through that North Korean armies had roared across the 38th Parallel; and as President Truman pledged the support of American might and the nation braced itself for the next world war, it looked for the coming weeks as if Donna's decision might be moot, since both Sparky and Al, unmarried veterans still of combat age, were automatically reservists.

On July 13, Al asked her over to watch TV, a novel way to spend the summer twilight in 1950, but she stayed home sewing and ironing, hanging back so that she could speak her heart to Sparky—although another version has her break the news to him over the phone at Art Instruction, forcing him to leave the building "just [to] walk around a little bit, because I was so upset and almost dizzy." That evening, from ten past nine to eleven, Donna and Sparky sat talking on the back steps of the Johnsons' house. Then Sparky drove away alone in his new car, only to return to 3245 Longfellow thirty minutes later, leaning out the car window to call, "I thought maybe you changed your mind."

Donna Johnson married Alan Wold at Holy Trinity Lutheran Church on October 21. Sparky waited years before including her in the story of his life. Among his strip characters, he first cast Violet, a frequent stand-in for Judy Halverson, as Charlie Brown's heartbreaker; in an early treatment of the theme, Charlie Brown asks, "You don't love me, do you, Violet?" and then calls after her, "Well, if you ever change your mind, let me know," to which she replies, "I'll do that!" After a beat, Charlie Brown runs after her: "CHANGE YOUR MIND YET?"

Writing twenty-five years later, he hinted for the first time that the object of Charlie Brown's longing, the Little Red-Haired Girl, had had a model in his own sufferings: "I have memories of a little girl, which have been translated into many defeats for Charlie Brown." But her identity remained concealed until 1990, when the first authoritative account of Schulz's life, licensed by United Feature Syndicate to celebrate the strip's fortieth anniversary, assigned to Donna Johnson and her alone the role of Charles Schulz's "first disappointment in love." Her predecessors Virginia Howley and Judy Halverson would be lost to myth. Though Donna herself reminded the world that "he had other girlfriends, not just me," the former redhead in accounting—still Mrs. Alan Wold of Minneapolis, in 1990 a "61-year-old grandmother of seven"—was henceforth known to the world as the model for the Little Red-Haired Girl who continually left Charlie Brown an abandoned, lovesick calf.

Curiously, the chief quality of Sparky's experience of Donna—being thrown over after a brief, chaste courtship that yet saw him surpassed by a more passive rival—is all but absent from Charlie Brown's singular pining for the Little Red-Haired Girl. Charlie Brown's unfulfilled wish—to break through self-isolation long enough simply to speak to the shimmering creature who never notices him—echoes back more clearly through Sparky's history with such unapproachables as Jane Gilbertson, Lyala Bischoff, and Naomi Cohn. But distant princesses are not as newsworthy as heartbreakers, and as time went on and Charles Schulz became both the public's laureate of lovesick yearning and the most highly rewarded cartoonist in history, it became increasingly accepted, especially in the idiom of tabloid renown, that the dismissive young lady who had left Sparky Schulz to pull indecently profitable yearnings out of his wound for half a century had received her comeuppance as the "Red-Haired Girl [who] Missed Out on $30 Million a Year by Jilting 'Peanuts' Creator."

The more salient characteristic of Donna's rejection—as had been the case with his mother's death—was that he himself was determined never to put it to rest. "You never do get over your first love," he would say when he was seventy-five. "The whole of you is rejected when a woman says: 'You're not worth it.' " Yet he did not care to examine the source of his unhappiness because it would not serve his art nearly so well as the tale he had established instead.

For the rest of his life, just as he would cast himself as a pawn in the syndicate game, so would he pose as the unappeasable Gatsbyesque lover of the golden—or, in his case, red-headed—girl. In one supposedly definitive account of their breakup, Donna would be made to sound as if, Daisy-like, she had rejected Sparky for lack of a bank account: ". . . He had too many failures, as far as I was concerned, and he had tried so long to sell his cartoons."

But if worldly enterprise, or even its potential, had been what Donna Johnson was looking for in her man, she would not have chosen Al Wold over Charles Schulz. Even in July 1950, Sparky was a qualified success; his fortunes as a newly syndicated cartoonist were not yet secure, especially in the eyes of an Art Instruction employee, but when his score of triumphs as a national gag cartoonist were added to his coup in New York City, he had already shown that he could win against the odds. Al Wold, toiling in the parts department at International Harvester and studying for his firefighter's test, had fixed his ambition no higher than solid municipal security. It was Sparky, not Al, who had an eye for the main chance.

But by her own later assessment, Donna did not have any "high career plans" for herself or her mate. She wanted to be a housewife, raise a family, attend church, get on with life. She "didn't care what Al did," nor was she much concerned with money or social position—she had never set her cap, she would emphasize, for "any rich boys." In 1950 her friends were marrying and settling down and having families, and she wanted to do the same: "Just digging in the dirt would have been nice." Sparky, if anything, was *too* ambitious; a popular cartoonist was not going to let Donna Mae Johnson live the plain, decent Lutheran life on which she was set.

Sparky took the barber's son's pride in his earnings. Profits from his first year of national distribution would exceed what his father had made in any given year on the corner of Selby and Snelling—a point he confided to friends in the Educational Department, who later recalled how "he was very proud of that." And not he alone: when Sparky returned home having clinched the deal, his father made a special trip to announce the news to his sister Alma and brother-in-law William L. Wegwerth, on the east side of St. Paul. Sparky's cousin Bill would remember how his uncle walked into 923 Conway Street and lit up a cigar, puffing and beaming, all but popping the buttons off his double-breasted suit. "Well, Sparky just got picked up by the syndicate and now he's going to make two thousand dollars a week." Sparky would, in fact, net $90 during the first month of syndication, $500 the second, but Carl's exaggeration bespeaks the small businessman's wonder at someone so taken for granted having entered the national marketplace.

Ironically, Sparky would blame love's hard decision having gone against him on the ambitions of Donna's mother. Even though Donna always contended that her mother had liked and trusted Sparky and certainly would not have objected had her daughter chosen him, he persisted in his depiction of the artist's garret being spurned for bourgeois comfort: "I loved that little girl but her mother convinced her I would never amount to anything," just as he would insist that Dorothy Halverson believed he would never amount to anything and had turned Judy against him, a rationalization that would be put to solid professional use when Lucy Van Pelt refuses to play on Charlie Brown's baseball team ("This team will never amount to anything! It's just going to lose, lose, lose, lose!!!"). Likewise, Snoopy, presented with a feast heaped high in the crowning glory of a brand-new supper dish, takes a special satisfaction in thinking as he gets down to some serious eating, "And my mother always worried that I'd never amount to anything."

He could not let go of the subject, insisting at every telling of the tale that "Mothers always liked me, except *her* mother, and she couldn't stand me." When honors became commonplace in later life, Schulz would say, "Oh, well, just another small thing to show the little red-haired girl's mother she was wrong about me."

But of course it was Dena Schulz, his own idealized mother, whom he could never have the satisfaction of proving wrong. Moreover, the success that Charles Schulz eventually attained was on a scale so vast—an "amount" so much in excess even of the wealth imaginable by people in the world from which he sprang—that it required an endlessly retold tale of early defeat and hope deferred to give full dramatic context to his mother's dismaying inability to recognize her son's extraordinariness.

"You know why that little red-haired girl never notices me?" broods Charlie Brown. "Because I'm nothing! When she looks over here, there's nothing to see! How can she see someone who's nothing?!"

At first sight, Charlie Brown does not so much fall in love with the Little Red-Haired Girl as he steps briefly out of his habitual invisible aloneness to imagine himself asking her to join him at lunch. But she will laugh, so he believes, "right in my face." Years later, when the Little Red-Haired Girl moves away, he dares to write and ask if she remembers him, knowing full well that the only chance of giving himself the faintest substance will be to explain that they sat in the same classroom: "I was the plain ordinary-looking boy in the fourth desk." Out in the world with his mother, Sparky could hide behind a willfully "ordinary appearance" the truth overlooked by his mother—that he was extraordinary—but as long as the Little Red-Haired Girl is nearby and yet will take no notice of him, Charlie Brown will remain alone and unseen because "she's something and I'm nothing."

Donna was, in fact, a manageable sorrow. Some years he would think of her constantly and recall her wistfully to his closest friends—so much so that they would feel sorry for his wife. Some years in his heyday she would send him a birthday card signed only with a heart. And there would come a time in later life when he would again reach out his arms to her. But always she eluded him, and always he was thrown back on the strip and the ever-mounting conviction that, in his case, the work was always going to repay more than the life. Even when, over a stretch of several years, he was beset by recurring nightmares in which he found himself "back at the Bureau of Engraving, and she was there, but there was no hope," he would still assert, "I had those terrible dreams for years, but I've made use of it all, of course."

As Henrik Ibsen came to terms with his predatory young admirer Emilie Bardach by using her as the model for Hilda Wangel in *The Master Builder* ("She didn't get me," said Ibsen, "but I got her for my writing"), Schulz made the most of Donna Johnson. To Sherman Plepler, Sparky would reveal the hard-nosed merchant within: "I got my money's worth out of that relationship."

WITH THE SYNDICATE GEARING up to push his strip as "the Greatest *little* Sensation Since TOM THUMB!" there was no time to pine for lost love. Directly on the heels of Donna's rejection came another of that summer's surprises.

Two days after the trade press announced the fall release of *Li'l Folk*, Tack Knight, creator of *Little Folks*, a defunct strip of the 1930s, saw fit to claim exclusive rights to the title for use in films, television, and radio, arguing that although "the spelling of the Schulz feature is different, the sound is definitely similar and with the subject the same, it seems like [a] conflict." Sparky replied to the retired San Francisco cartoonist on July 18, admitting that "one of the reasons for the contraction to *Li'l Folk* was to avoid such conflict," but added that the final decision was in the hands of the syndicate. Three days later, after a search of the U.S. Patent Office, attorneys confirmed that *Little Folks* had been a registered trademark since 1931; and so, on July 26, Larry Rutman telephoned to say they needed a new name.

To Sparky's ear, trained in comic strip vernacular, *Charlie Brown*, or even *Good ol' Charlie Brown*, sounded appropriate. In the expected pattern of an ensemble strip, the name of the lovable main character, sometimes coupled with an epithet—Krazy Kat, Little Orphan Annie, Li'l Abner— passed naturally, if sometimes only after years, into the feature's title. Now was the chance to speak out with a title that was a manifesto in itself. But the syndicate passed over these suggestions, and Jim Freeman then informed Sparky that they had "the perfect title."

In New York, each UFS executive had been asked for suggestions. While assembling his list, the production manager, William Anderson, happened to notice an article about *The Howdy Doody Show*, the children's television program at that very moment gaining fabulous popularity, on which an audience comprising exclusively boys and girls sat under a white banner loudly emblazoned PEANUT GALLERY. The term, first used in segregated theaters in the 1880s to designate the upper balconies to which blacks were restricted, here took on a further twist of stereotyping when Doodyville's founder and resident Native American, Chief Thunderthud, played by Bill LeCornec, opened every broadcast by approaching the forty privileged children in the gallery with his signature greeting: "How, Peanuts!"

Anderson added *Peanuts* to his list, the executives huddled at a brief staff meeting, and Rutman telephoned Schulz with their decision.

"Dignity" was the word to which Sparky time and again resorted in later years to catch the cardinal quality of the comic strip he had always yearned to draw—a strip with dignity. He had never heard of children being called "peanuts." "Peanut" might imply small size, but *Peanuts* sounded trivial, indeed trivializing, and his strip was going to be anything but that. Sparky was reported to have challenged Rutman: "What does it *mean*?" to which Rutman is said to have replied, "Little things." Sparky stubbornly insisted, "Yes, but little insignificant things—things of little value."

*Peanuts*, he believed, was nothing but "a tricky title" that might sell a few newspaper editors on the strip being marketed to them, but was all too likely to confuse readers, who, Sparky predicted, would almost certainly think it was the nickname of the strip's main character.

"I don't think with a name like that it will go very far," he told Frank Dieffenwierth bluntly.

"Isn't that an awful name for a strip?" he would complain to anyone who shared his love of comics.

"Well," Rutman told him in August, "the salesmen are ready to take the feature on the road, and we think it's a title that will catch the attention of editors."

The syndicate had meanwhile budgeted the not inconsiderable sum of $338.88 to promote the launch.

"What could a young unknown from St. Paul say?" Sparky later reflected.

"He went along—he was smart enough to," Harry Gilburt added.

The syndicate was willing to make one concession. If Sparky would agree to start out under the hated title, then Rutman would see to it that this could be changed if it proved a bad draw—provided the strip survived the initial setback of having to change its name in the first place.

"I gave in," sighed Sparky.

His friends at Art Instruction tried to buck him up. "To us it looks sure-fire and we are convinced it will be one of the nation's top cartoons," wrote Walter J. Wilwerding that summer, adding, "We are, of course, proud as Punch over the whole business," and predicted "PEANUTS and SCHULZ will be two names to remember."

One other name had to be changed before publication. The nameless little white-and-black dog who had appeared in *Li'l Folks* and several *Post* cartoons was now slated to reappear in the strip as Sniffy. Then, one day during his lunch hour at Art Instruction, as Sparky was walking around the Powers department store in uptown Minneapolis, he passed a magazine stand displaying a new comic book about a dog of that very name. "Oh, no, there goes my dog's name," and he started back for the office, where he could imagine himself sitting at his drawing board under a thunder-cloud, trying to gin up alternatives.

Then it came to him as he walked. His mother had said that if the family ever had another dog, they should call him Snoopy.

UNITED FEATURE SYNDICATE UNVEILED *Peanuts* on October 2, a bitter Monday in Minneapolis.

About a half-mile uptown from Art Instruction, there operated a large out-of-town newsstand, and Sparky set out through gusty rain with his friend and supporter Jim Sasseville to buy every paper that carried the strip, which was running, besides its hometown access in the *Minneapolis Tribune*, elsewhere just in the *Chicago Tribune*, the *Washington Post*, the *Evening Chronicle* of Allentown, Pennsylvania, the *Globe-Times* of Bethlehem, Pennsylvania, the *Denver Post*, and the *Seattle Times*. But when Sasseville asked the newsdealer if he had any papers with *Peanuts* in them, and the newsdealer said, "No, and we don't have any with popcorn either," Sparky's worst fears about the title came crashing down.

The more he thought about it, the angrier he became. Such exchanges were "doubly and triply obnoxious" to him, "because I hated the name, and I knew that things like this were going to happen." And he was right. Again and again in these early years, the question would arise, "Who is Peanuts, anyway? Is Charlie Brown Peanuts? Is Peanuts Snoopy? Is, perhaps, Schroeder Peanuts?" Sparky was acidly gratified when readers raised the issue on postcards that he passed along to the syndicate: "Dear Mr. Schulz: There seems to be quite a controversy concerning the true identity of 'Peanuts.' Please, sir, who is 'Peanuts'?"

"This is a legitimate question and is asked with justification," wrote one magazine editor. "Peanuts never appears in the strip, none of the characters ever mention the name, no reference is made to him, or it, in any way." A college humor magazine in Colorado was especially sympathetic to the puzzled reader: "We don't blame you for wondering exactly who is Peanuts."

Schulz never stopped resenting the cute label forced on his creation, whose unresolved riddle would become a symbol of the powerlessness of his early years. He never stopped insisting that it was "the worst title ever thought of for a comic strip." Nothing that the syndicate ever did over the next half-century could atone for the original wrong; yet if their first compromise, *Li'l Folk*, had stuck, it would have locked his characters into place as children—not what they became, and not what he wanted them to become; *Li'l Folk* was unendurably nice and precious. By borrowing a faddish cry from the revolutionizing medium of television, the syndicate was actually making a leap toward the new.

Sparky would refuse even to come out with the albatross title. When someone asked what he did, he would always reply, "I draw that comic strip with Snoopy in it, Charlie Brown, and his dog." But he would tell anyone anywhere anytime why he hated the wretched hand-me-down tag *Peanuts*, and in the midst of one rant forty-two years after the strip debuted, he came close to revealing why his anger had so long endured: "They didn't know when I walked in there that here was a fanatic. Here was a kid totally dedicated to what he was going to do. And to label, then, something that was going to be a life's work with a name like *Peanuts* was really insulting."

No matter what glory or riches accrued to the strip or to himself, he clung to this self-image of the unknown young midwesterner casually degraded by imperceptive eastern mandarins. "We all know that Christmas is a big commercial racket," Lucy would tell Charlie Brown. "It's run by a big Eastern syndicate, you know." To acknowledge in later decades that *Peanuts* had long since transcended its title—that it had become that rare cultural object whose name stands for the thing itself—would be to admit that Larry Rutman had been right. But even when Sparky was forced to accustom himself to his strip's exceptional place in people's lives, he could never apply the same to himself, and when he discovered that before Rutman died he had asked his son to notify Sparky personally, Schulz exclaimed, out of a half-century's insistence that he was just United Feature Syndicate's cannon fodder, "Isn't that astounding, that a businessman like that should have become fond of me, a nothing young man from St. Paul?"

In the end, the strip itself would be acclaimed an epic cycle. Cultural historians would describe "the saga of Charlie Brown, Snoopy, Lucy, and Linus" as "arguably the longest story told by a single artist in human history" and as "a whole different way of telling a story."

But for all the will to see it as a continuum of melancholy sweetness, it began with a precise declaration of feeling, shocking in its candor for a "children's strip" in 1950: "Here comes ol' Charlie Brown," says Shermy, the straight man—named for Sparky's old pal Sherman Plepler—who is sitting on a curb as his friend passes by: "Good ol' Charlie Brown . . . How I hate him!"

IN JULY 1949, JUDY Halverson married a doctor, Warren Noble Sheldon, and with the 1950 winter holidays fast approaching, she invited the Art Instruction gang to a party at the Sheldons' new place at 914 South Eighth Street, opposite Elliot Park, a block from where Sparky was born.

Sparky always felt strangely at home among the Halverson sisters. Their mother, Dorothy, plied him with her tapioca pudding, and after his court-

ship of Judy, he briefly dated Judy's older sister, the dutiful, levelheaded—
and redheaded—Ruth. Years later, Judy joked with her sisters, perhaps
rather seriously, that it was not so much the Halverson daughters whom
Sparky had really wanted as it was "to have Mother be his mother."

Taken together, the Halverson women were models for his strip's first
two female characters, Violet and Patty,★ who took turns serving as Charlie Brown's comedic foil. He had not yet crossed paths with the third and
youngest sister, Joyce, said to be the prettiest of the Halverson girls but also
headstrong, venturesome—"a little crazy," in the general opinion of Judy's
friends at Art Instruction. About herself, Joyce often said later, "At nineteen, I was naïve," or "I grew up in the Depression," or "I'm a Viking"—
cameo self-portraits that concentrated all that was bold, proud, resourceful,
and determined about her character.

In 1948, the nineteen-year-old Joyce had run off to New Mexico,
fallen in love with a cowboy, married, gotten pregnant, been abandoned by
her husband, and come home to Minneapolis to have the child—all within
twenty months. When Sparky met her at the party, Joyce was twenty-two
years old, divorced, with a baby and a curfew. Pulled away from a pretty
face was her strawberry-blond hair.

He found her doing the dishes at her sister's kitchen sink, and came
over to help.

---

★Schulz consciously named the first Patty in *Peanuts* after his cousin Patricia Swanson,
whose temperament more closely resembles that of the more substantial character
Peppermint Patty, but after revealing this to Patty Swanson, and especially after lesbian
groups claimed Peppermint Patty as one of their own, Schulz kept his cousin concealed as
his source, partly out of respect for Patty's privacy.

# CHAPTER 14

# SAGA

*Ah, to thee will I tell of my wrath!*
—VOLSUNGA SAGA

JOYCE'S FATHER, A STONEMASON'S son, spent most of his life in a futile search for love and success. The fair-haired, blue-eyed child of divorced parents, Henry Halverson, at seventeen, was left by his alcoholic father to fend for himself on Minneapolis's South Side. He rose through the ranks of book-keepers and clerks at the Boyd Transfer & Storage Company to become the firm's secretary—the only officer of the company not a member of the founding family, the Harlow Chamberlains, determinedly respectable Minneapolitan Baptists. In that door-opening position he met and married Dorothy Hamill, a twenty-year-old niece of the firm's founding brothers.

Dorothy and her sister Ruth had been left orphaned by illnesses that claimed their parents, a brother, and a sister. She was as much a survivor as Henry—both were deeply stubborn and willful—and their marriage in 1915 seemed to promise each a healing of old wounds. But though three daughters and a son were born to them, family happiness was made impossible by a mutual sense of deprivation, with Henry blaming Dorothy for withholding the love he craved, and Dorothy attributing their chronic financial instability to Henry's grandiose dreams of success. A similar strain in both their natures worsened this struggle. Each thought he or she was better than the other; Henry's self-righteous sense of injury mingled disas-trously with Dorothy's fearful snobbery. Their weaknesses securely hidden under a hard shell of Baptist moralism, both suspected—and accused—the other of being the one who would shake them and their children from their precarious position in the world.

Two blows shattered the Halverson family: the death of the blond, sweet-faced, five-year-old David from polio in the summer of 1925, which Henry blamed on Dorothy's casualness about the children's safety, and the collapse of Henry's new business in the fatally promising summer of 1929, when, over Dorothy's silent but furious dissent, he left the safety of the family firm, borrowed $10,000, and started a distributorship for Willys-Overland touring cars under the name Halverson Motors. He had just opened for business in October when the Great Crash buried his and so many others' dreams.

They struggled to have another child, but when Dorothy did get pregnant, the treatment she received at the hands of the Chamberlain family physician was, according to Henry, insufficient, and the baby died unborn. But then fate reversed itself, and on September 26, 1928, a third daughter was born to them, whom they named Joyce Steele.

Joyce's childhood was burdened by crushing poverty. Flight—sudden escape from one place to another, often into worse circumstances—became the family's way of life, as Henry and Dorothy moved their daughters from Minneapolis to Carthage, Texas, to El Dorado, Arkansas. Henry's belief in his future swept the family off on an empty odyssey of fruitless quests and get-rich-quick schemes, which always left Dorothy struggling to put food on the table. The Halverson girls learned to soldier on. Ruth helped to keep the family going with odd jobs, and by the age of twenty-two was able to support her mother and sisters from her earnings as cashier in an insurance company.

Joyce loved the wide-sky freedom of Texas and Arkansas; she had a tomboy's girlhood, digging up termite nests, cadging rides on a neighbor's old white horse, investigating the town dump. No stray dog could appear without Joyce's adopting it; she filled the house with animals, so many by memory's count that one wonders how the impoverished family fed them: thirty-three dogs and cats, two goats, a crow with a broken wing, and a turkey no one could bear to eat for Thanksgiving. "Her every wish was for a pony," her sister Ruth recalled, to the point that Joyce would gallop up and down the road, whinnying and tying herself to fences.

Moving back to Minneapolis during Joyce's junior high school years, the Halversons entered upon what Joyce still remembers as the most miserable time of her life, squeezing into "one gloomy apartment after another." The first of these afforded room enough for Judy to sleep on a Murphy bed in the dining alcove, with Henry on a cot by the bedroom window, and Joyce sharing the master bed with her mother, who snored, "sometimes with a light whistle," Henry noted, "but very frequently with a loud snort"—all of which meant that Joyce had to get to sleep in a hurry before Dorothy began the constant racket that often kept father and daughter awake all night.

Joyce's high school years saw decades of entrenched rage come to a climax. For if Dorothy was a brick wall, Henry was a fortress; the close-quartered, fiercely divided household was under continuous siege. Meals were eaten in uniform silence until Henry, wrapped in wounded isolation, made for the door, slamming it behind him as he finally burst out, "You know I don't like that for breakfast," no matter what Dorothy had set before him. Night brought the worst of the agony, as Dorothy's snoring and Henry's indignant complaints inevitably rounded out the daily stand-off with a final, fiendish exchange. Joyce would later recall that in these years, she was "a nervous wreck." One night before an exam, sheer lack of sleep left her hysterical and uncontrollably weeping, which in turn awak-ened and further upset the entire family. She still attributes the chronic insomnia of her later years to these crowded, come-down-in-the-world nights in Minneapolis.

Joyce sought escape in daydreams. Trapped in the apartment, she would project herself into wilderness vistas. The film of *The Lone Ranger*, which she saw when she was eleven, had awakened her senses and affirmed her passions; it was always white steeds and the Great West of which she dreamed, never love and marriage and children. And yet she did bring one kind of man into her secret world: "some gallant knight" who would carry her away from her domestic misery.

Early in 1948, Joyce got a job as a clerk at a real estate firm specializing in farmland, mortgage loans, and exchanges. Nineteen years old and still living in those crushing rooms at 3943 Bryant Avenue South, she strained against her mother's hard-and-fast rules and curfews. That summer, Joyce followed her passion for horses, her daydreams of vast distances and a gal-lant knight, to west-central New Mexico and the Whitewater Lodge, a dude ranch for vacationers who wanted a taste of romance and adventure in the Land of Enchantment, just open for business. Joyce cleaned cottages on Apache Ridge, washed dishes in the Moundhouse, and met Bill Lewis, the wrangler in charge of the lodge's riding program. "He was handsome, personable, and I fell in love with him."

Lewis, part Native American, a superb horseman, was also an accomplished guitar player and singer, playing at the bar and dance hall in Glenwood. He took Joyce on trail rides up the nearby canyons in the evening, roasting chicken over a fire. They fished Elephant Butte Lake and hunted for gold. Lewis was thirty-eight—twice her age—and matters proceeded swiftly when she moved into his place, a tarpaper shack where food was kept cool under a wet rag in the rear window. She hurried home to Minneapolis to announce her engagement, expecting to fly back to New Mexico for the wedding, and soon enough to have her mother and sisters visit her. But Henry, adamantly against her being married without her mother's presence, borrowed the $125 (at 3 percent interest) needed to send all the womenfolk down to Glenwood by car.

On July 13, 1948, still more than two months shy of twenty, Joyce married Newton William Lewis in Silver City, New Mexico, sixty-four miles to the southeast. Even her father, Joyce's great advocate within the family, would term it a tragic union, with an "unfortunate sequel." For after finding herself pregnant in June 1949, she returned to Minneapolis to share the joyous news and visit with her parents one last time before living, she thought permanently, with her husband in New Mexico. But a telephone call to Bill left her stunned: she was not to come back to Glenwood—he wanted out of the marriage. Vowing nonetheless to win him back, Joyce hastened to Glenwood, where she worked for room and board at the general store. Lewis kept his distance, but she hung on, finding a position as a nanny on a nearby ranch. In her final month of pregnancy, her father got together enough money for her to come home. Before she left New Mexico, she signed divorce papers in Deming; Lewis paid $50 in support of their almost-born child, then disappeared from their lives, never to be heard from again.

No sooner had Joyce returned to Minneapolis to have the baby than she irreversibly offended Aunt Ruth by declining a significant invitation. Ruth, acting as if Joyce's divorce was a black mark on the family name, then declared her a charity case and enjoined the Chamberlain relatives to treat her niece as if she were carrying an illegitimate child. Bill Lewis's abandonment had debased her in the eyes of right-thinking midwesterners—she had "failed to keep her man," as the idea was expressed in the women's columns of the day. Joyce was to hang her head and admit defeat. She refused.

On February 5, 1950, in Minneapolis's oldest hospital, St. Barnabas, she gave birth to Meredith Sue Lewis, whom Henry pronounced the most beautiful infant he had ever seen. "And she was," Joyce later agreed, recalling Meredith's brown curls, long dark eyelashes, and broad-featured face—an older inheritance in America than either what the Halversons' Viking kinsmen had brought or the Chamberlains' Anglophile graspings.

But with the shades of Chamberlain thus polluted, Dorothy, now supporting herself selling Singer sewing machines, had united with her sister to pillory Joyce. The fact that Joyce's child, while fatherless, was not illegitimate, did nothing in the sisters' eyes to palliate her real offense: taking the family down a peg.

Meredith was born, but Lucy Van Pelt was being conceived.

By the time Joyce met Charles Schulz the following year among her sister Judy's friends from Art Instruction, Inc., she had no hesitation about dating a newly syndicated cartoonist whose very name would aggravate her relatives' determinedly old-order stereotypes. In the worldview of Aunt Ruth (who had "lowered herself" by marrying a grocer's son), "Schulzes were always grocers or butchers."

JOYCE HAD JUST BEGUN a new job at the Minneapolis Recorder of Deeds, earning enough to afford a babysitter, when Sparky invited her to a Schumann night at the Minneapolis Symphony. She found him thoughtful and fun. On their next date, they went skating, but to Sparky's horror, Joyce skidded on a candy wrapper and down she went, only to pick herself up, unhurt.

Pretty girls and tomboys had always scared him, and Joyce was both. Slender, deep-breasted, her down-to-the-shoulders reddish-blond hair bracketing flashing blue eyes and the saddle of freckles that bridged her nose and burning cheeks, she was not so much the passive, tenderhearted girl next door of prom-date dreams as a GI's sweater girl, her heart calloused from hard knocks but still effervescent—perhaps the more so for a sense of having to seize the day.

Sparky was immediately attracted by her nervy wit. One evening when he invited some of his friends from Art Instruction over for a bridge evening at the North Snelling apartment, he included Joyce, who arrived out of breath. She had taken the streetcar and someone had come after her, which, she declared with a comic high tone, made her a "chased woman." But with Schulz she was less the pursued than the pursuer. One observer of their early courtship claims to have seen her "zero[ing] in on Sparky long before he realized what was happening." Nevertheless some of the Art Instruction circle noticed that he was "ready for marriage. He was looking for someone."

And he must have known immediately how much he, in his turn, could lean on her: "You must like me a lot to want to skate with me, Charlie Brown," says Violet, to which her wobbling swain replies, "Well, I guess so . . . But what I really want is someone to hang onto!"

A youthful single mother, so full of zest that she looked nineteen until she was forty, Joyce rode on her nerves, overflowing with vitality—although at twenty-two, for all her energy, she was not at all certain what talent or means would carry her forward, except restlessness itself. Unlike Donna Johnson, she did not intend to become submerged by ordinary life and its routines. Sparky might hide insecurities beneath a cool surface—and both of them showed the price exacted in hand tremors—but Joyce masked self-doubt behind an incandescent exterior. One cousin who knew her in adolescence recalled her as a "firecracker," a friend from adulthood called her a "fireball," and another, who met her when she was forty, characterized her as "fun and fire." Snoopy, after dancing with Lucy in a 1958 strip, would think, "Boy, how that girl can dance! She's really a ball of fire! Yes, sir! She's quite a girl!!"

Later, when wretchedly ill-matched couples had become his stock in trade, Sparky would be asked what he had first seen in Joyce and would single out her delight in culture. In childhood, music had moved her; as a teenager she had daydreamed of one day "being great," and had wept over the profound ways in which Rachmaninoff's second Piano Concerto "touched . . . my soul." She imagined becoming a concert pianist, as had her mother before her.

Joyce possessed, free and clear of her mother's reach, the gift of gab. During her senior year in high school, she had even handled a telephone company switchboard on the night shift, sometimes fielding calls from people who "were lonesome and just wanted to talk."

On their first dates, Sparky found that, as with Judy, he could relax: Joyce did all the talking. She had an acute sense of the ridiculous, and no end, it seemed, of opinions to declare and topics to initiate and effortlessly to follow through on, chief among them the year-old Meredith, who often had to accompany them on dates, since neither Joyce's mother nor her sisters would babysit (though Sparky's aunt Marion did volunteer). Joyce needed a father for her child and, as one of their friends of this period later put it, "Sparky saw a chance to be noble."

As he took his first steps toward becoming the good man in Joyce's and Meredith's lives, Joyce was amazed to see how he could handle Aunt Ruth, and handle her masterfully. Ruth regarded Scandinavian heritage with distaste: Dorothy's having married Henry Halverson had placed Joyce and her sisters in a lower caste from the rest of the Chamberlains, and the Halverson girls suffered Aunt Ruth's contempt for their "being Swedes." Joyce had furthermore been made to feel that she was the lowliest of the girls, and not only by Aunt Ruth. "My parents always said that Judy had all the talent, all the looks. . . . And I really loved my dad, but he thought Judy was the only smart one." One friend who knew both sisters in these days recalled that Joyce was "always trying to keep up with Judy."

In years to come, Joyce would say that she had been invited to her sister's party only because, Cinderella-like, she did the dishes; and would only be delivered from the malignancies of her aggressively judgmental aunt by the noble young man she met at the party. This turned out to be a natural role for Sparky, who admitted in later life that he had grown up wanting to be a heroic protector; in fact, the white knight archetype thunders into a dissonant romantic fantasy of 1952 in which Violet dreams about a man appearing on a great white stallion: "Suddenly he galloped toward me, and it was you, Charlie Brown!"

Charlie Brown starts off a Sunday page telling Lucy about a dream dominated by "this big castle," before which he himself appeared as "a knight on a great white horse," while Lucy, in her simplistic, predatory way, clings to the logic of fairy-tale endings: one of the storybooks she inflicts on her little brother describes a frog that turns into a prince, marries the princess, and lives happily ever after. From a wealth of experience, Linus observes, "I'll bet she started complaining the day after they got married," but he can't shake Lucy: "If it says here that they lived happily ever after, then they lived happily ever after!"

Reconstructing his first responses, Sparky later told a close friend that he realized that Joyce was "in a terrible situation." But, as a gallant boy in *Li'l Folks* says on bended knee to his six-year-old true love: "I tell you it's the future that counts . . . I don't care anything about your past!"

Sparky never asked Joyce about Bill Lewis. He had no wish to intrude, and as Joyce saw it, "that part of my life was so far beyond anything that Sparky could have understood that I rarely talked about it." The truth about her marrying Lewis, she later said, came down to her having been "terribly naïve and really falling in love with the 'horsy' life."

According to Joyce, Sparky came into the courtship "very naïve"—a virgin up to their wedding day. "He was very old-fashioned and romantic; he liked the idea of romance, but he didn't really know what romance was." He may not have aroused her passions as Bill Lewis had, but neither was he running away from her, or running around with other women. He was, in fact, truly kind to her, and as Joyce told it, "I had been through a traumatic experience. My mother wasn't the kindest person. Judy had a new baby. . . . After Bill had deserted me, having Sparky show up and ask for a date, and because things at home with Mother and Judy were not the greatest, I developed a real love for him."

She took him as he was, disregarding his looks. "I really loved Sparky, even though he was homely. . . . He had very bad skin," she emphasized, "terrible skin. . . . *So what's the matter with me?* I saw past that."

THEY WERE QUICKLY ENGAGED. Joyce would later say of herself and Sparky, "We're the kind who make rash decisions." But when they made their announcement, it seemed "sudden" even to many who knew them. It came as "a shock" to his church youth group because they had encouraged Sparky to invite whomever he wanted to their social gatherings, yet "[h]e hadn't said one word to us about her."

"That sure went fast," thought a startled Donna Johnson Wold.

His friends at Art Instruction noticed that while courting Joyce he preferred to be a loner, never double-dating, and some were certain that it was Joyce who had maneuvered Sparky into marriage. The women at church thought Sparky had proposed "out of sympathy for Joyce." In the opinion of one church couple, it was not Joyce who had made the conquest: "He fell in love with Meredith. If Meredith hadn't been in the picture he wouldn't have married Joyce."

Did Carl approve of the match? "Joyce was Sparky's choice, and Carl respected Sparky's decisions," said a close friend of Carl's. "They were very close and anything that Sparky did was OK with Carl."

But Aunt Marion was wary, said her daughter-in-law Ramona. "She was very cautious about his marriage. She didn't want anyone to hurt him. He was so vulnerable and she was protective of him."

Among the women in her family, Joyce found little support for the match. Her mother warned her against marrying a German—underneath their sentimentality, insisted Dorothy, Germans were cold, unaffectionate. Amid later claims and counterclaims, Joyce asserted that "Judy hated him by that time and so did Ruth," adding, "Judy must have known what he was really like. Both Judy and Mother said, 'You're making a big mistake.' " But neither Judy nor Ruth can recall opposing the engagement.

Perhaps Judy had come closest to the truth when she remarked that it was not so much any of the Halverson sisters whom Sparky wanted for a wife as it was Dorothy whom he really needed as a mother.

Henry Halverson, intensely identifying with the code of the Christian gentleman—courtesy, reverence, respect, dignity—considered his future son-in-law a "wonderful man." He admired Sparky's successful start as a cartoonist, almost as an exemplification of the success that he felt should rightly have been his. Henry had reached his peak in 1946, when, as advertising manager for the St. Paul Terminal Warehouse, he had coined a slogan that won first prize in a nationwide contest conducted by the American Trucking Association. The man who believed that his son had died as a baby from his wife's inattentiveness to their children's safety had come up with "Safety Is No Accident," and the governor of Minnesota himself, Edward John Thye, had crowned the achievement by present-ing Henry with a jeweled watch. But his life's greatest disappointment, as he saw it, was not the failure to achieve financial success or a position of power through the realization of his ideas (he had dreamed up rental cars and the soft-rubber finger pad to save people time when collating docu-ments long before either became ubiquitous) but to have been deprived of the loving marriage he had dreamed of as a young man abandoned by his own family.

By the time of Joyce's engagement to Sparky, even the skeleton of Henry and Dorothy's marriage had collapsed, and he had gone to live alone in a small Minneapolis apartment, a split that made an eerie prologue to Sparky and Joyce's wedding.

ON APRIL 18, 1951, with the earthy scents of spring suddenly in the air, they married at 1380 West Minnehaha Parkway, a brick-and-stucco Prairie-style house set on a rise two blocks above Lake Harriet, its front picture window looking out onto Minnehaha Creek. Just as her mother had been married from the grander residence of well-to-do relatives on Pillsbury Avenue, so Joyce took advantage of the warmer, more welcoming household of her cousins George and Colleta Town, for when her mother declared that Joyce did not "deserve" a second ceremony—"You've already *had* a wed-ding," Dorothy snapped—Colletta said, "You certainly do deserve one, and you're going to have it at my house."

Some twenty guests attended, mostly family, including Joyce's estranged parents, with a few good friends. Joyce ever after remembered how abominably her mother treated her father that day ("She really was nasty") as well as the absence of Judy and Judy's husband. Sparky's aunt Marion and uncle Buster witnessed the wedding certificate; Carl and Annabelle and Carl's sister Alma and her husband, were on hand too. Sparky's cousin Bill recalls the occasion as being "very subdued," almost perfunctory.

Joyce swept down to the living room on her father's arm and joined Sparky at a flower-sprayed mantelpiece adorned with two lighted candles, where bride and groom spoke their vows before Marvin Forbes and exchanged rings, inside both of which was engraved a single word: *Forever.*

A color photograph shows Sparky and Joyce cutting their wedding cake with eyes aglow. The groom wears a silver-colored two-button suit with buttressed shoulders, a white carnation in his lapel, a white shirt, and a foulard necktie patterned in '50s hepcat jazz style with crimson-and-light-blue-striped squares. His arm closes around his bride as he smiles down at her in radiant delight.

Joyce is a dish: thin and pretty, high-colored; across her peaches-and-cream complexion, a gash of red lipstick complements the red and white carnations in her roan hair. Instead of the traditional white wedding gown, she is wearing black—a sleeveless shirtwaist dress trimmed with white lace at the throat, and a seductive peekaboo black chiffon bodice over the lace at the bosom. But the design of the daringly contra-colored dress is lady-like and pretty, and this captures all that Joyce is saying about herself as she marries for the second time: she can't wear white, but she'll play the genteel game and meanwhile have some fun with everyone, reminding her mother and Aunt Ruth just how forcefully different a Halverson girl can be . . .

Leaving Meredith with Aunt Marion, they made their getaway in Sparky's Ford, now prankishly rigged by Art Instruction pals; the windshield painted to look as though it were broken, hidden marbles clattering in the hubcaps, they drove out West, to a brief honeymoon in Colorado Springs, of which Joyce remembered little, understandably, except the moment when Sparky turned to her on the drive out and said, "I don't think I can ever be happy."

"How do you like that for a honeymoon?" she said later.

But what he was forecasting was a life not in which happiness would have limits, but in which unhappiness would be a legitimate choice. Charles Schulz did not need to be happy—he needed to be loved; he imagined that he needed to work for that love, and yet no matter how hard he worked or how widespread and enduring the appreciation of his art, true love seemed always to elude him.

But for Joyce, even the first glimmer of understanding him was still in the future. At that moment, in the Ford, heading west, she was "a little bit shocked," and she thought to herself, "Well, I'll just *make* you happy.'"

Upon returning to St. Paul, the newlyweds reclaimed Meredith and moved in with Carl and Annabelle at Annabelle's house at 1163 Edgerton, where they were hilariously forced to shoehorn themselves into the only spare bed, a narrow single. Each morning, Sparky cheerfully descended to the basement, where he had set up a card table on which to draw, his arm jostled every once in a while "by women trying to get by me with big baskets of wash."

Joyce lived with her in-laws on sufferance—hers more than theirs. So far as she was concerned, the whole arrangement was "weird," although it served its purpose: a curious tug of war had broken out over Meredith, with Joyce's mother and her sister Ruth on one side, insisting that Meredith should stay with them, and Joyce and Sparky on the other, keeping her with them at Carl and Annabelle's. Sparky now stepped forward and legally adopted Meredith, and from then on, as he was called upon to tell the story of his life to an eager public, he and Joyce lied about the year of their wedding (1951) in order to assimilate and protect Meredith's place in their marriage. Even in official notarized documents, they ever after gave April 18, 1949, as their nuptial day, placing Meredith's birth (on February 5, 1950) just within the bounds of propriety as Sparky's daughter. They maintained this fiction for the next eighteen years—it endured even after his death—hushing up any talk of Joyce's first marriage, to keep the truth not just from the public but also from Meredith herself, and perhaps even to keep her safe from such claims as might be made by Bill Lewis, who had never known that it was a daughter he had fathered.

"I WILL NOT LIVE in Minneapolis," Joyce had warned Sparky when they first decided to get married. No one was going to bridle her into the quiet life of a Minnesota homemaker. She was going west, whether her husband liked it or not.

Joyce had no use for the old; to her, the past was the proverbial bucket of ashes, and she was set on putting the heavily defended Pillsbury Avenue world of her mother's clan behind her and finding her way to the new and the now. She was, moreover, an outdoors person; Minneapolis, with its vast flour mills, grain elevators, and looming skyscrapers, made her feel anxious, pressed. But more than anything, or anyone, it was Aunt Ruth who drove Joyce to get up and go. "I truly hated her. . . . She was so abrasive, so insulting."

But now that she had mobilized even Sparky, where would they live? For all his initial love of New York, he had no inclination to move East, the South and Southwest were strange, the Far West seemed remote, and the Pacific Coast looked to his eye almost as exotic as Hawaii. He always maintained that he was "just what in the United States would be called an ordinary Midwesterner."

To Sparky, the Upper Midwest was the real America, and he was grateful to have been born and raised there. St. Paul's provincialism comforted and reassured him; by 1958, he made a point of telling newsmen from the East that living in the Midwest and "being a little naïve" was an advantage; he was glad to be a young cartoonist in "a place as relatively calm as St. Paul, Minnesota . . . where my interests were not too sophisticated and yet not too bland." He thought of his humor as "very much middle-America" and later said that for a comic strip artist it might even be "an actual drawback if you were to know only what is going on in New York City or San Francisco."

Minnesota was for him no frozen hinterland; it was "the center of the United States"—home to a tradition of radical individualism that he would now recast in funny pictures and, one day, export around the world. Sparky

had no artistic need to leave behind his homeland on the Upper Mississippi. Left to himself, he—and his art—would have remained rooted in the
needling wit and snowy angularities of St. Paul. But this diehard home-
body had hitched himself to an optimist, a self-styled "Viking," a nomadic
adventurer who "never gave up."

Many years later, when Meredith was an adult, Sparky revealed to her
that they had moved in order to give her the best chance at a life without
the stigma attached to adoption. "In those days, what other people thought
was so important," Meredith recalled her father saying; and "because they
had covered up the fact of the adoption and made me out to be his daughter, the only way they could get away with that lie forever was by moving
away from St. Paul, where the societal pressure was intense. For my mom
and dad, it was the driving force."

The restless, west-going impulse of their new life meant that for
Sparky there would be no supportive routine as in St. Paul. His life had
direction—*one* direction: the comics—but little vitality outside his sole
ambition and his local friendships and his faith. Joyce pried him out of the
Cities, away from the Family Barber Shop and the Church of God, off the
unchanging tracks of his streetcars and morning routines at Art Instruction, Inc., and pushed him west, with Meredith in tow, in the direction of
her own formless dreams—music, art, design, the wind on one's face—and
in so doing, charged Sparky and his young strip with her optimism and
energy, and Meredith's, too.

In direct consequence, his anxiety bloomed, for here was another great
separation: "It was ridiculous," he would say of the move to the mountains. "There was no sense in us being there. And it took me away from
everything that I loved." Joyce would never forget that when they said
their good-byes on Edgerton Road, Sparky and his father turned away
from one another, both men choking back tears.

# PART FOUR

# PUSHING WEST

*I'm an optimist. I never give up.*

JOYCE SCHULZ

# CHAPTER 15

# TO THE ROCKIES

*For a moment, at the frontier, the bonds of custom are broken and unrestraint is triumphant.*
—FREDERICK JACKSON TURNER

DRY BUFFALO GRASS STRETCHED hundreds of miles to the limitless horizon, threaded by creeks, broken by scrub.

Beyond the western edge of town, spiny peaks thrust up to close the rolling prairie—the Front Range of the Rockies, on whose winter snows sunup played pink, sundown purple. In summer, sharp, red sandstone spires etched themselves against spotless blue skies. Here was a real-life duplicate of the world that Joyce had daydreamed back in Minneapolis: "mountains and deserts, a lot of room for riding my horse, and no relatives around."

With scant rainfall and six of every ten days dry and sunny, Colorado Springs had earned its title "City of Sunshine," and in May 1951, when the Schulzes arrived with Meredith in tow, it was becoming the fastest-growing town in America. They settled in Bonneville, a newly constructed tract of tidy bungalows lining smooth, paved streets devoid of trees or shrubbery. Erected by the developer John Bonforte as low-cost housing for veterans and their young families, Bonneville's well-built, affordable efficiencies stood on the edge of what just a year before had been open prairie, each white cottage starkly flanked by a peaked-roof garage and backed by a trim, unplanted yard: a place in which literally to put down roots—or to draw the lines of a new world.

Sparky secured 2321 North El Paso Street with a veteran's loan at 4½ percent; when he and Joyce moved in, he bought for her, also on a payment plan, a small upright piano—the Wurlitzer spinet. For Meredith, he painted a mural so that from her crib she could see her very own Charlie

Brown jumping nimbly over a lighted candlestick; her own Snoopy, barking on all fours; her own Patty, carrying a plaid balloon; and a throng of random figures—Miss Paro's triplicates reduced to singular presentation—including a smiling locomotive, a laughing elephant, a dancing fox, a bug-eyed rabbit, a fireplug, an upper- and lowercase alphabet, the numerals 1 through 10, the moon and the stars, two fish (one red, one green), a yellow duck, a blue note, a yellow and a blue butterfly, a shade tree growing behind a white picket fence, and, most meaningful of all to Meredith, at the bottom of the wall, like something that might lure Alice along in the rabbit hole, a mysterious little red door opening onto anywhere.

Here truly was a fresh start. Everything in the four-room cottage was brand-new and clean, not yet touched by mere living. A picture window in the front room framed a vast, open view of 14,110-foot Pikes Peak; the radiant, health-giving Colorado springtime shone all around, and with the good news from their pediatrician that Joyce was now a month pregnant, the whole world seemed freshly remade for the newcomers and their hopes.

IMMEDIATELY THERE CAME A problem. Sparky tried working at home but found himself distracted. "He was amazed at Meredith's gregariousness—and mine," Joyce would recall. "Meredith was forever getting herself *involved* in things." And if it wasn't their toddler's doings, or his wife's alarms when Meredith fussed excessively, or his mother-in-law's extended visits, then it was his own feeling that, perched in a bedroom like a tamed seal, he was not really at work.

His strong sense of duty exerted itself, and he continually felt divided between professional and domestic obligation. When the morning's drawing slowed, the original inspiration having dried up and no new spurt of energy forthcoming, he found it easier, rather than to doodle the afternoon away, just to go out to the backyard in his white T-shirt and khakis and check to see if the new grass seed had taken hold.

Syndication was proving to be a strict master. His sales, as Harry Gilburt had predicted, were slow. In later decades, as *Peanuts* became an ever-expanding powerhouse, its beloved characters licensed to appear in dozens of other media around the world, its triumphant growth as a brand would make its popular appeal as a strip seem inevitable from the first. But after a full year, the feature was still a pipsqueak whose prospects remained very much in doubt. "It just didn't seem to catch on," recalled Gilburt. By October 1951, its roster of daily subscribers had increased from the initial seven to a scant thirty-six newspapers, but for the syndicate to break even on expenses, the sales manager had set the bar at a hundred.

The trouble, according to Gilburt, lay in the sheer abundance of Schulz's characters: "People had trouble remembering who was who." Gilburt devised an ingenious promotional plan in which subscribing news-papers would run small ads, at no cost to the syndicate, each day introduc-ing another member of the *Peanuts* gang to readers.

Every morning Sparky would sit in his bedroom brooding about how to recruit subscribers: "I didn't think that I would ever get to a hundred." He followed the success of Walt Kelly's *Pogo*, another thinking-man's comic strip, whose appearance in paperback collections was just then wid-ening its readership, in newspapers as well. *Time* reported a new bench-mark: " 'Eighty newspapers!' " Sparky blurted. "How did he ever get to eighty newspapers?" In 1951, Kelly, darling of the intellectuals, won the cartooning world's highest honor, the Reuben, named for Rube Gold-berg—a prize on which Sparky had set his sights but did not expect to win for many years. He kept tabs on another rival closer to home, Ernie Bushmiller's *Nancy*, which continued to appear in more newspapers than any other strip owned by United Feature Syndicate: "Four hundred! That's unbelievable!"

On one of her visits, his mother-in-law urged him to get an office out of the house, and though he himself would not have considered such an extravagance, he soon had reason enough. On February 1, 1952, at the hospital in Colorado Springs, Joyce gave birth to her second child, a boy. Sparky was "awed," Joyce would later recall, "that he had a son." They named him Charles Monroe Schulz, Jr., calling him by the old Halverson family nickname "Monte."★

Joyce later recalled that Sparky "was very proud of the way he could put a tight diaper on the baby, [and] that was the time of safety pins and

---

★He later changed his legal name to Monte Charles Schulz.

cloth diapers. . . . [Nor] was he beyond giving the baby his bottle. On the contrary, he enjoyed it."

He rented a small room on the second floor of the Golden Arrow Building downtown, establishing a habit, which would endure to the end, of fulfilling his daily duty to *Peanuts* in as businesslike a setting as possible. Beside the room's single window overlooking the courthouse square he set up his drawing table and, with no telephone and no secretary to help answer what was beginning to be a steady trickle of fan mail from Los Angeles, Chicago, New York, Boston, Philadelphia, San Francisco, Evanston, Lake Forest, Glendale, and Scott Air Force Base, he built his strip.

"I was still searching for what I was going to do with it. The characters were beginning to develop and the ideas were changing"—and changing so quickly that when, on February 7, 1952, John Selby, editor in chief of Rinehart & Company, proposed the first *Peanuts* collection and asked to see the strips from 1950 to 1951, Sparky replied, "I am a bit ashamed of the earlier drawings, and hope that you do not intend to go back to the very beginning for reprints. My search for style both in drawing and humor had led me down various paths with the result that the shape of poor Charlie Brown's head suffers a good deal. I am sure that you will notice this when you view the earlier gags."

In his new studio, the stark simplicity of the early strip no longer satisfied him. The drawing, he decided, "needed a little more detail," and the particulars he now imparted to his panels came directly from the four rooms in Bonneville: the efficiency floor plan, the picture window in the living room, the '50s-modern curtains, the hallway leading to Meredith's room, her crib, from which one night she fell straight onto her head—all provided a real and ultracontemporary setting.

As he added details of daily life, opening his eyes and ears to the clean, uncluttered world of Bonneville, his settings remained spare. Most cartoon drawing is about distraction: popular masters like Walt Kelly and Al Capp crowded their panels with characters and activity; *Pogo* and *Li'l Abner* are dense with what actors call "business." *Peanuts*, full of empty spaces, didn't depend on action or a particular context to attract the reader; it was about people working out the interior problems of their daily lives without ever actually solving them. The absence of a solution was the center of the story, and, as Schulz insisted at the time, "ninety percent of the humor is in the drawing."

The ingredients of much of what was to become *Peanuts* mixed together with Sparky's new life in Colorado Springs during the first year of marriage and of fatherhood. They had moved in the very year that Louis Kronenberger, in *Company Manners*, wrote, "The Moving Van is a symbol of more than our restlessness; it is the most conclusive possible evidence of our progress," and the move itself, so optimistic on the face of it (this was the period of the Welcome Wagon and of IBM standing for "I've Been Moved"), was, for Sparky at least, a wrench away from all that he felt secure in—a "big move," as he later looked back on it.

In the strip that appeared October 17, 1951, Patty wants to show Charlie Brown her new-model sandbox, and he smugly goes along, saying, "Charlie Brown is always interested in progress . . . Show me to it!" But once he has climbed into what appears to be no different from the sandbox on any playground, he learns the profound difference between the two—as a happy Patty looks on without lifting a finger or calling for help.

The American assumption was that children were happy, and childhood was a golden time; it was adults who had problems with which they wrestled and pains that they sought to soothe. Schulz reversed the natural order of this universe (as he had reversed the dominance of the sexes) by showing that a child's pain is more intensely felt than an adult's, a child's defeats the more acutely experienced and remembered. Charlie Brown takes repeated insults from Violet and Patty about the size of his head, which they compare with a beach ball, a globe, a pie tin, the moon, a balloon; and though Charlie Brown may feel sorry for himself, he gets over it fast. But he does not get visibly angry.

"Would you like to have been Abraham Lincoln?" Patty asks Charlie Brown. "I doubt it," he answers. "I have a hard enough time being just plain Charlie Brown."

Children are not supposed to be radically dissatisfied. When they are unhappy, children protest—they wail, they whine, they scream, they cry—then they move on. Schulz gave these children *lifelong* dissatisfactions, the stuff of which adulthood is made.

Readers recognized themselves in "poor, moon-faced, unloved, misunderstood" Charlie Brown—in his dignity in the face of whole seasons of doomed ball games, his endurance and stoicism in the face of insults—because he is willing to admit that just to keep on being Charlie Brown is an exhausting and painful process. Charlie Brown reminded people, as no other cartoon character had, of what it was to be vulnerable, to be small and alone in the universe, to be human—both little and big at the same time.

The chesty Charlie Brown of 1950 and 1951, a "flippant little guy," as Schulz described him, had derived from the boy Sparky had been when he bullied his immigrant grandmother with spelling tests or played practical jokes on his neighborhood pals and, later, his Art Instruction colleagues—the boy whom Sherman Plepler recalled being "capable at times of *not* so humorous practical jokes, and [of showing] a devilish glee towards others which some may interpret as a mean streak"; the colleague with whom David Ratner would recall once teasing their friend Charlie F. Brown, whose touch of snobbery, social pretension, and taste for white turtlenecks and pipes made him seem "less of a guy" among the male art instructors: "It was like Ping-Pong: First Sparky would say something to Charlie Brown, then I would say something to Charlie Brown—we taunted him—until he cried."

But in 1952, a new character appeared who would sweat the cold cheekiness out of Charlie Brown, just as Joyce would help Sparky to restate his prankish, teasing side by demanding that he defend himself against *her* aggressiveness with a variety of counterpunches. The experience of being a stoical Everyman—a decent person in a world hostile when not indifferent—was essential to the quality of fortitude that lies at the heart of Charlie Brown's character. For although he dramatizes himself through increasingly powerful forms of negativity—self-reproach, the cult of vulnerability, the listing of one's own defects—his sense of what he lacks is honest and engaging, never self-referential or narcissistically dull.

He is ennobled by how well he handles being a person whom no one else would wish to be. He never cries. At most he vocalizes his feelings with a new outburst of Schulzian dismay. As Schulz worked hard to give his characters—and his readers—a language of their own—a "little language," to borrow Jonathan Swift's term—earlier laments such as "That's the way it goes!" or "I'm beat!" or even such standards of comic strip disgust and rage as AAGHH! and AARGH! boiled away, leaving Schulz's soul-baring catchalls, *AAUGH!* and *SIGH* as the *Peanuts* gang's signature expressions of frustration.

But on March 3, 1952, a month after Meredith turned two, a little girl entered the strip who did not just make sport of Charlie Brown but demolished him, and before too long would change everything.

AT THE START, LUCY Van Pelt was no more than a toddler with big, round, doll-like eyes. "She didn't do much at first," recalled Schulz. "She came in as a cute little girl and at first she was patterned after our own first daughter," ambling through the house in her Dr. Denton sleepers, speaking of herself in the third person, falling out of her crib, fussing. Lucy's ploys— waiting until *after* her father had tucked her in and returned to his easy chair and newspaper before demanding a glass of water—were Meredith's. Schulz would remember calling Meredith "a fussbudget" when she was very small, "and from this I applied the term to Lucy."

Increasingly outrageous, disconcerting, with rules of her own (usually framed five seconds before), Lucy came to *Peanuts* in the lineage of Lewis Carroll's Queen of Hearts and James Thurber's controlling wives,* but with a shining unreason all her own. She did not yet have the reserves of authority with which her predecessors had first been endowed, but as time went on, Lucy began, for example, to misinterpret nature with the same self-assurance that gives a magical adult realism to the characters of classic children's literature.

She is at once logical and illogical, both reasonable and unreasonable, as accepting as she is denying—whether she is possessed by the sudden joyful realization, as she counts stars and strains to see the "teeny-weeny

---

*In postwar America, Lucy became the new model for an existing genre of character: the young woman with nerve. Gore Vidal noted that, as a type, the strong-willed Dorothy Gale of L. Frank Baum's Oz books "is still with us in such popular works as *Peanuts*, where she continues her steely progress toward total domination in the guise of the relentless Lucy."

ones," that standing on a chair "makes all the difference in the world!" or when she duplicitously encourages Charlie Brown to have faith that she will believe anything he tells her, even his deliberately fanciful notion that "the world is made of snow," only to betray just this "idea" and its creator to public ridicule.

Before Lucy, *Peanuts* had been relatively quiet. Except for an occasional KLUNK when someone took a pratfall, or a yelled "FORE!" on the golf course or a subdued yet heartfelt "RATS!" on the tennis court, the words inside the speech balloons remained in the small, tight, all-capital lettering, drawn by Schulz's C-5 chisel-point Speedball pen, which he had been forced to adopt in *Peanuts*' early, space-saving days. All this changed with the arrival of Lucy, who exercises a simple fury at things as they are. When she is "doing some loud shouting," as Schulz put it, he inked up a B-5 pen, which rendered lines heavier, flatter, and rounder ("CAN'T YOU EVER BE QUIET?!" she yells at her gentle younger brother, her mouth as vast as the Gulf of Mexico); eventually he came to deploy a third pen, the B-3, for very heavy lines "to indicate maximum screams."

Lucy enabled Schulz to "do new and special things" with the characters. Her aggressiveness threw the others off balance. Not only could they now shout at each other at the top of their lungs, but with Lucy setting the tempo, one character's sudden rage might reach a level of force that could literally bowl another over, spinning the victim backward out of the frame. Lucy had only to toss a bug into Charlie Brown's lap to somersault him into the air for the first time. But Schulz added words to the sight gag—a misheard homophone—that precisely defined the difference in character between Charlie Brown and his new antagonist: Charlie Brown was sincerely prepared for Lucy to offer him a *hug*, not a bug.

But, for all her bluster, Lucy is a fairly direct and literal person, and only Charlie Brown would be taken in by her. She depends as much on Charlie Brown as he depends on her. Only Charlie Brown, frantic for someone to trust, believes her—is even, indeed, at times bewitched by her. The very fact that she has no other patsy showed readers in the early '50s that for all her noisy self-assertion, no truly threatening figure would emerge from *Peanuts*. It was the nature of things that was scary—not anyone or anything with a face. Disillusionments and ambushes came aplenty, but none set by an enemy. Schulz enlarged his characters—and his readers' expectations of the funny pages—by sharply contrasting the very human littleness of Charlie Brown with the huge surrounding universe. Simultaneously, he recognized the phenomenal number of small things into which the big questions can be dissolved.

Before Lucy, the strip had been a brilliant ongoing marginal doodle; Schulz saw it as a "tiny world." Drawn in Colorado Springs at the edge of the Rockies, *Peanuts* gave a sense of America the way *Huckleberry Finn* does. Americans believe in friendship, in community, in fairness; but in the end, they are dominated by their apartness, their individual isolation—an isolation that went very deep in Schulz, in his new household, and in his characters, who turned from the disappointments dished out in the strip's fourth frame to look directly at the reader.

FROM HIS STUDIO AT the Golden Arrow Building, Sparky sought no companionship with other professionals, and though the arrangement there was "fairly pleasant," the circumstances were "lonely," especially at the lunch hour: "I did a lot of reading." He never did quite adjust to their new life and could find "no sense in us being there," especially not when, as he often told it, he and Joyce had moved out of St. Paul to keep from the neighbors the facts of Meredith's birth, and then Joyce had ended up in Colorado Springs telling the new neighbors that Meredith was adopted.

Isolated by their determined self-sufficiency, they never got out into the mountains or into the social swim of the town. Staying close to home, as Sparky preferred, he and Joyce were more likely to host neighborhood kids at a Halloween party in the garage—a tightly controlled set-piece production of pumpkin carving and apple bobbing—than to risk finding their way into adult friendships, either as individuals or as a couple. "It took us time to get acquainted," Sparky would say, for the truth was, much as he and Joyce might have liked to expand their circle, both felt more comfortable keeping to themselves. In fact, four months went by before they made their first friends in Colorado Springs, Philip and Louanne Van Pelt.

Philip, known as Fritz, had been the bugler in the Twentieth Armored Division's headquarters platoon, but Sparky did not know him when Fritz and his wife, Louanne, happened to pass Schulz one morning as he was in conversation with an acquaintance on the Golden Arrow Building stairway. He let Fritz go by, and that would have been the end of it. "You know how it is with guys outside your own platoon," observed Sparky to Frank Dieffenwierth. "We each thought we recognized something familiar about the other." But after the Van Pelts had continued up the stairway, Sparky went on talking, and "it took [Fritz] to turn around" and say "Twentieth Armored?" for Sparky to find his voice. "Wait for me at the top of the stairs," he replied with the suddenly recovered authority of Staff Sgt. Schulz.

Fritz, twenty-six, was now a schoolteacher in his first year at Whittier Elementary School, moonlighting as a jazz trumpeter; Louanne, twenty-two, was looking for a job, and an employment agency shared the building's second floor with Sparky's studio. The Van Pelts were an attractive, witty couple around whom laughter and conversation came easily. Midwesterners—from Mariemont, Ohio, on the Little Stonelick River—they, too, were newlyweds, renting an upstairs apartment near the mountains, still a few years away from their first child.

The Van Pelts were the happy exception to the Schulzes' mountain-town solitude. Joyce and Sparky hosted Lou and Fritz and their pet parakeet three and sometimes four nights a week for supper, including Joyce's specialty, pear halves in green Jell-O topped with a dollop of mayonnaise and grated cheddar cheese, followed by an evening of auction bridge to a background of Beethoven symphonies. Sparky and Joyce loved the game, a more permissible version of bridge for a devout Church of God believer and his wife. "They just went crazy for bridge," recalled Fritz. Playing as a couple, "they became very good at it," and although church doctrine proscribed contract bridge, they presented themselves in a 1952 newspaper profile as "bridge fanatics." Joyce remarked one evening that Sparky's religious convictions had certainly loosened up in Colorado Springs.

Not for long could he resist the forbidden version of the game, after which he invested in the latest books about bidding and play for himself and Joyce. On the endpapers of that bible of modern contract bridge, Ely Culbertson's *The New Gold Book*, Sparky recorded their joint ownership, inscribing their names and the date, February 1, 1952—an interesting time to consult and mark a games manual, for that was the day Monte was born.

Lucy's little brother first appeared in September 1952, remaining a toddler until well into 1955. He began as an experimental doodle—"this little character with some wild hair straggling down from the top of his head"—whom Schulz named, as he had Charlie Brown, for an Art Instruction colleague (this time, Linus Maurer), but also using the family name of his friends in Colorado Springs. "I thought the fact that his name began with the letter 'L' would help to fit it with Lucy's name," he later wrote to Fritz.

Linus Van Pelt would bring intellect, reflection, and a sublime self-possession to *Peanuts*, speaking with simplicity and force about literature, art, classical music, theology, medicine, psychiatry, sports, the law, and life itself. The perfect foil to Charlie Brown, whose early cockiness would steadily fall away to leave him the strip's Everyman, Linus employed a subtle sense of morality and ethics to probe such themes—taboo to a comic strip—as faith, intolerance, depression, and despair. For all Linus's abstract intellectuality, he was stunningly competent with his hands. While Lucy was struggling with a snowman or Charlie Brown with a sand castle, Linus could toss off a full-scale *tableau vivant* of Leutze's *Washington Crossing the Delaware*, or a sand fort as big as the Alamo.

He was Schulz's favorite character to draw. Starting his pen at the back of Linus's neck, his creator would bring it down and pull it across, the point fanning slightly to thicken the line as the marks leapt onto Linus's shirt. He took a special pride in his skill at drawing the hair in all its different angularities, and found that Linus was not just consistently "the most fun to work with," but also the most adaptable: "[He] can be very smart, he can be dumb, he can be innocent, he can be all knowing, he can have the blanket and be completely dependent upon it, but then again, you can take it away from him." To the end of his life he would say, "I still am searching for that wonderful pen line that comes down when you are drawing Linus . . . and the pen line is the best pen line you can make."

A NATURAL TENSION EXISTS in the comics medium between the ideas, usually gags, that fuel a strip and the drawing that gives it visual identity and makes it pleasing to the eye. Most cartoonists, driven by the market, rely more heavily on effectiveness of gag than on subtlety of pen line. *Peanuts* had both. With each character, Schulz established a visual device that enabled him to articulate universal truths that made the strip's ideas organic to the drawing and vice versa. For Schroeder it was the piano, for Linus the security blanket—a term that Fritz Van Pelt would later take credit for passing to Schulz, recalling a bridge night at the Bonneville bungalow when Meredith, then known as Mimi, was scuttling around with a toy rabbit to which she was devoted. Sparky took it from her and, as Fritz told the story, "treated her a little unmercifully"—hiding it altogether too thoroughly for her to find. Fritz was taking an extension course in psychology from the University of Colorado, where he had absorbed the groundbreaking ideas recently advanced by the English psychoanalyst D. W. Winnicott in his paper "Transitional Objects and Transitional Phenomena" (1951), which posited as universal the phenomenon of a child's "first 'not-me' possession." But Fritz added a deeper existential tone to the construction: "Sparky, you're messing with her security."

Schulz never agreed that Van Pelt had been the original source for the idea; yet in 1955 Winnicott himself requested permission to reprint one of Schulz's security-blanket strips. Fritz Van Pelt, smart, caustic, with a dry sense of humor and a fine-tuned appreciation for the art form, was constantly trying to give him ideas. "I was after Sparky to use more socko, boffo gags—vaudeville jokes—and he didn't want that at all. He ignored me."

"One of the reasons cartoonists suffer a lot is that as soon as they have a reputation they are bombarded with ideas by people at parties and dinners," Art Buchwald once noted. Indeed, "I've got a wonderful idea for a cartoon!" would be identified as a common American saying of the period. "The ideas are usually lousy," Buchwald added, "but the cartoonists have to pretend they're brilliant. If they tell the person who suggested it the truth, the person will retort, 'I knew you were a sonofabitch . . .' "

Schulz repeatedly declared that he hated receiving suggestions, always replying, "That's good. Why don't you draw it up yourself, and send it in?"

"I hate to tell people, 'That's a lousy idea.' But I have to kind of weasel my way around it. All my friends know that I never take anybody else's idea. And I never take suggestions. And most of the time, if they say, 'Say, I got something funny,' I say, 'Don't tell me, because if you tell me, I'm not going to use it.' "

To himself he would think but never say aloud, "This is the only thing I can do, so let me do it." He explained, "When I have something that I know is good I feel wonderful. I have a good time doing it, I enjoy the drawing, I enjoy making every little line as perfect as I possibly can and I'm very proud of *a lot* of the ideas that I think of; and as I'm drawing them I'm thinking what a great idea this is, and I'm so proud of the fact that *I* thought of it and nobody else thought of it."

Over fifty years, he insisted that he only ever took one idea from a reader, a man in Florida, who wrote: "I had a funny thing happen with my little girl the other night. I was teaching her how to count, and I was showing her a book. And I said, 'See all the sailboats on this page? Now how many do you see?' And she says, 'All of them.' "

He never allowed more than "one" idea. His closest friends and colleagues—even Joyce—over the years would each be able to point to a single strip that contained a punch line that had first appeared on his or her own lips. Even though they could identify and show their own hands in the making of a number of strips, they loyally submitted to Sparky's program by limiting themselves to an assertion of one credit per head. Joyce's one idea came when she "inadvertently mentioned" in February 1951 that "birthdays should be retroactive." It's easy to imagine how the notion came up; Joyce's birthday would have been a few months past when she first met Sparky, and by February 1951 they were engaged; thus, he had "missed" the magic moment. Why not give Joyce a present now—*retroactively*?

Always he would make light of this one acquisition, teasing especially those friends, like Fritz Van Pelt, who routinely peppered him with suggestions, by sarcastically inscribing the original of the "one" honorary strip to "Fritz, my good friend, who gives me all those great ideas." "If you get any more ideas, send them to Walt Kelly," he would add. Or to a friend in later life, Clayton Anderson, "who gives me all my best ideas—Like one in thirty-five years."

Despite his stiff-arming of Fritz Van Pelt, he made a lifelong habit of keeping his ears open when friends came over for dinner. Anderson noticed that Sparky would appropriate a funny line if it dropped from a story, as when Anderson related how he had gotten poison oak while walking through the woods near the Pebble Beach golf course hunting for lost balls to sell. Sparky asked if he had made any money. "Just enough to pay for the poison oak shots," sighed Anderson.

Schulz questioned friends closely over the course of the most casual lunches or dinners. "I like to get people started talking, and probe them gently with questions to see what makes them tick. Some of my best lines—or perhaps I should say the strip's best lines—are the result of these conversations." "He got his ideas from everything around him," recalled an editor at the syndicate, "but I never acknowledged that he did that: It had to be his."

Meredith's "one" idea was that snow comes up from the ground:

But the story changed as the kids grew up. He was deadly serious on the subject and sometimes he maintained that his children had "never been the inspiration for my characters." Sometimes they had contributed only one idea each: Meredith, the concept of being a "fussbudget"; Monte, the Red Baron; Amy, the one-off strip "Am I buttering too loudly for you?"; Craig, the character of Joe Cool; Jill, the idea that if you hold your hands upside down, you get the opposite of what you pray for. Sometimes he told reporters that three of the five Schulz kids had dragged around blankets, "so I decided to give Linus one"; other times only two of them had. Sometimes Meredith had merely gone through "a stage" as a fussbudget; it had not been part of her permanent character. Sometimes he kidded about it all: "In thirty-two years, they only gave me six ideas."

By 1980, Schulz could finally discuss the possibility of his having drawn on his children for inspiration: "I may have borrowed a few ideas from my own children when they were small, but now that they are grown, I no longer have the opportunity. I don't mean that I actually stole specific ideas from them, but I did borrow broad themes such as Linus and his security blanket and Lucy being a fussbudget."

Yet later the same year he said, "Very little of what my children do has gone into the strip."

He wanted to be sure that people knew that the strip was his and his alone. "Far more of the strip depends on my own observations and memories than it does on the actual present-day experiences in my family."

Instead of binding himself to friends and family and associates through these transactions, he kept himself and his work at a safe distance. In the first flush of *Peanuts*' popular appeal in the '50s, when the press reported that readers of the strip who also knew the Schulz family "seem to see the Schulz children depicted as characters," Sparky heaved a sigh: "It isn't that easy," he told a reporter in 1956. "However I do use more actual incidents since the birth of the kids; direct quotations and adaptations. Most of these things I could never have done before I was married."

But even as he invested the evolving relationships between Charlie Brown and Lucy, and between Lucy and Schroeder, with the emotional difficulties of his marriage, he insisted that Joyce was giving him nothing. He maintained with equal firmness that he would "*never*" model any characters after people he knew, but without explaining why an alert cartoonist would not derive material from the lives around his own, indeed from the whole world, and at the same time acknowledging just as firmly that the entire population of *Peanuts* exhibited his own traits and characteristics.

He gave his wishy-washiness and determination to Charlie Brown, the "worst side of himself" to Violet, to Lucy his sarcasm, to Linus his dignity and "weird little thoughts," his perfectionism and devotion to his art to Schroeder, his sense of being talented and unappreciated to Snoopy. "I am completely at home with all the characters," he told Dieffenwierth that September 1951, "and can get as sarcastic as I wish, which gives me a sublimation for my desires, the necessary thing according to the now popular psychiatrists. (That's hard to spell when your [sic] not very intelligent.)"

As publicity for the strip became a more regular part of his life, the syndicate would warn him against identifying any character too closely with a living person who might make a legal claim. Even among friends—and even during *Peanuts'* first relatively modest years—proud, personal assertions were made, none more often than those of Charlie Francis Brown, whose name Schulz had borrowed at Art Instruction. The real-life Charlie Brown saw "so much of Charlie Brown in himself" that he found it hard to separate his own fate from that of his fictional counterpart and spent the rest of his life alternately attaching himself to and distancing himself from his comic page proxy.

In the 1960s, *Peanuts* would become so pervasive, Charlie Brown so supreme a figure in the culture's folklore—and Schulz, his creator, so quiet a voice at the very peak of *Peanuts'* fame—that a vacuum was created into which "the real" Charlie Brown could naturally step as a kind of media spokesman. At intervals of five and ten years, newspaper and magazine editors kept perfect time with the anniversaries of *Peanuts*, and whenever they could find "the real Charlie Brown" in his latest incarnation—as a social worker, as a program director at a juvenile detention center, and as a "sandy-haired bachelor"—they ran long, gratifying profiles. Brown also appeared on local television talk shows as "the real Charlie Brown," and on the syndicated game show *To Tell the Truth*, where he stumped the panel, although, true to form, he turned triumph into rejection, lamenting, "No one picked me."

Eventually he wrote his autobiography, an Augustinian-style confession and atonement, entitled *Me and Charlie Brown: A Book of Good Griefs*, which he narrated in the third person, making it difficult for the reader to know which Charlie Brown was which. He proposed to complicate the story further by bringing Schulz into the project to illustrate "Charlie Brown's" text with freshly drawn cartoons of "the 3 Charlies" holding hands. Charlie Brown, wrote Charlie F. Brown, was "our name now."

Schulz, however, did not participate, for he had chosen to remain as opaque as possible whenever he was asked if his characters were patterned on living people. He dismissed as "complete nonsense" the reports that Charlie F. Brown was the model for Charlie Brown, and he was appalled to read an article that referred to *his* comic strip character as Charlie Francis Brown's "clone." He always maintained that the only thing he borrowed from Charlie F. Brown was his first and last names and their indivisibility—"I regarded Charlie Brown as too good a friend ever to play on him in any other way." The rest belonged exclusively to the comic strip and his own pen.

But as Charlie F. Brown struggled with a variety of Charlie Brown–like misfortunes, including loneliness, romantic rejection, and a chronic wish to be liked, his personal confusion over the un-Charlie-Brown-like problems of sexual identity, alcoholism, and manic depression mounted to the point where Charlie F. Brown began to believe that his own life was somehow a part of Schulz's psyche. Once, at a party, inebriated, consumed by hunger, Charlie F. Brown grabbed what he believed to be a jar of nuts from a table and devoured a handful. The jar turned out to contain his hostess's dry cat food. Later, he would remember coming across a new *Peanuts* strip in which an angry voice says, "Charlie Brown, you don't even know the difference between dog food and cat food." In fact, no such strip exists; Charlie Brown, all out of dog food, serves cat food to Snoopy on several occasions, and even tricks Snoopy into thinking that Snoopy is eating cat food, but no voice ever remonstrates with Charlie Brown about dog or cat food. Charlie F. Brown nevertheless believed himself a conduit to the imaginary world. "I've never told Schulz about it," he said after the cat food incident at the party, "but you can almost see something psychic going on."

Into the 1970s, scarred by various episodes of mental illness, or what the newspaper profiles about him called "painful realities," he attempted suicide, later making a "Charlie Brown"–style confession of each struggle in his autobiography: He tried a rope in the laundry room but the knot came apart. He tried the car and a closed door in the garage but forgot to check the gas gauge and woke up with a headache and an empty gas tank . . .

But in the beginning Charlie Francis Brown's claims to Charlie Brown seemed purely lighthearted. In the Educational Department in the mid–1950s, for example, as a colleague's birthday card went around the room, Brown drew Schulz's Charlie Brown with a cartoon balloon saying "Madame Bovary!" thus staking his claim by reapplying "*Madame Bovary, c'est moi,*" Flaubert's classic statement of the artist's identification with his fictional creation. Indeed, Brown would seize every chance he got to remind Schulz—and others—that, in effect, "Charlie Brown, *c'est moi!*"

Sparky, in his turn, would never stop feeling the need to counter-claim: "This is me in the strip, absolutely me . . . I am all of the characters because everything that I am goes into the strip . . ."

Again and again, he presented himself to the public on these terms: born into the world as "just an ordinary person from the Midwest," but possessed of intelligence and native talent, which he had the wit and will to harness, he had come to intuit his destiny at an early age. No one in his upbringing had the vision or sensitivity to grasp the extraordinary nature of his quest—except for his silent sidekick, a wildly uncontrollable dog. Offstage, meanwhile, his loving yet intellectually disadvantaged parents could provide a secure home and moderate support for a dream they could not grasp, but could offer nothing more to its fulfillment than uncompre-hending practical advice and a leg up to correspondence education.

From then on, the story of his development finds no one but himself meaningfully present. As he told it, he took nothing from anyone; no more than one measly idea that worked to the fulfillment of his dream had come from any one particular human being. Loneliness gave him his first lessons in the elations and regrets of the artist; his mother's early death and the world's incapacity to notice his pain taught him the rest. But, always—and always from the very beginning of his time on earth—he alone had known what he was going to do; he alone understood, as part of the framework of his life, that he would succeed. There would be doubters who tried to deflect him from his goal, but in the end he would have the last word, and all along the way he would contend that every single word, every single deceptively simple penstroke in every single hard-thought-out frame, was his and his alone.

He knew full well that if *Peanuts* caught on he would be drawing these panels for the rest of his life. He had resolved never to depend on a col-laborator or assistant. Every future installment of *Peanuts* would be his own exclusive refinement of the original vision. Every idea for every strip would be his because, as he never stopped believing, the strip was all that he had, all that he truly was.

SPARKY AND JOYCE'S INITIAL isolation persisted past the first mountain win-ter, despite the Colorado Van Pelts. To Sparky, it was Needles all over again, only with better weather: "Colorado Springs was a pretty lonely place for us." And: "There was a feeling of temporary [living] there." And further: "I'm surprised I survived that period, really."

But the old mountain resort was not without its appeal—horse shows and rodeos for Joyce, golf tournaments on the famous Broadmoor Golf Course for Sparky, skating and a summer ice carnival at the Broadmoor Ice Palace for them both; among the many Minnesota-style attractions were the Pikes Peak Winter Festival, one of the country's top winter sports events, which included the National Indoor Speed Skating Championships and National Collegiate Ice Hockey Championships. "I suppose if we [had] hung on for another six months," Sparky reflected, "the possibility exists we would still be there." He later told Fritz Van Pelt that he wished he could have stayed. But he resisted growing in their new life; as always, he wanted to go back.

Whereas Sparky and his father had cried at their parting in St. Paul, Joyce's father had wished them happily on their journey, "delighted to see [the newlyweds] break away from home ties." To Henry Halverson, it had been "a very great satisfaction" when Joyce announced that she and Sparky were going to move to Colorado Springs. He would have liked to watch his grandchildren grow up, but he declared himself "far more interested in knowing that my little daughter and the new son are setting out right for a long and happy married life together."

He acknowledged that "the hardest thing for some people is to mature—to become adult. Childhood allows dependence upon parents"— a dependence that Sparky was still very much in the grip of, as Henry had surmised. Whereas Joyce, in Henry's analysis, had been "subject to [the] domination" of her parents and older sisters, leaving her "consciously or unconsciously [to] resent authority," Sparky was "an only child, and almost invariably an only child learns to depend on parents and be directed by them and [to have] his wants and desires satisfied by them. . . . Often an only child has been so protected at home that he or she is actually hesitant or even timid about facing the problems of the world alone. Even meeting new people becomes a chore."

Henry warned Joyce and Sparky against the dangers of relinquishing their newfound Western self-reliance in order to move back to Minnesota. Alone together in Colorado, they would be forced to mature, and, as stronger adults, they would come to understand each other better, to establish a spiritual and intellectual companionship, "and most important,"

Henry concluded, "you will never be lonely [as a couple alone together]." He ended this "epistle" by predicting that, once back in the Northwest, Joyce's well-founded resentments of authority would naturally reawaken: "I hope you stay there. If you don't, welcome back. Decide thoughtfully and wisely. Follow the hard path if it is wise. Don't try to escape from reality, from the harder things of life, by trying to 'escape.'"

In the end, Sparky's uneasiness made the difference, and on March 5, 1952, only nine months after they had arrived, he announced to John Selby at Rinehart, "In about two weeks my family and I will be moving back to good ol' Minnesota." Whatever the empiric truth of this sudden about-face, Joyce later told her children, with a force that made it a family legend, that the Schulzes went home to the Twin Cities because Sparky "couldn't handle being away from his dad."

As they decamped from Bonneville, they had not yet decided where to live in the Cities, so he gave out the address of his father's barbershop as his next mail drop. Packing up Joyce's Wurlitzer spinet, they ran afoul of a Colorado law that forbade any piece of furniture still covered by a payment plan to be taken out of the state. Sparky asked to borrow $300 from Fritz Van Pelt to settle the remaining payments, and Fritz said he would find it somehow, but then discovered that Sparky had only been testing him—as he would now so often test his friends to see if money or fame had changed the compact of ordinariness he maintained in all his relationships. For barely had Sparky asked than he explained that he didn't need the money: "I just wanted to see what you would say, and I was very gratified."

They were home in "good ol' Minnesota" three weeks shy of their first wedding anniversary. "I think I'll stay right [here]," wrote Schulz. "I like to see the seasons change and don't mind cold weather."

They moved into a simple two-bedroom ranch house at 5521 Oliver Avenue South, in Minneapolis, but by August they were ready—and could now afford—to move again. "Security is owning your own home," he wrote a decade later, but behind the formula was a truth.

Back when he bought his 1950 Ford, Sparky had admitted to one of his cousins that, above all else, he hoped he would be able to pay for it. At the same time, as he mused about his future, he declared that he would ultimately consider himself successful if he could ever make $100,000 a year—at a time when a "$10,000-a-year man" was a big success and $100,000 was the salary of the president of a large bank. Within seven years of setting this goal, there would be just 235 business executives in the entire United States who earned more than $100,000. "I was," he later realized, "unbelievably determined and ambitious."

The twenty-nine-year-old Sparky Schulz had come home to make money—"a lot of money."

Both he and Joyce had been brought up in households where pancakes had been served for dinner during hard times. They moved to Wentworth Avenue South, buying a two-story colonial in a neighborhood of bungalows, with a lawn out front, a yard in back, and a two-car garage that was the envy of their church group. "I always wanted," he would say that August of 1952, "a yard big enough for croquet in the summer and skating in the winter."

# CHAPTER 16

# PEANUTS, INC.

*If you give your customers fair treatment, friendly service, and good merchandise, they will remain your customers.*
—CARL F. SCHULZ

AT ART INSTRUCTION, INC., Schulz was welcomed as a returning hero and given plenty of breathing space. "These were happy days for me," he said later, "for I was back with my old friends and in the midst of those invigorating surroundings."

Now that he was an established cartoonist, the Buckbees, the conservative Baptist family that co-owned and administered the company, made him a member of the advisory board and assigned him a special studio atop the Bureau of Engraving, "a wonderful little room" that his Educational Department colleagues called "the Penthouse," as much for its position on the roof as in teasing recognition of Sparky's new status as the one among them who had gotten within reaching distance of the top.

His success had earned him an only child's preferred status within the company, including an exemption from the daily grind of the envelopes; its full scope would eventually write the most glorious chapter in the school's history—a "real-life success story," as Art Instruction's quarterly magazine would bill it, noting with satisfaction even as early as 1954 that Schulz "enjoys a larger yearly income than our cabinet members in Washington, D.C." The owners went so far as to groom Schulz to become an officer of the company, but he declined, preferring, he said, to concentrate on the strip.

He was already thinking about additional features, an action strip and a bridge strip, and when Jim Sasseville came back from nineteen months of active duty in the navy, they collaborated on fourteen trial episodes of *Joe Cipher*, an adventure story that Sasseville, with his clean pen line, had begun to develop in the manner of Roy Crane's *Captain Easy*. Schulz had long admired his colleague's confidently loose style, but was now doubly impressed by Jim's ability to draw chaste but sexy young women—the sort of cleaned-up girlie cartoon that Dena had urged him to sell as a beginner, forever shutting him down on "spicy gals." It was common in that era for cartoonists to collaborate, especially when the team comprised one established artist who would write and one still aspiring who would draw; Al Capp and the lesser-known Bob Lubbers, who penned *Tarzan* for United Feature and had a talent for drawing luscious women, were just starting such a strip (*Long Sam*) with United Feature. So Sparky proposed to pick up the writing and leave the drawing to Sasseville, for whom he would make the necessary introductions.

The proposal was met with an unequivocal NO! Harry Gilburt meanwhile advised Sparky directly: "Please don't attempt it if it cuts into *Peanuts*, my first love."

HE FELT CAPABLE OF anything—and so, it seemed, did the country. As the Eisenhower years got into quiet, steady gear, almost everyone appeared more prosperous than ever before. To his intense surprise, *Peanuts* showed signs of taking off. "The sales have been looking good lately," he wrote Harry Gilburt in September 1954. "At least the monthly check sure is adequate." His per-month share of profits had jumped to $2,500—at a time when the *annual* earnings of a middle-income family were $4,000. "That's an awful lot of money for someone who was only a staff sergeant," he added. The syndicate, moreover, expected his earnings to increase "substantially" each year; indeed, by 1956 Schulz was bringing home $4,000 a month, a milestone marked by a photograph in *The Saturday Evening Post* showing Sparky in his father's chair at the Family Barber Shop "as they gaze fondly" at one of the freshly cut checks. Only ten years had passed since *Life* magazine had pictured Frank King's weekly $1,000 paycheck and the men in his father's shop had waved away Sparky's boyish dreams.

Now, the big money was fighting over him. One morning in 1954, with more than a year before his contract with United Feature Syndicate was to run out, Sylvan Byck, comics editor of Hearst's King Features, telephoned Schulz and dangled before him some of the funnies' biggest names—*Krazy Kat, Barney Google, The Katzenjammer Kids, Popeye, Blondie,*

*Prince Valiant*—the very pantheon under which Schulz had grown up. In 1950, King Features had added *Beetle Bailey*, the new strip about army life by Schulz's popular rival, Mort Walker, who had been handpicked in a final display of prescience by none other than Old Man Hearst himself.

Would Schulz be interested in "severing relations" with United Feature and joining King? Byck promised a better deal than Schulz's current fifty-fifty split, and hinted at the probability of his coming to own the actual copyright to *Peanuts*—a tempting offer, for by jumping ship and gaining full rights over his work he would change the future and fortunes of *Peanuts* at the stroke of a pen. But Sparky did not for a moment hesitate to tell Byck that he "liked the way the feature was being handled" and "had no thought or intention of trying to do anything about his contract."

On a recent visit to the syndicate's offices in New York, he came away with a new sense of attachment. He had grown fond of the syndicate's people, none more than its vice president, Larry Rutman, who treated him, Schulz would always say, like a son. He wasted no time before reporting King Features' maneuver to Rutman and pledging his loyalty: "I now feel like I am working with a group of friends rather than with an organization."

The very next week, Harry Gilburt wrote to say that he had placed *Peanuts*, both daily strip and Sunday page, with the Santa Ana (California) *Register* and the Amarillo *News*, while the editor of the Denver *Rocky Mountain News* had authorized offering the feature to the Laramie (Wyoming) *Republican-Boomerang*, deep in *News* territory. "Judging by the call you had from King Features," Gilburt went on, "your popularity is spreading, but not fast enough to suit us. So we are pushing *Peanuts* that much harder worldwide."

Over the next four years the syndicate sold *Peanuts* to dozens of foreign and English-language newspapers, from the United States Occupation Zone in Germany, to American-occupied Okinawa, to Saigon. A batch of proof sheets was flown weekly out of San Francisco to the navy task force at Amundsen-Scott Station at the South Pole, and a Spanish translation sold well in Latin American countries under the name *Carlitos*—"Charlie."

The strip also took hold on American campuses, often sponsored by student petitions to the editors of the college newspaper. In May 1953, *Pea-*

*nuts* replaced *Li'l Abner* as the featured comic in the Cornell University *Daily Sun*, although Schulz still trailed Al Capp in a popularity poll. By 1956, he had pulled even with Walt Kelly in the eyes of eighteen thousand students at the University of Texas. In 1957, while on one coast, *Peanuts* characters appeared on stunt cards during the halftime presentation at the University of Southern California's homecoming football game, on the other, the Rhode Island School of Design Museum of Art mounted sixty-five originals in a ten-day exhibition alongside a collection of Picasso graphics—the first of its kind for Schulz's work, although anything but the last. A year later, the thirty-six members of the editorial board of Yale's monthly *Record* designated him Humorist of the Year, in apostolic succession to S. J. Perelman, Ogden Nash, Al Capp, Charles Addams, Walt Kelly, and Steve Allen.

College textbooks laid claim to *Peanuts*, appropriating the strip as no cartoon had been before, to illustrate themes as various as empathy, receptivity to new ideas, and "the characteristic sin of our culture . . . the horror of standing out—of being one's self." In November 1956, the director of psychological research at the Kaiser Foundation Medical Center in Oakland, California, asked permission to reprint in a forthcoming book on personality assessment a strip that illustrated a common psychological phenomenon: "the tendency to say one thing about oneself and to act in a way which may be quite different."

"This cartoon presents a masterful illustration of a psychological device which I have discussed in a pedantic and scientific manner," conceded Dr. Timothy Leary. Then only four years away from his Harvard-sponsored "Study of Clinical Reactions to Psilocybin Administered in Supportive Environments," the future "grand shaman of psychedelia" could still believe that Schulz's "witty and wise creations" were the only extra ingredients needed to "enlighten" the reader.

The moment when Charlie Brown became a national symbol—an Everyman who gains strength by admitting in his confrontations with the self that the most one can do is the best one can do with what one has—can probably be triangulated from certain entries on Schulz's 1954 desk calendar, but nowhere more clearly than the strip itself for Monday, February 1: Charlie Brown, dropping in on Shermy, looks bereft as his smiling friend, apparently unaware of his visitor, loses himself in a model train set whose tracks spread so Union-Pacifically far and wide across the living room that the railroad's complete dimensions cannot be shown in a single panel. Charlie Brown pulls on his coat and walks home to sit down alone in his own living room beside his own characteristically modest branch line: a single, closed circle of track, no bigger than a man-hole cover.

But no rage boils up, no self-pity spills over; no tears are shed, no punch line squeezed out—just silent endurance.

*Peanuts* spoke directly to a student generation absorbed in irony and tension, paradox and ambiguity. When Charlie Brown first confessed, "I don't feel the way I'm supposed to feel," he spoke for Eisenhower's America, especially for that generation of solemn, cynical college students—the last to grow up, as Schulz and his contemporaries had, without television, who read Charlie Brown's utterances as existential statements about the human condition.

"Someday," predicted a young public relations man named Gene Shalit, in a May 1957 fan letter, "people are going to talk about these daily doings in tones of awe, as they do now about *Krazy Kat.*"

AMONG HIS FELLOW CARTOONISTS, Sparky was still the odd man out. *Beetle Bailey* had debuted a month before *Peanuts*; Hank Ketcham unleashed *Dennis the Menace* only a few months later. Both strips grew faster than *Peanuts*, causing Sparky "great consternation in those lean early years." He envied both men the integrity of their strips' titles, especially Ketcham's shrewdly rhyming *Dennis*, which Schulz suspected "helped to sell some newspapers."

He hoped for a bid from the National Cartoonists Society, the clannish organization that met in New York City, at which Sparky could still dare to rub elbows with those childhood idols Roy Crane, Harold Foster, and Rube Goldberg, whose cartoons he remembered first glimpsing on his father's lap. But when Mort Walker had put Schulz up for membership in 1950, Otto Soglow, the *New Yorker* cartoonist serving as chairman of the membership committee, rejected his candidacy on two counts: Walker could not sponsor a man he did not know personally (Walker and Schulz had only exchanged a letter or two), and, besides, candidates needed two additional endorsements. Schulz had no other friends or acquaintances in the club.

At first glance Walker and Schulz seemed to have much in common. Both were dedicated to cartooning; they had launched syndicated strips that would become their life's work within a month of each other. Each, if in very different ways, was a typical product of the GI generation; both achieved success in and because of the changes in the postwar world. In their midwestern childhoods the comic strip had been the country's sole mass-market entertainment medium. Then in the '30s and '40s came the challenges of radio and the movies; now, in the '50s, television would give the tiny square its most serious competition yet, offering a full adventure story in half an hour. Comics editors saw less and less need for lushly drawn adventure strips that required the reader's studied attention.

What *Peanuts*, with its spare rendering and ever-widening cycle of small incidents, and *Beetle Bailey*, with its simple, abstracted human forms and elastic visual exaggerations, shared with great success was a reassertion of line as the artist's expression of authority against the visual and verbal allure of television. Their creators, however, could not have been more different. Walker was socially confident, gregarious, "instantly friendly"—a professional "funny man" and clubby drinker who liked to trade off-color jokes with his fellow penmen or to tell how one of them had pulled an editor's leg by imposing a trick nude-girl overlay onto a weekly submission. "Childish perhaps, but a certain amount of childishness is necessary to be in this business," he contended.

He later recalled feeling sorry for Schulz. "Even to me, a hayseed from Missouri, Schulz seemed naïve—a hayseed's hayseed. . . . I never would have figured him as the most likely to succeed." And yet he argued to Soglow that the National Cartoonists Society was not a social club but rather a professional association, and therefore, if Schulz was making his living drawing comics, "you can't keep him out." Before a year had passed, the society's Old Guard admitted him.

Monthly meetings of the Cartoonists Society, held at the Lambs Club in Times Square, were still old-fashioned stag affairs gleefully featuring belly dancers, nude models, cigars, highballs, martinis, and champagne prizes for "best nude sketches." "There have been no major scandals," one observer reported in 1959, "but the general level of mischief has been high, and the banshee might rightly be considered a cartoonist's muse."

Sparky had no use for jolly jokers at banshee luncheons—or for *Beetle Bailey*'s antic, gag-a-day view of army life. Walker had made the cruelty of army life sweet and eccentric: after a braining by Sarge, Beetle is left as a formless puddle, yet we know that overnight he will reappear full-bodied and unscathed. Walker allowed Beetle to become incorporeal—to come out of his skin and avoid the pain. Schulz drew Charlie Brown absorbing internally (therefore far more threateningly) the attacks of his most bullying, brutal character, Violet. Charlie Brown must absorb the blows without falling apart.

For Schulz, the art of cartooning was "a deadly serious business." He deplored the joy-buzzer style in American humor and abominated cartoonists who drew their characters to overreact to punch lines. "I'm a great believer in the mild in cartooning," he often repeated. In the years since syndication, Sparky had left behind not just gag cartoons but gags in their crudest forms. Drinking, a traditional storehouse of stock "laffs," never became part of Schulz's life or work, although it was integral down to the technique Walker had devised for developing gags for *Beetle Bailey*. To find his way to a punch line, Walker once explained, he would simply imagine himself at a cocktail party, the kind at which bons mots and witticisms flowed spontaneously. Asked what made Schulz different from other cartoonists in the club, Walker replied, "He didn't drink. That separated him from the group I was in."

The truthfulness of children had given *Peanuts* its earliest dominant tone and made Schulz representative of a then still-subversive trend in the culture. "Even in this happy-ending nation, Schulz's strip rarely ends happily," noted *The Saturday Evening Post*. *Peanuts* was not just "full of kids and kidding," as its earliest marketing put it, but because of its subtlety and apparent mildness, it "sort of snuck up on us," Shel Dorf recalled. "This little three seconds that we had reading Schulz every day was a little amusing, gentle, or even a little cruel."

"Aren't all kids egotists? And brutal?" Schulz asked, acknowledging in 1964 that "maybe I have the cruelest strip going." It was the same cruelty that was deeply embedded in the Minnesota world from which Schulz sprang; an anonymous author in Garrison Keillor's fictional Lake Wobegon, taking account of the traits his parents have taught him, lodges ninety-five complaints about his Lutheran upbringing, including: "I say vicious things to people's faces and then explain that I was kidding."

Sparky was frequently critical toward the New York cartoonists. Consumed with petty dislikes and harsh judgments—a "no-nonsense man of many peeves," as the wife of one cartoonist later characterized him—he especially resented it when colleagues suggested that he join them for a drink when he came to town. Alcohol became the focus of his contempt even when Dr. Frances R. Horwich of Chicago, known to millions of preschoolers as Miss Frances of television's *Ding Dong School*, hoped that he might "have time to have a cocktail." Schulz's response—indeed, reproof—to such invitations was curt and sometimes indignant. "It doesn't seem to occur to some people," he would say, in the mildest of mild-mannered voices, "that I wouldn't want a drink. And I *wouldn't*."

In such situations, he was invariably asked, "Why not?" These were the years, after all, when "Let's have a drink," was common social and business currency. At least once, intending sarcasm, or what, later, for the record, he recast as "sly humor," he answered, "I'm a religious fanatic."

Not surprisingly, some of Schulz's fellow cartoonists explained his abstention from drink, tobacco, and swearing as part of the moral arsenal he had taken up from fundamentalist Christianity. In fact, he refrained from alcohol and tobacco and profanity for strict, but highly independent, motives, which stemmed not from religious law or doctrine, as people invariably assumed, but from a lifelong fear that he would lose control to a habit, as had his mother's relatives.

He brought the same unending intensity to his hurts and grudges, especially to the certainty of being passed over. Each year, the National Cartoonists Society awarded its trophy to the year's outstanding practitioner at a banquet—a bronze cast statuette, designed by Rube Goldberg, featuring four contorted cartoon figures beneath an ink bottle. Another of Schulz's heroes, Roy Crane, had won the Reuben in 1950; the following year, it went to Walt Kelly. In 1952, Hank Ketcham was honored—*Dennis the Menace* had been an instant hit. Next year, Mort Walker and *Beetle Bailey* were on top. In 1954, Walker and other members "thought Schulz was next in line," and the word got out. He came east by train for the spring gathering. The moment of presentation arrived. Rube Goldberg stepped to the podium, eponymous trophy in hand. Schulz and Walker were at the same table. "He was all excited, thinking he was going to win," recalled Walker. And then the grail was passed to a sports cartoonist, Willard Mullin. "He just got up and left," Walker went on. "He didn't say anything, didn't say goodbye. He was out of there." Back in Minneapolis, he complained to a fellow cartoonist that he had been treated like "someone's poor relative." As he had done with his own disparaging kinfolk, he vowed to settle the score.

Many of the profession's Old Guard could not at first see *Peanuts* as anything but an oddity. "No one knew what it was or whether Schulz would be a flash in the pan," reflected one of the National Cartoonists Society's historians. Even contemporaries did not completely understand what he was up to. "His work puzzled me in the beginning because he didn't have any gags," Walker later admitted. "He was doing something different, and it was hard to understand. I'd read *Peanuts* some days and at the end it was just 'Sigh.' I'd think, 'That's not a gag line. What's he doing?' "

The last thing the cartoonists were clear about was the man himself. "Schulz defies all tradition," wrote a comics historian in 1959, going on to sum up his "defiance" in three sentences: "He does not drink. He does not smoke. He does not swear, even at syndicate editors." In a profession "crowded with screwballs and eccentrics," Schulz was seen as "a paragon," with "no eccentricities, no neuroses, no seething hatreds beneath the calm exterior." *The Christian Science Monitor* insisted that "the worst side of Mr. Schulz, you feel quite certain, must be so completely pleasant that you wouldn't mind changing bad sides with him at all."

As he had kept his aggressive side concealed from teammates in sports and games, he hid his ambition from colleagues. But Walker correctly saw that Schulz "was competitive with everyone." Or, as another colleague saw it: "His sights were set on being great. One of his mantras was: *Be the best.* He was a merciless competitor. He gave no quarter."

At Art Instruction, old friends like Charlie F. Brown had noticed the scope of Sparky's ambition, his "great desire" and "enormous drive" and "rush to success"—all of it, in Brown's eyes, "akin to an obsession," and partly understandable on those terms, especially at a time when, as George

Letness recalled, "We didn't talk about the inner feelings of people; we discussed art."

Brown detected the cold, untrusting side of Schulz, which flared whenever Sparky's inner workings were exposed to view. When, after receiving yet another rejection from one of the professional markets, he announced to the entire Educational Department that he, Charlie Brown, was giving up his "cartoonist career," Brown recalled that Sparky's reply was, "Good. That will make one less cartoonist I will have to compete with."

Brown took this as uncalled-for callousness from a friend, but still excused Sparky without challenge, seeking to put the most positive possible construction upon the snap: "I think he meant to spur me on, but his reaction only leadened my defeat." On the one hand, Schulz was paying Charlie Brown the compliment of treating him as a possible competitor. On the other hand, he knew how insecure Charlie Brown was and how vulnerable he was to rejection, as he himself had always been, but now had less and less often to endure as he rode his success.

His inability to acknowledge the scope of his ambition or to accept responsibility for the pain he gave others are double-helix themes that run through the postmortem recollections of Schulz's colleagues, business associates, family, and friends: "Sparky could be so insensitive sometimes." "He would never say 'I'm sorry.'" "He was never one to apologize."

Increasingly hidden over time by the scale of his success and the corresponding protectiveness and rationalizations of well-meaning, or perhaps just dazzled, friends and business associates, he himself would come to acknowledge that he continually wrestled "with something dark and unloving."

"Melancholy is the best word to describe it," he once said. "I've always been lonely." And he often pointed out that a comic strip was an ideal medium for revealing that "we are all made up of contradictions," because in comics "you are not required to be consistent—you can say anything you think of, even if there are contradictions."

Cartooning allowed him to harness his melancholy as the alternative to exploring what was making him so mad or, more pertinently, confronting what was hurting him.

SCHULZ ALWAYS INSISTED THAT he was "an uncomplicated man with ordinary interests," who had "no head for business," claiming that every opportunity to market his work had "[come] along by accident" and that any financial rewards had been "unplanned, unsought, and mostly peripheral" to the real work of drawing a comic strip.

But to read his business correspondence in the mid-1950s is to see how closely he collaborated (though never by modifying his subject matter) with the executives and salesmen at United Feature Syndicate to build the strip's circulation. "I have rejoiced with each new reported sale of *Peanuts*, and have appreciated your taking the time to write to me about them," he told Harry Gilburt. The correspondence also reveals how hard he worked to please advertisers and marketers, manufacturers and entrepreneurs, national magazine editors and corporate promotion managers, answering every request in the same cheerful, crisp, sometimes sardonic, sometimes ironic way.

Every couple of weeks, as Gilburt traveled from coast to coast, hawking *Peanuts* and reporting back to Schulz every new outlet no matter how small or large ("You'll have to learn the names of a great many small newspapers if you hope to keep up with me"), the two put their heads together by mail or telephone to devise tactics to flatter those editors who were "still dubious," such as at the Saratoga Springs *Saratogian*, where the managing editor admired *Peanuts*—his children also liked the strip—but "his wife doesn't" reported Gilburt. "We've got to get her eating out of your hand, too."

The *Los Angeles Times* started publishing *Peanuts* on Sunday, March 13, 1955, Gilburt proudly telling Sparky, "It looks good between two busier comics." The Reidsville (North Carolina) *Review* sent in an order to commence publication on Monday, April 4, and the *New Orleans States-Item* took up the strip on Sunday, April 10; the Tacoma *Tribune* became a subscriber as of Sunday, April 24; the *Dallas Morning News* and the *Fort Worth Press* unexpectedly made room for the daily in May; and, on Sunday, June 12, thirteen new clients came onboard, including the *Poughkeepsie New Yorker*, the Ada (Oklahoma) *News*, the Gallup (New Mexico) *Independent*, the Oregon City (Oregon) *Enterprise-Courier*, and the Pampa (Texas) *Spokesman*, which joined the list at weekly rates of $9.60, $4.36, $1.49, and $5.75, respectively. Gilburt was especially pleased with a deal he had struck to publish *Peanuts* on Sundays in the *New York Herald Tribune* at $35 a week, "with a good chance for more money later." By midsummer 1955, *Peanuts* finally passed the hundred-paper break-even mark.

From his father, Sparky had learned that building a business meant catering to the customer, one haircut, one nickel, at a time. One by one, in 1956, the Erie (Pennsylvania) *Times*, the Ontario (California) *Report*, the Grand Forks (North Dakota) *Herald*; the Santa Barbara (California) *News-Press*, the Martinez (California) *Contra Costa Gazette*, and a score of other papers that still served their towns and villages almost in defiance of the chokehold television was beginning to exert on prime advertising revenues ordered *Peanuts*, bringing the total to 125 subscribers by May—and then the landslide began, another 125 rolling in by October, 75 of them featuring the Sunday page.

Each week throughout 1957, another two newspapers added themselves to Schulz's list of subscribers, boosting the total in forty states and Canada to 230 dailies, 102 Sundays, with 16 college newspapers besides. By the end of 1958, *Peanuts* had reached a grand total of four hundred, including every ship and station newspaper in the navy. "Now if we can get *Peanuts* into submarines," Gilburt wrote in November 1958, "we'll only have the other planets to strive for."

Sparky was never satisfied, always working harder. "I never give up," he told Gilburt after sending off to *Life* magazine a third rough sketch of Charlie Brown and Snoopy to illustrate an article about the astounding growth of *Peanuts*. When a second collection of daily strips, *More Peanuts*, was published, he had "high hopes for many sales"; yet while telling the publisher that he was very pleased, he privately found the book "filled with so much bad work" that he could not bring himself to present a copy to Walt Kelly, to whom he wrote: "After the first book came out, I wish[ed] that they would put out another so that my more recent work would show up. Now that the second one is out, I'm just as much ashamed. Where does it all end?"

By 1958, these doubts had renewed themselves. The characters had "begun to look a little bit overweight," and he didn't like his rendering of Snoopy with an elongated nose—"I'm appalled at the way I drew him, I don't know why I did that—I suppose I was searching," he said later.

But, through ever-advancing technique and self-demands, he had begun to master issues of pacing and design, especially in the panels of the Sunday pages, where he had learned that the reader's glance tended to drop at once to the lower right-hand corner, spoiling the whole page by reading the payoff first. He learned to offset the American rush to the last panel by taking care that the beginning panels were interestingly enough designed to keep the reader from skipping. His title-panel cameos, often highly abstract pieces of whimsy, called for immediate decoding. Another of his secrets for seizing and controlling the reader's attention was to "plot" the sequence of panels as the unfolding of the will of a single personality: *Peanuts* became a strip of declarations, not of ripostes, and once Schulz had decided which character would be given the final word, no one could come back with an additional retort.

In ever-increasing numbers, readers took *Peanuts* as a gentle counter-weight to the "wars, rumors of wars, clamor and controversy, which make up the intruding realities of today," clipping and sending to loved ones favorite strips that found their way onto army bulletin boards in Korea, bulkheads at the U.S. Naval Base in Newport, Rhode Island, and refrigerator doors in probably a million homes. Asked why the strip appealed to so many people, Schulz answered, "Well, it deals in intelligent things—things that people have been afraid of."

Until 1956, when demand became too heavy to keep up with, any one of Schulz's by then more than twenty million readers could get an original just by asking the cartoonist or the syndicate. To a degree soon to be unknown in the comics business, Schulz and United Feature went out of their way to oblige every fan. According to one United executive, Sidney Goldberg, Sparky was "too accommodating—he gave away too many originals." They hung in hospitals, libraries, colleges, medical schools, churches, seminaries, fraternity houses, research laboratories, plants, community centers: "Everybody wants a *Peanuts* drawing," sighed Jim Hennessey.

"I thought you might be interested in my attempting to maintain goodwill toward readers," Sparky told Harry Gilburt, whom he reminded that he had addressed and mailed a reply to each sender of a Valentine or Christmas card to buck up Charlie Brown—some four hundred personal replies.

The thornier, teasing side of his humor could also be found in his answers to fan letters, especially those that dared make suggestions about the direction of the strip. In 1955, he replied sardonically to a reader in Pittsburgh, who had written with a slate of friends to ask if Schulz would drop a loudmouthed character of aggressive personality and definite opinions—Charlotte Braun, who had appeared in the strip fewer than a dozen times, and preceded Lucy as the strip's pot-stirrer. "I am taking your suggestion," Schulz told the twenty-one-year-old fan. "Remember, however, that you and your friends will have the death of an innocent child on your conscience. Are you prepared to accept such responsibility?" At the bottom of the sheet he drew Charlotte Braun with an ax blade falling on her curly head.

When it came to the needs of more powerful admirers, however, Sparky retreated into boyish innocence, doing his duty to the syndicate by signing the August 2, 1954, original about fingerprints for J. Edgar Hoover but ducking a request from Hennessey to add a word of his own to the country's most famous crime fighter: "I don't think I'll include a letter, for I wouldn't know what to say to a big man like that."

Sparky was inundated by "people seeking favors, originals, and," he added, only half-kidding, "ways to cheat us out of all our money." Hollywood producers, pursuing the rights to coin this unassuming phenomenon into movies, animated cartoons, weekly television shows, and television commercials, tossed around figures of $50,000, $75,000, and $100,000, until finally settling down to business and offering Schulz a preposterously low $100 per feature. He received requests for endorsements from manufacturers of men's and boys' underwear, canned fruit juice, Eagle pencils, and Goldenberg Peanut Chews. A New Hampshire paper company hoped to put out a "Peanuts party paper set" complete with tablecloth, napkins, plates, and cups; while a San Francisco biscuit company proposed to bake a peanut butter cookie packaged in a white bag printed with Schulz's characters, a million of which would be sold through Safeway stores.

"The Eagle pencil offer seems all right to me although I certainly don't use Eagle pencils," he told Hennessey. "Art materials and any discussion of art materials have always frightened me. I guess that's one of the reasons I have liked comic-strip work over other kinds of commercial art; the materials are simpler, and require no planning. However, if the syndicate is in dire need of money, and wants to split five hundred dollars with me, I suppose I can begin using Eagle pencils and erasers."

The commodification of *Peanuts* occurred gradually and without his having to leave the drawing board. "It comes upon you so slowly, you're not even realizing that it's happening," he later reflected. "And also you're young, you have a family to raise, you don't know how long this is going to last." He put his dealings in the responsible, paternal hands of the syndicate chief, Rutman, and at his urging kept open the option of accepting a corporate product endorsement that would guarantee "some kind of a reasonable income" for the rest of his life.

In 1955, Rutman persuaded Schulz to illustrate Eastman Kodak's *Brownie Book of Picture-Taking*, letting his characters run loose from the strip for the first time. The syndicate required from Kodak an advance payment against which royalties would be applied at the rate of 5 percent of a camera's selling price. Sparky happened to be in Rutman's office in New York on the day when he used nothing more complicated than what he called "the flinch system" to establish these "licensing" fees. When John Schnapp of Eastman Kodak asked how much it would cost for Schulz to provide eight four-panel strips and twenty spot drawings, Rutman answered, "Well, perhaps, one thousand dollars," and when Schnapp didn't demur, he then stated, "It will be an *additional* thousand dollars to have Mr. Schulz make the drawings for Kodak's exclusive use." When, again, Schnapp took this in his stride, Rutman explained that *domestic* rights to the characters in photography manuals would cost yet more. "And," as Rutman told it to Schulz, "I keep going up until he flinches, and that's the figure."

THE MORE SUCCESSFUL HE became, the more humble he wanted to prove himself. He yearned for the dignity his father had achieved in his trade;

Art Instruction gave this to him, and not only in the form of a penthouse studio atop the Bureau of Engraving. Art Instruction imparted professional standing to the business of cartooning, and for the five years (1953–58) during which *Peanuts* first took off as a comic strip but had yet to reach critical mass as a brand, the rewards of a steadily improving new business gave Charles Schulz the dignity he craved as an artist.

Later in life, whenever Schulz revealed that he had been trained through the mail, audiences and interviewers would laugh. The television host Larry King guffawed at his account of working as an instructor at the school that conducted the ubiquitous "Draw Me" contests. "You were in that?" snorted King, as if Schulz had been in the Mafia or the 1950s quiz show scams.

For Charles Schulz, Art Instruction would always be the institution that had helped make his long-held dream possible by prodding him to fuse his natural conscientiousness as a craftsman with a kind of entrepreneurial drive that he would have been too afraid to assert if left to himself. Art Instruction modeled for Schulz the kind of popular entertainer he would be: first and foremost a professional, never an artist only. For if art was the keynote, even in such half-arts as wallpaper and greeting card design, the underlying theme was earnings. The smart young people in the Educational Department had initiated him into the finer forms of art, music, and literature, and he would always credit them for having done "much to affect my later life." But the company itself had as great an impact, for it is impossible to understand the commercial phenomenon that would cast *Peanuts* into a consumer brand, or to see Schulz's part in it, without first placing his history against the business practices of Art Instruction, Inc., and the lessons he drew from them.

The truth was that Art Instruction's chief "product" was commercial rather than artistic. Most students dropped out long before completing the course, many getting no further than the third set of lessons.★ The Art Instruction system produced standouts—Schulz himself was one—but it also caught in its net a much larger rabble of dropouts. One postwar instructor estimated that out of every hundred students, probably no more

---

★A dropout rate of two-thirds of those enrolled was a home-study industry standard; in the postwar years, this would climb as high as 90 percent.

than three or four finished. Clearly, what made mail-order instruction profitable in the long run was not the rare professional successes of its graduates
but the more predictable failures of its dropouts. If, in any given year, all
enrollees finished all twelve divisions in the suggested amount of time, up
to ten thousand student assignments would have arrived at the school every
single weekday morning, not just keeping the school's twelve instructors
"busily engaged in reviewing and appraising students' lesson work," as the
school pictured it, but burying them.

As it was, the duties of instructors in the postwar era exploded when
the entries for the "Draw Me" contests poured into "Dept. 8973" at 500
South Fourth Street. Schulz and his colleague Charlie Brown were called
on to judge the entries that had passed the grading sieve of the second-
floor clerks. "Anything seventy-five and over had their names go to the
salesmen," Sparky recalled, "and anything ninety-seven and above was
set aside, so there would be fifteen or twenty [entries] that would come
upstairs, and then we would have to make the final judgment." Describing the process as "brutal," he said, "It was a *terrible* thing to have to judge,
because you'd have about twelve of these beautifully, perfectly drawn girl's
heads from the side view, and to try to pick out the one that was the most
perfect was almost impossible."

Nevertheless, to Sparky, the "Draw Me" contest offering "$1,275
in Prizes" was nothing more than a "great sales gimmick" that put the
names and addresses of prospective customers directly into the hands of
the school's salesmen. If they exaggerated claims to make a sale, what of it?
They were not devious or scheming; they were salesmen. They did not set
out to lie; they did mean to make sales.

Sparky saw nothing underhanded in the promises of the school's commission agents, or in the pursuit and all-too-probable disillusion of semi-
literate students, but most of his colleagues in the Educational Department
looked on the business side of Art Instruction as an embarrassment. Fifty
years later, they would shake their heads and their voices would tighten
when they spoke of it. "The business part was a real racket. It was pretty
sleazy down there on the second floor," said David Ratner. "They sold
the course to kids who couldn't read, and the pressure they put on those
people [to keep up with their payments to the school] was terrible." "The
collections department," said Harold Lamson, "was probably more impor-

tant than the Educational Department." "It was kind of a paradox," said George Letness. "It was a good course: If you had talent, it gave you a lot. But the way it was sold wasn't really ethical. They sold the course to kids who couldn't write or spell; and they didn't care if the kids finished the course, but they did care if they paid for it."

To the Charles Schulz whose name appeared on the company letterhead, all this was pardonable. Sparky never doubted the integrity of the home-study course or the sincerity of the company's owners and officers. He entertained no judgments against the Buckbees, who co-owned the company. A colleague would reflect that the shareholding executives were "the most respectable people. They didn't think they were doing anything wrong. . . . They weren't touched that they were conning the poor and the uneducated. [They] lived in the right neighborhoods and went to the right churches. They were pompously correct and righteous in everything they did."

Schulz viewed the gentlemen in the higher offices as pragmatic businesspeople, like his father, with handkerchief squares neatly folded in their suit-coat pockets, polished wire-rim spectacles on their noses, gleaming pen sets on their desks, and their hearts in the right place. They gave their most faithful employees gold watches after twenty years' service. Sparky's championing of Art Instruction set him against what he viewed as the aesthetic indulgences and elitism of the art academy. "I'm always astounded," he would say, "that people somehow think that these correspondence courses are a racket. There's nothing more of a racket with a correspondence course than there is going to a resident [art] school, have any instructor come in, put the model up, and say, 'Draw that,' and then have him disappear and not come back until class is over. That's what I call a racket."

Always, he emphasized that he had learned to draw at a correspondence school. Anyone, in other words, could grow up to be Charles Schulz—he had become the classic figure of the very bourgeois democracy on which Art Instruction had built and marketed its business. To the end of his life, serving on the school's awards committees, he remained unselfconsciously loyal to the institution.

ON MARCH 1, 1955, United Feature Syndicate formally announced that it intended to exercise the option on extending Schulz's contract. Whereupon, on the strength of his trust in Larry Rutman, as well as Rutman's promise of a "more fruitful financial return" over the next five years, Schulz bought a grand house overlooking Minnehaha Creek, paying $32,000, twice as much as the national average and considered "a fortune" by his friends. He moved on April 13, bringing his family to their new neighborhood south of Fiftieth Street and north of the creek, where the streets shook loose of Minneapolis's stern grid and began to twist and curve to give the neighborhood its nickname of Tangletown.

Set atop a terraced lawn, 112 West Minnehaha Parkway looked as tall as a cliff—three stories of white stucco crowned with a steeply raked red tile roof, half-hipped at the ends. A stand-alone stucco arch, also roofed with red tiles, met the visitor at the foot of a flagstone walkway. The house and its broad front lawn faced Minnehaha Parkway, whose elegant windings plunged through a landscaped valley down which Minnehaha Creek made its bubbling six-mile passage from Lake Harriet to the treasured Minnehaha Falls.

This was the better part of town. The best lakeside places lay still farther to the west, but "to be on the parkway was certainly nice," a neighbor recalled. "It was an address that commanded attention." Perhaps too much attention: observing that the Schulzes had bought "a much larger home," and "materially . . . appear to have prospered," the *Minneapolis Star* took note of the purchase in an article reporting that Schulz was now tithing one-tenth of his income to the Church of God. Downplaying the significance of his move, Schulz took note of his new situation as it would appear to others in his correspondence—"112 West Minnehaha Parkway, Minneapolis 19, Minnesota"—and offhandedly remarked, "That's really an all-Indian address, isn't it?"

Two cars stood in the driveway, though Schulz made a point of joking that he would not ride in Joyce's prized pink convertible because it made him feel silly. Indoors was a "showcase of upper-middle-class comfort," according to *The Saturday Evening Post*, for here were six air-conditioned bedrooms, plus a music room for Joyce, a studio for Sparky, a breakfast room for everyone, and a pool table in a finished basement. As Schulz had done for Meredith in Colorado Springs, he painted the walls of Monte's bedroom with murals of Charlie Brown and Snoopy. Joyce had a set of wooden train cars, big enough for a child to sit in, constructed for the basement playroom. They borrowed a book on bricklaying from Larry Rut-man and taught themselves how to build a full-scale barbecue pit behind the house. "So it's a little crooked here and there," reflected Joyce. "We'll call it 'rustic.' "

Their third child, Craig Frederick, had been born on January 22, 1953, and Joyce was expecting a fourth. Years later, a relative who knew them closely in these Minnehaha Creek days would think of it as the Schulzes' Camelot—a "brief, shining moment" in their life as a family. "They were happy there," said Ramona Swanson, "and it was a true happiness that they may not have experienced before and may not have had again."

On August 5, 1956, at Swedish Hospital in Minneapolis, a block away from where Sparky had been born, Joyce gave birth to a daughter, Amy Louise, to whom in times to come Sparky often would recall how on that Sunday morning, "The sun was shining brightly and it was a beautiful day." Joyce recalled her own happiness at having a second daughter.

Amy's birth was announced in a Twin Cities newspaper under the headline "PEANUTS" GETS NEW "CHARACTER," and—also typical of the change that overtook the family in that watershed year—was characterized as "an addition to the 'Peanuts' home on 112 West Minnehaha Parkway."

NOW FAME WAS UPON him, and for good. On April 26, 1956, the National Cartoonists Society finally voted Schulz the outstanding cartoonist of 1955. He was surprised to be recognized by his colleagues: "It wasn't as if they were voting for a friend. They didn't even know me. Wonderfully, they were voting for the work itself."

He attended the annual banquet at the Hotel Astor in a rented satin shawl-collar dinner jacket; Rube Goldberg called his name, and he went forward to receive the Reuben from the seventy-two-year-old master. The occasion was crowned by the presence of Harold Anderson, the syndicate executive who nine years earlier in Chicago had so decisively brushed away his early submissions. Sparky was polite but unfoolable; as he came down off the dais, the big winner bearing the big prize in his hand, he saw Anderson looking on aglow with satisfaction, as if he, Harold Anderson, had somehow played a part in this triumph. The unheeding editor had been brought to the bar of justice and made to witness what kind of young talent he had passed over. "There he was sitting—and that made me feel good." Going by Anderson's table, Sparky acknowledged the older man's friendly congratulations, but did not pause for an amiable exchange and declined in any way to put harsh memories aside. When describing the moment afterward, he would say, "Revenge is sometimes pretty sweet."

In just five years, he had reached the top of his profession. He made the necessary victory appearances in New York, and then promptly took the train home. Waiting on the platform at Pennsylvania Station, he found himself alone with his odd, homely looking trophy and could not quite accept that the National Cartoonists Society—still an awe-inspiring institution in his eyes, whatever he thought of its individual members—had honored *him*. It was, he later said, the happiest and the loneliest triumph of his life.

# CHAPTER 17

# THE CALL OF CALIFORNIA

*A better place for ordinary people.*
—KEVIN STARR

HE WAS HAUNTED BY the fear that he might yet slide back. "I've been dreaming about this thing since I was about six years old. Now I have it and now all I have to do is try to keep it."

The great calamities had been overcome: the Depression, World War II, his mother's death. The big questions of adult life had been addressed as he passed through the postwar rites of passage: job, friends, faith, marriage, fatherhood, family, career. Everything he had dreamed of as a soldier in France he had achieved within ten years of returning to civilian life.

By 1957 Schulz was earning more than $90,000 per year—twice as much as the highest-paid college president in the country. His prosperity was so out of proportion to the expectations and lives of his family and friends that he appeared to have achieved not so much the American Dream as the Adolescent Fantasy: *They can't get me now.* Indeed, he responded to every sign of achievement as if he had never left high school.

As at Central High, he now tried to cast as little shadow as possible. Calm, quiet, "exceedingly sober-sided," as one reporter described him in 1956, Schulz had a way of standing, as another observer noted, by which "he tends to melt into the landscape." Although portrayed by journalists— men and women alike—as "handsome" and "charming," with looks and a voice supposedly reminiscent of the young Charles Lindbergh, Schulz presented himself as plain and uninviting. To the suggestion that he appear on the popular television program *What's My Line?*, he asked Harry Gilburt, "Do you think that should be pursued, or am I too homely, or would it be worthwhile?" He then laid out the details of his schedule, offering to go out of his way "if such a thing was lined up," but ducked back under cover by the end: "Can I say all this without appearing as if I thought I really did belong on that show?"

As he had done at Central High, he made a point of camouflaging his true intellectual ability. Built up in the press—as "semanticist," "psychologist," "man of culture and letters," "superintellectual," and "the leading intellectual comic strip artist"—he scoffed at the whole business: "I'm as far away from an intellectual as you can get." When the Democratic National Committee came courting on behalf of Adlai Stevenson's presidential campaign, attempting to flatter Schulz by designating him "the youngest existentialist," Sparky played dumb, declaring ignorance of philosophical trends.

Camouflaging intellectual ability with humor is an American strain that goes back to the folksy masks that Abraham Lincoln and Mark Twain intended to disguise high intelligence and disarm potential opponents. But Schulz's off-the-page humor was beyond easy measure. Asked if he had been shy as a boy, for example, he made a deadpan routine of answering that, yes, "shy" was not a bad description, but he preferred *stupid*. And in a typical comic reversal, he would famously write, "Happiness is finding out you're not so dumb after all."

But, as so often with the self-invented, it was not "unimportance" or "dumbness" that actually defined his sense of himself; it was a sense of illegitimacy—of being an impostor. Charles Schulz had no family background to reinforce his position in the world, no story accounting for his eminence as an artist. He had to make one up.

Whenever called upon to discuss his life, he made a point of proclaiming himself a failure in all but his work. He reminded anyone writing about him that he had been "the youngest and smallest and most ignored boy in the eighth grade," and he designated his very own creation, Charlie Brown, as "author" of a print advertisement for Ford Motor Company— "How I Sold 1,000,000 Falcons (In My Spare Time)"—to introduce him to the public as a man whose "sense of unimportance developed in earlier life." Without otherwise crafting his blandness—his teetotaling, for example, was honestly bland—Schulz presented himself to a suddenly interested world as a "nothing young man from St. Paul" who had "parlayed his own frustrations and disappointments into wealth and fame."

The first national account of his rise to the top of his profession was published by *The Saturday Evening Post* in January 1957. In "The Success of an Utter Failure," Hugh Morrow declared, "All this might never have come to pass if Schulz hadn't been such a miserable failure." The "loser" legend was soon seconded by *Look* and sealed forever as the one true story by *Life* and *Time*, leaving unanswered the question of how a dumb, dull, meek, flat-footed businessman was becoming a success like no other in the history of his field. To what degree he had actually been recognized for his talent or skills, or had gone unsupported through the back halls of Central during the worst of his mother's cancer, he was not about to give a strictly honest accounting. To grow would have been to grow out of being Charles Schulz, and that would have been fatal. He had to market a Charlie Brown version of himself because he knew that hurt, and the anger that sprang from it—and the mildness that masked the anger—was the taproot of his life's work. At the height of his first fame, he went on *The Tonight Show* and told Johnny Carson, "I failed everything in high school," adding, "and I was kind of lonely, but mainly it was a matter of stupidity."

Over these years of tentative early triumph, he gradually discovered that he could disarm the public and deflect reporters from probing beneath the surface by agreeing to be Charlie Brown—or, more exactly, to being Charlie Brown's second fiddle. A typical magazine profile of these years would begin by stating that Charlie Brown "is practically flesh-and-blood real to readers of some four hundred newspapers today. But the man who hatches out all these comic situations is not nearly so real. For instance, when Charlie Brown got sick recently, he received two get well cards. But when Charlie's creator, Charles M. Schulz, fell ill, he got only one card."

Actually, some fifty to seventy-five fans now wrote Schulz each week, but when he flew a kite in his front yard for the photographer from *Look*, the magazine's writer did not note how effortlessly the kite soared in the breeze. The more famous the fictional Charlie Brown became for losing kites, the more satisfied reporters were to come back from Minneapolis with the news that "Charlie" Schulz was "not only young Charlie's creator but also his soulmate." He learned that the new medium of television preferred the simplest answer: "I guess I'm . . . Charlie Brown" (1958). "Mainly I'm Charlie Brown" (1961). "I'm just about one-hundred percent Charlie Brown" (1964).

Then came a shift in 1968, the year of convulsion and transformation for the adolescents who had done so much to make Charlie Brown a national presence: "I think of myself as Charles Schulz, but if someone wants to believe I'm really Charlie Brown, well, it makes a good story." In 1969, he made the change startlingly clear in the *New York Times*: "I don't do Charlie Brown and the friendless bit so much any more. There was a time when I didn't have any friends but now I have a lot."

"Is Charlie Brown really Schulz's alter ego?" he was asked, for the umpteenth time, in 1972. "Not really," he sighed, "although it makes a good story."

Looking back after ten years had passed, he reflected that reporters "invariably will ask, 'Do you think you are Charlie Brown?' Well, that has so many ramifications and you can talk about that at so many levels, and they don't want to hear it. But if you say, 'Yeah, I'm a lot like Charlie Brown,' that's what they want to hear, that makes the headline; and [then] they don't care about anything else. They've got their answer and that's all they care about for their article. So why go into it?"

But Sparky himself was far too willful, too much in control, to be Charlie Brown. In the "round-headed kid," Schulz was creating a state of mind; saying, this is *him*, this is *us*, and, as seldom as possible, this is me. Charlie Brown allowed Schulz to speak ever less *as* himself in real life, ever more *of* himself in the world of line.

Another crucial element of his public persona as a sincere ordinary fellow derived from his faith as an evangelical Christian. Whether presenting his chalk talk before five hundred Rotarians in Detroit or 3,500 sailors aboard the aircraft carrier *Coral Sea* in New York Harbor, he always began the same way, drawing Snoopy in a few quick strokes. Then he would stand back and face his audience. "That's just to show you I'm not a fake." The talk covered the evolution of the strip and his philosophy about its characters, but when he addressed overflow audiences such as those at a Youth for Christ rally at the Chase Hotel in St. Louis—scene of his army furloughs with Elmer and Margaret Hagemeyer—or at the evangelical Bethel College in St. Paul, his approach was "evangelical but sort of gentle," recalled one member of the audience. "He was certainly not a noisy fundamentalist, or anything of that sort, but he definitely brought in his Christianity."

As his confidence improved, he surprised himself and others by enjoying himself onstage. Before one of his first chalk talks in public—at the Walker Art Center in Minneapolis—the Twin Cities press speculated doubtfully "about what a man as shy and retiring as Schulz might do when faced with a large crowd." The next morning, a local columnist delivered the verdict: "In his quiet way, he was a sensation."

"Tell Larry to cancel my contract," Sparky wrote gleefully to Harry Gilburt. "I am going into vaudeville."

Yet for all his popularity among eighteen million daily readers, cartooning still had not made Sparky a member of a dignified profession. Even as a syndicated practitioner of the older, more regulated form of comics, Sparky never knew quite where he stood as a strip artist with the burghers of mid-1950s Minneapolis. "One moment you are praised and the next moment you are pushed aside. You don't know whether to think you are good or not."

His dedication to the dream of cartooning puzzled some of his church friends. Comics were not what a man with children devoted his life to. Comic books were seen as a threat to home and family. Mobilized by wartime sales (servicemen preferred comic books to magazines like *Life* and *The Saturday Evening Post* by a ratio of ten to one), the still-young comic book industry had established a beachhead inside the postwar American household in such numbers (sixty million per month in 1947) that Dr. Fredric Wertham, senior psychiatrist of New York City's Department of Hospitals, sounded the alarm in the *Saturday Review of Literature*, warning parents that comic books, "the marijuana of the nursery," would lead their innocent children into a life of degradation and crime. By 1954, with annual crime rates among juveniles spiking by as much as 50 percent above the historic trend, Wertham took the fight into congressional committee hearings, a comic book burning rally in Chicago, and a children's crusade petitioning President Eisenhower to impose a ban.

Wertham, born in Germany before the turn of the century, misjudged the extent of adult interest in comics, claiming that 75 percent of adults disapproved of comic books (in fact, 41 percent of men and 28 percent of women were regular readers), insisting that parents must shield their children even from Superman (a symbol of "violent race superiority"), Batman and Robin ("a wish dream of two homosexuals living together"), and comic art itself (a "corruption of the art of drawing").

The most serious voices of proportion about comics in this period had to concede to the judgment of publications like *Teachers' Digest* that "the so-called comic is crude, unreal, and generally trivial. Likewise overdrawn, and to a mind anywhere near adult, rather boring." Interest in comics as an aesthetic form was dismissed as "a sign of poor taste." And if they had to be present in a Christian man's life, then they were distinctly relegated to his premarital years and to the world of what the Apostle Paul called "childish things," which, like all true believers, Sparky had followed the apostle in putting away.

As long as Sparky fooled around with such trivialities as little boxy strips in newspapers he was not embarked upon a serious life. Although this confirmed the popular view of professional "funnymen" as perennial adolescents, Sparky did not fit the image of the ink-slinging misanthrope who hated to answer his mail, pay his bills, or use the telephone. On the contrary, he had chosen Christ, and having confessed the only Son of God as his Lord and Savior, quoted the Gospels word by word from memory to support his unselfconscious call for a good, clean, friendly spirit in the nation's daily humor, proudly proclaiming that he was an active churchman who ardently believed in "holy living."

When J. Clifford Thor, the new young pastor of the Minneapolis Church of God, introduced Sparky to his wife as the man who drew *Peanuts*, Jean Thor replied, "Oh—well, what other work do you do?" His answer is unrecorded, but he certainly picked up her implication, and knew, too, that she had most likely never before met a cartoonist and was too busy with her family and children and the church to pay attention to such literally marginal scribbles.

Looking back on his life in the Twin Cities in the '50s, Schulz recalled that while he knew that "there were a lot of people" who thought he would succeed, "I also knew a lot of people didn't. They just thought it was all foolishness and I wouldn't get anyplace." Most of all, "there were people in the church that thought that it was a useless endeavor and that I could have been doing something more worthwhile."

Since returning from Colorado Springs he had been increasingly active in the Church of God, both nationally and locally: establishing a scholarship fund in Anderson, Indiana, with the royalties from *Young Pillars*, a church-published book of his *Youth* cartoons, and serving locally as treasurer, Sunday school teacher, member of the Board of Christian Education, the Board of Deacons, and the Board of Trustees, as well as lay preacher at Sunday services. By 1955, Schulz was turning over one-tenth, or about $3,000, of his posttax *Peanuts* earnings to the Church of God; by 1958, when, according to church authorities, Schulz's "financial support was by now greater than all the rest of the [Minneapolis] church's income," he was tithing some $9,000 annually.

Under his leadership, the church had bought land and broken ground for a new Church of God—the first of its kind in Minneapolis—at East Thirty-eighth Street and Thirty-eighth Avenue South; while the twenty-eight-foot-by-forty-foot whitewashed chapel was going up, the congregation met in good weather along the Mississippi riverbank and in bad weather at the Schulzes' house. His old friend Marvin Forbes became the first pastor of the new church, to be succeeded by Clifford Thor in 1953, with Sparky serving as assistant pastor until 1958.

But with her superficially absurd, but in church terms searching, question, Jean Thor had shown him the impatience of the respectable—absurd because, after all, it was Sparky's comic strip that was funding her own church; searching, because to those who lay their work at God's feet some toil is more hallowed than others. But the new pastor's wife had almost casually tried to highlight the distance between his work, however productive, and God and goodness. The general opinion was that newspaper comics stood far below those things that brought one before God and could not be reckoned among His work. To Sparky, already, they were fused, and always had been. He himself saw no inconsistency in drawing a comic strip with, in his words, a "clean reputation." In his own eyes he could be a successful cartoonist, a responsible adult, and a tolerant Christian all at once.

IN AUGUST 1957, DURING a business trip that overlapped with the evangelist Billy Graham's sixteen-week "crusade for souls" in New York City, Schulz joined the throng of thousands crowding three bunting-draped tiers of seats gathered under a dozen American flags in Madison Square Garden to hear the Reverend Doctor Graham preach his mass ministry. People by the hundreds heeded the impassioned call to come forward to make "decisions for Christ"; altogether, by summer's end, more than fifty-five thousand men, women, and teenagers had made the pledge. Sparky was "amazed to see all the people going forward to receive Christ."

Watching the thirty-eight-year-old Graham at work, Schulz, at thirty-four, could see a contemporary creating his audience, one by one. Tall, blond, ruggedly handsome, Graham was an impressive man. The clear, pale blue of his eyes shone as he delivered himself of his vision. But Sparky concluded (as would the preacher himself) that it wasn't so much the spell cast by Graham personally as it was "the result of earnest prayer, and of the working of the Holy Spirit and the building up of love."

"Sparky was very high on Billy Graham," recalled the painter Hal Lamson, his colleague at Art Instruction, who had listened to Sparky's recapitulation of a Graham sermon, complete with the evangelist's distinctive hand and head gestures, as the two stepped off a Bureau of Engraving freight elevator by themselves. The power of Sparky's passion took them both by surprise. "It was just a little uncomfortable for me because he was not ordinarily emotional about something that was personal. His voice was kind of trembling.

"There was no doubting the depth of his faith. He lived by it. We all respected him for it."

ACCORDING TO HIS GROWING legend, Charles Schulz—the "Father of Peanuts," "Peanuts' papa," "Charlie Brown's Father," "Snoopy's pappy," all of which he hated to be called—loved small children. "His fondness for the six-and-under set . . . has made him one of the most admired cartoonists of the day," bubbles a typical bit of '50s mythmaking, of the kind in which Sparky was only too happy to collude when *Peanuts* was struggling to get off the ground: "Sure, I like kids. Got one of my own. Daughter. Twenty months old. Named Meredith," he told the editors of the *Rocky Mountain News* in 1951.

Twenty-six years would go by before Sparky could finally say, "I have never been especially fond of children. I really haven't. I adore my own kids, but I'm not a children lover." During the height of his fame in the 1960s, he confided this truth to no one; not until the end of his life would he publicly admit, "I never had any interest in children at all before we had our own children; and then I began to see the joy you could get from having your own children."

The cartoonist Virgil Partch could have been speaking for a multitude in the early '60s when he applauded Schulz for "[loving] children. . . . You can tell that he loves them just by the cartoons." Schulz, after all, was no W. C. Fields, who had wrung a special humor from a curmudgeonly contempt for little rascals, although, in truth, Sparky took great pleasure in the jaundiced eye that Fields had cast over children, and while watching *The Bank Dick* with his son Monte, relished imitating the great child-hater's classic jab, "Get away, kid, you bother me." "He loved the snickering language of those movies," recalled Monte. And indeed *Peanuts'* most often snickering character, Snoopy, has a grumpy contempt for the kids in the strip.

Over the next ten years, as the nation's accepted wisdoms came under attack, gradually eroding the sense of postwar order and certainty, Schulz would be turned to for his old-fashioned decency and his self-effacing dignity, and would always be seen as "an individual of human niceness," as one visitor summed him up. It was universally assumed that the cartoonist who gave the nation's households their "security blanket" had to be a naturally warm, protective guy. As with no less a laureate of contemporary children's literature than Dr. Seuss—Theodor Seuss Geisel, who did not like being even in the same room with children—the public took for granted that Schulz had to favor kids. On a popular television talk show in

the late 1970s, the host framed it as a matter of good and evil: "If Charles
M. Schulz doesn't like children, I'm Adolf Hitler."

"Oddly enough," he later remarked, "I have fought against children's products all these years because I do not consider it a children's
strip. I have always said, 'If you have to do something for children, that's
fine, but let's not forget that our main reading audience is out there
among the college kids, and in the fathers and mothers and grandmothers. Let's not forget all of *those* products; I just don't want a bunch of
children's things out there. But . . . I have not been able to close the
floodgates. The children's products just keep coming. And I guess it's
all right; it doesn't hurt anything. But that always has been a personal
problem with me."

The problem was that, as with Donna Wold and the Little Red-
Haired Girl—whom it was assumed he also loved in one-to-one proportion—Schulz in real life suspected that children would not like him,
would find him boring, would reject even his sincerest hello. And he,
being unconfident and nervous, decided that he couldn't get them to
like him; so, at the drawing board, he became a user of nominal child
figures for the sake of adult commentary embedded in art, not a lover
of children for their own sake. From the beginning, boys and girls had
been useful "because they were what sold," even though, as he would
confess, "I had only a meager interest in drawing little kids." And to the
very end of his life, even when he was surrounded by children during his
daily routine in the snack bar at the Redwood Empire Ice Arena in Santa
Rosa, he would say, "I still don't pay that much attention to children.
But at least I've learned how to talk with them. And I'm always amazed
when they do like me."

He liked his own creations best of all: "I know them very well. . . .
And I like them. If I didn't like them, I wouldn't use them. . . . I really
like Charlie Brown. I think he's just the neatest little kid and I would
like to have had him for a next door neighbor when I was small, because
I know we would have gotten along well, because he's an innocent little boy who just wants to play ball and be left alone . . . never mean to
anybody." And Charlie Brown was similarly awkward in the presence of
little kids:

To Schulz at the drawing board, his characters were "practically as real and alive as his own children," in an oft-repeated trope of the mid-'60s, but there were limits to his affection, as he admitted once in later years: "I could never say, 'I love my characters.' I find that a difficult sentence to speak." And he never dreamed about Charlie Brown or Snoopy or Linus and Lucy. Once, in 1956, he reported awakening in the middle of the night to "a disturbing thought: *Who are these little people? Must I live with them for the rest of my life?*" Otherwise, he would only go so far as to say, "They're my second family, I feel responsible for them," and sometimes he would get the gang from *Peanuts* mixed up with his own family. His daughter Amy would recall hearing an interview with her father later in life, in which he was asked, "How are your kids?"

"And he thought they meant his characters, and he started talking about them. And the interviewer said, 'No, Sparky, I mean your five kids.' And I'm, like, 'Oh, great, he thinks of his characters before us.' But now that I'm older, I understand that about him. Were we his everything? No. His strip was his everything."

The pressure on Schulz to make appearances, autograph the latest collection from Rinehart, give a chalk talk—drawing freehand with a felt-tip pen on large sheets of newsprint as he delivered an updated form of an old-fashioned cartoon technique demonstration he had learned at Art Instruction—entailed more and more trips out of Minneapolis.

Pelted with miscellaneous requests and still without any secretary or assistant to help with his mail or his schedule, he burst out with a touch of weariness before one trip to New York, "As usual, everything is getting crowded, and I haven't even left home yet." Once he was launched on the journey, the smallest thing could unnerve him; if he heard a child cry in a railroad depot or on an airplane, "it would destroy my whole trip," he later recalled. "I would become terribly depressed, because I would miss my own kids so much, and I would wonder . . . *What in the world am I doing here?*"

Within a decade, he would be able to tell a reporter, "This uneasiness at being away from home has been diagnosed as a fear of being out of control. Perhaps that is why some of the shorter vacations, such as simply going down to play in the annual Crosby Pro-Am [invitational golf tournament], bring me such satisfaction. I have done it often and I am among friends, and there is a wonderful gratification in being invited."

But a few years after that, he had barely got to the Crosby than he suffered a panic attack and had to leave Pebble Beach after only a day of practice.

When the same thing happened the following year—this time, Sparky wanted to bail out on the very first day—Joyce told him, "You can't go home. Our friends have all come to see you play." Schulz was a scratch golfer, with a five handicap, who shot consistently in the low seventies.

"I don't have to do anything I don't want to do," he answered.

"We're staying here and that's all there is to it," she said.

Joyce later recalled that he "did this over and over and over again." When the Yale *Record* offered him its Humorist of the Year award in 1958, he tried at the last minute to back out of attending the magazine's annual dinner in New Haven, despite advance notice that "Mr. Schulz will be there"—headlined UP AT YALE, THEY'RE NUTS ABOUT OUR "PEANUTS"—in the New York newspaper that carried the strip. "You can't *not* go," said Joyce. "You've got to go." Sometimes she left the airport, having just put him on a plane, only to have Sparky beat her home in a cab.

In April 1965, when the National Cartoonists Society announced that Schulz had once again won the Reuben—the first time in the society's twenty-year history that any cartoonist had been given the profession's highest award twice—Sparky declined to go to New York for the banquet at the Plaza Hotel; Harry Gilburt accepted the award for him. "I am shying away from these trips more all the time," he had told Gilburt five years earlier. "I just hate to say 'Yes' now, and then find next fall that I'd wish I hadn't."

Always, he kept the true nature of his anxiety to himself. "It took me years to learn to talk about it, that it was nothing to be ashamed of," he revealed, but without the least insight or curiosity about its cause. Sometimes Joyce would flush him out, breezily remarking in front of a reporter that traveling "makes Sparky insecure," but in truth, the increasingly stiff resistance that now preceded any scheduled trip, and the sulky withdrawal that followed his final refusal to board the plane, infuriated her, even as she could also understand it: "He just didn't want to be away from home. . . . He grew up in the apartment over his dad's barber shop, and all he ever did was sit there and listen to classical music, draw his cartoons, and play golf."

And even when at home, he now had to receive reporters, give interviews, stage *Peanuts*-like situations involving the whole family for photographers from *Look* and *Life*, even from *Playboy*, Hugh Hefner's new magazine for men, and at the same time from *Conquest*, "A Magazine for Christian Youth." When *The Saturday Evening Post* sent a reporter to spend the day with the Schulzes, Joyce felt invaded and called Elaine and Harold Ramsperger for reinforcements: "We need somebody else over here. We're tired of this guy following us around with his pad and pencil." No sooner had the Ramspergers arrived than Joyce left Harold with Sparky and the reporter, to take Elaine shopping: "I have to get away from here because it's just questions, questions . . ."

The question she most disliked was: "Are you Lucy?"

"Sparky is really Charlie Brown, and I guess I'm Lucy," Joyce said in April 1962, "though I don't like to admit it." Usually, she would concede that because she herself was fond of Lucy, "I suppose that means something," and brush off the issue with a laugh, adding, "But *someone* has to do the hollering." Yet when *The Saturday Evening Post* wrote her up in 1964 as the "no-nonsense boss of . . . this matriarchy," she was surprised and hurt to find herself described, even with an appeasing modifier, as "endearingly shrill."

AS LONG AS LUCY Van Pelt was the wide-eyed child pattering around the Bonneville bungalow in her sleepies, she invited comparison with Meredith. But as Lucy grew out of toddlerhood into a girl—"an interesting girl . . . sort of a fun type," as she describes herself in *Peanuts*, or "a wild little thing," as her creator amiably described her, she more and more took on Joyce's characteristics—first as Joyce had been when Sparky was courting her ("Boy, how that girl can talk!" says Charlie Brown of Lucy, expanding in the next panel: "Talk, talk, talk, talk," and amplifying in the third: "Talk, talk, talk, talk"), and then as she was in their marriage: matter-of-fact, direct, blunt, forever busy with the details of one or another project; saying what she thought, pulling few punches, and sometimes rubbing people the wrong way.

Operating under rules of her own, Lucy became ever more outrageous, disconcerting, a disturber of the peace, "important because most of the other characters are basically decent," as one early observer of *Peanuts* noted. As Schulz assigned her more and more attributes of his wife, he gave Charlie Brown and Schroeder and Linus his own responses in marriage; and once that became a pattern, a bridge between the worlds, Lucy became the pivotal character in *Peanuts* for that period, her aggressiveness fomenting the conflicts that drove the strip, and perhaps discharging some of the tensions that her original was pumping up in the three-dimensional world.

As when the newly married Joyce prodded Sparky out of Minnesota, there is something unsparing about Lucy: she denies people the chance to get back into their own skins. Yet just as there would be far less energy in *Peanuts* without Lucy, there might also have been a lesser *Peanuts*—a limited, briefly enduring, local strip, far from the planetary phenomenon it would become—without Joyce.

Sparky, inclined like his mother to be fearful of the world, and as resistant to change as his father, needed someone to get him out of himself, someone (outside of Art Instruction, Inc.) who would compel him to legitimize the grand scale of his own ambition, although his dependence on such strength terrified him. Clearly, this was Joyce, for as Meredith would later reflect, "He was afraid of strong women—they were threatening to his very being—and he used Lucy to exhibit that. It was a direct slam to me and my mom, although I always wondered if it really could be me because when he started drawing Lucy, I didn't have a personality: *How could that be me?* It had to be my mom, but he kept telling people it was me, because, of course, he would not have gotten anywhere saying Lucy is Joyce: His marriage would not have stood for that. He was protecting himself there, and I didn't disprove it publicly, so it worked."

In private, the Schulzes' friends nevertheless could not but discern

Joyce's drive, temper, sharp wit, strong opinions, and flat statements in Lucy. When the family came to live an hour north of the Golden Gate Bridge, one of Joyce's most memorable declarations was: "Whenever we want to go anywhere, San Francisco is in the way." But Lucy's obstructions are Charlie Brown's opportunities: to keep his antagonist right where he wants her, off the field and back in the house.

In Colorado Springs, Meredith had a next-door playmate named Susan who one day bit Meredith on the arm. Joyce let Susan's mother know about the incident, but when next Susan came over to play she bit Meredith again. This time, Joyce did the disciplining herself: she took Susan's arm and bit *her*, not to break the skin, but to show her how it felt.

Lucy also bears close relation to the women from whom Joyce was in flight; the Lucy who is resisting growth and who is the worst kind of small-town clubwoman, filled with the community's suffocating certainties, owes much to her aunt Ruth.

Joyce's mother, too, endowed Lucy with conviction; indeed, as Joyce would later reveal, "My mother's favorite expression was 'Snap out of it.' That was her answer to anyone's complaints. That solved it."

Dorothy Halverson, insensitive and indirect, could not tolerate depression in others; she pretended that she could not understand how anyone could suffer from it, and was always ready to dish out the hard "truth," thus becoming the perfect model for the "doctor" who was "in" when she was out, and out even when she was in.

When Sparky discussed Lucy's character and personality, his friends could hear him talking about Joyce:

"She has a way of cutting right down to the truth. This is one of her good points."

"She's not as smart as she thinks she is. Beneath the surface there's something tender."

"She really can't help herself."

"She is annoyed that it's all too easy. Charlie Brown isn't that much of a challenge."

In the strip, Sparky depicted Joyce's drive and ambition as nothing less than presidential. On June 6, 1960, three weeks after Senator Hubert H. Humphrey—of Minnesota, and half Norwegian at that—conceded the Democratic race to Senator John F. Kennedy, Lucy sets out to boost an alarmed Charlie Brown into the executive mansion. She naturally has nothing but contempt for the idea of this perpetual dupe's holding power—it is she who will stand on the ultimate plinth, and she fantasizes how the two of them, "as husband and wife," will sit by the television on election night, watching the "votes pile up." Already she has "the plans" at her side. "For what?" he asks. "Redecorating the White House," she responds impatiently.

He even gave Lucy Joyce's sleepless nights, as well as her wakeful sensitivities: "I can't stand to have anyone touching me while I sleep; I regret it but I can't help it."

And to Joyce herself he gave a St. Bernard, whom they called Lucy. Yet Schulz would always insist, whether with an old friend or a reporter, that Lucy had no one real-world original.

It was as a couple that Sparky and Joyce most clearly had their analogs in Charlie Brown and Lucy, whom Walt Kelly called "a perfect parody of what American life is supposed to be—the ineffectual male and the domineering female." In the Schulzes' marriage, one visitor noticed, there was "a nice balance. He was all warm and gentle. She was a tough broad."

In 1957, when he was visiting St. Louis for a speaking engagement, Sparky introduced Joyce to his army buddy Elmer Hagemeyer, who noticed then, and on their next visit, that Schulz was unusually quiet with Joyce. "She liked to be the big cheese, the big person in the deal all the time." Elmer did not like her; she gave vent to a boast during that visit that he did not care for, and never forgot: "She had a sister who was married to a doctor, and she bragged that this doctor made so much money. And that Schulz would eventually make much, much more than this doctor ever thought about making."

But it wasn't as easy as that. Even if Joyce could have known in 1957 that Sparky's touch would be Midas-like, she honestly did love the things that money could buy ("She loved money for what money could build," recalled Chuck Bartley, a closer friend of Joyce's than Elmer Hagemeyer) and made no secret of her passion: "I love appliances!" she would admit to a reporter. "Refrigerators, dryers, stoves . . ." Friends in Minneapolis who heard her say such things would chuckle and shake their heads. "She sure could spend his money." One of Sparky's pet stories was about the time the light went out in the refrigerator: he would tell people that Joyce was the only person he knew who could go to the hardware store for a replacement lightbulb and come home with a whole new icebox.

To understand this, one has to recall what life was like before appliances, back at the sink during Joyce's Depression childhood. And not just Joyce's—the whole nation's; Americans in the 1950s were buying 75 percent of the appliances on earth. The first decade of the Schulzes' marriage was "one of history's great shopping sprees." With the nation's gross national product doubling between 1940 and 1960, it was, as American advertising reminded everyone, "a time to buy, buy, buy." And not just for oneself, but for the general good: a depression-seared society, deeply afraid for years after the war that any drop in public demand would cave in the economy—hence the emphasis upon what cold war spending was doing to nail prosperity in place—saw investment in consumer goods as virtuous confidence. Buying the new and throwing out the old was now the thing to do. "Why be tied down to yesterday?" asked the Ford Motor Company.

Joyce had also taken over important roles once played by Sparky's father. Before the war Carl had done Sparky's banking for him, just as he had done the talking on social visits. Now Joyce did both, and as she managed their personal finances, she allowed Sparky the kind of freedom from visibility he had enjoyed under his father's roof. She framed him much as Carl had. "He is a sensitive person with an artistic personality [who] works hard—seven hours a day, five days a week," all of which provides an ambiguous portrayal: "sensitive" was not Joyce's prime compliment, and a thirty-five-hour week in a beautiful studio wasn't exactly a U.S. Steel mill schedule.

He asserted himself at the drawing board, but less so in the household, and even less in his role as husband. "He would never criticize her," said one of the church group. "Most men, in those days, wanting to be kings of their castle, would not have tolerated Joyce, but Sparky did, and that's why it worked." Recalled an Art Instruction colleague, "She and Sparky were a fun couple, and they were fun to be with, but there were times when she was pretty nasty to him. And he would just simply take it, and not respond."

Throughout her life, Joyce was known to a few very close friends as an exceptionally thoughtful and caring person. But beyond those stalwarts, her manner could seem brash, arbitrarily changeable. Her energy and drive—the willingness to initiate the next good thing and indeed to press it upon others—would give way in the twinkling of an eye to an untrusting stiffness and a self-absorbed shyness that seemed to belong more to Sparky than to her. "Joyce was the kind of person, who, if she liked you, she would do a lot for you. If she didn't like you, forget it," recalled one of the Schulzes' friends at Art Instruction. Even her self-presentation varied. One day she would look warm, sympathetic, concerned; another day, her face had hardened, the chin knobby, blue eyes cold and hooded.

She and Sparky "struggled," he later admitted, and for all their "joy with the raising of our children," they were a young family in a time of anxiety and intensity—"this disturbed age of ours," Schulz called it. They still did not know much about each other, making what discoveries they could in successive testing moments; it would be years before Sparky came to realize that it was not just he who felt alone.

If he got angry with Joyce, she got angrier, and things came to a showdown. But if he kept his anger in and instead made it silently clear that he was downcast, Joyce's anger was neutralized by his "depression," and they returned to a stalemated middle ground. In this way, he learned that there was nothing Joyce could do when he let himself turn black; "being depressed" gradually became the weapon with which he could express his anger while disorienting Joyce's.

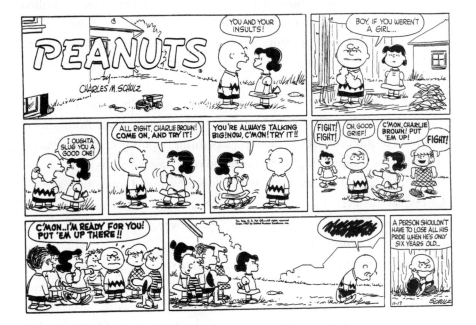

He could also turn the tables on her by putting his head down and losing himself in the act of drawing, as Schroeder had done from the moment Lucy first fixed on him from across his keyboard.

UNTIL HER THIRD CHILD came along in 1953, Mrs. Charles Schulz had no help with the infants or with housekeeping. Joyce raised the children, consulting Dr. Benjamin Spock's *Baby and Child Care*, managing the family's finances, running the household, doing the cooking, cleaning, washing, and folding by herself. Her father had written to her in Colorado Springs to remind her that "a successful life must be a life of study. . . . You will not soak in wisdom from the sunshine and fresh air." Joyce had "a high grade of intelligence," Henry carefully asserted before coming to the point: "What are you going to do with that mind?"

In 1955, with Meredith five, Monte three, Craig two, and Amy to be born next summer, Joyce bought a Baldwin baby grand piano and enrolled in a four-year program at the MacPhail School of Music in Minneapolis, majoring in piano and minoring in violin—four mornings a week, up to two each afternoon. She stayed behind that April, when Sparky went to New York for meetings at the syndicate.

Joyce's father praised her ambition "to become really good in music," and could not help noticing that her mother discouraged Joyce from pursuing a level of professional excellence, "frown[ing] upon [the music courses at McPhail] and approv[ing] Judy's method of taking lessons with no desire to do more than play reasonably well." Dorothy urged Joyce to reach no higher than the level at which her own ambition had been curbed in childhood by a rival's superiority. "But that," said Joyce, "wasn't what I had in mind—playing hymns for people."

Sparky, meantime, was "proud of me," Joyce recalled, "and wanted me to be a great pianist." But in her class at MacPhail she discovered a young woman her own age who had perfect pitch. Faced by a score, Joyce would have to take minutes working out notation that Gloria Mattson could knock off in seconds. "It was so discouraging to me that I quit." It did not matter that Gloria could play anything but without much feeling or expression. When Joyce realized she herself would not ever be anywhere near a great pianist, she stopped playing altogether.

Lucy is the most ambitious figure in *Peanuts*. In this, too, she was like Joyce: set on high objects, although no one can say exactly what. As Schulz once told a reporter, "Joyce studied violin and piano at the Minneapolis Conservatory of Music [*sic*]. Now she bowls." Lucy is simultaneously formidable and ridiculous because she will be denied her ambitions, but she is a powerhouse nonetheless. "Charlie Brown is too vulnerable," Schulz reflected a few years later. "Lucy is too sharp for him, and she is full of misdirected confidence. You have to give her credit, though. . . . She can cut through a lot of the sham and she can really feel what is wrong with Charlie Brown which he can't see himself."

Like Joyce, Lucy is highly successful on her own terms. Even as she throws herself at Schroeder, however much she will always fail to arouse him directly, she uses jujitsu technique to penetrate his defenses, igniting his true passion by belittling his "ol' Beethoven" to his face. In similar fashion, her succinct insight into the essential Charlie Brown will always get him up for one more charge at the football.

Without Lucy, Charlie Brown might have remained the cocky prankster he had been at the strip's outset; her drive sobered and deepened him, opening him up to life's ambushes and disappointments. Colleagues and friends who knew Sparky and Joyce on Minnehaha Parkway believe that, without Joyce, Schulz would have remained in Minneapolis. Monte later recalled, "He wanted to raise us in Minnesota, but Mom made him move." In fact, the time and the place—and Joyce and Sparky's response to Minneapolis in the late '50s—were equally responsible for the Schulzes' restlessness.

IN MARCH 1957, SCHULZ mailed off to Harry Gilburt the beginnings of a new project that he had conceived with Gilburt's sponsorship—a single-panel bridge feature, to be called *It's Only a Game*. Gilburt agreed to be its advocate within the syndicate, but once the sales manager saw the initial sketches, he doubted that enough editors would devote daily space to a feature limited only to the bridge-playing constituency. "Could you broaden the entertainment value among the majority of the public who would not understand and appreciate the finer points of bridge? We'd like to reach a maximum audience for general appeal, particularly now that editors are being pressured to reduce feature content to only the essentials because of rising costs from all directions."

In June, the syndicate signed Schulz's new enterprise to its standard five-year feature contract without further discussion, and on Sunday, November 3, *It's Only a Game* debuted in twenty-eight newspapers, paying weekly rates as high as $35 (the *Washington Post*) and as low as $5 (the Fort Wayne, Indiana, *News-Sentinel*), running as a single black-and-white panel on Mondays, Wednesdays, and Fridays, and as a color triptych on Sundays. The "new and delightfully different comic feature by gifted artist Charles M. Schulz, the creator of 'Peanuts' " was aimed at people who played bridge, golf, shuffleboard, checkers, "or just plain hammock-loafing."

For the first time outside his church cartoons, Sparky had license to focus on a single theme close to his heart—the screwball aggressiveness and sheer competitive nuttiness running beneath any game governed by the social contract—and he happily drew the panels himself for the first three months. But then, unable to find the time to keep producing finished work that met his standards, he turned once more to Jim Sasseville.

Earlier that fall, Sparky had cut Sasseville in on one of *Peanuts'* newest subsidiaries, a full-length, "extended play" comic book published by Dell, which Sasseville agreed to draw and write for the next two years as a direct employee of Schulz's. From ghosting *Peanuts* comic books at a weekly salary of $100, it did not seem too steep a slide into dependence for Jim to take pen and ink to Sparky's weekly set of penciled roughs for the sports panels. Sasseville had, after all, fulfilled the duties of an assistant at least once before—one week in August 1955, when Schulz had to be away, Sparky had asked the syndicate to send Sasseville the weekly color chart for the October 9 *Peanuts* Sunday page. Most important of all, Sasseville had become the one cartoonist besides Schulz himself who had mastered Charlie Brown's head.

For decades to come, amateurs and professionals alike would discover what a difficult job it was to draw the round-headed kid. Charlie Brown's gallery of Chaplinesque facial expressions were hard enough to capture in themselves, but his head had to be rendered with precision to save it from grotesquery. As the next-generation cartoonist Matt Groening recalled of his own and his friends' earliest imitations: "In our wobbly hands, Charlie Brown's big round head turned into a macrocephalic oval. No matter how much we practiced, our Charlie Browns looked like freaks." Chris Ware, another preeminent cartoonist of a later generation, remembered the particular problem of finding the right pen lines for Charlie Brown: "He always comes out looking so *wrong*, a lurid joke, like someone dressed up at a costume party." And nothing seemed to improve the imitator's result: "Even if you think, after repeated attempts, that you've 'got it,' and then look over at one of Schulz's actual drawings to compare—only then do you see how far off you still really are."

By January 1958, Sasseville had learned to copy Charlie Brown's head "with ease" and was sharing Schulz's office atop Art Instruction. The finished art and lettering in *It's Only a Game* had become his official, if uncontracted, anonymous responsibility, for which Sparky paid him 50 percent of his own half-share of the net cash proceeds, amounting to $514.47 in the month of December 1957, which Sasseville considered "great money." Schulz's byline appeared alone on the feature, and he had the "final look at everything." Sasseville obtained approval from Schulz even when he roughed out and then executed his own ideas for certain panels in which Sparky had little personal interest, especially when the theme was football or rodeo.

They met daily in the penthouse studio, and while Sparky drew *Peanuts*, Jim tried to copy Schulz's "adult style" as he took over more and more of the duties of *It's Only a Game*. It was a curious collaboration, less from any difference between Schulz and Sasseville than from their very visible similarities: both were brilliant, insecure, and competitive, with slight but reciprocal variations—Jim could be irritatingly deferential to Schulz, where Sparky could be maddeningly self-deprecating to Sasseville. "You draw so well, you'll sell a strip long before I will," Sparky had always said—right up to the day he left for New York to sell what became *Peanuts*. Even after the failure of their first collaboration, *Joe Cipher*, Sparky routinely let others at Art Instruction know that, between him and Sasseville, he considered Jim the better cartoonist.

Five years younger than Sparky, Jim had grown up Catholic in South Minneapolis. In boyhood Jim had thought himself a "predestined genius . . . fit to rub shoulders with Einstein, Picasso, Stravinsky and the rest of them." His mother had wanted him to be a priest. His father, an alcoholic postal clerk, had belittled Jim's talents, scoffing at his ambition, telling him during one bender, "You don't have the chance of a fart in a whirlpool." By twenty-two, while applying for a job at Art Instruction, Inc., Jim had realized, "here I am just a plain ordinary person."

Their ambition similarly camouflaged, he and Sparky were also alike in boyishness—or, as Sasseville saw it, "both kind of afraid of growth." They had what Sasseville considered a "very close attitude towards sexuality." Like Schulz, Sasseville specialized in relationships with women to whom he was the supplicant—polite, earnest, silently beseeching, frightened at the thought that he might be taken seriously. He was most comfortable with a very attractive woman who kept herself at exactly the most tantalizing distance, who knew "how to handle men"—a "don't-touch-me type" like Charlie F. Brown's sister, Catherine, after whom he had modeled Ginny, Joe Cipher's heart's desire, the curvy rendering of whom so delighted and impressed Schulz that from then on he was set on having Sasseville as a collaborator.

Meanwhile, as the junior partner and pen-and-ink finisher on *It's Only a Game*, Jim found Sparky's flattery frustrating because, as he told himself, the original rough-handed pencil sketches conveyed their ideas better than even his own most carefully rendered work possibly could. But Sparky, bending over backward not to put Jim in the position of an underling, would come into the studio, cast one glance over Jim's latest panel, and say, "Well, you've taken my insignificant little sketch and made a masterpiece of it." ("Don't believe him," Jim's wife, Helga, told him.) Jim's confidence was further eroded by the fact that the syndicate had not been able to sell the feature to a single additional paper after Jim had started to draw the panel himself. "My drawing," he believed, "was failing the whole thing."

What Sasseville understood clearly was that Schulz used self-doubt—his own and others'—to keep people at a distance. For the truth was that, if Sparky had believed in himself, he might have seen that his own freehand improvisational rough sketches from the 1950s indeed met the renowned graphic artist Chip Kidd's later assessment of them: they *were* "worthy of *The New Yorker*." But Sparky never considered his work good enough to offer up at the temples of intellectual humor—*The New Yorker* would be forever "hopeless"—and remained as stuck in self-dismissal as his junior partner, though Schulz's version was the more complicated, because, as Sasseville also discovered, "Sparky had a certain amount of contempt for other cartoonists. He knew that he was better—he even said to me that he was a better cartoonist than all those guys combined. And he really was. He wasn't humble: he knew that he was good."

JOYCE HAD NEVER WANTED a lot of children. It was Sparky, she later contended, who wished for a big family. On April 20, 1958, when she returned to St. Barnabas Hospital to give birth to their fifth child, Jill Marie, the baby presented in breach position, and as Joyce later told it, despite the best efforts of two obstetricians, she almost died. When at last the nearly nine-pound newborn was safely delivered, she immediately elected to have a hysterectomy. "Five kids was enough," she said. "Sparky would have loved to have had more, but I had had it."

Not long after Jill was born they got a letter from a neighbor who had moved to California, describing the orange tree in her new front yard. Joyce was electrified. Sparky would always say that he would have been happy raising the children in Minneapolis, but "Joyce was fed up with living in the snows of Minnesota, putting the kids in snowsuits every time they went outside." He cheerfully admitted that, while "it was a chore, dressing the children in all those clothes," as Joyce was the parent in charge of such duties, "it didn't really matter that much to me."

Joyce wanted to move, but at first she knew only what she wanted to move from, not where she wanted to move to. Both she and Sparky, in their different ways, were painfully misplaced outside a small, immediate circle of friends. Each took life on his or her own terms, and their marriage had done little to ease the awkwardness each felt in any world other than his or her own, though each had immense capacity for community service and for getting a job done.

In their life on Minnehaha Parkway, Joyce had kept her distance most notably from the church, although she had genuine affection for Marvin Forbes, "a wonderful person." But she rarely attended services, and while her proclaimed belief in "a supreme being" was no affectation, she had been unable to find an identity among the tightly knit group of married members with whom Sparky each week attended as many as three services, two or three meetings, and a social event or two.

The women at church found it easy to know Sparky—or thought they did—but hard to know Joyce. Where Sparky was seen as "totally faithful," Joyce's involvement was considered "spasmodic," her outlook "worldly." One pastor's wife recalled, "You could just get so close to Joyce and then she'd kind of back away; I couldn't quite break through the wall." "Joyce wasn't uncooperative—she just wasn't part of the group," reflected one parishioner.

At the Church of God, she noticed that although Sparky's aunt Marion and uncle Buster faithfully attended the Sunday-morning service, certain of the younger members let it be known that Marion, as a divorced woman, had no place in their congregation—an attitude that could only have piqued the former Mrs. Bill Lewis in the first instance. But with Joyce, who loved Marion, it was the principle. Joyce and some of the married women from the church went to help out a German carpenter living in North Minneapolis with eight children; trained in the metric system, he had been unable to make the jump to U.S. equivalents and find work. On returning from the squalor of his quarters, particularly the bathroom, one of the women remarked, "At least they could have had soap." Joyce, who knew poverty, did not hesitate to tell her fellow churchgoer, "If there's a choice between food and soap, you don't buy soap," and went on to coax new shoes for the children out of Dayton's department store.

She shared with Sparky a credo of duty and obligation to the common good tempered by a nearly radical individualism, which he once put this way: "Someone says he's not a joiner? I'm not a joiner either, I don't belong to anything, but I think we all have an obligation." If called upon, Joyce would always step up to twist arms at Dayton's on behalf of a needy family, but she did things her way.

One holiday season, at the close of the church's children's program on the last Sunday before Christmas, she shocked the congregation by hiring a Santa Claus to appear from the back of the church, booming out his ho-ho-hos and scattering candy among the children from a big sack slung over his shoulder. "I just about died," recalled one of the congregants. "It ruined the program, the spirit of it," said another, "but everybody knew Joyce." Characteristically, she had kept it all a surprise, consulting neither the pastor nor the program committee, not even telling Sparky.

But by 1955, with their extraordinary tithes, the Schulzes held a unique place in the congregation. "You might say that God owns a one-tenth share of the comic strip 'Peanuts,' " remarked the *Minneapolis Star*. No other tithing families in the First Church of God in Minneapolis were able to give increasing sums every year, starting at $3,000—or, taken together over the Schulzes' last four years in Minneapolis, a total of as much as $20,000, the 2007 dollar equivalent of $144,155. Sparky became the local church's chief financier, his weight in the small congregation being such that when he commissioned a colleague at Art Instruction to execute a rendering of Christ for the altar, the painting went up in the sacred place without objection, even though certain members of the congregation silently resented the artist for depicting a "Jewish-looking" Savior. "It was an awful picture," Dolores Edes remarked in later years. "Nobody liked it, but nobody would say anything: nobody would cross Sparky, and that's not good for a small church."

"Sparky himself realized that that was not a healthy thing for the church," recalled Kenneth F. Hall. "At the same time Joyce was uncomfortable with the Church of God connection and seemed to resent the responsibilities he was carrying with it."

As some members saw it, Joyce exerted pressure to move him away from his formal church affiliation. "His personality would allow her to do this," added William Edes. "He really never did stand up to her when she pushed." But more than fifty years later, Joyce would maintain that "it was ultimately the attitude of some of the congregation, not approving of his divorced Aunt Marion and their narrow-minded view of the world of those less fortunate which turned me away from them, and possibly Sparky also."

Sparky hoped that Carl and Annabelle would follow them to California, as Joyce's mother and Sparky's aunt Marion and uncle Bus eventually did. He would later say that his "only regret about leaving Minnesota, and it was a strong one, was my dad. My dad and I were close and I know he was just destroyed when we left. But I was one of those husbands who just went along."

They were not certain how to look for a place in California. They knew about Atherton "because Shirley Temple lived there," and about Carmel and Pebble Beach, home to the Bing Crosby Invitational professional-amateur golf tournament, and they had agreed that Southern California, with its movie stars, was "out of the question." Sparky wanted to be near San Francisco and have at least five acres, but also to live in a "real community"; Joyce wanted a place where she could keep horses. Her sister Judy spotted an ad in *The New Yorker* for a real estate company that sold big properties, and Joyce and Sparky flew to San Francisco in late January 1958 and met a realtor from Santa Rosa.

They explored Atherton, Carmel, and Woodside, grew discouraged, and were all set to fly home, when the agent suggested that, just for fun, they have a look in Sebastopol, about sixty-five miles north of San Francisco. There was a place up there in Rancho El Molino, deep in the apple country of Sonoma County—an L-shaped cottage inspired by the rustic Bay Area style of Bernard Maybeck and featuring a studio, stables, and corral, sited on 27.6 acres of rural hillside backed by tall pines and redwoods. The owner of 2162 Coffee Lane, Rolla B. Watt, a photographer, had built the place in 1952, dubbing it "the Coffee Grounds." The asking price was $70,000, more than twice what they had paid for the house on Minnehaha Parkway—and with five fewer bedrooms. Neither Sparky nor Joyce had ever heard of Sebastopol, but it was raining and they had nothing better to do that day, so they went.

SEBASTOPOL'S ORCHARDS AND CANNERIES stood at the center of California's apple industry. In the surrounding valley, the land was covered with growers' trees and veined with railroads carrying produce to market. Fog rolling in over the fifteen miles that separate Sebastopol from the Pacific protected the fruit from too much sun, "sizing up" the fragile Gravenstein, a tangy eating apple prized by bakers and also good for applesauce and apple juice.

In April, snowy blossoms drifted along the roads; in late August, the harvest filled the air with its spicy perfume, and visitors driving through West County neighborhoods were engulfed in the fragrance of baking.

In January, the nostrils of any outsider driving along the Occidental Road would have filled only with dust. But as Sparky and Joyce turned onto Coffee Lane, dropping down into a swale on the far side of a long pasture, dust and bare orchards and railroad crossings were shut away behind them as they entered an enclosed green world, fragrant with pines.

Decades later, Sparky still remembered that as soon as they reached the driveway, he and Joyce knew that this was the place.

# CHAPTER 18

# COFFEE LANE

*Cartoonists don't live anywhere. They aren't real people.*
—C.M.S.

THE PROPERTY WOULD STAMP its name on a whole period of family life. When the Schulz children later spoke of Coffee Lane, they meant more than an estate rolling up a hillside, bordered by windbreaks; thick with blossoming fruit trees; lush with lawns; host to a bedlam of children, pets, livestock, and transplanted relatives; harbor to a constant stream of visitors, friends, business associates, and well-wishers from the world beyond.

Monte remembered Coffee Lane as a time as much as a place—a decade in which the Schulzes seemed to be the center of everyone's life, when Sparky and Joyce formed a complementary couple, and art, comedy, and the latest pop music filled the house—the newest Tijuana Brass album "going full blast" on the record player—and Sparky, a proud father, "whether playing softball, or Ping-Pong, or tennis, or shooting pool, or just sitting around telling jokes . . . beamed and beamed."

Joyce had landed him in "America's America." As the United States stood as the globe's promised land, so postwar California was for millions of Americans the destination to which they journeyed to live out their dreams—never more than in 1958, on the upward swell of one of the largest mass migrations in American history, which by 1962 would make the Golden State the most populous in the nation. Television and major league baseball joined the surge to the farther ocean, and the rest of the country looked on enviously as young middle-class families swarmed into the country without a fear or care, not to reinvent themselves but to dream themselves along in a sun-spangled land of split-level suburbs, station wagons, swimming pools—of "clean family living" as a way of life. One father spoke for thousands when he told *Life* magazine: "My kids have a better chance to be healthy here than anywhere else." On television in 1961, a crew-cut

Schulz downplayed the material luxuries of Coffee Lane, emphasizing, "It's an especially fine place to raise the children. . . . That's what counts."

SUNSHINE FALLS ON SEBASTOPOL 250 days each year, while the rainfall averages thirty-six inches, although the Schulzes' first year at Coffee Lane, which saw sixty-six inches come down, proved to be the wettest since 1941. But farmers turned up bearing baskets of Gravenstein apples, and Sparky and Joyce right away made friends with their nearest neighbors, Pancho Medrano, a garage mechanic, and his wife, Mercy, and the Schulz and Medrano children played enthusiastically together. Upon arriving, Sparky and Joyce were also invited to join a Thursday-night bowling league. With no Church of God nearby, they took a break from church membership, while enrolling the older children in Sebastopol's Methodist Sunday school, where the minister greeted Sparky warmly, inviting him to teach there. "It didn't take us long to figure out that people were friendlier than in Minnesota," Sparky recalled. In the village, no one seemed to care one way or the other that Schulz was a cartoonist, though one tradesman asked, "Can you make a living at it?"

The first years at Coffee Lane coincided with the biggest windfall of *Peanuts* licensing income so far. The paperbound reprints by Rinehart, the games by Selchow & Righter, the comic books by Dell, were all well and good; they kept *Peanuts* in its original two-dimensional world, while greatly extending it. But in 1958 the Hungerford Plastics Corporation created the first set of statuettes deriving from the strip's characters—six-inch-tall figurines molded from Geon polyvinyl, a versatile new material from the B. F. Goodrich Chemical Company of Ohio, whose own national advertisements wasted no time letting people know that "Toys prove there's profit in 'Peanuts.' "

It had taken only ten years for his characters to attain complete reproducibility outside the panels of the strip. In 1960, Hallmark Cards of Kansas City, Missouri, introduced *Peanuts* greeting cards and paper goods. Over the next few years, as Charlie Brown and Lucy and Linus papered the country and sales jumped from $20 million to $50 million, Schulz himself produced some fifty greeting card designs to meet every occasion, even some for which no sentiment had yet made itself felt. Detroit, meanwhile, turned Charlie Brown to even greater profit.

Starting in November 1959, the Ford Division of the Ford Motor Company paid an annual licensing fee for the exclusive right to have the *Peanuts* gang speak for their new compact model, the Falcon, in all media, including magazines, billboards, and animated television commercials. "That's when we first started making what you'd call a lot of money," Sparky later recalled. *Peanuts* commanded an initial fee of $75,000, rising the following year to $82,500, increasing again to $86,000 in 1961, and reaching $90,000 in 1962 and $100,000 in 1963. Schulz's aggregate share of the first five years with Ford amounted to $216,750 (at least $1.3 million in terms of today's buying power), with additional payouts from the century-old J. Walter Thompson advertising firm, still dean of the industry, for special art.

The boy who had drawn the family Ford winding around a mountainside on the first day of second grade in Needles, California, was now working closely with one of Madison Avenue's top white-shoe outfits to produce each print advertisement for the campaign, consulting on every animation storyboard with the art directors and on every word of every script with the writers, while also approving the agency's final selections from among dozens of real children auditioning for the characters' voices in New York and Hollywood—all to make sure that Charlie Brown, Lucy, and the rest would be, as Ford assured the nation, "faithfully reproduced and as amusing selling Ford Falcons as they are in their comic-strip escapades."

Ford, a "man's" outfit, was an index of Sparky's having arrived. He had "always tried to turn out a product of dignity," and he was "glad that we could team up with an advertising client who also had a dignified and respected name." A business associate of Schulz's would recall that both Sparky and Joyce were "very proud of the Ford situation. The feeling was never the same about Dolly Madison cupcakes. But Ford—that was upscale."

Month after month, a steady flow of Schulz-drawn ads passed under the gaze of the combined readerships of *Life*, *Look*, and *The Saturday Evening Post*—an aggregate audited circulation more than 19 million strong. These print ads, together with "Peanuts Love" and other two-minute animated television commercials directed by the former Disney animator Bill Melendez, now of Playhouse Pictures, won J. Walter Thompson a dozen of the industry's highest honors and awards—and helped Ford, which had taken much grief from the steely assertiveness of GM's large-finned luxury cars, to fight back with its compact. The Falcon proved to be "a huge success, profitwise," Ford's then rising star, Robert McNamara, later recalled.

This partnership—extending through seven years of deadlines, meetings, Screen Actors Guild strikes, and continual correspondence and telephone calls between New York, Detroit, Hollywood, and Sebastopol—proved unusually successful and did far more than provide Schulz and his family with the "annuity" that the paternalistic Larry Rutman had been seeking to spin out from the first ten years of licensing offers. Rutman had believed that an "agreement with someone like Ford, or Procter & Gamble for one of their more acceptable products, or General Motors" would put Schulz and *Peanuts* "in pretty good company," and when Ford made its offer, he pushed hard to negotiate a deal to Schulz's advantage.

The lucrative partnership was also the wellspring of a current of criticism that would beat against him until the end of his life, to his unending puzzlement. In November 1959 United Feature Syndicate and Schulz shook hands with Ford and J. Walter Thompson; two months later the Newspaper Comics Council, a trade organization sponsoring events for cartoonists, splashed the first cold water when it invited those attending a forthcoming meeting to a discussion of "How Greedy Can You Get?"

Schulz received notice of the meeting as he sat down to work on Thursday, January 14. "Since 1950 when I first began to draw PEANUTS I have not become angered with anything like I was this morning," he confided to Larry Rutman an hour or two later. "We don't have to read very deep to see what recent deal has sprung this into the open. I highly resent being called greedy by people who have never even met me, and know nothing about me."

In five single-spaced paragraphs—by far the longest, most impassioned letter he had ever written as the creator of *Peanuts*—Schulz analyzed the situation ("The attitudes here are what are disillusioning[,] especially since we were so careful during our negotiations with Ford to do what we felt was right toward our newspaper property") and hammered out his credo:

"The duty of the comic strip is to bring readers to the newspaper as a whole, and I have many letters from readers who say that the only reason they buy certain papers is to read *Peanuts*. If that is not fulfilling an obligation, then I don't know what is." He insisted that "we are primarily in the newspaper business, and will always attempt to make *Peanuts* a feature that will help readers to decide to buy the paper in which it runs. We have not become advertisers first and comic strip dealers second.

"I am thoroughly happy," he summed up, "to be doing what I have dreamed about doing since I was six years old, and this is drawing a comic strip, but I don't think that I am greedy, and I don't think that you are either, Larry."

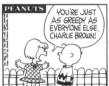

AS TELEVISION FLOODED AND united the nation's homes, transforming the daily habits of millions who had previously acquired their sense of the larger world as readers or listeners, not as viewers, it threatened to sweep away the local institutions on which cities and towns had depended for decades—from the city room to the public library. Newspapers grasped at *Peanuts*, now uniquely valuable, in the words of one managing editor, as a "good hot feature for holding on to readership." As Harry Gilburt crisscrossed the country, he no longer had to sell the leading newspaper in any given territory on *Peanuts* so much as he had to arbitrate disputes over which paper deserved exclusive rights. Struck by how often bitter competitors embraced the comic itself as more than a commercial advantage—the loser in a territorial fight might well be found afterward with a *Peanuts* strip still displayed beside his desk—Harry wrote Sparky: "Evidently Peanuts breaks down all barriers."

And as one or another character rose to prominence, the standout members of Schulz's repertory company—first Snoopy, and later Peppermint Patty, and Snoopy with Woodstock—achieved a star power great enough to stabilize a newspaper's circulation. The executive editor of one such regional institution, William P. Steven of the *Minneapolis Star* and *Tribune*, suspected that using characters as appealing as Schulz's in an advertising program would diminish their power in the newspaper by confusing the public "as to when it can believe the message of *Peanuts*." When Steven heard through the grapevine about the Ford deal in early November 1959, he immediately asked Larry Rutman how United Feature could justify commercializing such a top feature. Rutman replied that after considering all the possibilities "very carefully," the syndicate concluded that licensing the *Peanuts* characters would "not hurt the property nor the interests of the newspapers who are using it," but would instead "enhance its value by the proper usage and broader distribution by a top-flight American corporation."

There was so much money at stake in the television marketplace that the *Peanuts*/Ford issue sharply divided syndicates and cartoonists. But earnings from newspaper syndication were minuscule compared to the multimillion-dollar profits now on offer from TV's corporate sponsors; moreover, the very size of the coast-to-coast and impending global audiences meant greater payouts than ever before from the associated merchandising of licensed toys, games, accessories, and books. By 1960, with television sets in 90 percent of American households and more than a hundred million casting their glow worldwide, every previous form of mass entertainment was scrambling to attain symbiosis with the triumphant new medium.

Over the next five years Schulz's share of licensing income amounted to more than a million pretax dollars, and, starting in 1967, United Feature paid annual premiums of $26,675.50 to insure their forty-five-year-old star's life for another million (the syndicate to be the sole beneficiary), with a double-indemnity clause in the amount of $500,000 in case of accidental death.

But money was only part of what made Schulz an object of jealousy and resentment among his fellows. More than any other of his readers, his peers held *Peanuts*, the first mainstream comic strip ever to regularize the use of the word "depressed," to a higher standard. Jules Feiffer, for one, had initially seen in Schulz a fellow subversive—within the comics world, Schulz would be called "the goyishe Jules Feiffer"—even though their styles and audiences could not have been more different. "I have been giggling for three days over Linus asking Santa Claus to define what is good and what is bad. I have stopped people in buses and subways to tell them about it," wrote the creator of Bernard Mergendeiler to Schulz in December 1959.

Feiffer, the enthusiastically melancholy Jewish intellectual living in Brooklyn, aimed his weekly satirical strip *Sick, Sick, Sick* at a megalopolitan, bohemian readership; Schulz was drawing for everyone everywhere, even when his language and Feiffer's coincided, as in this strip from April 1958:

But in the mid–1950s a large part of his public consisted of good, plain people who felt guilty at being discontented in an epoch of unprecedented prosperity. *Peanuts* struck a chord with those who had thought they had everything they wanted only to discover that they didn't, and needed an acceptably gentle reminder of this insight.

Schulz uncovered topics that in anyone else's voice would have come out as impieties. Linus's wistful reverse-English on W. C. Fields—"If you can't trust dogs and little babies, whom can you trust?"—would have paid off in bitter laughter if Mort Sahl had tried it out at San Francisco's neonihilist North Beach nightclub, the hungry i. Schulz found that by substituting melancholy for anger he could give voice to a kind of sorrow at once inescapable and yet endurable:

In an era when youth was struggling toward still-unmapped freedoms, *Peanuts* made sense.

Schulz did not believe that children were going to be like their parents; he knew, and clearly indicated, that children are highly autonomous. (He treated his own children this way, never dictating to them, not forcing even Sunday school on the younger ones when they showed little interest.) Even before the term "generation gap" came into vogue, a distinct and deliberate separation showed itself between the generations in *Peanuts*. The characters said certain otherwise unsayable things, not to *their* invisible adults, but to one another, inner child to inner child—and this was another of Schulz's impieties, although he never confronted the reader with them. He put things in subversive, not confrontational, terms.

"Nobody was saying this stuff," reflected Feiffer. "You didn't find it in *The New Yorker*. You found it in cellar clubs, and, on occasion, in the pages of the *Village Voice*. But not many other places. And then, with *Peanuts*, there it was on the comics page, and it was the truth."

As *Peanuts* advanced from selling cars and games and toys and dolls and clothes and greeting cards to a broad media front of books and plays and television programs and movies, reshaping, in some cases, the way whole industries sold their products to children (and their ever more child-oriented parents), the adult, college-educated audience that had first embraced the strip's gentle originality began to express distrust of—indeed, alarm at—the brand's persuasive power over the marketplace.

*Peanuts* had been a favorite of the writer William K. Zinsser. "But my affection no longer runs as deep, and it is not because Charlie Brown is any less my alter ego or the truths in *Peanuts* are any less true. It is because the sub-product is smothering my love of the product." Zinsser argued in *Look* magazine that Schulz "took a part of Charlie Brown away from me when he used his *Peanuts* characters" in the Falcon ads, claiming to feel "hurt and puzzled to open a grown-up magazine and see my small friend touting a grown-up automobile. And why wouldn't I be? If there was one quality about Charlie Brown that particularly binds him to us as a character, it is his own hurt and puzzlement when innocence is betrayed. Few figures in fiction are so pure in heart."

Schulz was not alone in leasing his characters to Detroit. In the '40s, Crockett Johnson (*Barnaby, Harold and the Purple Crayon*) had drawn ads for Ford, using his *Little Man with the Eyes*; in the winter and spring of 1959, cartoonists no less august than Rube Goldberg, Charles Addams, and George Lichty had produced visually sophisticated panels in their distinctive styles for American Motors' Rambler. In postwar American society, commercial meant real. If a comic strip did not become commercial, it had failed, and for good reason: in cartooning, the public's was the truly sovereign voice.

The first *Peanuts* commercial for Ford aired in 1959, and the ensuing campaign did more than make Sparky financially secure; it placed his creation at the center of the postwar American economy—one of every seven workers in the United States was in some way dependent on the auto industry—and at the forefront of a trend that would revolutionize the way that Hollywood, Madison Avenue, Main Street, suburbia, and especially that newest force in American life, the baby-boom generation, produced and consumed mass entertainment.

By 1960, with the vogue for Davy Crockett coonskin caps and Hopalong Cassidy six-shooters having run its highly profitable course, TV producers on both coasts were betting that animated cartoons would soon replace Westerns as the basis of television's next fad, and even the most conservative syndicate executives found themselves "just waiting for the right deal to come along." Neither Schulz nor United Feature was yet ready to commit to a producer, director, or team of animators, but as the marquee characters from the most popular newspaper comics of the '40s and

'50s—Dick Tracy, Li'l Abner, Dennis the Menace—began to transcend mere advertising and appear in their own television series sponsored by no less venerable corporations than General Foods, it was now clear that in "a medium of entertainment which permits millions of people to listen to the same joke at the same time, and yet remain lonesome," as T. S. Eliot said of television, "Good ol' Charlie Brown" could be king.

THE GROUNDS AT COFFEE LANE presented a rough, unfinished aspect when the Schulzes rolled up from Minnesota in two cars packed with dogs and relatives and all the paraphernalia of small children. "It wasn't much," Joyce would recall, but for her, Coffee Lane was the place where she could design without a degree and spend money without Lutheran reproach. In California, no one was watching—at least, not in that spirit. The restrictions of the Scandinavian Midwest did not apply out here among the redwoods and apple blossoms. Sunny California gave no thought to the past; it put newcomers in mind of home just sufficiently to feel at ease, then allowed them to unite energy with forgetfulness to create the good life for themselves and a better childhood for their children.

To Sparky, Coffee Lane looked "like northern Minnesota," especially where it rose into a knoll behind the house, thick with evergreens, two Douglas firs overtopping the rest. Back in the Twin Cities he had been labeled a rich man; here in apple country, as one visitor observed, he could "attempt to be ordinary."

Drawn to the old photography studio with its traditional north-light window, he made it his headquarters; with a wing added on, it easily accommodated additional drawing tables for his assistants. But the ugly little redwood board-and-batten ranch house sitting on a concrete foundation was too small for all seven Schulzes, even with the two bedrooms added when they moved in, and so, with plans in hand and now cash in the bank, Joyce, the stonemason's granddaughter, began to build.

At a cost of $20,804.75, she rolled out a tennis court, lighting it for nighttime play (a novelty at that time, when even night baseball games were new), and put in a heated swimming pool, bathhouse, children's wading pool, and stone waterfall, all enclosed by an Anchor fence braced on clean-cut square terminal posts. By the spring of 1960, she had bulldozed a new driveway and car turn, and then began raising a five-thousand-square-foot redwood ranch house some fifty yards from the smaller original dwelling.

"You will be amazed at the progress of the house," Sparky wrote Larry Rutman on April 18, "and at the deterioration of my mind."

"Isn't it a little early in the game to have your mind affected?" replied Rutman. "I can usually coast through three-quarters of the construction period before I see my tailor to be measured for that white, long-sleeved jacket!"

The split-level layout followed the design trend of the era: the "open plan," a union of air and light, eleven spacious rooms flowing easily one into another, each of six bedrooms (the children's rooms decorated in themes compatible with each child's interests) opening onto an extensive redwood deck. A formal dining room flanked a forty-foot, two-level living room, which Joyce carpeted in beige up to a breathtaking wall of picture windows commanding the hillside. In the adjacent music room, she set her black baby grand piano on a raised floor and decorated the walls with landscapes painted in the impressionist manner. She fanned magazines over the coffee table: *Life, Paris-Match, The Reporter, Show, Saturday Review, The New Yorker,* in any one of which on any given week there might be mention of Sparky or his characters.

The kitchen was her command post, and she designed it as "a housewife's dream," with up-to-date conveniences and appliances: two ovens, two refrigerators, and a separate deep-freeze unit for stocking meats, plus a hair dryer, a shampoo sink, a drinking fountain for children, and a breakfast nook. Meantime, the old main house became Sparky's new studio, with an additional apartment for Joyce's mother; the former studio, with its tremendous north-light window, became a two-bedroom guesthouse, soon to be occupied by Aunt Marion and Uncle Bus.

With frontier forcefulness, Joyce cleared tracts of woodland to spread seven acres of lawn watered by a buried sprinkler system and created a park by enclosing irrigated pastures in rustic post-and-rail fences. She rolled out tarmac pathways for bikes and installed a playground with standard school-yard equipment including a slide, swings, and climbing bars; she bulldozed woods to claim a Little League–sized baseball diamond and dammed a spring to form a pond into which she extended a dock. Soon enough, Sparky himself got into the act, putting up a barbecue pit, brick by brick. With a pool in his life, he finally taught himself to swim. "I can even dive for pennies now," he told *The Saturday Evening Post*. "It makes me feel so good."

One sweltering day that first summer—some remembered it as Sebastopol's hottest day in years—with the kids tracking dirt into the newly finished pool from the unplanted edges of the raw deck, Joyce found a local nursery under "B" in the Yellow Pages, and without any hesitation, Violet Bassignani, her son, Tony, a freshman in high school, and his cousin Leroy came over to plant golden juniper around the pool. "If you guys'll come over on a hot day like this," said Joyce, "I'll work with you."

She laid out a formal garden with miniature box hedges inset within the more unbuttoned grounds, and thronged the rolling landscape with flowering plum trees and shrubs: azaleas, camellias, pyracantha, and rhododendrons. Agapanthus flourished along the driveway. "Trees and planting material were sacred to her," Tony Bassignani recalled. "She knew what she wanted; and if she didn't like it, you changed it."

Behind the stables and riding ring, she erected a cow barn with a hay-loft, tack room, and feed room, opening one pasture for a herd of four cows and another for horses and ponies. No fewer than five dogs would eventually inhabit the place, along with ten cats, several ducks and turtles, a pet mouse, a pink-eyed white rabbit for whom she built a hutch, plus assorted birds that filled the Joyce-designed aviary with twittering song. "We had all sorts of animals—one of everything," recalled Craig Schulz.

The splendor of Joyce's creation lay in how clean it all was—and new. At that high note of America's postwar hurrah, within that singularly home-oriented decade, every cycle of the Amana dishwasher, every blade of grass in the Scott's turf, every drop of chlorinated water in the Esther Williams pool, served as warranty of the grace and favor of a non-denominational God who surveyed His children's works and saw them to be good. The most popular form of upward mobility, the embrace of the breathtaking latest—new appliances, new cars, new clothes, all with a mint-fresh gleam—was the Schulzes' strongest indulgence. Joyce's designs would be praised for absence of ostentation and "an easy-going unpretentious quality."

Bigness—that other American indulgence of the 1950s—along with an original but still self-conscious whimsy, were Coffee Lane's chief characteristics. Even in the absurd vocabulary of postwar real estate agents, by which any split-level Georgian on a lot larger than one-fourth of an acre was dignified as an "estate" and anything bigger than half an acre was called a "farm," the rolling acres of the Coffee Grounds were beyond counting. The place sprawled so wide, its plenitude of natural and man-made wonders affording such a kick to the imagination, that it almost had to be cataloged to be brought down to size. Anyone setting out to describe it on paper naturally found himself reeling out a list. Magazines describing Charles Schulz's manorial life invariably rehearsed in awe "his attractive blond wife and five children, three cars, five dogs, calico cat, horse, rabbit, cows, tennis court, swimming pool, formal gardens, and billowing lawns."

Schulz himself would lapse into these rosters of wonder as he gave visitors the "fifty-cent tour," often leaving the sense that "each time he himself is impressed."

Under Joyce's close supervision, Coffee Lane dedicated itself to family-style recreation. No guest was served anything stronger than root beer; no futuristic ashtrays invited smokers to light up; no swearing or crude jokes or monkeyshines were tolerated from visiting cartoonists. When by spontaneous combustion some oily rags in the basement ignited and burned down the original house in 1966, Joyce raised up a toyland on the bereft cement foundation—a nine-hole miniature golf course designed as an around-the-world tour, a veritable Alps rising at its center. Players chose one of two paths through the glacier, skirting a waterfall and playing through a Southern plantation; a five-par Norman castle with a moat and motor-ized drawbridge, which invited golfers to putt through the gate into a tiled courtyard; a hamlet of Bavarian cottages; a Low Countries windmill; a tiled street of Mediterranean houses girt with real wrought-iron balconies and planted with stunted living palm trees; a working waterwheel gristmill; a covered bridge, painted an appropriate Yankee red; and a New England church with a Palladian window and a steeple, atop which perched a glow-ing copper sphere that had started life as the flush ball from a toilet tank. Joyce's originality and resourcefulness with materials—as a child, she had once made an igloo out of a coconut, rolling cotton over the half-shell—was on full display, including the flanged sewer pipe she had reworked into the castle turrets. She had even plaited a splendidly straw-seeming fabric onto the thatched-roof English house by interweaving strands of a masonry brush with nylon thread.

Children and adults could further lose themselves in a privet maze or stroll across the tiny footbridge overarching a little creek that ran through the property. The Schulz sons—Craig, always muddy, a Pig-Pen proto-type; and Monte, sometimes a Linus model, sometimes Snoopy, dream-ing through boyhood in Union-soldier blue—took their adventures into a four-story tree house erected in a grand old fir. After a swim or a few holes of golf, visitors would be challenged to a game of Ping-Pong or pool in a hexagonal, high-ceilinged recreation room called "the Kiosk," which fea-tured its own independent kitchen so that the Schulz kids and their friends could have snacks without walking over to the house seventy-five yards away. Lunchtime guests were invited to picnic at a circular wooden table on whose top carved *Peanuts* characters danced around a lazy Susan.

With road signs pointing the way down "Charlie Brown Boulevard"—a shaded road variously put by reporters at fifty or a hundred yards or a full quarter-mile—and whole swaths of landscape given to the fairways of what Joyce ballyhooed as "the hardest four-hole golf course in the world," its greens flags embroidered with faces from the strip, Coffee Lane unfolded into what *Family Circle* called a "private Disneyland." To Amy Schulz, indeed, it was "our little Disneyland"; Monte Schulz recalled a "western never-never land" and Schulz's secretary, Sue Broadwell, said it was "like a state park, only . . . nicer."

It never stopped surprising Sparky—or his guests from back home—that this was where and how he lived. One day, Fred Shackleton, former pastor of the Merriam Park Church of God in St. Paul, and his wife, Doris, dropped by the Coffee Grounds.

"Sparky, this is nice," called Fred as he climbed out of the car.

Schulz swung an inclusive arm. "Behold," he said, "the power of the American comic strip."

The idea of an ordinary man becoming so rich overnight that he could now foot the bill for any of his wife's appetites, however fantastic, was itself a comic strip theme. The humor of George McManus's *Bringing Up Father*, also known as *Maggie and Jiggs*, was grounded in the mismatch of Maggie, the socially ambitious wife of a newly rich Irish workingman, set on doing everything she can to be Mrs. Big, while Jiggs, nostalgic for his simple life, desires nothing but to be small potatoes again.

Sparky was determined to give wealth the least visible power over him, but Coffee Lane forced him into a lot of fancy footwork to demonstrate that as nearly as possible he was the same Charles Schulz who as a young man had always considered himself "just an ordinary fellow" and had to flood the backyard to skate on. One visitor recalled how Sparky and Joyce were constantly hopping up from whatever they were doing to skim the pool or sweep the tennis court, "doing stuff that middle class people do. They were killing themselves. It took them a long time to learn how to live [their new] life."

But they could still let go and have fun. One never-to-be-forgotten time became known in the family as the Huge Water Fight. It started when Meredith, doing the dishes, sprayed her father, and he wrestled the sprayer away and doused Joyce. Monte and Craig entered the fray with squirt guns, but then Craig filled a bucket from the laundry sink to heave over Meredith and Sparky, and soon everyone was soaking everybody else, using any receptacle they could find. "It was quite a thing to do in a big, expensive house like that," Meredith recalled. "It showed me that my mom and dad could still play."

In the June 1960 strips about Lucy's plans to run Charlie Brown for president, positioning herself to remake the executive mansion, Schulz had anticipated, by eight months, the sweeping restoration on which Jacqueline Kennedy would embark soon after her husband took office. Joyce, meantime, was sailing effortlessly into the First Ladyhood of Sebastopol. In her role as Mrs. Charles Schulz, rebuilding and redecorating at Coffee Lane, her every landscaping decision became a potential boon to the local economy. "You might say they have kept the depression away from Sebastopol," one storekeeper told a *Newsweek* reporter in 1961. "Every time you see a bulldozer going by these days, you know that Charlie and Joyce are making some improvements to their place."

They both gave absolute primacy to the magic of an estate—the building of a dream—and for more than ten years, from 1958 to 1969, including one of the stock market's strongest bull surges, they would end up investing only in Coffee Lane and its improvements, never buying a stock or bond—nothing extramural, in fact, but life insurance and a small house in the St. Francis Wood area of San Francisco, supposedly picked up as a pied-à-terre so that Sparky could avoid hotels during overnight visits to the city, but actually for the benefit of Joyce's childhood friend, Jean Donovan, and her family. Not until 1969, as the great '60s boom began to disintegrate, did an accountant helping Joyce with her taxes become the first to advise her to invest in stocks.

Sparky's father suggested that Sparky and Joyce buy an apartment building as an investment—to Joyce's eternal annoyance, for although she liked Carl, his lack of financial know-how infuriated her almost as much as Sparky's shortage of mechanical prowess. "Your son," she told her father-in-law, "doesn't even know how to turn a key in a lock, let alone fix a broken boiler."

AT THANKSGIVING 1960, THE Schulzes celebrated their first holiday in the new house, Joyce inviting as many as thirty relatives, friends, neighbors, and strays to a feast for which she had spent days baking pies; and she designed Christmas, too, as she would every year, mobilizing a new color scheme—midnight blue and silver, or red and gold—so that everything from wrapping paper to ornaments came in the chosen colors. And to this particular Christmas, Sparky, proud of his family and new home in the first flush of the Ford deal, invited his surrogate father, Larry Rutman.

His own father could scarcely believe his eyes. Carl and Annabelle traveled by train and Greyhound bus from St. Paul in February 1960 for a month's vacation, inscribing themselves in the guest book as "Grandma and Grandpa Schulz." Carl stood in proud awe of his son's success. His one great hope for Sparky had been that he earn enough to own a semi-detached house with a garage. Now here he was, a *land*owner: master of weedless lawns and redwood groves, tennis court, pool, stables—"an establishment to boggle a boy from Selby and Snelling, grander even than the houses on Summit Avenue," as one visitor noted. Why, Sparky's wife had even stocked the pond with forty bass; Carl could pursue his fondest pastime without having to face his alarms at leaving home.

He had thought that Sparky might starve; he had certainly never conceived that anything like this would come of drawing things. Even after Sparky had signed his first contract back in 1950, Carl wondered how his son was going to think of enough ideas to meet payments on the 1950 Ford Tudor. Now he was Ford's spokesman, producing a comic strip that appeared in 614 newspapers, read by thirty-eight million people in thirty-five countries, including, as Carl was quick to say, "by the top people, like in Washington." Then, to shut himself up, he would add, "I don't really like to be talking this way too much, because people put you down as bragging."

But in a strip following his father's visit, Sparky enumerated just how far his own attainments—and Joyce's grand designs—set him apart from the quiet, cautious life of a street-corner barber:

At Sparky and Joyce's invitation, Aunt Marion and Uncle Buster had upended their lives in the Cities and moved into the old photographer's studio at Coffee Lane. "Marion and Bus went with us, and that made it easier," Joyce recalled. "I think Sparky was lonesome for family," reflected Marion's daughter-in-law, Ramona Swanson. "And with the size of their place, they needed extra pairs of eyes, just to keep the kids out of trouble. Bus was going to help with the horses, Marion was going to help with the kids."

But Marion, forced out of her job at the telephone company by a stroke in 1959, now suffered a second one, which made it hard for her to walk more than a step or two. Still feisty and opinionated, a fighter first and last, she started physical therapy, hoping to recover movement in her arms. In August 1959, her daughter, Sparky's cousin Patty, came up to the Coffee Grounds from San Francisco with her roommate, Elise Gallaway; they would serve as models for one of the strip's most significant future duos, Peppermint Patty and Marcie. But on this visit, they made a more immediate contribution. Pat, Elise, Sparky, Joyce, Marion, and Bus were all sitting around the kitchen one evening and found themselves talking about what made each of them happy; one after the other, they took turns defining that elusive condition. "Happiness is a baby who's well," said someone. "Happiness is a yacht," said another. And then, with uncanny confidence, Sparky threw in: "Happiness is a warm puppy."

Eight months would pass before, on April 25, 1960, Lucy delivered that soon-to-be famous line to the nation from the daily *Peanuts*. And nine months after that, a petite and utterly persuasive young woman—five feet, or at most an inch over; her body soft and rounded, her personality tough and edgy; with pale blue eyes, long blond hair worn in a French twist, red lipstick, big round eyeglasses—presented herself at Coffee Lane accompanied by her partner, the quieter, more modest but no less original graphic designer James Young. "Hi," she said, "my name is Connie Boucher and I want to do a *Peanuts* date book calendar."

CONSTANCE KLINGSBORG BOUCHER HAD BEEN born in Minnesota in 1923 to a family of Swedish ancestry on both sides, the daughter of a perfectionist furniture maker who lost his woodworking business during the Depression. In 1959 she had been a window trimmer at I. Magnin's department store in San Francisco, married to her high school sweetheart, John Boucher (he pronounced his name BOW-chur; it was she who decided that the correct form was boo-SHAY), and the mother of two young sons, when she saw the possibilities for a well-drawn coloring book on high-quality paper. Flying to New York to meet Shirley Slesinger, whose late husband had bought the merchandising rights to A. A. Milne's Pooh-cycle characters from the author, Boucher made a deal for $500 ("Coloring book?!" said the widow Slesinger), ran up a prototype, and paid no attention when every publisher she approached in New York told her that no market existed for such a product.

With her husband for a business partner and her store colleague Jim Young as designer, she mortgaged her house, printed and marketed the *Winnie the Pooh Coloring Book* herself, and by the end of Christmas 1960 had sold fifty-two thousand copies at the then unheard-of price for a coloring book of $3 each, netting $40,000. The following year, again using Jim Young's designs, and now with Schulz's and United Feature Syndicate's blessing, she produced the *Peanuts Date Book*, itself an original idea—calendar-sized date books did not exist, let alone one that featured bold graphics, bright solid colors, and the beloved characters and bite-sized nuggets of "impassioned philosophy" from a truthful comic strip. Twenty-five thousand copies sold out immediately. Determined Productions—and a new age in character licensing—was born.

Although Schulz always put the strip first and "never wanted to be another Disney," he was genuinely proud of the things the brand brought forth, and yielded to their variety and multiplicity: Snoopy not just in plush, but in sterling silver, in gold, in platinum, even with a diamond nose; Snoopy as a hair-curler caddy. He went along because, in America, a barber's son does not pass up such opportunities. He did not turn away a force of nature such as Connie Boucher, with her soft goods and merchandise, her lasting commitment to high-quality materials and workmanship, her new gift ideas, her items. He did not say no to Norwich Mills (T-shirts), or Simon Simple Originals (fashion accessories), or the J. Chein & Co. (toys), or Sawyers of Portland, Oregon (Viewmaster scenes), or Carolyn Chenilles (rugs), or King-Seeley (lunch boxes), or Schmid Bros. (music boxes and lamps), let alone Wilson Sporting Goods (baseballs). All else aside, it would appear standoffish and sniffy and undemocratic not to embrace such natural parts of the American scene. If he wanted to be successful in America, he had to play the game on America's terms: *The barber not only serves the public; he has something to sell.*

Boucher immediately followed the calendar with another new idea, suggesting to Schulz one day in 1961 that Lucy's moment of revelation in the original "Happiness is . . ." strip would make an ideal starting point for a little picture book further illustrating the theme. Sparky liked the idea, but doubted that he could think of enough representations of happiness to fill a book.

But Connie's appreciation of his drawing flattered him—Rinehart, the publisher of his books, now merged with Holt and Winston, had never shown interest in anything original from his pen, only strip reprints—and after Connie had left for San Francisco later that day, Sparky remained at the drawing table, sketching and writing page after page of cameos. The happy times in his life, he realized, had come not from "the artificial delights you paid a lot for, but [from] the simple things—like getting together with a few friends." By nightfall, he had composed every gentle page of *Happiness Is a Warm Puppy*.

BOOKSELLERS HAD NEVER SOLD a hardcover quite like the offering that Determined Productions (itself a new and rather different voice in publishing) shipped to stores in November 1962, only weeks after the United States and the Soviet Union had come to the brink of thermonuclear war. The Cuban missile crisis had just died down, and people were again remembering to shave, when Schulz's small, square volume—complete with mocha-shade dust jacket, shocking-pink endpapers, and brightly colored pages—arrived in bookshops accompanied by a letter that closed, "It won't change the world, but we hope it will make things a little more pleasant for us survivors."

*Peanuts* offered no solutions to the world's problems—rather, it made them more visible; neither did Schulz's strip depict, or seek to depict, any final overcoming of life's anguishes. In *Happiness Is a Warm Puppy*, the familiar *Peanuts* troupe served only to illustrate, as Schulz explained it, the "little moments you remember when you stop and think back over your life." But would comic strip fans, or even established book buyers, settle for a tiny, tile-shaped volume offering slices of newly coined folk wisdom at the astonishing price of $2 (the equivalent of at least $12 today)?

*Happiness Is a Warm Puppy* quickly proved itself to be that rarest of publishers' dreams, a favorite of all constituencies, reaching the national best-seller lists on December 2, where it remained for forty-three weeks, becoming the fifth-most-bought book of 1962 and the nation's number one nonfiction—or whatever it was—choice of 1963. Everything that puzzled booksellers—the odd format; the single theme, explored with childlike sincerity through limitless variations; the unnumbered tinted pages through which Linus and Lucy and Charlie Brown and Snoopy romped, not as strip characters but as picture-book archetypes—made it the "gift item" (a new term in retail sales) that people bought for one another to commemorate the most personal of occasions.

A second microbook, *Security Is a Thumb and a Blanket*, with a first printing of three hundred thousand, became the number two nonfiction seller of 1963, ahead of Victor Lasky's *J.F.K.: The Man and the Myth* and even the slain president's Inaugural Edition of *Profiles in Courage*. Even Minneapolis's ruling house, with its *Pillsbury Family Cookbook* at number seven for the year, could not top the barber's son from St. Paul. Schulz observed with justified pride that it was the first time that an author had produced the year's top two best-selling works of nonfiction. To visitors at Coffee Lane, he would offhandedly mention that someone had "figured out statistically that there's a sale of one of my books every ten seconds." Pausing for a few heartbeats, Sparky would cock his head, then snap his fingers: "There goes one now."

Holt, Rinehart had made a success of the first twenty paperback reprints, selling four and a half million copies through 1966— or one every *thirty* seconds. Meanwhile, Fawcett split each Rinehart book and divided the contents, publishing double the original twenty titles as mass-market paperbacks at forty cents each, to sales of more than ten million copies. But it was the steady popularity of Determined's hardcover books that entitled *Peanuts* to shelf space of a breadth that the American bookstore had never dreamed of conceding to any previous cartoonist. By 1967, *Happiness Is . . .* would sell 1,350,000 copies in three languages; *Security Is . . . ,* 500,000; *I Need All the Friends I Can Get*, 175,000; *Christmas Is Together-Time*, 125,000; and no fewer than thirty *Peanuts* titles could be found alongside such best-sellers as William Styron's *The Confessions of Nat Turner* and Robert K. Massie's *Nicholas and Alexandra*.

And there was more to come: reaching beyond books and calendars, Boucher introduced a thirty-two-page children's album that offered puzzles, songs, scissors projects, "*Peanuts* Pencil-Pal letters-postcards-stamps," a *Peanuts* play, masks, a baseball hat, a recipe for "Snoopy cookies," secret codes, painting, charades, a do-it-yourself flip book, and *Peanuts* cutouts to hang on the Christmas tree, as well as eighteen-inch-tall *Peanuts*-character dolls—"the soft, cuddly, pillow-kind that 'you can't find in the stores anymore,' " as Determined quickly let its customers know.

What set Boucher apart, and, with her, *Peanuts*, in a field where marketers had routinely produced cheap merchandise to cash in on a fad—Shirley Temple dolls, Davy Crockett coonskin caps—Determined Productions lavished only the finest, most durable materials and workmanship on its designs: Snoopy dolls "plush enough to make any adult want to suck his thumb," sweatshirts and nightshirts and pillows marketed not to vanish from shelves within weeks but to catch any eye roving over the special in-store *Peanuts* outlets, month after month, year after year.

Quality was of the highest. The only product safety risk was exhaustion—for there was to be still more. Before 1965, when Determined introduced the "Peanuts Sweatshirt" at Brentano's bookstores, from Constitution Plaza, Hartford, Connecticut, to Rockefeller Center, New York, and thence by way of the Mall at Short Hills, New Jersey, to Washington, D.C., no one had thought to market sweatshirts to book buyers. Sweatshirts were sporting goods items worn to warm up before or after team athletics. They were gray or putty-colored, with college names and insignia flocked to the cotton in raised letters, until one day in 1959, a hip San Francisco adman, volunteering to help save a local classical radio station, touched off the Beethoven sweatshirt fad. Howard Gossage's innovation set the stage for the *Peanuts* sweatshirt, which took a highbrow advertising gimmick and broadened it by introducing bold colors—Peacock Blue, Ridiculous Red—and begetting a family of products that included nightshirts, dresses, and pillows all made of sweatshirt material. The front of each garment featured one of the strip's beloved characters (depicted in the huge black graphic style made popular by the Beethoven sweatshirt), while the back spelled out that character's most familiar refrain in all-capital lettering that revived the graphic styles of nineteenth-century circus posters.

Packaged by Boucher, designed by Young, *Peanuts* merchandise in 1965 defined for the curious, clean-cut mainstream the dividing line between the old and the new. The look that Determined Productions gave to its output—crisp lines standing out among ornate Edwardian motifs designed to contrast amiably with the daring colors of the psychedelic '60s—signaled a connection to San Francisco and the mix-and-match of counterculture aesthetic. By the mid-'60s, the voice of Determined—snappy, knowing, sharp—was vox populi. Connie Boucher's finger-jabbing persistence ("If you don't find PEANUTS PROJECT BOOK or PEANUTS CHAR-ACTER DOLLS at your favorite book, toy, or gift store, complain to [1] the store and [2] us, in that order") articulated for consumers the era's first sounds of enlightened grievance.

In the spirit of the age, Connie Boucher sold *Peanuts* as if it was a consumer cause, marketing Schulz as the unlikely point man for everyone "under thirty" and over nine, while Jim Young gave the books and products a look that was at least one half-stroke ahead of no less potent pop culture avatars as the Beatles. A full four years before the Fab Four revolutionized the record industry, printing the lyrics of *Sgt. Pepper's Lonely Hearts Club Band* against a Chinese-red background on the back of the album, so that the words seemed almost to vibrate, Boucher and Young zapped the customer's eye with design schemes that, as John Mack Carter reported, "have virtually taken over Carnaby Street."

William K. Zinsser had no way of knowing how prophetic would be his suggestion that "the time has come for Schulz to take his merchandise out of the bookstores and open a separate outlet for them—like Sears, Roebuck—in every major town." By 1967, Boucher had launched special *Peanuts* boutiques with nursery-sized doghouses in department stores around the country, Selfridges of London had opened a "Snoopy House" in time for Christmas, and the *New York Times* reported that the *Peanuts* industry (which was as much as to say Connie Boucher, who now owned the licensing rights to 90 percent of *Peanuts* products) was "one of the major phenomena of the time . . . running along at a rate comparable to the color TV industry and a great deal faster than trains." Meanwhile, along Parisian boulevards, Frenchmen were heard proclaiming, *Le bonheur est comme un petit chien chaud.*

The "Happiness is . . ." formula permeated mass culture, not for a season or even a year, but throughout the rest of that difficult, splintering decade. "Happiness is a warm puppy" became the phrase launcher of the times. Advertisements, party games, newspaper and magazine headlines, crossword puzzles, grade-school assignments, bumper stickers, campaign buttons, lapel pins—all bore the mark of Schulz's 1962 book and the supposedly vanishing values that it and its sequels extolled in their signature minor key.

In sequel after sequel to *Happiness Is a Warm Puppy*, Schulz embraced the sweet and sincere as comfort and consolation. As seen in—and on—Determined products, *Peanuts* characters no longer endured their souls' individual trials, but instead served as quiet lay figures for a universal review of common dreams. Instead of speaking for all of us simply by being themselves, they became none of us by dressing up as everyone.

By their repetitive and syrupy tone, the little books showed how subtle and many-sided the strip actually was. When Lucy famously embraced a warm puppy that springtime morning in 1960, Snoopy let himself be nuzzled. The next time Lucy tried to cuddle up—specifically, on October 12—she came at Snoopy with open arms and a beatific smile. Immediately he drew back, determined not to buy whatever this fanatic was selling. In the second panel, he breaks into a sweat as Lucy envelops him in the heat of her sincere sloganeering: "There's nothing cozier than cuddling up to a nice warm puppy on a cold morning . . ." But it turns out that for Snoopy there is something all too real and unsafe about a world in which people like Lucy run their emotions hot and cold. "PHOOEY!" he thinks in one uncontrolled convulsion that hurls Lucy backward onto the ground and, "warm" puppy or not, stalks off in a cold fury, warning: "My mother didn't raise me to be a heating-pad!"

ONE DAY JOYCE TOLD Sparky, "Some of the things you're doing show the kids as being very sweet. But always remember it's the contentiousness that makes this thing go." Others agreed. The critic Richard Schickel, a fan of Schulz's who declared *Peanuts* to be "one of the few pop-culture achievements of the desperately dreary Eisenhower years," measured his words as carefully as he could when he reviewed the *Happiness Is . . .* and *Security Is . . .* sequel *I Need All the Friends I Can Get*, but could not help delivering "the sad truth . . . that *Peanuts*, in this book as well as elsewhere, has gone public. The merchandisers have moved in and converted what was once the private preserve of the cultural in-group into a firmly established, national fad." He went on to say that by "cleverly packaging the least attractive, but most popular, element of his cartoon strip—its sentimental cuteness," Schulz "loses the virtues that used to be the great joy of the strip"—"a loss," Schickel explained privately to Schulz in a follow-up letter, "of your delightful tartness."

In the face of such criticism, Schulz would insist that "I don't think it's overly sweet or sticky or cute," often repeating through the years, "Anybody who says *Peanuts* is cute is just crazy. It's not cute. There [are] a lot of bitter and sarcastic things in [it]. I think it's very real. I think you can be real without being vulgar."

Schickel reserved his strongest public critique for the final panel of *Security Is a Thumb and a Blanket*, which pictures Linus kneeling beside his bed saying his prayers—the drawing captioned "Security is knowing you're not alone," which prompted the critic to recall that "since religiosity, along with patriotism, is the last refuge of the tired entertainer, I was prepared to agree with those over-zealous, over-serious people who kept telling me that Charles Schulz had 'sold out.' "

Another commentator took Schulz to task for pampering his audience with his "little books of pop uplift": "They are too easy. No truth worth knowing will surrender without a tussle. . . . If we love a Bach fugue, say, or a Picasso painting or a Nabokov novel, it is because we have teased its meaning out—slowly and with a certain reverence."

"Happiness is not a warm puppy. It's work," the newly appointed Master of Churchill College, Cambridge, Sir William Hawthorne, who developed the jet-engine combustion chamber, sharply observed to the poet May Sarton one morning in 1968. And when yet a fourth critic expressed polite skepticism, suggesting that perhaps life was "more complicated" than the "Happiness is . . ." formula allowed for, Sparky counterpunched, his voice crackling with just-restrained anger: "This is an outrageous accusation. I never said that it wasn't more complicated. But I will defend to my dying day the statement that happiness is a warm puppy. I defy [the critic] to give me a better definition of what happiness is. It may take him a twelve-volume set of books to do it, but in one sentence let him try to tell me better what is more happy than a little kid putting his arms around a warm puppy. If that isn't happiness, I don't know what is."*

His fans knew exactly how complicated life was becoming. In every week's mail could be heard the sheer relief that readers took from their morning's ration of *Peanuts*. Readers of his generation almost always

---

*By 2004, studies would seem to prove Sparky right: "Playing with a dog appears to increase the level of happiness-inducing hormones oxytocin and phenylethylamine," reported *Men's Journal*.

thanked him for having "given us so many happy moments in a worry-torn world." For them as for him, the Eisenhower years had been a time for the celebration of American values. But with Kennedy's assassination and the start of the Johnson years, just as Schulz was pulled center stage, such certainties began to erode. Yes, it was still nice to cuddle a puppy—but as the decade went on and Snoopy stood up and began to think and act like a willful being, his protests offered a sad recognition, even a resigned acceptance, that other *people* were not to be relied on as the source of one's happiness.

"What's so happy about a warm puppy?" asked Linus in June 1964, when Snoopy showed himself to be fed up with unwanted attention. Linus's ability to raise clear, hard issues had become one of the sources of the strip's power. Linus's conversations with Charlie Brown demonstrated that pain, voiced through humor as loneliness, disappointment, rage, had a proper place in the daily culture of comics. But in the Determined Productions library Linus now appeared behind a glazed smile that made him look like the Linus doll made by Hungerford in polyvinyl. *Peanuts*, retextured through plastics, plush, chamois, cotton, and crepe, was becoming an affordable comfort, which is no business of art, but which can make art into big business.

But since businesspeople always came to Schulz, it appeared as if he were the one being acted upon. He let them come and negotiate for franchises, being fair, honest, and uncommonly generous in the deals he made, and actually turned many of them into partners sharing equally in profits. His choices were pragmatic; his self-interest was their self-interest, but he made it look as if it was he who was along for the ride. In fact, Schulz's knack in business came from stepping back and letting talented people find new ways to mint *Peanuts* while getting more from them in the coin of reputation than they took from him in their share of winnings.

"He liked the idea of more money," said one of Connie Boucher's assistants. "But I don't think he really understood that there was [eventually] going to be an army of people banging on doors everywhere just to bring more money in for the corporation."

Ambivalent about the ever-increasing interdependence of the strip and the marketing of the brand by Determined Productions, Sparky put complete faith in Jim Young's talent and judgment. Young's and Boucher's collaboration on plush toy Snoopy won a Massachusetts Institute of Technology design award for excellence in materializing a two-dimensional drawing. But it was the specific artist in the team whom Sparky trusted, as would also be the case at Hallmark, and as time went on, his suspicions of newer designers would come sharply to the surface at the monthly approval meetings: "He was overwhelmed by the samples and product and catalogs and magazine layouts," recalled one assistant who worked at Determined in later years. "It was hard for him to grasp that people had to take his work and then do overlays or expound on it or revise it or change it. It drove him crazy to think that anyone was associated with this, which was an extension of him, as if he were saying, *This is mine, don't touch it.*"

"I don't mind how the *Peanuts* idea is used," he told *Life* magazine for its cover story entitled "The Peanuts Craze," "as long as I feel that it has come directly from my head." He enjoyed discussing the film rights to *Peanuts* with producers who came to Coffee Lane. "But the moment they start talking about 'their writers' I kind of get chills. I want it to be my words in everything I do."

Hard as it was for Sparky to credit anyone else for whatever part he or she played in his larger success, he always emphasized the originality of Connie Boucher's ideas and her high standard of quality as crucial elements that established *Peanuts* in the world outside the comics, not just as a motley crew of drafted spokespersons selling the products of others, or as a craze, but as an enduring international brand in its own right. Boucher— "our Number One licensee," he ever after called her—proved to be the hinge figure, not just in his material fortunes, but in his way of thinking about how the original enterprise should separate itself from the supremacy of the cartoon into the newfound worlds of licensing.

No longer would it be enough just to pull an idea from the air and reify it in the strip. Now began an era of Schulz's life in which everything he thought of was applied by other talents to successive media, from records to stage and screen and television, onward to ever more goods and services. "It's nice," he would eventually say, "to be able to get double action from things."

CHAPTER 19

# GOSPEL

*There will always be a market for innocence in this country.*
—C.M.S.

NO ONE WAS READIER than Charles Schulz to write a parable about commercialism when Lee Mendelson telephoned one Wednesday in May 1965 to announce that he had just sold a Christmas show to Coca-Cola.

For ten years, Schulz and United Feature Syndicate had been turning away offers to put *Peanuts* into film and television animation. Children wrote constantly to ask when Snoopy would be on TV, and he gave each the same brisk reply: "There are some greater things in the world than TV animated cartoons." Then in late 1963 Lee Mendelson, a thirty-year-old independent producer in the San Francisco suburb of Burlingame, persuaded him to sit for interviews as part of a documentary about his life and work, *A Boy Named Charlie Brown*—a kind of ironic companion piece to Mendelson's first film, *A Man Named Mays*, about the San Francisco Giants' great centerfielder.

Mendelson had gotten his start in television in 1960 as a production assistant at KPIX-TV, the CBS station in San Francisco. His Willie Mays film had been broadcast to acclaim on NBC in October 1963, and he hoped to bring that production's level of originality and imagination to the Schulz documentary by including the *Peanuts* characters in a brief segment of animation, for which, at Sparky's insistence, he had brought in Bill Melendez, the Disney animator who had earned Schulz's respect by *not* Disneyfying the *Peanuts* gang when he made the Ford commercials. Melendez, an animator on numerous Mickey Mouse cartoons and films such as *Fantasia*, *Pinocchio*, *Bambi*, and *Dumbo*, had established his own production company in Los Angeles by 1963. Schulz trusted him to place Charlie Brown and the others into animation without changing their essential qualities, either as "flat" cartoon characters or as *his* cartoon characters.

Melendez had never before produced a half-hour program, but when he met with Mendelson and Schulz in Sebastopol over Memorial Day weekend to flesh out ideas for the script—to be written by Schulz, storyboarded by Melendez, and animated by Melendez's team of fifty artists—they had six months and a budget of $150,000 with which to create a running film from more than ten thousand hand-painted cels—a production that would usually be completed over the better part of a year.

Theirs was a highly productive collaboration, each bringing something characteristically valuable to the work. They made production decisions immediately: whether to hire adult actors to imitate children's voices, as was traditional in animated children's programs, or to find children with Screen Actors Guild cards and just enough experience to read the parts. "This is where Schulz was smart," Melendez later said, "he let us do it"—leaving Lee and Bill to audition some forty-five kids, ages six to nine, and then train the cast of seven principals, some of them too young to read, yet who, under Melendez's close direction, delivered their lines with startling clarity and feeling. The children's voices paid off most strongly when addressing the show's more adult themes; children, after all, are consumers at heart—what child ever worried about the commercialism of Christmas? But the aloneness and isolation of being lost in melancholy thoughts at a compulsorily happy time would come through in *A Charlie Brown Christmas* with limpid authenticity, enunciating those heartaches that are peculiar to childhood.

The show's soundtrack was among its most original and powerful strengths, the children's voices projecting over a spare, uncluttered background that imposed no ambient undernoise and no uproarious prerecorded laughter—something Mendelson had suggested at the Memorial Day weekend meetings "to help keep it moving along." Schulz loathed the hyena hilarity of canned merriment and rightly judged that an audience would not have to be told when and where to laugh; Mendelson countered that all comedy shows used such tracks. "Well, this one won't," said Sparky firmly. "Let the people at home enjoy the show at their own speed, in their own way." Then he rose and walked out, closing the door behind him.

Mendelson, shocked, turned to Melendez. "What was that all about?"

"I guess," replied Melendez, "that means we're not having a laugh track!"

Mendelson later called it their one disagreement; Schulz termed it the production's biggest decision. Melendez recalled that in their frequent meetings over the months and years ahead, as more than seventy animated specials were matched to the calendar of national holidays and rituals, Sparky "was very sensitive and you had to be very careful not to open that window for anything. You could make fun of something, but if you hit home, he would really withdraw."

On the subject of scoring and music for *A Charlie Brown Christmas*, however, Schulz put aside his own tastes—indeed, his prejudices—and, fortunately, deferred to the producer. Two months later, he told a reporter, "I think jazz is *awful*"; he had once said to his friend Philip Van Pelt, who himself played trumpet, that "the only kind of jazz that I really like is that sort that has a trumpet in the combination." But for the Christmas show he agreed that they should try to mix traditional hymns with "that jazz music" that they had used in Mendelson's documentary *A Boy Named Charlie Brown*.

Left to himself, Sparky might well have chosen only traditional music for the special (Schroeder plays Beethoven's "Für Elise" in the school auditorium), but, as with so many other matters in his life as creator of *Peanuts*, jazz would simply happen to Charles Schulz—a bubbly, childlike, but also sophisticated and bluesy jazz. The Grammy Award–winning composer Vince Guaraldi was known to jazz musicians as "Dr. Funk." Like others whose talents became layered in with the *Peanuts* phenomenon, Guaraldi gave Schulz's work a contemporary musical signature that proved to be exactly right for his characters. The catchy rhythm of "*Linus and Lucy*," a modest but witty piano piece that Guaraldi had composed for the Mendelson documentary and played at the Monterey Jazz Festival, became the centerpiece of *A Charlie Brown Christmas*, and eventually a pop music standard. But it was the slower, mixed–mood, improvisational pieces in Guaraldi's jazz suite, especially *"Christmas Time Is Here"* (lyrics by Mendelson) that elicited the unarticulated emotions lying below the holiday's joyful surface.

Mendelson and Schulz initially agreed that the show would include outdoor winter scenes and that staple of children's Christmases, the school play, Sparky recalling the terrors of having to memorize lines for such roles as his performance as the letter "A" in the D Street School's pageant in Needles. Lee and his wife had read Hans Christian Andersen's "The Fir Tree" to their children the previous year, and when he suggested that the show somehow involve a comparable motif, Sparky seized upon the idea: "We need a Charlie-Brown-like tree."

In the pool at Coffee Lane over Memorial Day, Schulz remarked to Mendelson that the true meaning of that holiday—called Remembrance Day in his childhood and observed as a time to honor the nation's war dead—had been lost in the general good-time frivolity. The same had become increasingly true of the religious observance of Christmas, but Sparky insisted that the season's true meaning could be found in the Gospel according to St. Luke, and they agreed that the show would somehow work in the Nativity story.

But Mendelson had not realized just how much of the Gospel Schulz intended to include in the movie. When Sparky began work on the script, he "proudly announced," as Lee recalled it, that there would be "one whole minute" of Linus reciting the Gospel (not reading it, as in the strip).

"But this is an entertainment show, Sparky," said Mendelson ("gingerly," he later recalled).

Network broadcasting in the three-channel world of the early 1960s was driven by a single, impossible mission: to please everyone and offend no one. Not only would the show have to pass muster ahead of time with its commercial sponsor and network executives, but it would also be vulnerable to the aftershocks of government regulation and popular taste, all of whom and which pretended that, so far as the world of national entertainment was concerned, religion—or, more exactly, religious differences—did not exist.

Sparky insisted: "We can't avoid it—we have to get the passage of St.

Luke in there somehow." He looked at them for a moment in silence, and then turned his "strange blue eyes" on Melendez, and said, "Bill, if we don't do it, who will?"

THE CHURCH OF GOD had given him both a home and a family in the war's lonesome aftermath. Yet in the years since moving to northern California he had ceased to be a churchgoer, although he taught Sunday school at the Methodist Church in Sebastopol and contributed a youth cartoon panel every two weeks to the Church of God magazine. But he consciously dodged questions about his faith and, when asked why he had stopped attending church altogether, said only, "I don't know where to go. Besides, I don't think God wants to be worshipped. I think the only pure worship of God is by loving one another, and I think all other forms of worship become a substitute for the love that we should show one another."

Prayer also began to puzzle him ("I find it very difficult to know how to pray sometimes," he said in 1977) and he complained in 1963 that the ceremonies of church were empty of the essence of true belief: "Many people attend church on Sunday with the same feeling that they attend a theater. They just sit there and enjoy what is going on . . ." Even the sacraments were misrepresented: "You cannot 'take' communion. You are *a part of* the Communion."

He read the text of his Standard Revised version of the Bible word for word at least four times with study groups, but as time went on, he found himself looking at his own markings in puzzlement: "I know that the underlined passages served some purpose, but here and there are verses that have no special meaning to me. It is almost as if a friend had secretly opened the book and made some markings just to tease me. What was the spirit trying to say to me then that I no longer need to hear? Or, what was I listening for then that I no longer care about?"

More telling still, in Schulz's copy of John Updike's 1972 story collection *Museums and Women*, he marked the page number, not of Updike's reference to a Snoopy decal in one story, but of a more interesting, perhaps equally self-applicable passage: "He was not, as he understood the term, religious. Ceremony bored him. Closing his eyes to pray made him dizzy. He distinctly heard in the devotional service the overamplified tone of voice that in business matters would signal either ignorance or dishonesty."

Between 1965 and 1975, Schulz underwent a transformation. "I have changed my views completely," he said in 1971, reluctantly explaining that he was "quite certain [that] Jesus had no intention of establishing a new Church. I'm quite convinced man isn't saved through sacraments." He did not go further than this in public, nor did he formally recant, but he began to exercise his extremely independent turn of mind, often saying, "I'm not an orthodox believer, and I'm becoming less of one all the time."

In later years he tried to put the change onto Joyce, saying that "my first wife didn't care much about getting involved in the church once we got out here [to California], so we sort of drifted away from it." But Joyce countered still later that she did not believe that it was her "refusal to continue in the church that turned him away." She could not explain exactly what had happened but maintained that Sparky had always been "more a scholar of religion" than a dogmatic believer.

More and more he operated in the tradition of his prairie poet hero Edgar Lee Masters, a freethinker who despised hypocrisy in fundamentalist preachers. "My own theological views have changed considerably over the past twenty-five years," he wrote in 1975, "and I now shy away from anyone who claims to possess all of the truth." He had come to think of evangelical Christianity as a danger to independent thinking. "I am fearful of an overly organized church and I am *very* fearful of a church which equates itself with Americanism," he said as early as 1967, identifying it as a "frightening trend: people who regard Christianity and Americanism as being virtually the same thing."

He kept a sober and irreverent eye on the world around him, seeing through the very things that many people thought him too conservative even to question. Yet to the end of his life he was known to the public as a quietly reverent Christian, who "even in a bright green striped sport shirt looks like a minister or a priest," as goes a typical newspaperman's description of the famous cartoonist onto whom people more and more easily projected what they wanted to see: "You keep picturing his ascetic face above a clerical collar. He doesn't look Schulzy at all. . . . His hands form a gothic arch beneath his chin. The studio is monastery-quiet. It's a study, a scriptorium. . . . It's like a sanctuary . . ."

When another of the strip's stunningly varied subsidiary successes, Robert Short's *The Gospel According to Peanuts*, came along in December

1964, many readers took this new theological spin on Charlie Brown as proof that a cartoonist who had long identified himself as an active church-man in an evangelical "movement" would naturally take this extraordinary, surely God-given, opportunity as a medium for occasional witness. As it turned out, *The Gospel According to Peanuts* became another number one national best seller in hardback, snapped up at the rate of four thousand copies a week, with more than ten million of its paperback edition eventually scattered through the world.

Christians of strict faith held up Schulz as "a devoted Christian and dedicated churchman . . . a model Christian professional artist, a loving family man, an unabashed witness to Christ as his Lord and Savior." *Christianity Today*, which saw itself as "ideologically in accord with Schulz's [*sic*] own evangelical Christian convictions," embraced the cartoonist as "a devout evangelical." The secular press, meantime, found it "rather incongruous" that the cartoonist worked at his drawing board with a small picture of Christ hanging above his left shoulder.

People on all sides of religious debates made such sharply personal assumptions about Schulz and *Peanuts* that he could respond only with a sigh. In the course of the most innocuous newspaper interview he was now routinely asked, "Do you think it's necessary to believe in Christ to go to Heaven?" To which he would reply in his mildest voice with a brief, ambiguous statement, and then afterward, among friends, protest the idea that such a question could be answered by anyone.

"His positions were much more liberal than he had let people know when he wrote for Billy Graham," Robert Short observed. "Sparky could talk with the conservatives and sound like the conservatives, but in his understanding of God, there was always this very humanistic liberal strain that was beneath the surface."

The article of faith that most sharply divided Schulz from strict fundamentalism was his belief that *everybody* was destined for salvation. "He believed that very strongly," said Short, "but he had to be careful that he didn't offend a lot of his audience, because he wanted to be the world's most popular cartoonist, but he knew that he would be drawn into these questions, and he didn't want to disappoint people or upset them with his own theology."

For all its steady reference to the Gospels, *Peanuts* turned its back on revealed religion. "It's not an evangelistic strip," said Schulz. "In fact, I'm anti-evangelistic." But even in the mid-'50s, when he was still tithing at the Church of God, he lampooned the kind of street-corner evangelizing, or "giving of testimony," that he himself had engaged in as leader of his Church of God youth group at the Union Gospel Mission, even indirectly drawing on such placard sloganeering as could be found at such Twin Cities outreach centers as the Gateway Mission in Minneapolis, which in the 1940s posted on its walls: JESUS NEVER FAILS! The cult of Beethoven, the cult of suppertime, and the cult of the Great Pumpkin all served to show how the exclamatory avowal of one's beliefs could only place more obstacles between man and God.

The strip refused to say that suffering was the consequence of sin. When Snoopy's doghouse burned down one night in September 1966, Schulz treated the fire as an inferno, drawing the blaze as a high-contrast tableau in which the night's blackness is as threatening as the fire's white plumes.

The next morning, the doghouse's skeletal, still-smoldering carcass hulks wretchedly among puddles, as Snoopy examines the blackened ruin from all sides, then sits down and cries. Soon Lucy is on the scene, casting judgments. "You know why your doghouse burned down? You sinned, that's why!" The voice of every punitive Lutheran that Joyce and Sparky grew up with runs gleefully on: "You're being punished for something you did wrong!"

The theme of questioning and faith, which was central to his life, had emerged in the strip's Great Pumpkin sequences, where Linus, smart but simple, had gotten ahead of himself in holidays and begun to believe that an omnipotent pumpkin would appear on Halloween to serve good little children as Santa Claus did on Christmas. But, of course, the Great Pumpkin does not come to lavish toys on all good little children. Linus performs a mitzvah every Halloween in going to the pumpkin patch to do what he must to be betrayed again. The reader does not discern any radiance of certainty; the worshipper is not alight with enduring faith—he's hopelessly hyped up: enthusiasm is a more modulated and cheering emotion. Linus is keyed to the highest pitch as he marches out with his placard: WELCOME GREAT PUMPKIN! His willed mania demonstrates that people would rather live drunk on false belief than sober on nothing at all, at whatever cost in ridicule. Schulz is saying: be careful what you believe.

From *Peanuts*' language of broadly understood terms, he could side-step any truth about which he was called upon to give unequivocal testimony simply by blinking modestly, chuckling lightly, and saying, "I'm wishy-washy." As Violet and Patty sum up "Good ol' wishy-washy Charlie Brown": "He seems to get along with everybody . . . Nobody hates him . . . Everybody likes him." "That was a part of his cover," reflected Bill Melendez. "Schulz behaved like that, but *he* didn't want to be considered wishy-washy, no, sir." Another defense, still available from school days, was "to play dumb," as Robert Short frequently observed in this period. "He would try to be an ordinary Joe and say that all these things were beyond him, and they weren't, and I don't think he was dumb for one minute."

One Sunday in October 1963, Sally had hidden behind the living room sofa to confess to Charlie Brown that she had prayed in school. Both sides of the school-prayer debate wanted to reprint the strip, each seeing in it an affirmation of their position. Sparky himself later came out and said that he personally was opposed to prayer in the schools. But he did not actually care that both parties could find their message in a single strip—this happened over and over to *Peanuts* with any number of public causes. Schulz's artistic disinclination to involve his strip in politics would have been understandable, but again and again he protested that *Peanuts* was a commercial property and could therefore not be accused of "selling out" or going commercial. And yet the same did not apply to politics or to moral or religious confrontations. When the time came to decide to whom Charles Schulz and United Feature Syndicate would grant permission to reprint the Sunday page in which Sally whispers her secret, Sparky simply denied permission to both parties.

That same year, 1963, Schulz talked about "Christian living" for the Reverend Billy Graham's publication *Decision*, but later admitted that he had answered the magazine's questions out of a sense of obligation. "I really didn't want to," he told an interviewer in England in 1977. "I answered in a rather wishy-washy manner, I suppose. I said the things that they wanted to hear, and if I had said other things, they wouldn't have printed the article, I'm sure."

Yet Schulz's spell over religious groups became so powerful in these years that both the visual and the verbal imagery of the doghouse provided an idiom for faithful people to express their own struggles in life and love. In April 1966, Thomas Merton, a Trappist monk at the Abbey of Our Lady of Gethsemani in Kentucky and an internationally famous spiritual writer, fell into a romance with a student nurse in Louisville, a relationship partly founded in a shared passion for *Peanuts*. Their correspondence rehearsed Merton's struggle with his feelings over whether to leave his order and used Snoopy to express the conflict. In one four-page letter from the nurse, Snoopy became a monklike figure who stubbornly refused to leave his solitude. The doghouse became a working abstraction for the monastery, with Snoopy on the roof like an abbot or knight on his tomb, thinking "It's nice to have a friend."

Commenting on changes in the nation's iconography, John Updike noticed, by the end of the decade, that the illustrations in church pamphlets and broadsides "look more and more like *Peanuts*":

Charles M. Schulz, America's leading cartooning Christian layman, has engendered a race of anonymous imitators in the ranks of ecclesiastical publicity; the crucifix and the bearded shepherd have yielded to a new, evidently more potent image—that of the round-headed, childlike Everyman with a worried look. That worried look, we suppose, contains the residue of Original Sin, or at least guilt, or at least angst, or at least the suspicion that one should stay off the golf course on Sunday morning.

What Schulz had been doing on Sunday mornings in the early years at Sebastopol was studying the Gospels: first, by himself, alone in his yellow chair in the library at Coffee Lane, consulting his favorite reference text, Abingdon Press's twelve-volume *Interpreter's Bible*; then an hour or two later with twenty-five adults at a Sunday school class at the Sebastopol Methodist Church, to whom Schulz would raise a topic, "something he was questioning or had read," but would never comment himself. "He sat and listened to what the rest of us were saying" recalled one of those regularly present. "He was always searching, always questioning."

The life of Jesus remained for him a consuming subject, but Joyce no longer attended church, and though he had enrolled Meredith, Monte, and Craig in Sunday school, they had shown little interest. As Amy and Jill grew older, he did not try to interest them in Sunday school either—indeed, with his younger daughters, he was shy even of talking about what he called spiritual values: "There are a lot of things I'd like them to know that I'm afraid to tell them, because I just don't know how," he said in 1967. "I don't like to lay those down in black-and-white terms, because I don't believe in that. So it's a mystery to me. I don't want to be a lecturer—I think there's nothing more boring than being lectured to by an older person—and my greatest fear in life is that I'll be a bore."

"I'm not a teacher," he often insisted. "I don't like teaching anybody."

Amy never forgot her father reading the Scriptures in his yellow chair, but more vivid still was the fact that "he never read [them] to us kids and he never took us to church. He didn't share it with us." Amy was twenty-two before she ever opened a Bible. After her own conversion to the Latter-Day Saints, she told a church publication, "I wish I had learned all this before, when I was growing up."

At Christmas, the Schulzes decorated the Coffee Lane house with a tabletop crèche made of wood. "But," Amy recalled, "no one ever told us what it was for."

WHEN THE SCRIPT WAS finished in June 1965, Lee Mendelson made one last stand against Linus's recitation of the Nativity story, insisting that religion and entertainment did not mix on television.

"He just smiled," Mendelson later wrote, "patted me on the head, and left the room."

With that, the plot of *A Charlie Brown Christmas* was set: Charlie Brown is searching for the true meaning of the holiday. He doesn't understand why he should feel depressed, with Christmas only days away. The untroubled, childish greed of his amateur psychiatrist, his little sister, and his nutty dog, each of whom has found a way to make money from the holiday's excesses, only adds to his dismay. In consultation with his analyst, Lucy, he decides that what he needs is "involvement," and takes on the job of directing the school's Christmas play, the rehearsals for which play as comedy when Charlie Brown tries to master a cast that includes Linus as a shepherd who hangs on to his security blanket by turning it into a burnoose, Pig-Pen as the dusty innkeeper, Frieda as his dirt-allergic wife, and Snoopy, ever the company's scene-stealer, as all the animals at the manger. The actors' foolishness threatens to corrupt the play's very theme, and when Lucy tries to get Charlie Brown to face up to the reality—hers, at least—that "Christmas is a big commercial racket . . . run by a big Eastern syndicate," he decides that a Christmas tree is what the show really needs. Alas, the sad little fir that he brings back to the set provokes jeering, scorn, and personal insults; yet just as he is about to give up on Christmas altogether, Linus takes the stage, asks for the auditorium lights to be dimmed, and recites the story of the birth of Christ.

The clean and forceful words of the Gospel revive Charlie Brown, and, his faith in the sacred meaning of the season renewed, he takes the little fir home to his backyard to decorate it properly. But when the weight of a single scarlet ornament borrowed from Snoopy's crazily decorated prize-winning doghouse threatens to snap the frail tree in two, he gives in once more to self-loathing and despair, and shambles away. Only the love and attention of his newly forgiving friends bring about the final miracle.

With Charlie Brown offstage, all gather quietly around, as Linus swaddles the ugly, unwanted branches in his now-magic blanket, while Lucy and the rest of the gang, emphasizing the spiritual virtues of modesty, turn their backs to the audience and take down the ornaments from the garish secularist doghouse to transform them into the proper trimmings of a gently beautiful, unassuming monument of faith. When Charlie Brown reenters to behold this awesome sight, he, too, becomes part of the miraculous transformation. The children—even Lucy acknowledging that although Charlie Brown is a blockhead "he did get a nice tree"—burst out in united chorus "Merry Christmas, Charlie Brown!" and he joins his little world's soft caroling of "Hark! The Herald Angels Sing," around the now magnificent tower of light and beauty, as snow begins to fall.

WITH A WEEK TO go before the show's prime-time airdate—and more than $25,000 over budget—Melendez turned over the first "answer print" to Mendelson, who delivered it to Coca-Cola and its ad agency McCann-Erickson, and then to CBS.

In a screening room at network headquarters in New York, two CBS vice presidents watched the show in silence. "Neither of them laughed once," Mendelson recalled. When the lights came on, the executives shook their heads and shrugged. "Well," said one, "you gave it a good try." "It seems a little flat," said the other. "Too slow," said the first, "and the script is too innocent." "The Bible thing scares us," said the other. The animation was crude—couldn't it be jazzed up a bit? The voice talent was unprofessional—they should have used adults. The music didn't fit—who ever heard of a jazz score on an animated special? And where were the laughs?

Frank Stanton, president of CBS since 1946, later recalled that after he himself had screened the show, he "had a difficult job selling [it] to some of my associates. They thought I had really flipped." Stanton, "the Statesman of Broadcasting," had built his reputation on turning CBS founder-chairman Bill Paley's big dreams into clean, orderly, corporate reality. He claimed no special instinct for what would go over on the air, but a doctorate in psychology from Ohio State plus ten years in CBS's research department had taught him that respectability and cleanliness were essential values of the American television audience of that time. He also had a pure visual sense, a love of design. The son of a manual arts teacher in Dayton,

Stanton had created the CBS network's simple logo (Paley had wanted the CBS eye to have a cloud passing in front of it), and he had overseen Eero Saarinen's choices for "Black Rock," the austere modern CBS building, even selecting the granite himself.

Stanton knew the power of a classically clean line; but it was his friend the timelessly stylish furniture designer Florence Knoll who "thought that Schulz was the beginning and end of everything" and had pushed *Peanuts* across the network president's uncluttered desk at least as early as 1959. Stanton and his wife, Ruth, had also been friends with Milton Caniff since grade school in Dayton, and Stanton would have liked to have turned *Steve Canyon* into animation for CBS, but he could see why Charles Schulz would translate to television in ways that the "racy" characters and essentially illustrative draftsmanship of his old friend Milt would not. *Peanuts*, however, "didn't have the class that some of my associates were looking for, and of course, that was just one of the reasons that it was so great." Schulz, Stanton would later say, was a "pure cartoonist," and although "Charlie Brown didn't have fancy sets, and the specials at that time were real Hollywood productions—simplicity wasn't known to them—you just had to have an idea."

*A CHARLIE BROWN CHRISTMAS* was broadcast as scheduled at 7:30 P.M. on Thursday, December 9, preempting *The Munsters*. Almost half the people watching television in the United States tuned in—some fifteen and a half million households—and found themselves breaking out in gooseflesh as Linus walked in silence to center stage, dragging his blanket, called out "Lights, please?," and filled the empty auditorium with his clear recitation of the Gospel's tidings of great joy to all people. For years, viewers would be surprised to find themselves once again moved to tears by Linus's unadorned rendition of the Nativity. The simple, lisping authority of his exit line, "That's what Christmas is all about, Charlie Brown" would forever bind Schulz and his characters to the pure heart of the season.

The next day, "all heaven broke loose," as one adman in New York summed it up. *Weekly Variety* called the show "fascinating and haunting," the *Philadelphia Inquirer* declared it a "Yule classic," and United Press International's Rick DuBrow correctly foresaw that the "*Peanuts* characters last night staked out a claim to a major television future." Across the country, reviewers raved about the "special that really is special," hailing the children's voices as an innovation, and praising Vince Guaraldi for giving *Peanuts* what no other cartoon had ever had on television: a score sophisticated enough to translate into sound the poignant, joyous, mixed-mood quality of the beloved strip; the melodies seemed almost to "commiserate with you," one critic observed. The *New York World-Telegram* proclaimed Linus's recitation "quite simply, the dramatic highlight of the season," and letters poured into CBS, thanking Charles Schulz for "keeping Christ in Christmas."

Four months later, *A Charlie Brown Christmas* won television's most coveted honor, the George Foster Peabody Award, but faced stiff competition for the Emmy Award for Outstanding Children's Program from CBS's *Captain Kangaroo.* The awards ceremony in May 1966 was broadcast simultaneously from New York and Hollywood, and when, in New York, *A Charlie Brown Christmas* was declared the winner in its category, a moment's stunned hesitation followed at the Mendelson-Melendez-Schulz table before Lee and Bill, in sleek black tuxedos, rose from their seats. Sparky remained in his chair, and Lee paused beside him, urging him to accompany them to the stage. With a stiff smile, Sparky waved him on his way.

At the podium, Lee accepted the award from Danny Kaye with the solemn words: "It is our great pleasure to introduce to you the man who's brought so much happiness to so many people—Mr. Charles Schulz!"

Sparky appeared in a moment, resplendent in shawl-collared tuxedo, smiling nervously. Lee, meanwhile, pressed the Emmy on Bill, who urged it on Sparky, who looked up shyly and, accepting on behalf of his character but not himself, sealed the Charlie Brown–Charlie Schulz myth forever by saying, "Charlie Brown is not used to winning, so we thank you."

HIS FATHER AND ANNABELLE, on a vacation trip to the West Coast, attended the Hollywood ceremony.

Since 1958, after Sparky had left Minnesota for good, he and his father had come to keep in touch only rarely, and months often went by without either of them calling or writing. Later, Sparky expressed regret that he had failed to tell his father certain important things, such as how proud he had been of Carl's serving as an usher at the Gloria Dei Lutheran Church that Carl and Annabelle attended. In the end, however, he had the satisfaction of knowing that his father had seen him at the very pinnacle of American entertainment.

After the Emmys, Carl and Annabelle visited Coffee Lane to savor the triumph. Monte Schulz remembered it as "a weekend of clouds and the darkest skies."

Carl, at sixty-nine, was thicker, his face jowly, his hands hammy. He had hung up his white tunic and put down his clippers two years earlier. He had been a neighborhood institution at the corner of Selby and Snelling for almost five decades, rising to high office in the state and national associations of Master Barbers and Beauticians, indeed serving as national president. Even in retirement, he kept up his license, and went on barbering a few old regulars by appointment. But an era was passing. "The Beatles put an end to the golden age of barbers," recalled one of his colleagues. "Guys wanted their hair styled, not cut."

Bedeviled by angina, Carl gobbled nitroglycerin tablets all the way from Minnesota to California. Joyce recalled that Sparky was upset with Annabelle for having pushed his father to make the trip by car. Why, for heaven's sake, hadn't they flown? Annabelle offered two excuses: one, that she had brand-new white luggage and wanted to keep it clean, and the other, that she had somehow come to believe that on a Minnesota-to-California airliner she would not be allowed to get up and go to the bathroom even once. "On Annabelle's part, it was total naïveté," observed Joyce.

That Saturday afternoon, May 28, Carl took a walk around the grounds with his adored grandsons. Before dawn on Sunday morning, Sparky, awakened by Annabelle's cries, rushed to the guest suite off the basement playroom where Craig, now thirteen, had some friends sleeping over, to find his father stretched on the floor. Struggling to find his pills, Carl had died of a heart attack before anyone could help him. Joyce, not realizing that he was already gone, ordered Sparky to give his father mouth-to-mouth resuscitation. It was not enough that his father had died—he had to place his lips on his father's and try to breathe life back into them. "He did it," she recalled, "but it upset him." Finally, he rushed Carl to Sebastopol's Palm Drive Hospital, only to have him pronounced dead on arrival.

Sparky turned over local arrangements to the Analy Funeral Chapel in Sebastopol before returning the body for burial to St. Paul, where a wake and funeral services were conducted at the Carlson Funeral Home on Payne Avenue. Two hundred and fifty-five mourners came to pay their respects, including Sparky's friends from the old neighborhood, from the Church of God, and from Art Instruction.

At the wake, Lloyd Neumann, who had worked with Carl since 1937, was presumed to know more than most about the family. "They all come to me and said, 'Where is Sparky? . . . Where is Charles Schulz? . . . Where is Charles . . . Where is Charlie?' 'Well,' I said, 'He'll be here.' I stayed there until eleven-thirty that night—a lot of people came to Carl's wake; he was a well-liked person—and Sparky never showed up. So I told a lot of 'em, I say, "Oh, well, if he didn't get here tonight, he'll probably be here for the funeral tomorrow.'

"The funeral came, the funeral went; and he never showed. He was an only child. His mother was gone. Now his dad is gone. He's got nobody. So when I was out to his home, I couldn't help but bring it up to him—I just said, 'Sparky, I went to the wake and the funeral and everybody was asking for you. How come you didn't come to your dad's funeral?' "

Sparky put his failure to escort his father's body—or, indeed, to attend the wake or burial—down to fear of flying. At least that was how he explained it. But there was more to it, and he himself could not identify the anxiety that spiked at times of real grief or the source of the psychic pain he lived with practically every day. Talking to an interviewer two decades later about the general, chronic sense of dread that afflicted him all his life, he said, "It's so complicated. I suppose I've always felt that way— apprehensive, anxious, that sort of thing. I have compared it sometimes to the feeling that you have when you get up on the morning of a funeral."

He also had hard feelings toward his stepmother. To his great and unending disappointment, Annabelle buried his father in St. Paul's Forest Lawn Cemetery, under a stone that bore Carl's full name and dates and left blank spaces for *her*. Sparky had wanted something else for his father's grave—a wish, without much logic or practicality, that his parents be rejoined in death, Carl beside Dena, in Roselawn Cemetery. But the plots adjacent to his mother's grave had long since been filled, and Carl would have to have been cremated to squeeze in beside her. In any event, Sparky had not gone back to St. Paul to make any such arrangements, not even calling Annabelle to make his wishes clear, let alone asking her what she wanted.

Carl responded to life's sudden shake-ups by cutting hair. Sparky did the same with pen and ink. "I would feel just terrible if I couldn't draw comic strips. I would feel very empty if I were not allowed to do this sort of thing." His answer to his father's death was to resume the daily routine. The methodical creation of six daily strips and a Sunday page oriented him, channeled his anxieties. The word his secretary, Sue Broadwell, used to sum up his life in the year following his father's death—the year of *Peanuts* as an international fad—was "steady."

# CHAPTER 20

# THE DAWNING
# OF THE AGE
# OF SNOOPY

*I'm the first dog ever to launch a human being!*
—SNOOPY

MORNINGS HE WAS AWAKENED by roosters crowing in the Medranos' chicken yard.

Rising with the sun, he showered and shaved, and then called gently through the children's bedroom doors, much as his mother had whispered to him, *Sparky, it's time to get up.* Joyce did not like to get up early, but up she rose to fix breakfast, turning out stacks of pancakes from a recipe she had learned from a ranch cook in New Mexico. Sparky took pride in her cooking; in 1966, when the Newspaper Comics Council published *The Cartoonist Cookbook*, he sent in Joyce's special trick (maple syrup added to the batter to add flavor to the pancakes), remarking, "Our family has never gone in for fancy cooking and I, personally, can cook nothing, but I am very fortunate in having a wife who can make the simple things, like apple pie, roast beef, etc., the way they should be made."

At twenty minutes past eight, he climbed behind the wheel of the family's Country Squire station wagon and drove the kids to Pine Crest Elementary School in Sebastopol, stopping at the bottom of Coffee Lane to pick up the Medranos' children. He took deep pleasure in his role as neighborhood chauffeur, using the minutes spent commuting down Occidental Road to pass along to his passengers a lifetime of lore about cars and driving, both of which he adored. The all-steel Country Squire, trimmed with imitation wood, served as a kind of mobile family room; for Sparky, it was the place he felt most intimate with his children. "That was the joy of my life," he later mused. "I discovered that my place was to be with the kids." This also kept him at a safe remove from responsibility: "I used to love taking the children to school in the morning—I guess because I knew I didn't have to go myself. It's like taking someone to the airport knowing you don't have to get on the plane."

With the kids off and running, he took his usual booth at the Roberts Café in Sebastopol, to breakfast over the *San Francisco Chronicle*, comparing his work with other strips and panels. "I like to look at it in the way that I think the reader will be looking at it as he or she picks up her morning paper." By 1967, with *Peanuts* entrenched in 745 daily and 393 Sunday newspapers in North America, Schulz was read by half the people of the United States and much of Canada, as well as in a hundred newspapers on the other continents. In the larger cities, most editors had moved Schulz to headline their Sunday comics section; in all but a few Podunks, *Peanuts* had bumped *Dick Tracy* as the supreme page-one feature. Schulz regarded the comics page "almost like a Stanley Cup or a tennis tournament like Wimbledon," every morning a championship match. "I don't think you have to be number one," he would say, "but you have to work hard if you're going to stay up there."

Then back to Coffee Lane and the studio by nine-thirty. "I never thought he had a job," recalled Amy, "because he didn't seem to have to be anywhere." Joyce respected his need to get away behind the drawing board every weekday morning, gladly taking charge of the house, the grounds, and their minimally ambitious social life, with its weekend visits from neighbors and friends, the occasional overnight drop-ins of business associates, and even more infrequent set-piece luncheons for a visiting celebrity like Jack Lemmon—for whom Joyce went all out, serving the finest filet mignon, only to see her helper, a French girl working as the Schulzes' au pair, drop the whole platter in a fit of nervousness.

But increasingly she felt distanced from Sparky, for the more she designed new projects and supervised their construction, the less joy it gave her to transform Coffee Lane alone. "The golf course, the kiosk, the ball field were all things she built to pull him out of the shell of that comic strip," observed Meredith. "She tried to do everything she could to try to get him interested in more than one thing."

In 1965 the *Christian Science Monitor* reported that she had even tried to coax Sparky to accompany her on trips around Sonoma County to sketch weathered barns, fishing boats, and wharves. But for Joyce, it always ended up the same, as Meredith recalled: "A project she thought she was doing for both of them became *her* project. He wouldn't enjoy it with her, [but] he usually enjoyed the finished product."

Nowhere was this truer than with parenthood itself. Devoted as each was to their children, and similar as were their values, Sparky and Joyce had different styles, which in time only grew more pronounced. ("He was gentle, saying to them, 'Tell me about it,' " a family friend recalled, "and she was, 'You go do this and you do that.' She told them what to do; Sparky was more their friend.") "He did enjoy the kids," said Joyce. "He enjoyed them when they were little, but when they got a little older, or had problems, he didn't want to be involved."

"To me, raising children is a complete mystery. The older they get, the more it baffles me," he admitted in 1967. In tune with the changing times, he conceded that parents should "talk with children more than we do," But with their older kids well into their teen years, neither Sparky nor Joyce opened up to any of the usual questions. Meredith, at twelve, had come across a tampon in her mother's bathroom closet, but when she asked what it was for, Joyce replied that when Meredith was old enough to know, she would tell her. "Neither one of them would talk," recalled Meredith. "All they said to me was, 'You're paving the way for your brothers and sisters, you have to set a good example.' " But Meredith didn't always know what that entailed, and in seventh and eighth grades, as she began to be interested in boys, she "didn't have anything to go on except rumors circulating on the subject." She would recall searching her parents' library for "sex books" and "the closest thing I could find was these African books with naked people in them." She recalled asking her parents about the facts of life and each time being rebuffed: "You're just a kid, you've got plenty of time."

Joyce was strict about dress, outfitting Meredith in conservative thick wool suits when she wanted to wear miniskirts: "I was dressed like a thirty-five-year-old woman." But Meredith, a tomboy to the age of twelve, had entered a new world of boys and socializing with her girlfriends at Analy High School; the same seven girls who had once come over to Coffee Lane for a weekend sleepover and eaten ninety-six of Joyce's pancakes for breakfast on Saturday now wanted to wear fashionable clothing to school. Miniskirts made headlines in late 1966: the aptly named Twiggy popularized the new flat-chested, skinny look, and although the other girls were allowed to hem their skirts up to the middle of their thighs, Joyce did not allow Meredith more than one inch above the knee.

Sparky took Meredith's side, in public, at least: "I don't see anything wrong with mini-skirts," he told a reporter in the summer of 1967. "If a girl can wear one well, then I think it looks very nice. I am all for experimental changes in fashion if they make a person have a nice appearance, make them feel good." But in private he would not take Meredith's side to challenge her mother; he and Joyce maintained a unified front on such issues. In this case, it took Dorothy to step in and help her granddaughter make her own flowered skirts.

Meredith also wanted to wear her hair long, but Joyce "never helped me be a girl"—she didn't want Meredith to grow up too quickly, as she had.

Joyce, in charge of the children's meals, clothing, and activities, also set the house rules, adjudicated punishments, enforced groundings. "Out of necessity, she ruled that roost with an iron hand, because Sparky was so mild-mannered he didn't like to raise his voice to anyone, but Joyce wasn't afraid to tell those children how the cow ate the cabbage," recalled one visitor. "He would not discipline or make a decision," recalled Amy. "Mom did all the hard emotional stuff with us, and Dad enjoyed all the fun cute stuff."

"This is not a father-dominated house," he told *Family Circle* with a wry smile, and only in later years would he come straight out with it: "I'm no disciplinarian. In fact, I don't think I've ever disciplined the kids. Probably should have, but I didn't."

Passivity ran counter to Joyce's every instinct. She seized the moment, made her decision, then acted upon it. Schulz let the same moment pass in escapist indecision or pointless discussion or even a lighthearted remark, once summarizing the problem by saying that Joyce was "like a surgeon, while I was more a doctor of internal medicine." She cut with a knife; she had nerve. He handed out diagnoses, prescriptions, lollipops.

His abdication pressed Joyce by default into absolute authority. "She wanted to be a wife and a mother, but she turned out to be the father, too," observed a close family friend of this period. "Sparky wasn't there for her. He couldn't discipline. There were some real times with Meredith. She put them through it, and Sparky was never there. He couldn't cope with things that weren't positive. He didn't like confrontation."

Passivity and anger are circular-feeding devils. Leaving Joyce to do the hard parenting by herself only widened the rift between them as a couple. "That was always a contest between him and Joyce," recalled Chuck Bartley, a family friend. "She wanted him to discipline the kids, and he couldn't do it. Their arguments, and they had many, were all over discipline."

"Can't you do anything?!" the Bartleys would recall Joyce shouting at Sparky. "Joyce dictated to Sparky in front of other people," another friend remembered. It was what she had watched her mother do, ordering Henry around "like a section boss." But Sparky "was confused by all that," another visitor said. "It may be aggravating living with me," Joyce herself admitted to her husband, "but it's never boring." At the marriage's outset, Schulz had been Charlie Brown to Joyce's Lucy, but as time went on, he was ever more Schroeder, immersed in his art, aloof, withholding.

Schroeder—the German name was no accident—is subject to the constraints of hero worship, but his internal discipline is an affront to Lucy, who lives to dominate others. A creature of externals, Lucy can't exercise the control that Schroeder can exercise in art; she can merely be his girl Friday, playing timeless second fiddle to his daily routine:

With his toy piano, Schroeder is building a real wall of music against the world, the frets and bars of sheet music appearing as solid and substantial as the brick and mortar of Charlie Brown's "meditation wall." There is no question of his getting married or falling for Lucy; he can happily do without her. For Schroeder, ambition trumps dependence. If he turns out to be a first-class composer, the music will justify his isolation, and he will be able to hold the whole world at bay. And there is no diffidence here; he *knows* he will be a great composer, as Sparky knew he had it in him to be a great cartoonist.

If Schroeder is Schulz at the drawing board, the music emanating from the toy piano is a ciphered strip comic, its miniature scale representing the way that comics were measured by the culture that Schulz grew up in.

Sparky later recalled that when he was a boy, "it just didn't occur to me that drawing had value." Compared with the Pastoral Symphony, comic strips were playthings, toys. But, as Schulz never ceased to point out with relish, Schroeder transcends the mechanical limitations of his instrument. Just as *Peanuts* stretched its shrunken black-and-white panels to introduce themes never before presented in the funny papers, Schroeder "somehow manages" to elicit everything from sonatas to jazz suites from his dingy painted-on keyboard.

Unable to draw Schroeder's attention from the disciplines of art, Lucy is one day driven to recognize that "this piano is too much competition for me" and snatches the instrument right out from under Schroeder's hands—clean, like a weight lifter—and runs out into the street, yelling, "It's woman against piano! Woman is winning!! Woman is winning!!!" and tosses the wretched instrument down the sewer.

★ ★ ★

HE BEGAN WORK BY going through the day's mail—as of June 1967, about five hundred letters a week from all around the world. For years he had made a point of personally answering every letter. He felt he had "an obligation to be nice to people." But after Charlie Brown and Snoopy appeared on the cover of *Life* magazine in March 1967, he could no longer keep up with the many polite but specific requests for special favors: a drawing "for the priest in our church who is retiring and uses your cartoon"; "for my grandfather who's retiring"; "for a crippled kid."

"Just do a quick sketch of Snoopy," each one would ask—for a birthday, for a high school dance, for a worthy charity—"it'll only take five minutes."

"And they're right," he would admit. "But they think their letter is the only one on my desk. The five minutes have to be multiplied by hundreds—thousands. They forget that I not only have to do some drawing, I occasionally have to do some thinking."

His routine required that he sit by himself at the drawing board and follow his thoughts as he doodled in pencil on a piece of paper. "If you're going to survive on a daily schedule you survive only by being able to draw on every experience and thought that you've ever had. That is, if you're going to do anything with any meaning. Of course, you can grind out daily gags but I'm not interested in simply doing gags. I'm interested in doing a strip that says something and makes comment on the important things of life." "You're drawing mainly memories," he once explained. So he would "just sit there and think about the past, kind of dredge up ugly memories and things like that."

If this failed to produce an idea that could carry a daily strip, he resorted to a second procedure: "Starting little arguments with yourself," he called it—in which he would imagine Lucy coming in and saying, "Charlie Brown, you blockhead," to which Charlie Brown would reply, "What?" and she would say, "Get away from in front of that TV set . . ." On some days their opening volley was enough to trigger a daily strip and, if the idea expanded, a whole Sunday page, or a series of dailies; but the very next morning, yesterday's theme might prove to lead nowhere, whereupon he would switch characters, this time imagining Snoopy on the doghouse, looking up at the sky, which always had the effect of freeing the cartoonist himself to tilt his head back and think and doodle.

He was deeply ambivalent about his relationship with the reader. On the one hand, "I draw my comic strip for myself. I don't do it to bring joy to the world. That's insane"; on the other, "I would be satisfied if they wrote on my tombstone, 'He made people happy.'" Either way, he knew that if he got too close to his audience, he would be destroyed—readers now identified so closely with his characters that they responded with the almost mystical belief that "Charlie Schulz did this cartoon just for me." The qualities that for hundreds of thousands of readers carried J. D. Salinger's novels and stories over from the purely literary into a realm inescapably personal were, in these years, present to some extent in *Peanuts*, too. Like Salinger, he wanted his readers to identify not with him but with his characters' temperaments.

Every so often, the mail would crest to flood level when a particular strip touched a nerve or brought widespread pleasure, or when such annual conjunctions as the absence of valentines in Charlie Brown's mailbox would bring dozens pouring into Schulz's studio. He received few serious complaints—no more than a dozen over the course of *Peanuts'* first fifteen years. One, in 1965, had come from a woman who asserted that the Great Pumpkin was sacrilegious. Schulz wrote back saying that he was "basically on [her] side, that the real sacrilege is Santa Claus, and that [he had been] trying to show this in the Great Pumpkin strips."

After dictating replies to redheaded Sue Broadwell for half an hour, Schulz turned to his drawing board, the same varnished model he had bought for $24 in 1946. It had been his first step up from a card table, and that was where he wanted to remain. Looking around the large and luxurious workshop Joyce had built for him up on the edge of the redwoods overlooking his four-hole golf course, he would say, "I've simply graduated from a card table to a very comfortable place to be."

Repetition itself gave him comfort. The process of going in every day, sequestering himself in the studio, and regaining contact with the energy and force of his imagination made him feel real and alive. The routine, which began with taking off his glasses the moment he sat down, anchored him in the engrossing repeated sameness of the creative process, where the newest strip was always under way. He had no interest in being a mere curator of his creation or a guardian of its business; he was its builder. He had to make it again every day.

At the drawing board he was a different presence from the man people knew outside the studio—and not just because, in his own transformation from ordinary citizen to extraordinary cartoonist, he followed the Clark-Kent-to-Superman routine of freeing himself from his specs. Here, there was no scratching of the head, no kneading of the neck, no biting of the lip. "It is one of the few situations in my life where I feel totally secure. When I sit behind the drawing board I feel that I am in command." An interviewer noticed that when Schulz engaged with others, he was "gentle and casual." But when sitting down to work, "he changes. He becomes integrated, intense, concentrated. His right hand never makes a wasted motion."

He had an absolute faith in his craft, at the core of which was the belief that "a professional cartoonist has to have the ability to take a blank sheet of paper and out of absolutely nothing come up with an idea within five or ten minutes. If you can't deliberately do that, then you're never going to make it. You just have to be able to do it cold bloodedly."

It was jeweler's work: shoulders forward, elbows tight, head bent, eyes sharply following the progress of pen or brush. When he had a good idea, or when a doodle that had been sitting for months to one side of the drawing table suddenly took shape, he could hardly get the ink down fast enough. "I have a very light feeling and I feel that my drawing hand is moving very quickly and lightly and my mind is working very quickly and lightly, and the words just come out . . ." He was always afraid that inspiration would dry up before he could pin the whole idea down onto paper, but when he did get something fresh and original into the panels, his thrill, especially at seeing the words come out exactly the way he wanted them, gave him such a powerful jolt of satisfaction that his hand would literally shake from excitement.

HE USUALLY HAD LUNCH in the studio—almost always a ham sandwich and a glass of milk fixed by Sue Broadwell, sometimes a dish of tapioca pudding made by Joyce's mother—and then returned to the drawing board. Some humorists of this era might have milked a mother-in-law like Dorothy Halverson for gags and one-liners. Schulz depended on Dorothy, perhaps more even than he cared to admit. He had sent her with his father's body to St. Paul, and, earlier in 1966, on the night when the basement combustion burned down the studio at Coffee Lane, he had stood by—"helpless," as Joyce later told it—while Dorothy "ran into the garage and saved the car."

Seventy-five years old in 1967, the former Mrs. Henry Halverson went on living in the apartment over the garage at Coffee Lane, earning a place in the strip, and filling the void left by Sparky's beloved Aunt Marion, who, "skin and bones at the end," had succumbed to colon cancer in the old photographer's studio on July 30, 1963. Marion was buried in a military cemetery in San Mateo County, south of San Francisco; as Sparky sat on the verge of tears in the chapel, he put his head on Joyce's shoulder. His cousin Patty, Marion's daughter, ever after remembered the gesture—and how Joyce lifted her hand to pet him.

Marion's widower, Buster, remained in the studio, working as a janitor at the Sebastopol Elementary School. But it was Joyce's mother who stayed longest and left the deepest imprint on the family: bathing and grooming and properly dressing herself every morning with the discipline of one who had survived everything, including the damage she had done herself. "Dorothy was so much like Joyce," reflected Broadwell. "She was very firm in what she thought, what she said, and what she [did]. There was no gray area—Joyce was like that, too. And they would constantly do battle." Asked in the mid-1960s whether the strip's blanket-hating grandmother was supposed to symbolize conformity, Schulz answered, much more pointedly than usual: "The grandmother represents all grandmothers who are ashamed of kids with blankets and think their daughters should be able to handle the child better but who couldn't handle it any better themselves at the same age."

With coolly aggressive righteousness and stoicism as her weapons, without ever showing actual anger, Dorothy would calmly and insistently rebuke Joyce about the way she was raising the children, preach to the gardener, find fault with the housekeeper, browbeat Sparky's secretary. The one time that Broadwell ever heard her boss raise his voice was when, after Dorothy had been dressing her down for some minutes on some minor point, all at once Sparky rounded the corner of the guesthouse kitchen and barked, "Dorothy! Would you just leave her alone?"

With Sparky, her technique was never explicitly to assert that she considered herself his better; she would merely belittle him, his work, and his beliefs, by withholding. On Sunday mornings, she attended the Sunday school class he taught at Sebastopol Methodist Church; on the way home together, Sparky would stop to pick up doughnuts and the Sunday paper, wrapped by the color panels of the comics—*Peanuts*, the nation's one indispensable feature, the anchor of nearly every comics section, leading the page above the fold, being therefore unmistakable. But Dorothy would pull away the comics without a glance, tossing them into the back seat as she turned with higher purpose to the inside pages.

He took his revenge by working her into *Peanuts* as Linus's unseen "interfering," cunningly manipulative grandmother, whose relentless intrigues against his security blanket leave him sighing, "That foxy old lady has put me in a corner."

Around four, the kids began to come home from school, busting in to see him, often to invite him into their games, a practice he encouraged. He wanted the studio to be a place his children could come anytime. Although it was quietest in the afternoon, with nothing much louder than the wind blowing in the redwoods or the boom of high-flying F-101 fighter jets training from Hamilton Air Force Base ten miles away, he was never one to say, "I'm drawing now, don't bother me."

"I don't want the children to feel the studio is an unpleasant place. I hope that one or two of them might develop along the line. There is no indication so far. But drawing develops slowly."

At the time that Schulz hinted at this oldest of fatherly dreams—February 1961—Meredith, eleven, Monte, ten, and Craig, eight, had all shown signs of wanting to please him, and none more persistently than Meredith. From earliest girlhood, she had stood enthralled alongside her father's drawing board and, moved to emulation, had drawn horses for him in pencil on construction paper—well-formed equines in medieval harness. By the time she was eight, in the family's first year at Coffee Lane, she had begun to try her hand at copying the *Peanuts* characters, turning up one day to present her father with a batch of her own Lucys and Linuses and Charlie Browns, consciously meant to let him "know that I was the one who would carry it on."

"These are very good," she remembered him saying, and she would never forget her excitement, which turned in the next moment to shock, when he let her know that he wanted one of his sons to carry on his comic strip. He did not ever say which son, but it left Meredith hurt and mad. Both Monte and Craig did attempt cartooning, but only in the most casual way. Monte's panels were populated by characters stylized to look like actual peanuts in their shells. "We showed them to Dad, who basically told us we weren't good, which was not a big defeat because we knew we were no good."

When Jill was born, Larry Rutman had sent a wire from United Feature in New York: IF SHE IS LEFT HANDED AND CAN DRAW WE WANT FIRST OPTION ON SYNDICATION RIGHTS. But Jill, a slim, sweet-faced blonde, had no interest in cartooning; at nine, she was adventurous, adaptable, uncomplaining, and would spend long afternoons by herself at Coffee Lane, riding her horse around the neighborhood, bareback and barefoot. Later, with children of her own, she wondered at being left to herself without adult supervision. When asked, Joyce shrugged it off: "I raised you to be responsible. You knew how to handle the horse." But Jill still wondered, "Where was Mom?"

During the emergency of Thanksgiving Day 1968, when Jill's pony stepped on her face and broke her nose, Sparky and his close friend of these years, the ophthalmologist Ward Wick, rushed Jill to the hospital, but Joyce did not go along to comfort her little girl. "Jill is much better now," Sparky wrote to his stepmother on December 5, 1968. "We had her to the doctor yesterday and he removed the stitches and the cast from her nose, and it looks like you will never notice that anything happened. She has stayed home from school all this week, however, to prevent anyone from accidentally bumping into her. . . . I think this whole experience made Jill think a little bit, because she said to me the other night, 'I wonder what life is all about. It seems to me we have a few tragedies or we win a few prizes and then it is all over.' I really didn't know what to say to her."

Craig Schulz—at fourteen a jug-eared boy with a lopsided grin—was inclined to go his own way. Known as the quiet son, he taught himself to ride dirt bikes; in the afternoons at Coffee Lane, he would still just as soon jump off a roof as he would take part in activities that interested his father and brother, such as baseball or reading and discussing books. He was on his own, or loosely allied with the family's other independent, Meredith, and would later recall being aware that from 1967 on, parents and children in the Schulz household lived increasingly separate lives: "They never knew where we were at."

Sparky deplored the continual suggestion that he retire from the drawing board so that he could spend more time with his family or out on the golf course while someone else did the drawing. For some comic strip artists the notion of deputizing another cartoonist or team of cartoonists to handle mechanical duties was the fulfillment of the whole career. Time and again, he was asked, "Why don't you have an assistant?" and would simply and not always amiably reply, "Would Arnold Palmer have somebody hit nine-irons for him?"

He never talked the strip over with Joyce. "I don't discuss it with anybody," he insisted. "I work completely alone." At most he would concede, "I would hope that she'll like it. I always hope that everyone will like it."

ONCE OR TWICE A month now, Connie Boucher would drive a station wagon load of layouts, samples, and prototypes up from San Francisco, unveiling each new design to the axis of the *Peanuts* universe, always finding him "kind of quiet" at the start of each meeting; but as soon as she and her assistant had unpacked the latest samples and begun laying them out for Sparky's inspection, item by item, banner by banner, Snoopy by Snoopy, "things started to liven up." "Once he gets interested," noticed Boucher, "he lets go."

He adored the stuff—he who had wanted nothing so much as a Mickey Mouse watch for Christmas and now commanded the power to turn that same little key in millions of hearts. Cartoon characters had always had mass appeal, as Sparky was fond of reminding reporters in the new age of television, but with everyone searching for himself in a world now made more complicated by new freedoms, people needed to "express themselves" by fusing a beloved character with their own actual possessions. "They'll put anything on their refrigerator or on their car that they happen to like." Or on their ears, throats, fingers, and lapels: another pioneer licensee, Aviva Enterprises, authorized to sell *Peanuts* jewelry, zoomed from a $10,000 start-up to sales of $2.8 million in its first three years.

Even before he won from United Feature Syndicate the contractual right to inspect new *Peanuts* products, Schulz insisted upon doing so. What about a Charlie Brown baseball glove? "What kid would want one?" said

Sparky. "He couldn't catch a thing with it." Not since Beatrix Potter sewed the first Peter Rabbit doll herself had there been a writer and artist who so consciously controlled the transition from the page to the plastic world of three-dimensional product: "I wanted to make sure everything we did was right, that the products, the language, were all in character with the comic strip, although my old contract really spelled out no rights in that regard. I probably was the first cartoonist who watched over licensing . . . and I did it only because I wanted to."

Several of the earliest *Peanuts* products had been letdowns, especially a snow-dome paperweight that showed Snoopy skating, the prototype of which had so excited him that he planned to give the very first off the line to all his friends at Christmas, only to find the allegedly finished work so shoddy that he tossed it into the trash, putting Jim Hennessey at the syndicate on notice that more careful attention would henceforth be needed, and that he himself wanted to see every new item whether or not he had the power to disapprove it.

In his meetings with Boucher in early 1965, Sparky remained initially downbeat, worrying about the prospects of each proposed new product, especially those of a new book—a seemingly curious tic from an author whose cumulative sales through February 1965 had amounted to some five million copies, but understandable in light of his suspicion that the pressure of Determined Productions was compelling him to "[turn] out too much too fast." When California's new governor, Ronald Reagan, proclaimed May 24, 1967, Charles M. Schulz Day, he presented Sparky with a scroll that read, in part, "Happiness is having Charles Schulz as a California resident—all those bucks rolling in."

He was whipsawed by his fortune. He wanted the world to appreciate and honor him as a great cartoonist, yet he felt that at a million dollars a year, his income had grown "embarrassingly large." On the one hand, as he would tell a Christian youth magazine, "no one can be worth all this money." On the other: "You can't help it. You're just in a business where there are a lot of people who want the drawings and it makes money, and that's all. But it makes money for a lot of other people, too."

So he let the businesspeople come and get their franchises, and he was fair and honest—indeed, uniquely generous, dividing licensing income in thirds between himself, the syndicate, and a licensee. "When a fourth party came in," recalled a licensing executive, "he would say twenty-five [percent]—twenty-five—twenty-five—twenty-five. Boy, you talk about a generous point of view: this was unbelievable." But the licensees provided a hidden function: by taking an equal share, along with the syndicate, they shouldered some of the burden of his unease that his success was being measured by money. "I've never quite been able to resolve this," he said in 1967. "I cannot *help* that the comic strip brings in a good deal of money. I do not draw the comic strip to make money. I draw it because it is the one thing which I feel I do best, and I can see no reason why I should give up drawing the comic strip in order to go to the mission field, for instance, and become a terrible missionary or to study for the ministry and become a terrible minister, merely because the ministry would seem to be closer to spiritual things. I think it's much better to be a good cartoonist than a terrible minister."

Under the enthusiastic peppering of Boucher's presentations, he eventually lightened up, flashing nervous grins and murmuring approval. "She was a brilliant woman, a merchant *extraordinaire*," recalled an executive at the syndicate. "She would take product in, schmooze Sparky, show him how great he [was], and work on him. Of course, too, she'd take one of her good-looking assistants, and everything would be rosy."

One morning at Coffee Lane, Boucher came into the studio to find Sparky poring over the photographs of four beautiful women—candidates for a high school beauty contest that he had agreed to judge. Picking his favorite, he remarked, "When I was in high school, if a girl like that even looked at me, I would have died."

Now he found himself regularly surrounded by Boucher's miniskirted assistants. Connie herself was very much a woman of the moment, with her full figure and French twist hairdos—"at mid-decade," as the 1960s social historian Geoffrey O'Brien notes, "the Swedish blonde was, along with the liberated airline stewardess, the primary sexual icon." And indeed, as one Schulz friend said, "Sparky did like good-looking women, but he was always timid around them." With Boucher and her assistants in the studio, Sparky turned shy, excessively self-deprecating, even more soft-spoken than usual, all according to his boyhood pattern. For in Boucher was yet another of his relationships that crackled with female dominance and pulled him away from the quiet control won at the drawing board, thrusting him into a frantically expanding marketplace—where, nevertheless, as even he had to admit, once he had "let go," it was nice to hear what he would have Lucy phrase as "that beautiful sound of cold, hard cash!"

Here, in other words, was yet another of his life's Lucy Van Pelts, the more unsettling for becoming visibly successful as his adjunct—and Boucher certainly had as much of Lucy's will as any of the Halverson women. "Yes, I think Sparky is Charlie Brown," she said in 1965, "though he's certainly not a loser these days."

As an older man he would learn charm, becoming skilled at indirect flattery and flirtation, and would discover that it was not as hard as he had always thought to be at ease with himself and his appetites; instead of having to settle for the suppressed longings and contained infatuations of earlier years, he would find himself welcomed into intimate friendships with romantic overtones. Nevertheless, even in the mid-'60s, still married to Joyce, he would continue to camouflage himself. A woman friend who knew him then later reflected that he preferred to think of himself as unattractive because if he *were* attractive, "maybe the girls would fall for him and then he'd be in a dangerous situation." Thinking of himself as a wallflower was still a safer place from which to love.

In 1965, Sparky presented himself as a Chaplinesque little-man figure caught between the greater grinding cogs of Joyce's get-up-and-go gusto: "I had a restless wife," was his stock explanation of why the Schulzes had moved westward, eastward, and westward again. His image of himself in these years of marital sparring accords with the view of friends: "Sparky was never the macho man. He was the Milquetoast man. He'd smile and shake his head and say, 'Well, that's Joyce.' He never crossed her."

AFTERNOONS IN THE EUCALYPTUS-SCENTED air, people came to the Coffee Grounds: old friends on vacation, friends of old friends, third cousins of old friends, fans, and well-wishers—they would all swing into the driveway in their campers and station wagons, and for the next hour he would be taken prisoner. The lucky ones—those who caught him in an expansive mood—would later recall their life-changing hour with "a remarkably sincere and shy man with a quiet magnetic charm and wit."

His midwesterner's sense of being encroached on rose with each new arrival, especially when total strangers roared uphill, in plain defiance of

the sign on the electrically operated gate—SORRY, NO UNEXPECTED VISI-
TORS, PLEASE—and drove up, waving their Kodaks and autograph books,
expecting to be warmly received. In such situations, he was "always afraid
of being called temperamental—I have a horror of that." And he cheerfully admitted that he did not know how to handle such intrusions: "I don't
know whether to be like Frank Sinatra and yell at them, or be polite."

His innate courtesy most often won out, especially when people took
the time to write ahead, civilly asking to stop by on a certain date, when
they dotted their "i's" and crossed their "t's" and spelled his name correctly in their careful Palmer penmanship. "What are you going to tell
them," said Sparky, "that you're too busy?" He would admit that he was "a
softie who can't turn anyone away."

As all ages and kinds of people came to his work, they yearned for
more information about *him*. "Who is Charles Schulz?" was the question in every Sunday supplement. More and more, he had to choose what
he wanted the world to know about him, and he kept telling the world
what he was *not*: not a teacher, not a philosopher, not a preacher, not an
entrepreneur, not an artist (neither a Disney nor an Andrew Wyeth), not
a celebrity. "I like being a cartoonist," he said one afternoon on *The Mike
Douglas Show*. From that he never wavered. Being a cartoonist was still
the only role in which he could truly accept himself. "I can't do anything
else," he insisted.

As it turned out, he would become all the things that he said he was
not—for instance, an entrepreneur on a global scale heretofore unknown
in the comic strip business—but always because other people carried him
into new territory. He never put his own foot forward, except at the drawing board, because if he changed anywhere else, he would lose his power.
If he expanded—if his life and outlook were enlarged by even a micron—
he would lose the familiar, the magic of the ordinary. "I never think of
myself as being successful," he typically said, "but people keep telling me
I am."

"Heck, no cartoonist can become a millionaire," he insisted in 1967,
when he was well on his way to a million a year and therefore, since he was
no spendthrift, must have already been one several times over, "but that's
what [*Life*] magazine said and now I'm getting requests for money from all
over the world." Three years later, his income having more than doubled,
he would just as adamantly contend that "reports that I'm a multimillion-

aire are ridiculous. How can you become a multimillionaire by drawing a comic strip?"

When asked if he enjoyed his fame he said, "I enjoy being recognized by people when I go into stores. I enjoy the little extra-nice treatment that you get merely because someone likes what you draw." And yet at the same time he conceded, "It's really more of a disturbing element in my life than anything else, I think, especially because of my Christian belief. I've never quite been able to resolve this."

The more people wanted to know about *him*, not just about the "miracle creation," as one reader described *Peanuts*, the more they wanted him to be extraordinary, to be "blessed." One reader marveled, "He helped raise me."

When their father's transfer forced Lucy and Linus to move (temporarily) out of the *Peanuts* neighborhood, a little girl from Stockton, California, wrote "sob" on a sheet of paper 100 times. Another fan wired Schulz: PLEASE DON'T LET LINUS LEAVE, HE IS LIKE A SON TO ME. (Schulz wrote back: "Don't panic. Time heals all wounds.") One reader reported that all twenty-seven thousand students at Berkeley were "extremely upset" and another wrote to say that her mother had "a very insecure feeling about the whole situation" and worried that if Schulz did not return the children to their rightful home her whole family was "going to crack up." A doctor agreed and sent a telegram: HEARTBROKEN OVER CURRENT DEVELOPMENT. BAD FOR PSYCHE OF YOUNG. PLEASE ADVISE. One fan, Rachel Gonzalez of Mastic, New York, asked Schulz if he had "any idea how precious your creations are to so many people you have never met." They were "more real to me than many of my acquaintances," wrote Virginia Shearer. Another fan told him that *Peanuts* was "part of me"—"almost a part of my personality."

*Apollo 10* linked Charlie Brown and Snoopy with the nation's highest aspirations, but it took the private reflections of an official at the National Aeronautics and Space Administration (NASA) to give Schulz a hint of a broad-based national identification far beyond his characters: "While at NASA, my ideal patriot was always John Glenn," deputy public affairs officer Al Chop related in a letter to Sparky. "We used to call him 'Mr. Clean' because he was the perfect role model for America. Well, I always rated you right up there with John Glenn, as a shining example of what our country is all about—or at least should be."

Logically, with so much to live up to, he worried that if people thought and wrote and talked this way about him, they would inevitably see through him, discovering that he was boring and inarticulate, that he had gotten away with a small talent spread thinly. At the turning points of his early life, he had taken comfort in the dream of becoming a cartoonist—he had even, occasionally, fessed up to his ambition—but he had never for a moment imagined himself as a man of consequence. In fact, he had always been a highly deferential person, but now he found himself the equal, or in the comics business even the superior, of people to whom he had previously deferred.

The biggest names in show business now wrote fan letters—Frank Sinatra, Bing Crosby, Yul Brynner, Jack Lemmon, Carol Burnett, Charlton Heston, Sammy Davis, Jr. (who used "Charlie Brown" when calling his Swedish fiancée at her hotel)—and he was stunned to find himself in correspondence with such movie legends as Shirley Temple and Sonja Henie, the Norwegian skating champion, or out for an after-theater supper in San Francisco with Kaye Ballard, whose cabaret act at the hungry i incorporated gags from *Peanuts*, and who introduced Sparky to Mike Nichols, Elaine May, and Bette Davis.

Without leaving home—from the drawing board itself—he exercised a magical allure: simply by framing the incident of a daily strip around the name of one of his heroes or crushes—Sam Snead or Andrew Wyeth, Sonja Henie or Peggy Fleming—he could elicit from that star a letter or phone call, or, in the mail from Wyeth's studio in Chadds Ford, Pennsylvania, a drawing of the artist's dog, which Schulz hung in his own studio and kept close by him for the rest of his life.

Beyond wealth and fame and celebrity, achievement increasingly filled him with dread. Year by year, awards and honors piled up, but as much as he was genuinely thrilled by formal recognition, he was afraid that the more he was acknowledged, the more likely it was that it would all be swept away. He could not celebrate his achievements; gripped by a sense of foreboding that "someone is coming along to knock me off," he spoke more and more often of the day when another, younger cartoonist would be the most popular, the most beloved. "Oh, I dread that day," he had begun to say as early as 1964. In the meantime, nothing but drawing eased his sense that "there's no place to go but down." The fact that every morning millions of people opened their day with his drawings was, for him, the achievement, all the proof he needed that he counted.

He needed to hear from his readers. He was afraid of alienating ordinary people by appearing to be bigheaded, and dreaded being thought arrogantly unapproachable. He saw himself as a regular citizen—a phone call away from whosoever cared enough to check the book, pick up the phone, and call him at VAlley 3-6444. One day a teenage girl telephoned him from New Jersey and asked Schulz to send her $65,000. He replied that he could not do that, and she claimed to be surprised—she said she thought she must have gotten the wrong Charles Schulz; she had been told that he was kind and generous; she didn't understand why *Charles Schulz* wouldn't send her $65,000. He asked her why she wanted the money. "Oh, there are a lot of things I can do with it," she said.

At times, Coffee Lane unmanned him. If the driveway crunched with ceaseless comings and goings, the car turnaround was a virtual motor pool in itself. To the five family cars of the mid-'60s had, by 1967, been added a herd of brand-new Mustangs. But as he presided over this paradise, where everyone had the freedom to go anywhere at any time in any direction, he could not find lasting contentment.

The grounds, tightly supervised by Joyce, were increasingly beyond his command. When some of the Schulz kids burst open one of the two lawn-sprinkler systems while riding a mower, they rushed into the studio. Bill Melendez, visiting from Hollywood, immediately dashed to the main water valve, while Sparky stood frozen to the floor, staring out the plate-glass windows and muttering to himself that this was what he hated about the place.

He did not care to know how things worked: the strip was his job; the grounds and buildings were Joyce's; the horses were for her and for Meredith, Amy, and Jill; the baseball diamond and tree house and redwood groves for Monte and Craig. To maintain the property's tax status as a ranch, the Schulzes kept livestock; but, although Joyce tried to enlist Sparky at feeding time, he was afraid of horses, and still did not like cows. Nothing had changed since he had abandoned Joyce's sister Judy to the charging herd of heifers in a Wisconsin pasture. And so the ranch's responsibilities fell to Joyce also, especially when animals got loose. As she told a reporter, "There are emergencies all the time!"

The more visible Schulz became, the more threatening the world seemed. "He worries all the time," Connie Boucher noticed in March 1965, "he's never sure about anything." He worried about his children: how would they cope with the world outside Coffee Lane? And as people of all kinds now came to beg him to involve himself in their extreme behavior, he feared for his children's safety. He had become "afraid of all the goofy people in the world" and since 1961 had been voicing his fear that "someone might grab one of the kids."

He worried so much about so many things that he peopled the strip with a whole phantasmagoria of terrors, but he himself resisted formal diagnosis. "How do you account for someone being unhappy when he has nothing to be unhappy about?" But "cartoonists," he said, "are strange people. I don't think we're especially happy people. Most of the cartoonists that I know are kind of depressed, or they're melancholy. I think a lot of us are very melancholy. But from that feeling comes humor."

His one clear symptom was a chronically upset stomach; the more he brooded, the more it turned on him. "I've been trying to cut back on all my extra activities until I begin to feel better," he said in May 1965. "If I try to write too many cartoons and write too many books it results in my stomach hurting, and nobody loves a cartoonist whose stomach hurts." But no one knew how much he really hurt—only that Charlie Brown had decided to "dread one day at a time" and that Schulz's "philosophy" was available on T-shirts, buttons, and bumper stickers "for those of us who are having a little trouble dealing with the zeitgeist these days." Asked from the floor at a meeting of cartoonists and comedy writers in San Francisco in 1969, "Does it frighten you sometimes to see that the times reflect you rather than the other way around?" Sparky "looked up sheepishly," according to one observer, and said, "Everything frightens me."

Attacks of panic came more frequently now; nonetheless, he refused to consult with any kind of doctor and was increasingly afraid to go anywhere. As soon as he started to keep other people's schedules, he felt profoundly threatened. The roster of events at institutions to which he was invited to speak, the timetables of airlines and trains, the whole world of strangers on airplanes, appointments in distant cities, nights away in hotels filled him with a physical weight of doom. Eventually, he found that the only invitations he could not refuse, or the only trips he was prepared to make for Joyce's or the children's sake, must fall into the category of those that would not prevent him from being home by bedtime. "Happiness," he wrote in 1962, "is sleeping in your own bed."

But he could not go to New York and back in a day, so the irresistible force met the immovable object. Here was a contradiction he could not easily resolve. Staying at home was one way to ensure the continuity of the work; the other was to remain who he had always been. His was now one of the most influential voices in America, but as long as he kept alive the feeling of midwestern nothingness—the sad, bitter, Selby-and-Snelling melancholy of the 1940s—then he could remain the person he had always known himself to be, and the strip went on today as it had yesterday and would tomorrow.

The "security" Schulz had written about in *Security Is a Thumb and a Blanket* was a child's comfort in things remaining unchanged, while, of course, the child changes at stunning speed. As the inventor of the "security blanket," he had become the inevitable subject of profiles entitled "Schulz: The Man Who Wouldn't Grow Up" and "29 Years of Being 8 Years Old," or even "Don't Grow Up," but it was true that even in his forties he found little incentive or ability to let go of long-held insecurities and dreads. "Schulz doesn't seem to want to be sophisticated or to change the basic pattern of his life," concluded one reporter in 1965. "Rather he seems to seek mostly to fortify it."

The more Joyce called on him to take responsibility for himself as a man, the more "unhappy" he became. "He was always sad," Joyce recalled. "Who knows why? And I said to him, 'You should go to a psychiatrist,' and he said, 'No, I don't want to go to a psychiatrist because it will take away my talent.' "

DESPITE SCHULZ'S EFFORTS TO keep it for adults, *Peanuts* was becoming, and would now remain—in the public's mind—family entertainment passed on from parent to child. The "Charlie Brown specials"—more than seventy in the end, sixteen of them with music by Vincent Guaraldi—had recast *Peanuts* as a holiday tradition for children while refashioning the national calendar for adults, drawing attention to the highly marketable role of the *Peanuts* gang as stand-ins for Americans at all their year-round rituals: consuming too much on New Year's Eve, exchanging valentines, planting trees on Arbor Day, hunting Easter eggs, celebrating the Fourth of July, all this climaxing at the consumer high holidays, Halloween, Thanksgiving, and Christmas, now defined as a *Charlie Brown* Thanksgiving, a *Charlie Brown* Christmas, and especially Halloween, to which Schulz had given new meaning. In his own generation, carving jack-o'-lanterns and fashioning costumes for trick-or-treating had been a hit-or-miss neighborhood observance lasting one night only (as Valentine's had been a one-day ritual in the classroom), but, in the baby-boom generation's embrace of the Great Pumpkin, becoming a full-blown, nearly weeklong national festival.

*A Charlie Brown Christmas* would become over the years the longest-running cartoon special in television history, its soundtrack a multiplatinum recording whose themes became showbiz standards. The generation now growing up with the specials—for many it was their only experience of Schulz—marked the calendar of their childhood with the shows' cyclical appearances and the sweet-sad sound of its score. Older newspaper readers still engaged the seasons and their passage accompanied by the slow, regular beat of the daily and Sunday *Peanuts* and its intramural traditions—Woodstock's New Year's Eve party, Snoopy's bales of Valentines, the Easter Beagle, Peppermint Patty and Marcie at summer camp, Lucy setting up the football, Linus in reverent vigil for the Great Pumpkin, Charlie Brown finding himself as he finds purpose and meaning for the sad little Christmas tree . . . but more and more, *Peanuts* would evolve into a world of video and plush.

Critics noted the change from a *Peanuts* that was primarily a commentary for adults to one that was a brand for children: "After all those years of 'Have you seen Peanuts this morning?' and clipping out those capsule expressions of guilt and inadequacy to pin to office bulletin boards or magnetize to family refrigerators, it was hard to trail off. We kept trying to be amused," wrote Judith Martin, also known as Miss Manners, in the *Washington Post* in 1972. "But the little bursts of identification became less and less frequent. Partly it was the repetition of ideas. Once you knew the *Peanuts* calendar—Beethoven's birthday, baseball season, summer camp, opening of school, Great Pumpkin night, football season—it began to get tedious."

"Should one blame him for milking all the commercial advantage he can out of the system which, it should be remembered, he had to embrace before he could claim our attention? Really, it is too stupid," concluded Richard Schickel. "That we of the middlebrow audience are no longer compelled to clip his cartoons and pin them up on the office bulletin board, quote them at parties, and discuss their hidden depths with fellow cultists is not, finally, his fault. He did not go into the cartooning business just to please 'we happy few.' He would, indeed, have failed if we were his only audience. No, he went into it needing, for economic success, all the friends he could get."

"I hate to think about it," Charlie Brown says when faced in 1966 with Snoopy's real needs as a dog. "The responsibility scares me to death."

The unprecedented success of *Peanuts* as a brand (with gross earnings of $20 million by 1967, $50 million by 1969, and $150 million by 1971) initiated an inner schism that would endure to the end of Schulz's life, profoundly dividing him: "I'm torn," he would say, "between being the best artistically and being the Number One strip commercially."

Strip and brand pulled Schulz in different directions, stretching him between the roles of cartoonist and entrepreneur, making him feel strong, indeed omnipotent, at one creative moment, dependent and vulnerable at the next executive juncture. But in 1967, as *Peanuts'* broad-based audience began gradually to come to terms with the nation's unease about civil rights, the war in Vietnam, sexual freedom, and so much else, Schulz regained control by turning to the one character in his strip who could single-handedly reestablish the personal quality of his making.

SNOOPY HAD COME A long way from the puppy who, despite being "very smart"—indeed, "almost human"—had entered the strip as an ordinary domestic pooch, not even yet a beagle. By the early 1960s, as Connie Boucher was rendering Snoopy the cuddliest dog on the planet, his tougher image served, with Schulz's permission, as war eagle for the United States military: in Vietnam as a talisman on American fighter planes and on the short-range Sidewinder air-to-air "dogfight" missile; in California, as an emblem emblazoned on aircraft spearheading the flight test program of the GAM-77 Hound Dog strategic missile; and in Germany, as a flight shield for the "Able Aces" of the Air Force's 6911th Radio Group Mobile, patroling the skies over Darmstadt.

Typical of Snoopy's many-sided appeal, he also served in deliberate violation of army regulations on the helmets of assault–helicopter pilots, alongside such emblems of antiwar sentiment as rainbows and slogans like "Bum Trip." More than Rin Tin Tin, Lassie, Trigger, and even Old Yeller, Snoopy had taken his place as the American fighting man's most trusted friend when going into combat.

Of all Schulz's characters, he was the slowest to develop. Not until January 26, 1955, had he finally come out with his essential dilemma, announcing to himself that he was tired of depending on people for everything and wished he were a wolf. Then, like a frustrated child breaking a long, moody silence, he declared: "If I were a wolf, and I saw something I wanted, I could just take it." To make his point, he growled a human-sounding AARGH!! through a set of distinctly lupine fangs; whereupon, the earnest, smiling, everyday presence of Charlie Brown immediately dislodged him from this wild new height of power, and he ended the episode hanging his head, his face cross-hatched with embarrassment.

"There's nothing more stupid than someone trying to be something they aren't," Charlie Brown repeatedly reminded his all-too-human dog, only to be foiled repeatedly by Snoopy's bravura talent—a gift for silent comedy so great as to turn instruction in a simple party trick into a Chaplinesque commentary on the human condition.

Ever the subversive comedian, Snoopy could not resist uncanny impersonations of Violet, Lucy, Beethoven, a baby, even a certain mouse:

Schulz's satiric take on the supreme cartooning figure of his youth (drawn two months after a chuckling, affable "Uncle Walt" had welcomed some ninety million viewers—more than half the nation's citizens—to the televised debut of Disneyland) shows one of many strengths that one day would enable Snoopy to challenge his Disney rival for universal stardom: Mickey's ears were as rigid as sharks' fins, whereas Snoopy's yielded to a wide range of expression, reshaping themselves in response to cold and heat, insults and rewards, food and music, joy and sadness, fear and shock, surprise and shame, pride and disgust.

Mickey Mouse had no capacity for states of mind. As a supremely representative figure of the American world of action—pluck personified, modest but mischievous, a dancing World War I doughboy maturing into the age of Lindbergh—Mickey had become a Fairbanks-sized movie star from the moment he uttered his first words in 1929: "Hot dogs!" As bust followed boom, Disney extended his action star into situations that proved time and again throughout the Depression that Mickey was indestructible.

But the more Disney became an entrepreneur of technique and spectacle, the more his cartoonists and animators called on Mickey to do little more than play straight man to newer comedic pacemakers like Donald Duck and Goofy. Then, in 1955, with the simultaneous rise of *The Mickey Mouse Club* on television and the opening of Disneyland, Mickey once again became the franchise star, his very ears the icon of worldwide commerce, while he himself revealed so little individual personality, his mind such an affable blank, that the viewer could not know what was going on *between* those ears. To be sure, from the beginning he had had energy and an unconquerable heart, but never did he seek an inner life. Schulz never tired of pointing out that nothing that Mickey Mouse had ever said, much less *thought*—no word or phrase—had passed lastingly into national consciousness.

In *Peanuts*, energy made Snoopy lovable, but thought made him human. Schulz perceived that although we cannot possibly know what a dog is thinking, the impulse of all dog owners is to imagine that we alone know what *our* dog is thinking, and the proudest of dog owners will often explicate with great subtlety what their sidekicks are now "saying."

Snoopy's stardom grew out of Schulz's ability to create an intimate bond by letting the reader in on the dog's continual awakening to his most human thoughts. The basis for this bond was trust: the reader could count on Snoopy to be himself, even when he was being someone else. The cartoonist, meanwhile, could be depended on to turn to comedy Snoopy's dominant traits—an almost arrogant commitment to independence (and its flip side: a deep-seated fear of dependence); a grand dreaming self continually deflated—not by mediocre vaudeville gags pulled out of the filing cabinet by a studio bureaucracy, but by the more exacting and individualistic physical comedy of the silent movie clowns of Schulz's boyhood Saturdays at the Park Theatre.

Snoopy extended body and mind into identities that conveyed the restless spirit behind them: rhinoceros, pelican, moose, alligator, kangaroo, gorilla, lion, polar bear, sea monster, vulture—all of which would eventually give way to the serial "World-Famous" archetypes who would illuminate his sardonic spirit behind a showcase of false fronts as sportsman, lover, spy, pilot, art aficionado, magician, attorney, surgeon, and on and on. In each of Snoopy's masterfully seized, casually discarded roles, Schulz's drawing became looser and rounder.

Snoopy was distinctly—defiantly, so far as Schulz was concerned—different from Mickey Mouse in one regard above all. Where Mickey embodied the gutsy "little guy" of American myth in the 1930s, followed by the "brave regular Joe with a rifle" of the war years, and was therefore an adult, no matter how childish were the worlds Disney pitched him into, Snoopy was distinctly a postwar, even a 1960s, phenomenon: he was purely adolescent—grandiose, revolutionary, with a mind of his own and feelings to match. Often, he acted like a very badly hurt person, except that, precisely because his innermost thoughts were open to view, his wound, and its shame, were exposed for all to see. The more he tried to live by his own rules, and the louder Charlie Brown remonstrated ("BE HAPPY WITH WHAT YOU ARE!! . . . YOU DUMB DOG"), the more human he became, as each experiment in living a life fully his own landed him right back on the floor of the doghouse, or in the parental lap, once more dependent.

As Snoopy's rebellions developed, his personality as a player in the *Peanuts* repertory company evolved. In this world without adults, he now behaved for all intents and purposes like the one and only child—the *real* child—joyous one minute, cast down the next; now magnanimous, now petty; by turns critical, tactless, cunning—"a little selfish, too," Schulz noted, identifying a whole range of controlling, testing qualities, starting with a "mixture of innocence and egotism."

Snoopy often treated Charlie Brown and his friends as if he were their intellectual superior; none of them could appreciate his talents, while he, in his turn, tolerated the foolish things they did. Lucy might play along with his fantasies (as mothers, or keepers, will), but she nonetheless let Snoopy know exactly who was in charge: "Any piranha tries to chomp me, I'll pound him!!"

Snoopy is the one character in the strip allowed to kiss, and he kisses the way a child does: sincerely, and to disarm. As the rest of the *Peanuts* gang struggles to love and be loved, they find themselves stuck in the incompatible romantic pairings of classical comedy. Lucy's definitive acceptance of Schroeder's rejection, for example, would be a relief to both; instead, she subjects herself to ongoing cold, even brutal, indifference. Snoopy, meanwhile, becomes the one between them, dancing on the piano, smitten by the beauty of the music, licensed to enact real feeling, inserting himself between the couple like a child whose family's emotions are kept forever under restraint.

Throughout the late '50s, Snoopy's doghouse was depicted in three-quarter view. Located on the side of Charlie Brown's house, it had a peaked roof, a simple, unseen, one-room interior, and its owner's name written over the arched opening. It was nothing more than a real doghouse for a real dog. This rarely varied until early 1960, when, as the grand side of Snoopy's personality began to stretch the dimensions of reality itself—one day he demanded to eat "on the terrace"; on another he installed an air conditioner—there came, Schulz later recognized, a turning point. Snoopy was now, he realized, "a character so unlike a dog that he could no longer inhabit a real doghouse."

And so, on February 20, he turned the doghouse broadside and presented Snoopy sleeping on the roof. Seen from this angle, powerfully alone in a horizonless world, dog and house merged to form a continuous line.

There would be occasional reversions to the old form, but never again would Snoopy be a dog in any conventional sense, and the rendering of his house would now be simplified to the point where, sometimes, such as when Snoopy is composing at the typewriter, it almost loses its identity altogether. Seeking to keep the doghouse even marginally real, Schulz found that if he tilted the tip of his pen in a certain way, so that "a little bit of the ink drops below the line," he could suggest the feel of wood in the roof and side-planking.

But it was more than elements of craft and design that demonstrated Schulz's new conquests in the medium. The reader listening to Snoopy's rooftop meditations was, in fact, overhearing Schulz's thoughts, but instead of ascribing them to the cartoonist (as he might with Charlie Brown's speeches), the reader took the interior monologue for his own, somehow coming to believe that he was hearing his own innermost jokes and quirks, worries and hopes.

In Al Capp or Walt Kelly, an intense editorialist was always at work. Feiffer could say crazy things because the reader understood him to be the ambassador from Greenwich Village. Mort Walker and Hank Ketcham were still gag cartoonists pulling the reader's leg one more time. But once Schulz began to let his strip's dog think aloud on top of a doghouse, "all hell broke loose," as Ketcham recalled it, for only a genius could speak for himself and have the world believe it was overhearing the voices on the edge of its heart.

For Snoopy to become a universal partner of the race with which he shared the planet—to overleap his present assignment as a radical individualist in the Minnesotan tradition—he had to *become* the hero, a tragicomic figure of such absurdly grand and revolutionary capacities that only he—and we—could see him transfiguring his doghouse into a flying machine sent aloft against the ultimate unseen enemy, the German ace Manfred von Richthofen, the infamous Red Baron. Snoopy threw himself so fully into an action fantasy that he by now had earned a title as powerfully mock-heroic as that of Cervantes's Knight of the Rueful Countenance.

The World War I Flying Ace took off one day late that summer of 1965 while Sparky was at the drawing board and the thirteen-year-old Monte came in with a model plane. Sparky's recollection was that as they talked about Monte's Fokker triplane, it crossed his mind to try out a parody of the World War I movies *Hell's Angels* and *The Dawn Patrol*, which had gripped him as a boy at the Park Theatre. He thought he might take off on the classic line, "Captain, you can't send young men in crates like these to die!" And then it came to him: Why not put Snoopy on the doghouse and let *him* pretend he's a World War I flying ace? But Monte always claimed that it was he who first suggested the idea of Snoopy as the pilot. Sparky denied it just as frequently, only conceding in the last year of his life that Monte "inspired it." Either way, Schulz admitted, "I knew I had one of the best things I had thought of in a long time."

UNTIL NOW, *PEANUTS* HAD been commentary on the world as seen and heard by Charles Schulz—recognizable everyday problems transposed into the key of little-old-adult children. Unintentionally, Schulz's themes raised the larger social questions that the civil rights movement and Lyndon Johnson's Great Society initiatives had put on the table: Who was entitled to happiness? Was the security of "owning your own home" and of "having a few bones stacked away," as Snoopy put it, the birthright of prosperous white America only? Were black and poor people going to go on being excluded from the expectations spelled out by Schulz's universal mantras for "Happiness" and "Security" and "Home"? When the Southern Christian Leadership Conference (SCLC) brought what was popularly known as the Poor People's Campaign to Washington, D.C., to lobby Congress for a $30 billion antipoverty bill in May 1968, the placards that rose over Resurrection City on the Mall came all but directly from Schulz's drawing board: "HAPPINESS IS . . . A Warm Dry House . . . No Rats or Roaches . . . Lots of Good Food."

As doubt and distrust crept into people's lives, Schulz's plain commentaries on the comics pages and in Determined Productions' small, square hardcovers set him up for a role he never intended or wanted. "I'm not a philosopher," he insisted, sometimes adding, "I'm not that well-educated." But the country had just reached the end of an era in which it considered itself the land that boasted the world's most distinguished philosophers. For thirty years, every high school principal read Professor John Dewey, or thought he ought to, and every college president salted his speeches with the aphorisms of George Santayana ("Those who cannot remember the past are condemned to repeat it") and Oliver Wendell Holmes, Jr. ("Taxes are what we pay for civilized society"). But the era of Professor Santayana, Justice Holmes, and Dr. Dewey was closing, and middlebrow culture reassigned the role of philosopher. Henceforth, the general public would take philosophy in capsule form through novelists (Hemingway, Vonnegut), journalists (Kempton, Baker), social scientists (McLuhan, Galbraith), and cartoonists (Capp, Kelly, Schulz), although Al Capp and Walt Kelly were drawing allegory that tartly commented on politics and society, and Schulz was creating the kind of myth in which everyone could find his or her own story: "Myths and fables of deep American ordinariness," as the writer Samuel Hynes construed *Peanuts*.

In a very midwestern way, Schulz reversed the American pattern of winners and losers, making a virtue of the fortitude required to endure blowing a hundred ball games in a row. The very notion embedded in *You Can't Win, Charlie Brown* turned the traditional East Coast orthodoxies of American children's literature inside out; in the creed of Louisa May Alcott, everything came out right in the end, but in *Peanuts*, the game was always lost, the football always snatched away. In Charlie Brown's world, the kite was not just stuck in a tree, it was eaten by it; the pitcher did not just give up a line drive, he was stripped bare by it, exposed.

Now, in 1966, as Snoopy pantomimed people to themselves from the doghouse roof—no longer through the merely subversive impersonations of the '50s but acting out the Flying Ace's full-fledged crusade—*Peanuts* acquired an explanatory as well as a descriptive character for thousands who burned draft cards and protested an unjustifiable war.

While mission upon mission of B-52 bombers hammered North Vietnam's capital and primary port cities, Snoopy's mania, his single-minded pursuit of the enemy and his hatred of losing, epitomized the America haunted by an always victorious John Wayne, the postwar U.S.A. that was racing to beat the Soviets to the moon.

As Snoopy soared—and danced—*Peanuts* once again led the culture. If the World War I Flying Ace mocked the martial spirit of the Great War, Snoopy's spontaneous, soul-satisfying dances of the '60s made him a genuine free spirit whose only commitment was to ecstasy itself.

His flutter-footed step kept time to bliss itself, lifting him so high above the "over-thirty" concerns of his strip mates, he hardly seemed to notice that he was leaving reality—and petty old Lucy—in the dust:

*Peanuts* in the new age of Snoopy was bolder but still quietly dissident, laying claim to joy, pleasure, naturalness, and a self-glorifying spontaneity without the ferocious exhibitionism that most radicals and rebels of the period deemed necessary to bring attention to their causes. Snoopy's basic desire—to transcend his existence as a dog by altering his consciousness—typified a central urge of the era and caused alarm among the strip's authority figures no less than its analogs did in the "real world":

"The strip's square panels were the only square thing about it," reflected the novelist Jonathan Franzen, who, "like most of the nation's ten-year-olds," was growing up through those "unsettled season[s]" of the '60s by taking refuge in "an intense, private relationship with Snoopy"—a stronger attachment than that which the reader could have with any of the other *Peanuts* characters because Schulz was now making us Snoopy's accomplices in transcendence. We alone can see what the Flying Ace is seeing; everyone else in the strip, even Charlie Brown, remains blind to the identity and miraculous feats of the "Masked Marvel," the Easter Beagle, the World-Famous Astronaut, the World-Famous Wrist Wrestler, Joe Cool, Flashbeagle, "Shoeless" Joe Beagle, and the Scott Fitzgerald Hero.

Snoopy had his origins in Spike, the dog of Schulz's youth, whom Sparky called "the wildest and the smartest dog I've ever encountered," and as long as Snoopy was treated as a pet—an eccentric, even a lunatic, household dog—by the *Peanuts* gang, he evinced Spike-like behavior. But now he left the kids behind.

Lucy had fantasized about the White House, but in the presidential elections of 1968 and 1972, Snoopy was embraced by actual voters as a write-in candidate, prompting the California legislature to make it illegal to enter the name of a fictional character on the ballot. Brought down behind the German lines in the Red Baron sequences, he operated in a larger, more threatening world than did anyone in the secure suburbs of the *Peanuts* neighborhood. Unique among the gang, he was allowed, in romantic encounters with a "country lass," to enter just ever so slightly into adult sexuality; Schulz once again having it both ways, for Snoopy also kisses like a child.

Back at home—again, uniquely—he had adult possessions, and not just books and records and pinking shears. The multilevel rooms under the A-frame roof of the doghouse now included a front-hall rug, a cedar closet, a lighted pool table, a stereo, and a Van Gogh, which, after a fire, had been replaced by an Andrew Wyeth. Snoopy's tastes were like those of every college kid in 1966, who, with a folk guitar and a tattered paperback copy of Herman Hesse's *Siddhartha*, had hung the dorm room with a Wyeth print—a magical-realistic picture unsettling because it transcended the ordinary rural life it seemed faithfully to be depicting—as an emblem of the searching, melancholy, considered life toward which he or she believed himself/herself, perhaps the whole troubled world, to be tumbling.

This was the first time in the comics that an animal had trumped its humans. Never before had an animal taken over a human cartoon, and "it did more than change *Peanuts*," said Walter Cronkite, "it changed all comics." Schulz's fellow cartoonists read and reread the Red Baron episodes to figure out how Sparky was getting away with it. His rival Mort Walker looked on, dismayed. The gag-minded creator of *Beetle Bailey* had been able to follow along with Schulz when Snoopy was perched in a tree, pretending to be a vulture. But, a dog . . . flying a Sopwith Camel that was actually a doghouse, which he couldn't sit on, anyway? "That's when I realized I didn't know anything about the comic business," said Walker. "What does a dog know about World War I and the Red Baron? Where did he get the helmet?" Most astonishing of all: what was Schulz doing showing actual bullet holes in a doghouse? "Good golly," Walker said to himself, "this has gone beyond the tale."

Hidden from no one except Charlie Brown and his friends, the visual and verbal idiom of Snoopy's fantasy universe became common to both the younger and the older generation through the 1960s. One of the very few "enemies" that Americans could agree on in those years was the Red Baron. In college fraternities and motorcycle gangs, rock groups and combat units, communes and airmen's hangouts, people nicknamed one another Snoopy and Red Baron and Flying Ace and Pig-Pen (this last including the Grateful Dead's keyboardist Ron McKernan). There was even a San Francisco band calling itself Sopwith Camel.

Free spirits in the counterculture loudly asked the very question that Schulz had been whispering in mainstream comics pages for more than ten years: *What would it be like to feel happy?*

A 1967 *Time* cover story had cited Schulz's characters as "hippie favorites" and placed Schulz in his Shangri-la on Coffee Lane as the admired neighbor of the infamous Morningstar commune. By 1968, six years after *Happiness Is a Warm Puppy*, John Lennon would retort with a song on the Beatles' *White Album*, "Happiness Is a Warm Gun," and two years after Schulz wrote the scene in *A Charlie Brown Christmas* in which Linus decides that Charlie Brown's wretched little tree is "not a bad little tree—all it needs is a little love," the Beatles hammered the same message around the world: "All You Need Is Love."

The lexicon of *Peanuts* filtered through the culture, middle to top, top

to bottom. As "security blanket" found its way into Webster's dictionary and "Happiness is . . ." into *Barlett's Familiar Quotations*, "Good grief!"
became the all-purpose refrain of Candy Christian, the innocent, infinitely
corruptible heroine of 1964's most notorious book, *Candy*, an erotic satire
written by the expatriate hipsters Terry Southern and Mason Hoffenberg.
The next summer, members of the Jefferson Airplane had heard that children in the neighboring studio were recording the voices of the parentless
*Peanuts* characters for a Christmas television special and, treating the *Charlie Brown* cast as if they were an enlightened prophetic microcosm of the
whole youth culture, came over to get *their* autographs.

Unbeknown to Schulz, another rock group, the Royal Guardsmen, a
sextet from Ocala, Florida, was on its way to selling three million copies
of a hit single called "Snoopy vs. the Red Baron" ("Finally, a hero arose/A
funny-looking dog with a big black nose . . ."), Schulz hearing of it only
when a friend remarked, "Great song you wrote." As soon as cartoonist and
syndicate had been cut into the royalties, the group added a string of sequels
and produced four LPs, on one of which they loosely fitted an anti-Vietnam
message to the "fascinating allegory" of Snoopy and the Red Baron calling
a Christmas truce in no-man's-land, with which the Guardsmen intended
"basically [to] expose the futility of never-ending conflict."

As early as 1959, two Convair B-58 supersonic bombers, designated
*Snoopy-1* and *Snoopy-2*, took to the skies with their namesake painted "in
his most supersonic pose" on their noses. By the mid-'60s, whole squad-
rons of F-100 pilots took their craft into action in flight suits decorated
with diamond-shaped patches featuring the Flying Ace; officials at NASA
named Snoopy the symbol of a new safety and morale-building program.

From 1966 to 1969, Snoopy could be found pursuing—or being
pursued by—the Red Baron wherever America explained itself to itself,
whether in a rock formation on the rim of the Grand Canyon, nicknamed
"Snoopy Sleeping on His Doghouse" or as a Goodyear blimp or inflatable
balloon in Macy's Thanksgiving Day parade. In form and function, the
doghouse could now take Schulz and his beagle anywhere the nation was
going, including the moon. And on March 10, 1969—four months before
man's first lunar landing—the World-Famous Astronaut was dispatched
into space.

Two months later, in a command module named *Charlie Brown* and its lunar module, *Snoopy*, Captains Eugene A. Cernan and John W. Young, of the U.S. Navy, and Commander Thomas P. Stafford, U.S. Air Force, piloting the *Apollo 10* spacecraft on a scouting mission to the moon, descended to within almost eight and a half nautical miles of the Sea of Tranquility in a final rehearsal for the history-dividing *Apollo 11* landing in July. To the astronauts, Snoopy was more than mascot: as "the only dog with flight experience," he served as guardian and guide; about halfway to the moon, 128,000 miles from Earth, Cernan held up a drawing of Snoopy, goggled, helmeted, and scarved, to the color TV camera on board for transmission to Earth. "I've always pictured Snoopy with the old World War I aviation helmet and goggles and silver scarf, and I think we sort of fashioned ourselves that way in those days," Cernan recalled. NASA estimated that more than a billion viewers all over the world saw Snoopy at that moment.

On May 22, after the two spacecraft recoupled in a tense docking procedure on the far side of the moon, mission control in Houston broke out a large cartoon showing Snoopy kissing Charlie Brown, and newspapers around the world ran banner headlines: DOPO LA MISSIONE VICINO ALLA LUNA: 'SNOOPY' RITROVA 'CHARLIE BROWN'—and when they splashed down in the Pacific: 'SNOOPY' SAFE AFTER PERILOUS MOON TRIP.

*Peanuts* had sprawled out of the old comics page to hit a new nerve. "Something was touched," Renata Adler wrote years later. Never have a cartoonist and his characters so consistently captured so much of the culture and the times. In the previous decade, *Pogo* had identified the true enemy power in McCarthyism: *He is us*. But *Pogo*, for all its brilliance, remained fixed in the McCarthy-Stalin era. Now, in the '60s, *Peanuts* was the one imparting messages and meanings to the hurtling moment, with one significant difference. Instead of ending after two decades, *Peanuts* had just begun.

# PART FIVE

# ZENITH

*All right, I'm extraordinary. What of it?*

T. E. LAWRENCE

# CHAPTER 21

# A GOOD MAN

*It was a shrewd move, to keep being the boy, as Robert Frost kept being the farmer.*

—ADAM VAN DOREN

TRY AS HE MIGHT, Sparky could not elicit from Joyce the love he wanted, nor could he make her feel loved and desired.

At first, Coffee Lane had been enough. "They were Midwestern-ers," observed their friend Betty Bartley. "Family meant everything. Joyce cooked, Joyce cleaned, even though she was building, and Sparky loved that. He loved being home, and with his family most of all, and then creating his strip. That was his world."

"We didn't pay much attention," he later said, "when people talk about the fifties and sixties and seventies. I frankly don't even know what they're talking about. . . . We lived out there in that Coffee Lane, and we had our life out there." It was, by design, "kind of an isolated life."

But as early as March 1963, five years after buying the Coffee Grounds, they put the place up for sale, at a price of $440,000. Although the Schulzes did not find a buyer, *Happiness Is a Warm Puppy* still topped the best-seller lists, so one newspaper ran the story under the headline BUSY CARTOON-IST QUITS "HAPPINESS" ESTATE, asserting that "growing business enterprises" were keeping Schulz in San Francisco, when, in fact, neither Sparky nor Joyce ventured into the city more than once a month, if that. According to another press account, Schulz was tired of his "showplace in Sonoma County" because too many freeloaders were dropping in. And there was a real element of truth here—complete strangers felt entitled to barge in on Charles Schulz. But there was another reason behind the Schulzes' inten-tion to sell, as Joyce would reveal more than forty years later: "Sparky and I were not getting along."

To a newcomer they seemed a happy enough couple: "The sense you got when you first met them was that things were reasonably idyllic," recalled one of the Schulzes' employees. But to a friend and constant visitor like Robert Albo, "It wasn't warm there. She seemed to go her way, and he went his—he spent all day up at the studio. We'd play baseball; Joyce never played baseball. We'd swim at the pool, but Joyce never went swimming. The household wasn't as warm and wonderful as it should have been."

One Christmas Sparky gave Joyce a St. Bernard puppy that he named Lucy; another year, a yellow Ford Mustang was waiting for her in the garage. And she gave him elaborately thought-out presents: a restored army surplus Jeep, in which he conducted tours of Coffee Lane, and a rolltop desk that recalled the miniature from his childhood. But, as a couple, they were not tender.

He had no pet name for her. He invested no time in imaginative cards or illustrated notes or letters—"no poems, no flowers, no special jewelry," Joyce recalled. Even when his annual income had reached nearly a million dollars, he did not present his wife with some memorable ring or necklace; Joyce wore nothing beyond the engagement ring and wedding ring with which she had started their marriage. He took the trouble to pass down family stories to their children, but never told the story of his courtship of their mother, or of their engagement or honeymoon. His most cherished memories centered on his father and the barbershop and his baseball days on the sandlots of St. Paul.

"Sparky was surely a Romantic in his thoughts and aspirations, but certainly not 'romantic' in the true sense of the word," Joyce reflected. "Even my Mother noted his complete lack of tenderness toward me when he would return from a golf game or a time away. She would say to me 'the Germans are just not an affectionate race.'"

He scarcely kissed Joyce hello or good-bye, and did not kiss his children good night. There were few, if any, hugs between father and child in the Schulz household of those years. When Monte was a very little boy, Sparky would sing to him before bed, "Little Man, You've Had a Busy Day," and he would bring glasses of milk on request to any of his children, but he avoided physical closeness. With family, as with friends, he stinted on displays of affection. "He was not an affectionate man: he never put his arm around the kids and said 'I love you' to them," one close friend noticed. Monte recalled his father embracing him but once in his life—when he was twenty-six and leaving home for graduate school. Amy had no memories as a child of physical affection from her father. Jill said, "I don't know if it was his conservative Minnesota upbringing, but we weren't the type of family that grew up with hugs and kisses and 'I love you.' "

Sparky himself felt awkward being embraced and resisted raising his arms to reciprocate. "I had a hell of a time trying to hug him," his cousin Patty recalled. "Hugging him was like hugging a tree—he never moved." His daughter Meredith would try to embrace him "all the time, and he wouldn't hug me back—he wouldn't get his arms all the way around. If you were lucky you'd get his arms on your shoulders. It was like he didn't know how to be warm." Even so, she added, and all the more poignantly, "Somehow we knew he loved us."

Little wonder that the returning soldier whose father had gone on cutting hair ("No one gave me a hug") had grown into a man unprepared for open arms. The last thing he expected was for someone who loved him to show it. "He always seemed kind of surprised that he was getting hugged," reflected Meredith, who eventually "learned to hug from other families." Amy, too, would use the same construction when, in later life, she recalled that she had had "to learn how to do it" from the members of her church community. Not until his daughters had reached their twenties would he take them in his arms when they said hello and good-bye; but even then, as Amy recalled, "It was never comfortable." Or as Meredith added, "He got a little better as he got older but not much." By then, perhaps, his fears of being unloved had diminished, but as a husband and father in his forties, Schulz was a man for whom most statements of affection were a confession of need: to say "I love you" demanded reciprocation, and as his cousin Patty observed, "He always felt that no one really loved him."

Years later, when asked with whom, of all the people in his life, Schulz was most intimate in the years at Coffee Lane, Joyce reflected, "I think Sparky was closest to his memories of the people in his family who were gone." Joyce had no use for yesteryear. "I am a person who lives for the present and the future. . . . I don't relish the past. What is gone is gone."

AS SNOOPY'S DREAM WORLD more and more dominated the strip—by 1975, Schulz noted, "It has certainly been difficult to keep him from taking over the feature"—*Peanuts* became a world obsessed with Snoopy's preoccupations, which, consciously or unconsciously, were Sparky's in miniature, right down to the Western Front getups, which had been transformative talismans in his school days, from the aviator helmet he had worn tightly buttoned among alien classmates in Miss Kelly's fifth-grade classroom to the Sam Browne belt of the school safety patrol that had been denied to him, but which had turned his male peers from "nobodies" into "somebodies"—and beyond this, the continual fear of nameless playground bullies.

The sense of being in enemy territory, the feeling of being menaced, the romantic possibilities of flirting with waitresses (as Carl had, when he met Dena), the unseen, distant, excitingly alien quality of a desired girl—all were themes from Sparky's life: as a city boy among farm cousins; as a lonesome high school senior fighting for his identity among "Thumb Tacks" classmates; as an army dogface advancing from France into Germany; as an aspiring cartoonist shot down by one editor after another; as an ambivalent celebrity in the '60s ("One minute you're being built up and the next minute you're being dashed back to earth"); as an eternally boyish, eternally lonesome man wondering whether he had been loved.

In Snoopy, Schulz repeatedly worked through his own inner cycles at a safe remove. He had still not resolved one of the central struggles of his own growing up: where, beyond the fortress-safety of a steeply raked drawing board, would he find *himself*? Should he just stay home, or did he dare to go out into the world, risking rejection and failure?

On the one hand, the drawing board provided a clearly invocable reason for staying at home. Carl had modeled this "work-as-love" solution for him, telling Sparky more than once how he loved to get up in the morning and go to work, and Sparky had always admired his father "for being a self-employed person who . . . was totally at home in the barber shop as I am off doodling in my studio." But as an adult Sparky "began to realize that a lot of this being at home in your place of work is not necessarily because you love it so much, but because you're secure there, and [Carl] probably had the same travel fears that I have. But he was incapable of expressing them."

The wider world, where as an adult Sparky was actually powerful, made him feel anxious and small. His mother, in her own fear of the world and withdrawal into her clan, had left him to struggle in boyhood to find his place, but he felt powerless, undermined, angry, especially at finding himself so dependent on her. Later, in his shy, introverted young manhood, she let him know that he was not masculine enough—his cartoons not sufficiently "smutty"—to be worthy of a woman's desire. And then she had died, foreclosing the satisfaction he might have found in proving her wrong.

At every life stage from youth on, the mainspring of his character had been the belief that no one would care about him or pay attention to him or even love him if he did not get out into the world and perform. To be loved—to show someone he was "something, after all"—he had to *become* someone or be clearly seen *doing* something; he could never just be himself. By himself, he was not lovable. If not for the daily reaffirmed achievement of his comic strip, recast now in a thousand somethings—in an endless flying circus of Snoopys—no one would even know he was alive.

But at Coffee Lane, even with the release of an occasional game of golf, his limitations oppressed him, and he found himself newly demoralized in his old search for true love, insight, understanding. Should he just stay home and settle for what little he got there—and what little he gave—or did he dare to go out into the world, risking rejection and failure and hurt? And if he did find someone who made him feel handsome and funny and understood, what then?

As in Thurber's "The Secret Life of Walter Mitty," imagination and dreaming had long lifted him out of a purely domestic sphere. Joyce had never objected to his escaping into the strip; she tolerated the fantasy world into which his work enabled him to retreat at any moment, leaving her to discipline the children and run the household alone. What galled her was that the more famous he became, the more passive he remained, except when cute young women actually made their way into his territory. "Sparky was big on anyone who stroked his ego," said Joyce. "His ego just got carried away."

BETWEEN THEM, THE DISTANCE had grown gradually. Sparky developed away from Joyce without really noticing it. All the activity of creating and maintaining the parallel worlds of Coffee Lane and *Peanuts* concealed a lack of commonality. Sparky was not interested in—indeed, was fearful of—two of Joyce's passions: riding and travel. Joyce had never been a devotee of the comics. "I never grabbed the funnies to see Al Capp's latest. I was a *Nancy Drew* fan." Sparky did not enjoy tennis with his wife ("I wasn't good enough," she said), and even after she took golf lessons, in hopes of improving sufficiently to keep up with Sparky, he went right on playing with his regular foursome of men, finally suggesting that Joyce play with a group of women.

They no longer played bridge but still enjoyed many of the same novels and stories, both were devoted followers of fiction in *The New Yorker*, and both were autodidacts committed to lifelong self-education, although when, in the spring of 1965, they both signed up for extension courses to continue their formal education at the local junior college, their goals could not have been more different. Joyce took French and American history, and put in five or six hours a day studying, struggling in one instance to translate three pages of French from an essay about existentialism ("I can't even understand it in English") and to learn about the Colonial navigation acts. Sparky, meantime, plodded through Tobias Smollett's *Humphry Clinker* with no ambition for a degree—simply out of "need to do something else with my mind"—while Joyce worked toward her bachelor of arts not just "for something to do, but also as a sort of insurance policy in case I ever have to work for a living."

With *Peanuts* earning the Schulzes a fortune—no longer simply good, exciting money, it was now serious money, unexpected riches, their annual take reaching $1 million in 1969 and more than $3 million by 1971—Joyce nonetheless did not believe that she was financially secure. She was always preparing herself for a return to the lean years. Her work in music school only revealed how much further she would have to go if she were to become self-sufficient in a career of her own. Yet throughout her marriage to Sparky she insisted that, between the two of them, she was the artist with the multiplicity of talents; Sparky, she contended, knew how to do "only one thing."

Joyce rebelled in her youth, but her rebellion failed, and though she redeemed herself in her second marriage, her capacities had found no outlet beyond the creation of Coffee Lane. Now, approaching midlife, she felt unsafe as Mrs. Charles Schulz and insecure in her skills. At forty she had no unifying cultural ambition, outside of her free-ranging contact with "the many facets of art." One magazine writer would take note of her "scatter-shot interests," the insufficiently harnessed energy that she would one day deploy in public-spirited projects—never mere exercises in civic beautification but always grand designs, magnificently executed.

Sparky had conformed in youth. He did as he was told, in everything except his determination to be a comic strip artist, and in that he was motivated by a feeling of being underestimated and misunderstood: *I'll show them!* Their marriage depended on this shared ambition. Each in his and her different way held the same dream of the future. "I never give up," he had told Harry Gilburt in 1956. "I'm an optimist," she would say all her life, "I never give up."

Their favorite Broadway musical was Meredith Willson's rags-to-riches-to-life-jackets love story, *The Unsinkable Molly Brown*, which opened in 1960. Inspired by the "true story" of scrappy *Titanic* survivor Margaret Tobin Brown, "Molly" contained echoes of Joyce's life and character: born to a struggling family during a flood in Hannibal, Missouri, Maggie Tobin, with visions of Rocky Mountain riches, lights out, at nineteen, for Colorado, where she sings and plays piano in a Leadville saloon, and despite a repertoire of only one song, she attracts the attention of James Joseph Brown, who is working his way up in the local silver mines. Brown marries Molly and the couple opens a soup kitchen to help the less fortunate in the mining community; then James strikes it rich, and they move to Denver, where Brown's newly minted millions are not enough to gain entrance to the well-guarded gates of society. Molly's ultimate ambitions are unfulfilled until, off to Europe to "buy herself some class," she returns on the maiden voyage of the *Titanic*, on which she becomes the real article, a truly classy woman, by saving souls whom the snobbier grande dames are too afraid to pull into the lifeboats.

In 1960, Sparky and Joyce took Molly Brown's bold and brassy anthem, "I Ain't Down Yet," sung by the raspy-voiced Tammy Grimes, as an expression of the shared hopes that had brought them over the Rockies to California. But by 1967 few of those in the Schulzes' world realized how tenuous Joyce felt her position had become. Outwardly, she was a very attractive woman—as one family friend described her, "gregarious, outgoing, flirtatious. But she really worried about losing Sparky."

★  ★  ★

YOU'RE A GOOD MAN, CHARLIE BROWN comprised little more than a dozen musical vignettes and a few extended scenes organized, as its composer and lyricist Clark Gesner and director Joseph Hardy conceived it, "around little moments picked from all the days of Charlie Brown, from Valentine's Day to the baseball season, from wild optimism to utter despair, all mixed in with the lives of his friends (both human and non-human) and strung together on the string of a single day, from bright uncertain morning to hopeful starlit evening."

Sparky first heard the music in early 1965. Gesner, an earnest, clever, twenty-eight-year-old composer-lyricist-librettist, was modest and shy in the manner of Schulz, and with a similarly quirky, droll sense of humor. With a talent for burlesque and parody, Gesner composed two numbers rooted in his love for popular song forms and for Schulz's comic strip characters: "Suppertime," a syncopated rag sung and danced by Snoopy in a kind of Jolsonesque delirium, and an ensemble march, "You're a Good Man, Charlie Brown." He wrote three additional tunes, each spotlighting a *Peanuts* character in a playful parody on a standard musical form, including a hymn for Linus to his blanket and, for Schroeder, a counterpoint melody, according to the *Moonlight* Sonata.

Schulz was so enthusiastic about the young composer that in April 1965, as CBS weighed ideas for presenting *Peanuts* on television—a month before Lee Mendelson sold Coca-Cola on the one-page outline for the special that became *A Charlie Brown Christmas*—the network came close to approving an outline and partial script that proposed to televise Schulz's strip in the form of an animated musical revue centered upon Gesner's songs. But an intramural feud among CBS executives grounded negotiations for that plan, and Gesner, on the verge of flying to the West Coast to meet with Schulz and Lee Mendelson, returned to his more modest original notion of a "Peanuts in Song" record album, which Metro-Goldwyn-Mayer eventually produced, in October 1966, as *You're a Good Man, Charlie Brown*, an "original MGM album musical," starring Orson Bean as Charlie Brown. "It's perfect!" Schulz told Gesner. "I am very pleased for both of us and hope that it sells a million."

Through Christmas 1966, Gesner's record played almost continuously on the turntable at Coffee Lane, and both Sparky and Joyce agreed, as they had upon first hearing the test record, that it would make a wonderful Broadway show. For the time being, however, they were alone in their opinion. When the producer Arthur Whitelaw secured the rights to adapt it for an Off-Broadway musical, even Gesner had his doubts, pointing out to Whitelaw over lunch at Sardi's restaurant that all they really had was "a record score and not a show, and the one does not necessarily guarantee the other."

Transmuting cartoon into theater had a long history on Broadway, but the very nature of the comics meant that an audience brought to the theater an intensely personal set of expectations about what their favorite cartoon characters should look and sound like. How could an actor play Snoopy? Or Charlie Brown, with his enormous head? Or Linus and his security blanket? "It's not like casting Dolly Levi," Gesner said years later. "There's always a way to turn an actor into a familiar role, but assuming the personality of a comic strip character is different."

During the four weeks allotted for rehearsal, Gesner was constantly grumbling that it could not be done, while the director, Joe Hardy, without so much as a written page to work from, directed his six actors to wander around a bare stage reading to each other out of *Peanuts* books. When Arthur Whitelaw, joined by a second producer, Gene Persson, announced that the curtain would go up on a Charlie Brown musical in the new Theater 80 St. Mark's, alarms and suspicions swept the United Feature Syndicate offices. Did these theater people really know what they were doing? How were they going to put a dog onstage? Why wasn't there a script to approve? How would the strip's fans know that these were *Peanuts* characters when the actors' costumes deliberately did not resemble any of Schulz's renderings of Charlie Brown and the others? And what about the neighborhood—what would happen to good ol' *Peanuts* when plopped down among hippies and Ukrainians in a renovated nightclub in the East Village, whose management served champagne during the intermission on opening night?

When the curtain came down on March 7, 1967, sustained applause and enthusiastic early reviews from the radio and television critics followed the cast to a restaurant in the Allied Chemical Building at One Times Square, where they waited until after midnight to telephone Sparky with the all-important *New York Times* notice—a rave. Walter Kerr reveled in the show's simple, untroubled innocence and joy, praising Schulz for "pulling off the small miracle of opening up one end of his comic-strip frame and letting his people out." The *Peanuts* characters had "marched clean off that page of pure white light in which it always seems to be high noon with invisible snowflakes falling, and right onto an actual wooden stage, onto actual teeter-totter equipment, and into forthright, fuming, explosively funny conversation without losing a drop of the ink that made their lifelines so human."

Overnight, the show became an Off-Broadway hit, unanimously praised for its fidelity to the "unique, delicate quality of Mr. Schulz's humor." For the next four years, through 1,597 performances at Theater 80 St. Mark's, all 199 seats sold out each evening and matinee—a gold mine yielding some $2.3 million in ticket sales. The show reopened on Broadway and closed in a month, but proved to be one of Off Broadway's hardiest exports, with thirteen touring companies in the United States and fifteen abroad (*Tu Es Un Chic Type, Charlie Brown*). Despite rumors in the New York press that Schulz would soon attend his hit show, he did not see *You're a Good Man, Charlie Brown* until it began rehearsals at San Francisco's Little Fox Theatre; on opening night, June 1, 1967, with Joyce in evening dress, gloves, and a fur piece, and he in a tuxedo, they drove in from Coffee Lane. A standing ovation greeted the curtain, and as Sparky came up the aisle, he was mobbed.

WITH THE COAST-TO-COAST SUCCESS of *You're a Good Man, Charlie Brown,* there followed a period in the summer of 1967 when Sparky could not remain at Coffee Lane striking his Jack Benny pose and saying, "All of the things that we have done have happened because somebody came to us. I never went out and searched for anything like that."

This time he could not be passive; he had to be Charles Schulz, creator of *Peanuts*, and drive into town on successive days in July to join several cast members for press interviews, TV advertising spots, and local midday television shows, including the Gypsy Rose Lee program (important enough to be broadcast "in color"), on which he appeared with Janell Pulis, the San Francisco cast's Lucy, and Roy Casstevens, who played Schroeder, all of them conveying to the television audience a spirit of winsome, energetic wholesomeness. Whenever Schulz, or the show, or any of its San Francisco cast appeared in local media, the emphasis was on good-hearted whimsy—two members of the cast even collaborated with a state trooper and a cow named Bossy to stage a "Drink Milk If You're Driving on New Year's Eve" public service advertisement, written by Schulz.

Needing a suit for the Gypsy Rose Lee program, he asked Janell Pulis to go suit shopping with him at Bullock & Jones on Union Square. They had become fast friends during rehearsals when they found how much they had to say to one another. Janell was a free spirit, dramatic, declamatory, adorable, in the mold of Christopher Isherwood's Sally Bowles. With dark hair, dark eyes, a Mediterranean earthiness and a sparkle in her eye, Janell, at twenty-three, had "turned Lucy Van Pelt into a surprisingly sexy five-year-old," San Francisco's legendary columnist Herb Caen reported. She was warm, fun; she touched Sparky's elbow as they spoke, reached for his arm as they walked, and called out to him, "Sparky—my darling Sparky," whenever he entered the theater in his plaid shirt, beige slacks, and matching beige belt and shoes.

Janell was always authentic, always herself ("I think he liked me because I'm a great walker and talker and cuddler and kiss-you-on-the-ear type of person"), and he could converse with her for hours, tracking back and forth between personal history and literature. He took pleasure in Janell's low, musical voice, and liked to hear her talk about books: they compared notes about Thomas Wolfe, he had recently read Pasternak, and she shared his love of *Spoon River Anthology*. She liked that he could be silly, "coming up with all this goofy stuff: making up names for roses that were ridiculous. He had a wicked sense of humor, and he made little observational quips that made you want to top him."

For Sparky, this was a step past "sophisticated" into a wild unknown—and certainly a long way from the Men's Brotherhood group and the class of hard-of-hearing old folks he had taught in the First Church of God in Minneapolis. Janell was single, a working actress, playing Lucy in the San Francisco production of *You're a Good Man, Charlie Brown*. He was nearly twice her age, the most famous, most beloved cartoonist in America, living on an estate in Sonoma County with his wife and children. Rumors circulated coast to coast among the *You're a Good Man, Charlie Brown* companies; in New York, producer Gene Persson heard talk from San Francisco that

Sparky and Janell were involved: "It was common knowledge that things were going on there that no one ever saw." But Persson dismissed the gossip, telling himself, "Sparky would never do something like that."

For her part, Janell would never be quite sure how to explain their relationship. "We never had an affair but something much more touching," she said years later. "I hate to sound so Victorian, but I always called it an affair of the heart."

Starting on the suit shopping day, when he bought her a gardenia at a flower stand on the corner of Stockton and Geary, they established their routine: in the late afternoon, they took walks—strolling downtown to Union Square and to the antique book shops on Post Street, or wandering the San Francisco waterfront. In the weeks ahead, they extended the ritual, walking all over old North Beach, with its mix of small family restaurants, old businesses, and new tie-dye, candle, and incense shops, stopping in the Italian delis and bakeries, eating lunch at a favorite table in a German restaurant under the Coit Tower on Telegraph Hill.

Often on their walks, they held hands—a theme of the show: "Happiness is walking hand in hand"—and Janell would sometimes be recognized as Lucy by passersby. "They knew me, but they never knew him. And I'd say, 'But this is Charles Schulz,' and they never knew him."

His fame was a curious thing: Charles Schulz was far more *present* in people's lives than he was a famous person, and that was the way he wanted it. Few if any passersby recognized him in the context of bohemian North Beach, but cast pictures of *You're a Good Man, Charlie Brown* had been plastered all over town, and Janell was enjoying a moment of celebrity such that, as she and Sparky took their walks, people would jokingly call out to her as if she were Lucy at her psychiatric booth and ask whether "the doctor" was "in," putting Sparky in the awkward position of having to be introduced—and once identified, he would be on the spot, almost always asked to draw something. "It was very hard for him to say no," Janell recalled, "and he usually did a little drawing but he didn't like to—it was like having someone ask me to sing off the street corner."

Joyce had no such artistic sensitivities. The Red Baron craze had elevated Sparky to a yet higher peak of celebrity, and now when he and Joyce attended hockey games with friends at the Oakland Coliseum, as many as twenty-five or thirty *Peanuts* fans would line up for his autograph between periods, presenting any bit of paper that could bear ink. He would graciously comply with every request, but then, wearying of the interruptions as the game resumed, he grumbled, "Why can't they just leave me alone?" And Joyce would answer that these were the people who had made him famous and that he had an obligation to them. "You want fame and fortune," she reminded him, "but not some of the things that go with it."

The only way he knew how to handle it was by withdrawing. To avoid autograph and doodle seekers when he was with Janell, they developed a hand signal: if Sparky preferred not to be introduced to the person who had stopped Janell, he was supposed to squeeze her hand once; twice, if he did want to say hello. "And he never did. He preferred to be incognito."

On their walks, Janell and he made a point of noticing the moment that twilight came down over the city, especially in North Beach, where the breeze off the bay carried a tang so sharp with salt that it touched the back of the tongue. As Janell later recalled, Sparky "would always get very quiet then. The tempo of the day was changing. He usually stayed to see the show but the quiet time was over."

He took immense satisfaction in the audience's delight in the play. Seated in the third row of the gilt-and-gesso theater—and beyond it, the flower-power culture, topless bars, and saucy nightclubs of North Beach— he heard for the first time his own lines spoken out loud and getting laughs, as six actors in their early twenties turned the pen-and-ink lines of his cartoons into flesh-and-blood characters. "I think it's changed him a little," Janell said at the time.

Of necessity, he had been self-sufficient at Coffee Lane, making do without an immediate response to his work; Joyce was not a comics reader, his mother-in-law was covertly hostile to *Peanuts*, and the children's interest was variable. The mechanics of comic strip publication—daily strips had to be finished and mailed to the syndicate eight weeks ahead of publication; the Sunday page had an even longer lead time, as much as twelve weeks—meant that each week as he sent off the latest batch of strips and at the same time received the latest surge of fan mail, he was completely out of sync with his readers' responses and had no direct way of knowing how the strip was going over. And so the tiny world of the Little Fox Theatre gave him something he had never had before.

After the evening's performance, he would go out with the cast to

Enrico's sidewalk café, a San Francisco institution. "He loved going there after the show," recalled Janell. "This was something he'd never done before. He loved hanging out. It was like a gang, a little family." The cast fussed over him; the waiter fawned. Janell and Sydney Daniels, who played Patty, tried to "turn him into a hippie," beribboning his turtleneck with love beads, tousling his crew cut. Men of his generation were now beginning to loosen up and wear their hair over their ears, but Sparky stuck with the buzz cut, which, as his aunt Marion had always told him, made him look younger. "Why don't you let your hair grow long?" the cast would ask, and he replied, "I don't want to be a conformist!" And Janell, roaring with laughter, said in her Lucy voice: "He turns me on, this man!" "He's a true flower child, the most beautiful, peaceful man," she told the newspapers. "He's what all the hippies would like to be: kind, helpful, tolerant."

Over supper, they would all wind down by reviewing the highlights and miscues of that evening's show: "Aren't Don and Earl getting a little up tempo on 'Ballgame?' "—"Hey, Al, great 'Blanket' "—"Good 'Happiness' tonight"—and Sparky would sit quietly, listening. One night, the question was, "What would you do if you weren't doing the show?" Each went in turn. Janell said, "I'd be having babies." Sydney said, "I'd be in movies." Austin O'Toole, who played Snoopy, said, "I'd be a gentleman farmer."

"It was all fun and easy," Janell recalled. Then it was Sparky's turn, and the silliness around the table fell off suddenly. He was being serious. Janell posed the question: "If you weren't doing the strip, Sparky, what would you be doing?"

He looked her in the eye. "I would be dead."

DRAWING WAS PROOF OF his very existence. He drew, therefore he was.

In January 1968, he reported to his old friend Fritz Van Pelt, "I am much more gray-haired than I used to be. I am gray on the left side of my head from the daily strips and the right side of my head from the Sunday pages."

In the turbulent spring of 1968, the ground underfoot cracked with every headline: six thousand marines surrounded and outnumbered at Khe Sanh; President Johnson stepping down; the surprise victory of the antiwar candidate in the New Hampshire Democratic primary, that other

Minnesotan with the needling wit and sardonic national presence, Senator Eugene J. McCarthy; Martin Luther King, Jr., cut down in Memphis, and riot-set fires consuming the inner cities. Needing someone steady and stainless to look to, the country turned to Schulz, its gentle distracter, with the special devotion reserved for national figures who capture the public's heart and trust in terrible times.

At the moment of winning the California presidential primary, Senator Robert F. Kennedy was shot in Los Angeles and died barely twenty-four hours later, early in the morning of Thursday, June 6. The very next day, his sudden widow, Ethel, sent word through a friend that her children would be comforted if Mr. Schulz would make each of them a drawing of Snoopy or Charlie Brown. On July 1, Sparky sent ten drawings, one for each child (the Kennedys' eleventh would be born in December), to the mourning family at Hickory Hill. A month later Ethel Kennedy replied: "It is very cozy to have Snoopy and his pals on our walls, mixed up with photographs of the family, which we think of them as anyway."

It was always the characters, never the cartoonist himself. When *Peanuts* appeared on the cover of *Time*—an honor awarded to a cartoonist only twice since the newsmagazine's founding in 1923, Schulz did not take his turn to be painted or photographed to appear within *Time*'s red-bordered frame. He drew his own cover, which, characteristically omitting himself, disposed a group portrait of his characters, his only presence, as usual, being his signature.

From 1968 to the end of his life, Charles Schulz would be universally cast as one of the few remaining good guys: "an individual of human niceness"—"a really sweet guy along the line of your favorite uncle"—a "good man." And because his public appearances were known to be few and far between, his mildest observations drew awed, appreciative laughter. His opinions on subjects ranging from the miniskirt to the sexualizations of *Peanuts* were surprisingly tolerant, indeed hospitable.* Although he remained politically uncommitted, refusing to come right out in direct opposition to the war in Southeast Asia, despite the rising denunciatory chorus of prominent Americans (Walter Cronkite had added to the fraught-

---

*When Dick Cavett asked Schulz on his television program if anyone had ever come up with a "porno *Peanuts*," Sparky replied, "All the time." Cavett: "Seriously? I'll be darned. Does Snoopy seem to enjoy this sort of thing?" Schulz: "We all need a little of that."

ness of the year by breaking the newscasters' code of neutrality to oppose the war on national television), Schulz's statement on the *Today* show in November 1968 clearly set him on the same side: "We're gradually, finally, coming down to the point where we're really beginning to realize how unspeakable war is, and that we simply have got to learn to stop this."

Fame distressed him and he would not allow it, which left Joyce—at the dawn of the women's liberation movement in mainstream America—neither as the wife of a famous man nor as a woman in her own right, nor even as a model for one of America's best-known cartoon characters. "I just can't be satisfied in being Mrs. Charles Schulz, I have to be ME," she told a reporter, with enough emphasis that Santa Rosa's *Press Democrat* capitalized the word.

This was March 1968, and Joyce may have said more than she meant to, especially when, after a quiet moment during the interview, she "suddenly" revealed, "I get so depressed sometimes. I look around and think: what have I accomplished? Then I realize I do all the footwork. I like business and wheelings and dealings. . . . Most of all, I love building." Dressed in slacks, sweater, and a beehive hairdo, she appeared under the headline SHE LIVES WITH A FAMOUS PERSON . . . BUT KEEPS HER INDIVIDUALITY—a title addressed to thousands of women who were just now realizing how much of their individuality they had sacrificed over the years. Two months later, Joyce turned up in *Family Circle* saying, "It's hard to be an individual with a famous person in the house. I know that *I* wanted to do things that were mine alone, and as the children get older, they begin to feel the same."

All this would have been enough to put a strain on a marriage even if everything else had been working. But both Sparky and Joyce were about to have creative epiphanies that would pull them further apart rather than put them back together.

# ARENA

*It was a miracle of rare device,*
*A sunny pleasure-dome with caves of ice!*
—SAMUEL TAYLOR COLERIDGE

FEW PRIVATE PLACES WERE more public, few public places more personal—
and almost nothing of real importance in Charles Schulz's life was less
explicable at first glance. Until a carved wooden sign heralded the newly
built Redwood Empire Ice Arena in the spring of 1969, motorists flashing
by on Steele Lane might have thought they were passing some campy new
roadside attraction—a Tyrolean inn or faddish fondue restaurant done up as
a monstrous cuckoo clock.

The press coverage of its grand opening on April 28, 1969, referred to
it as "Snoopyville," "Snoopy's town," "Snoopy's new skating home," and
"Snoopy's Ice Palace." Locally, it became known as "The Arena," or, by
Schulz's closest friends, as "Sparky's rink"; its first letterhead proclaimed it
"Charles M. Schulz's Redwood Empire Ice Arena." No one spoke of it
as Joyce's, although she was its prime initiator and supervisor, first business
manager, and constant guardian, while Sparky had been really no more
than a shadow partner in its creation.

In time, his game (hockey), his interests (the annual ice shows, senior
hockey tournament, and Sweetheart Ball), his merchandise (the Snoopy
Gift Shop)—even "his" table at the arena's coffee shop, the Warm Puppy
(by the window, closest to the front door)—would all be commemorated
by Joyce's creation, while her part in it remained unacknowledged, her
name completely absent from the official history of "Snoopy's Home Ice."
Yet without Joyce, none of it would have come into being, and without
the Redwood Empire Ice Arena, it is hard to imagine in what material
world outside his daily-evolving comic strip Charles Schulz would have
lived his real life over the next three decades.

But the story could not be told because it was a tale, as Sparky saw it, of failure—failure at the peak of *Peanuts'* popularity; a unique failure in a life of unending adult success.

For Sparky and Joyce, the arena's coming into being in 1969 marked the end and the beginning of family life. The world that Joyce and he had made together with the children on Coffee Lane soon gave way to new attachments, and, as the dust settled, Joyce moved on to larger projects and greener worlds, but Sparky anchored himself to the arena, making it his home, the one place outside the studio where he could be most nearly what he could allow himself to be. And in this reversal, which made Sparky the guardian and Joyce the shadow partner, the history of their failure to remain successful together would be recast to fit his myths.

Some said he built the arena so that his daughters could become professional skaters. Others swore that he used it as nothing more than a tax write-off. Some believed it was for the sheer love of hockey; others saw in it "the love for humanity." Still others would construe it as a last-ditch effort to save his troubled marriage, while some claimed that its very construction brought the marriage to an end.

Near the end of his life Sparky would tell the world, "I built it because I was raised in Minnesota," and then chuckle at the irony, because, to a Minnesotan, having a sheet of backyard ice is as ordinary as owning a pool is to a Californian. But there was nothing ordinary about this transplanted Minnesotan's home ice or the troubled romantic—or perhaps just romance-haunted—age in which it was built.

WHEN JOYCE AND SPARKY reinvented themselves as Californians, ice skating was the one thing they both missed from home. Since moving to Sebastopol in 1958, they had "despaired at the thought of giving [it] up," until one evening in 1966 they discovered the Santa Rosa Ice Arena, a modest but well-run rink where the Baxter brothers, Meryl and Lloyd (known as Skippy, a professional ice star and member of the 1940 United States Olympic team), had been teaching children figure skating since 1961.

With their own kids on the ice and the thrill of a rekindled passion upon them, Sparky and Joyce became enthusiastic boosters, joining the other families in the Santa Rosa Figure Skating Club, in whose annual ice revue all the Schulzes performed in June 1967—all, that is, except Meredith. Their idyll might have gone on indefinitely had not the county safety inspectors found a serious flaw in the roof and condemned the place. But the Schulzes liked the brothers; so when Joyce asked Meryl how he proposed to handle this disaster and he just shrugged, she explained the situation to Sparky, who would ever after recall saying, "Gee, I wish there was something we could do about it."

Until now, Joyce had been building on instinct—schooling herself in design as she moved from project to project, each scheme more ambitious than the last, each a grander-scale venture in family-scope entertainment. But with Coffee Lane all but fully developed—Sparky's new studio, buried among pepperwoods on the rim of the redwood forest, was completed in September 1967—and with their marriage under strain and their oldest daughter heading for trouble and the Baxters' rink shut down for good, Joyce conceived an enterprise so audacious as to seem capable of solving all their problems at once.

When she first spoke of building an ice arena, no one understood what she was talking about. In California, ice rinks were warehouses—rectangular, flat-roofed, and "sort of blah inside," as Charlie Brown might have put it if Joyce hadn't said it first. The leading architects and zoning-board planners of Sonoma County barely grasped the most elementary basics of conventional rink construction, let alone the peaked-roof marvel that Mrs. Schulz was talking about: a 33,600-square-foot family entertainment center, featuring a coffee shop, gift concession, box office, locker rooms, and mezzanine complete with lounges and administrative offices overlooking an Olympic-sized ice surface that would convert to a carpeted concert auditorium. If built, it would be the largest structure of its kind between Berkeley and Portland.

On August 21, 1967, the Schulzes bought two parcels of land on the wooded fringes of town—six and a quarter acres in all—and broke ground on Steele Lane the following April for "the Redwood Empire's Largest Ice Arena." They expected construction to take four months and to cost, by contractor's estimate, $170,000.

MEREDITH'S ABSENCE FROM THE Figure Skating Club's ice show in June 1967—and from the household itself that year—was an outward and visible sign of the trouble that was to be a prime force in Joyce's drive not just to build, but ultimately to run, a multipurpose civic center. The word she emphasized over and over as she expounded the central theme of the arena's operating philosophy was "wholesome." She was equally set on her creation's being beautiful, certain that "if young people have a beautiful place to go, they are not likely to be destructive, but will turn their energies toward the joy of accomplishment in ice skating and playing hockey"—a center, she argued to the balky zoning board, that would "keep children off the streets."

Meredith, seventeen that spring, a junior at Sebastopol's Analy High School, was, as Joyce saw it, running wild: keeping bad company, taking drugs, sneaking out at night to meet a boy. Meredith had, in fact, tried marijuana once and did not like it, and though she was indeed hitchhiking along West County roads to keep trysts late at night with her high school boyfriend, Gordon Anderson—who, somehow to make it worse, happened to be the rhythm guitarist in a local rock band, the Bystanders—it did not register with Joyce and Sparky that Meredith and Gordon were the group's acknowledged "straight" kids.

Like a bewildered myriad of other American parents who had grown up in the Depression and come of age in the war, the Schulzes knew little about what they were actually up against with their oldest child. In Sonoma County, "those were tough years," recalled their contemporary Betty Bartley. "The drug scene was coming in and the music and all these other things, and children were being exposed to things that we weren't familiar with." Most typical of the GI generation as it faced the 1960s, Joyce and Sparky felt certain that they were uniquely alone in their troubles and should remain silent about them.

From the start, Joyce and Sparky had gone to great lengths to keep the secret of Meredith's biological parentage; even when, at eight, during the family's first year at Coffee Lane, her curiosity grew to the point that she dug out her adoption papers from a drawer in Sparky's closet, they turned away from the challenge. Meredith did not know what the papers were, only that her name was on them, alongside the word "adoption," but when she asked if the document meant what she thought it did, Sparky and Joyce denied it. Her intuition told her otherwise, and though she pressed the point again and again, each time they lied to her.

The more her parents covered up, the more Meredith stripped away—

or tried to strip away—her legal and practical father's defenses. She grew up craving Sparky's affection. "I'm a very warm, huggy kind of person, and he was not," she recalled. While all the Schulz children described their father as reserved, Meredith took it personally. It seemed to Meredith that Sparky "didn't like me as much as he liked the other kids," although she would be years putting this intuition fully to the test. But it was not just her unacknowledged status as an adopted child that complicated their relationship, as she would come to realize after years of struggling to feel close: "He was so cold and so distant, but not because he didn't like me, but because he was afraid to love." First, however, she "had to find out what was the matter with me that my dad wouldn't hug me. That sent me down the path I went down."

If Sparky felt uneasy before a demonstrative, high-strung teenager, Joyce made it her mission to set Meredith on the straight and narrow. But when, in the eighth grade, Meredith first showed signs of being boy crazy, Joyce sent her away to a girls' boarding academy, the Katharine Branson School, in Ross, California, which only served to certify her in the role of rebel. So Joyce brought her back to Analy High as a ninth-grader and went on permanent, and probably very wearing, alert for Meredith's next infraction.

One night that fall, when Meredith was supposed to be listening to records with three girlfriends, Joyce found them dancing in the basement with some boys whom the girls had invited in without the Schulzes' permission. Meredith swore there was "no hanky-panky going on," but Joyce yelled for Sparky to come and see for himself, and "for once in his life" to enforce retribution. But when he found empty beer bottles and an empty whisky bottle under the pool table, it was Joyce who picked up the phone to call the police, hanging up only when Sparky calmly sent the boys home and sat the girls down for a stern talking-to.

Rarely did he enter into such confrontations, however. "My father was always kind of out of things, out of touch with me or what was going on," reflected Meredith, "and I felt I was kind of a threat to his social status, and I wanted to be accepted by him, and I wanted to be accepted by my mother. It got to be kind of a distorted thing because I didn't feel any security with either of them." Sometimes Joyce and Sparky would sit Meredith down on the hearth to talk to her, Joyce bitterly, Sparky clearly and calmly—she fire, he ice—to the point where Meredith could no longer take in what they were saying but would "sit there and become part of that fireplace."

Over and over, Joyce chastised Meredith for the company she kept. "Avoid people who do nothing" was Joyce's constant refrain.

Finally, after the summer of 1967 and more unauthorized late-night parties, Joyce decided that the time had come to "get Meredith straightened out." Backed up by her own mother and a family friend, she bore Meredith off to Switzerland, where, after a two-week tour, which proved a prime inspiration in designing the ice arena, she enrolled her at The American School in Switzerland, on the outskirts of the sober city of Lugano. "I thought they'd be strict in Lugano and that that would be good for her," said Joyce.

But, lest Meredith feel singled out for punishment, Joyce decided that Monte, fifteen, and Craig, fourteen, must also be packed off. "It wasn't right to send Meredith off and not the boys," she contended.

Sparky did not like transferring Meredith to some cosmopolitan holding pen, nor did he wish to farm out his sons to a prep school. But he had lost his will to resist Joyce. "Dad was crushed and angry but went along with the plan," recalled Monte. "He may not have agreed with her but he just didn't say anything," said Meredith. In any case, Joyce prevailed. Amy, eleven, and Jill, nine, remained at home, enrolled at the 3-R School in Santa Rosa, but Monte and Craig were never told why they were being sent away, and it fell to Sparky alone to deposit the boys at the Cate School.

Dispirited himself, he tried to soften the blow with an overnight stop at the Madonna Inn in San Luis Obispo, and took them to a drive-in across the highway—John Wayne playing Sheriff Chance in Howard Hawks's *Rio Bravo*. But even the "big guy with the battered hat" and Winchester rifle couldn't bolster their fortitude; the next morning's journey hung heavy over all three. "He hated to see us go," said Monte half a lifetime later.

Meanwhile, back in the Swiss Confederation, Joyce's plan had backfired. Her untrusting heavy-handedness got Meredith's back up: "I knew full well that I was straight, that I was upstanding, that I had all the morals she wanted me to have; and I felt I was being punished, so I figured if I was being punished for it, I may as well do it." Within a day of landing on the school's sunny hillside she took up a classmate's offer of some Paris hashish—an irony, since such an exotic substance was virtually unknown to high schoolers in Sonoma County in 1967, however commonplace to teenagers on the fringe of Switzerland's Eurotrash circles—and was soon using regularly and sneaking out of her dormitory at night to meet a graduate student down the road. Come spring 1968 and just eighteen, she was pregnant.

This would have been a crisis for any family, but for the Schulzes several factors complicated this ordeal—especially the fact that, by the time Meredith returned home in June, she was already into her third month, yet had told no one except her old boyfriend, Gordon, with whom she had again become close. She then further delayed breaking the news, not willing to risk the wrath of parents who "looked like they were going to kill me if they found out one more thing," while reviewing the alternatives with Gordon, with whom she settled on a plan: They would marry, Meredith would have the baby—whereupon, in an eerie echo of her own birth just eighteen years earlier, Gordon would adopt the child. But when Meredith got back to Coffee Lane at two in the morning, after hours of such soul-searching, she found Joyce waiting up.

Abruptly, she showed Meredith straight to the door with a curt offer of $500 a month. If she could not live by the rules of her parents' house, then she must leave at once.

"Well," Meredith shot back, "I just hope that five hundred dollars is enough for me and the kid."

"What did you say?" asked Joyce, firmly, evenly, and, one suspects, despairingly.

Meredith repeated herself, and Joyce sat down hard in a chair. "What 'kid'?"

"The one I'm going to have!"

Crying out for Sparky, Joyce plunged upstairs to make sure that this time at least he put in an appearance. Of the ensuing hullabaloo, Meredith would most recall that he asked her why she had told her mother.

"Well, it's the truth," she replied.

And now, indeed, her parents faced a grim choice. They did not want her to marry Gordon, or for Gordon to become the nominal father of the child, or for the episode to become known in any way. By morning they had decided to send Meredith back to Minnesota to have the baby and give it up for adoption. But almost immediately Joyce had doubts. So far as she was concerned, no matter where or how Meredith had the child, she was destabilizing the family, and though Joyce later came to agree that Meredith should have married Gordon and had the baby, at the time she had little confidence in either one's capacity for responsible parenthood—and what was more, should the Minnesota solution come to light, it would put Sparky in a bind with his public that is almost impossible to imagine today.

And so, three days later, after consulting with a friend—the markedly original physician Robert Albo, early specialist in sports medicine, highly accomplished magician—Joyce and Sparky determined instead to send Meredith to Japan, a veritable archipelago of abortion mills while legislatures remained entrenched against the procedure in America. Joyce would accompany her; Sparky would hold the fort at Coffee Lane. "Mom was terrified when we had to go by ourselves," Meredith later reflected.

In Japan, Joyce took Meredith to a hospital—or what passed for such in Kyoto: one shabby little cottage, the shoes all lined up at the door—and gutted out the wait. Happily, Meredith came through safely and recovered in Kyoto; but she returned home with clipped wings, "tainted," as she later recalled, "and so completely humiliated, I didn't care anymore." She was soon getting high on a variety of drugs every day, and moved out to live with Gordon Anderson. Within another year, she had met another young man, Gary Fredericksen, and, as had her mother before her, married against her parents' wishes at nineteen. "I felt like I was following in her footsteps right down the line; the only thing was, Gary Fredericksen never became Charles Schulz."

For Meredith, a rough time was coming. And no less would this be true for Sparky and Joyce.

When Joyce had shepherded Meredith safely home, they had barely said their hellos to Sparky when, without so much as one question about the ordeals that mother and daughter had just undergone, he asked Joyce whether she had seen anything of the Japanese countryside: "What was it like?" inquired the minimalist pioneer of the cartoon panel about the land of the woodblock print.

"I could have killed him," she recalled.

For a long time, Joyce had tolerated his passivity, his absence even when present, the colorless camouflage of his settled inaccessibility. She had grown accustomed to being the parent who made the tough decisions. But after this worst journey, something had to change.

Declaring 1969 to be her year, Lucy proclaimed herself tired of being ignored, and in short order threw Schroeder's piano up a tree—not just any tree, a kite-eating tree, which devoured the instrument. But Lucy was far from satisfied ("Maybe I should have thrown *him* up a tree!"), and her complaints and questions about and for Schroeder mounted through the year: "I'm sick and tired of the way you ignore me!" (January 21). "I hate your piano!" (January 22). "You never pay any attention to me . . ." (January 23). "All I want is for you to notice me once in a while . . . Is that asking so much?" (January 31). "It's been a long time since you said you liked me" (February 20). "I have a lot of questions about life, and I'm not getting any answers!" (March 17). "You dislike me, don't you?" (April 18). "Do you know what love is?" (November 4).

Finally, she takes her search to the night sky. "Poets tell us that the answers to life can be found in the stars . . ."

★   ★   ★

STUPID CARTOONISTS! THE ANSWERS in life and love could be found not at the drawing board but at a construction site—not in pen and ink but in steel-reinforced concrete.

Joyce was at the arena's building site every day now, supervising every detail, as brilliant yellow bulldozers transformed Steele Lane. "No point, however fine, was too small for her attention," recalled one observer. "Joyce liked men," observed her friend Betty Bartley. "I don't mean that the wrong way. I mean, she liked to watch things go up and construction work be done." "I admire the artisan at work," Joyce herself said at the time.

The roof, raised by three cranes and pitched at the thirty-degree angle characteristic of Alpine design, arose according to a plan unprecedented in Sonoma County. Costs at this stage mounted to $1.5 million—an increase of 780 percent. Sparky never balked at the overruns, but neither did he join her in her enthusiasms at the building site. The architect who drew up the plans for Schulz's new studio recalled the couple's different visions of the building: "All he cared about was a place to put a drawing board and a chair; he didn't care about anything else. Joyce was the builder, and she was the one that knew that he needed a staff and space for them and meeting rooms and all that kind of stuff. But Sparky never came in; I never did see him. All he wanted to do was draw, and he just needed space for that, and a place where he could rest once in a while."

All three structures had been put up by Edwin V. Doty, a general building contractor, whose family had farmed the land around Sebastopol for generations. Ed had been in the construction business since 1956; he and his wife, Ruth, both of them blond, handsome, and outdoorsy, had been among the young couples invited to the Schulzes' November 1960 open house for the new residence at Coffee Lane. Joyce worked well with Ed—he could somehow accommodate her determination to be consulted on even the smallest detail, and her habit of making highly specific changes even when the work was far advanced, all without losing face with his men or falling behind schedule. John Van Dyk, the Santa Rosa architect who had drawn up initial plans for the arena, openly doubted whether Doty Construction, a small contractor based in small-town Sebastopol, was up to the job and suggested that Doty at least pair up with a Santa Rosa builder. In her turn, Joyce suggested that she might need a new architect, threw all her weight behind Ed, and got him the contract.

Joyce, the stonemason's granddaughter, prized talented craftspeople and had deep respect for building materials, especially the beautifully craftable lava that clothed the slopes of Mount Lassen—volcanic stone would become a signature of every structure she built with Ed Doty. To create persuasive trees for her Swiss village, she hired from Hollywood the designer whose special effects had made *Planet of the Apes* that year's surprise hit. She sent a noted architectural photographer, his wife, and 250 pounds of equipment to Switzerland; Don Meacham's pictures of high mountain meadows in the Bernese Oberland and the wind-ruffled Lake of Thun framed the main arena in four panoramic photomurals, each thirty-eight feet long. She urged additional photographs on her carpenters as points of reference in constructing the chalet fronts that would line the walls of the arena and hired "only the finest artisans in house painting" to impart the weathered tone of a time-hallowed wood-beam Alpine village. Cabinetmakers spindled balcony railings and elaborated gingerbread shutters, each to its own design; Joyce herself took pains with the flowers in every window box and the planters hanging over the forecourt. "She wanted it to be right," recalled Thomas Tomasi, her architect on later projects.

"She never did anything part way," said an employee. "It was first class and done right, and it was beautiful."

She hired a painter from Carmel to bring out the vivid scenery by tinting the black-and-white photomurals with oils, and she found far subtler alternatives to the cold glare of conventional rink lighting: over the main arena, not a single fluorescent tube could be found; decorative border lights of clear glass twinkled like stars glimpsed between mountain peaks. When not in use, spotlights for concert performances were carefully shuttered behind the chalet windows, and the average temperature was a comfortable sixty-eight degrees, as eight miles of coiled subsurface piping kept the rink frozen.

"This is California," she said. "It shouldn't be cold."

"Warmth was the thing Joyce was after in the arena—she didn't want a cold place," Sparky agreed.

WITH JOYCE BUSY ON Steele Lane, Sparky experienced a new sense of freedom that burst upon the strip that year and the next in two new characters and a full house of new devices: Franklin, a black boy whose father was serving in Vietnam, became Charlie Brown's new pal at the beach; Lila, Snoopy's first owner, named for Lyala Bischoff, his secret streetcar crush in high school, came back to haunt Charlie Brown. Snoopy, his days as a second banana far in the past, was more and more the strip's superstar: entering and winning the Wrist Wrestling Championship in Petaluma; going to the moon; tossing off a novel or, anyway, its first paragraph; celebrating Veterans' Day with a root beer at Bill Mauldin's; foiling Lucy at every turn with preemptive displays of affection—his kisses, seasoned by a new life in Parisian cafés, having become a potent counterforce against Lucy's aggression.

Schulz often remarked later on the freshness of his work in these months, but as to why this period was so especially productive, he never ventured a guess beyond stating the fact of Joyce's preoccupation with the arena, and then reflecting, "I suppose what's going on in your life has something to do with it." Robert L. Short, who visited with the Schulzes on several occasions in 1968, hazarded his own opinion: "This unhappiness they were enduring gave the strip a dimension and a depth that you don't find except in the life of an artist who is enduring that kind of unhappiness."

They had six season tickets for Seals hockey games at the Oakland Coliseum, initially going as a family with the four kids still at home, often adding an extra ticket for Joyce's mother. But now Joyce went to the Coliseum for the express purpose of comparing notes with the management on arena design and maintenance, so they more often left the children with a sitter and took along another couple, such as their friends Don and Donna Fraser.

At some point in the evening, recalled Don, Joyce "would start to needle Sparky, or would want to be [center]-stage, and it would make you feel sad for them both because together they were having a hard time but separately they were terrific. By herself, Joyce was a lot of fun; she was creative and quick and fun. But together they were the kind of married couple that made you uncomfortable."

"I think there is nothing more depressing," remarked Sparky in January 1968, "than to see a married couple out in public where the wife is cutting the husband down all evening. She is ashamed of him and of everything he says." With company at Coffee Lane, they followed the same script; Joyce "just took him apart," a friend of Sparky's recalled from several visits. Or she put him down by comparing him to other men, as she did with Chuck Bartley after bridge nights at the Bartleys', picking on Sparky on the drive home to the advantage of Chuck, "a man's man."

He thought he knew what Joyce wanted, and with an intense passive-aggressive stubbornness he avoided giving it to her, because to become what she wanted would entail compromising himself. "It is quite obvious that women would prefer some sort of leading and domination," he observed in 1968, "and when they don't get it, then they have to compensate for it in some way." But, as he continued to tell an Aesopian version of his marriage by highlighting the story of couples in general, "in their struggles to try to get their husbands to be stronger, they probably end up making him [sic] even worse than ever."

For her part, Joyce "wanted a *man*—a romantic man," said a friend, "but Sparky was not the man she wanted him to be."

"He was never completely comfortable with Joyce, and she was never satisfied," observed their friend the actress Kaye Ballard, who, having met Sparky in 1958 when recording her own cabaret version of Lucy and Charlie Brown's relationship, *Good Grief, Charlie Brown!*, often visited Coffee Lane. "I really felt that he was *so* unhappy and that was why: he was totally suppressed by her; it was obvious that he felt trapped. He was very uneasy around her, or he was trying to please her too much."

He knew how dissatisfied she was with him, but took no responsibility for any part he might play in her unhappiness. "My wife is a very nice person," he said in 1968. "But I'm afraid that generally women never find the man who is ideal enough in their estimation so that they can continue to be dominated by him and accept his decisions and his leading all the time, which is, after all, only human because no one is ever going to find anyone just perfect anyhow."

Joyce and Charles Schulz on their wedding day,
April 18, 1951, Minneapolis, Minnesota.

Sparky and Joyce, visiting the Hagemeyers in
St. Louis, Missouri.

In the backyard with Meredith, called "Mimi," at 2321 North El Paso Street, Colorado Springs, Colorado, 1951.

Charles Monroe Schulz, Jr., called "Monte," was born February 1, 1952, Colorado Springs, Colorado.

Christmas 1953.

With Craig, their second son, in the breakfast room of the big house overlooking Minnehaha Creek, 1958.

As a young man in the army, Schulz had considered himself "one of the staunchest opponents of classical music." At thirty-six, at home with his family, he enjoyed listening to a large collection of recordings of Beethoven, Berlioz, Haydn, Mendelssohn, Mozart, and his favorite, Brahms.

Schulz receives the profession's highest honor—the Reuben—from Rube Goldberg himself, at the National Cartoonists Society Award Dinner, Hotel Astor, New York City, April 1956. Schulz won an unprecedented second Reuben as the outstanding cartoonist of 1964.

By the mid-1950s, *Peanuts* was a campus phenomenon. Here the cartoonist signs copies of the first strip collections published by Rinehart.

During the presidential campaign of 1956, Schulz was dubbed "the youngest existentialist."

Coffee Lane, Sebastopol, California, 1961.

*Peanuts* made the cover of *Time* on April 9, 1965, a triumph that Sparky and Joyce could share together in the world they were building at Coffee Lane.

Schulz on skateboard, with (*left to right*) Amy, Monte, Jill, Craig, 1965.

The world-famous cartoonist at the drawing board.

June 1968: Nearing their zenith of 1960s popularity, the *Peanuts* gang were photographed with their creator for *Look* magazine.

Joyce, 1968, photographed inside the ice arena during construction.

The Redwood Empire Ice Arena opened to the public on May 6, 1969.

Meredith, 1969, dressed for work in the uniform of a Warm Puppy Café waitress.

Schulz and sons: Monte (*left*) and Craig (*right*), posed at the ice arena, 1969.

Sparky signed this photograph to Tracey Claudius, the twenty-five-year-old Pacific Telephone executive with whom he fell in love the day he met her, March 16, 1970. He immediately declared it "one of the great days of my life."

Tracey (*at right*), photographed as a bridesmaid, before she moved to California in 1969. Sparky later said that he fell in love with the sparkle in her golden-green eyes and the excitement in her low, musical voice when she described the way that a philosophy course in college had opened her up to the world of ideas.

Sparky with Jean Forsyth Clyde, September 1973. "Sparky always took me in his arms, and there wasn't a night that we were together—to the last night of his life—that we didn't cuddle before we went to sleep."

Sparky and Jeannie, jogging outside the studio at One Snoopy Place, circa 1975.

Sparky, at home in his favorite chair, with Andy, the wire-haired terrier whom the Schulzes adopted in 1988. "Up until then, I always just liked having the dogs, never really paying much attention to them," Sparky observed. "For some reason, I have never liked a dog in all my life as much as I like little Andy. . . . I developed a fanatical love for this funny little fuzzy dog."

Into his final decades, Schulz was a scratch golfer with a respectable 8 handicap. He regularly shot scores in the 70s, and in August 1995, at the age of seventy-two, he sank his first-ever hole in one.

The master, photographed in the studio at One Snoopy Place, September 16, 1999. Advanced cancer was diagnosed two months later; strokes followed its treatment, and his eyesight blurred. On December 14, 1999, he announced his retirement, releasing his grip on a worldwide multimedia enterprise yielding annual sales of more than a billion dollars.

The last portrait of Charles Schulz at the drawing board.

Where did Sparky and Joyce connect in this period?

"The arena seemed to be the tightest bond between the two of them," one friend observed. "Joyce's real interest and her real love—everything—was centered around the arena."

In truth, the marriage had gone dead in the bedroom. In their early days together, Sparky, though "not oversexed by any means," Joyce recalled, "was as exuberant as any young guy having sex for the first time." But nineteen years had passed, and "it got very boring at the end, and we just drifted apart."

Their incompatability went at least as far back as August 1964, when Sparky and Joyce had taken the children, Joyce's sister Ruth, and a friend of Meredith's, for a two-week holiday to Hawaii—their first trip as a family since 1958. "We hardly ever took a vacation," said Amy, "we just stayed at home at our little Disneyland." Sparky's fear of travel—or, anyway, his wish to be home by dark and soon asleep in his own bed—blocked any trip farther than half a day's drive from Sonoma County. But with the strip three weeks ahead of deadline, he assented to the expedition, although, as he later told it, he went to Hawaii not for Joyce, or for the sake of the marriage, or even for his own relaxation, but "for the kids."

Indeed, as Joyce recalled it, despite four days at sea and the promise of "golden hours under the sparkling Pacific sun" on the Matson liner *Lurline*, Sparky would not make love to her. And no sooner had they arrived, festooned with leis at the Hilton Hawaiian Village, than Sparky started feeling deeply uneasy. Most likely he was having an anxiety attack, as he did so often when separated from home—a predicament made the worse when the hotel doctor gave Schulz a complete examination and declared him healthy and fit.

Sparky diagnosed the trouble as loneliness, pure and simple: Joyce had brought Ruth; Meredith was teamed up with her best friend of that period; Amy paired off with Jill; Monte and Craig, in their collarless surfer shirts, had each other. "Now everybody has a pal—everybody but me," Sparky lamented, for the benefit of a local newspaper columnist, Cobey Black, a handsome woman who had come to interview the Schulz party over breakfast—during which, according to Black, "a sunkist [*sic*] coed in a white bikini drifted by," and Schulz wistfully turned to his French toast "with an expression familiar to all admirers of Charlie Brown."

On the four-day voyage home, he at last had real reason for worry. The purser had begun the trip by running the passengers through a safety drill, warning them that the worst thing that could happen was a fire at sea—and, of course, three nights later, under a star-speckled darkness that would also have been familiar to Charlie Brown's and Lucy's admirers, that is exactly what happened: still twenty-four hours from San Francisco, the *Lurline* was ablaze. In the Schulz staterooms, Monte and Craig were playing a late-night game of Monopoly, when Sparky came in and told them that a fire had started in the kitchen, smoke was pouring up the elevator shaft, and they might have to abandon ship. He then went back out for further word. With the lifeboats swinging out on their davits and the Schulz boys revving up at the prospect of being castaways, the flames were smothered, and the crisis passed. But Craig would later say that he had never seen his father so visibly anxious.

Joyce had no patience with his worrying, no inclination to soothe when he fretted; this was the daughter, after all, of a woman whose solution for any complaint was "Snap out of it."

The Schulzes' friends took note of Joyce's refusal to put up with Sparky's melancholy, which would descend upon him without warning, like the plunge in temperature before a storm. When he iced over, she burned up. "He was perpetually sad, and he had no reason to be," she contended. "He got everything he wanted. Here was a life where everything worked out. Everything progressed. The dailies, then the Sunday page, the comic books, the Reuben, Yale: everything he wanted! It just went, went, went."

One day she said to him, "I don't understand why you're depressed, I'd be ecstatic." But, to her recollection, "He was always depressed. I think he liked being depressed. And he said he wouldn't go to a psychiatrist because it would take away his talent."

Instead, he "went" to Joyce: "He would say, 'My mother and the war,' and I would say, 'There are worse things than that. You were not eleven, for instance. It's tragic, but everyone loses their mother.'"

The older he got, the more his anxieties paid him a dividend that depression scarcely ever does.* "Depression," he insisted, was "the wrong term. I would say 'melancholy' would be a better term for myself. Perhaps 'fearful.' Perhaps 'anxious.' Although this may make life itself rather uncomfortable it is certainly a good and maybe even necessary trait for a cartoonist to have."

If there was to be happiness in life—in Aristotle's sense of the fulfillment of one's capacities—for Schulz it would grow out of yearning and seeking and working and dreaming; it would be a product of the Romantic imagination and of his brand of mordant humor. To be beloved for drawing *Peanuts* was as close as he could come to winning love: the readers' devotion would fill the emptiness for a moment and then be gone, leaving

---

*The 1969 *Peanuts* collection, *You've Had It, Charlie Brown,* was later published under the title *My Anxieties Have Anxieties.*

his heart to yearn for the romantic fulfillment he had believed in all his life but, it seemed, had never found.

On these terms, he was not so much depressed as he was romantically disappointed, and he consciously welcomed romantic agony as artistically useful. For people of his work capacity—especially his capacity to harness doubt (especially self-doubt), anxiety, frustration, and the dark night of the soul—misery is a strategy. "Unhappiness is very funny," he would say whenever people needed reminding of his purpose. "Happiness is not funny at all."

BY THE TIME THE arena opened on April 28, 1969, with a charity benefit ice show for 1,700 spectators, the Schulzes' marriage was "just about [over]—it was pretty bad," recalled Chuck Bartley.

The finished building presented itself as a Swiss chalet. Framed by fir, birch, and redwoods transplanted from Coffee Lane, the facade's white stucco and dark wood cladding caught the morning sun full on. Beside the front doorway, Joyce hung a small sign: COME ON IN—SPECTATORS FREE.

The Warm Puppy's huge stone fireplace blazed, flowers brightened the windows, "Snoopy Specials" (for people) appeared in souvenir dog dishes, the cheery young waitresses sported dirndls and white blouses, and the climate-controlled temperature really did stand at a comfortable sixty-eight degrees.

Inside the main arena, the air was dry and bracing, communicating the zip and crackle of moonlit northern nights and the body-lifting zing of skate blades on hard ice. Visitors felt that they were gliding on a perfect sheet of ice at the bracing heart of a mountain village. Authentic Alpine chalet facades, built to scale, beamed over what was surely a lake, their character emphasized by gingerbread balconies; window boxes thick with wildflowers reached out behind tiered rink seats, masking the crassly technical apparatus of a twentieth-century American ice arena. At the far end of the ice, the ceiling dropped to a simulated village inn whose shuttered windows flew open to display the hockey scoreboard, while at the near end, flags of the Swiss cantons overhung plate-glass windows looking out from the coffee shop.

The press hailed the arena as "unique in its field," "matchless in beauty and perfection," "grand in overall concept and exquisite in every detail." Reporters exulted over the authentic Alpine design ("If someone yodeled you'd look for an avalanche . . ."), acclaiming the exterior rock gardens "laced with hanging flower baskets" and the "imported interior carpeting." Newspaper stories praised its taste and style and its excellent acoustics, and gave the Schulzes high marks for "the subtle intrusion of the *Peanuts* gang"; except for Schulz's spot drawings in the coffee shop menu and the list of rink rules, Snoopy, that year's hottest planetwide commodity in character merchandising, had been limited to a series of stained-glass appearances at the coffee shop (designed by Schulz and executed by a friend).

The grand opening, a $25-per-ticket benefit for Sonoma County's Family Service League and the Santa Rosa Junior Hockey Club, billed as the "most spectacular social event in the history of Santa Rosa," turned out the town's social stalwarts, who hosted friends at preshow cocktails and hors d'oeuvres and dinners and postcurtain midnight suppers. Every work-man employed in construction of the building was also invited, each with a guest, and Joyce, wearing her hair in braids and a jaunty ankle-length dirndl over a white blouse, greeted them all. When she was introduced in the opening ceremonies, the crowd rose to applaud her, marking the first time in their married life that she was recognized for her own achieve-ment, independently of Sparky. Friends recalled him adding a few brief, quiet remarks to the acclamation, but Joyce was by no means the presiding light of the ceremony.

The night belonged to Peggy Fleming. Witty Joe Garagiola warmed the crowd up; the San Francisco company of *You're a Good Man, Charlie Brown* sang two numbers from the still-popular show; Skippy Baxter per-formed his world-famous backflip; Vince Guaraldi and his trio played a suite still so fresh that to Santa Rosa society it sounded more like "good jazz" than the show-business standards that Guaraldi's *Peanuts* tunes would become; Judy Schwomeyer and James Sladky, ice dancing champions, flew across the ice as one, followed by even younger bright-eyed hopefuls for whom the audience cheered wildly.

But it was the Olympic gold medalist who held Santa Rosa in dead silence. She had bewitched the whole country. The previous year's Winter Olympics, broadcast by satellite from Grenoble in the Alps, was the first ever televised live and in color, and two shades in particular saturated the viewer's eye: the royal blue of French skiing champion Jean-Claude Killy's sweater and the chartreuse of the minidress, trimmed with rhinestone cuffs and lace choker, that Peggy Fleming wore as she skated her way to the United States Olympic Team's only gold medal.

Fleming became an overnight star, a national sweetheart in a sour time, sugarcoating the cover of *Life* when the magazine's alternate lead story had been the siege of Khe Sanh. The attention Fleming drew to her sport also made her a highly charged conductor for the idea just coming into vogue of women not only as the partners of men but as champions in their own right. Still, for all the voltage that Fleming brought to the new cause of women's sports, the descriptions of her in the press as "a package," a "coed," a "shy Bambi-like teenager," combined with the green minidress and all that it revealed as she twirled curvaceously on the flat cold whiteness, turned her into the most up-to-date incarnation of an American type. No longer would London girls swinging down Carnaby Street in their Mary Quant minis be the only ones baring their thighs for the whole world to see. With Peggy Fleming, the American Girl Next Door burst into the 1960s just before they swung closed, and men of Sparky's generation were invited for the first time outside the pages of *Playboy* magazine to look without restriction at a young sportswoman's legs, knees, thighs—"more thigh than any presixties girlwatcher could ever have hoped to see in public," noted cultural reporters Jane and Michael Stern.

Sparky was not alone in his crush. But here was Peggy Fleming, stealing hearts in his own ice arena, none more than his own, as she skated a number entitled "Snoopy's Girl," and he, Sparky, no longer doomed to yearn across a streetcar aisle, brought the show to its climax by stepping onto the ice and presenting Miss Fleming with a large plush embodiment of the Dog Himself.

Back at the drawing board, he let his surrogate do his dreaming for him. "He let Snoopy be in love with Peggy Fleming," observed Judy Schwomeyer Sladky, "but he was in love with her."

Snoopy's showboating for his ice princess turned into abject worship:

Lucy, of course, was on hand to deflate the fantasy:

NINETEEN SIXTY-NINE WAS supposed to have been Joyce's year—as Sparky himself announced, through Lucy, on January 1:

But in no single example of the press accounts that greeted the arena's opening was Joyce's name mentioned half so prominently as Sparky's. The *Sacramento Bee* made it clear that Joyce was "the brains and drive behind the project," but only after headlining the article ICE ARENA IS BUILT IN SANTA ROSA BY CREATOR OF "PEANUTS." Local columnists acknowledged that "Charles Schulz's new combination ice arena and concert hall" was "her creation," but Joyce routinely found herself identified only in terms of her husband's fame and achievements—"the dynamic wife of 'Peanuts' creator Charles M. Schulz" was as good as it got. To one well-intentioned Sonoma County reporter it came naturally to ascribe some "credit . . . to his wife Virginia, too, who is really the organizer . . ."

It made her mad. Understandably, recalled a friend of Sparky's, "she was jealous of him." In 1972, Santa Rosa would confer its Civic Art Commission Merit Award for "her contribution to the cultural advancement of the City of Santa Rosa," but by then it would be too late. "Joyce wanted to be recognized," recalled one observer close to both Schulzes, "but most of all she wanted to be recognized by Sparky."

But 1969 turned out to be the year that Charles Schulz reached some kind of apex. "Personally, I feel the strip is at its peak," he said in February.

*Peanuts* had registered social tremors with seismographic accuracy over Schulz's first two decades of syndication. His had become the prevailing mainstream comic voice on social change, precisely because his answers were less smart-aleck certain than his competitors', and his panels, consistently but quietly topical, had illuminated up-to-the-minute questions about the currents and personalities of the real world—nuclear testing and the H-bomb, smut and gore in comic books, 3-D movies, excessive vigilance by the FBI, global overpopulation, hazards of the jet age and the sonic boom, Rachel Carson, the nationwide adoption of Zone Improvement Plan (ZIP) codes . . .

More recently, hippies and long hair, police brutality, teachers' strikes, Tiny Tim, love beads, "these troubled times," and the teargassing of campus protests had all found their way into the strip, and people on all sides located themselves and their causes in the morning strip. "No matter how rough things get, *Peanuts* gets my morning off to a pleasant start and I find myself chuckling all the way to the Capitol," Governor Ronald Reagan would write after a series of dailies in which Snoopy had been heckled and teargassed while making a speech at the Daisy Hill Puppy Farm. "It is a great comfort to know that other Head Beagles are having problems, too. I was beginning to think that they were all my own." Reagan, who loved *Peanuts* and regarded Schulz's characters as personal friends, noted his delight that "my hero Snoopy has also experienced the joy of a campus disturbance."

As the framing institutions of everyday life took hit after hit, and decency itself seemed threatened, the reputation of Charles Schulz reached its full stature. "*Peanuts*, we venture to say, is not only part of the American scene but also the American psyche," observed the *Today* show one morning in November 1968.

Cartoonists and their creations might occasionally make news, but they certainly hadn't—until then—grabbed headlines or made history; in March 1969, as *Apollo 10* sank into "the harbors of the moon," Schulz and *Peanuts* did both. "That had to be the supreme compliment," Johnny Carson observed to his guest, and, indeed, having a historic spacecraft named for his characters would be among the highest honors of his life—a distinction that even President Kennedy, for whom so much was named in the late 1960s, could not match.

That spring and summer not an inhabitant of North America but knew the *Peanuts* gang by sight. Come July 24, 1969, when Neil A. Armstrong and Edwin E. Aldrin, Jr., landed on the moon, *Peanuts* seemed to be standing beside them on the lunar plains, so loaded were the stores with tie-in merchandise: pennants, pillows, and tote bags showing Snoopy in his space suit (ALL SYSTEMS ARE GO! THE MOON IS MADE OF AMERICAN CHEESE!) and Space Beagle dolls fully equipped with "authentic [*sic*] space suit and flight safety kit."

With *Peanuts* now running in a thousand newspapers, Schulz had an estimated ninety million readers—a hundred million by 1971. As a humorist and observer of human nature, he had no equal. He was the number one cartoonist in a way that none had ever been before. As the public had taken Robert Frost as its one great poet, Albert Einstein as its one super-scientist, and Arnold Palmer its one golfer, Schulz was now its one grand cartoonist-philosopher. But instead of being grand, Sparky set out to make himself insignificant. Who could possibly be interested in Charles Schulz? "Who wants to look at me? All I do is sit at the drawing board," he would say when someone close to him suggested something that might improve his appearance.

"How do you feel," asked a reporter in October 1969, "when you consider that at this very moment, millions all over the world are reading your material?"

"I don't know. It's OK, I guess," he shrugged, spreading his hands.

"Isn't it about a thousand papers and ninety million readers?"

"I don't know. I guess so. Sounds right. Something like that."

As the calendar 1960s came to a close, on one single night in December, when fifty-five million Americans watched *A Charlie Brown Christmas,* and *You're a Good Man, Charlie Brown* played to sold-out houses off Broadway, and a feature-length film, *A Boy Named Charlie Brown*, set attendance records at Radio City Music Hall, grossing $300,000 a week in the process, and the *Peanuts* strip was read around the world, there still had to be reckoned the books: with 36 million copies in print, Schulz now placed fourth in sales figures for all twentieth-century authors, behind Erle Stanley Gardner (creator of Perry Mason: 135 million copies), Mickey Spillane (49 million), and Erskine Caldwell (43.8 million), but ahead of John Steinbeck (28.8 million), John O'Hara (21 million), and Pearl Buck (13 million). Schulz had reached a larger readership and audience than any other artist in American history. Over and over he cast himself as a dwarf in a land of giants: "All I want to do is draw. . . . I don't like to see things get too big."

But into the Redwood Empire Ice Arena tourists now poured daily from all over the country, just to see "Snoopyland," as visitors began to call the place. In 1971 Walt Disney World would open on forty-seven acres in Orlando, Florida, stretching Disney coast to coast; the popularity of the Redwood Empire Ice Arena, sitting on its seven acres at the edge of Santa Rosa's Coddingtown Mall, raised the question of how big the Schulzes' enterprises would become. A reporter for the *Los Angeles Times*, watching Jill skate in a Snoopy costume to Burt Bacharach's music, asked if Schulz intended to emulate Walt Disney.

"Walt Disney was a producer," Schulz replied. "I'm a cartoonist."

The reporter pressed Schulz for his ultimate ambition. "I would like to be known as one of the greatest comic strip artists who ever lived." The strip would always be his core, his anchor. Joyce, meanwhile, went into show business, recasting the arena as "Northern California's top live entertainment center," and carpeted the ice each month with a fabric called Heugatile, the latest in auditorium accessories, to present headliners like Bill Cosby, Liberace, Victor Borge, Bob Newhart, the New Christy Minstrels, and Rod McKuen. That October, she appeared in a Heugatile ad with a cartoon balloon coming from her mouth: "Turn my ice skating rink into a theater every month? Good grief!"

She promoted rock concerts on Friday nights, turning the Warm Puppy into a showcase for local bands, and sponsored three summer concerts to prove that the arena was not afraid "to get involved with an activity which is rapidly becoming unpopular with the Establishment." By featuring popular groups The Reaction and Evolution, plus a light show by Prismatic Revenge, she threw down a challenge to Meredith and her contemporaries in Sonoma County: "Can you go to a rock concert without getting stoned? Can you go just to dig the sounds and groove on the dance floor with a good-looking chick?"

But the bands were duds, and the headliners were not the big success she had hoped for. Numbers were disappointingly small. During its first complete calendar year of operation, the arena lost $98,000. Revenues would have to increase 50 percent before a profit was turned.

Worse was to come. The big squares of Heugatile had barely been installed for the first show of the new concert season when the Internal Revenue Service sent an agent to reckon with Mr. and Mrs. Charles Schulz. The trouble was that the arena's original estimated cost of construction, $170,000, had first jumped to $250,000, and then in the end had proved to be $2,143,000. Joyce, moreover, had not just overspent (the Schulzes' tab for the gala opening alone had come to $20,000), she had failed to set aside sufficient funds to pay Sparky's and her estimated and final tax payments on their personal finances.

The IRS's district director in San Francisco came personally to meet with Joyce at the law offices of the Schulzes' attorney and friend, Edwin C. Anderson—one of those meetings at which, as Anderson recalled it, "you have a hard time representing your client," for no sooner had the official opened discussion on the Schulzes' tax bill than Joyce was dressing him down for spending the taxpayers' money on the war in Vietnam instead of on wholesome, civic-minded places like the Redwood Empire Ice Arena. Eventually, they established a payment schedule for their overdue obligations, but not, as Anderson recalled, "before Joyce gave it to him . . ."

The Schulzes owed the government more than $630,000, and since *Peanuts'* earnings placed them in the 70 percent bracket for federal and state income taxes combined, Sparky would now have to earn between $2 million and $3 million in order to settle the debt. The trouble with the IRS added turmoil to their already strained relationship. Sparky had never grown accustomed to paying a hefty tax bill. "The Federal Income tax is killing us," he wrote in 1961 to an old friend in Minnesota. "I personally paid for Commander Shepherd's [*sic*] trip into space, and I think they are also charging me for his trip to Washington." But he was conscientious, and Joyce's lack of control disturbed him. In a September 1971 strip, Sally Brown reports attending a show at a theater where the man at the box office has told her that his theater cost $2 million to build but he doesn't mind, because he is now going to charge her $2 million for her ticket, "and that way he'd get it all back at one time." Sally thinks that he was teasing her but isn't quite sure whether he was or not.

In April 1970, Joyce hired two young men away from Shipstad and Johnson's Ice Follies to help her run the arena and straighten up the Schulzes' finances: Warren Lockhart, twenty-nine, a marketing and sales executive, and Ron Nelson, a twenty-five-year-old Minnesota-born accountant, who went on bended knee to assure Wells Fargo Bank that he had been hired to slow Joyce's spending.

Their debt would not be settled until December 1972, but Joyce nonetheless was laying plans for expansion. As always, building had only been a start. In February 1970 she flew with Skip Baxter to Yugoslavia to attend the World Figure Skating Championships in Ljubljana, but also to take notes on the operation and maintenance of Olympic-magnitude arenas. Returning to Steele Lane with new eyes, she saw that Redwood could be broadened to include a whole training village, centered on the arena, with facilities to house visiting athletes for up to several months and a headquarters for TV Channel 50. On March 19, 1970, the Redwood Empire Ice Arena Corporation bought ten more acres of property across Hardies Lane.

By July 1971, to give himself increased control over the licensing of *Peanuts*, especially his television and theatrical interests, Sparky had shifted Warren Lockhart and Ron Nelson from the business side of the arena to the business side of the studio, and had formed the Charles M. Schulz Creative Development Corporation with Pat Lytle as his personal secretary, Lockhart as president, Joyce as vice president, Nelson as manager, and Evelyn Ellison as receptionist. Lockhart was now Schulz's right-hand man, negotiating licensing arrangements, running interference with the syndicate, and serving unofficially in two additional roles: substituting for Joyce as Sparky's gatekeeper to the public and succeeding Howard Roberts, his darkly handsome cousin in the 1920s and '30s, Uncle Buster, his Captain-Easy-type of the 1940s, and Tony Pocrnich, his Robert-Mitchum-lookalike assistant of the 1950s, as Schulz's beau ideal for the consciously stylish '70s.

Lockhart, a handsome California native with "a suntan an inch deep," was often mistaken for an actor and was fawned over by female visitors to the studio, whereupon Sparky took him aside to ask, "What's that like? Women aren't interested in me." Lockhart, meanwhile, noticed that women visiting the ice arena *were*, in fact, attracted to his boss, and not so much because he was Charles Schulz as by "that combination of his being shy and yet capable of coming up with just the right words at the right moment." But Sparky stubbornly cast his younger sidekick as the operation's heartthrob and himself as the aging runner-up, repeating in humorous refrain that he wanted women to act around him the way they did with Warren.

Again and again he insisted that he was not attractive to women and that those who were interested would not give him a second look if he were not famous. He repeatedly quizzed his new "friend of friends" (Snoopy's recently minted epithet for Woodstock carried straight over to Lockhart): How did it feel to magnetize the opposite sex? How did a handsome man talk to a woman who was interested in him? What did he *say* to make her interested? In later years, Warren summarized Sparky's entire battery of questions as, "How do I loosen up?"

WITH THE ARENA UP and running, Sparky and Joyce seemed to have the chance to be a couple again. Into the bough of a tree "growing" alongside the rink, Joyce had seen to it that a heart appeared in which was carved the legend: LUCY LOVES SCHROEDER. A couple-encouraging bench had been built around the trunk. "Everything in the rink was romantic," one of the professional ice dancers who skated there remembered. "It had to fulfill the feeling that everybody who was in that rink was dating or in love or a family with their kids and they were skating on a pond."

It was romantic—if the fulfillment of romance is frustration. For all the arena's whims and fancies, there was something willfully distanced at its heart. Sparky and Joyce never set out to gather the romantic hints into a truly sustaining ambience, and they did not have the time or inclination to plunk themselves down on the couples' bench together, though Sparky would often urge that very offer upon friends on the ice: "Come on, let's go have a root-beer float and sit under the tree," as Judy Schwomeyer Sladky would recall. Or he might whisper, "Look, someone's cut a heart in my tree." "He just oozed romance," Judy recalled.

Their friends came on weekends and skated in pairs, to old waltzes and new show tunes crackling over the public address system, but the arena's First Couple could not rekindle their passion for—or on—the ice. No one could remember ever having seen Sparky and Joyce skating together on their own frozen playground, though three of their five children recalled their mother bawling out their father before the whole rink.

Joyce would not allow herself a moment to sit down. She was operating the ticket office, directing her talent agents' negotiations for bands, orchestras, and comedy acts; as business manager, hiring and firing personnel—and even at the outset there had been fifty full- and part-time employees. Somehow she found time, every weekday night, to bake more than a dozen pies for the coffee shop. One day, while Sparky was lunching with a friend at the Warm Puppy, she shot through the front lobby and into the main arena. "When I see Joyce," observed Sparky, "I think of a speeding bullet."

Typically, he assigned it to Snoopy to enact with Lucy the dramas playing out between Joyce and himself:

He may have wanted to believe that Coffee Lane was still home, but in truth even there the ground was shifting.

The non sequitur "flower-power" gag in the January 17, 1969, strip could not disguise the real love-me?/love-me-not? dilemma behind the scenes at Coffee Lane. With the arena up and running, Joyce spent less time at home, leaving with her fresh pies for the Warm Puppy first thing in the morning and arriving back at Coffee Lane only after supper. More often now, it was their housekeeper, Eva Gray, who fixed the kids an early supper. As Monte remembered it, "Mom was obsessed with what she was doing." And now, with Joyce striving not just for recognition but for "Olympic recognition," Sparky was left free to find an actual Daisy.

JOYCE HAD BEEN BACK from Yugoslavia for a week when two young women called upon Sparky at the Warm Puppy on Monday, March 16, 1970. A woman named Maggie (whose last name no one would remember) was sent by the headquarters magazine of her company, Fairchild Semiconductor, a microchip manufacturer in Mountain View to interview Charles Schulz on the subject of effective communication, and, so far as Sparky knew, her companion had come to photograph him for the article. Her name was Tracey Claudius, and he knew her voice right away, as if its low pitch and musical amusement had registered years earlier. She was twenty-five years old, single, quick, cute, with chestnut hair, a trim, athletic figure, and unusual golden-green eyes—"an odd color," a friend later recalled, "but it's not the color that is remarkable, it's the light from within them—an animation that comes from the inside."

He liked the confident way Tracey flirted. Her independent streak attracted him, too. As the "interview" went on, he asked each woman what the women's liberation movement meant to her; Tracey, who had been raised a Roman Catholic in Philadelphia and graduated from St. Mary's Academy, a church school, had gone on to Rosemont, but after only a half semester found the curriculum of a Catholic women's liberal arts college pointless and that her real reason for enrolling—"to get my M.R.S. degree"—was false:

"No man was worth endless lectures and reading on topics wholly unrelated to my life." She dropped out, only to return after a stint as a stenographer at the FBI awoke in her a genuine impulse to learn for learning's sake.

A few months later, Sparky would say that he fell in love with Tracey that very first afternoon because of the excitement in her voice as she spoke of how she had explored the philosophy of Descartes.

In her eyes, Sparky was an idol, whose trim grace greatly appealed to her. "His face wasn't beautiful; the crew cut made him beautiful, all-American, athletic." But for her, as for him, it was the suggestion of intellectual pursuit that was most compelling. His heavy, black-rimmed glasses, quick smile—and equally quick frown—made him look like a professor. Tracey dreamed of marrying a professor, with summers off to read and write together; Sparky indulged this fantasy in days ahead by saying that maybe he would quit cartooning and go and teach, and together they could live the life of the mind.

As much as anything that fueled their intense attraction was the sense that they were two of a kind. Each had a teasing, competitive side; each suffered anticipatory anxiety when leaving home and panic attacks when out in the world; each placed staying put, reading books, talking about art and music, above any journey. He dreaded Sunday afternoons; she dreaded Sunday nights. Both were racked by intense self-consciousness—the kind of shyness in which, recalled Tracey, "you can't stop thinking about yourself; but he had it more than I did. He, more than I, never got over himself. I guess no one had made him the center of the world, so he became the center of his own world."

When lunch ended, he made it clear how much he had enjoyed the conversation, but added that he had no idea why people were interested in what *he* had to say. "I cannot comprehend that anyone would be in awe of me. I still have that inferiority feeling," he said into Maggie's tape recorder. "I cannot imagine that people would get a kick out of meeting me, would enjoy sitting and talking to me. I cannot get over it."

He walked her out to the parking lot, each of them talking about particularly beloved books and authors, and they laughed when the name F. Scott Fitzgerald came to their lips at the exact same moment.

TWO WEEKS LATER, TRACEY and Maggie returned to the arena, at Sparky's urging. At their first meeting, she had thought him charming, witty, handsome, "as warm and fuzzy as his little comic strip characters." Now, she was struck by what a good listener he was. "He wrapped his attention around every word that came out of your mouth. He made you feel that everything you said was important. You couldn't be more fascinating."

He was indeed fascinated by her idiosyncratic skills. For one thing, she could make herself sneeze anywhere, anytime; for another, she was completely ambidextrous and had earned a penmanship certificate, as had Sparky, but she had also learned to write backward in looking-glass script, so that she could pass notes in class without getting caught by the sisters.

After dinner at the Warm Puppy, he supplied skates, but Tracey was daunted by her own inexperience and turned him down, looking on as Sparky led Maggie around the ice. Then, jealous, she got up her nerve, scraped across the rink, and hooked arms on his other side. "Skating between two pretty girls," he said. "If I'm asleep, please don't wake me." After Maggie excused herself with cold toes, Tracey remained at his side for a few wobbly turns, then sat down.

"How did I do?" she said.

He grinned. "Let me just say that when I refer to you in the future as Ol' Rubber Legs, know that I mean it in the nicest possible way."

She countered that he hadn't seen her at her best, because *skating backward* was her specialty.

"Living backward is mine," he said.

Hunched over the drawing board the next day, he sat taller when a call came through from Maggie with a few more points, she said, for her article about effective communication. He knew from the blatant intimacy of her final question that Maggie meant for him to know that it was Tracey, not she, who needed the answer: "Is effective communication more difficult in a personal relationship, like marriage, or a business relationship?"

He sighed—and answered more candidly than anyone at Fairchild Semiconductor Corporation would ever have expected: "Don't ask me. My wife has met someone else and is filing papers for a separation, so I'm obviously no expert on the subject."

This was a curious bombshell to lob out of his usual deeply guarded trench. Joyce, in fact, had not yet shown signs of moving on or of serving him with such papers, but when Sparky called Tracey the following morning, he came right to the point, declaring himself all but free of his marriage and apologizing immediately for not having clarified his situation earlier.

A week later, they met at a bookstore on Ghirardelli Square, where they made a distinctive couple: Sparky in his "Arnold Palmer hand-me-downs," as Tracey called them, his crew cut a gray brush; Tracey in hot pants and leather vest, an acceptable turnout for a young professional woman in those days. Months later, he recalled that evening on Ghirardelli Square in a letter: "I have never been happier than when we were prowling together through the stacks of books, holding hands and teasing."

They teased about everything. He was such a prig about good grammar, she nicknamed him "Mr. Whom." Tracey had been penalized by the nuns at St. Mary's for her "lack of cooperation" in sacred studies class, and whenever Sparky and Tracey discussed issues of belief ("We had some of our best fights about religion"), Sparky would say that he was not going to argue about such matters with anyone who hadn't cooperated in sacred studies. His Halverson relatives had shown affection with scorn and joshing and ridicule; Sparky's delight in needling Tracey took him straight back home, and when he observed the niceties of an old-fashioned courtship by opening and closing the passenger door for her, she came right back, reaching over as he rounded the car to lock him out, then smiled out at him with a wrinkled nose.

But the central trend of all this byplay was Tracey pulling Sparky out of a funk. She recognized that he needed someone to buoy him up out of self-preoccupation and melancholy. He had neither the disposition nor the training to pull himself out. Now, with his marriage in free fall, he needed not just someone, but a woman, to anchor him. From the start, the unspoken assumption between them was that Tracey was going to make him happy. "He just needed somebody who didn't make him feel alone."

But something also happened that first evening together in San Francisco that he would remember, and draw, and return to again and again in thought to the end of his life. Behind the open trunk of her MG, she told him that he was adorable.

SPARKY IMMEDIATELY MEMORIALIZED THE founding events of their romance in an entire series of drawings fired off to Tracey's apartment in Mountain View.

A small, unusually smiling Charlie Brown peers out from blue construction paper to say, "Remember?"

Then he comes forward from a green backdrop to announce: "March 16th was the day we met."

The sequence is now in flow. He leans against a tree, smiling: "April 1st was the second time I saw you." Then, seated alone at a restaurant table, he beams into beloved absent gold-green eyes: "On April 8th we dined alone for the first time."

Next, on shockingly red paper, Charlie Brown up and kisses a startled Tracey on the nose: "On April 15th, we went to the top of the Fairmont."

The hotel's famous glass elevator, built in 1961, climbed the side of the building twenty-four floors above Nob Hill, to bring into successive view Chinatown, Coit Tower, and, away to the right, the entire South Bay Peninsula. It was four-thirty in the afternoon, they were alone, and as the lift soared into the sky, Tracey pressed her nose to the glass, ecstatic. "Isn't this magnificent?" she asked, only to hear over her shoulder a tight, colorless voice, facing away from the threateningly enlarged world: "The elevator door is nice, too."

The danger passed, Sparky regained his equilibrium at a table on the garden terrace, and as they sipped Diet Cokes and told each other their lives, he gave her an openmouthed kiss. Other firsts followed on successive Wednesdays: "On April 22nd you squeezed my hand in the dark, remember?" A week later: "We drove through the hills of Mountain View."

And then one Friday, the first of May, they planned to attend a Shakespeare festival in Santa Cruz, but Tracey got the date wrong, so they drove to Monterey, ate dinner at Calista's Place, where a man played guitar and people joined in to sing folk songs. Calista herself emerged from the kitchen, a glass of wine in her hand, to urge this dish or that upon her guests, and Tracey, swept up in the free and easy mood of the evening, had some wine, which she never did; Sparky as always remained teetotal sober. In the hills over Monterey they found a hotel with a homey atmosphere, and he took her to bed—their first night together, a happy, rousing night, as Tracey recalled it well after everything was over. Sparky, recovering the part of himself that he had lost in these last grinding years with Joyce, felt a reawakened confidence. "He was," said Tracey, "a healthy, red-blooded, American man."

The next morning, they drove to Mountain View and, with Tracey's roommate, Maggie, off for the weekend, spent a lazy day at her apartment on West Middlefield Road: "We got to be together, you know, like a real couple . . ."

The enchantment of their first night together was still upon him when he drew a smiling, sated Charlie Brown leaning against a leafy, toothless tree and murmuring, "May 1st and 2nd were so neat I can hardly stand to think about it."

The drawings were something almost new in Charles Schulz's life. Not since his courtship of Donna Johnson had he commanded a visual language of passion and romance. When he listed Tracey's "good points"—"BEAUTIFUL, CHARMING, CUTE, BEEPABLE, SUNSHINY, HUGGABLE, BUGGABLE, SWEET, SENSITIVE, ADORABLE, [crossed out] (THAT'S ME), WONDERFUL, ATHLETIC, BOOKABLE, SESA-MYABLE, TEASEABLE, AVAILABLE(?) MOUNTAIN VIEWABLE . . ."—he was using the language of the strip, as in these dailies of 1970 and 1968, respectively:

In May, he began writing letters—addressing her, as he always would, in triplicate:

> Tracey—Tracey—Tracey,
>     Dark hair and a perfect nose. Soft hands that are sometimes cool and sometimes warm. Cute . . . Pretty . . . Beautiful.
>     The most musical voice you have ever heard.
>     She hugs you in the doorway and when you say to her, 'If you move just six inches closer, I'm going to kiss you,' she moves closer, and you kiss her and the whole world is nice.

His letters and drawings show how natural it seemed to him to have her in his life, but we cannot tell how he viewed his affair in the light of his marriage and family—he acted no differently than usual and kept these feelings entirely separate from his obligations to Joyce and the children.

He conducted the secret romance in the presence of the one person whom he already trusted. Charlie Brown stood in for him in the unfolding private realm to which he had admitted Tracey. Now he wanted to let that most faithful of his companions, the daily reader of *Peanuts*, into this new magic. For anyone who still doubted that homely, "big-nosed" Sparky Schulz could attract a girlfriend, he hid proof in plain sight.

In July, Tracey's soft hands were translated into the strip. Snoopy, invited to make a distinguished-grad speech at the Daisy Hill Puppy Farm, finds himself caught up in a riot protesting the drafting of dogs to serve in Vietnam. True to the times, the riot is televised; Charlie Brown and Linus watch from home as Snoopy, at the podium, is hit with a dog dish, then teargassed. As Snoopy gropes through the billowing fumes and chaos, he encounters a girl dog. The old romantic switches on, his gallant "You have a soft paw, Sweetie!" bursting from the heart of the gas cloud. Love will find its way; but the smothering murk screens out the love story.

Other strips in the sequence brush the real-life turbulence:

Schulz himself often mused during lunches at the Warm Puppy that what married people really needed was a three-day pass:

Not surprisingly, Snoopy's life as a writer, which had begun on the doghouse roof the previous July, took new shape in the first springtime weeks of his creator's startlingly awakened passion. Snoopy turned to auto-biography in the week that Sparky and Tracey met. By July, as the private letters to Tracey reached new peaks of intensity, Snoopy initiated his public for the first time into the language of adoration:

These irruptions of the deepest heart—whether human or canine becoming ever harder to distinguish—had become installments in the unseen story. It was as if he were testing Joyce and the autograph hounds and the millions of people who loved his strip to go on loving him despite what he was doing behind the frames.

He trusted his readers above all. When this new love came into his life, it was only natural that he bring her home to the reader, if not exactly to the reader's direct attention. It was the great regret of his life that Dena Schulz had not survived to see her son achieve his great good fortune. So he had made all his readers do duty for that one ultimate reader he could never draw for. Daring to introduce his secret love only by indirection is the act of a boy still not willing to dislodge his mother from first place in his heart. But drawing and indirection were ways of summoning Dena Schulz into the present.

FOUR MONTHS AFTER THE seismic meeting of March 16, he, Joyce, and the Bartleys went to Hawaii, consciously to save the Schulzes' marriage. Sparky and Chuck shared equally in the arrangements, the Bartleys paying the airfares and the Schulzes securing the rooms. The party stayed at the luxurious Kahala Hilton on Oahu, a celebrity hideaway near Waikiki known to cater to the special needs of the extremely rich and very famous—an interesting concession by Sparky to the actual scale of his wealth and reputation. So they arrived at the resort's palm-girt enclave, their luggage was whisked away, and they were shown upstairs in their private elevator to the red-carpeted Presidential Suite on the tenth—and top—floor.

Whatever the Hawaiian vacation's intent, on July 16 a postcard left for Mountain View: "Aloha. Like Gatsby I am pursuing the green light. Hope to see you soon. I miss you very much." Roses also arrived to commemorate their "four-month anniversary," which left Tracey baffled: who celebrates an "anniversary" after a third of a year? She would have to wait until he returned to learn that this was a significant length of time for him because exactly twenty years earlier Donna Johnson had decided to marry Alan Wold after the romance with Sparky, which had lasted precisely from March 2, 1950 to June 24, 1950—three months and twenty-two days. So he was savoring the fact that Tracey had kept her commitment longer than Donna. "It was really more a milestone for him," Tracey recalled realizing.

Meanwhile, the *Peanuts* of that very same day, July 16, 1970, carried a peculiarly pointed secret message of which Sparky, once back in his own territory, would send her the original, very specially signed.

In Hawaii, meanwhile, the do-or-die expedition was already turning into a disaster. Sparky woke up early every morning, tiptoed across acres of presidential red carpet, and slipped out. "He blatantly ignored me," recalled Joyce, who felt sure that he was going down to share secrets with Betty Bartley. "Betty was thick with Sparky. She was a turncoat." But Chuck, as she recalled it, "was good to me."

Betty, for her part, tried to understand Sparky on his terms: "He romanticized everything"; she knew that because he was "the kind to walk down the beach with you and say, 'Let's run away,' " he was therefore less likely to act on such doghouse impulses. What was more, once the thrill of desire had been unleashed—*Let's run away*—he preferred to savor its never-realizable potential. Rather than have to continue the story, let alone build it to a climax and a satisfying resolution, he found the greater delight in unconsummated anticipation of the ever ominously exciting beginning: *It was a dark and stormy night . . .*

Chuck, meanwhile, taught Joyce to enjoy a good glass of wine; she had never indulged in so much as a sip during the years at Coffee Lane. Chuck's company, Bartley Pump, was the kind of Santa Rosa business with which Joyce worked on a regular basis these days; a man who knew how to dig a well and bring water to the surface by way of a fully welded system was now closer to her heart than a cartoonist who commanded a resort suite that since 1965 had entertained Hollywood stars, European royalty, sporting legends, presidents Johnson and Nixon—and in which he himself was no more comfortable than anywhere else outside his tiny fiefdom of the mind four thousand miles away.

The pivotal moment came when the producer of a touring company of the long-running Broadway smash *Man of La Mancha* sent a Cadillac for the Schulz party. They had all just settled in when the producer, sitting on the jump seat, turned to inquire of Joyce, "How much did you pay Liberace when you booked him at the Ice Arena?" "Fifty thousand," she said, and he replied, "Oh my God, did you get screwed!"

Once exposed this way in front of Sparky, Joyce was embarrassed and enraged; she seethed all the way to the theater and could not wait to return for an avenging call to her talent agents from the hotel. But she had to hang fire through "The Impossible Dream" and all the rest, and when at last they got back to the Presidential Suite and she had the satisfaction of firing the agents, she turned the full force of her fury on Sparky when he suggested that this was the end of the fight.

"That was just the beginning," recalled Chuck Bartley—because Joyce wanted to sue to recover the bloated overcharges, while Sparky just wished to eat the loss and drop the whole matter.

"That was the beginning of the end," recalled Betty Bartley. "She was really upset about it."

"That's the closest the marriage ever came to getting back," reflected Chuck Bartley, "because after that it was just one thing after another." The Bartleys came home thinking, "There was no chance of holding that marriage together."

Indeed, things went from bad to worse as soon as Joyce returned to the arena. Mad at Sparky, as well as at Ron Nelson, her new accountant, who also advised against a lawsuit, she was now furious with the city of Santa Rosa—vandalism was persistent; no one appreciated what she was doing for the kids of Sonoma County.

That month's telephone bills brought another jolt. One of the phone lines showed numerous calls to Redwood City—as many as ten in one day. Joyce did not know anyone there, and ordinarily Sparky would not call anyone that often, not even Connie Boucher; nor did he phone his closest associates, Bill Melendez in Hollywood or Lee Mendelson in Burlingame, more than twice or three times a month. Thirty-five years later, Joyce would still pale a little as she recalled, "I wanted to know who that was."

She need only have read the July 15 *Peanuts*:

IN AUGUST SPARKY HAD sprung a surprise on Tracey at her office in Redwood City: it was their anniversary—five months—and she was to leave work (it was a Sunday) and meet him in San Francisco. From that point on, the daytime would be hers; he had a plan for the evening, but in the meantime she could choose all her favorite places.

They spent hours riding the cable car runs from beginning to end and back again. They climbed Telegraph Hill and strolled down to Fisherman's Wharf and took in the Museum of Modern Art. She "bullied him" into taking her beloved glass skylift at the Fairmont, in which, as before, Sparky turned halfway around and faced fearfully away from the view. Tracey kissed him from behind and put her arms around him, and the more he protested, the more she let him have it. "Sparky was not into public displays of affection."

But it wasn't because he was afraid of being discovered—on the contrary, that same night he took her to the Tonga Room, a choice that made her deeply uneasy, for though it might be tucked a safe two floors below the Fairmont's grand lobby, the nightspot was a frequent haunt of San Francisco's ubiquitous columnist and chronicler Herb Caen. As they approached the entrance, Tracey begged him to be discreet—only to hear him tell the maître d', to her horror, that they were Mr. and Mrs. Charles Schulz, that they had reservations for 9 P.M., and that they would like a special table: "It's our anniversary."

The dim room fell into the shadow cast by a single hurricane bar glowing from the banks of a rippling jungle lagoon over which the Tonga Room orchestra floated on a bamboo raft. At their table for two in the bamboo-village darkness, Tracey hid behind the cocktail menu of Mai Tais, Bora-Bora Horrors, and other Pacific paradise potions.

"I do not want to be known as the other woman in your life," she whispered furiously. "I do not want to be the woman who ruined the innocence of the *Peanuts* characters."

"You're so naïve to think they're innocent," said Sparky reasonably. "Children are not innocent at all. Children are cruel."

"Children aren't cruel. They're learning from *us*."

And on it went, Tracey unable to stop herself from imagining that Herb Caen would pierce the expensive consumers' twilight to alert all Hearstdom to their idyll; Sparky either feigning or, worse, feeling indifference ("to him it was a lark"); Tracey concentrating her alarms into the fear that she would contaminate the strip; Sparky relishing the diminishing propriety of the well-dressed couples as they gave themselves up to the high-charged South Seas dimness. "I know I was a little overblown," she reflected later. "But that's what I thought: This was holy stuff. This cartoon was holy to me. And I would be the one that would ruin his image for the world? God! If I'd found this out when *I* was reading it, I would have been crushed. Charlie Brown wouldn't be innocent to me any longer."

Twice every hour, commercial lightning dutifully flared above the huts, thunder growled, wind machines roared, and a sudden tropical downpour safely agitated the pool. Sparky and Tracey cycled damply through two or three storms before getting back into one of their regular conversations about their respective reading, during which the orchestra floated across the pool, and the bandleader stepped to the microphone. "We are dedicating our first song to Mr. and Mrs. Charles Schulz, who are celebrating their anniversary tonight." Applause from the other tiki huts, the first strains of "The Anniversary Waltz," and the evening conclusively knocked off track.

Five days later, he sent her on tropic-green paper "A Kiss in the Garden": Snoopy bussing Tracey's cheek "SMAK" amid the Tonga Room jungle, backed up by a folded red sheet of construction paper that said "Happy" on the outside, "Anniversary" inside, "From all your friends in the Tonka [*sic*] Room," with the defensive follow-through:

> Who else do you know who brings you one perfect Jaguar,
> notices that your eyes don't match, squeezes your arms, takes
> all those insults, beeps you, removes the tomatoes, let's himself
> be bossed around and bullied and tormented and attacked in
> elevators? Who else? No one! That's who. (Whom?)

"I was not dominating and bossy," Tracey later maintained. "I let him dictate the relationship. Most of the relationship was on his terms."

> Here I am again still following Gatsby's green light but mine hangs
> not near Daisy's dock but rather near Mountain View. I was sorry
> to hear sadness in your sweet voice last night for I feel that if I had
> the chance I could make you very happy, for you're wonderfully
> good. You are a person so special that most people simply cannot
> comprehend you. You are out of their range. You are Tracey,
> Tracey, Tracey. I love you Tracey. Please don't doubt yourself.

On their next date she tried to resume their discussions about books and music and art, but he did not want to take in anything except Tracey. "He would just sit there and stare at me." No one else had ever noticed so much about her—that her arms were large and muscular, for instance, or that one of her eyes was bigger than the other—but his worshipful gaze fell on these asymmetries and made them part of his repertoire of teases.

She discovered that he, meantime, was extremely sensitive about his nose—and his skin, with its memory of ancient acne scarring the jawline beneath his right ear. Tracey had the identical scarring, as soul mates do, but where his nose was, to him, a "proboscis," Tracey's was "perfect," and he never let her forget it, just as he never stopped drawing attention to the size of her arms.

For Sparky the transcendent new element was his confidence in being beloved; no matter what he threw at Tracey, no matter how he teased her, she adored him in a way no other woman in his life had. He had always been the beloving one, but to Tracey, he was a towering figure. He had never allowed himself to see himself in that light, and certainly he knew that he did not so appear to Joyce. What was more—and more complicating— was that this also made him vulnerable, and dependent, because it put him at Tracey's mercy: were he really that sky-filling a presence, then he would have to work to live up to her image of him and indeed might well lack the skill or the will to do so; should he turn out not to be what she thought he was, then he would not be just hurt but totally shattered.

On Wednesday evenings in the fall, he would pick her up in his Jaguar at Mountain View. "Say the word and the Jaguar is yours," he offered one night. She didn't take him seriously, but he repeated the suggestion often enough that she came to answer routinely, "I don't want anything but your company—and books." On one of their dates, he gave her a paste-diamond and faux-pearl brooch, which only upset her: "You could give it to me when we're married." Another time, he bought her a gray and blue suede belt with a pocketbook attached. "Sparky," she said, "I think we better go upscale again." She was horrified by the importance he placed on pressing lumpish, material things upon her: "You don't have to bring anything. I don't want anything."

"I won't try to buy your kisses," he promised in his next letter. "Why can't I walk by your side and hold your hand forever?"

After one evening when they stayed up late talking about the meaning of existence and all that, Tracey went to bed thinking that it had been one of the best nights of her life. She imagined a future "filled with books, learning, laughter, love, and, of course, *Peanuts.*" The only discordant note had sounded when Sparky had asked whether Tracey had meant to draw a parallel to him when she described the suicide of a lonely and anxiety-ridden friend.

Waiting one day for a tennis court at a city park in Mountain View, he grew impatient. Having to sit on the sidelines reminded him of his childhood, and he burst out to her about the bullies who had hammered the smaller children off the St. Paul playgrounds. To distract him, Tracey offered an idea she had for some time entertained: that Snoopy should take up speed writing, playing with the funny shorthand words, such as she had once seen in a subway advertisement at Broad Street Station in Philadelphia, "Gt gd jb . . ."

"I don't take ideas for the strip," he replied icily.

She thought he was kidding. This was the first time she had seen him stern—"and this was in the joy of new love! He changed—like that—on me."

Another day he sent her James Thurber's *Men, Women and Dogs*, marking his favorite drawings, one of which showed a woman in one bed, a man in the other, his finger cocked at her like a gun. "These were little hints. But at a time when you're feeling romantic about somebody, you think you're going to change them. I was going to make him happy. Then I recognized he would have changed me."

In October, he took her to San Francisco to see the admired musical revue *Jacques Brel Is Alive and Well and Living in Paris*, which, with its laments and stirring anthems and nostalgia for lost love, was as mood-mirroring of this moment in Schulz's romantic life as Powell and Pressburger's *The Red Shoes* had been in 1950. They sat at their table holding hands, letting the French cabaret songs hold them in a spell. He kissed her fingers, and she knew he was thinking of asking her to marry him, and then he said, "I would marry you tomorrow, if you'd say yes."

After a pause, she said, "Yes. Now let me think about it."

From then on, she knew that all she had to do was say yes and he was ready. At work, she was constantly being advised by her closest colleagues to marry the mighty Schulz. But she had her doubts. "I didn't know if I could make him happy because he was so sad underneath."

IN NOVEMBER, WHEN JOYCE confronted him with the roster of calls to Redwood City, Sparky wrote to Tracey: "My phone calls were discovered and a bad scene took place, so I have been forced to live without the sound of your nice voice, and, much worse, the sight of your marvelous face." Then Snoopy comes in, eyes closed, three-quarter profile, saying out of his left side: "With the perfect nose." And out of the right: "We nose types are very conscious of noses."

Then, Sparky resumed his other, less eloquent, voice:

> Do you still like—[*crossed out*]—love me? I miss you very much, and I don't know what to do. Please be happy, but don't forget me.

When Sparky and Joyce went to bed that night at Coffee Lane, they lay in silence until Joyce said, "How could you do this? Don't you know I go over the bills?" He had no answer. "He didn't say, 'I'm sorry,' " recalled Joyce, "he didn't say, 'But I love *you*.' "

"Don't you even feel sorry about it?" she asked him.

According to Joyce, Sparky said, "No."

"The thing that hurt me," Joyce explained later, "was that he never said he was sorry."

# CHAPTER 23

# DOGHOUSE

*I've been trying in the last couple of years to show how these little kids are searching for something.*
—C.M.S., 1972

AFTER DISCOVERING THE AFFAIR, Joyce consulted a therapist, never revealing to Sparky the depths of her hurt or vulnerability. "I did all my crying in the psychologist's office," she said years later. He, meantime, did not express remorse, or show sympathy, but he agreed to give up Tracey—or at least he promised himself to cover the issue up more carefully.

When she went home for the holidays, he kept track of her through calls from a pay phone, and he sent her a specially crafted ring—small diamonds enclosing a garnet—to replace one she had lost on a date. It arrived at her parents' house in time for Christmas.

Sparky and Joyce carried on through the rest of that grim year as if nothing had changed, or was changing, or probably could change. Sparky ended the dailies for 1970 with this strip:

Joyce never learned the full extent of Sparky's secret. So far as she was concerned, the real threat to their marriage and their family future—Sparky being Sparky (and sometimes Schroeder)—was not so much his involvement with "a gal in Redwood City" as the more continuous and damaging problem that "Sparky was involved *with himself.*"

He had no intention of losing Tracey, or of leaving Joyce and the children, although how to sustain both simultaneously remained a puzzle. He had the strip in which to work out, or at least exhibit, his unending sense of rejection and abandonment, while Joyce, similarly haunted, had to contend with the memory of her first marriage as she came to terms with Sparky's betrayal: "I was dumped once. I wasn't going to be dumped again."

So it was she, at first, who resolved to keep the marriage together, and thus went no further than the telephone bill in facing the truth. She did not call up the telltale phone number to warn off that "gal in Redwood City." And she never saw the utility of turning to the morning's *Peanuts* to gain some purchase on what might be going on inside Sparky, missing always and entirely the personal implications hidden in plain sight.

On January 6 and 7, 1971, in these early weeks of his doubly secret double life, he flirted on successive days, first and overtly with Tracey, in a strip whose punch line he had already tried on her in private:

Then with Joyce, obliquely, and rather cruelly:

The top-earning movie of the previous year, *Love Story*, based on the number one best-selling novel by Harvard classics professor Erich Segal, had given a jittery public a melodramatic tearjerker about the doomed young couple whose manifesto, "Love means never having to say you're sorry," replaced "Happiness is a warm puppy" as the catchphrase to exchange between sincere, if bleeding, hearts. By 1970, so many people had misbehaved in their experiments with the new sexual freedom that they needed a slogan that made them unaccountable. "Love means never having to say you're sorry" got everyone off the hook; no one had to take responsibility for the ugly mess he or she had made at home or at the office. It also meant that if you really loved someone, you would let them do anything—even, as Schulz pictured it, letting a "friend of friends" have one more good cry over a bad movie:

For Sparky, hope was very much alive. Tracey was not dying of leukemia, but Sparky, who had grown up, like *Love Story*'s competitive, hockey-playing narrator, Oliver Barrett IV, with the notion that he always must be number one, now enjoyed his perfect girl in an almost equally safe state of suspension. "He loved an ideal," said Tracey. "I matched the ideal."

CONCEALMENT HAD BEEN IN his nature when he pursued Donna Johnson in the accounting office at Art Instruction, keeping her identity from his closest friends, lest she be judged less than perfect by anyone other than himself. By March 1971, having promised Joyce that he would give up Tracey, he chose instead to live in secrecy, to newly painful levels, and so resorted once again to "living backwards."

In letters "full of longing," he now reopened his heart to that distant princess of his Minnesota youth, Donna Mae Johnson, letting her know that his marriage was in trouble and that he still found himself wishing that he had been with her all along. But Donna, still married, still living in Minneapolis, and now the mother of four children, was content in a stable relationship. She recognized that Sparky's wish to put their old love to the test had been energized less by her than by "the idea of it."

In the annual Valentine strips of 1971, Donna takes first place among Snoopy's admirers, edging out Schulz's daughters, as well as another new passion for Sparky—the author Joan Didion, recently come into renown, who filled a role that became standard in the fan of female figures he forever spread before him: the literary starlet. In this case, several visits to Didion, her husband, John Gregory Dunne, and their daughter, Quintana Roo, while in Los Angeles, mounting to an exchange of letters, left Schulz yearning for a novelist's life; Didion, he often said, was the kind of writer he would be if he were a writer and not a cartoonist only.

"I haven't stopped loving you," he wrote to Tracey at the end of 1970. "I have simply been forced to stop calling and seeing you. My only consolation was the wonderful knowledge that you always understand, which is one of the thirty million reasons I fell in love with you . . ." But the temporary suspension of their romance meant that he could relax his will, giving vent to his sleepless yearning:

> Someday I'll see you again but I don't know how. I want to sit across from you and hold both of your hands and look into your eyes and tell you that I love you and that I shall always love you, and then just talk and giggle and tease you and be with you. Tracey—Tracey—Tracey—I can't tell you to wait for me, but if you don't fall in love with anyone else, I'll be around.

Tracey, meanwhile, had come to see Sparky's gushing letters through the eyes of an ambitious but ambivalent young woman who now knew what it took to keep one's edge in the corporate world and had just begun to wonder if she really belonged on the fast track. She still believed herself, at heart, to be a born social worker, or, anyway, a smart woman with a social conscience. If the virtually all-male management program did not make her feel sufficiently displaced from her true path, her boss had just confided to her that he had hired her a year earlier because he was in love with her and, having revealed himself, hoped that she too would catch fire.

That spring of 1971, Tracey later said, was a difficult time in her life, and with her troubles at work unresolved, she would happily have married Sparky had he been ready to propose. She believed that he really was Charlie Brown, just as she wanted to cling to her belief in Charlie Brown's "innocence," but it was getting hard to ignore the simple fact that instead of sympathy, understanding, and love, she was getting the same letter over and over—and not letters so much as incantations:

> Tracey, Tracey, Tracey, Golden eyes and a perfect nose. The nicest smile the world has ever seen . . .

She read on, hoping. . . . But Sparky seemed to have delegated composition to Snoopy, pecking out his cycle of sentences on the doghouse typewriter:

> You are a very pretty girl. You are the most fascinating girl I've ever met. You are the girl I would most like to sit across from in a cozy booth and hold your hand and admire those two beautiful eyes. I love you very, very much. The green light is driving me crazy.

Early on, he had been "the world's greatest listener." And yet now, as she later recalled, "I could say stuff and he wouldn't hear me." The more direct she was describing her confusion at the office, the more easily he glossed over it, resuming his worshipful rhetoric.

IN JUNE 1971, SPARKY took Tracey, with her friend Kathleen Hendrix serving as cover, to a production of *You're a Good Man, Charlie Brown* at the high school in Millbrae; that evening she had a sense that for the first time he felt somehow free of his marriage and had come to a decision: "From that time on, he really pursued me again. It was now my reluctance."

Tracey was apprehensive. "It wasn't all roses with Sparky. There were things that gave me great pause." Ever since their talk of marriage, she had worried that he loved her—needed her—more than she loved and needed him. Every week at work, friends told her, "You have to marry him—you'll be rich." But, as she later recalled, "My main concern was: I love him. Money would be nice. But: Money versus Knowing-You-Don't-Love-Him-As-Much-As-He-Loves-You?"

She was also cautious about the way he shut down around children. "He had no feeling for kids. He didn't see the wonder they had." And she was especially hesitant when thinking ahead to life with a man who did not seem to like *people* very much. Two of her heroes were famously gregarious men, Will Rogers and Jimmy Durante; Rogers had "never met a man he didn't like" and Durante had a gentle way about him in his good-hearted sign-off "Good night, Mrs. Calabash, wherever you are." But Sparky's gentleness, she felt, had "fooled" her. "Sparky really didn't give a damn about people. Charity was not uppermost in his mind. He had on blinders. He had no larger feeling for humanity."

"I think the weakest part of my personality," Schulz told a reporter that year, "is not showing enough concern for individuals and maybe even for great causes." He pictured this part of himself in Snoopy, who takes a stand against the way human beings are ruining Earth for all animals by standing on his head on the doghouse. "He's going to stand on his head until these wrongs have been righted!" Charlie Brown explains to Lucy. She abruptly pronounces the whole protest stupid, which is all it takes to topple Snoopy from his pose. "That's what I thought all along," he admits, "but I didn't want to say anything!"

Another woman friend to whom he drew close in later years concurred: "He didn't think anyone cared because *he* didn't care for anyone. First to last, his *Peanuts* characters trumped his feelings toward real people. Why should he love anyone? Snoopy and Charlie Brown were delightful; people loved them, they didn't love him. People always disappointed. Once the *Peanuts* ensemble became Sparky's constant companions they took over his life. With them, his ambitions were fulfilled."

One evening, he and Tracey were talking about commercialism, and she let it fall that she mistrusted *Peanuts*' being used to further the ends of big business. Why should honest Charlie Brown sell unsafe products made by a corporation like Ford? She mentioned the allegedly deadly design defects of the Ford Pinto gas tank and Ford's culpability in rushing the car into production to compete with Japanese carmakers despite evidence that rear-end collisions could easily trap motorists to roast inside.

"Sparky had a way of turning his back on that."

But Schulz was both owner and possession; the system possessed him and yet he was unquestionably an owner, or perhaps manager, of America— one of the hundred or so people who had a grip on how the nation imagined and projected itself. He emphasized that he did not pretend to have the answers. He was no guru telling people how to live their lives, but merely a cartoonist suggesting how to come to terms with the way things were—just another hardworking, God-fearing man who repeatedly reminded his public that "it takes a certain kind of person to do what I'm doing. If I were a social activist I wouldn't be able to sit in a room all day for twenty-one years drawing silly pictures."

He had his father's example. Carl Schulz, a lifelong Republican from Minnesota—the state that had produced the Democratic Farmer-Labor Party—had a deep suspicion of the demands of labor. In 1978, at the height of the biggest labor/management struggle in two decades, *Peanuts* bedding products were manufactured by J. P. Stevens, a southern textile corporation known since 1963 for breaking labor laws and firing employees who wanted its plants to be organized by the Amalgamated Clothing and Textile Workers Union (ACTWU). In 1976, after its workers in North Carolina voted for the ACTWU to represent them, management once again refused to bargain, igniting a five-year international consumer boycott against the firm, which proved ineffective—in part because *Peanuts*, stitched into the textile giant's sheets and towels, masked the corporate identity. People had no way of knowing that they were buying the products of one of the most egregious labor-law violators in America. They thought they were only buying Snoopy.

Schulz typically warded off the general charge of commercialism by saying that he had a responsibility to the people whose jobs and families depended on manufacturing *Peanuts* products.

Yet the strikers at J. P. Stevens considered anyone who did business with their high-handed company irresponsible. Moreover, *Peanuts* was in a special position of influence with both the company and the consumer. According to Determined Productions, which licensed *Peanuts* bedding products, the J. P. Stevens *Peanuts* line, which grossed $10 million in sales annually, was in 1978 the "single biggest-selling sheet pattern ever produced in the history of the domestics industry."

But neither Schulz nor Determined Productions took steps to persuade J. P. Stevens to negotiate with the ACTWU. Finally, it was pressure applied by a campaign against the directors of banks and institutions that supported J. P. Stevens, including that future pillar of *Peanuts* licensing, Metropolitan Life Insurance Company, that forced Stevens to settle.

WHEN TRACEY WAS HONEST with herself, she saw that she was living their affair in three dimensions and he was not. She thought she had made contact with a great man who had played an important role in her life. But then gradually she discovered that he was like the tourist photographer's life-size cardboard cutout of the president that stands outside the White House. "When you put it all together, he wasn't who I thought he was."

His feelings about her, meanwhile, showed no sign of developing. After eighteen months, his latest letters sounded just as had those written eighteen days into the relationship. He sentimentalized her to the point of invisibility. She later described them as "wonderful, romantic, flowery words," while recalling her impression that behind them Sparky was "there and yet not there." Worst of all was her sense that she had been idealized; even after

all this time of talking about fiction and poetry and issues of contemporary politics, the figure she had left in his imagination was that of a passive
beauty whose brains and character should be kept out of the picture.

His letters awoke in him an urgent need for her to reply; again and
again he asked her to affirm her love. Over and over he asked why she
liked him. "He sort of pulled it out of you." Meanwhile, what was she
getting from him? Talk and laughter and books, yes, which she later rated
as among the best of her life; his letters—in the main delightful, especially
with their drawings; his phone calls, which were "like sitting through *Dr.
Zhivago*: Everything was a drama, everything was a parting." And he called
more often than he wrote: she found herself one day slumped on her bed,
gripping the phone like an enemy, pleading, "Sparky, I can't fulfill that
need you have for someone to be there holding your hand."

During their first months, Tracey had known what to do about Sparky's
intense sensitivity. His struggle did not frighten her. She knew how to bring
him back to his dreams: by letting him feel that he was able to please her
with something he had accomplished, some small victory—the A on his
paper, his ace serve in a tennis game, even the "long letter" he sent as a joke
(a single, elongated letter "A").

The only control he seemed to have over his own capacity for self-
affirmation came when he could feel that he was in command of her
admiration. When he lost this, he seemed to lose his whole purpose. If
she failed to boost him, he could plunge in ten seconds flat from being
"something" in his own eyes to "nothing at all" in his sense of the world's
view of him:

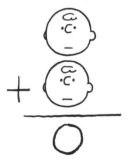

More than his melancholy, more than the occasional flare of anger
behind his sadness, it was this incapacity to live in himself with confidence

and joy that made her doubt that she had what it would take to make him happy. If true happiness is built from the self-forgetfulness embodied in many small acts of compassion toward others, Sparky seemed unfulfilled in his hopes for intimacy.

One day came a drawing of Charlie Brown sitting at the foot of a tree, eyes closed, beaming: "On Thursday, I'm going to get to be with Tracey for 10 hours!"—an occasion whose sweet sadness he commemorated by drawing Charlie Brown, desolate in a parking lot under bright stars and a half moon overhead, as he says, "I can't [take] all these parking lot good byes."

JUST AFTER CHRISTMAS 1971, Snoopy lay atop the doghouse, wondering at the double nature of the heart:

Nearly twenty years later, Schulz returned to the theme of duplicity, this time without the indirection but in a mirror image that heightened the contrast—Charlie Brown and Snoopy, his own two personae, on either side of the tree of life:

Two days later, Charlie Brown discovers that "being in love with two different girls can make you do strange things" and notices that "You feel confused . . . You do things that ordinarily you would never do . . ."

In June 1971, Joyce and Sparky had put Coffee Lane up for sale. A daily strip in September seemed to hint at a coming upheaval in domestic geography, to say nothing of disputes over ownership:

In October Sparky moved his workplace out of the studio Joyce had built for him up along the redwoods.

The real estate market was soft, but Joyce was determined to sell: "My husband was not with me—he was not with me at all. It was too much: Trying to keep that property going and the ice arena."

But Sparky clearly had his doubts about his side of the change, as the November 14, 1971, Sunday page may indicate:

When no buyers appeared, a tax write-off began to look just as beneficial as a sale. By the end of December, the Schulzes deeded the entire property to the First Assembly of God of Santa Rosa (soon to become the Agape Force), which agreed not to transfer it to any other owner for three years after the date of gift, and, indeed, farmed the land and preached in the woods for four years before it sold the property for more than $800,000.

In June 1972, Sparky and Joyce bought a thousand acres on Chalk Hill Road outside Healdsburg. If Sebastopol had been rural when the Schulzes moved there from Minneapolis in 1958, Healdsburg in 1972 was the boondocks. Chalk Hill Road cut through undulating country south of the Russian River, the property being reachable only by a rutted track winding through a mile and a half of dusty oak, madrone, and manzanita trees up to an old white clapboard ranch house built in a hollow by cattle farmers who wanted a quiet place out of the wind.

This square mile and a half of rough country lay half an hour's drive from a quart of milk. Sparky's Norwegian relatives might have made do on such a place two generations earlier, but it was hard to imagine Charles Schulz driving his 1972 Jaguar E Type Series to and from his drawing board every day; indeed, he traded in his prized green sports car for a brown Ford Pinto, enduring the exchange as a visible sacrifice to his marriage. In any case, Windy Valley Ranch, as Joyce christened it, did not seem to be Sparky's home, even after Joyce put in a swimming pool in the shape of Snoopy's head. Monte later reflected that his father had no interest in going to live there: "He allowed the move to be made to keep the marriage together." Craig remembered it as one of the major sorrows of his father's life, and could understand why: "You're driving this junky Ford Pinto. Your marriage is going bad. You've just left paradise. It must have been turmoil for him."

The move was made in June 1972. A month earlier, he and Tracey met at a bayside restaurant in Sausalito, and he asked her to marry him. The intensity of his feelings—or his desperation—may be measured by another meeting he had arranged with Donna Johnson Wold a month before.

In April 1972, on one of his rare trips back to Minnesota, he decided that he had to meet with Donna and, without her husband, "just talk to her and see if there was a spark in her eye," as one friend later summarized his motives. He agreed to give a speech at the Seventeenth Annual C-400 Founders Day Dinner, at Concordia College in Moorhead, Minnesota, where his elder son was finishing freshman year—the very kind of occasion that he so often agreed to speak at and just as often backed out of at the last minute. But the combination of its being Monte's college and Donna's having agreed to meet him triumphed over his usual horror of leaving home.

On Thursday evening, April 27, he met Donna in the lobby lounge of their hotel. Two decades had fled by, yet as Sparky recalled these first moments of being with her again, "It was like not a day had passed." She was still pretty, still blue-eyed, her strawberry hair tinged with soft gray— still Mrs. Alan Wold, but that did not stop Sparky from asking her to dance. Years later, with her husband very much still on the scene, Donna insisted that the meeting was uneventful. She downplayed the strength of her own feelings at this interlude, just as she minimized the scope and duration of their earlier romance, always leaving Sparky alone to make "something" out of "nothing."

HE RETURNED TO CALIFORNIA on Saturday, April 29, and a week later asked Tracey to marry him. They were sitting outdoors at a restaurant overlooking San Francisco Bay.

She did not immediately say yes or no but instead replied that she did not think that she could make him happy. She also had her own news to report: in these recent long intervals apart, two other men had crept into her life—a volatile former boyfriend whose proposal she had turned down in college, and a steady Eddie she had met through business contacts in San Francisco. She had come to lunch intending to tell Sparky that she loved *him* but that she could not be responsible for the rest of her life for not bringing him joy, and that she would probably end up marrying one of these other two men, although she did not know which.

But when she saw his sad, sweet face—"If a face could continuously cave in while you're talking, his face did"—she doubted that she had the courage to break off with him.

Just then, a towering sailboat drew up alongside, and her heart froze, because she could see in his eyes that the yacht embodied a new way to break open their stalemate. "If you married me," he said, "you could have anything you want. I make four thousand dollars a day."

It was the paltriness of the new gambit that was so shocking. Years later, Tracey recalled thinking, *Why did you say that? A romantic soul like you?* And to her further surprise she then burst into tears at how desperate—but how unimaginatively, out-of-touch desperate—he was to marry her. It was a plea as much as a proposal. And she cried because he was asking her to be a bird in a gilded cage; after all this time he still did not know her, or seem interested in knowing her; did not know that money would not entice her; did not understand that she wanted to be his real partner.

She had no illusions about Sparky now. She adored him, but that was not enough. He raised enormous conditions for being loved, and she knew that nothing that she could do would ever be enough—the endlessness of longing in romance would turn into endlessness of demand once enclosed in marriage. In the end, his nourishment would always come from his creation first, such nourishment as it was—because there he need not have, would not have, real people as partners.

A PASSAGE IN LITERATURE once again determined the course of his life. The hard clarities of the Gospel of Luke—eight sentences describing the miracle of God's coming to earth in human form—had raised *A Charlie Brown Christmas* to the standing of a deeply felt perennial classic and given *Peanuts* new life in a new medium for generations to come. Then the closing sentences of Fitzgerald's great national romance, in which "the fresh green breast of the New World" contracts and coarsens as the frontier closes, had brought Sparky a golden girl named Tracey, and was now taking her away. But if not the golden-eyed goddess, then who—or, as he would have reminded her, then *whom*?

A CREEK RAN THROUGH the new property; one day that first summer Joyce insisted that Sparky roll up his sleeves and help Cliff Silva, their gardener, reinforce its banks against erosion. The job entailed manhandling large rocks into place above the creekbed. It was a hot day, he was nearly fifty years old, his marriage was dissolving, his adoring Tracey had turned him down, he had no idea how or when all this would end, and now here he was humping rocks around a muddy ditch out in the Healdsburg sticks.

"I wonder why I'm doing this," he said.

That summer, Joyce lavishly redecorated the new ranch house. When Bill Melendez saw her work, the thickness of the carpeting, the richness of the materials, the shine of the new his-and-her master bathroom, he saw a woman—"a real feminine woman, with a gorgeous figure and great big boobs"—trying to seduce her man back. "She did everything she could, and he was not reacting. He was cold as a cucumber." So he took Sparky aside to offer some perfectly disinterested suggestions.

"Sparky, you're missing the boat. That woman is trying to woo you. . . . Look what she's doing; she's building that place. So I tell you what you do: I think you're a little bit too cold and you've got to change your way of life and your relationship with her. Tell you what you do. When you go home tonight, you go into this gorgeous bedroom that she built for you. You go in there, you grab her by the arm and throw her on this huge king size bed—[it's] surrounded by mirrors for Christ's sake—[and] you throw her in there and you bang the hell out of her. Then you grab her and you drag her off that thing and drag her to the little sitting room, and you toss her on that waterbed in front of the fireplace, and you bang her again and just give her hell."

As Melendez recalled it, "He never reacted. He was thinking about it, but most likely his mind was far away." Yet that evening Sparky went home and tried to counter-seduce Joyce just exactly as mustachioed Bill Melendez had blocked the moves out. But his heart was not in it, he resented Bill's meddling, and the rising voice of Joyce's flustered dismay—"What are you *doing*? What's the *matter with you*? *Are you crazy?*"—only made him confess the faster: "Well, Bill told me this is what I should do." And with that, Joyce's fury spiked.

Sparky and Joyce's old friend Frieda Rich visited that summer, and so did Robert L. Short, who recalled, "Frieda was encouraging Sparky to get out of the marriage, and she was more open with him than I had the courage to be." One night, Joyce "proceeded to take Sparky apart" quite regardless of Short's presence. The next day, Schulz confided: "If things don't change pretty soon, I'm getting out."

Friends and associates noticed their wavering. "By that time they were just kind of going sideways." "Both of them were having mixed feelings about what to do." "I didn't think he'd ever leave her." "I couldn't believe that Sparky could exist without Joyce." "Divorce wasn't his language, but it finally occurred to him that that might be the best route." "I never thought Joyce wanted to divorce Sparky. You start down that road, and pretty soon you've got lawyers involved, dividing up property. I never thought that that's what Joyce wanted." "He was lost and lonely and he had a lot of kids and it was not a good marriage, and he was overwhelmed by everything."

HE KEPT TRYING TO leave her. Once, after a fight, he got in the car, intending to drive away and never come back. But no sooner was he behind the wheel than he realized he had a dentist appointment within the hour— which he kept—and went back to the studio to finish the day's work, then came home as usual.

After another fight that summer, he was again on his way out the door, when one of his sons came in, asked for the car keys, and drove off in Sparky's one means of escape.

One morning, Jill noticed her father sleeping on the couch. "It made me sad. But I never said anything to anybody."

"What would you think if I were to live in the studio?" he asked Amy.

"That would be dumb," she replied, and thought to herself, "My life is over."

In the evening, after everyone had gone to bed, Monte could hear his mother yelling at his father in the quiet ranch house, *"I know you think I'm a shrew!"*

THEN CAME AN AFTERNOON—he always remembered that it happened in the afternoon—when he and Joyce fought once more. This time, he made it to the front door, actually passed through, and headed outdoors, walking toward his silly, dangerous little Ford Pinto. He pulled the keys from his pocket—everything looked unreal, even the car keys—when, without warning, Joyce's head popped out a second-floor window.

"You don't have the guts!" she called after him.

He answered with silence.

"You won't do it!" she taunted.

He put the key in the ignition and started the car. He put the stick in gear and drove down the long driveway, not stopping to close the gate, as she always told him to do . . .

And so he left her. After twenty-two years and four months of marriage to Joyce Steele Halverson, he did not go off to seek Tracey or Donna. He left Joyce the way a good midwestern man would leave his wife: he went to live for a while with his mother-in-law in her apartment on Hardies Lane.

UNCERTAIN ABOUT HIS NEXT move—who would make the final break, he or Joyce?—he did the only other thing he knew how: he left it to Charlie Brown. And therefore on August 2 of that awful summer, Charlie Brown kicked Lucy off the baseball team:

"I used to think if I went back and read all the strips before the divorce," reflected Amy in a less fraught world, "I would see what had gone wrong."

On August 7, Schroeder thinks that, without Lucy, the team has a chance. "Isn't it nice not having her around?" beams Charlie Brown. "Isn't it nice not hearing her voice?"

A MONTH AFTER MARRYING Joyce, Sparky had introduced a new motif into the strip, opening up a subject that became a theme through all his years with her:

"My stomach hurts," Shermy tells Patty.

Not long after, Charlie Brown's stomach gets upset while he watches Patty play marbles; every time she hits a marble with her shooter, Charlie Brown cries out in pain. But, finally, Lucy becomes the consistent source of wrenching internal distress; all she has to do is discount his correct answer to a simple math problem, while insisting on her own willfully wrong solution, for him to grasp his stomach.

Lucy's charades of unreason—lectures on oak trees and how they are used for "knotty-pine recreation rooms" or on palm trees, so named "from the fact that the average person can put his hand clear around it"—acquire that systematic a power of getting Charlie Brown "so worked up" as to revolt his belly.

His colleagues at Art Instruction had been aware of this chronic wretchedness. "He had indigestion quite a bit," recalled Hal Lamson. "I think it was turmoil. There was a lot boiling under the surface, which had to do with his wife. I could understand it: He did not get much peace or rest at home; and he complained one day to me that he hoped he'd be able to control that before it was too late."

"I'm not a relaxed person," Schulz readily admitted. "I'm a worrier."

All the Halverson women, with the exception of the steady Ruth, seemed at one time or another to have had a visceral impact on him: he had spat out Judy's coconut cookies; now he argued about religion with Dorothy, often saying that he had ended up with nothing more than a headache.

The hurt stomach motif almost always appeared in a boy's venting his discontents to a girl, even in the gags Schulz drew for the Church of God's *Youth* magazine. "How can you be a good Christian when your stomach hurts?" a baffled teenage girl asks her soured boyfriend. In *Peanuts* through the next ten years, Lucy's masterful irrationality would tie Charlie Brown's stomach into anguished knots, most often when she taunted him on the baseball field. Around 1962, Joyce herself acknowledged a change: "Sparky is really Charlie Brown, or rather, he was," she said. "Before we were married, he was shy and reserved. He felt he could never do anything well. He's different now. But he's still quiet and kind of reserved." And his stomach still hurt "all the time." Finally, in 1965, after suddenly losing some twenty pounds in two months, Sparky consulted a doctor; although his symptoms seemed to indicate an ulcer, neither X-rays nor other tests could confirm the diagnosis. He was put on a bland diet and advised not to worry, though he often suspected privately that this siege of miseries must be the first sign of cancer.

After 1972, watershed year of the marriage, the theme vanished entirely, and Charlie Brown never again invoked his gut to express dismay or anguish over Lucy's behavior. In fact, his stomach hurt in only two more strips in all the rest of *Peanuts*. Near the end of his life, Sparky told Monte that he was having one of those days when he was disgusted with the "whole Halverson thing." He was glad to be rid of the entire family: "They were a miserable lot," he said. "They bickered all the time."

BY AUGUST HE HAD moved into his office at the arena.

The new studio that Joyce and Ed Doty were building for Sparky on Hardies Lane was not ready until the first of December. The moment it was finished he moved out of Dorothy's to set up housekeeping in the upper half of his workshop, sleeping on a hideaway bed, eating cereal from Styrofoam bowls bought at the supermarket, and once again finding himself alone.

But, within weeks, without ever having to leave home or go beyond the confines of the Warm Puppy, he had met another young woman, and this one, though married herself, seemed to be prepared to love him as he had always longed to be loved.

# CHAPTER 24

# HAPPINESS

*He walked on a few more steps, and before him opened the skating rink, and at once, among all the skaters, he recognized her.*

—TOLSTOY

SHE SKIMMED THROUGH THE Warm Puppy three mornings a week that summer to drop her daughter off at the rink at five-thirty.

While he waited for Amy and Jill to finish their skating practice so that he could drive them to school and start his own day, Sparky watched this cute, compact young woman bustle out of the sunshine and into the ice arena, her slender, tanned arms and legs showing richly brown against a well-cut, bright-white tennis skirt. Her vitality each time seemed to light up the room.

In the end, he had to raise a hand: "Wait a minute. Every morning I see you coming in and going out. What is your name?"

"My name is Jeannie," she replied, and he later reflected that had she been factually formal and used her married name, he could not decently have initiated another conversation.

When he next saw her at the Warm Puppy, and once again she smiled directly at him—an inquisitive smile, conveying an acute fascination to know everything about him—but at the very same moment went shyly on her way, he stopped her again, and said, "Wait a minute. You come in. And you go there. And then you go there. . . . What are you doing?"

She explained that she had left off her eleven-year-old, Lisa, for skating, and was now off to play tennis—and was nearly away again, so that once more he had to pull her up in her tracks just to keep the conversation going.

The next time she breezed in, he lit up and asked her to sit and have a cup of coffee; he already loved seeing her and would soon get in the habit of turning to whomever he had been talking with to ask, "Didn't I tell you she was beautiful?" Joyce was still very much on the scene at the Warm

Puppy; and one day, she later recalled, Sparky turned to her when Jeannie breezed in and said, "Isn't she cute?"

On another occasion, later in the morning than usual, he stopped Jeannie at the Warm Puppy counter, and it was she—not Sparky—who lifted the relationship to a new level by saying, "I'm so glad that you like me."

There was something he very much liked in Jean Clyde: he liked it that she basked in his liking for her. Everything he said, every word he spoke, seemed to fascinate her; he could not have bored her had he tried.

To Jeannie, they seemed "meant to have come together." She was thirty-three, married, with two children, and later said that whereas Sparky's marriage had definitely ended by the summer of 1972, hers was not yet over: "I wasn't thinking of not being married, but Sparky swept me off my feet." He, meanwhile, told *Peanuts* collectors, "I'm lucky that Jeannie found me," as if he had been lost and she had scooped him up.

To Sparky, the deep good fortune of their encounter was magical: "You could sit in the coffee shop at the arena and look across and see someone and know right away that you would just like to go over and sit down and talk with that person. And yet dozens of other people will walk through all day long and you wouldn't care if you ever saw them again. But suddenly one person comes in, and you want to meet that person. What is it?"

ELIZABETH JEAN FORSYTH had been born in Germany in 1939, the third child of educated English parents. Her father, Archer Baxter Forsyth, left Downing College, Cambridge, at the outbreak of the Great War to join the Bedfordshire Regiment, in which he rose to the rank of captain. He had been married and divorced when he met Pamela Mary Green in Paris, where she was attending the Sorbonne before going up to Oxford. They married in 1933 and settled in Mannheim, where they ran the Berlitz Language School until the British government advised British subjects to leave Germany in August 1939, when Jeannie was six months old.

The Forsyths considered moving to Southern Rhodesia, but emigrated instead to the United States, and were by 1940 teaching at the Berlitz School in San Francisco, before they established themselves in the real estate business in Marin County. Jeannie later described hers as "an English family—non-demonstrative, can't cook, don't care about eating, oblivious to a lot of comforts." Real estate for the Forsyths was a matter of social engineering; her mother, a problem solver, saw home ownership as one of society's great solidifiers; her father believed that he was helping people to make the most important financial decision of their lives accurately.

Pamela was strong-minded and independent. In 1947, when Jeannie was nine, her parents divorced, and she was brought up by her mother in Southern California, on an avocado ranch in Fallbrook.

She was intelligent, and, among the women in Charles Schulz's life, comparatively well educated, liking school and loving to read. Raised on A. A. Milne, she did not begin reading the comic strips regularly until later in life. In 1955 she threw herself into college life under the red-tiled roof-tops and towering eucalyptus trees of Pomona College. In her sophomore year, she met Hunter Brooke "Peter" Clyde, Jr., during a drama production, and was soon engaged. That August they married in Ross, California, honeymooning in Hawaii. Jeannie set out "to work on the Perfect Little Family," and a year later, had her first child, Hunter Brooke Clyde III, whom they called Brooke. Their second child, Elizabeth, called Lisa, was born December 27, 1960.

The bright, cynical Peter Clyde, his frowning, querulous expression half-hidden by wire-rim glasses, thinning blond hair parted off center above a narrow face and full lips, looked like a junior professor at a small college. In July 1959, he moved the family to Hawaii and found work at the *Honolulu Star-Bulletin*—a period Jeannie recalled as "the carefree days . . . when our children were babies" and in which she drove a convertible Morris Minor and began taking classes at the University of Hawaii. When the Clydes moved back to Santa Rosa in 1962, Jeannie continued her studies at Sonoma State University and Peter went into real estate.

But, as Jeannie later reflected, "I wanted Pete to be more outreaching, more ambitious. [He] was smart, and I wanted him to do something with his smartness." A friend and neighbor would later recall: "No one took Pete Clyde as seriously as Jeannie. Pete was fun—he played guitar and sang songs at parties." By 1967, Jeannie had told a friend that she wanted to marry someone who would make a difference in the world.

In 1968, she was given the key to the City of Santa Rosa for serving two years as cochairperson of the Building a Better City Committee, which had got the bond issue through for a new city hall. She was dedicated and curious; when she participated in a blood drive, she gave not once or twice but systematically; when she took up Spanish, she fashioned labels marked with Spanish equivalents for every object in the house, down to the mirror in the hallway. She had artistic tastes; she wrote poetry—but books, stories, were not where she lived her life. She was too active for that, although her father's searching, metaphysical side had taught her to appreciate the nuanced pursuit of ideas.

Like Sparky, Jeannie had grown up feeling special—destined, as she put it in earlier years, "to *do* something." But as she matured and married and had children, she struggled, as had Sparky, with feelings of being "not really anyone." Both had a social gift—Jeannie perhaps more than Sparky—but each was well acquainted with aloneness and with the sometimes daily battle to control chronic "impatience at the imperfections of others," or at her own powerlessness to correct this, as Jeannie described her puzzlement in a 1960 letter to her father.

Both Jeannie and Sparky placed great value on being seriously right on a range of issues; each concealed struggles beneath a calm, unflappable manner. Jeannie could have been speaking for both when she wrote, "I don't feel like a very good family person—in fact, I tend to be too much of an individualist."

And indeed, in snapshots of Jean Clyde's small-city 1960s activism, we can catch glimpses of the future Jean Schulz. Jean Clyde, that whirlwind of civic chores and errands for social betterment, was not just Another Mother for Peace, even when most of her friends had not yet taken a stand on Vietnam. "Jeannie wanted to experience everything. She was looking for somebody who would help her change the world."

And yet that was precisely the role that Sparky had been sidestepping all these years. By 1972, people wanted—were desperate—not for a delineator but a solver. Yet Sparky had always known that if he ever came out and said, "The message is—," there would be no need for his comic strip. One afternoon Monte played a Graham Nash song for his father— "Chicago"—and when they reached the chorus, "We can change the world/ Rearrange the world," Monte recalled, "Dad, very vigorously remarked, 'No, you can't. You can't change the world.'"

In late October 1972, Sparky kept a scheduled appearance before a group of dentists at the Masonic Auditorium in San Francisco. Inspired perhaps by Jeannie's willingness to come along, or perhaps just carried away in the moment, he told his listeners something of a kind that he had never tried out on an audience: that Snoopy was at work on a new book, his second, to be entitled (as a parody of a then-popular best seller) *The Sensuous Dog*, by "S."

Afterward, he took Jeannie to Ghirardelli Square, the scene of his first date with Tracey ("He knew where he was going," recalled Jeannie), and bought her a present on the square, an interlocked pair of mushrooms wrought of metal: "That's me and that's you, and I'll always look after you." Then they stopped somewhere and kissed—"a kiss not so much of passion but of yearning, longing. . . . He just had the softest lips."

SPARKY AND JOYCE'S SEPARATION legally began on November 15, although no part of the split was made public, and no explanation was given to the children. Eleven days later, Sunday, November 26, was Sparky's fiftieth birthday, but on his calendar the day remained blank.

So soon after his zenith he had sunk to his nadir, or, anyway, the lowest point in his life since his mother died just as he approached twenty-one. With the half-century milestone upon him, he was astonished to consider that he was now the same age his mother had been when she died. "Realizing this saddens me even more," he wrote, and when he now thought about himself in the world without Dena, it seemed to him that he had never recovered from losing her.

As he tested the idea of marrying Jeannie, he sometimes drove along St. Helena Avenue, just to pass Number 1120, a snug two-story house with brick trim and a deodar cedar shading the front lawn, where she and Peter were raising their children. What was she doing right now? What was she thinking?

But he still called Tracey several times (giving her an impression of "fishing") and Donna also; during one of these conversations he floated the idea of the two of them meeting up in Hawaii. We don't know Donna's response to the proposal, but Jeannie later recalled Sparky debating such a trip for days and finally deciding not to pursue it.

ON THE FIRST OF December, Ed Doty completed his twenty months' work on the new studio, a spacious one-story building with Joyce's and Ed's signature design features: redwood and Modoc stone. The post office and city consenting, the building was formally designated One Snoopy Place; Sparky moved right in, and two weeks later was served there with a summons in *Schulz v. Schulz*. About a week later, he drew this daily:

Joyce executed and filed divorce papers on December 11, 1972, requesting the Superior Court of California, Sonoma County, to award her custody of the children, support for them and herself, her rights in shared property, and her attorneys' fees and court costs, later explaining to the children that "I really didn't want to be a spectator at your dad's life, and that's what I was," although to Bill Melendez she confided, "I just couldn't take the betrayal."

When the news broke on the radio on December 14, this was the first the children had heard of it. Jill, stopped by the traffic light near the Roy Rogers at Coddingtown Mall, heard on her car radio: ". . . Joyce Schulz is suing Charles Schulz for divorce . . ." and the word "*suing*" knocked her back in her seat. "It was as if he were a criminal," she said.

Craig, who heard the same broadcast, later recalled the next part of the bulletin, which Jill did not hear because the first part had already deafened her: "*—and it won't be for 'peanuts'!*"

Monte heard the news as he pulled into the driveway at his girlfriend

Bunny Peterson's house on Dyer Avenue outside Graton; someone in her household had been listening to the radio and Bunny came out in alarm and confusion to tell him.

Amy took it hardest; she was the daughter to whom in childhood Sparky's refrain had been "You're so sensitive, if I look at you wrong, you cry." On the ice in recent years she had grown from a completely inexperienced "rink rat" into a graceful but temperamental skater; in moments of defeat Sparky would try to comfort her by saying, "This world is just too hard for people like you and me, Amos. We're just too sensitive." Now, she had rightly perceived that it was her father who had left the marriage to date Mrs. Clyde, and she confronted him with her dismay, which rose so quickly into hysteria that she saw no reason not to let him know that his choice of a young woman—not just sixteen years younger, but, as Amy put it obliquely, a "bippety-boppety" young woman—sickened her.

The others came to terms with the split in various ways; Monte believed that no discussion or explanation was necessary: "It was clear that it was coming. They weren't getting along." Meredith had overheard fighting behind closed doors for several years and, whenever the yelling resumed, had taken her brothers and sisters into another room, out of earshot.

One night in the jumble of messy weeks that followed, Sparky and Monte were on opposite hockey teams, Monte's team having the upper hand, and Monte danced away from Sparky during a play, whereupon father slashed son across the backs of his legs so hard that Monte had trouble walking to the locker room. "He really injured my leg—an unbelievable welt." After the game, in the parking lot outside the arena, Monte was sitting at the wheel of the MG his father had given him—which made things, for Monte, even more awkward. Deciding that the best form of defense was attack, he said to his father: "You're lonely, I come and visit you all the time. Now you've maimed me." But he does not recall his father apologizing until two days later.

One thing after another came to an end that December. *Apollo 17* splashed down in the Pacific, closing out the moon-landing program. The idealism of Sparky and Joyce's halcyon days at Coffee Lane, when *Peanuts* could not put a foot wrong and Snoopy had taken to the skies, ultimately beating Armstrong and Aldrin to the Sea of Tranquility—suddenly it all seemed far away. *Life* magazine, which for three decades had pictured the nation's lives, theirs included, published its last issue on December 29, a victim of hubris and television. Harry Truman died the day after Christmas, and the car radio never seemed to stop playing Don McLean's "American Pie," with its lament for the "day the music died."

Sparky himself could no longer listen to his records. "For a long while after my separation and my missing of the kids for a little bit, it was so depressing that I just didn't listen to any. It would make me sad."

The day came when he decided to remove his gold wedding band, never to wear it again. But it was stuck below the knuckle and would not come off. His old pastor from the Merriam Park Church of God, Frederick Shackleton, and his wife, Doris, happened to be visiting the new studio that day and found themselves bearing inadvertent witness to Sparky's sense of shame: "It makes you feel like a failure." The ring, with its dishonored engraving, *Forever*, adding a morbid envoi, finally had to be hacksawed off.

Around Christmas, Jeannie shocked her husband with the news that she was in love with Charles Schulz and that they planned to marry. The Clydes separated on January 2, 1973. Sparky called Tracey to announce his engagement, not knowing that on July 1, 1972, in Reno, she had gotten married to the steady fellow from San Francisco whom she had known for only five months. He let her know that Jeannie was pretty, like her. Tracey wished Sparky well, with a hopeful insistence that "this is a new start for you." Years later, she said, "I was really happy he wasn't going to be alone."

JOYCE HAD BEEN THE aggressor in the marriage, the disciplinarian with the children, and now she had to be the bad cop in the divorce. Sparky could say nothing about his affair with Tracey, nor could he publicly acknowledge his new feelings for Jeannie. The arena could talk of nothing else. "Everybody assumed that since he was Charlie Brown," one observer summarized, "then it had to be Joyce's fault." Joyce's role as "the dynamo of the duo," in Bill Melendez's phrase, made people think that it was she who was leaving "poor Sparky." Even those who knew Schulz best could not accept that it would be Sparky who would leave the marriage. Surely Joyce was to blame, and therefore who wouldn't sympathize with Sparky?

To old friends, he appeared trapped and helpless. When he came to explain the breakup in casual telephone conversation with his former fellow parishioners in Minnesota, he seemed to take the high road, omitting any mention of scandalous behavior, and simply, quietly, lamenting that Joyce "was getting to care about me less and less." "I don't think she even liked me," he often repeated, or "She just didn't like me anymore," saying as little as possible about his own feelings or inability to live up to promises. And they colluded with him in this withholding: "We didn't think that Joyce was really the right companion for him," agreed his old friends at the Church of God. And: "He was afraid that he hadn't been a good husband, but it was more her than him."

Among friends and associates and acquaintances in California, it became generally accepted that Joyce had all but single-handedly made the break by leaving Sparky for Ed Doty. The arena spoke of it as fact: *Joyce ran off with her contractor! The man who built this place!* "Between you and me," went a typical piece of arena gossip, "I'm quite sure that the reason she kept building was so she could keep that contractor around."

Edwin Doty was a virile outdoorsman, a hunter and a fisherman. He split wood, smoked a pipe, operated bulldozers, drove a twenty-year-old GMC one-and-a-half-ton truck, and took his work and his customers seriously. "Sparky had everyone believing that Joyce and I were having an affair before him and Jeannie, but that was the furthest thing from the truth: [ Joyce] was my best customer, and I wasn't about to mess that up."

He had been an Army Air Corps pilot and flight instructor, flying B-25s during the war, and when, at last, he asked Joyce out on a date, and she accepted, he took her flying in a Cessna in which he owned a one-third interest—first to Monterey for lunch; then into the skies over San Francisco Bay on the Fourth of July 1973. Joyce was ecstatic about soaring *above* the fireworks to gaze down into the bursting skyrockets. Another evening they flew to a secluded Pacific beach, where he had prepared a pit for roasting hot dogs. There was in this new romance more than a little of Bill Lewis's trail rides in the Land of Enchantment . . .

Brought up on the land in Sebastopol, Ed was first and foremost a working man, with sun-darkened hands and stained fingernails and a broad, easy friendliness, all without emotional self-consciousness. With Ed, Joyce could return now to open spaces, the outdoors, to freer living. "Ed could do all the stuff that Mom really liked," recalled Monte. "She always wanted to dance and Dad would never dance," said Jill. "She wanted to travel and he wouldn't."

Meredith, at a rebellious remove from family conventions, saw that Sparky had emotionally starved Joyce: "The difference between Ed and my dad was that Ed stroked my mother emotionally; and my dad had not learned that women need that first. How would he? In a Norwegian family of that magnitude—in which women's only purpose is propagating their own kind—how could he have learned to stroke women emotionally?" Meredith also saw the divorce as a liberation for Sparky; where before he had been a sensitive, easily hurt human being who had used his routines and patterns as a shield, his new life "allowed him to come out of himself in a way."

Jeannie's daughter registered new growth in her mother, too: "In a way, she grew up. She wanted to respect someone. She wanted someone intellectual and philosophical. She looked up to Sparky. My dad is smart, but she has a will—she was too much for my dad; Sparky was quietly confident and accomplished, and she needed someone like that."

HE MADE HIS CHOICE, but was not sure if it was the right one. Indeed, doubt gnawed at Sparky even as a more fulfilling life seemed ready to catch him up and sweep him forward, and he fretfully signaled his predicament as an eye-catching stand-up movie poster in the title panel of the February 18, 1973, Sunday page:

Living alone in the studio, he woke up early, often wondering where he was, and had to hunt around for the simplest utensils to put some cereal into his stomach. He "was so upset with everything that was happening to [him]"

that he declined to play in the Crosby golf tournament, one of the high points on his yearly calendar. The next day, January 4, Tracey's birthday, he called her in San Francisco and found her in wretched spirits; she might theoretically be married, and she certainly was pregnant, but her husband had already made it clear that he did not intend to support her or their baby.

For the first time, Sparky marked "birthday" in the February 23 panel of the New Year's *Peanuts Date Book*, although he omitted Jeannie's name—that would not be safe to display until the following year.

Most often he did not know who to turn to except the strip itself:

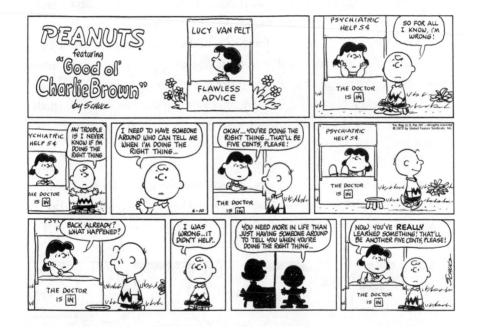

The strip was rarely as challenging or fresh in its last three decades as it was when he was forced to take so many truths into account. "Some of the best work he ever did was when his own personal life was [in] turmoil," observed an associate. "He would withdraw from that world and go into the other world and be more creative than ever. He could just kind of shut off the rest of it."

The strips of February and March 1973 had been no edgier than usual, though Snoopy showed more than his ordinary coldness and stinginess as he campaigned with conspicuous unsuccess for the Daisy Hill Puppy Cup.

Woodstock had hurt himself on a barbed-wire fence. Linus's blanket had been recalled. Lucy had dominated a debate about how it feels to step on the pitcher's mound for the first time each spring, steamrollering all Charlie Brown's delicacies of sentiment before her blank insistence that it would give anyone a feeling of raw power. The kids had, meanwhile, planned and then canceled a testimonial dinner, leaving the guest of alleged honor—of course, Charlie Brown—waiting at the head table, when they realized that it was simple hypocrisy to pretend that Charlie Brown had been a good team manager.

"Why, Mr. Schultz [*sic*]?" asked Mrs. Robert B. Maye of Orrville, Ohio, occasioning a long defense of the melancholy in *Peanuts*, which concluded, "Actually, I am very fond of Charlie Brown myself, and I don't like to see him hurt. I am afraid, however, that a happy comic strip is almost impossible to draw and would be as unrealistic as a completely happy and carefree life." Happiness, he insisted, was not a source of humor. In this observation, he echoed Tolstoy, who wrote that ". . . happy people have no history."

IN APRIL, HE DREW his own history, unleashing from the drawing board a story sequence that began running on June 11, in which Charlie Brown awakens to find that the rising sun has become a baseball:

He naturally, and therefore self-destructively, resorts to Lucy for reassurance:

Then the moon also manifests continent-long seams and a chilling smoothness.

In fact, everything he sees has turned into a baseball,

until finally he himself falls into the dreadful pattern: the back of his head develops a rash whose lesions are sporting-goods stitches,

and Charlie Brown has to go off to camp as Mr. Sack:

"I thought of the idea while working on a Sunday page. Instead of the sun rising I drew a baseball on the horizon in the title panel, which is dropped by most newspapers. I worked on the idea and just thought of things as I went along." Two years later, he wrote:

> I don't know which story has been my favorite, but one that worked out far beyond my expectations concerned Charlie Brown's problem when, instead of seeing the sun rise early one morning, he saw a huge baseball come up over the horizon. Eventually a rash, similar to the stitching on a baseball, began to appear on his head, and his pediatrician told him it would be a good idea if he went off to camp and got some rest. Because he was embarrassed by the rash, he decided to wear a sack over his head. The first day of camp, all the boys held a meeting, and someone jokingly nominated the kid with the sack over his head as camp president. Before he knew it, Charlie Brown was running the camp and had the admiration of everyone. I don't pretend there is any great truth to this story, or any marvelous moral, but it was a neat little tale and one of which I was proud.

Schulz could never explain "where the idea came from"—"it just happened, that was all."

It was the story of Sparky before, during, and after the army, starting on the morning he awoke to find that his mother had died and the world he knew as a boy had ended. No longer a son, no longer the solar power around whom all the other planets orbited, he could not rise, he could not shine; he was bound to Earth. It was literally hard to get out of bed. Stitches had been left to mark his wounds. The trauma was so severe that his life was at once postsurgical: he had to be patched up to go on. What was more, he had to report to camp—Camp Campbell, Kentucky—and hide his shock and grief under a sack, which itself draws on a self-deprecating cartoon image of that grim time and place—George Baker's famous GI cartoon, in which the eponymous hero is a *sad sack*.

But then, in a transformation that exactly mirrors Charlie Brown's experience in summer camp, he became powerful—he followed Carl's barber strategies for success—and was elected by his peers to be their leader. But just as Staff Sgt. Schulz of Company B was not a leader who goes out front but the leader to whom people come—just as his mother had been a kind of squad leader in the Halverson clan—Mr. Sack's leadership in camp amounts to his being a faceless ear to tent mates.

The next part of the sequence tells the rest of the tale of Charles Schulz: success attends the grotesque "sack," or mask, that is supposed to keep our hero in safe anonymity. If we listen to Schulz narrate the action at Charlie Brown's summer camp, it is exactly as if he were describing his own life from 1950 to 1973: "It seemed that no matter what he did, it turned out well, and he became known as 'Sack' or 'Mr. Sack,' and became the best-liked and most-admired kid in camp. Unfortunately, he could not resist taking the sack off to see if his rash was cured, and once he had removed the sack, he reverted back to his old self."

THAT SPRING, HIS NEW love began visiting the studio regularly, and he brightened whenever Jeannie walked in, giving her a big hug. He took pride in showing her the latest freshly inked strip and pleasure in watching her delight in the panels. But he might also share the most recent irritations of the week: an extravagant request from a fan who nonetheless could not be bothered to learn the correct spelling of his name; a waiter who, on realizing that he had Charles Schulz at his table, tried to be funny for the rest of the meal; a cartoonist whose characters overreacted to a punch line . . .

Most people are embarrassed at having to complain; he wasn't. He felt secure in defining his relationship with the world as one of frustration. It was a mark of security—the new security of his life with Jeannie—that he *could* complain. " 'Poor sweet baby' is what I used to say to Sparky to deflect his complaints," she remembered. On Sunday, April 8, she entered *Peanuts* to stay:

ON AUGUST 7, 1973, divorce proceedings were heard in Superior Court before the Honorable Lincoln F. Mahan. Schulz did not contest the divorce, and the marriage was dissolved. The court, however, reserved jurisdiction on the questions of child custody, child support, and division of property.

The next day, Joyce Schulz married Edwin Vernon Doty in Kenwood Community Church. "I didn't invite any of the kids to my wedding," she later recalled. "I thought it would too traumatic for them."

"WHERE DO YOU LIVE NOW?" he was asked in late August.

"I don't have any place to live. I'm trying to get reestablished."

"Where do you sleep?"

"Right here on the couch. I've been living here about six months. Joyce has remarried and I have to start my life all over. Strangely, I've drawn better cartoons in the last six months—or as good as I've ever drawn. I don't know how the human mind works."

Exactly a month after this exchange, on Saturday, September 22, 1973, at two o'clock in the afternoon, Charles Schulz married Elizabeth Jean Forsyth Clyde at their new home in Santa Rosa. Sparky was fifty, Jeannie thirty-four.

# PART SIX

# EMPIRE OF ONE

*Maybe I am meant to dwell alone behind*
*a drawing board.*

C.M.S.

# CHAPTER 25

# POOR, SWEET BABY

*I'd like a girl who would call me, "Poor, sweet baby."*
—CHARLIE BROWN, APRIL 1973

AND SO HE RISKED opening his heart again. This time he might be loved.

But why in Santa Rosa? He was asked constantly, when the world was his oyster, why live with his new wife in a drowsy, formerly beautiful garden city that had allowed the freeway to mutilate it? He always answered that this was where Jeannie lived. "Her kids were still teenagers and were still going to school, so we just bought a house in Santa Rosa." In her eyes, the ice arena had an equally strong anchoring influence.

He bought a bishop's residence in fashionable Montecito Heights from the Roman Catholic diocese—a twelve-room house on four acres, with a swimming pool, three-car garage, guesthouse, cabana, prayer grotto, including a private chapel with stained-glass windows in which he and Jeannie took their vows that September 1973, and afterward remodeled as a "combination gym and game room."

For Sparky and Jeannie there followed an expansive time of sunlight and ease. The disarray of the late '60s rolled away, to be replaced by a decade of jogging and other innocently egotistical, California-friendly pursuits that united Jeannie's athleticism and Sparky's seemingly unending quest for happiness. "It felt as though I opened up a whole new world for him," she later reflected.

Before they met, Jeannie had been "pondering the problem of how essentially alone man is," notably in letters to her father, for though she had felt herself "special," she told him, and was "certainly not one of the herd," she had come to see that by standing apart there was a price to pay not just in internal loneliness but in identity itself: "Now I feel that in addition to aloneness, I'm not really anyone."

Sparky came out with similar feelings at roughly the same time: "I have the feeling I don't belong any place. I guess everyone feels like an outsider sometimes. I don't belong to Rotary Clubs because I feel out of place with businessmen. I'm not an artist . . . I don't know what I am. . . ."

Many years later, he said to Jeannie, "You and I have the same problem: We don't fit in."

They fitted with each other. Jeannie evoked his thoughtful, searching side. And with Jeannie there could be sexual fulfillment. "He was very playful about sex—and sometimes silly," a point that she later emphasized "because people would be totally surprised: People thought of Sparky as prudish, but in fact he was anything but prudish. Sex was an important part of love for him."

In those first glad, confident years of marriage, Sparky dropped his four-handicap golf in favor of Jeannie's sport of tennis. They took lessons, playing occasionally in tournaments and regularly during lunch hours at courts built specially beside Sparky's studio. "Golf was too time-consuming," he contended. "I really got kind of bored after a few holes."

He was suddenly sociable, happy to go out in the evening, delighted to greet Jeannie's friends at dinner parties at home, and always pleased to introduce her to his old friends: "Didn't I pick a winner?" he would ask, taking special pride when Jeannie and a partner won the Nevada State Senior Mixed Doubles Tournament.

Jeannie had also earned a pilot's license with commercial and instrument ratings. Flying as copilot with her petite, silver-haired mother, Pamela Vander Linden, she was already a veteran of women's transcontinental air races—the Powder Puff Derbies of 1972 and 1973; their third entry, taking a 185-mile-per-hour single-engine Bellanca from Riverside, California, on July 4, 1975, on a four-day, 2,600-mile course to Boyne Falls, Michigan, with seven intermediate stops, passed in real time into *Peanuts*, starting on June 19.

★ ★ ★

JOYCE AND ED DOTY HAD honeymooned in Ed's camper, revisiting the uplands and rivers around Hambone, California, where Ed had hunted and fished in his youth, returning to Windy Valley Ranch to breed and train mules. Joyce had liberated herself. Mule breeding, albeit on the grand scale she had made her signature, proved to be an ideal counterpoint for the new plain ways she was embracing. "I consider myself the publicity agent for mules," she explained, "because they have had such bad publicity all of their life"—in sharp contrast to Sparky, who had "never had a day of bad publicity in his life."

Sparky kept his distance from Joyce in these years; if they saw one another, as they did once at a bookstore in Santa Rosa, they nodded politely, but they did not seek each other out to talk about the children or of the past that was now submerged beneath 8,143 comic strips—one per day for the whole of their marriage, whose substance was fuel that the strip had consumed.

The court awarded Joyce custody of the children, but all except Meredith seemed to prefer to live with their father. Amy, seventeen, called 3699 Montecito Avenue home for a year, then moved out and found her own place. Jill, fifteen, also lived with Sparky, Jeannie, and Jeannie's children, Brooke, fifteen, and Lisa, twelve. Monte, twenty-one, briefly joined in when he was transferring from Concordia College to Jeannie's alma mater, Sonoma State University. Craig also resumed residence under his father's roof, only to put immediate pressure on Jeannie by filling the house: "Every night there is a mass of friends in," reported Sparky, "and kids dropping in at all hours."

But their children did not fit together. The Schulz kids maintained that Brooke and Lisa resented them because, as the Clydes allegedly saw it, Sparky had broken up their parents' marriage, but Brooke and Lisa later denied having had such suspicions.

With so much to resolve in their relationships with their own children, both Sparky and Jeannie made clear that they were not serving as surrogates to others. "I don't consider myself a stepparent," Jeannie told the authors of a popular late-seventies text about stepparenting, *Your Child? I Thought It Was My Child!* "I'm just somebody who is in the house. That sounds like I'm putting myself down, but I don't mean it that way. I just think I'm somebody married to their father. They're too old for me to try to tell them what to do." Sparky fell in comfortably with this withdrawal: "And I don't have to be a father to Jeannie's kids. I'm there and I try to help, but I don't have to be a father. And I don't cross her children in any way."

When he was asked "What happens if one of Jeannie's children makes you absolutely furious?" Jeannie answered for him, summing up Sparky's whole history of emotional hurts kept under cover, with all its chapters of repeatedly finding it impossible to trust himself and others to be honest: "No one ever does anything that makes Sparky absolutely furious."

Sparky was "a quiet, gentle presence," as Lisa Clyde remembers her new stepfather. He made her feel welcome in his world and had a knack for making Brooke feel special and cared for. Having told his stepchildren that he would not try to take the place of their father, he also avoided the parenting required of any issue that built up an authentic emotional charge; he never got involved in sibling disputes and refused to set limits, or help enforce them, when Jeannie drew the line (though she would later recall no lack of emotional support from him), even as he refrained from the kind of decision making that might help clear up discontent and withdrew into his distancing daily routine rather than be disliked.

Neither Sparky, the only child, nor Jeannie, the only girl in her family, had strong clan attachments. "We both felt that we didn't belong anywhere in our families," Jeannie later observed. "I really don't think I fit in anyplace," he said. "I've always felt like kind of an outsider, even though I have a lot of friends, and I think I have some good friends. I still feel like an outsider—that people would really rather be around somebody else—that I'm not that interesting."

He confided to Jeannie that he felt lonely for friends, cut off by fame, trusting only a very few. "He doesn't know 'who he is,'" she wrote, recording her own puzzlement: "Is he detached? He only engages with a few people. Says he likes 'attractive' people—wants to know about them. Feels most people who 'want to know' him wouldn't even pay attention if he weren't famous." And she reflected, "The artist, in some way, stands back from society so he can report on it."

She felt a strong defensive instinct toward her new husband. She wanted at all costs to avoid hurting him herself, and that included never showing any of her hard feelings to him. "He wanted a companion, and he wanted someone who wanted him," said Jeannie. "He wanted to be adored; and I was happy to do that." But of a time only a few years beyond these joyous beginnings, she would add, "It was important that I not be needy."

Neither did he want her making suggestions about how to run his business. When he first showed her his most recent work, or shared some of the hundreds of letters that poured in each week, he valued her opinions. Then, in 1972, she suggested that he publish a book of letters to Charles Schulz. Sparky himself had illustrated just such a volume, *Dear President Johnson*. She later admitted that behind the notion was a fairly innocent hidden agenda: "I thought it would be a way to work with him." But he very carefully explained to her that he did not think it was "right" to publish people's letters, and she agreed with him and respected his decision.

On the surface, Jeannie appeared to be more feminine and accommodating than Joyce. She was nicer than Joyce, and better educated, a more competitive athlete, and she radiated an inscrutable Anglo-genteel mystique. But she, too, had a strong will, yet unlike Joyce—more like Dena Schulz or Donna Johnson—she kept her feelings, especially any frustrations with or about Sparky, to herself.

As Sparky's new wife, Jeannie was going to great lengths to shield him from aggressiveness. "I understood how easily he could be hurt, and I never wanted to say or do anything to hurt him. I imagine if I hurt him at all it was because of what I didn't do." Part of his relief and pleasure in her "niceness" was in direct proportion to Joyce's infamous bossiness. When reflecting in later years on why she and Sparky had been so well suited to one another, she said, "I've never had an inner Lucy. Lucy wants to hurt people. Lucy gets personal. Even in the beginning, Lucy was mean. I'm not mean. That came before me."

Sparky and Jeannie founded their marriage on a nonaggression pact: "I honestly think that the reason Sparky and I had a wonderful life together wasn't because we never irritated each other, but [because] neither one of us wanted to hurt the other." But Sparky had spent most of his life engaging in a daily contest of wills, and without a Lucy to challenge him, he could do nothing but turn against himself. Joyce's open aggressiveness had activated feelings that he had learned to cover up and then bring out in the strip; her fury made his own anger accessible, more comfortable to live with.

The Lucy of the 1960s lived in a world of fools and incompetents and one genius who didn't want her; Charlie Brown was no contest, and her little brother was too heavily defended; only the dog would stand up to her. Lucy's every glowering mood, such as this from 1965, had charged him toward active resistance:

"Look at Lucy after our marriage," observed Jeannie. "She lost a lot of meanness. She mellowed somewhat." But he more than mellowed her; he shuffled the pack and dealt out a new Lucy:

In these later years, Schulz made everything about Lucy smaller; even her infamously peppery baseball-team taunts to Charlie Brown had boiled down to compulsive, solipsistic list making.

Dedicated Jeannie always had causes, projects, a busy schedule. Inevitably, he suspected that he was becoming just another item on her schedule, another thing to do—so much so that the family jest went that Jeannie's evening schedule had a slot in it that read: "9:15–9:30: Comfort Sparky."

When the old Lucy reappeared, it was now as a visitor to the strip, removed from the present, consciously picking up on old insults from the past:

Using her lungs, fists, elbows, lips, even her teeth, the earlier Lucy had habitually overdisplayed her will, even in issues where it wasn't necessary. Lucy was three-dimensional because she was the one character in *Peanuts* who had authority to order around her equals. She had been the strip's channel to the adult word: a matron brilliantly disguised as a little girl. The Lucy of 1996 had become that matron, but she had lost the power of her girlish disguise:

The Lucy of 1966 was a controller of others, not a pesterer. The last thing she would have done to get her way was to pester. A queen or a general does not *need* to pester; in the 1950s, children pestered, wives pestered, mothers pestered:

Here is the quintessential Lucy, at the top of her game, confident to the point of casualness, almost of boredom, on the last April Fool's before Sparky and Jeannie married:

And then here is the penultimate April Fool's strip in the *Peanuts* canon, twenty-six years later, featuring a wan, wispy Lucy and an ineffectual Rerun, who is more of a young son to Lucy than a younger brother:

What had once been a masterfully played chess game, a continually renewed power struggle between Lucy and each of the other characters, became a world-weary exercise in filling white space, and, stunningly, even Charlie Brown exercised a measure of executive authority in this new world:

In small but important ways, the central *Peanuts* characters had become rather dull and adult: Snoopy as scoutmaster was a grown-up to the birds, just as Lucy was parental with Rerun, Marcie was the adult in her duo with Peppermint Patty, and Linus had become a passive-aggressive crank, dodging Sally's latest show of affection with a harsh scolding.

Schulz resented critics who said that his best work was behind him and protested that he now worked "just as hard on every strip, every idea." But he granted that the strip was now "a little more mild than it might have been years ago," and even Jeannie conceded that with Lucy "less a crabby monster," the work was "less biting." She wondered if, because Sparky was "a measure happier, did it reversely affect the strip?" She found herself considering that perhaps he had "gotten mileage from the discord at home—pouring it into his work," but then dismissed that notion as too simplistic. "I'd like to think that having a modicum of peace at home and some fun allowed him to continue to do what he loved."

But Sparky's love for cartooning was not what set *Peanuts* apart from other comic strips; any number of cartoonists shared such passion for the craft—or even what had lifted it from being merely good into greatness. Schulz's *dis*passion—his ability to transmute raw joy and pain as well as unassimilable events and moods from his own life into line—had molded the characters. The sadness of the strip in these years of Schulz's aging is the absence of feeling. To judge by the 1988 model of one of his most reliable annual set pieces—Lucy coming up with a fresh explanation for the routine of pulling the football away from Charlie Brown—Schulz's work had fallen victim to its own best trick:

Schulz originally drew the football-kicking episode to show that Charlie Brown was incapable of combating Lucy's shrewdness. "This is a parody on the fact that little boys and little girls generally are not equal at that age," he said in 1968. "It's also a parody on how society sometimes views the struggle that goes on between men and women and between different kinds of people."

From first (1952) to last (1999), each setup of the football encouraged Charlie Brown to one more act of determination and, ultimately, martyrdom. In the very last of the annually recurring setup—how will Lucy disappoint him this time?—Schulz took his creation into a new century by pulling the football away from Lucy . . . and from the reader himself:

WHEN HE TRIED NEW ideas for the strip on Jeannie, she was warmly appreciative. The school building that befriends Sally, sharing its thoughts and feelings, for example, took shape during the first summer of their marriage. He characterized the building as a world-weary old lag, one of the demimonde figures of the Minnesota neighborhood that had made Sparky—one of Carl's customers, or Billy DeBeck's denizens of the track. But, of course, it was Sparky himself, the older partner in the couple, wondering how he was going to get through to Monday:

In the series, as in so many strips of this halcyon period, his themes and jokes are about health, exercise, tennis, acupuncture; the viewer can feel the California glow of Jeannie and the mid-'70s and the new hope-fulness of their marriage: "You've changed my whole life," Sally tells the building, hugging its corner. The school, for a change, at least feels cared for: "I can't believe it. Somebody loves me!"

But, finally, the building became Jeannie. In the daily strip for October 24, Sally brings the unfairness of life and the misery of not being under-stood to her protector. She confides in it—Schulz reprises the sensitive theme of fingers "falling off"—and lets her head rest on the "shoulder" where concrete masonry meets brick. The building comforts Sally: "Poor, sweet baby." James Thurber had turned a house into a horrifying image of devouring womanhood. Schulz had transformed his peripatetic new wife into bricks and mortar, set firmly in place:

ONE SUMMER DAY IN 1975 he unburdened himself of his real feelings to a stranger.

Sparky was sitting at a picnic table overlooking the tennis courts in Howarth Park, on the east side of Santa Rosa, when a young man approached the water fountain alongside the table. Mark Doolittle was a trim, dark-haired twenty-six, Sparky a slender, silver-haired fifty-two.

Doolittle had just won a tournament match at Howarth Park and sat down to take a break. Sparky asked how his game had gone, saying that he had seen Doolittle's cannon serve and figured he would do well, and for the next few minutes they traded tennis palaver until it somehow came up that Doolittle was finishing his doctorate in clinical psychology at Berke-ley. At that, Sparky locked glances with an expression of "sincere, hopeful interest" and said, "So you have an interest in psychology?" Then, as Doo-little recalled it, "He got this twinkle in his eye. The minute he found that out, he was on an expedition."

Without any hesitation, he asked Doolittle what he knew about pho-

bia, and in such a way that the younger man knew the question was neither casual nor academic but rather serious and personal. So Doolittle
asked what sort of phobia this "waifish-looking older guy" was wondering
about, and Sparky explained that he had an overwhelming fear of traveling
away from his home, going out in the world and being around people, and
that this was making it very hard for him to function.

Up to this point, Doolittle had no idea that his interlocutor was
Charles Schulz, but as he began to ask about his life and work, and how
these fears had come to be, Sparky very matter-of-factly explained that he
was the cartoonist who drew *Peanuts*, and that his fame was bringing great
pressures to travel, socialize, leave the comforts of his home and studio. He
also told Doolittle about his divorce, which he characterized as "painful
and difficult," discussing "many conflicts during that process which ate at
him," and "spoke of his new wife in glowing but somewhat apprehensive
terms." Her outgoing nature attracted him, but he was uncertain if his
phobia would get in the way of their relationship.

As Schulz spoke about his wives, Doolittle saw the transition from
Joyce to Jeannie as "out of the depressing fire and into an exciting, anxiety-
producing frying pan." "He was frank about saying that he was hooked up
with a live wire," and told Doolittle with his covering laugh, "She won't
let me stay in the house!"

Lucy's outdoor, middle-of-anywhere psychiatric booth had sprung to
life, and after listening to Sparky for the better part of an hour, Doolittle
offered a summary of the standard current thinking on fears and phobias, as
well as clinical approaches to lessening them and some of the more inventive and creative responses. But more than this, Schulz wanted to know
how Doolittle handled his own fears, and would leave an indelible memory
of "how sincerely interested he was in comparing our experiences, despite
the difference in age and background."

It was this, as much as anything, that warned Doolittle that "something
was wrong here," the signals being unmistakable in the very way Schulz
had conducted this whole interaction: "Here's this man reeling from a
divorce, uncertain about his live-wire new wife, can't leave his house, says
he's shy and full of fears, but he isn't just curling up in a ball—here he is,
talking about all this in a public place."

The future Dr. Doolittle thus rendered Schulz a real service by challenging the concealed pride and resistance of the hurt and angry spirit he sensed behind Schulz's quiet, thoughtful front.

"So if you are so afraid, how did you get divorced, remarried? And how did you get here today?"

Doolittle had never heard a laugh such as the one that now burst from Schulz. "The bluntness of my youthful question somehow snuck past his reserve, and his comic sense of the absurd kicked in. There was a visible sense of relief on his face, not enough to erase the fact of his fear, but it suggested that there was far more to the story, and that the story up ahead could change, even if only a little, even if only for a short time, even if only in fits and starts."

They never spoke again. Whenever he later crossed paths with Dr. Doolittle in a social situation in Santa Rosa, Sparky just nodded in his quiet, careful way, no further connected to this stranger than to a donor from whose body he had been given the brokered blood of an emergency transfusion.

HE MARRIED TWO DYNAMIC, individualistic women. Joyce he tagged as restless, while Jeannie he termed energetic—"a suntanned package of energy 16 years his junior," as *People* labeled her in 1989. In fact, Joyce put in long hours at home and would be remembered by houseguests for her cream pies. Handy with a needle, she had sewn the first Snoopy costume, and knew her way around a sewing machine. Jeannie, who curiously combined the hectic and the serene, wanted to see every corner of the globe— "Nothing exists," she once said, "until I have seen it." Between 1973 and 1993, she traveled the world, most often with her children—China (1978), Australia (1979), Kenya (1980), Peru (1981), Russia (1983), Mexico (1986), Nepal (1987), Czechoslovakia (1991)—her friends describing her in these years as "hard to catch" and "nothing but vapor trails." While Sparky encouraged Jeannie on her way, he didn't understand her need to travel. "I'm getting where I don't even like to be home alone," he said in 1986, acknowledging that "it's really a problem," and that he had "done a couple of psychiatric sessions on it." At the same time, "he never wanted to hold me back," Jeannie recalled, "and he always had company."

But what was the exact trouble, now that he was happily remarried, now that his children were grown and starting out in careers and families of their own?

"I wonder," he reflected in a candid mood, "if I don't have a fear of being damaged by outside forces all the time—the things that I have no control over. I like a secure life of knowing what I'm going to do each day. I like coming to the studio and drawing and I don't like to have my life disturbed by sudden outside interruptions. It could spoil everything. Maybe, after five years of psychiatry, you might find that it would be simply a fear of death, I don't know."

Jeannie had a hard time understanding how he could get so queasy about her absences; after all, at those times, he was staying exactly where he wanted to be: at home. But when the prospect of his going away began to bring on the same dread, she could not understand why he didn't just cancel the trip outright, rather than "torture himself as the time got closer and then [feel] bad." When he accepted invitations to speak, he was "always very enthusiastic" when the invitations arrived. But then, as the date approached, as plans for the particular trip firmed up and phone calls from organizers began to light up the studio lines, the idea of breaking with his daily routine disoriented him. Anxiety about abandoning his drawing board mounted daily, and he grew increasingly resentful.

A visiting reporter who followed Schulz through his routines for a couple of days noticed, "The entire time I was there he was fretting over an upcoming trip to New York City. 'I have to go to New York soon,' he said as we whizzed through Santa Rosa streets in his butterscotch-colored Mercedes coupé. His voice is morose. 'I don't like to travel,' he goes on, pausing only to reply to a roller-skating teen-ager who yells, 'Hi, Sparky!' to the passing car. . . . Back in the car, he speaks again: 'I wish I didn't have to go to New York . . .' He sighs. 'I just want to stay here and draw.' Just before we left the next day he was still fretting and saying, 'How can I get out of going to New York?' "

His fear, as he explained it to Jeannie in 1973, "was that he would panic on the plane—that he would lose control, start screaming."

"I'm afraid you'll think less of me," he admitted, and she sympathized, saying, "A lot of times I didn't care if we were [going to take the planned trip] or not, but I hated him to have that feeling of embarrassment."

Sometimes, Jeannie was left feeling sharply disappointed. She had made plans for them to see people; she had gotten her hopes up about the place and the occasion. But it was hard for her to say so directly—she risked further entangling Sparky in his own guilt and resentment.

On a couple of trips, he tried Valium, which enabled him to fly to France in 1977, to revisit the ancient Château de Malvoisine, where he had been a young, frightened soldier, and again in 1978, to film a documentary about his personal memories of the war. "It enabled him to go, but I don't think he liked taking anything," recalled Jeannie, "and later on, he was very resistant: he didn't want to do it. His rationale was always, 'Why do I have to do things I don't want to do? Other people don't do things they don't want to do.' "

In 1978 he and Jeannie were staying with her aunt. Schulz woke up, disoriented, lost. What was he doing here in England, when all he wanted was to be home? What was England? How had he let himself get into this? "He woke me up," Jeannie recalled. "I got in bed with him. He was saying, 'I just can't stand it. I just can't stand it.' " Jeannie suggested that he try one of the Xanax that he had brought with him. He did, fell back asleep, and felt better in the morning.

On trips that had no overt business purpose, "Sparky's ploy was to get a lot of people to go. We never went anywhere alone. He invited all those people because then he would say: 'Well, I can't let *them* down.' Then, too, he was entertaining them, and having people around could change his mood." To research the third full-length *Peanuts* movie, *Race for Your Life, Charlie Brown*, he rode a rubber raft down Oregon's Rogue River in July 1975, putting himself in the hands of Jeannie, Lee Mendelson, and sixteen friends, the whole group laughing and humming the mantra "om" as they floated downriver in pouring rain.

By 1989, Schulz had come to recognize his father's behavior as agoraphobic: "He would never have guessed what he was feeling had a name, but I'm convinced that's what it was." Sparky's own anticipatory anxiety before most travel, the occasional instances of panic escalating into a full-blown attack, but most of all his attempts to grow out of phobic reactions that "came close to paralyzing him," as one of his assistants recalled, are all the more poignant for his attempting to go as far as he dared, without help. In 1999, he told Steve Kroft of *60 Minutes*, "I would love to be unanxious. And I don't know how to go about doing it. . . . But I would love to be a little more carefree. But I can't. . . . I have this awful feeling of impending doom."

It came over him, he reported in 1982, immediately on awakening: "a very disturbing quality. . . . I seem to be living with what you might call the feeling of impending doom. It may be something that could be attributed simply to the low blood sugar in the morning. I don't know. I hope that that's all it is. Maybe some electrical fault in my head, too. But when I wake up in the morning I wake up to a funeral-like atmosphere as if today is the day I'm attending the funeral. But once I get up and start moving around, I generally feel better. . . . I think activity is good for all of us when we have those kinds of feelings."

For several years he found real pleasure in taking dance lessons with Jeannie on the arena's mezzanine level, played hockey and golf in weekly rounds with his regular groups, and made annual pilgrimages to the Crosby golf tournament and to the Santa Barbara Writers Conference, held each June at the Miramar, a rambling Pacific coast resort with a campuslike atmosphere, where some 350 writers and aspirants gathered for a week of seminars. Run by the writer Barnaby Conrad and his wife, Mary, the conference featured a handful of master storytellers; Ray Bradbury almost always delivered the first Friday-evening lecture, and Schulz followed in the important Saturday-night slot. He stayed each year for just four of the seven days and enjoyed himself immensely, talking about books with writers, meeting admirers who recognized him as something more than a cartoonist, soaking up the applause for his annual speech, and proudly attending the workshops conducted by his writer son, Monte. One year he told his conference audience that he had "always hoped that [his own] love for books and for reading would filter on down to my five children." Only Monte, who by 1991 had staked his claim as a novelist with *Down by the River*, a crime story set in a California river town, fulfilled his wish for some intellectual companionship among those coming after him.

Trying to break the chronic hold of what he always described as his "melancholy," he found ways to make daytime business travel bearable: his son Craig, a licensed pilot, took on the job of commanding the small jet that Schulz had bought for business trips, relieving him, at least temporarily, of some anticipatory anxiety. But he found the core of his fears hard to explain. "All I know is that I don't really like going places." Or: "With me, it's almost a form of security that when everything else in life seems difficult and you have fears and anxieties and everything, I feel most at home sitting here in this room drawing these silly pictures." When his dread of travel intensified to the point where he was "forced to give up many wonderful opportunities," he felt ashamed and strove, as he put it, to be "more mature."

Whatever was bothering him, it did not keep him from his responsibilities. He functioned exceptionally well, astonishing his associates and friends with what he accomplished on any given day. As both he and they understood it, he was not depressed: he was unhappy, and for him, unhappiness was consciously seen as useful; unhappiness paid him a dividend that depression scarcely ever does. A depressive with a franchise like *Peanuts* at his disposal would have long since abandoned the demands of the drawing board and fallen back on the franchise. But for someone of his work capacity and intellectual curiosity—especially his capacity to do things with unhappiness itself—unhappiness became part of a strategy; indeed, it became his life:

"You could probably go to a psychologist and get some form of medication now to relieve you of these anxieties," suggested an interviewer.

"Yes, but that would take up Monday, wouldn't it? And then there's Tuesday, when you have to go have your teeth cleaned. And then you have to have the oil changed in your car on Wednesday. And then Thursday is a golf day, and we play hockey on—when am I going to draw the strip, you know?" And he laughed lightly. "So, that's the way my life is."

Asked in 1996 to name his greatest regret, Sparky had said, "I could have been more adventuresome." But he also recognized the restrictions of the disability for the gift they also gave him: "I don't think you can tie yourself down to a drawing table and a dedicated schedule and still be the sort who is running all over the world."

Agoraphobia, literally "fear of the marketplace," can now be defined, as Allen Shawn pictures it in *Wish I Could Be There: Notes from a Phobic Life*, as "a restriction of activities brought about by a fear of having panic symptoms in situations in which one is far from help or escape is perceived to be difficult." The condition's sources, though still disputed, are rooted in heredity and upbringing; among sufferers, writes Shawn, "imitation of a phobic parent is almost universally present."

Carl Schulz had taken refuge from his fears by being a burgher, a townsman. The arena on Steele Lane offered Sparky his one place to enjoy a community outside his hermetically sealed life as a cartoonist. The arena surrounded him with people of all ages. He hated the idea of being confined to his own age group "all day long every day," and took real pleasure in a variety of friendships in this happy village centered upon the ice.

At the arena, he surprised himself with moments of energetic silliness, and found warmth and gaiety trading good-natured insults with his senior hockey teammates over coffee at the Warm Puppy. "When he was in a good mood, he was funny as hell. He had the quickest wit," said Larry James, recalling that when bad moods struck, his male friends recognized "how hard he'd be to live with" and expressed sympathy for Jeannie, identifying her as "the best thing that ever happened to him." He enjoyed it when children approached him at his table for anything other than an autograph; even a short burst of conversation with a smart, engaging child made him feel better, more self-assured—they liked him! They called English muffins "Sparky toast."

At the arena, he sponsored and played in an annual senior hockey tournament in which, by 1989, he was hosting fifty-eight teams in five-year age brackets from forty to sixty-five ("It's one of these things that keeps getting bigger and bigger, and I can't let go of it"), and also found deep satisfaction in finding new and better ways to present family variety entertainment in two ice shows, one in July, one in December, the second of which had become a Sonoma County holiday tradition that drew as many as forty-one thousand people to its thirty-seven performances. For five out of fourteen years between 1986 and 1999 the shows were completely sold out, lines forming early in the day tickets went on sale and stretching around the arena.

Each year he attended rehearsals, offering suggestions on everything from sets to costumes, and working closely with choreographer Karen Kresge, even dreaming up a version of *War and Peace* on ice, as well as adaptations of *Henry V*, Ken Burns's *Civil War*, and a "Gatsby number" in the Christmas show of 1991 that featured Jill Schulz as Daisy, arriving on the ice in a vintage car. "He always taught me that you must give the audience moments," recalled Kresge. "You must give them laughter, you must give them a little poignancy, you must give them romance; maybe come close to a tear—certainly, lots of humor. And . . . when I create the shows, I find that they really do relate to the philosophy that's behind the comic strip."

The arena was a daily rush of energy, a fountain of youth, replenished each morning at five-thirty by mothers delivering young girls to the ice; a surge of flame pulsed through the gas jets that lit the fake log in the lava-rock fireplace of the Warm Puppy coffee shop as Sparky looked on from his table, like Degas watching the ballerinas.

"I'm where I want to be," he said about his table by the window at the Warm Puppy. "I don't want to be anyplace else. So I'm perfectly content to come here. I love going to the arena in the morning, having an English muffin, a cup of coffee, reading the paper and talking to my friends. I look forward to that every day. And I resent it when these moments out of the week are taken from me."

He spoke in much the same way about his split-level workshop in the studio around the corner: "This is my ship, and I have my own captain's quarters here, and I have the people that I like [administrative staff] outside, and over at the arena and everything, and yet it's all on my terms. I can go home anytime I want to and I can do anything I want to."

IN OCTOBER 1980, HE and Jeannie finally shifted to Upper Ridge Road, three years after buying the land, high in the foothills above Santa Rosa, where they built a multilevel hillside house on a spot so magical, as Jeannie told it, the place could "be both in the clouds and above them." On radiant weekend mornings in the new house, she later recalled how they would "lie in bed with that beautiful view and talk about philosophy and life."

Then, on July 1, 1981, Sparky awakened with a strange tight feeling in his chest. At first, he attributed it to having slept crooked during the night. As he dressed and then went into the kitchen, the feeling persisted, and he mentioned it to Jeannie and a houseguest; both were optimistic that he would feel better once he got going, but driving down out of the foothills into Santa Rosa, he almost turned around—the strange tightness wouldn't go away. A few deep breaths seemed to help, however, and he went on driving. At the studio, he tried to begin work, but as he sat at the drawing board, the tightness began again. He called Dr. Lundborg whose nurse said he should come over immediately. A few quick tests convinced Lundborg to call a cardiologist, who ordered Schulz directly to the hospital.

The morning's tests showed that one of his arteries was completely closed and others were 50 to 90 percent blocked. Surgery was recommended, and Lundborg told him that he must make a decision: undergo a quadruple bypass operation or give up ice hockey, golf, tennis, and all the activities that he enjoyed.

For a month he debated, finally deciding that this was the only way for him to get back to normal. And so, having built up a two-month lead on his deadline, he submitted to the knife, entering Santa Rosa Memorial Hospital on the afternoon of September 1. The operation was scheduled for eight the next morning; Jeannie helped settle him in his room and went home that evening at ten o'clock.

As soon as she was gone, he panicked: "Suddenly everybody had left and I was lying there alone in the room knowing what I was going to face and thinking, you know, I really don't have to go through with this. This is still just my own idea. I could work this out and go home and just take the medication and live a very mild life, and not play hockey anymore or tennis or anything, and just do my work and probably survive quite well. I wonder what would happen if I just got in my clothes and ducked out. But, no. I thought I'd make a total fool out of myself, disgrace my family, and I just can't do it. So I kind of put it all out of my mind and settled back. And I suppose pretty soon a nurse came in and asked me if I wanted anything. And now I'm glad I didn't do anything, but I came close to it."

After surgery, he spent eight days in Room 233 at the hospital. The operation left him with pronounced tremors in his drawing hand, but on the fourth night he picked up a felt-tip pen left on his nightstand by a nurse who had asked him to draw something on the blank wall opposite his bed before he went home. He had disliked the suggestion ("I am not one who goes around drawing pictures on the wall"), but now, in the quiet of the evening, with Jeannie reading the newspaper beside the bed, it suddenly came to him, and he got up and went to the wall and straightaway drew a sequence in which Snoopy struggles postoperatively to regain his lung power by making three balls rise to the top of a spirometer before collapsing in exhaustion and triumph.

His sense of audience was as acute as ever ("All patients could identify with this frustrating exercise, devised to keep the lungs clear and get them back to good working order"), but as always it was the return to the two-dimensional world that restored his power, and as the thick black lines looped across the blank white wall, he had a passing fear—*Drawing on walls: I better get it right*—but the pen felt strong in his hand, and when the five sequential poses had come out to his satisfaction, he got back into bed, looked at what he had done, and said to himself, "Maybe, somehow, drawing cartoons really was what I was meant to do."

# CHAPTER 26

# PLUSH

*I've decided to be a very rich and famous person who doesn't really care about money, and who is very humble but who still makes a lot of money and is very famous, but is very humble and rich and famous.*

—LINUS

PEANUTS was now a merchant empire, spreading tens of millions of plush Snoopys the world over, from Argentina to Zimbabwe, Congo to Togo, Norway to New Zealand, Cameroon to Canada, growing fastest in Europe, Latin America, and the Far East, where Japanese companies ended up owning 40 percent of all worldwide licensing agreements, and for which the syndicate mapped an expansion campaign in April 1985, marshaling its forces to establish a "country plan (on paper) and go after China as a *market*."

Domestic sales briefly dipped in the 1980s, but it scarcely mattered. *Peanuts* was now so many things to so many people—an "ongoing parable of contemporary American existence," a "distillation of modern childhood," a "comic opera," a "personal work," and at the same time a "universal language," and there were so many commercial markets in which to quantify *Peanuts'* success: as a daily and Sunday comic featured in a world-record number of newspapers; as the longest-running animated Christmas special on television; as the most-produced musical in the history of the American theater, with more than forty thousand productions of *You're a Good Man, Charlie Brown* (some 240,000 performers had played Schulz's characters and the show had trained a generation of actors—every actor in the country, it seemed, had at one point early in his or her career played Charlie Brown or Snoopy, Linus or Lucy); as a jazz album of show business standards; as best-selling books, both original and reprinting the strip; as advertising for cameras, cars, cupcakes, and life insurance in an ever-expanding fan of media, including hot-air blimps; and, not least, as an internationally renowned brand of character merchandise with more than twenty thousand officially licensed products and countless pirated knock-offs—there seemed no end to it.

By 1989, annual revenues from *Peanuts'* global worldwide merchandising empire topped $1 billion. Over the next dozen years, the brand name appeared on over one hundred million packages of consumer goods annually, and Schulz split with the syndicate a 5 to 10 percent royalty on the wholesale price of every item. This ranked him among the nation's highest-paid entertainers, topped only by the pop singer Michael Jackson, the movie director and producer Steven Spielberg, the prizefighter Mike Tyson, the talk-show host Oprah Winfrey, and the comic Bill Cosby. When Sparky introduced himself to a stranger, he no longer mentioned Charlie Brown or *Peanuts,* instead saying, "I'm the person that draws Snoopy."

The character whom Schulz once described as the most adorable in his strip—but who at the same time was "not to be trusted"—now was universally embraced. On every continent Snoopy made *Peanuts* second only to Disney in the sale of merchandise: clothing (30 percent of sales), books (15 percent), toys and accessories (15 percent), greeting cards and other *Peanuts* items (40 percent). Schulz proudly informed visitors, "He is the most recognized character in the world, much more so than Mickey Mouse." An oval, a smiling mouth, a pair of lopsided ears, and two jelly-bean eyes were all that was required for most people anywhere, of any age down to three, to respond "Snoopy."

As the undisputed totem of the *Peanuts* brand—"less a brand than a U.S. government seal of approval," said one critic—Snoopy had so thoroughly replaced "Good ol' Charlie Brown" as the top-billed *Peanuts* character that his name now led the inventory of Schulz's creations in all legal documents protecting the property. Snoopy appeared high on any list of all-American icons alongside Mount Rushmore, baseball, the Big Mac, and the Grand Ole Opry—a final ratification of the young Charles Schulz's acute sensitivity, as first expressed in his high school art teacher Miss Paro's triplicates, to symbols that speak for American values.

Even as Schulz led Snoopy into new strip situations, often by way of such sports as were emerging into wide popularity in the 1960s, '70s, and '80s—surfing, skiing, figure skating, tennis, golf, ice hockey—each new incarnation spun off its own line of merchandise, drawing specialty consumers deeper within an ever-expanding catalog of products. "Versatility is the key," Sparky had come to learn about the power of his brand.

When Snoopy appeared on national prime-time television in January 1985 as a "spokescharacter" for Metropolitan Life Insurance Company, followed in February with the first of innumerable print ads in an enormously popular $30 million campaign ("Get Met. It pays") everyone's favorite all-arounder became an advertising icon as familiar as Prudential's rock and Allstate's hands. And not just the beagle; by signing up the whole *Peanuts* gang, Met Life could advertise its business insurance (Lucy's psychiatric booth), home owner's coverage (Woodstock's nest), and group insurance (Charlie Brown's All Stars) in ads slated to last well into the next century.

Sparky's income rose from $4 million in 1975 to $12 million by 1980, soaring to $62 million in 1989 and settling into an annual flow of between $26 and $40 million over the following ten years—sums of such incomparable magnitude that on one New Year's Eve in the '80s, Schulz's old friend from Art Instruction, George Letness, the former "Bureau's top drawer," calculated that by twelve minutes after midnight Sparky had already made more money than he would make the rest of the year.

He had achieved a stunning autonomy, becoming something so dif-

ferent from any cartoonist who had gone before him that he was now saddled with the additional job of having to rationalize what had happened to him. Upon meeting Patrick McDonnell, his favorite among the new, young, thinking-person's cartoonists, he shrugged at the absurdity of it all: "Do you know anyone else who owns two Zambonis?" For that matter, what other cartoonist had ever seen his characters speak in Arabic, Basque, Catalan, Latin, Malay, Serbo-Croatian, Tlingit, Welsh, and a dozen and a half more languages? And since *Peanuts'* homely annual patterns would never end—Lucy had snatched away the football with the regularity of the sumacs changing color in New England, Schroeder had been celebrating Beethoven's birthday every December 16, Snoopy strained the mails every Valentine's Day, Charlie Brown had yet to win a baseball game on the Fourth of July, and yet one more chill Halloween night found Linus waiting in the pumpkin patch for the Great Pumpkin—the reader, or viewer, or all-purpose consumer could endlessly put his own embroideries on them.

In *Peanuts*, the atmosphere of unfulfilled dreams that Schulz was coaxing from his own heart freed the onlooker of any age or race or nationality to try to fill the same spot in his or her own emptiness. For the average child beset by midnight terrors, Snoopy on the doghouse became Snoopy on the night-light and Snoopy in the hospital ("When I was about eleven years old I had to go into the hospital and I was very scared," wrote a fan. "My mother had to leave me after visiting hours, but my stuffed Snoopy didn't. I held it all night long")—even, ultimately, Snoopy on the tombstone: in one case, a cutout of the beagle was seen hastily propped against a young father's grave like a kindly guide into the underworld; in another, a mother and father who had lost their daughter to cancer asked for and immediately received the cartoonist's permission to have Snoopy's image chiseled onto her grave.

Little could Dena Schulz have known when she reached back into her Norwegian childhood that the endearment "Snupi," later recast by her son's pen into a cartoon and followed on by an industry of subsidiaries, would become a global symbol, a mascot, a name for everything from spacecraft to pets with strong personalities or high intelligence or for any animal who seemed to act human.

AS THE CREATOR OF the most widely syndicated cartoon on the planet, read by 5 percent of the world's literate population and watched in animated television specials by more than 4.4 billion viewers over the previous twenty-five years, Sparky could have maintained his presence at the top just by hiring a team of assistants to ring changes on his themes, but instead he made a strict point of getting himself to the drawing board every morning and consciously striving to be a better cartoonist.

He still wanted *Peanuts* to be everyone's favorite strip, still regarded the comics pages as a competitive arena where, as he saw it, "each cartoonist fights for attention." He read his rivals' strips "the way all cartoonists do, looking to see if they won, if they beat everyone else that day," recalled the cartoonist Cathy Guisewite, who once watched Schulz study the Sunday funnies in the *San Francisco Chronicle*. "He liked to win on the page."

It was not enough that he had "revolutionized the art form, deepening it, filling it with possibility, giving permission to all who followed to write from the heart and intellect," as Garry Trudeau pointed out. It did not matter that he achieved a success of dreamlike dimensions, or that *Peanuts* had been the most popular comic for years in newspaper readers' polls. Sparky had to get the better of everyone else on the comics page every day. "In the thing that I do best, which is drawing a comic strip, it is important to me that I win."

In January 1978, United Feature Syndicate's outgoing president William C. Payette (who had succeeded Schulz's great mentor Larry Rutman in 1969) accepted a new strip about a fat, mean-eyed cat with an appetite for lasagna, and on June 19, 1978, with United Feature Syndicate now consolidated with Newspaper Enterprise Association under an umbrella company called United Media Enterprises, the new chief executive, Robert Roy Metz, unveiled *Garfield*, which made its intentions clear at once. "Our only thought is to entertain you," declared the strip's main human character, the cat owner Jon Arbuckle. "Feed me" was Garfield's last-word rejoinder. Clearly, this cartoonist had taken Schulz's simplicity as his guide, and in *Garfield*'s first week, the young midwesterner Jim Davis proclaimed his homage when the cat curled up and reflected, "Happiness is a warm television set."

It proved to be one of the most successful launches in comic strip history. As Schulz had done thirty years earlier, deliberately fashioning *Li'l Folks* from the marketable children he had developed in one-off cartoons for *The Saturday Evening Post*, Davis, a thirty-three-year-old Hoosier who had cut his teeth as assistant on the popular *Tumbleweeds* strip, had made "a conscious effort to come up with a good, marketable character." Within two years, Davis was vaulted to national attention when his first collection, *Garfield at Large*, held out as number one paperback best seller on the *New York Times* list for nearly two years. As time went on, Davis ever more consciously took more than Schulz's artistic success as his model—the *Peanuts* licensing program had become "a template that I could apply to *Garfield*."

At first Schulz and Davis shared an editor at the syndicate, Roberta "Bobby" Miller, who recalled that whenever Sparky telephoned he would find a new way to "bring up Jim without bringing him up. . . . He would ask how many papers Jim had now, and he never believed it. Jim was rivaling him, paper for paper." By 1982, *Garfield* had the emblematic one thousand subscribers that it had taken *Peanuts* twenty years to attain. In 1983, a record-setting seven *Garfield* titles appeared simultaneously on the *Times* best-seller list; so far, *Garfield* books have sold more than 130 million copies—a third fewer than *Peanuts* to date—and by then Garfield had stormed the cover of *People* and was appearing in 1,400 newspapers in twenty-two countries. The next year, the fat cat was a full-fledged nationwide fad, pushing Snoopy out of Macy's Thanksgiving Day parade.

*Garfield* let loose the insecurities that lay behind Schulz's competitiveness. "Sparky had been king of the mountain and suddenly he had a competitor," recalled one syndicate executive. He had a competitor at home only. Taking final domestic sales figures for 1985, we can see that *Garfield*, with receipts of $6,486,838, was edging up on *Peanuts*, at $8,036,464. In the global marketplace, however, it was still no contest: *Peanuts*, a whopping $12,053,409; *Garfield*, a mere $1,526,843.

*Garfield*, with $8.3 million in sales overall, was already far ahead of *his* nearest competitor at United Media—*Robotman*, with far more average annual receipts of $81,466—but *Garfield* was not about to supplant a $20.2 million champion like *Peanuts*. As a comic strip, *Garfield* also had a much narrower range than *Peanuts*; whereas Schulz swung between the intellectual and the warm and cuddly, Jim Davis was uniformly middlebrow. The humor of *Garfield* had no concealing subtleties; it was plainly aggressive, with a clear edge of malice. *Garfield* took no consideration of real human pain; Davis's character Jon was so obtuse as not to register his multiple rejections, so no tragedy lay in his predictably endless humiliations at the hands of his dates. Above all, the drawing was crude, empty; Schulz took every opportunity in private to belittle Davis as a cartoonist. Davis's smug cat celebrated laziness and cynicism, and Sparky loathed it: Garfield, he often said in private, was the "ugliest, most insulting, and vicious" character he had ever seen.

To Davis, meanwhile, Schulz was a fatherly presence and an artistic conscience at the drawing board—"kind of like having Dad there," said Davis. "It would have meant a lot to Davis, especially now that they were both with the same syndicate, to have some sign of Sparky's approval," recalled the syndicate's president, Bob Metz. But Schulz remained stingy—the best he could manage was to give Davis tips on how to draw Garfield's feet—and when the syndicate let him know that *Peanuts* and *Garfield* would soon be sharing more than an editor— the salespeople who had once devoted their exclusive energies to selling Schulz's strip would now be turning their attention to Jim Davis's work—he didn't just bristle, he was genuinely troubled.

With domestic sales figures for *Peanuts* reprint books and licensed merchandise leveling off in 1985, both the strip and the brand needed to be revitalized in the United States. Syndication was flat; editors at big-city newspapers were taking the strip off the front pages of their comics sections, no longer treating it as a major property, shrinking it from half to a third of a page and stuffing it inside, or dropping it altogether. The syndicate had not put any real salesmanship into the property for years; it had forgotten how to sell Charlie Brown and his friends in their own country.

By 1987, nationwide comic strip polls showed that Snoopy and Charlie Brown tied for first place as the favorite comic strip/cartoon characters among all American comics readers, but among teenagers Snoopy for the first time ranked behind Garfield as the favorite. Snoopy and Charlie Brown shared the number one slot among girls ages six to seventeen, and Charlie Brown ranked number one as the most popular cartoon/comic strip character among adults over fifty.

Schulz had reason to be suspicious of the syndicate. Under their old four-times-amended agreement, the latest iteration of which dated back to 1959, United Feature was the absolute owner of copyrights and trademarks relating to the strip. But in October 1974, Schulz had decided that, after twenty-five years, he wanted all *Peanuts* copyrights and trademarks put under his name exclusively. He also wanted the right to final approval of all future *Peanuts* licenses and to have complete editorial control over the feature.

Syndicate president William C. Payette and the E. W. Scripps attorneys objected to his terms. Payette, tall—six feet, four—and authoritarian in manner, considered cartoonists little more than spoiled children, and he held out during initial discussions of Schulz's latest demands, unable to understand what was bothering Sparky when he was making more money than any other cartoonist in history. "Yeah, but I *earn* more, I've done more," countered Schulz.

Frustrated, Payette sent out his associate, George Downing, to reason with the "greedy" cartoonist.

"How old are you?" asked Sparky.

"Well, I'm fifty-seven," replied Downing.

"You know, all my life I've been pushed around by your kind," said Sparky, "and I've been told, you have to do this, you can't do that, and all that—well, no more. From now on, I control the licensing myself and what I say goes. . . . I don't want more money, I just want control so you guys can't ruin it. I want to own this thing. I'm tired of you selling Charlie Brown razor blades in Germany without telling me. I want to be able to do what I want to do. So either I get my way—exactly what I want—or I'm going to quit."

In 1977, as negotiations deadlocked, Payette made clandestine arrangements for the veteran backup cartoonist Alfred J. Plastino to draw several months of *Peanuts* Sunday strips and dailies against the day that Schulz refused to sign a new contract. Plastino discovered that he liked drawing *Peanuts* as well as or better than superheroes and had just "started to enjoy it," when the contract was settled and the experiment was shut down. Although Payette had no further need of the backup strips, he stashed Plastino's work in a big safe in the syndicate offices on Park Avenue, where they were meant to remain a secret; word of their existence circulated for years at United Media, hovering between rumor and urban legend, and when at last one of Sparky's editors came across them, she was horrified by their quality, later pronouncing them "ghastly, absolutely third-rate."

When Sparky learned about Payette's betrayal several years later from an editor at the syndicate, he pretended to take the whole thing in his stride, saying that "it's disappointing that somebody thinks that it's that easy" and that he "couldn't believe Bill Payette would be so dumb," but that was the word he had applied to the teachers in St. Paul who had not understood his true value. Underneath he was deeply wounded.

But Sparky came out the winner of the Plastino debacle, the *Garfield* wars, and the contract fight. Soothed by the higher purpose and greater diplomacy of Payette's successor, Robert Metz, who took over in June 1978, Sparky made an ally of the former newspaperman, and in the end, with 61 percent of its $84.9 million in revenues coming from *Peanuts* comics, TV shows, and merchandise licensing, United Media had to concede that the strip was his creation. By 1980, everyone involved in negotiations between cartoonist and syndicate had resolved that Sparky deserved to control the future of the strip and that in the event of his death or disability no successor would be appointed.

WITH THE SALE OF *Peanuts* to its two-thousandth newspaper (in Needles, California) in 1983, Schulz had no equal. The only modern cartoonist given a retrospective at the Louvre, he was now in a class by himself. His characters could go from being pitchmen for cars and life insurance, their huge heads and tiny bodies stretched across blimps at golf tournaments, to being the inspiration for a *Peanuts* concerto by contemporary composer Ellen Taaffe Zwilich, which premiered at Carnegie Hall.

When an interviewer confronted him with a straightforward summary of his great good fortune, he replied, "Have I had enormous success?
Do you think so?" When a trusted friend told him that he loved him, he
responded, "You do?" His reaction to a simple, uncomplicated hug from a
daughter was genuine surprise. "Innumerable times all through our marriage," recalled Jean Schulz, "I'd come up to him and kiss him on the forehead, cheek, hand, shoulder; he didn't make a big thing of it, but I know
he liked it, and if I'd say, 'I love you,' he'd say, playfully, 'Me?' "

Anyone who worked closely with Schulz came to understand the contradictory nature of his personality, for in truth he was neither excessively
needy nor stingy—he was something else. Dale Hale, his assistant from
Coffee Lane days, remarked: "If you really loved him and you said 'I really
love you,' he wouldn't believe you. He'd think 'Why?' " Since Sparky did
not believe that people really loved *him*, he felt no need to reciprocate.
"That was the maddening thing about him," said the cartoonist Cathy
Guisewite, who briefly became a protégé of Schulz's in these years. "You
never felt like anything you said or did would ever make him feel really
loved."

How much was his own mother in his thinking in these years? His
children remembered him talking about her constantly; his first biographer
recalled that he "did get misty-eyed" when he spoke about Dena. "He
would choke up when he thought about his parents. He had made them
into almost mythical people by the time I talked to him, and would talk
about how popular his father was. He was so impressed by his father's daily
routine and perseverance in the barbershop."

Crowding sixty, he was suddenly greedy, as a child is greedy, for his
parents. His wishes were a child's wishes: he wanted to have them back.

He did not want *his children* to be children again. *He* wanted to go back to being a child—the only child. He talked more and more often about wanting to be in the backseat of the car while his parents were driving home. "There are times when I would like to go back to the years with my mother and father—the times when I could have them bear all my worries."

He had articulated this wish before on a Sunday in August 1972—the month he moved out of the house on Chalk Hill Road:

Almost everyone who knew Schulz in his later years felt the need to protect him. Jeannie had shielded him from the very start. Cathy Guisewite recalled how Sparky had "made us want to put our arms around him and tell him everything was okay. That he wasn't really that big of a failure." "You always felt like protecting him," recalled Edna Poehner, his administrative assistant and Jeannie's sister-in-law, "even when he made you mad." The men on his every-Tuesday-night hockey team "were very protective of him," always playing with the idea that "you don't hit this man."

Tracey, listening to him talk by the hour about his childhood, had never been convinced that his mother had loved him. Those to whom he drew close in these last two decades watched as, before their eyes, he became a boy once more, unfulfilled, uncertain—the very boy who had feared in his deepest heart that his mother would get off the streetcar and forget him and let him go on alone. People who met him for only a few minutes felt it, too: "We talked about a range of things, including books," one woman remembered, "and I left feeling very honored and moved, but saddened, too, by the sadness this man who had made legions of people happy clearly felt."

A reporter in Santa Rosa recalled, "There are people who go through life thinking everyone else has a bigger piece of the pie than they do, and Mr. Schulz was the only person I ever met who felt he had no piece of the pie at all. He was just so vulnerable in a querulous way. He seemed always to be saying, 'Please be my mom, please understand, please take care of me.' "

Of all the themes of his life that remained unresolved, none gave him greater personal difficulty or more long-lasting professional success than loneliness—"aloneness," as he himself referred to the side of his character that seemed incomplete. In *Peanuts*, he called it "deep-down, black, bottom-of-the-well, no-hope, end-of-the-world, what's-the-use loneliness." And from it he drew the profoundest themes in the strip. In life, he rarely spoke of it, and tried to rise above it, most often with charm and humor and a measure of hard-won wisdom. "The difference between how he spoke of it and the impact it had on him was profound," recalled Cathy Guisewite. "I tried to have a conversation about it, but he wouldn't go there at all. He needed to keep it as a surface kind of experience."

To the novelist Laurie Colwin, with whom he spent several days in Santa Rosa, in May 1982, examining his feelings, to the furthest extent of his wish to enter into analytic review of his life, he admitted, "I've been alone so much in my life."

"That's an odd remark for someone with five children," she observed, and he tried to slip away—"No, this was before five children"—but Colwin rightly pointed out that by 1982, he had been a father for the greater part of his life. However, he would not ponder his sense of loneliness. Once again he deflected the freshness and truth of Colwin's observation by resorting to a set-piece statement of his own that by now he had lived longer with his children than his mother had lived with him. And there—after insisting once more that he had been "alone a lot when I was small," but

without seeking to understand that early sense of alienation and deprivation, even with his mother always close by—he let the matter drop.

From childhood on, and especially in the hurtful years of his mother's
dying, the atmosphere of things left unsaid had been a dominant influence
on his evolution as a comic strip artist. "It is difficult to talk about what
I do, because I do it so I don't have to talk about it," Sparky told Peter
Joseph in 1972. "If I talked about the things that I draw, I'd probably be
a lecturer or a novelist, but I draw comic strips because somehow I have
feelings way in the back of my mind that come out in little pictures and in
funny little sayings."

"I know what it is to have to spend days, evenings, and weekends by
myself," he reflected in 1975, "and I also know how uncomfortable anxiety can be. I worry about almost all there is in life to worry about . . ."

On a trip to Half Moon Bay with Jeannie, he explained away a sharp
drop in his mood by saying, "I just feel strange. I don't mean it as any insult
to you, but I feel lonely. I just have this lonely feeling."

It kept recurring, no matter how well loved he was, no matter how
often he attempted a fresh start.

# CHAPTER 27

# STILL LOOKING

*Here I am again . . . still looking for the answers!*
—PEANUTS

AS HE TURNED SEVENTY, Sparky noticed that his relationships with women had changed. For one thing, his lifelong wish ("I'd like to be somebody that would be instantly attractive to women") had at last come true. Women adored him, found him attractive, loved being with him. To his great surprise, he found that he got along with such admirers with greater ease than at any other time of his life. "I enjoy talking with them and I have lunch quite frequently over at the arena with different ladies, whether it's an interview or just somebody who likes to ice skate. I enjoy that."

He had always been a capital-R Romantic, but now he no longer had to try so hard to impress, and, as with the art of conversation, he had acquired the art of flirtation. "In the same way that Archie Leach became Cary Grant, Sparky became the person he always wanted to be," said Amy Lago, who became, at thirty-two, his editor at the syndicate in 1994. "Sparky was very good at flirting."

"Sparky could make you feel like a princess," said Lynn Johnston, who had immediately preceded Amy Lago as Sparky's latest light romance, although, as Jeannie pointed out, with great good humor, "He really didn't have one at a time—he was an 'equal opportunity' person." Jeannie saw these multiplex interests for what they were, later remarking that for Sparky "it was all performance and play," and "none of it detracted from his love or attention to me."

"Sparky fell in love with every girl," recalled Judy Schwomeyer Sladky, the champion skater who had made a career of costumed appearances as Snoopy. "If they were blonde and pretty or cute he would just fall in love with them and stay in love with them—to the point where I almost considered Jeannie a saint." Schulz had a playful relationship with Judy in which, as Snoopy, she played the part of his sidekick. Walking around together, he would confide in her about women he found attractive. "As his dog I would hear him say to me: 'Isn't she gorgeous?' It was safe."

One of his techniques was to say, "Nobody likes me." To which the woman involved would usually say, "Sparky, what do you mean nobody likes you?" And he would then enumerate a lifetime of rejections, finally eliciting from his new friend: "Well, I like you . . ." And that would start him off.

"He had this absolutely old-world charm," recalled Johnston, "the kind of thing that you see in a Shakespearean film where the courtesy and the choice of words were nothing short of charming. He was like that: he could say little things in a manner that made you feel romanced."

Into his seventies, he grew more confident and better-looking, with an imposing physical presence that filled the driver's seat of his big Mercedes, his broad shoulders set off by a rainbow array of well-made, often expensive, sweaters as he drove to work. "A lot of people shrink as they age, and he didn't at all," observed his friend Mollie Boice. "He had the most amazing carriage." At Reuben awards dinners, he was seigneurial in a dinner jacket, pointed up by hair now as white as his smile, his latest honor on a brightly colored ribbon at his throat.

In everyday life, too, he appeared handsomer than he ever had before, but of course he did not believe it. "How I liked his face," Federico Fellini wrote to Jeannie after meeting the Schulzes in 1992. "It's the face of an aristocrat: trustworthy, the ideal friend. I imagine he's often been offered to take part in some movie, in the parts that once belonged to Leslie Howard." Turning away the compliments evoked by one appearance on national television, he expressed surprise at people liking his looks: "I've never looked attractive for a moment in my entire life." His syndicate editor realized that he "had no idea how photogenic he was—he still had an image of himself as awkward and unattractive." Even when at his most graceful—on the golf course, where his stepdaughter one day in 1986 told him how good he looked—he replied, "No, I look like an old man."

His first grandchild was born September 1, 1974, and when he went to visit Meredith and the baby in the hospital and learned that she named the little girl for his mother (with Jill's middle name)—Dena Marie Fredericksen—"he got real soft. His eyes started to well up, and he said,

'Thank you.' " In the aftermath of heart surgery, when he found real savor in his children's lives, his first grandson, Craig and Judy's child, Bryan, born on October 25, 1981, reminded Schulz of the newborn Monte. Two years later, Amy delivered Stephanie Anne Johnson on October 16, 1983; although Sparky had known Amy to be a single-minded, acutely sensitive, often anxious teenager (at seventeen she had declared in a school report that her biggest fear in life was the obligations of motherhood), Sparky looked on amazed as over the next thirteen years, Amy and her husband, John, brought nine children into the world, the first seven of whom were colicky as babies. And as Stephanie, Brian, Chuck, Melissa, Emily, Marci, Michael, Heidi, and Daniel each grew out of hollering infancy, Amy presented her brood on visits to Santa Rosa, where her father was "pretty short with my kids—he didn't want anything to go wrong—but he was a great grandfather for an hour, drawing Snoopys and playing blocks."

The inescapable experience of Sparky as a grandfather signaled a shift in the strip. For the first time, he acknowledged the passage of time when Charlie Brown began telling the stories of a "grandfather" whose concerns about aging and whose generational memory could only be Schulz's. In 1954, Charlie Brown's grandfather remembered dunking the girls' pigtails into the school-desk inkwells. In 1979, he considered that the smartest thing he ever did was *not* to have followed 1960s fashions and bought a Nehru jacket. By 1986 Linus has a great-grandfather whose chief characteristic is borrowed from Schulz's childhood in the 1930s:

Aging—the body's slowing—had troubled him since his late forties. In the army he had taken great pride "at being able to run forever," and so when a grounder zipped past him in a pickup game in the late '70s, it struck home hard: "Suddenly I realized that I could not bend as fast as I could have done even five years before that." In the early '80s he tried to play softball with the arena's team, composed mainly of twenty-somethings. Now the ball not only zoomed by him, it was also out of focus: he could no longer follow the flight of an infield fly. "And so," he related afterward, "I gave up. It was a setback. I don't enjoy that sort of thing."

The surest sign of aging showed in his feelings for his children. "It upsets me [that] the kids have to grow up and be so big," he lamented after they started lives of their own. "Once they become adults, it's like they've died." He had resisted holding his children in his embrace when they were young, but now that they were pulling away to start families of their own, his arms opened after his departing offspring. "I think it was very difficult for me to face up to their leaving," he said later.

With his children, he was often fun and silly (signing off after visits with his trademark "chipmunk wave"—hand under chin, knuckles up, fingers wiggling), correct and courteous, considerate and kind, amusing and witty: "Each one of us will tell you that our dad was wonderful company at every stage of our lives," said Monte. "He was such a fun dad to have." But now, Schulz admitted in 1987, he "somehow felt left out."

"It's a little sad when you see that you have drifted away," he reflected. "When I used to get together with the kids, even in their early twenties, we had them all up to the house, laughing, joking, and I always felt part of the whole thing. But a couple of years ago I had them up and now almost all of them are married, some had kids, and suddenly I realized that I was out of it. Now I'm a grandfather; they all had their own conversations about their own married lives and their own kids and babies and things. That was a little depressing. But you have to make your own life. I think one of the great tragedies is to become a burden to your kids."

On his bad days, he grumped that life was passing him by. "He hated getting older," recalled his stepson. "He didn't think it was fair. He used that word"—but not as a lament for the human condition so much as a reflection of his apparent belief that he had somehow been granted a special out.

Aging became a source of friction between himself and his friend and younger peer Lynn Johnston, whose power and success was now such that by 1999 For Better or For Worse was winning readers' polls. "She always beats me. But I like her anyway," Sparky told reporters. And he firmly kept the upper hand: when Lynn reached another milestone—1,600 papers—he congratulated her, but when she said, "Yep, I'm catching up to you," he replied, "Call me when you're in the Louvre."

At the start of their friendship, he had acted as mentor, telephoning her at home in North Bay, Ontario, to tell her that he liked her work. *For Better or For Worse* had debuted in 1979 and was well on its way to the top of the comics pages when they finally met at the 1986 Reubens award ceremony, where she became, at thirty-eight, the first woman and first Canadian to win the profession's highest honor.

Johnston later recalled the grace and grandeur of Schulz's presence when she met him—his "regal" bearing impressed her. "I was charmed because he was the dad I never had, the teacher who approved. He was handsome. He was a hero. He was funny."

A number of factors drew them instantly together. They "recognized each other as The Best," observed the editorial cartoonist Herbert Block. They also saw mirror images in each other: "When he smiled his full smile, I could see my own smile in his face, as if we were related. We have the same dentition," said Lynn, whose husband, Rod Johnston, is a dentist. They felt as if they had already known each other a long time and found themselves telling each other things they would normally have kept inside.

"Drawing has saved my sanity and meant more to me in my life than most things," Lynn wrote Sparky. "If I couldn't draw, it would be devastating." Both "had no self-confidence," as Lynn put it, "even though I had tremendous self-confidence." Both had had mothers from whom it was hard to get a hug. Both grew up in households in which, as Lynn recalled, "If you were angry you didn't talk about it." Both had suffered from bullying. Both knew that their strips set a new standard for their peers. Both saw themselves triumphing over the doubters and deprecators in their childhood; each had declared, "Someday I'm going to show everybody." Both had been divorced and remarried: the first marriage, painful and mismatched; the second, untroubled. Both succeeded beyond their dreams and both drew in later years against illnesses, with shaking hands.

Both were romantics at heart. During the first years of their friendship, Sparky would telephone every couple of weeks on a Tuesday during their studio hours, and without even saying hello, he would sing Lynn the first line of an Oscar Hammerstein song: "Why do I love you? Why do you love me?" To which she would reply, "Why should there be two, happy as we?" Although, once, when he tried out "Kiss me once and kiss me twice and kiss me once again," she carried the next line—"It's been a long, long time"—only to hear him stop short and say, "Darn! You got that one!" as if humorous competition was what this was really all about.

"Know what I really love?" Lynn wrote Sparky after one of their early visits. "It's the rare and fleeting times we sit and actually talk about drawing!" They both understood—beyond words—that the images in comics grew in force when "the pen wasn't just an extension of the hand and that the pressure on the paper wasn't just a means of transferring ink to board, but our way of actually touching the character . . ."

At the outset, Johnston's feelings for Schulz were akin, she maintained, to "the kind of crush you would have on your first-grade teacher: this is my teacher and my teacher approves. And he was terribly affectionate. And Jeannie, who understood his need to have crushes quite often—because they kept him young—didn't discourage these things. She'd say, 'Why don't you and Sparky go have a walk?' Or if we were at a book fair, he would take my hand and we'd hold hands. And I'd say to Jeannie, 'I'm holding hands with your husband, you know.' And she'd say, 'Or maybe he's holding hands with you.' And she would let it go. And I'm thinking: I'm holding hands with Charles Schulz. This is the hand that draws *Peanuts* . . . Wow!"

But as cartoonists, they could not have been more different. In *For Better or For Worse*, Johnston encouraged her readers to look on with affection as ordinary people grew up, one generation succeeding another. Her strip characters, the Pattersons, aged more or less in real time and thus repeatedly had to tackle issues that Sparky never took on, such as the human struggle to acknowledge time's passage and accept with grace and maturity the ordinary transit from aging to death—all the things that a human being must confront to become the person he or she is destined to become. Even the Pattersons' family dog, Farley, a big, fluffy English sheepdog, began to age, although Johnston did not realize it until a friend called her up to say that Farley, then twelve, had begun to reach the upper limits of realistic survival among his breed. But she let another two years go by, and more people noticed and wrote to her, and finally, when Farley was about to turn fifteen, she knew she had to act.

Farley had to die and, by the example of his death, might attain the transcendence of other magically real animal-kingdom martyrs such as

E. B. White's gallant spider, Charlotte, or C. S. Lewis's noble lion, Aslan. The technical question that Johnston as artist had to work out was: how to kill off a beloved creature?

But before she went ahead and did it, Johnston wanted Sparky's advice, and she was completely unprepared for him to say what he said from the other end of the phone: "You can't do this. You cannot kill off the family dog."

He was still working with an old rule of the comics: there are no unhappy endings. Or the cardinal rule: there were no endings at all. And Johnston, who "desperately did not want to write" the story of Farley's death, explained that her strip ran chronologically and that if she was going to be true to the strip, even the dog had to live out his life in real time. Moreover, she had to plan ahead for an offspring of Farley's to be born.

To buttress her case, she laid out the story she had planned, and Sparky listened, and when she was finished explaining how Farley was going to die trying to save the Pattersons' youngest daughter, April, from drowning in a spring-freshened river, there was silence on the phone, and then Schulz said: "If you do this story, I am going to have Snoopy get hit by a truck and go to the hospital, and everybody will worry about Snoopy, and nobody's going to read your stupid story." As if to prove that Snoopy was still the biggest newsmaker, he added, "And I'll get more publicity than you will! So there!"

At first, Johnston thought he was kidding. For one thing, it would have been out of character to have any one of the *Peanuts* gang hit by a truck. Schulz had been sensitive to issues about child safety since his first strip; he had never drawn his kids "in any position where they could be injured in any way, where a car could come along and run over their feet" and remained vigilant into the 1990s, withdrawing from publication a November 1996 strip that seemed to him, with so much violence occurring in the nation's school system, only to make matters worse.

But Johnston took his threat seriously and did not tell him when the story of Farley's death was going to run. In early February 1995, only her husband and her editor knew when she submitted the series of strips to Universal Press Syndicate—eight weeks ahead of print time. Then, in the second week of April 1995, when the story of Farley's heroic death appeared, Sparky went on the air, and in response to the interviewer's questions, he went out of his way to mock Johnston, describing what had happened in the "Farley strips" not as a heroic death but as a "killing."

"We can say Farley 'died,'" he deadpanned, "but he died because of the stupidity of that little girl." Then, with stunning vehemence, he declared that the "killing of Farley" personally annoyed him no end, and he announced that he was holding Lynn responsible for the tragedy, as if Lynn were April's careless mother: "I'll never forgive her for that," he insisted, "because April never should have done it. And now the dog died." He let his bitterness gather for a moment before he added, "Well, I hope she's happy. I don't think she should have done that, but, after all, Lynn is Lynn, and I am me, and we're different, that's all."

HE BECAME THE ELDER statesman of the comics, but he never ceased to be competitive with his fellow cartoonists. "He could be really brutal when he disliked someone's work," said his editor, Sarah Gillespie, "and everybody wanted to know what Sparky thought of their material." He described himself in the morning at the Warm Puppy, reading the other comics and thinking, "Oh, why do they do that? Why don't they work harder? Why do they put down their first thought? Why don't they think about it a little bit longer and break beneath the surface a little better and try to make it better? Why do they settle for those first easy ideas?"

He found it flattering, he said, to see his influence on younger cartoonists, "and for the good ones I think that's fine. It's a little bit sad when I see some of the others that are imitating, or at least think they're imitating, what I am doing, by having little, sly, philosophical remarks in the last panel which are neither sly nor philosophical but are just plain dumb. They don't have the touch to know how to do that. And I think if you don't have the touch, you shouldn't do it. I see this so often."

In the top ranks of comic strips, others now counted in ways that he had once counted. In 1985, after executives at United Media had offered a development contract to a twenty-seven-year-old midwesterner named Bill Watterson, only to reject as unmarketable his offering of a stuffed tiger that comes to life in the imagination of a little boy, Universal Press Syndicate of Kansas City launched *Calvin and Hobbes*. The strip proved to be not just full of life, but funny, literate, honest, and, by August 1987, the nation's fastest-growing comic strip—everyone's new favorite, as its invitingly big and vividly rendered Sunday panels shared the front page of more than three hundred comics sections with the headliner *Peanuts*. When Watterson's first collection, with an approving foreword by Schulz, soared to the top of the best-seller lists with five hundred thousand copies coming off the shelves in its first year, when the Pulitzer committee awarded its 1987 prize for editorial cartooning to a second strip artist, the thirty-year-old Berkeley Breathed, for the off-color, sharply satiric, and wildly popular sentiments of *Bloom County*, and when Gary Larson's brilliant, sometimes wonderfully lunatic panel sequence *The Far Side* established itself nationally, eventually reaching 1,900 newspapers, it looked for a moment as if Schulz had real heirs to greatness in the funny pages, and as if newspaper comics, having at last come into their own as a true American art form, might enter a new golden age when once again, as their historian Lucy Shelton Caswell put it, "opening the newspaper every day was an adventure."

Like Trudeau and Larson and Breathed just before him, Watterson embodied his generation's reverence for early *Peanuts*. For Watterson, born in 1958 and growing up in Chagrin Falls, Ohio, *Peanuts* "had a magic that other strips didn't." No other strip "presented a world so relentlessly cruel and heartless," and he "instantly related to the flat, spare drawings, the honesty of the children's insecurities, and to Snoopy's bizarre and separate world." But the most important lesson for the future cartoonist was that "a comic strip can have an emotional edge to it and that it can talk about the big issues of life in a sensitive and perceptive way."

For most baby-boom cartoonists, Schulz *was* the comics. Starting as a subversive in the 1950s—"the Brando" of the funnies, said Ivan Brunetti—he had given four exemplary decades of what a contemporary strip could be. Even when, every few years, someone piped up to say that *Peanuts* was a "shadow" of its former self, or "isn't as funny as it was," or had "gotten old," some young defender like Watterson stepped forward to say what Sparky himself could not: "I think what's really happened is that Schulz, in *Peanuts*, changed the entire face of comic strips, and everybody has now caught up to him. I don't think he's five years ahead of everybody else like he used to be, so that's taken some of the edge off it. I think it's still a wonderful strip just in terms of solid construction, character development, the fantasy element—things that we now take for granted: reading the thoughts of an animal, for example."

Following Schulz's example in one important way, Watterson rejected it in another. He devoted himself to the comics as an art form, taking his readers' daily attention as "an honor and a responsibility," and tried each morning to give them the best strip of which he was capable. Because he regarded cartooning as a highly personal form of expression, he, too, refused to hire assistants, working alone, drawing every line himself and painting special art for each of his books. But this was also why Watterson refused to "dilute or corrupt" his strip's message with merchandising. "I want to draw cartoons," he said, "not supervise a factory"—which declaration he later expanded: "I went into cartooning to draw cartoons, not to run a corporate empire."

Schulz had long been held up as the native genius who had come out of nowhere and done the most with the least, creating a revolutionary comic strip out of space-saving necessity. He was the first minimalist of the comics page, striving for exactly the right number of words and the right phrasing, never putting in more detail than was needed—indeed, showing with unprecedented economy how much more less could be—and structuring gags to omit all less-than-essential words, every note sounding on beat. And as the decades rolled on, his determination to stay on the job, turning out every strip by himself alone, canonized him in the eyes of younger cartoonists. To work without assistants had become the industry standard.

For all of that, however, Schulz emphasized the inconsequential nature of his accomplishment. In October 1997, during a long, candid interview with *Comics Journal* editor Gary Groth as his seventy-fifth birthday approached, Groth had only to mention the word "art," pointing out that Schulz made good use of his army experience later in life by transforming war's intense loneliness and desolation into artistic achievement in *Peanuts*, for Schulz to reply, "What a waste of time."

"How do you mean?" said Groth.

"To spend all of your life drawing your comic."

"You don't really mean that, do you?"

"Sure."

Under pressure from the disconcerted Groth, Schulz insisted that he really did mean what he said. "Well, you know: what have you done? Drawn a comic strip. Who cares?" He laughed his mirthless laugh. "Now I'm seventy-five years old."

"But don't you feel like you have an enormous achievement behind you, a lasting legacy because of that achievement?"

"No," said Schulz, and laughed again. "Because I know that I am not Andrew Wyeth. And I will never be Andrew Wyeth." In the next breath, he admitted that he was proud of one thing: "I think I've done the best with what ability I have. I haven't wasted my ability . . . I haven't destroyed it, I haven't misused it in any way."

He returned to the theme of assessing his limitations to another interviewer a month later: "I'll never be an Andrew Wyeth, and that's kind of sad. I wish what I did was fine art, but I doubt it is. It's well researched and authentically drawn, but I do not regard what I am doing as great art. Comic strips are too transient. Art is something so good it speaks to succeeding generations. . . . I doubt my strip will hold up for several generations to come."

When November 26, 1997, rolled around, he passed his milestone birthday quietly, astonished by an enthusiastic phone call from the eighty-year-old Andrew Wyeth, his hero in art and fellow stay-at-home genius, who was still painting every day at Chadds Ford. Jeannie noticed that Sparky "seemed to be in great shape, but then, increasingly, he began to talk about being tired. But it wasn't a tiredness you'd worry about. He was still playing hockey, tennis, golf . . ."

He wrestled with the idea of taking a sabbatical—an unheard-of luxury, even for the most successful, when Sparky had started in the profession. "Do you think I should do it?" he asked Jeannie.

Twenty years earlier he had shown the first signs of fatigue: "The burden of drawing this becomes oppressive at times," he admitted to a reporter. "And I begin to think, do I really want to sit here for the rest of my life and fight this schedule? I see other people taking a vacation."

Jules Feiffer came up to Snoopy Place while opening a play in San Francisco, and sincerely mistook Schulz's studio for a branch office of some suburban bank. As they sat and talked, Sparky turned to his fellow craftsman, "in an almost wistful way," as Feiffer recalled it, to ask whether he ever got bored with drawing his comic strip. "I was quite surprised that he would say this," said Feiffer, "because to ask the question was to admit something." At that moment, Feiffer happened to be excited about his strip, but he had gone through stretches of weariness with drawing—having, in fact, branched out into theater and movies and children's books for just that reason: "I loved everything about what I did, and I certainly loved the success of it. But after a while, every element of what you love, if it keeps repeating itself on the same level, starts turning out to be a negative. Instead of moving on, you start to parody yourself. And you lose the freshness, because what was first fresh, and evolved from insight to style, turns from style into technique and formula."

Never before had Schulz said publicly that he might retire. But in 1986, he revealed that he had begun to think about it every day. The right hand that twenty-five years earlier had "never [made] a wasted motion" now shook uncontrollably. He found himself telling people, "I used to have a great pen line, you know. I had a pen line which I would match to Percy Crosby's anytime, but that was a long time ago." But with repeated effort and practice, he reconciled himself to the challenge of drawing slowly and awkwardly with one hand propped against the other, and, like Katharine Hepburn, who turned to advantage even the quaver in her aging voice, Schulz found new warmth in his tentative line.

By the middle of the 1990s, when old friends and colleagues telephoned or, less often, visited, some noticed that he "sounded genuinely depressed about growing old." To those around him, however, he did not age. "Sparky never seemed old," said Jeannie. An interviewer asked him if he was growing older gracefully. "No, no," he said, "I'm fighting it." He had, as he put it, "an almost obsessive fear about being ill," adding, "but I don't like being old." He admitted that for at least ten years he had been "looking at younger people and envying them." He noticed "how freely they [skate] and . . . the muscles in their arms and legs flowing and their flat stomachs." He also envied golfers of his own vintage the singular accomplishment of a hole in one and became obsessed with a sense of unfairness that he had played golf ever since seeing a series of Bobby Jones movie shorts when he was nine years old and yet had never attained every golfer's dream.

At the age of seventy-two, teeing off one day with Jeannie and Brooke at Bodega Bay, he drove to the right side of the green and his ball kicked to the left, rolled up twenty-five feet, and dropped into the cup. At last.

One evening of the second or third day at a golf tournament, he and Jeannie attended a buffet dinner at which they found places at a round table and introduced themselves around. An elderly woman sitting to his left said, "Charles Schulz—that's kind of a nice name, isn't it?"

"I never really thought about it," said Sparky,

Whereupon she said, "Isn't that the name of the fellow who's the cartoonist?"

And she said, "He's dead, isn't he?"

One night he had a dream in which he died. Later he told a younger friend, "When you're my age, everybody around you is dying." He kept count of his squad mates from the army; so many were gone. But it was his high school classmates over whom he kept a closer watch. Over and over in recent years, he opened the 1940 *Cehisean*, and, in his now always shaky handwriting, recorded the fate of some figure passed a thousand times in the halls sixty years before.

"I'm so scared of dying," he told his friend the painter Tom Everhart. "That's all I can think about. I've been thinking about it for days."

"Maybe you should take a pill."

"I take too many pills."

People spotting him at the arena or in the Coddingtown Mall called out, "Are you still drawing the strip?"

"Good grief," he wanted to reply—and sometimes did, "who else in the world do you think is drawing it?"

★ ★ ★

"I STILL DON'T THINK of myself as a Californian," he said in 1989, "but I sure have drifted away from Minnesota. I don't think about Minnesota at all. I have no regrets about it, no desire to go back." He had kept up a correspondence with Frieda Rich and several others but generally avoided the funerals of old friends at Art Instruction. When Charlie Francis Brown, after years of alternating alcoholism and sobriety, closeting his homosexuality, and other struggles, succumbed to cancer in a hospice at Metropolitan Medical Center in Minneapolis, Sparky noted in his date book, "C.B. Died," and circled it, but that was all.

In October 1994, he returned to his hometown only for the second time since he had moved to California thirty-six years earlier. He attended a weekend of tributes to himself. The Mall of America hosted "Around the World and Home Again: A Tribute to the Art of Charles Schulz." The mayor gave him the key to St. Paul, and the University of Minnesota conferred an honorary doctorate upon him. A lunch was thrown for him at O'Gara's Bar and Grill, on the corner at Selby and Snelling—the locus of so much that had made him. All through the weekend, at each event, he believed that no one would be there.

The strip on November 10, 1996, derives from the homecoming weekend. One of Schulz's rare explanatory captions records the fact that "even Linus himself was surprised at the huge crowd that had gathered to welcome him on his return . . ." He turned his old friends and relatives and hometown acquaintances into impassive figures—people of obvious goodwill but without anything to say.

Snowmen occupied a major place in Schulz's worldview from his earliest days of drawing. Throughout *Peanuts*, the snowman had appeared as a figure in uncountable numbers of daily and Sunday strips, rendered as playful commentary on the significant form of modern art:

and in the emerging idiom of Snoopy:

He even stood them on their heads:

cut them in half:

and, like a chef experimenting with the next dish, blackened them:

Snow is a temporal medium, and the creator working in snow is an old image of artistic achievement: Would Schulz's comic strip last? Would readers a hundred years later take meaning and pleasure from *Peanuts*? Or would today's daily strip melt as soon as the sun came up the next morning?

In the end, snowmen always disappointed. They represented unfulfillment—never getting what you wanted. When you are out in the cold, snowmen are friendly, reassuring figures. But every friendship with a snowman is doomed; it's best not to hope for friendship in the first place. With snowmen, hope is a heartbreaker. Snoopy becomes friends with one snowman over the course of a week and finally has to plead with the sun to spare his friend:

Snoopy is eventually abandoned by so many snowmen, he can no longer stand the possibility of loss and simply refuses to be hurt. Rerun, true to his name, takes up the theme more than thirty years later, standing bodily between his snowman and the sun, begging:

And from the snowman—or its absence in California—came an eerie variation on disappointment:

ON THANKSGIVING 1997, THE day after Sparky's seventy-fifth birthday, he took his first break in forty-seven years, explaining to his public, "My wife had noticed I was getting a little jumpy." The official five-week hiatus lasted until New Year's Day; in the meantime, the 2,600 newspapers subscribing to *Peanuts* received reruns from between 1987 and 1992.

He thought about a couple of days of golf in Palm Springs but found excuses not to go, and a longer trip was out of the question. So, at first, things remained much the same: he still woke up in the middle of the night with an idea; still went down to the Warm Puppy for breakfast; still kept a pile of doodled ideas at the ready.

Jeannie later recalled "how he loved getting new information . . . and could remember and quote the latest thing that he was fascinated with, and how he would discuss it with people whose opinions he sought to explore and expand his own."

It took only three weeks of his five-week sabbatical before Sparky had sneaked back and was working every day.

The arithmetic of daily intake—and output: 17,170 strips to date—kept him at the drawing board. "All you're trying to do is fill in those squares," he said in 1997. "Do something good for Monday, and then do something good for Tuesday, and then you do something for Wednesday. Where does it all come from?" He was almost cheerfully businesslike when he reminded people, "It says in my contract that when I die the strip ends."

Knowing how particular Sparky was about music, Jeannie asked him what kind of music he wanted at a memorial service. Brooke, irreverent about everything, would say, "Mom's planning Sparky's funeral." As with so many broachings of the otherwise unutterable, this became an acceptable, a useful, joke. Jeannie would ask if he wanted to have a service at the arena. He said no, and she didn't pursue it further.

At the end of each week, he went on marking his latest *Snoopy Date Book*, as he had for years, with the tersely crucial: "Dailies done . . . Sunday done."

He usually drew a week's worth of daily strips before giving them up to be scanned and sent to United Media, but did not always draw them in the order in which they would run. Only after finishing all six and then laying them out on a studio countertop did he establish their best sequence, and only then did he mark their corners with the dates of their eventual appearance.

So it was that on Tuesday, November 16, he was working on the daily strip for Friday, December 31, the last appearance of *Peanuts* before the much-anticipated rollover into the year 2000. He had already drawn the strip for Saturday, January 1, 2000, although he had not yet lettered it. After a total of 17,896 strips—15,390 dailies and 2,506 Sundays—here was one more installment of *Peanuts*.

SUDDENLY THE DOG REALIZED THAT HIS DAD HAD NEVER TAUGHT HIM HOW TO THROW SNOWBALLS..

Snow. The cold of a January day. Peppermint Patty and Marcie, behind the rampart of one snow fort, exchange volleys of snowballs with Charlie Brown and Linus. Snoopy sits behind the lines in Charlie Brown's camp, pondering a snowball. There are no voices in the strip and no thought balloon over Snoopy. Curiously, there is a caption; Schulz had begun experimenting with these in 1992. They freed him from traditional pacing and allowed him to draw a whole daily strip as a single set piece: "Suddenly the dog realized that his dad had never taught him how to throw snowballs . . ."

The strip—the last of his dailies, but not in any sense an ending or resolution to *Peanuts*—is nonetheless a coming to terms with fundamental constraints. Limitations had been his generation's theme, and here, in the final image of the strip, the dog who stood up on his hind feet and began to dream and so became both man and superman now faces reality and becomes close to an ordinary dog again. Reality here takes the form of a snowball—a symbol not unlike the snow-filled glass paperweight that gives us the first clue to the identity of "Rosebud" in *Citizen Kane*, the fable of a man of great power whose limitations have proved to be his fate.

Asked in 1989 to name his greatest accomplishment, Schulz chose not to speak of children or art or money or fame or power. His greatest accomplishment, he said, was "making the most out of what limited talent I have."

Limitations had been the theme of a number of strips in 1999, most notably Rerun's epiphany at the art museum that he did not have it in him to attain greatness. In that moment, the reality of Schulz's own voice and assertion—"I'll never be Andrew Wyeth"—disturbed the strip's carefully guarded preserve of characterization. Schulz's exact words, heard often in television, radio, magazine, and newspaper interviews during this year of retirement, and now ventriloquized into a character's mouth, diminished not only Rerun's artistic struggles but the whole world that had given him birth.

"To think that I've done this," he had recently remarked to a visitor, "considering that everybody thought that I would never amount to anything," then quickly added, "But I know my limitations."

For his part, Snoopy struggles in the final daily strip, as always, with the issue of identity. He has long since overcome his restraints by operating in a fantasy universe. Over the past forty years, he has cast himself as a pilot, a doctor, and so on. Now he is merely a dog who can't get his paws around a snowball. Once he could take a Sopwith Camel into the skies over France; now, at the end, he is earthbound. Literally downed, he sits slumped on the cold, lifeless earth. His crisis is all interior, it involves none of the other characters, and its sources are in the past . . .

The last strip is not about a father who hasn't taught a son to play but about a father who hasn't known how to help his son become the artist he yearned to be—a father who *couldn't* teach him how to play because he himself could not free himself to play. Carl Schulz always had to be doing something useful. He could not just go out and throw baseballs or snowballs with his son.

Drawing, even on a fogged trolley car window, had been the one area in which the son was free to play, to feel, to be a child, and to be creative; *Peanuts* had preserved that sacred grove for fifty years. And now it was to be cut down.

HE TRIED TO FINISH the batch of dailies for December 27 through January 1, drawing and lettering the first two panels of the Friday (December 31) strip:

He was having a hard time with the third panel, Charlie Brown's feet coming out strangely undersized, when a sudden sinking sensation in his flesh—a dropping away of his lower body, an absence of feeling in his legs—forced him to put down his pen and struggle to his feet. Gathering up the batch of strips, he started down the hall to his new creative director's office. Paige Braddock would finish the word balloons in the final panel on the computer.

In the carpeted hall outside Paige's office, he dropped several of the strips and forced himself to stoop and pick them up. When at last he straightened, he leaned against her office doorjamb, out of breath, and managed to say, "Oh, Paige, I am feeling really strange."

# CHAPTER 28

# DAILIES DONE

*I'm too me to die!*
—SNOOPY

RUSHED BY AMBULANCE TO Memorial Hospital in Santa Rosa, he was found to have a blocked abdominal aorta. During surgery to clear the obstruction, doctors found that cancer had overrun his colon.

In the intensive care unit, with chemotherapy begun, Dr. Bob Richardson told Monte and Craig that he had removed as many tumors as he could from Sparky's intestines, but that the reality of Stage IV colon cancer was that their father had perhaps a year or two to live.

Within a couple of days he was able once again to form words clearly, but his vision and his appetite were severely compromised. Lynn Johnston, just ending a book tour in Vancouver, hopped a jet to San Francisco and drove up to Santa Rosa to see him. "He was still in shock—it had all happened SO FAST," she wrote to Herbert Block, the *Washington Post* editorial cartoonist, who had been fond of Schulz through their careers. After even a few moments with Sparky, Lynn knew "that he wouldn't make it to Reuben time" in the spring. "He didn't have the will," she explained. "He kept saying WHY?!!"

The doctors moved him out of intensive care on November 19, and his cousin Patty came to visit. "Why can't I just be Sparky Schulz?" he asked her. "Why do I have to be Charles M. Schulz?"

"He wanted to go back before the fame, before the pressure," recalled Monte. "The mantra became 'Why can't I just walk on the beach?'"

"No one loves me," he said to Chuck Bartley.

"Sparky, everyone loves you," said Chuck.

"That's right," said Cousin Patty. "And you know why?" she said to Bartley.

"Why?"

"Because they don't know him." At which Sparky let out a big laugh.

On November 23, a week after the illness struck, he drew a shaky Linus and a tentative Snoopy on the lined notepaper with which his doctors charted his progress. He spent Thanksgiving in the hospital, as well as his seventy-seventh birthday the next day. His family gathered around his bed, ran relays for food, struggled to keep up a front. Jeannie spent every night with him.

Released from the hospital on November 30, he stopped by the arena to wish the cast of the holiday ice show good luck before Friday's opening. As the cancer broke him down, all restraints on his emotions collapsed, too. The day following, before attending a benefit performance of the show, he had just sat down at his table in the Warm Puppy, when all it took was for Amy Lago to walk in, and the shining tears spilled down his face.

With Amy was Stephan Pastis, a new cartoonist whose strip, *Pearls Before Swine*, was in development at United Media. Schulz asked, "How many papers are you in?" and Pastis told him, "None—yet."

"I hope it gets a good launch. I started in seven papers."

"That must be hard to make a living in just seven papers."

"It's never about the money," he started to say, and choked up on the sentence, then broke down in lasting tears.

To Amy he said: "This was taken away from me."

At the ice show, he tired quickly and had to leave at intermission. The house lights came up and the song, "You're a Good Man, Charlie Brown" swept over the arena PA system. People who saw him get up at his table began to applaud wildly. Once more he started to cry. And now they were standing and cheering him out the door. Before turning to go, he said to Pastis, to whom he had been giving career advice: "That's what you need to do"—cultivate that kind of direct, emotional connection to the audience. "You do that," he challenged Pastis. "You do that *for the next fifty years!*"

AT HOME, SPARKY WAS now unable to contain emotions that in the past he had kept under wraps. "Tears would come," recalled Jeannie, "and he didn't mean them to." The doctors put this "emotional incontinence" down to the effects of the stroke, and warned the family about such dislocation. Sometimes he formed a sentence in his mind, could not say it, and grew frustrated. Or he knew he was drooling and got disgusted with himself. During one of Amy's visits, he became irritable: "Everybody's sending me all these cards and letters."

"Isn't that great?" said Amy.

"Well, what good does it do anyway?" said the architect of Charlie Brown's empty mailbox.

When she had to return to Utah, Amy made a point of calling her father every day and telling him she loved him. And though, as she remembered it, "he didn't always say, 'I love you' back, he did so many other things and said so many things—terms of endearment—that said 'I love you.' I'd call, and he'd say, 'Ah, Amos.' That said 'I love you.' Or he'd pick up the phone and say, 'Ah, the girl with the golden eyes.' That meant more than those three words."

A week later, he threw another clot, had trouble in his right leg, and had to go back to the hospital. They shifted blood thinners and dissolved the clot, but he couldn't eat, was getting dehydrated, and became truly depressed when he realized he couldn't do anything. The last month's stroke had affected his vision. He would see a blooming of flowers to the left of someone's face but couldn't see the person. He would look down at a golf ball on the tee, but it wasn't there. He couldn't read, couldn't draw, couldn't drive a car. It was difficult for him to talk; he struggled to recall the words he needed. All that might have been tolerable, and he could have still hoped to return to the drawing board, but for two other factors: the chemotherapy had begun to nauseate him, and stage IV colon cancer afforded him only a one in five chance of survival.

ON DECEMBER 14, HE addressed a letter to his estimated three hundred odd-million readers in more than seventy-one countries, to colleagues, fellow cartoonists, and "friends near and far." He would retire in January "in order to concentrate on my treatment for and recuperation from colon cancer. . . . I want to focus on my health and my family without the worry of a daily deadline." The following year, John Updike ended *Rabbit Remembered*, final installment of his every-ten-years masterwork of middle America, on the day "after the day when Charles Schulz announced he was ending *Peanuts* . . ."

Mail poured into the studio by the boxload; bouquets arrived by the hour, dozens and dozens, maybe 150 in all. "It looked like a funeral parlor in there," recalled Evelyn Ellison, who had now worked with Schulz long enough to know that "when people admired or loved him, he didn't think [they] meant it. He thought they were just trying to flatter him and he didn't know why. It wasn't until he saw the world's reaction to his retirement that he thought, Well, I guess they do mean it."

Millions of fans felt that they were losing something precious and personal. Their letters vibrated to the single refrain: *I loved Charles Schulz*. Sometimes their affection and awe had been ellicited by the briefest, handwritten response to a fan letter, an equally brief encounter at a golf tournament, a passing exchange in a restaurant; sometimes it was simply a gesture, or the time he had taken to listen, or the check written to meet someone's need—all to people unknown, whom he had touched deeply, so often at some critical moment. His goodwill, his generosity, changed so many lives forever.

Still more devotees flooded the Internet with torrents of grief and adulation: *Charles Schulz is my hero. . . . Just to be in his presence would be like meeting the Buddha or Christ.*

Enfeebled but dignified, he held himself erect and made his way into the studio to find bushels of letters on his workshop floor. "What is all this?" he asked. "More love letters," replied Edna Poehner, who at last was able to say when it was all over, "He couldn't quite figure out why people liked what he did. But he did get a feeling for it at the end."

The sweet, sad melodies from Vincent Guaraldi's *A Charlie Brown Christmas* accompanied every story about his retirement—anthems to what was past and passing. People kept reaching out to *Peanuts* for the simple things that reminded them of what it had been like in a time of misunderstanding to feel understood. "This was a generation that really did fear the next day, sometimes wasn't sure if the next day was going to come," Schulz had said in 1973; in listening every December in those years to the "Charlie Brown music," they could hear that they had lost some part of their earliest, unchipped innocence, and yet feel how *Peanuts* had filled some of their most youthful yearnings. But now the young of 1973, who had left *Peanuts* behind, were returning in their middle age for a fond farewell: "Like most adults, I haven't read it for years in the papers," wrote *Time*'s Matt Cooper. "It was one of those things, though, you'd assumed would be there, the way you assumed that, well, 'the Year 2000' was the future."

★ ★ ★

ALL HIS LIFE HE had resolved problems by work. The taking away of his physical strength and his power to get things done destroyed his metaphysical balance.

Five days before Christmas, Al Roker arrived late in the afternoon from New York to interview Sparky a second time for the *Today* show. The first interview, shot in August, had run in November, coincidentally on the day that Sparky collapsed, and though none of his family or anyone at Creative Associates or United Media wished him to appear on national television in his present condition, Schulz was set on telling to the public that he couldn't draw anymore.

Jeannie suggested they do the taping in the studio at One Snoopy Place, but he said, "No, that's over."

He slept all day while they were setting up in the living room, and by the time the cameras rolled, the hills of Santa Rosa stood in shades of deep blue outside the window.

From the first question—"Why did you decide to retire?"—he had trouble formulating every sentence. "It's hard for me the exact remember," he began. "But we did found out—we did find out that we had the colon cancer."

The very sound of his voice was a surprise. It had been stripped of the polish of later life. He covered over the roughest patches with his trademark smile and chuckle, but the mask was as worn out as the rest of him. For though he was wearing a cheerful yellow golf shirt with its black-and-white-striped collar, he looked savagely transformed. The public that had seen the solid, sensible Schulz of Al Roker's August interview now met a decrepit, gushy ghost, and was as shocked as he was himself.

"I never dreamed that this was what would happen to me," he stammered. "I always had the feeling that I would probably stay with the strip until I was in my early eighties. But, all of a sudden, it's gone. It's been taken away from me. I did not take this away from me," he emphasized in an aggrieved tone. "This was taken away from me."

Roker tried to bring him out from behind the curtain for one final bow. He asked Schulz whether he wanted to say a parting word to the folks who had read and loved his strip for the last almost fifty years.

He was as reluctant now at the end as he had been at the beginning to acknowledge directly the powerful connection between himself and his readers. One last time, he evaded that intimacy by discounting himself and the work. "It is amazing that they think that what I do was that good," he said and then, his voice rising with emotion: "I just did the best I could."

Artists are supposed to say that anyone who thinks that the work was adequate to their vision doesn't know anything about art. But this was the parting word of the boy who had been deflated in his earliest dreams by the world around him, the young man for whom cartooning had been an act of angry self-vindication upon the people who didn't believe he could draw, the master of unfulfillment.

Roker offered his hand, as you would to an elderly man in a wheelchair, and Schulz grasped it and shook it and bowed his head and peered down at the floor, then shook his head as if distressed beyond dismay.

AFTER CHRISTMAS, ANOTHER CLOT in his leg sent him back into the hospital. One afternoon while Jeannie and the rest of the family were at the funeral of Craig's mother-in-law, Lynn Johnston visited Sparky in his hospital room. She sat on the end of his bed, startled to find that he "didn't seem at all like the Sparky I knew. Gone was the need to *win*. Gone was the feistiness—he was like a small child. He was absolutely terrified of death, even though he'd prepared for it all his life—through his religion, his philosophy, and desperate need to re-create his childhood."

He reminisced with Lynn, but all his memories seemed to be about being picked on as a boy, and about how he still wanted to meet the kids who had bullied him face-to-face and get even. "I'd always known that side of him," recalled Lynn, "but at a time when people usually resolve their unresolvable histories by making peace with the past, he was angry that he'd never changed anything. You could see the bitterness in him. . . . Nothing in all of his seventy-seven years had been resolved."

Cathy Guisewite visited him and recognized that his illness had raised "the same question as 'Did my mom love me enough?' Or 'Does this woman love me enough?' Now it was 'Does God love me enough?' "

As Lynn Johnston reported to Herblock, Schulz on his deathbed seemed "angry at God, angry with friends, angry with fate—angry [about] all the troubles he could never let go of." She sensed his helplessness as well: "He had had control over the [*Peanuts*] universe for fifty years, but he had no control over his death. He didn't accept it graciously. He wasn't ready."

The strip had allowed him an illusion of eternity. Comics never end, no story is ever finished, four more blank white panels await the next installment. When finally he fell ill, the fantasy was irrevocably broken, and he discovered that he was a creature of time, ordinary after all.

AT THE WHITE HOUSE, Schulz's illness appeared in early drafts of President Clinton's State of the Union speech. On February 2, California senator Dianne Feinstein sponsored Senate Bill S.2060 "to authorize the President to award a gold medal on behalf of the Congress to Charles M. Schulz in recognition of his lasting artistic contributions to the Nation and the world, and for other purposes."

Cartoonists and comedians outdid each other in acknowledging the power of his influence: "My career is all his fault," wrote *Doonesbury*'s Garry Trudeau, "but I'm far from alone. Study *B.C.* or *Feiffer* or *Calvin and Hobbes* or *Bloom County* carefully, and you'll see his influence everywhere—stylistically, narratively, rhythmically." Without *Peanuts*, there would have been no *Doonesbury*, no *Garfield*, no *Far Side*, no *Mutts*, no *Simpsons*; without a comic strip "about nothing," made up only of "little incidents," there would have been no *Seinfeld*; and only after the master was gone could *South Park* and *Family Guy* be recognized as "a kind of joyous unleashing of the weird, retentive genius of Charles Schulz."

When the *Press Democrat* was delivered on February 6, Sparky pulled out the Sunday comics. The section heading—COMICS—was aglow with color: orange turning yellow to green to blue to violet to purple to pink. His own Sunday page appeared in the first place above the fold on the front. He ran his eye over it and then compared the competition's drawing with his own. Then he said to Jeannie, "Look at my Sunday page. Every line is just perfect." At the very last he had got it exactly as he wanted it.

In the first ten days of February he talked on the telephone with practically everyone he had ever known who was still alive—even Donna Wold—the conversations almost always leaving him teary, sometimes filled with longing or sadness, sometimes just because he could not think of a word he wanted to say, such as "orthodox."

On Friday, February 11, he harnessed his regained strength and went off to skate with Jill and his friend Gayle Delaney at the arena. As they wound their way home through the foothills, Jill said, "Oh, by the way, Mom wanted me to tell you this: 'I Ain't Down Yet.' "

Sparky nodded with a little laugh. "That was from your mom's and my favorite show, *The Unsinkable Molly Brown*."

The next day—February 12, 2000—Jeannie went into San Francisco to see the matinee of a Tom Stoppard play that she and Sparky had long planned to attend together, leaving him to watch golf on television with his buddies, Larry and Dean James. Jill came over to pick him up and take him to her house for dinner. He watched the hockey game on TV, grew drowsy, and became exhausted over the meal. Wearing a red sweater and a look of mild bewilderment, he raised to his mouth a spoonful of baked Alaska, which shook and fell to the table. He scooped it up and tried again. This time he made it. Conversation passed along around him. He sat thoughtfully awhile, then said, "Forgive me," got up and headed a little uncertainly into the living room.

After dinner Jill took him home. It was a dark and stormy night. At the house, he felt some tightness in his chest and sat down in his big, wide, blue-leather throne of a chair, facing the TV and the fireplace. When Monte arrived, a doctor who lived nearby was taking his pulse. Schulz announced that he was going to throw up and asked for some Tupperware; soon he did so a second time, and felt a little better. Judging that the nausea was a standard consequence of chemotherapy, the neighbor doctor consulted by phone with Sparky's oncologist and suggested he go to bed. It was 8:59, and Jeannie said, "It's his bedtime anyway."

When Jill left, Schulz kissed her on the lips instead of the usual spot on her cheek, whispering, "Jill, I don't think I'm going to make it."

"Dad, you've got to make it," she replied.

Monte and he parted with a final word about the novel Monte had been writing. Looking his older son in the eye, he said, "Keep going, finish your book."

Jeannie came to lie down with him, and they cuddled for a while, then she got up to tidy the kitchen, whereupon he said that if she was getting up, he was going to roll over on his side; it was more comfortable.

When Jeannie came back, he was asleep—on his back, not his side. She changed and went to the bathroom, and when she came back to the bed, Sparky was still on his back, his hands holding the bedcovers to his chest, his eyes closed.

TWO MONTHS EARLIER, HE had dictated his retirement strip from his hospital bed to Jeannie to telephone to Paige Braddock. It was to be released as the final daily on January 3, 2000, but would appear again in February as part of the final Sunday strip, which Paige and Amy Lago composed with his supervision.

They began it by borrowing the title panel from the November 21, 1999, Sunday page, then added a throwaway panel in which Snoopy, head down, is typing a letter beginning, "Dear Friends . . ."

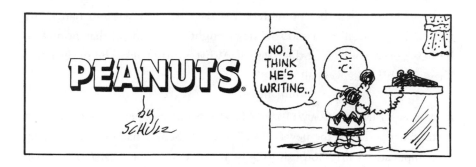

Then a big, wide-open double-height panel below carried the farewell letter in its entirety (one line had been dropped for space reasons from the daily version: "My family does not wish Peanuts to be continued by anyone else, therefore I am announcing my retirement"). Snoopy would appear in the lower right corner, reflecting at his typewriter, while in the pale blue sky above him floated cloudlike cameos of the strip's most cherished characters, taking a curtain call in their most iconic moments.

Paige Braddock laid out as many possibilities as she had the courage to choose by herself, but found it a struggle to pick from fifty years of *Peanuts*, getting only as far as Lucy and the football, Woodstock racing the Zamboni over his frozen birdbath, Peppermint Patty and Marcie in the classroom; so she strolled from the studio, cutting across the baseball field on the hidden outfield path, across Hardies Lane to the ice arena, where Sparky happened to be having lunch at the Warm Puppy, and asked him, please, to pick his own favorites.

He agreed with all of Paige's choices, quickly adding the obvious selections of Snoopy dueling the Red Baron, Lucy dispensing psychotherapy, Charlie Brown marooned on the ice. And he had always thought it funny that the baseball bounced off Lucy's head with the cartoon sound BONK! And he had liked drawing Sally Brown hanging off her brother's reading chair because her legs were too short for her to reach the floor and get his attention at the same time. And he loved it when Snoopy at full speed grabbed Linus's blanket with a CLOMP!, launching them both into flight.

But it was in the hospital, as he had composed the message to his "Dear Friends," that all his feeling for these figures at last found its way into his voice as he dictated the last sentence to Jeannie: *Charlie Brown, Snoopy, Linus, Lucy . . . how can I ever forget them . . .* Then, "right at the end," as he recalled the moment a few days later, "I wrote a name, my name. . . ." And all of a sudden, he thought: "You know, that poor kid, he never even got to kick the football. What a dirty trick—he never had a chance to kick the football."

IN THE MORNING, FEBRUARY 13, 2000, the Sunday paper carrying his last cartoon arrived with the news that Charles M. Schulz had died in his sleep of complications of colon cancer, just hours before the final *Peanuts* strip appeared around the world. To the very end, his life had been inseparable from his art. In the moment of ceasing to be a cartoonist, he ceased to be.

# ACKNOWLEDGMENTS

SEVEN YEARS AGO, WHEN I was granted access to Charles Schulz's papers, I placed my faith in the historical record. To my surprise and delight, it turned out that fifty years of *Peanuts* comic strips are as important to the study of this life as any document in an archive. So I must first thank United Media, the company that syndicates and licenses *Peanuts* in all its forms, for generously allowing me to anchor my narrative in Schulz's comic art.

My greater debt is to Jean Schulz. From the first suggestion of a full-length biography of her late husband, Jean gave her whole trust and cooperation to this project, opening the way to original research, unlocking doors in the world of Schulz, and leaving me free to my own discoveries and conclusions. I am grateful also to Monte Schulz, who championed the idea of an independent biography of his father, encouraging family members and friends to contribute to my research, making family papers available for study, while putting aside his own writing in order to answer my questions.

I am equally grateful to Craig Schulz, Amy Schulz Johnson, Jill Schulz Transki, and Meredith Schulz Hodges for their frank and thoughtful reflections on their father's life and work. Brooke Clyde and Lisa Clyde were no less clear-eyed in their understanding of their stepfather. Patricia Swanson supplied invaluable and original insight into the Halverson past.

This book would have been regrettably incomplete without the vivid recollections of Charles Schulz's first wife. I owe a great deal to Joyce Doty for permitting me the freedom to engage in a straightforward discussion of her early adult life as Mrs. Charles Schulz—the first such interview that Joyce and her husband, Ed Doty, had permitted since their marriage in 1973.

Sincere thanks go to each member of the Schulz family for his or her patience and trust. If I have failed to do justice to their lives in my telling of the story, the responsibility is entirely mine.

For permission to quote without restriction from Charles Schulz's unpublished letters and papers, I thank his heirs and estate; with special thanks to Edwin C. Anderson, Jr., trustee of the Schulz estate, and to Barbara D. Gallagher, family adviser and attorney.

I must express admiring appreciation to Laura Handman for her indispensable and wise counsel at several crucial stages in the course of this work. The book also benefited at the start from the advocacy of Mr. and Mrs. Andrew Wyeth and the interest of Lillian Ross. With the loving support of Clara Bingham and our family, I gladly began work.

Jean Schulz and I agreed in June 2000 that it would be vital for me to begin my interviewing while those who knew Charles Schulz in his earlier years were still alive. For their time and trust and generosity, I thank all who are named in the list of author's interviews in the source notes that follow. Among those who gave their recollections but did not live to see how helpful they were to the final work, a regretful envoi is offered to Justine DeMaio Anderson, Betty Bartley, Josie Bredahl Gish, Sidney Goldberg, Elmer Hagemeyer, Felix Holt, Larry James, Art Linden, Timothy S. O'Gara, Jim Sasseville, Dr. Frank Stanton, Lorraine Swanson Wentlandt, and Quentin Wentlandt; I must also remember, with wistful affection and gratitude, the good hearts and significant contributions of David Ratner, Clark Gesner, Patricia Plepler, Janell Pulis Kiechle, and Lloyd J. Neumann.

In September 2000, I found myself in the unusual situation of starting research in Charles Schulz's studio when he was only recently dead and with unprecedented access to his records, only to discover that Schulz had made a systematic habit of throwing out his professional papers. Sparky Schulz believed that to keep an account of his life and work was self-important. To the cartoonist, the finished strip was the thing—truer to who he was than the records of his working life. Even when the idea of a Charles M. Schulz Museum and Research Center had been established during his lifetime, and Jean Schulz, its prime founder, had asked him to save things, the secretaries in his office still had to pull his balled-up doodles out of the wastebaskets, smooth them out, and press them flat.

I am deeply grateful, therefore, to have been given access by United Media to the long-buried business correspondence, dating to 1950, between cartoonist and syndicate. No less privileged or vital was my admittance to the United Media Comic Strip Library, which saved me the labor of at least a year in the pits of microfilm. I thank Doug Stern, Helene Gordon, Rita Rubin, Jason Bannon, Melissa Menta, Jean Sagendorph, Kim Towner, Shauna McKenna, and, not least, Teri Rosenblatt, the office manager who led me to the tombs under Madison Avenue. No less important were those who had served the syndicate and Schulz in various earlier ages of *Peanuts*, including Robert R. Metz, Michael V. Georgopolis, Nancy Nicolelis, Liz Conygham, Mary Beth Croutier, Louisa D. Campbell, Barbara McLaughlin, Sarah Gillespie, and especially Roberta D. Miller. My unreserved admiration and thanks to Schulz's last editor, Amy Lago, who provided an invaluable education in the business of comic art.

United Media was not alone in its contribution to the institutional records of Schulz's life and work. I profited from access to the George Pipal Papers and the Lawrence Quinn Collection at Creative Associates; the Jules Feiffer Papers, Bill Mauldin Papers, and Roy Howard Papers in the Manuscript Division at the Library of Congress, where I have Jeffrey M. Flannery to thank for his careful attention to newly catalogued collections in which Schulz correspondence turned up.

Thanks go to the archivists at the Minnesota Historical Society; the Time/Life Archives, Time-Warner Incorporated; the Newsweek Archives; and to Steve Unverzagt at Art Instruction Schools, Inc., and Bob Cappelloni at Determined Productions, with a respectful salute to Arthur Lynch, editor of *Parade Rest*, newsletter for Company B, 20th Armored Division. I thank my dear friend Virginia Smyers Buxton and the staff of the Imaging Services Department in Harvard's Widener Library; Corinta Kotula, executive director, The Newspaper Features Council, Inc.; Dr. Paul M. Pearson, director and archivist, Thomas Merton Center, Bellarmine University; Sue Godnick, executive director, Needles Chamber of Commerce; the staff of the Needles (California) Regional Museum; Patricia Hanratty Wysocky, executive director, the Servicemen's Center of Minnesota; Vonnie Matthews, director of the News Research Center at the Santa Rosa *Press Democrat*; and Dr. Sioux Harvey, who while cataloging papers of Robert F. Kennedy at Hickory Hill, McLean, Virginia, unearthed Schulz treasure.

I am particularly grateful to all who provided letters, diaries, and notes that were written contemporaneously with events described in the text: Emil V. Abrahamian, Gordon L. Anderson, Betty Bissonette, James Bruner, Frank Dieffenwierth, Douglas and Nancy Erickson, Wallace Exman, Clark Gesner, Betsy Griffin, Elmer Hagemeyer, Priscilla Jenne Herzog, Deborah Humphries, Art Jacobs, Ethel S. Kennedy, Amy Lago, Bill Melendez, Roberta D. Miller, Charlene Neal, Lloyd Neumann, Lois and Walter Ortman, Stephan Pastis,

Michelle Pedersen, Sherman Plepler, David Ratner, Marc Ratner, Suzanne del Rossi, Martha K. Sabata, Jim Sasseville, Jeff Shesol, Robert Short, Steve Thompson, Louanne and Philip Van Pelt, Lorraine and Quentin Wentlandt. I am deeply grateful to Tracey O'Hearen for her grace and generosity.

Tom Everhart, Peter Guren, Lynn Johnston, Patrick McDonnell, Karen O'Connell, and Stan Pawlowski gave freely of their time and expertise and love for Sparky in order that I might better understand the art of Schulz from the inside out. I also benefited from expert appraisals on matters in the historical record of Schulz's life during consultations with Dr. Jerome Groopman, William Ivey Long, and Dr. Caroline C. Murray; my thanks to these professionals for their collaborative spirit.

In the same vein, the good-hearted and wise Rheta Grimsley Johnson, author of an earlier book about Schulz, shared unstintingly from her interviews and research files. I owe special thanks to Judy Jones McKinney for sharing documents from her original and unique work in Schulz genealogy; and to Ruth Halverson, dedicated genealogist of her branch of the Halverson tree; and to the faithful Victor Lee of the Peanuts Collector Club; and Derrick Bang, undisputed authority in all things *Peanuts*.

I never had the privilege of meeting Charles Schulz; for the sound of his everyday voice and the truth of his features, I relied on taped and videotaped interviews conducted, respectively, by Monte and Jean Schulz. Craig Schulz provided video conversions of old home movies as well as television footage from early in Schulz's career. For sharing transcripts and/or videotaped interviews, I owe a debt of gratitude to Karen and David Crommie, Meri Gyves, Ann Shields; and to Don Fraser for sharing the beginnings of his oral history project. Steve Kroft of CBS's *60 Minutes* generously allowed me to study outtakes and full transcripts of his interviews with Schulz and his family; Mark Miller of *Newsweek* was no less kind; Adam Van Doren, director of a documentary about Harold Ross for which he had interviewed Schulz, courteously shared with me his findings.

I want to thank four individuals whose questioning drew out Schulz perhaps as far as he wished to be known: Ken Martin in the 1970s; Laurie Colwin and Rheta Grimsley Johnson in the 1980s; Gary Groth in the 1990s. I have a special debt to Juris Jurjevics and Jeanne Heifetz, who went beyond the call of duty in order to bring to light the extensive and invaluable Colwin–Schulz tape recordings.

In Santa Rosa, I benefited from the many kindnesses of Lorrie Adamson, Kitty de Brauwere, Pam Drucker, Bev Fisher, Heather Orosco, Randy Pennington, Edna Poehner, and Erin Samuels at Charles M. Schulz Creative Associates, the creative and business management arm of the Schulz family estate. The cartoonist Paige Braddock was a selfless friend from beginning to end. My thanks also to Evelyn Ellison, Warren Lockhart, and Ron Nelson. In Sonoma County, I especially want to thank Gaye LeBaron for her interest in this book. At the Charles M. Schulz Museum and Research Center, my appreciation for the support of its current and founding directors, Karen Johnson and Ruth Gardner Begell, with special thanks to Sue Broadwell, Melissa McGann, and Lisa Monhoff.

Closer to home, my unqualified gratitude to the one and only Tracy Kolker, who aided me in scores of tasks with patience and kindness. Liz Perkins ably assisted me in the early stages of research; Andrew Fox deserves sleuthing credit as well. Nancy H. Olexa gave stalwart support, week by week, returning letter-perfect transcriptions of those of my interviews that were taped. Special thanks also to Nicholas Tarrant, to Duff Pacifico, to Pauline Wan, to Gene Taylor, to Amy Pearson, and to Mandeep Singh Sandhu, Matthew Kweskin, and Jesse Czarniecki, for their loyalty and technical help.

James Chace and David Halberstam were early friends to this book, as was Jay Kennedy, of King Features, who had high hopes for it as an advance in the field of cartoonists' biographies; I mourn the sudden and premature deaths of these three generous men.

For sage advice and indispensable encouragement at crucial points during the work, I thank Joel Achenbach, Peter Alson, Chris Benfey, Joan Bingham, Bob Boorstin, Katherine Bucknell, Libby Cameron, Sally Fisher Carpenter, Thomas R. Congdon, Jr., Anne Fadiman, Peter R. Fisher, Flora Fraser, Jackson Friedman, John Gerson, Michael Gilson, Ashbel Green, Jean Halberstam, Cully Irving, Walter Isaacson, David "Bemis" Johnson, James Kaplan, Deborah Karl, Andrew S. Karsch, Max Kennedy, Robert F. Kennedy, Jr., Matthew Klam, Steve Kostorowski, Darrell Larson, Terry Lenzner, Bevis Longstreth, Jennifer Maguire, Peter Michaelis, Michael Michaelis, Sally Munro Murray, Robert Nedelkof, Steve Ney, Laura Sass Peabody, Robert L. Peabody, Stephen Reily, Tom Rietano, Matthew Rogers, Robert G. Rosenblatt, Keith L. Runyon, Matthew Salinger, Sally Bedell Smith, Richard Stengel, Griff Thomas, Michael Van Vleck, Eugenie Voorhees, Robin West, and Ted Widmer.

Timothy Dickinson provided practical assistance during my research and gave detailed critical attention to the entire manuscript; I am very much in his debt not only for raising my sights but also for his encouragement and friendship. I have once again benefited from the experienced and gifted eye of Laurie Adams, whose astute appraisal helped me to shorten and strengthen an overlong manuscript. Lisa Chase also helped me to cut and edit with care and discipline. Paul D. Friedland made invaluable suggestions for improvements. The late Charles P. Spicer and Dr. Ordway Tead provided early inspiration in the new language of *Peanuts.*

At HarperCollins, the book's editor, Tim Duggan, had a uniquely challenging task. Tim guided me to completion with skill, patience, and editorial brilliance; I am enormously grateful for his accomplishment in bringing *Schulz and Peanuts* to its highest level without any sacrifice in its scope. Hugh Van Dusen's work also enhanced the book; I thank Hugh for his characteristic courtesy and forbearance as he shepherded the project through its early and middle phases. I owe thanks to Allison Lorentzen for many intelligent solutions and a sympathetic ear during production; to Virginia Carroll, who copyedited the text; and to Jonathan Burnham, Kathy Schneider, Tina Andreadis, Katherine Beitner, and Christine Boyd, for a superb launch. I was lucky to have Mark Jackson in my corner during all legal matters.

The world of publishing is a better place because of Chip Kidd; I am doubly fortunate to be writing books in the Age of Kidd and to have a manuscript of mine fall into his hands. My wholehearted appreciation to Chip, not only for the inspiration of his own volume on the art of Schulz, but for serving this book with wisdom and confidence to the end.

Melanie Jackson's good sense and sensitivity guided me at every step. With boundless energy and strength, Melanie protected and supported her writer.

I offer my greatest thanks to Betsy James Wyeth and to A. Scott Berg, who champion passion and excellence in the telling of American lives; and to Peter W. Kaplan and Nancy Steiner, who sustained me with their love.

David Michaelis
New York City
May 15, 2007

# SOURCE NOTES

Nearly all the documents cited here are now held in the collections of the Charles M. Schulz Museum and Research Center in Santa Rosa, California.

When I began work—in June 2000, four months after Schulz's death—much of this unexplored material was scattered around the country or located on opposite coasts. Archives within the Schulz studio at One Snoopy Place, Santa Rosa, were not yet organized, or even labeled as such; indeed, every drawer and cupboard in the master's workshop stood sealed behind bushels of mail—a double avalanche of condolence that had buried the studio in successive months after Schulz's retirement and death.

Meanwhile, in a basement below Madison Avenue, United Media had all but unknowingly preserved the papers of United Feature Syndicate, dating back to the start of the strip, including original manuscript letters written by CMS, carbon copies of syndicate executives' outgoing letters, and a steadily rising tide of inquiries from fans and collateral businesses around the world.

Significant personal documents and photographs remained in the possession of the Schulz family; additional letters and papers were stored in the attics and drawers of innumerable relatives and a few childhood friends and army buddies. Through the trust and generosity of Jean Schulz, Monte Schulz, and Brian and Amy Schulz Johnson, along with the goodwill of several branches of the Halverson, Borgen, Swanson, Bredahl, and Schulz families, and the kindness of individuals like Gordon Anderson, Frank Dieffenwierth, Clark Gesner, Elmer Hagemeyer, Louanne and Philip Van Pelt, and Tracey O'Hearen, these private collections also became available for study. The most substantial of these are designated here by the initials of their primary caretaker.

Charles Schulz's commitment to newspapers was second only to cartooning itself. He saw it as his obligation to give an interview to every editor who sent out a reporter, no matter how large or small or distant the paper. Across five decades he spoke through the press about his life and *Peanuts,* and in answering what were often the same old questions week after week, year after year, he charted major and minor shifts in his beliefs and opinions, all the while accumulating a vast treasury of commentary about his personality and character. The newspaper stories and magazine profiles from which I have borrowed Schulz quotations are designated with a (Q); the same applies to radio and television interviews. I have also benefited from several full-length interviews, published and unpublished; these are indicated by the initials of the interviewer. My interviews (I) are listed here by name and initials, and cited in the notes by initials and date.

The single greatest primary source for studying the life of Charles Schulz is his half-century of daily and Sunday *Peanuts* comic strips, begun on October 2, 1950, when he was twenty-seven, and ended on February 13, 2000, the day after his death at seventy-eight. The United Media Comic Strip Library, includes most, but not all, of the *Peanuts* canon; strips found elsewhere are noted as such.

## ABBREVIATIONS

| | |
|---|---|
| A | Advertisement |
| A&E | A & E *Biography* |
| AA | Annabelle Anderson (Schulz) |
| AP | Anderson Papers, CMSMRC |
| AII | Art Instruction, Inc. |
| ASI | Ann Shields interview with CMS |
| ASJC | Amy Schulz Johnson collection |
| BBC | British Broadcasting Co. interview with CMS |
| *CBS&M* | CMS, with R. Smith Kiliper, *Charlie Brown, Snoopy and Me* |
| C | Clipping |
| CFB | Charles Francis Brown |
| CFBMS | CFB, *Me and Charlie Brown: A Book of Good Griefs*, unedited manuscript |
| CGS | Clark Gesner Scrapbooks |
| CMS | Charles Monroe Schulz |
| CMSCA | Charles M. Schulz Creative Associates |
| CMSMRC | Charles M. Schulz Museum and Research Center |
| CS | Carl Schulz |

| | |
|---|---|
| D | Detail |
| DP | Determined Productions |
| DR | Drawing |
| DEP | Deposition |
| DIA | Diary |
| DHS | Dena Halverson Schulz |
| DTM | David Tead Michaelis |
| E | Epigraph |
| EM | E-mail |
| *FGA* | Judy Jones McKinney, *From Germany to America* |
| GG | Rheta Grimsley Johnson, *Good Grief* |
| GGI | Gary Groth interview with CMS |
| HG | Harry Gilburt |
| I | Interview by Author |
| JF | James Freeman |
| JH | James Hennessey |
| JFSI | Jean Forsyth Schulz interview with CMS |
| JHS | Joyce Halverson Schulz |
| L | Letter |
| LCI | Laurie Colwin interview with CMS |
| LIL | CMS, *Li'l Folks, St. Paul Pioneer Press* |
| LR | Lawrence Rutman |
| M | Memorandum |
| MCSC | Monte Charles Schulz collection |
| MCSI | Monte Charles Schulz interview with CMS |
| MNHS | Minnesota Historical Society |
| N | Notes |
| NCS | National Cartoonists Society |
| O | Obituary |
| P | CMS, *Peanuts* |
| PC | Postcard |
| *PD* | *Press Democrat* (Santa Rosa, CA) |
| *PDB* | CMS, *Peanuts Date Book* |
| *PGC* | CMS, *Peanuts: A Golden Celebration* |
| *PJ* | CMS, *Peanuts Jubilee: My Life and Art with Charlie Brown and Others* |

| | |
|---|---|
| P20 | Lee Mendelson, *Charlie Brown & Charlie Schulz: In Celebration of the 20th Anniversary of Peanuts* |
| P35 | CMS, *You Don't Look 35, Charlie Brown!* |
| P40 | Giovanni Trimboli, ed., *Charles M. Schulz: 40 Years Life and Art* |
| P45 | CMS, *Around the World in 45 Years: Charlie Brown's Anniversary Celebration* |
| P50 | CMS, *You Really Don't Look 50, Charlie Brown* |
| Q | Quotation |
| RM&GG | Rick Marschall and Gary Groth interview with CMS |
| S | Speech |
| SBWC | Santa Barbara Writers Conference |
| SKI | Steve Kroft interview, *60 Minutes* |
| T | Transcript |
| TMAT | LM, *A Charlie Brown Christmas: The Making of a Tradition* |
| TOHC | Tracey O'Hearen collection |
| U | Unpublished |
| UFSP | United Feature Syndicate Papers |
| UM | United Media |
| V | Video |
| YAGMCB | *You're a Good Man, Charlie Brown* |

## AUTHOR'S INTERVIEWS

Robert Albo (RA) • Clayton Anderson (CA) • Edwin C. Anderson, Jr. (ECA) • Justine DeMaio Anderson (JDA) • Frederick P. Angst (FPA) • Marcia Aoki (MA) • Tom Armstrong (TA) • Marcella Bakke (MB) • Kaye Ballard (KB) • Derrick Bang (DB) • Betty Bartley (BB) • Charles R. Bartley (CRB) • Anthony Bassignani (AB) • Lloyd "Skippy" Baxter (LSB) • Carol Benfell (CB) • Betty Bissonette (BBis) • Mollie Boice (MB) • Mary Beth Borré (MBB) • Paige Braddock (PB) • Sue Broadwell (SB) • Elizabeth J. Clyde (EJC) • Hunter Brooke Clyde III (HBC) • Dorothy Jane Comport (DJC) • Elizabeth Conyngham (EC) • John J. Creedon (JJC) • Mary Beth Croutier (MBC) • James R. "Jim" Davis (JRD) • Gayle Delaney (GD) • Suzanne Del Rossi (SDR) • Frank Dieffenwierth (FD) • Nancy Diez (ND)

• Raul Diez (RD) • Jim Doe (JDo) • Mark Doolittle (MD) • Beverly Hansen Dorsey (BHD) • Edwin Doty (ED) • Joyce Doty (JD) • Richard "Mr. Debonair" Dwyer (RDD) • Dolores Edes (DE) • William M. Edes (WME) • Evelyn Ellison (EE) • Nancy Ortman Erickson (NOE) • Tom Everhart (TE) • Wallace Exman (WE) • Jerry Fearing (JFe) • John G. Fee (JGF) • Jules Feiffer (JFeif) • John R. Finnegan (JRF) • Ruth Forbes (RF) • Don R. Fraser (DRF) • Donna Fraser (DF) • Bernard Friel (BF) • Carl F. Fuelling (CFF) • Barbara D. Gallagher (BDG) • Jennifer Gallagher (JG) • Jack "Pudge" Geduldig (JPG) • Donna Genck (DG) • Michael V. Georgopolis (MVG) • Clark Gesner (CG) • Victor E. Gibson, Sr. (VEG) • Ruth O. Gilburt (ROG) • Sarah Gillespie (SG) • William Glasser (WG) • Sidney Goldberg (SGo) • Leslie W. Greenig (LWG) • Jerome Groopman (JG) • Gary Groth (GG) • Cathy Guisewite (CGu) • Peter Guren (PG) • Meri Gyves (MG) • Richard Hackney (RH) • Elmer R. Hagemeyer (ERH) • Dale Hale (DH) • Nona Hale (NH) • Janine Hallisey (JH) • Gaylon "Corky" Halverson (GCH) • Lynos Halverson (LH) • Marcia Correll Hamilton (MCH) • Victor Hansen, Jr (VH) • R.C. Harvey (RCH) • Fred Heaberlin (FH) • Patricia Hefflefinger (PH) • Barbara Herzinger (BH) • Priscilla Jenne Herzog (PJH) • Thomas Hewson (TH) • Willie Hilliard (WH) • Meredith Schulz Hodges (MSH) • John Hohstadt (JHoh) • Felix H. Holt (FHH) • Barbara Bittner Hoppe (BBH) • Art L. Jacobs (ALJ) • Karl Jaque (KJ) • Larry James (LJam) • Sandy Terrado Janachowski (STJ) • Bill Janocha (BJ) • Amy Schulz Johnson (ASJ) • Hart Johnson (HJ) • John Brian Johnson (JBJ) • Randi S. Johnson (RSJ) • Rheta Grimsley Johnson (RGJ) • Lynn Johnston (LJ) • Polly Keener (PK) • Thomas Kelly (TK) • Jay Kennedy (JK) • Janell Pulis Kiechle (JPK) • Jim Klobuchar (JKlo) • Avis Kriebel (AK) • Steve Kroft (SK) • Mel Labovich (MLa) • Amy Lago (AL) • Harold K. Lamson (HKL) • Gaye LeBaron (GLeB) • Phil LeBrun (PLeB) • George Letness (GL) • Art Linden (ALin) • Marty Links (ML) Everett V. Little, Jr. (EVL) • Warren Lockhart (WL) • Gary Lombardi (GLom) • Arthur C. Lynch (ACL) • Kay M. Marquet (KMM) • Ken Martin (KM) • Linus Maurer (LMa) • Donald G. McClane (DGM) • James R. McDonald (JRM) • Patrick McDonnell (PMcD) • Judy Jones McKinney (JJM) • Barbara McLaughlin (BMcL) • Maggie McShan (MM) • Bill Melendez (BM) • Lee Mendelson (LM) • Robert R. Metz (RRM) • Roberta D. Miller (RDM) • Idelle Mitchell (IM) • Dave Mruz (DM) • Mary Murphy (MMur) • Lorrie Myers (LMy) • Bernetta Nelson (BN) • Ron Nelson (RN) • Shirley Spencer Nelson (SSN) • Wallace Nelson (WN) • Lloyd Neumann (LN) • Nancy Nicolelis (NN) • Karen O'Connell (KOC) • Timothy O'Gara (TOG) • Elizabeth O'Hara (EOH) • Maggie O'Hara (MOH) • Tracey O'Hearen (TOH) • Paul Olsen (PO) • Frank Oravetz (FO) • Lois E. Ortman (LEO) • Walter Ortman (WO) • Charlotte Carlson Ostlund (CCO) • Stephan Pastis (SPas) • Stan Pawlowski (SPaw) • Gene Persson (GP) • Mary Ramsperger Peterson (MRP) • Patricia Plepler (PP) • Sherman Plepler (SP) • Anthony Pocrnich, Jr. (APJr) • Edna Poehner (EP) • Elaine Ramsperger (ER) • David Ratner (DR) • John Riley (JR) • James Sasseville (JS) • Beverly Gish Savage (BGS) • Donald J. Schaust (DJS) • Paul Schlueter (PSch) • Craig Frederick Schulz (CFS) • Erin Schulz (ES) • Jean Forsyth Schulz (JFS) • Monte Charles Schulz (MCS) • Frederick G. Shackleton (FGS) • Donna Shaffer (DSha) • George L. Sher (GLS) • Jeff Shesol (JSh) • Ann Shields (AS) • Robert L. Short (RLS) • Clifford Silva (CSil) • Judy Sladky (JSlad) • Lettie Snider (LS) • Frank Stanton (FS) • Peter Sterner (PSt) • Tom Stuart (TS) • Jack Stuppin (JSt) • David Swanson (DS) • Patricia Swanson (PS) • Ramona Peterson Swanson (RPS) • Warren Taylor (WT) • Patricia Blaise Telfer (PBT) • Sandra Terrado (ST) • Roland L. Thibault (RLT) • J. Clifford Thor (JCT) • Jean Thor (JT) • Karen Kresge Titola (KKT) • Thomas M. Tomasi (TMT) • George H. Town (GHT) • Jill Schulz Transki (JST) • Polly Travnicek (PT) • Steve Unverzagt (SU) • Adam Van Doren (AVD) • Louanne Van Pelt (LVP) • Philip Van Pelt (PVP) • Ami Victorio (AV) • Art Volkerts (AVo) • Shirley Gish VonderHaar (SGV) • Mort Walker (MW) • Gordon Watson (GW) • William Charles Wegwerth (WCW) • Mary Welch (MWe) Lorraine Swanson Wentlandt (LSW) • Donna Johnson Wold (DJW) • Richard Wolff (RW) • Patricia Hanratty Wysocky (PHW)

## PREFACE

LIFE AND WORK: Charles L. Bartholomew and Joseph Almars, eds., *Modern Illustrating, Including Cartooning, Division 3* (Minneapolis, MN: AII, 1945), p. 38; *Charles M. Schulz: A Charlie Brown Life*, A&E *Biography*, 1995; (I) RW, Oct 23, 2003; (I) GLeB, May 18, 2001.

LEGEND: Mark Voger, "Now It Can Be Told!" *Asbury Park Press*, Feb 18, 2000, p. 25; Jennifer M. Contino, "Never a Blockhead: Jean Schulz on Peanuts" (http://www.comicon.com/cgi-bin/ultimatebb); (Q) Robert Digitale, "Charles Schulz: 'A Normal Person Couldn't Do It,' " *PD*, Apr 4, 1982, p. 2A; Pat Beresford, "Thirty Years and Still a Warm Puppy," *The American Kennel Club Gazette*, Dec 1979, p. 41; (V) (Q) John Cord, Peter France, BBC-Everyman TV, Jun 20, 1977; SKI, Jul 27, 1999, CBS News-*60 Minutes*, tape 13, (T) p. 16; LCI, Mar 15, 1982 (U), courtesy of Jeanne Heifetz and Juris Jurjevics; GGI, *The Comics Journal*, No. 200, Dec 1997, pp. 37; A&E; Ron Goulart, "Overrated/Underrated: Comic Strip," *American Heritage*, Oct 2004, p. 27; Walter Cronkite, Introduction, CMS, *The Complete Peanuts, 1953–1954* (Seattle, WA; Fantagraphics Books, 2004), p. xiii; Dan Harman, "Why This Book?" in CMS, *I Take My Religion Seriously* (Anderson, IN: Warner Press, 1989), p. v; David Blair, Letter to the Editor, *St. Louis Post-Dispatch*, Feb 15, 2000; LCI; Barbara McIntosh, "But We Love You, Charles M. Schulz," *San Jose Mercury News, West Magazine*, Jan 12, 1986, p. 7.

MODELS: JST, Jun 21, 2001; (Q) Teresa Exline, "Charles Schulz," *Art Product News*, May/Jun 1984, p. 14; (C) "Peanuts Creator Cartoonist of Year," *San Antonio News*, n.d., May 1955, n.p., UFSP; (Q) Rich Mellott, "Dreams and Disasters of Sparky Schulz," *Santa Rosa News Herald*, No. 40, Oct 2–8, 1974; (C) David Saltiel, "Charles Schulz: 'Plain Folks,' " *Stanford Daily*, n.d., 1972, n.p.; "Psychiatric Help, 5 Cents," *Suck*, Nov 30, 1999 (http://www.suck.com/daily/99/11/30); (Q) Terry Gross, *Fresh Air*, National Public Radio, Dec 18, 1990.

KANE: (P) Dec 18, 1968; (P) Sep 12, 1971; (P) Dec 9, 1973; "Literature and Movies in Peanuts" (Exhibition, CMSMRC, Summer/Fall 2004); (P) Jun 5, 1965.

## PART ONE

E: (P) Dec 18, 1991; (P) Dec 9, 1973.

## 1. SPARKY

E: RM&GG, "Charles Schulz Interview," *Nemo: The Classic Comics Library*, No. 31/32, Jan/Winter 1992, p. 18.

TROOP TRAIN: GG (New York: Pharos Books, 1989), p. 49; (I)

DJS, Jan 18, 2002; (I) JFS, Apr 29, 2002; (Q) Joel Goodman, "Up Close and Personal: Charles M. Schultz [*sic*]," *Laughing Matters*, Vol. 2, No. 1, The Humor Project, Inc., 1988; (Q)(C) Janet Motenko, " 'Peanuts' and Cracker Jack," Feb 7, 1988.

CANCER: Dena Bertina Schulz, Certificate of Death, Minnesota State Department of Health, Division of Birth and Death Records and Vital Statistics, Mar 5, 1943; (P) Sun, Oct 29, 1972; (I) ERH, Nov 2, 2000; RM&GG; CMS, *PJ* (New York: Holt, Rinehart & Winston, 1975), p. 24; ASI (U), Jun 25, 1989; CMS in Marshall B. Stearn, *Portraits of Passion: Aging, Defying the Myth* (Sausalito, CA: Park West Publishing, 1991), p. 95; CMS, with R. Smith Kiliper, *CBS&M* (New York: Doubleday, 1980) pp. 14, 18, 20; (Q) William Childress, "Charles Schulz," *Friends*, Vol. 32, No. 8, Aug 1975, p. 13; (Q) Peter Gorner, "Happy 25th Birthday, Charlie Brown," *Chicago Tribune*, n.d., 1975, n.p.

CHILDHOOD MEMORIES: (I) JBJ, Oct 15, 2001; (I) BF, Sep 5, 2003; GG, p. 40; (P) Jul 14, 1987; (PC) DHS to Mrs. L. D. Borgen, Mar 23, 1921, MCSC; (I) CFF, Apr 17, 2003; MCSI (U), n.d., 1989.

DENA: (I) PS, Sep 12, 2000; ASI; (Q) Hugh Morrow, "The Success of an Utter Failure," *The Saturday Evening Post*, Jan 12, 1957, p. 72.

PRE-ARMY LIFE: (P) May 13, 1970; William A. McIntosh, interview (U), National D-Day Memorial Foundation, Apr 1998; (Q) C. Robert Jennings, "Good Grief, Charlie Schulz!" *The Saturday Evening Post*, Apr 25, 1964, p. 26; MCSI; SKI, tape 13, (T) pp. 33–34; (Q) Brian Dunn, "Coming of Age: Charlie Brown became a man at Camp Campbell," *Leaf-Chronicle* (Clarksville, TN), n.d., c. 1999, p. D-1; (Q) Patricia Welbourn, "You're a Good Man Charlie Schulz," *Weekend*, Vol. 20, No. 11, Mar 14, 1970, p. 10; (I) PVP, Jul 12, 2001; RM&GG, p. 18; ASI; JFSI (U), Apr 28, 1997; (P), Jan 21, 1968.

## 2. RELATIVES

E: (P) May 15, 1965.

ANTI-GERMAN: Mary Lethert Wingerd, *Claiming the City: Politics, Faith, and the Power of Place in St. Paul* (Ithaca, NY: Cornell University Press, 2001), p. 163; RM&GG, p. 6.

CS: Judy Jones McKinney, *From Germany to America with the descen-*

*dants of Johann Friedrich Guenther: Includes the family names of Herms, Talbot, Seyer, Fricke, Witzel, Schulz. . .* (privately printed, 1995), pp. V32–V36; (I) CFF, Apr 17, 2003; CS Birth Certificate, Stendhal, Germany, certified Jul 6, 2001; Emma Seyer Schulz, Preliminary Form for Petition for Naturalization, Nov 24, 1942; CS retirement testimonial (Selby-Snelling Business Association, Nov 3, 1959), AP; (I) LN, Sep 12, 2002; (I) PS, Sep 12, 2000; (P) Feb 25, 1952; (L) Joan K. Peper, Liberty State Bank, to DTM, Feb 27, 2002; *75th Anniversary Album* (St. Paul, MN: Liberty State Bank, 1992), p. 5; (L) Walter Christian to CS, Feb 27, 1920, AP; (I) CCO, Apr 2, 2003; U.S. Department of Commerce, Bureau of Census, *The Fourteenth Census of the U.S.*, 1920; MCSI; RM&GG, p. 6; (I) FGS, Dec 6, 2002; GG, p. 99; CMS in Stearn, p. 93; (P) Mar 13, 1991.

DHS: (I) TOH, Jan 30, 2002; "Halvorson," family recollections and informal genealogy (U), courtesy of BHD; CS-DHS Marriage Certificate, AP; *Minneapolis City Directory*, 1922.

BIRTH: (PC) CS to Lars Borgen, Nov 27, 1922; *PGC* (New York: HarperCollins, 1999), p. 6; (Q) *Good Morning America*, Oct 2, 1996; CS records, AP; RM&GG, p. 8; Maurice Horn, ed., *100 Years of American Newspaper Comics: An Illustrated Encyclopedia* (New York: Gramercy Books, 1996), p. 49; Coulton Waugh, *The Comics* (New York: Macmillan, 1947), p. 53; PS, Jan 27, 2005.

SCHULZES AND HALVERSONS: CMS photo album, courtesy of JFS; (P) Jun 12, 1997; (L) Sarah (no last name) to Meloin Bredahl (Norwegian Lutheran Church, Spring Valley, WI), May 27, 1922, ASJC; A. B. Easton, *History of the St. Croix Valley* (River Falls, WI: St. Croix Valley Genealogical Society, 1909); (I) CFF, Apr 17, 2003; (I) PS, Sep 12, 2000; Sinclair Lewis, "Minnesota: The Norse State," *The Nation* May 30, 1923, p. 23; P. M. Wiff, *Is There Any Lutefisk and Lefse Left? A History of Martell Township: 1840–1994, With Genealogies of Pioneer Families* (Beldenville, WI: Helmer Printing, 1994), p. 259; (I) LSW, Jul 10, 2001; (I) DS, Jul 10, 2001; LCI; MCSI; *FGA*, pp. V32–V36, V45–V55; (I) WCW, Jun 9, 2002.

BORGEN FARM: MCSI; (I) PS, Apr 16, 2002; Lars Danielson Borgen, Petition for Naturalization, Jun 17, 1916, courtesy of Dorothy Zeuli; RM&GG, p. 6; *CBS&M*, p. 59; SKI, tape 13, (T) p. 4; (I) SGV, Sep 12, 2002; (I) DS, Jul 10, 2001; JFSI; CS records, AP; (P) Jul 7, 1951; (I) BHD, Feb 20, 2002; (Q) Mellott, "Dreams and Disasters of Sparky Schulz," n.p.;

(P) Nov 3, 1950; MCSI; (Q) Linda Witt, "The Soul of Peanuts," *Chicago Tribune Sunday Magazine*, Dec 22, 1985, p. 10; (P) Aug 31, 1980; (P) Apr 28, 1954; (P) Feb 2, 1967; (I) JPG, Oct 19, 2001; (I) PHW, Mar 22, 2001; (P) Dec 31, 1961; (I) MB, Sep 12, 2002; (P) Feb 17, 1994; CMS cited in JBJ, Family Group Record-54, courtesy of JBJ and ASJ; (I) LSW, Jul 10, 2001.

NORWEGIANS: F. Scott Fitzgerald, "The Ice Palace," *The Short Stories of F. Scott Fitzgerald* (New York: Scribner's, 1998) p. 74; (Q) Morrow, p. 71; (P) May 2, 1994; (I) PS, Jun 20, 2001, Sep 12, 2000, Jan 25, 2005, Apr 17, 2002; JFSI; GG, pp. 35, 125; MCSI; (I) LSW, Jul 10, 2001; (L) Lois Larson to ASJ, Aug 2 and 8, 2001, courtesy of ASJ; (P) Jul 19, 1956; (I) DS, Apr 24, 2001; "Halvorson"; ASI; (I) IM, Dec 11, 2002; RM&GG, p. 6; (P) Jan 21, 1990 (see also JBJ Genealogy Family Group Record-54: "Sparky said he didn't like his [Schulz] cousins too well. They were different and uneducated").

## 3. THE ART OF BARBERING

E: "Neighbors Honor Barber; 42 Years on the Corner," *Your Neighbor* (St. Paul, MN), Nov 4, 1959, p. 6.

BARBERING: (Q) "I'll be Back in Time for Lunch," *Los Angeles Times*, Mar 17, 1985, p. 16; (I) PS, Jun 7, 2001; (I) CFF, Apr 17, 2003; (I) LSW, Jul 10, 2001; (I) LN, Feb 15, 2001; CS records, AP.

CMS AND BARBERSHOP: (L) CMS to Joan K. Peper, May 27, 1992, courtesy of Joan K. Peper; (V) (Q) Karen and David Crommie interview, unedited footage, Aug 8, 1989, for *CMS—To Remember*; PGC, p. 54; (P) Sep 19, 1968; (P) Jan 27, 1968; *CBS&M*, p. 11; CMS in Stearn, p. 93; "Second General Vice President Schulz Dies in California," *Master Barber & Beautician*, n.d., 1966, p. 32; "Neighbors Honor Barber; 42 Years on the Corner," p. 1; CS retirement testimonial; ASI; A&E; L. Sherman Trusty, *The Art and Science of Barbering*, 3rd ed. (Pasadena, CA: Wolfer Printing., 1956), pp. 9, 106, 318.

MOTHER: *St. Paul City Directory*, 1928; (P) Jun 8, 1952; (I) PS, Jun 20, 2001; (I) SP, Dec 4, 2000, Dec 13, 2000, Jun 19, 2001; (I) SGV, Feb 14, 2002; (I) RH, Oct 22, 2001; (I) TH, Feb 25, 2002; (P) Nov 20, 1950; (I) PP, Jun 18, 2001; CMS, P45 (Kansas City: Andrews McMeel,

1984), p. 10; (I) CCO, Dec 3, 2002; LSW quoted in Meg Heaton, *Star-Observer* (Hudson, WI), Dec 30, 1999; see DHS in CMS photo album; (PC) DHS to Mrs. Lars D. Borgen, May 10, 1927, MCSC.

EARLIEST RECOGNITION: *CBS&M*, pp. 9, 10; *PJ*, p. 12; (I) LSW, Jul 10, 2001; Childress, p. 13; MCSI.

## 4. EAST COMES WEST

E: Tor Åge Bringsværd, "Bergen Guide" (http://www.bergen-guide.com/345.htm).

SIX: *CBS&M*, p. 17 (quotation from unedited manuscript); (Q) Kimmis Hendrick, "The Personal Equation," *Christian Science Monitor*, Oct 21, 1958, n.p.; Walter J. Wilwerding, "Sparky's Li'l Folks," *The Illustrator*, Summer 1948, p. 7; Kenneth F. Hall, "It Scares Me!" *Upward*, Feb 1, 1959, p. 18; (V) "Close-Up on *Peanuts*: Charles Schulz with Bob Quintrell," n.d., 1961; (Q) John Arms, "Charlie Brown, Linus, & Co," *Christian Science Monitor*, Aug 18, 1965, p. 13; (I) PS, Jan 27, 2005; (P) Nov 17, 1957.

LEAVING: (I) CCO, Dec 3, 2002, Apr 2, 2003; MCSI; *PJ*, p. 12; (I) VH, Apr 17, 2002; (L) CMS to Beulah Notley, Oct 15, 1996; (I) LWG, Apr 16, 2002; (I) PS, Apr 17, 2002; (C) *The Needles Eye*, n.d., 1910; *Footprints*, Vol. 29, No. 3, May-Dec 2001, p. 27 (Needles Museum, Needles, CA); (I) JHoh, Apr 5, 2002; *PJ*, p. 12; MCSI; GG, p. 32; CMS, "Comic Inspiration," *National Geographic Traveler*, Jul/Aug 1991, n.p.; RM&GG, p. 8.

NEEDLES, CALIFORNIA: Federal Writer's Project of the Works Progress Administration, *California: A Guide to the Golden State* (New York: Hastings House, 1939), p. 609; MCSI; "Needles," *San Bernardino City and County Directory*, 1887, p. 213–216; Paul Fussell places Needles on the next-to-lowest rung of American places in *Class: A Guide Through the American Status System* (New York: Summit Books, 1983), p. 36; Lesley Poling-Kempes, *The Harvey Girls: Women Who Opened the West* (New York: Marlowe & Company, 1991), p. 127; (V) *Charles M. Schulz: Und Seine Peanuts*, MarzFilm Production, 1990; U.S. Department of Commerce, Bureau of Census, *Fifteenth Census of the United States*, 1930, Vol. 177; (I) Sue Godnick, Needles Area Chamber of Commerce, May 22, 2002; Maggie McShan, "Profile of a Mother City," *2002 Needles Historical Calendar* (Needles, CA: Needles Regional Museum Association, 2002); GG, pp.

33–35; *Needles Nugget,* Aug 30, 1929; (for nearest date to Schulzes' arrival, see CS photographed in Wolf's Studio in Needles for California barber's license on Aug 26, 1929, AP); (I) LWG, Jan 25, 2002; (L) LWG to JFS and CMS, Nov 30, 1999; (I) LSW, Jul 10, 2001; George H. Foster and Peter C. Weiglin, *The Harvey House Cookbook: Memories of Dining Along the Santa Fe Railroad* (Atlanta, GA: Longstreet Press, 1992), p. 77; "Santa Fe Notes," *Needles Nugget,* Oct 3, 1930, n.p.; (P) Oct 2, 1952.

SCHOOL: William Stanley Knipple, *Historical Development of the Needles Elementary School District,* master's thesis, University of Southern California, 1957 (U), p. 28; MCSI; *Needles Nugget,* Aug 23, 1929; (I) MM, Apr, 5, 2002; GG, p. 34; (Q) Marie Schooley in Barbara DeGidio, "From the Information Station Desk at the Needles Branch Library," *Desert Star* (Needles, CA), Oct 16, 2002, n.p.; *Needles Nugget,* Dec 6, 1929, pp. 4–5; *Needles Nugget,* Sep 12, 1930, p. 3; (L) CMS to Beulah Notley, Oct 15, 1996.

IN THE DESERT: *The Harvey Girls: Women Who Opened the West,* p. 125; (I) LWG, Jan 25, 2002; (I) VH, Apr 17, 2002; MCSI; (P) Oct 3, 1975.

LEAVING NEEDLES: GG, p. 30; MCSI; *PJ,* pp. 12, 35; *Needles Nugget,* Sep 27, 1929, Oct 4, 1929; (P) Feb 1, 1963.

## PART TWO

(P): Feb 1, 1976; E: Fitzgerald, *The Great Gatsby* (New York: Scribner's, 1925), p. 118.

## 5. DISGUISED

E: *PJ,* p. 81; (Q) "Doing Business with Charlie Brown Is No Peanuts for 68 Publishers and Licensees," *Publishers Weekly,* Jul 7, 1975, p. 45

ST. PAUL: CMS, *Security Is a Thumb and a Blanket* (San Francisco: DP, 1963), n.p.; (I) LSW, Jul 10, 2001; *CBS&M,* p. 13; Gareth Hiebert (Oliver Towne, pseud.), *Once Upon a Towne* (St. Paul, MN: North Central Publishing, 1959), p. 30; Donald J. O'Grady, *The Pioneer Press and Dispatch: History at Your Door 1849–1983* (St. Paul, MN: Northwest Publications, 1983), p. 78; (I) PHW, Jul 9, 2001.

ELEMENTARY SCHOOL: MCSI; (L) Lois Martin Hefflefinger to Tony Hefflefinger to CMS, Dec 26, 1997; (I) PH, Aug 5, 2003; CMS in

Carter V. Carter photograph of Miss Kelly's B-5 class, Gordon School, St. Paul, 1932, AP; A&E; *PGC*, p. 129; (P) Nov 14, 1966; LCI; (L) Tony Hefflefinger to CMS, Dec 26, 1997; JFSI; GGI, pp. 5, 9; *CBS&M*, p. 34; CS records, Mar 24, 1965, AP; *PJ*, pp. 14, 81; Curt Brown, "Good Grief! You're 75," *Minneapolis Star Tribune*, Nov 23, 1997, p. E1; BBC; SKI, tape 13, (T) p. 19; (L) JPK to DTM, Jun 17, 2001; *GG*, p. 223; (L) CMS to Janice Blanchard, May 30, 1997; (Q) Mary Harrington Hall, "A Conversation with Charles Schulz: or The Psychology of Simplicity," *Psychology Today*, Jan 1968, p. 21; A&E; (I) SP, Jun 19, 2001; (P) Feb 17, 1966; "50th Anniversary of Art Instruction Schools Special Issue," *The Illustrator*, 1964, p. 10; (I) BF, Sep 5, 2003; (Q) "The World According to Peanuts," *Time* (cover story), Apr 9, 1965, p. 82; (Q) Gerald Jonas, "The 'Peanuts' Man Talks About Children," *Family Circle*, May 1968, p. 22; (P) Nov 12, 1979; (Q) Shel Dorf, "Charles Schulz," *Comics Interview*, No. 47, n.d., 1987, p. 8.

FATHER AND SON: P45, p. 10; Samuel Hynes, *The Growing Seasons: An American Boyhood Before the War* (New York: Viking, 2003), p. 237; WPA, *Minnesota: A State Guide* (New York: Viking, 1938), p. 63; MNHS, Barber Examiner's Board Case Files (see Amendment to Code of Fair Competition); A&E; (I) LN, Feb 15, 2001; SKI, tape 14, (T) p. 19; RM&GG, p. 6; MB quoted by Lois Larson to ASJ, Aug 2, 2001, ASJC; *CBS&M*, pp. 15, 34; (V) *Charles M. Schulz: Und Seine Peanuts*; LCI; (Q) Gross, *Fresh Air*; DJW quoted in RGJ, "Remembering the Embarrassed Genius," *Hogan's Alley*, Vol. 2, No. 8, 2000, p. 140; (I) JPG, Oct 19, 2001; (Q) Jud Hurd, "Charles Schulz," *Cartoonist PROfiles*, No. 44, Dec 1979, p. 54; (Q) Stan Isaacs, "Charles Schulz: Comic Strips Aren't Art," *Newsday*, Aug 28, 1977, pp. 15–17, 36, 38; (I) GL, Jul 11, 2001; Trusty, pp. 314, 347; *Oxford Classical Dictionary*, 2nd ed. (New York: Oxford University Press, 1969), pp. 451, 1038; (P) Mar 11, 1960; (I) PS, Jun 20, 2001; (P) Dec 22, 1976; GGI, p. 37; (P) Jan 13, 1958.

INTELLIGENCE THWARTED: (P) Apr 24, 1951; (I) CCO, Dec 3, 2002; (I) VH, Apr 17, 2002; (I) BHD, Feb 20, 2002; (L) SGV to DTM, Feb 14, 2002; (L) BGS to ASJ, ASJC; (V) Minette Paro on A&E; CS records, AP; Richard Marschall, *America's Great Comic-Strip Artists* (New York: Abbeville Press, 1989), p. 277; (LIL) Aug 29, 1948; CMS in Stearn, pp. 92–93; (S) CMS, SBWC, 1996; GGI, p. 18; (L) CMS to Pat Kerns, Nov 16, 1982; *GG*, p. 206; MCSI; (I) SGV, Sep 12, 2002; (L) SGV to

DTM, Feb 14, 2002; (P) May 14, 1965; (I) SK, Oct 4, 2003; SKI; (V) (S) CMS to Beaglefest, July 13, 1997; (LIL) May 8, 1949; (Q) "A Dialogue Between Jack Lemmon and Charles Schulz," *Redbook*, Dec 1967, p. 50; (Q) Gloria Bledsoe, "Breathing Life of Sparky into Peanuts," (Salem) *Oregon Statesman-Journal*, May 17, 1983, p. C-1; (DEP) CMS, *Skippy, Inc. v. CPC International Inc.*, Jul 22, 1980, p. 74; Elizabeth McLeod, "Amos 'n' Andy in Person: Radio's All Time Favorites and How They Got That Way—1928–1943" (http://www.midcoast.com/~lizmcl/aa2.html); Gilbert Seldes, "American Humor," in Fred J. Ringel, ed., *America as Americans See It* (New York: The Literary Guild, 1932), p. 353; William Manchester, *The Glory and the Dream: A Narrative History of America, 1932–1972* (Boston: Little, Brown, 1973), pp. 370–371; CS records, AP; CS Certificate of Citizenship, Feb 27, 1935, AP; CS, retirement testimonial, Selby-Snelling Business Association, Nov 3, 1959, AP; (P), Nov 21, 1963; *CBS&M*, pp. 11–12; (I) SP, Dec 4, 2000; (V) CMS, special presentation in *It's A Pied Piper, Charlie Brown*, 2000; (P) Oct 5, 1956; SKI, tape 14, (T) p. 31; CMS in Marvin Heiferman, Carole Kismaric, *Talking Pictures: People Speak About the Photographs That Speak to Them* (San Francisco: Chronicle Books, 1994), p. 88; (PC) Sophia Halverson to Augusta Borgen, Mar 25, 1903, MCSC; MCSI; CMS, P50, (England: Ravette Publishing Limited, 2000), n.p.; (P) May 4, 1975; (I) James R. McDonald to DTM, Oct 24, 2003; (I) PS, Jun 20, 2001, Jun 7, 2002; (L) RPS to ASJ, n.d., 2001, ASJC; (S) CMS, De Young Museum, Feb 20, 1992;

RIVALS AND DRAWING: (L) Lois Larson to ASJ, Aug 8, 2001, ASJC; (I) PS, Apr 16, 2002; JFSI; GG, pp. 16–17; RM&GG, p. 7; *PJ*, p. 13; (DEP) *Skippy, Inc. v. CPC International Inc.*, p. 6; A&E.

## 6. ORDINARY JOES

E: John Updike, "Cartoon Magic," *More Matter: Essays and Criticism* (New York: Alfred A. Knopf), p. 790.

THE COMICS: Robert Benchley, "The Newspaper 'Game,' " in Fred J. Ringel, ed., *America as Americans See It* (New York: The Literary Guild, 1932), p. 332; R. C. Harvey, *The Art of the Funnies: An Aesthetic History* (Jackson, MS: University Press of Mississippi, 1994), p. 69; Bill Blackbeard and Dale Crain, eds., *The Comic Strip Century: Celebrating 100*

*Years of an American Art Form* (Northampton, MA: Kitchen Sink Press, 1995), p. 27; Russel B. Nye, *The Unembarrassed Muse: The Popular Arts in America* (New York: Dial Press, 1970), p. 219; "Funny Strips: Cartoon-Drawing Is Big Business; Effects on Children Debated," *Literary Digest*, Dec 12, 1936, p. 18; Clare Briggs, *How to Draw Cartoons* (New York: Harper & Brothers, 1926), p. 107; Martin Sheridan, *Comics and Their Creators: Life Stories of American Cartoonists* (Boston: Hale, Cushman & Flint), p. 15; William Lass, "A Half-Century of Comic Art," *Saturday Review of Literature*, Mar 30, 1948, pp. 40–41; Gilbert Seldes, *The Seven Lively Arts* (New York: Sagamore Press, 1957), pp. 193–194; e. e. cummings, introduction, *Krazy Kat by Herriman* (New York: Grosset & Dunlap, 1969), p. 12; Blackbeard, "The Forgotten Years of George Herriman," *Nemo*, Jun 1983, p. 54; Seldes, "American Humor," in *America as Americans See It*, p. 357; Philip Nel, "Crockett Johnson and the Purple Crayon: A Life in Art," *Comic Art*, No. 5, Winter 2004, p. 8; "The Funny Papers," *Fortune*, Apr 1933, p. 47; Brian Walker, *The Comics Since 1945* (New York: Harry N. Abrams, 2002), pp. 22–76, 72–80.

SCHOOLBOY CARTOONIST: JFSI; P50, n.p.; GGI, p. 6; LCI; RM&GG, pp. 7, 10, 13; *PJ*, p. 13; *CBS&M*, pp. 17–18; Waugh, p. 225; (N) CMS, Studio Work Notes, n.d., 1990s; (Q) William Scobie, "Happiness Is . . . Snoopy," *Observer Magazine*, Aug 14, 1983, p. 77; (I) LSW, Jul 10, 2001; (I) SGV, Feb 27, 2002; (I) RPS, Sep 16, 2002; SKI, tape 14, (T) p. 6; (P) Jun 20, 1982; (L) SGV to DTM, Sep 12, 2002; ASI; (C) "Noted Comic Artists to Show Work Here," *St. Paul Dispatch*, Feb 5, 1934, n.p.; (S) CMS, DeYoung Museum, Feb 20, 1992; Stan Asch Papers, MNHS.

## 7. SPIKE AND THE GANG

E: Percy Crosby, *Skippy*, n.d., 1938, cited by Jules Feiffer in "Introduction to Skippy," Feiffer Papers, Manuscript Division, Library of Congress.

NEIGHBORHOOD: Hiebert, p. 43; *St. Paul City Directory*, 1937, MNHS; LCI; (Q) "Creativity forged in fires of 'loneliness and joy,'" *PD*, Apr 4, 1982, p. 1B; SKI, tape 14, (T) pp. 4–5; (Q) "A Dialogue . . . ," p. 134; (P) Aug 14, 1952; (I) TH, Feb 25, 2002; *Par Fighters, by "Stewey" and "Sparky"* (U), n.d.: CMS kept the stapled-bound work in a desk drawer in his studio; (L) CMS to GW, Dec 12, 1997, courtesy of GW; (L) SP to DTM, Dec 4, 2000, Jun 19, 2001; (L) GW to CMS, Dec 8, 1997; (L) GW to DTM, Jun 5, 2003; (P) Jan 22, 1961; CS records, AP; (L) CMS to Betsy Friesen, Feb 18, 1986, courtesy of TH; (I) GW, Dec 10, 2002.

ICE SKATING: (S) Stewart Wright, on receiving St. Paul's Walk of Fame honor in CMS's behalf, n.d., 1990s; (I) TH, Feb 25, 2002; *GG*, p. 217; (Q) Jim Phelan, "Penthouse Interview: Charles M. Schulz," *Penthouse*, Dec 1971, p. 38; (Q) (C) Dan Hruby, "Ice Warms Schulz's Heart," n.d., c. 1967; (Q) John Gilbert, "Peanuts on Ice," *Minneapolis Star Tribune*, Aug 14, 1993, E-1.

BULLIES: (Q) Jonas, p. 28; (I) JPG, Oct 19, 2001; (Q) (C) *PD*, Apr 4, 1982, n.p.; LCI; (L) SP to DTM, Oct 4, 2001; BBC; (P) Aug 8, 1974; GGI, p. 40; (Q) "Creativity forged in fires of 'loneliness and joy,' " *PD*, p. 1B.

CARL: (I) JPG, Oct 19, 2001; CS records, Mar 24, 1965, AP; MCSI; (Q) Charles Maher, "You're a Good Sport, Charlie Schulz," *Los Angeles Times*, Aug 28, 1973, pp. 1, 7; *PJ*, pp. 22–23; (L) GW to CMS, Dec 8, 1997; P50, n.p.; (P) Oct 2, 1952; MCSI; *GG*, p. 43; (P) Jul 6, 1951.

SPIKE: *CBS&M*, pp. 60–62; P45, p. 11; CS records, AP; (V) (Q) *The Dick Cavett Show*, Sep 2, 1978; (I) WCW, May 9, 2002; *PGC*, p. 7; (I) LSW, Jul 10, 2001; A&E; (P) Dec 4, 1960; (I) SP, Dec 4, 2000; Jan 7, 2001; (P) Sep 1, 1958; (I) CFF, Apr 17, 2003; Sheridan, p. 244. For the complete caption, consult the original *Ripley's* in *PGC*: the original has been bowdlerized and the noun "screws" removed.

## 8. CLASS OF ONE

E: "The World According to Peanuts," p. 82.

DENA: (I) PS, Apr 16, 2002; *GG*, p. 48.

CENTRAL HIGH: Program, Graduating Exercises, St. Paul Central High School Class of 1940, which graduated 558 students; CS records, AP; Paul Aurandt, *Destiny: More of Paul Harvey's The Rest of the Story* (New York: William Morrow, 1980), n.p.; B. McIntosh, p. 7; *Minneapolis Star Tribune*, Dec 5, 1981, E-1, SKI, tape 14, (T) p. 5; SKI, tape 13, (T) pp. 21–22; "A Dialogue . . . ," p. 134.

CERVICAL CANCER: DHS Certificate of Death, Mar 5, 1943; (I) JG, Nov 25, 2002; Jerome Groopman, "Contagion: Papilloma Virus," *The New Yorker*, Sep 13, 1999, p. 34; (I) JGF, Sep 8, 2003; (I) LN, Sep 3, 2003; (I) PS, Jun 7, 2001; (I) WCW, May 9, 2002; CMS, in Stearn, p. 95; (I)

RGJ, May 30, 2002; (I) SGV, Feb 27, 2002; CMS, *Security Is a Thumb and a Blanket*, n.p.

CENTRAL HIGH (cont.): Minette Paro, quoted in *Minneapolis Star Tribune*, Dec 5, 1981; CMS final report card in *PJ*, p. 15; (A) Ford Falcon, 1959, in Chip Kidd, *Peanuts: The Art of Charles Schulz* (New York: Pantheon, 2003), n.p.; (Q) *PD*, Apr 4, 1982, p. 1-B; LCI; (I) MCH, Dec 2, 2002; (I) JPG, Oct 19, 2001; *The Cehisean* (St. Paul, MN: Central High, 1940), p. 109; (Q) M. H. Hall, p. 21; "The World According to Peanuts," p. 84; (I) SDR, Sep 27, 2001; (Q) Cleveland Amory, ed., *Celebrity Register* (New York: Harper & Row, 1963), p. 556; (Q) Morrow, p. 71; (DR) CMS, n.d. 1940s, pencil on paper (U), CMSMRC; CMS, *I Need All the Friends I Can Get* (San Francisco: DP, 1964) (see also CMS's sketchbook in Kidd, n.p.); Dickens adapted by Maj. Malcolm Wheeler-Nicholson, *New Comics* (New York: National Periodical Publications, 1936); William B. Jones, Jr., *Classics Illustrated: A Cultural History, With Illustrations* (Jefferson, NC: McFarland & Co., 2002), p. 9; (O) (C) "Gertrude Borden," Mar 17, 1980; JFSI.

ART INSTRUCTION: (I) SGV, Feb 27, 2002; RM&GG, p. 13; Hynes, pp., 269–270; GGI, p. 6; *What Individual Instruction Means!* (Minneapolis, MN: Federal Schools Inc., n.d., 1930s); (A) "Cartoonists Make Big Money," *Picture Play*, Federal School of Applied Cartooning, n.d., 1920; *The Road to Bigger Things: Describing How Success May Be Won Through Illustrating and Cartooning as Taught by the Master Course* (Minneapolis, MN: Federal Schools, Inc., 1931), pp. 64, 65; Charles L. Bartholomew Papers, 1895–1941, MNHS; *Working Americans 1880–2003, Volume V: Americans at War* (Millerton, NY: Grey House Publishing, 2003), pp. 244, 263; A&E; BBC; JFSI; *PJ*, p. 23; CS records, Mar 24, 1965, AP; *Modern Illustrating: Including Cartooning, Division 7* (Minneapolis, MN: Federal Schools Inc., 1940); CMS's AAI records were later stolen: the present-day AII confirms that CMS was enrolled as a student from Feb 19, 1940 to Dec 1, 1941; (EM) SU to DTM, Jul 10, 2001; (Q) Bledsoe, p. C-3; CMS in Stearn, p. 92; (Q) M. H. Hall, p. 66; "Ingenue Visits 'Peanuts,'" *The Illustrator*, 1973, n.p.

GIRLS: "The World According to Peanuts," p. 84; David Burton Morris, Central High Class of 1940, "To the shorty of Central," holograph inscription, CMS's copy, *The Cehisean*, 1938; (P) May 22, 1995; RM&GG,

p. 10; (I) PHW, Mar 22, 2001, Jul 9, 2001; Grace Stewart Christensen testimonial to University of Minnesota, n.d.; (I) MCH, Dec 2, 2002; (I) LSW, Jul 10, 2001; (P) Jul 18, 1954; (I) LJ, May 8, 2002; SKI, tape 13, (T) p. 18; (I) JFS, Dec 7, 2000; (L) Lyala Bischoff Woods to CMS, Sep 19, 1970; (L) JPG to CMS, Sep 20, 1970; (I) JPG, Oct 19, 2001; (P) Dec 4, 1963; Holograph inscription, front endpaper, CMS's copy, *The Cehisean*, 1940, p. 40; (I) MCH, Dec 2, 2002.

FRIENDSHIPS: CMS, *Security Is a Thumb and a Blanket*, n.p.; (I) SP, Dec 5, 2000; (P) Dec 18, 1950; JPG, Oct 19, 2001; (I) DR, Feb 22, 2002; (I) PHW, Jul 9, 2001: I am indebted to Patricia Hanratty Wysocky for directing my attention to "Charles Brown" in "Camera Dodgers," *The Cehisean*, 1940, p. 38.

MISS PARO: (O) (C) n.d., 1984, courtesy of JFe; (L) Marjorie Neff Taylor to Schulzes, Feb 15, 2000; (I) JFe. Jul 18, 2002; (Q) *Minneapolis Star Tribune*, Dec 5, 1981, E-1; GGI, p. 5; Paro quoted in *PGC*, p. 8; A&E.

CANCER (cont.) CMS in Stearn, p. 95; (P) Jun 17, 1966; RM&GG, p. 10; MCSI.

CEHISEAN: (Q) B. McIntosh, n.p.; GGI, p. 6; *PJ*, p. 14.

# 9. ALONE

E: (I) SGV, Sep 12, 2002.

GRADUATING: *PJ*, pp. 15, 23–24; program for St. Paul Central High School Graduating Exercises, Jun 14, 1940; *Minnesota*, WPA Guide, p. 112; Hynes, pp. 269–270; (Q) "The World According to Peanuts," p. 82; (Q) Dorf, p. 8; CMS in Stearn, p. 92; (Q) "A Dialogue . . ." p. 135; SKI, tape 13, (T) p. 23; CMS in *The Most Important Thing I Know*, compiled by Lorne A. Adrian (New York: Cader Books, 1997), p. 16; (V) interview at the opening of Camp Snoopy at the Mall of America, 1992, courtesy of LN; (I) MCS, Aug 26, 2000; (Q) *The Charlie Rose Show*, May 9, 1997; (I) PS, Sep 12, 2000, Jun 20, 2001; (I) CFF, Apr 17, 2003; GG, p. 98; (I) AL, Mar 29, 2001; (I) DR, Feb 22, 2002; (I) LJ, May 8, 2002; LCI.

FIRST START: Walter Kerr, *The Silent Clowns* (New York: Alfred A. Knopf, 1975), p. 190; CS records, AP; Hank Ketcham, *The Merchant of Dennis the Menace* (New York: Abbeville Press, 1990), p. 50; SKI, tape 10, (T) p. 3; Jed Rasula "Nietzsche in the Nursery: Naïve Classics and Surrogate

Parents in Postwar American Cultural Debates," *Representations* 29, Winter 1990, p. 56; JFSI; (Q) recorded by JFS, Dec 23, 1998, courtesy of JFS; *GG*, pp. 22, 63–64, 123; (Q) "Creativity forged in fires of 'loneliness and joy,' " p. 1B; Kenneth L. Wilson, "A Visit with Charles Schulz," *Christian Herald*, Sep 1967, p. 63; GGI, pp. 6–7, 32; CMS, "Foreword (or Backword)" to Bill Nellor and Jim Molica, *Funny Fizzles* (New York: New American Library), 1978; Gurney Williams, ed., *Collier's Shares Its Wits* (New York: Robert M. McBride & Company, 1944), n.p.; P50, n.p.; (L) Albert Plepler to CMS, n.d., courtesy of SP and PP; RM&GG, pp. 8, 13; Frank Wing, "Caricature from Life," *Modern Illustrating: Including Cartooning, Division 8* (Minneapolis, MN: Federal Schools, Inc., 1924), p. 15; RCH, "Popeye, a Masterwork in the Medium," (http://www.rcharvey.com/hindsight/); (I) PO, Feb 27, 2002; (Q) Dorf, p. 8; O'Grady, pp. 74, 78; *100 Years in the St. Paul Pioneer Press 1849–1949* (St. Paul, MN, 1949), pp. 109, 111, 193; *PJ*, pp. 20, 30; Emile Gauvreau, *My Last Million Readers* (New York: E. P. Dutton, 1941), pp. 174–175; *Minneapolis, City of Opportunity: A Century of Progress in the Acquatennial City* (Minneapolis, MN: T. S. Denison and Company, 1956), pp. 112, 144; SKI, tape 13, (T) pp. 13–14; SKI, tape 15, (T) pp. 2–3; (L) Marie Lick to CMS, Aug 16, 1990, Dec 12, 1990.

DYING: (I) PS, Jun 7, 2001, Jun 20, 2001; (I) BF, Sep 5, 2003; DHS Certificate of Death, Mar 5, 1943; ASI; GG, p. 49; (I) BN, Feb 28, 2002; (V) CMS by JFS, St. Paul, MN, Aug 10, 1992; Morrow, p. 72; (I) ER, Jan 9, 2003; CFBMS, p. 18; (I) DJW, Jul 9, 2001; JFSI; MCSI; *CBS&M*, p. 14; SKI, tape 14, (T) pp. 2–3; BBC; CMS in Stearn, p. 95; (Q) Witt, p. 10; (Q) MJM Entertainment, "Interview with Charles Schulz," n.d. (www.mjmgroup.com); (I) WME, Sep 14, 2002; *This Fabulous Century: 1940–1950* (New York: Time-Life Books, 1969), p. 182; RM&GG, p. 18; *PJ*, p. 24; (I) ASJ, Jun 4, 2001; date of burial: *FGA*, p. 46; Hiebert, p. 55.

## GI INTERLUDE

E: *The Poetic Edda, Guthrunarkvitha I*, translated by Henry Adams Bellows, Princeton: Princeton University Press, 1936.

CAMP CAMPBELL: A&E; (I) DJS, Jan 18, 2002; (I) DGM, Oct 1, 2001; ASI; *GG*, p. 49; GGI, pp. 9, 32, 44; (L) CMS to Gishes, May 11, 1943, Jun 5, 1943, courtesy of BGS; Witt, p. 10; Charles Osgood, *Kilroy*

*Was Here: The Best American Humor from World War II* (New York: Hyperion, 2001), p. 18; (Q) "The World According to Peanuts," p. 84; Paul Fussell, *Wartime: Understanding and Behavior in the Second World War* (New York: Oxford University Press, 1989), p. 91; LCI; (L) CMS to Gishes, Jun 7, 1943; W. A. McIntosh interview, National D-Day Memorial Foundation, Apr 1998 (U); (Q) Dunn, "Coming of Age," p. D-1.

BASIC TRAINING: (DIA) Donley M. Swanson, Jul 10, 1945, *Parade Rest*, n.d., p. 9, courtesy ACL; *GG*, p. 43; (I) ERH, Nov 2, 2000; ERH on A&E; CMS in Stearn, p. 97; (L) CMS to Gishes, May 11, 1943; (P) Jun 12, 1965; (P) Jun 11, 1965; (L) CMS to Gishes, Jun 5, 1943; (S) CMS, DeYoung Museum, Feb 20, 1992; W. A. McIntosh interview; *St. Paul Sunday Pioneer Press*, Rotogravure Section, Jan 9, 1944.

LEADER: Morrow, p. 71; (I) ERH, Nov 2, 2000; Ken Martin, "Have It Your Own Way, Charlie Schulz!" *Nova* magazine (UK), n.d., c. 1972; (L) CMS to Gishes, Jun 7, 1943; Pfc. Charles Schulz: Bravo Company Roster of Enlisted Men, Sep 10, 1943, courtesy of ACL; *20th Armored Division in World War II* (Atlanta, GA: Albert Lowe Enterprises, 1946), n.p.; (I) FD, Feb 14, 2004; (D) CMS on envelope, S/Sgt ERH to Margaret Hagemeyer, Feb 11, 1944; (I) DGM, Oct 1, 2001; ACL, "Non-Commissioned Officers of Company 'B,' " *Parade Rest*, Sep 1988, n.p.; (I) ERH, Nov 2, 2000; (Q) W. A. McIntosh interview; (Q) Neil Steinberg, "Pen Pal," *Mature Outlook*, Sep/Oct 1987, p. 39; (I) DJS, Jan 18, 2002; (L) FD to DTM, n.d., Jul 2002; ALin, *Parade Rest*, Sep 1988, p. 3; (I) FD, Feb 14, 2002; AL, *Parade Rest*, Aug 2001, p. 3; FHH, holograph inscription, endpapers, CMS's sketchbook, *As We Were* (U); (I) VEG, Sep 9, 2001; (L) ACL to DTM, May 2, 2004; CMS, *Parade Rest*, Sep 1987, p. 4; CMS, "What the Last 20 Years Have Meant to Me," ms. dated Feb 25, 1993, for *Asahi Weekly*; S/Sgt. CMS's copy of General Field Marshal Erwin Rommel, *Infantry Attacks* (Washington, DC: The Infantry Journal, 1944); (L) CMS to FD, Oct 9, 1946; (I) DGM, Oct 1, 2001; (I) EVL, Apr 23, 2004.

LAST FURLOUGH: ASI: Until this 1989 interview, CMS never referred publicly to Virginia-Howley, and even here did not identify her by name: "[I] never really did what we call 'fall in love' until I was in the army and I had a nurse that I liked a lot"; CMS to RGJ, taped interview (U) for *GG*, n.d., 1989, courtesy of RGJ; (L) CMS to AA, Aug 17, 1944; *Cehisean*, 1938, p. 156; *St. Paul Pioneer Press*, Mar 23, 1941, p. 5; (I) JDA, land, and saw that they were good. We are created in your image

**All: To see good in the world**

Leader: So you created people to live on the earth, to love and be loved, to care for this creation and be fruitful and increase. And you saw it was good, very good. We are created in your image

**All:,To see good in each other**

Leader: And when we failed to praise you for harvests of plenty, to obey your commands and seek your Kingdom and care for the world that you put in our hands, you sent us your Son to show us the way. We are created in his image

**All: To see good in the dark**

Leader: So look at each other: we are made in God's image, to love and be loved, and find peace from that love.

**All: Thank you, Creator of All, that we can see you are good and find peace with each other. Amen**

Oct 12, 2001; (I) DJW, Jul 9, 2001; (L) CMS to AA, Aug 17, 1944; (I) SP, Dec 5, 2000; (L) CMS to AA, Nov 26, 1944; (V-Mail) CMS to AA, May 18, 1945; (I) CMS to ASJ, May 11, 1982; (L) FD to DTM, n.d., Jul 2002.

EUROPE 1945: (I) DGM, Oct 1, 2001; *20th Armored Division in World War II*, n.p.; CMS, *Parade Rest*, Sep 1987, p. 4; (I) FD, Aug 30, 2005; (DIA) Glenn W. Gintert, "A European Journey, GI Style," Jan 25–Feb 5, 1945 (U), courtesy of Vernon Sells; (I) FGS, Dec 6, 2002; Waverley Root, *The Food of France* (New York: Vintage Books, 1992), pp. 112–113; (P) Mar 1, 1987; (L) CMS to FD, Oct 9, 1946; (L) FD to DTM, Sep 16, 2002; (V-Mail) CMS to CS, Apr 6, 1945; *GG*, pp. 52–54; Belton Y. Cooper, *Death Traps: The Survival of an American Armored Division in World War II* (Novato, CA: Presidio Press, 1998), pp. 176–177; (L) ACL to Kevin T. Lynch, Oct 31, 1999, courtesy of ACL; *Parade Rest*, Aug 2001, p. 3; (I) EVL, Apr 23, 2004; Lord Byron, *Childe Harold's Pilgrimage*, Canto III: 55; Paul Fussell, *The Boys' Crusade: The American Infantry in Northwestern Europe, 1944–1945* (New York: Modern Library, 2003), p. 145; (DIA) Donley M. Swanson, Apr 29, 1945; (L) ACL to CMS, May 29, 1991, courtesy of ACL; (L) CMS to ACL, Jun 6, 1991; (L) ACL to CMS, Jul 31, 1990; (Q) Childress, p. 13; K. Martin, n.p.; Witt, p. 10; (Q) "The World According to Peanuts," p. 82; (Q) M. H. Hall, p. 21; Jim Dane, John Fox, Jim Watts, ACL (ed.), "Diaries by 3 Men in the 1st Rifle Sqd., 2nd Platoon," *Parade Rest* supplement, Sep 1988; (EM) ACL to DTM, Apr 25, 2004, May 2, 2004; (I) DGM, Oct 1, 2001; Fussell, *The Boys' Crusade*, p. 116; (I) MCS, Sep 12, 2000; (L) JFS to DTM, n.d., Nov 2002; (I) RGJ, May 30, 2002; (EM) JD to DTM, May 18, 2005; CMS to RGJ, taped interview for *GG*; (P) Jul 21, 1963; (P) Jan 10, 1952; (P) Mar 15, 1964; (P) Jan 10, 1952.

VICTORY: *Armor*, May–Jun 1993, p. 32; *Parade Rest*, Sep 1988; Manchester, p. 371; James Martin Davis, "An Invasion Not Found in History Books," *Sunday World-Herald Magazine of the Midlands*, Nov 1, 1987, p. 16; (C) Camp Cooke newspaper, Nov 1945, courtesy of ACL; *General Orders*, No. 6, May 17, 1945, Headquarters, 8th Armored Infantry Battalion, courtesy of Sells; Fussell, *The Boys' Crusade*, p. 103; (Q) *Vanity Fair*, Oct 1996, p. 310.

COMING HOME: (L) CMS to AA, Jul 1, 1945; (I) DGM, Oct 1, 2001; CMS to RGJ, taped interview for *GG*; (Q) Martha Sheridan, "Snooping into Charles Schulz's Private Life," *San Antonio Express-News*

*Sunday Magazine*, Sep 13, 1987; A&E; (C) "The Way Home," *Time*, Aug 7, 1944, n.p.; A&E; GGI, p. 10; CMS in Stearn, p. 95; B. McIntosh, p. 7; RM&GG, p. 10; (I) ERH, Nov 2, 2000; (Q) Goodman, n.p.; (Q) T. Glenn Harrison, "Soldier Home on Visit—Has Comic Strip Plans," *St. Paul Daily News*, n.d., 1945, (C) AP; (Q) Sheri Graves, " '65 Sheri Street," *PD*, Oct 24, 1965; (I) DJW, Jul 9, 2001; GG, p. 20; (I) JA, Oct 12, 2001.

LAST HITCH: (L) CMS to AA, Aug 17, 1944; (L) CMS to AA, Sep 20, 1945; Brian Walker, *The Comics Since 1945* (New York: Harry N. Abrams, 2002), p. 22; John Gunther, *Inside U.S.A.* (New York: The New Press, 1997), p. 277; CF holograph inscription, CMS Photo Album.

## PART THREE

(P) Dec 22, 1963; E: SKI, tape 13, (T) p. 16.

## 10. BREAKING THE ICE

E: (Q) Howard Hughes, "The Secrets of Success," [0cf2]News Herald (Santa Rosa, CA), Jan 10–16, 1984, p. 4.

SECOND START: GGI, pp. 5, 7–8, 10–11; (V) CMS by JFS, St. Paul, Aug 10, 1992; (I) LN, Jul 12, 2002; (L) CMS to FD, Apr 1, 1946; (DEP) *Skippy, Inc. v. CPC International Inc.*; (I) DR, Jun 1, 2004; *Minneapolis School of Art*, 1946, pp. 6, 25, 28 (Minneapolis College of Art and Design archives); (Q) Dorf, p. 13; (I) PBT, Jul 11, 2001; *St. Paul City Directory*, 1946; (O) Roman Dominik Baltes, *St. Paul Pioneer Press*, Jul 17, 1997; (I) JFe, Jul 25, 2002; *PJ*, p. 28; (L) CMS to FD, Oct 9, 1946; (L) CMS to FD, Feb 3, 1947.

CHURCH OF GOD: Merle D. Strege, *The Story of the Church for Children, 1880–1930* (Anderson, IN: Warner Press, 1987), Vol. 1, pp. 1–8; GG, p. 133; Jonas, p. 28; K. L. Wilson, p. 66; BBC; FGS in David Liverett, ed., *They Called Him Sparky: Friends' Reminiscences of Charles Schulz* (Anderson, IN: Chinaberry House, 2006), pp. 53–56; CMS, "Knowing You Are Not Alone," *Decision*, Sep 1963, p. 8; CMS in Stearn, p. 95; RM&GG, p. 18; (I) RF, Sep 20, 2001; (Q) M. H. Hall, p. 21; (Q) "The World According to Peanuts," p. 82; (Q) Jonas, p. 28; (I) FGS, Dec 6, 2002.

ART INSTRUCTOR: GGI, pp. 6–8; (I) PO, Feb 27, 2002; (I) SU,

Oct 31, 2001; *Introducing Your Art School* (Minneapolis, MN: AII, 1952), pp. 5, 24–25; Joyce Lain Kennedy, *Joyce Lain Kennedy's Career Book* (New York: McGraw-Hill, 1997), p. 349; Derrick Bang, "Jim Sasseville: The Ghost in the (Peanuts) Machine," (http://www.peanutscollectorclub.com); (I) DR, June 1, 2004; *Modern Illustrating, Including Cartooning, Division 2* (Minneapolis, MN: AII, 1945), pp. 2–3; (I) GL, Jul 11, 2001; (I) HKL, Sep 20, 2002; CMS to Max Harrison, Jun 23, 1948; CMS to ALJ, Oct 20, 1975; (I) PO, Feb 27, 2002; (I) DH, Dec 6, 2000; (I) JS, Jul 17, 2001, Oct 16, 2001; (I) LS, Feb 28, 2003; *PJ*, pp. 28, 30; (S) CMS, "On Cartooning," NCS, n.d., 1994; (Q) Dorf, p. 9; "S.S.R.," "Ingenue Visits 'Peanuts,'" *The Illustrator*, n.d. 1973, n.p., (V) CMS by JFS, St. Paul, MN, Aug 10, 1992; (L) CMS to FD, Jul 10, 1949; MCSI; P35 (New York: Holt, Rinehart and Winston, 1985), n.p.; (Q) Dorf, pp. 13, 15; *Is This Tomorrow?* Catechetical Guild Educational Society, Sep 1947, preview copy, courtesy of Dave Mruz; *Just Keep Laughing . . .* was published on the last page *Topix,* Vol. 5, No. 5 Feb 1947; (L) CMS to FD, Feb 3, 1947; *PJ*, pp. 31–32; *CBS&M*, p. 23.

MERRIAM PARK: *GG*, p. 133; (I) WME, Sep 14, 2002; (I) NOE, Feb 25, 2002; (I) LEO, Feb 25, 2002; (I) RF, Sep 20, 2001; CMS, *I Take My Religion Seriously*, p. 59; CMS to RGJ, taped interview for *GG*; (I) DE, Sep 14, 2002; Charles E. Brown, "The Visible and Invisible Church," in Warren C. Roark, ed., *The Church* (Anderson, IN: Warner Press, 1946), p. 68; (I) MRP, Dec 4, 2002; (I) ER, Jan 9, 2003; (I) PS, Jun 20, 2001, Jan 31, 2005; (I) JRM, Oct 24, 2003.

LI'L FOLKS: *Just Keep Laughing*, in *Topix,* Vol. 5, No. 7, Apr 1947, n.p., courtesy of DB and Mark Marz; (Q) Dorf, pp. 6, 8, 11; *CBS&M*, p. 22; (L) CMS to Boyd Lewis, n.d., 1971, courtesy of Brian Walker; (LIL) Jun 22, 1947; (LIL) Jun 15, 1947, *Minneapolis Tribune*; (LIL) Sep 21, 1947; (LIL) Oct 5, 1947; (L) CMS to Fred and Doris Shackleton, Jun 29, 1949, in Liverett, pp. 63–65; (LIL) Nov 9, 1947; (LIL) Sep 28, 1947; (LIL) May 23, 1948; (I) DJS, Feb 18, 2002; (I) MB, Sep 12, 2002; (P) Nov 10, 1966; (I) JS, Sep 13, 2001; DR, Feb 22, 2002, Mar 20, 2001, Sep 27, 2001; PO, Feb 27; *The Illustrator*, Summer 1948, p. 5.

CHICAGO: (L) CMS to FD, Jul 17, 1948; SKI, tape 13, (T) p. 4; SKI, tape 13, (T) pp. 5–6; *GG*, pp. 22, 154; RM&GG, p. 10; CMS, introduction, Kern O. Pederson, *Makers of Minnesota: An Illustrated Story of the Builders of Our State* (St. Paul, MN: Marric Publishing, 1971); Hiebert, pp.

102–104, 111–113; GGI, p. 24; Kenneth E. Eble, "Our Serious Comics," *The American Scholar*, Winter 1958–59, p. 26; (A) "Five Aces . . . ," Publishers Syndicate, *Editor & Publisher*, Aug 6, 1949, p. 35; *PJ*, p. 32; CMS to Hurd, n.d., 1972, taped monologue for *Cartoonist PROfiles*.

A NEW LIFE: (I) AL, Sep 10, 2004; LCI; Witt, p. 10; GG, pp. 22, 117, 135; GGI, pp. 3, 6–7, 24; (I) DR, Feb 22, 2002, Mar 20, 2001; (P) Feb 24, 1951; (P) May 15, 1952; (I) David R. Smith, Walt Disney Archives, Burbank, CA, to DTM, n.d., 2002 (see also Bill Peet, *An Autobiography*, Boston: Houghton Mifflin, 1989, pp. 73, 83); (Q) Dorf, p. 11; "School News," *The Illustrator*, Vol. 33, No. 4, Fall 1947, p. 23; (V) (Q) *The Charlie Rose Show*, May 9, 1997; (EM) JRF to DTM, May 30, 2002; O'Grady, p. 153; (I) JFe, Jul 18, 2002; (Q) Dorf, pp. 6, 17, 19; (I) LWG, Jun 21, 2001; Ketcham, p. 24; (EM) Ron Ferdinand to DTM, Feb 18, 2002; Bill Yates, "The Gag Cartoon Business," *Gag, Editorial, and Feature Cartooning* (Minneapolis, MN: AII, 1960), p. 23; RM&GG, p. 14; N.B.: no record exists of any Schulz submission in *the New Yorker* magazine collections, New York Public Library; "Reruns & Revivals," *The Comics Journal*, No. 141, Jun 1991; (I) MW, Jun 5, 2002; (I) PBT, Jul 11, 2001; Priscilla Jenne, interviewed by John Jenne, Sep 8, 2002, courtesy of Deborah Jenne Humphries; (N) (U) CMS, studio notes, n.d., 1990s; *PJ*, p. 32; (O) Eric P. Nash, "Bill Peet," *New York Times*, May 18, 2002, p. B15; (I) RF, Sep 20, 2001; Holly G. Miller, "The Church With a Mind of Its Own," *The Saturday Evening Post*, Nov 1985, p. 29; CMS on Feb 12, 2000, in telephone conversation with DR, related to DTM, Jun 1, 2004; CMS, "Charles Schulz—Drawing on Life," *The Illustrator*, 2000, p. 4.

## 11. HEADS AND BODIES

E: (L) CMS to Max Harrison, Jun 23, 1948.

EDUCATIONAL DEPARTMENT: CFBMS, pp. 7, 11, 15–16; JFS, Sep 14, 2000; (Q) Dorf, pp. 8, 9–10; (LIL) Aug 3, 1947; Jean Telander to CMS, Jan 1990; (I) PBT, Jul 11, 2001; *PJ*, p. 30; (I) PO, Feb 27, 2002; (L) HKL, Sep 20, 2002; (I) HKL, Oct 1, 2002; GG, pp. 200, 202; (I) LM, Oct 22, 2001; (I) JS, Jul 31, 2001, Oct 16, 2001; (I) DR, Mar 20, 2001, May 24, 2001, Sep 4, 2001, Sep 21, 2001; (I) LS, Feb 28, 2003; (I) GL, Jul 11, 2001; (EM) GL to DTM, Feb 22, 2002; (P) Aug 21, 1966; (L) Samuel

Hynes to DTM, Oct 15, 2005; *Introducing Your Art School*, p. 5; CMS in Bill Downey, *Right Brain . . . Write On!* (NJ: Prentice-Hall, 1984), p. 158; ASI; (L) CMS to FD, Jul 10, 1949; GGI, p. 3.

POST CARTOONS: *CBS&M*, p. 51; *PJ*, p. 32; (Q) *The Larry King Show*, Apr 28, 1988; Charles Schulz: byline on CMS's first published cartoon, *The Saturday Evening Post*, May 29, 1948, p. 116.

PROPORTIONS: Ketcham, pp. 111, 210; Frieda Rich, *Landmarks— Old and New: Minneapolis and St. Paul and Surrounding Areas: A Collection of Drawings* (Minneapolis, MN: Nodin Press, 1988); Jim Klobuchar, "Frieda was a model for more than just the 'Peanuts' strip," *Minneapolis Star Tribune*, Nov 22, 1994, p. 3B; (I) JK, Mar 17, 2003; (I) DR, Mar 20, 2001, Dec 3, 2002; Priscilla Jenne interview by John Jenne, Sep 8, 2002; Don Jardine, "Peanuts and Charles M. Schulz," *The Illustrator*, n.d., 1985, n.p.; Barbara Flanagan, "Peanuts Characters to Attend Fête in City," *Minneapolis Tribune*, May 15, 1964; (I) GL, Jul 11, 2001; (P) Mar 7, 1961; (I) HKL, Oct 1, 2002; (Q) M. H. Hall, p. 69; (Q) Hurd, p. 55; (DEP) *Skippy, Inc. v. CPC International Inc.*, p. 126; (P) Feb 24, 1964; (I) GLS, Feb 7, 2002; (I) WME, Sep 14, 2002; (I) LS, Feb 28, 2003; (I) PBT, Jul 11, 2001; (I) BBH, Dec 4, 2002; (L) HKL to DTM, Sep 20, 2002.

## 12. FAITH

E: (V) (Q) *The Mike Douglas Show*, Mar 7, 1979.

CONVERSION: (L) WME to DTM, Nov 16, 2002; (L) CMS to FD, Jul 17, 1948; (L) CMS to FD, Jul 10, 1949; *CBS&M*, p. 81; *PJ*, pp. 36, 90; (P) Apr 6, 1958. (I) DE, Sep 14, 2002; *This Fabulous Century, 1950–1960* (New York: Time-Life Books, 1970), p. 176; (L) CMS to Frederick, Doris, and Martin Lynn Shackleton, Jan 4, 1949, in Liverett, pp. 59–62; (L) CMS to FGS, Jun 29, 1949, in Liverett, p. 63; (P) Jul 8, 1952; (LIL) Nov 23, 1947; (LIL) Sep 5, 1948; BBC; GG, p. 134.

STATEMENTS FOR CHRIST: GG, p. 126; (I) FGS, Dec 6, 2002; (C) RGJ quoted in Michael Lollar, "Biographer Draws Schulz Out," n.d., c. 1989, courtesy DRF; (I) WO, Feb 25, 2002; CMS, "Knowing You Are Not Alone," p. 8.

THREE CIRCLES: GGI, pp. 6–9; ASI; GG, pp. 97, 134–135; (L) SP, Jun 19, 2001; CMS in GG, p. 97; (I) RF, Sep 20, 2001; FGS, "Memories of Sparky," in Liverett, p. 53; (I) GL, Jul 11, 2001; (L) HKL to DTM, Sep 20, 2002; (I) DR, Sep 27, 2001, Feb 22, 2002; (I) PO, Feb 27, 2002; (I) JS, Jul 31, 2001, Oct 16, 2001; JFSI; (P) Oct 3, 1998; CMS's accounts of street-corner preaching vary; I prefer the later account because by then he had discredited the veracity of his own account ("three golfing buddies") in the Reverend Billy Graham's *Decision*, Sep 1963, p. 8; "two" old friends are recalled by CMS on BBC-Everyman TV, Jun 20, 1977; (I) PBT, Jul 11, 2001; CFBMS, pp. 6, 18A; *PGC*, p. 28; (P) Dec 7, 1967; (V) CMS, interviewed by Joe Garagiola, *Today* show, Nov 18, 1968, courtesy CFS; LCI; (P) Dec 12, 1955.

MORE FALSE STARTS: GG, pp. 22, 135, 154–155; *PJ*, p. 36; (L) Ernest Lynn, NEA, to Joseph R. Fawcett, Jul 12, 1948; (L) CMS to FD, Jul 17, 1948, Jul 10, 1948; Boyd Lewis, "The Syndicates and How They Grew," *Saturday Review*, Dec 11, 1971, p. 68; " 'Peanuts' Creator Overcame Rejection," *Scripps Howard News*, Summer 1994; "Charles Schulz: Our Cover Artist," 35th Crosby golf tournament program, n.d., 1970s; (V) (Q) Crommie interview; (Q) Curt Brown, p. E1; CMS cartoons, *The Saturday Evening Post*, May 21, 1949, pp. 72, 166; (L) CMS to K. F. Hall, Oct 29, 1958; (I) FGS, May 23, 2003; (L) CMS to FD, Jul 10, 1949; (I) JFe, Jul 18, 2002; Bill Greer quoted in M. H. Hall, p. 67; (EM) JRF to DTM, May 21, 2002; (Q) "The World According to Peanuts," p. 82; CMS, *Young Pillars* (Anderson, IN: Warner Press, 1958), n.p.; K. F. Hall, "Memories of Sparky," in Liverett, p. 95; *St. Paul City Directory*, 1949; RM&GG, p. 11; (Q) "Charles M. Schulz, An Interview by Michael Barrier," Aug 1, 1988, n.p., (http://www.michael barrier.com/Interviews/Schulz/interview_charles_schulz.htm).

## 13. REDHEADS

E: Marcel Proust, *In Search of Lost Time, Vol. II: Within a Budding Grove*, D. J. Enright, C. K. Scott Moncrieff, Terence Kilmartin, translators, (New York: Modern Library Paperback, 1998), p. 512.

NEW LOVE: (I) CCO, Apr 2, 2003; SKI, tape 13, (T) p. 27; (V) DJW on A&E; (I) PBT, Jul 11, 2001; (I) GL, Jul 11, 2001; *Minneapolis City Directory*, 1950; (I) DJW, Jul 9, 2001; GG, pp. 86–88; Bill Milbrath, "Connected by More Than a Thread," *Holy Trinity Times: A Century of Change, 1904–*

*2004* (Minneapolis, MN: Holy Trinity Lutheran Church, 2004), p. 21 (see also pp. 10, 25); (DR) See DJW desk diary, Apr 11, 1950, in *GG*, n.p.; (I) LJ, May 8, 2002; A&E; *The Red Shoes*, theatrical trailer; (P) Jan 13, 1951; (P) Feb 16, 1952; (I) PS, Apr 17, 2002.

SUBMITTING STRIPS: Barrier interview; *PJ*, p. 36; *The Illustrator*, 50th Anniversary of Art Instruction Schools Special Issue, 1964, p. 11; Manchester, p. 246; *This Fabulous Century, 1950–1960*, p. 250; Allan Prior, *The One-Eyed Monster* (London: Bodley Head, 1958); William Laas, "A Half-Century of Comic Art," *Saturday Review*, Mar 20, 1948, p. 40; (Q) Dorf, p. 24; GGI, p. 31; CMS, interview with Morrie Turner (U), n.d., (L) CMS to Gail Rudrick and John Whiting, n.d., 1965; *GG*, pp. 23–24; (I) GL, Jul 11, 2001.

UNITED FEATURE: RM&GG, p. 11; *GG*, pp. 13, 31; (DEP) *Skippy, Inc. v. CPC International Inc.*, p. 117; CMS to RGJ, taped interview for *GG*; A&E; LR quoted in James L. Collings, "Rutman Explains Recent Failure of Some Strips," *Editor & Publisher*, May 5, 1956, p. 58; "Al Plastino," in *Legion Companion* (Raleigh, NC: Two Morrows Publishing, 2003), p. 19; *New York Times*, Jun 25, 1964, p. 47; (L) HG to CMS, Aug 9, 1956; (I) ROG, Sep 25, 2001; (I) SGo, May 31, 2001; HG quoted in Frances D. Williams, "Ex-Syndicate salesman helped put Schulz's gang in our homes," *Fort Myers News-Press*, Oct 8, 1985, p. 1D; Jane McMaster, "UFS Signs 'Li'l Folk,' 'Howdy Doody' Page," *Editor & Publisher*, Jul 8, 1950, p. 38; CMS, "Developing a Comic Strip," *The Comics Journal*, No. 250, Feb 2003, p. 107 (originally published by AII, 1959); *Peanuts* promotion pamphlet, 1950, UFSP; (Q) Dorf, p. 16; *Editor & Publisher*, Aug 6, 1949, p. 1; LCI; *PJ*, p. 179; CFBMS, p. 10; Laas, p. 40; (L) Joseph R. Fawcett to LR, Jun 20, 1950, UFSP; CMS-UFS Agreement, Jun 14, 1950, courtesy of ECA, BDG.

DONNA'S DECISION: *PJ*, p. 36; SKI, tape 13, (T) pp. 27, 29; *GG*, pp. 86, 90, 92, 164, 254; CMS quoting DJW, A&E; Garrison Keillor, *Lake Wobegon Days* (New York: Viking, 1985), p. 112; *CBS&M*, p. 27; *1950 Passenger Car Owner's Manual* (Dearborn, MI: Ford Division, Ford Motor Company, 1950), pp. 6–7 (see also *Life*, Jan 30, 1950: advertisement of 1950 Ford models, showing the two-door Tudor Sedan); (P) Sep 3, 1954; *PJ*, pp. 81, 87; M. Thomas Inge, "Two Boys from the Twin Cities: Jay Gatsby and Charlie Brown," *Comic Art*, No. 6, Spring 2004, p. 65; (C)

*National Enquirer*, n.d., 1980s; (Q) Curt Brown, p. E1; (I) DJW, Jul 9, 2001; (I) GL, Jul 11, 2001; (I) WCW, May 9, 2002; (I) ASJ, Sep 13, 2001; (P) Aug 2, 1962; (P) Jul 25, 1991; (Q) Dianna Waggoner and Roger Wolmuth, "Charles Schulz," *People*, Oct 30, 1989, p. 86; (P) May 25, 1964; (P) Nov 12, 1963; (P) Dec 11, 1970; (P) May 17, 1968; CMS to RGJ, taped interview for *GG*; (I) SP, Jun 19, 2001.

PEANUTS: McMaster, "UFS Signs 'Li'l Folk,' 'Howdy Doody' Page," p. 38; Tack Knight's *Little Folks*, 1930–33, Chicago Tribune-New York News Syndicate, aka Tribune Media Services; (L) Tack Knight to UFS, Jul 13, 1950; (L) Benjamin Shankman to UFS, Oct 30, 1950, and to LR, Nov 6, 1950; (L) LR to E. K. Bailey, Jul 26, 1950 (see also memorandum to Paul, Weiss, et al., Nov 1, 1950, UFSP); RM&GG, pp. 11–12; Stephen Davis, *Say Kids! What Time is It? Notes from the Peanut Gallery* (Boston: Little, Brown, 1987); P35, n.p.; *GG*, pp. 25, 23; (V) (Q) CMS on *Comics, the Ninth Art*, unedited footage, n.d., 1990; (L) CMS to HG, Oct 30, 1957, UFSP; (L) CMS to FD, n.d., 1950; (L) CMS to FD, Sep 17, 1951; (M) Nov 20, 1950, UFSP; "New kid cartoon by Schulz," *The Illustrator*, Fall 1950, p. 21; (Q) Curt Brown, p. E1; (Q) MJM Entertainment Group; see Isaacs, p. 16: Sasseville's name is misspelled "Sassaoill"; (M) George Pipal to CMSCA; (L) CMS to HG, Oct 30, 1957, with clipping attached from *State Times* (Jackson, MI), Sep 8, 1957, and *Publishers Weekly*, Jul 22, 1957, UFSP; "Peanuts Confidential," *Flatiron*, Mar 1953, p. 12; (M) to CMS, Nov 11, 1957, unidentified except by initials: J.R.W., W.E.W., T.D. (UFSP); *PJ*, p. 180; (Q) "The World According to Peanuts," p. 82; Lee Mendelson with Reflections by Bill Melendez, *TMAT* (New York: HarperCollins, 2000), p. 159; SKI, tape 13, (T) p. 16; (O) CMS by Sarah Boxer, *New York Times*, Feb 14, 2000, p. 1; (V) Robert Thompson quoted on "So Long, Charlie Brown," *PBS NewsHour with Jim Lehrer*, Jan 3, 2000 (see also Sarah Boxer misquoting Robert Thompson, *New York Times*, Feb 14, 2000); (P) Oct 2, 1950.

SISTERS: (C) Judith Halverson Sheldon quoted in *News-Tribune* (Oberlin, OH), c. 1956; (I) DR, Mar 20, 2001, May 24, 2001, Sep 4, 2001, Sep 21, 2001; (I) DJC, Feb 28, 2002; (I) MSH, Nov 8, 2005; (I) JD, May 9, 2005; (I) DR, Mar 20, 2001; Celia Ersland, "About Joyce Schulz . . . She Lives with a Famous Person . . . But Keeps Her Individuality," *PD*, Mar 3, 1968.

## 14. SAGA

E:"Of Brynhild's Great Grief and Mourning," *Volsunga Saga* (http://sunsite.berkeley.edu/OMACL/Volsunga/chapter29.html).

HENRY AND DOROTHY: Jonas A. Halverson and May Chase Halverson, Divorce Papers, quoted in Ruth Halverson genealogical research, courtesy of MCS; Dorothy H. Halverson to Miss Emma Chamberlain, Jul 20, 1909, copy in MCSC; H. H. Chamberlain, *The African in the Woodpile: A Foolish Fable with a Wise Meaning* (Minneapolis, MN: privately printed, 1921), pp. 94–95; (DIA) Henry L. Halverson, May 4, 1913, to Jan 21, 1956, MCSC; Dorothy to Henry, Dec 6, 1917, copy in MCSC; David H. Halverson, Certificate of Death, Sep 18, 1925, MNHS.

GROWING UP: (I) JD, May 9, 2005; (L) Ruth E. Halverson to MCS, n.d., courtesy MCS; (I) MCS, Nov 30, 2004; JD interview (U) by MCS, Jan 10, 1980, courtesy of MCS; (EM) Ruth E. Halverson to MCS, Feb 20, 1997, MCSC; (DIA) Henry L. Halverson, Jan 21, 1956, pp. 158–159.

FIRST MARRIAGE; MEREDITH: *Minneapolis City Directory*, 1948, 1950; (I) JD, May 10, 2005; (I) DJC, Feb 19, 2002; (I) MCS, Jan 8, 2001; (DIA) Henry L. Halverson, Jan 21, 1956, pp. 147–148; (L) Ruth E. Halverson to JJM, Dec 28, 1989, courtesy of JJM; JD interview by MCS; (L) MSH to JJM, Jan 5, 1990, courtesy of JJM; (P) Dec 22, 1954.

JOYCE AND SPARKY: (I) JD, May 9, 2005; (I) ASJ, Oct 15, 2001; (Q) "The World According to Peanuts," p. 82; (I) GL, Jul 11, 2001; (P) Jan 19, 1952; (I) DR, Mar 20, 2001; (I) PS, Jun 20, 2001; (I) MCS, Oct 5, 2000; (I) GHT, Feb 27, 2002; (C) Gaye LeBaron, *PD*, n.d., 1969; (I) BM, Dec 5, 2000; (P), Jan 12, 1958; (I) ASJ, Oct 15, 2001; JD interview by MCS; JD quoted on Na 'Aina Kai Botanical Garden website (www.naainakai.com 2002); (I) JD, May 10, 2005; (P) Dec 30, 1950; (I) JFS, Jan 30, 2001; (I) PVP, Jul 12, 2001; (I) DR, Mar 20, 2001, Sep 27, 2001; LCI; (P) Feb 28, 1952; (P) Mar 7, 1954; (P) Dec 18, 1994; (I) RDM, Mar 8, 2002; (EM) JD to DTM, May 18, 2005.

ENGAGEMENT, WEDDING, HONEYMOON: (C) JD quoted in Cobey Black, "Who's News: Life with Charlie," n.d., Aug 1964; (I) DE, Sep 14, 2002; (I) DJW, Jul 9, 2001; (I) JS, Oct 16, 2001; (I) GL, Jul 11, 2001; (I) LM, Oct 22, 2001; (I) BN, Feb 28, 2002; (I) WME and DE, Sep 14, 2002, Oct 23, 2002; (I) JDA, Oct 12, 2001; (I) RPS, Sep 16, 2002;

(I) JD, May 9, 2005; (EM) JD to DTM, May 18, 2005; (DIA) Henry L. Halverson, Jun 12, 1915, pp. 106–107, May 16, 1954, n.p.; (EM) Ruth E. Halverson to DTM, Nov 26, 2000; (EM) Ruth E. Halverson to MCS, Feb 20, 1997, MCSC; Marriage License and Certificate for Charles Monroe Schulz and Joyce Halverson Lewis, Book 590, p. 277, Marriage Records, Clerk of District Court, Ramsey County, MN; (C) *Minneapolis Morning Tribune*, Apr 18, 1951; (I) George Town (son of GHT), Feb 27, 2002; (I) WCW, May 9, 2002; GG, p. 103; (I) ASJ, Sep 13, 2001; (I) TOH, Jun 25, 2001; (P) Nov 14, 1958.

STARTING WEST: (Q) Hurd, p. 53; *PJ*, p. 158; (Q) Albert Morch, *Daily News Record*, (Harrisonburg, VA), Jul 14, 1965, p. 5; Barrier interview ("Well, that's a lie, too . . ."); (I) JD, May 9, 2005; "Gentle Genius," *People*, Feb 28, 2000, p. 56; (L) Ruth E. Halverson to JJM, Dec 28, 1989; JD interview by MCS; BBC; (Q) K. L. Wilson, p. 59; (V) (Q) *Charles M. Schulz: Und Seine Peanuts*; (I) MSH to DTM, Nov 9, 2005; CMS to RGJ, taped interview for *GG*.

## PART FOUR

(P) Nov 20, 1966; E: (I) JD, May 9, 2005

## 15. TO THE ROCKIES

E: Frederick Jackson Turner, "The Significance of the Frontier in American History," *The Annals of America, Vol. 2, 1884–1894* (Chicago: Encyclopedia Britannica, 1976), p. 478.

COLORADO SPRINGS: (I) JD interview by MCS; *Colorado Springs, Manitou Springs, and the Pikes Peak Region*, Colorado Springs Chamber of Commerce, 1941; Vernon Kilns plate depicting Colorado Springs, n.d., 1950s; (L) CMS to LR, Apr 2, 1951; Marshall Sprague, *Newport in the Rockies: The Life and Good Times of Colorado Springs* (Chicago: Swallow Press, 1980), p. 317; Rosemary Hetzler and John Hetzler, *Colorado Springs and Pikes Peak Country* (Norfolk, VA: Donning Co./Publishers, 1989), p. 183; (I) LVP, Jun 17, 2002; (P) Apr 13, 1952; (L) CMS to FD, Sep 17, 1951; (I) PVP, Jun 5, 2001, Jul 12, 2001; (I) MHS, Nov 8, 2005; *PJ*, p. 158; (I) JD, May 10, 2002; (Q) Dorf, pp. 15, 19; *GG*, p. 101.

FIRST SALES, FIRST SON: *GG*, p. 27; " 'Peanuts' Artist Visits the News," *Rocky Mountain News*, Oct 10, 1951, p. 6; (I) JD, May 9, 2005; CMS and JHS's copy of Ely Culbertson, *The New Gold Book of Bidding and Play: Contract Bridge Complete* (Philadelphia: John G. Winston), 1949; (I) PVP, Jun 5, 2001; (6 pounds, 8 ounces: see photo montage made by JHS, MCSC); (EM) JD to DTM, May 18, 2005.

DEVELOPING THE FEATURE: (EM) LVP to DTM, May 3, 2003; (L) PVP to CMS, n.d., 1999; Nell Womack Evans, "Cartoonist's life isn't all funnies," *Colorado Springs Sun*, Apr 24, 1980, p. 5-D; CMS to RGJ, taped interview for *GG*; CMS to John Selby, Feb 7, 1952, RGJ files, courtesy of RGJ; (N) LVP about the Schulzes in Colorado Springs, n.d., 1951, courtesy of LVP; RM&GG, p. 7; (Q) *Youth*, Mar 24, 1968, p. 13; (N) CMS quoted in LVP; (P) Oct 11, 1951; Louis Kronenberger, *Company Manners*, quoted in *This Fabulous Century, 1950–1960*, p. 181; (Q) Dru Wilson, "You're a Good Man, Charlie Brown!" *Gazette Telegraph* (Colorado Springs, CO), Mar 1, 1979, p. D-1; (P) Nov 23, 1950; (C) John Cavola, "And, Please, Don't Ever Give Up 'Peanuts,' " *Press-Scimitar* (Memphis, TN), n.d. 1956; United Feature Syndicate promotional materials, May 1956, UFSP; *PJ*, p. 81; (L) SP to DTM, Jan 7, 2001; (I) DR, Jun 1, 2004; John Bayley, "Not Just for Children," *The New York Review of Books*, Mar 27, 2003, p. 5; Scott Long, "Schulz's Endearing Kids Have Book to Themselves," *Minneapolis Sunday Tribune*, Oct 3, 1954.

LUCY VAN PELT: CMS quoted in P20 (New York: World Publishing, 1970), p. 35; "City Man Creator of 'Peanuts,' " *Minneapolis Star Tribune*, Jul 31, 1952; *PJ*, p. 81; (footnote) Gore Vidal, "The Oz Books," in *United States: Essays 1952–1992* (New York: Random House, 1993) p. 1112; (P) Feb 14, 1954; (P) Feb 20, 1955; (P) Apr 25, 1951; (P) May 29, 1951; CMS quoted from earlier source in GGI, p. 30; (P) Jun 6, 1952.

LOUANNE AND FRITZ VAN PELT: CMS to RGJ, taped interview for *GG*; (I) MSH, Nov 9, 2005; (I) PVP and LVP, Jul 12, 2001; (Q) D. Wilson, n.p.; (L) PVP to DTM, Jun 5, 2001; (L) CMS to FD, Sep 17, 1951; (L) CMS to PVP and LVP, Feb 1, 1957, courtesy of LVP; (I) JD, May 9, 2005; (EM) LVP to DTM, Aug 19, 2005; (N) LVP; "Meet Charlie: The Man Behind 'Peanuts,' " *Sunday Free Press* (Detroit), Aug 31, 1952; *PGC*, p. 23; K. L. Wilson, p. 64; (L) CMS to PVP, Jun 20, 1989, courtesy of PVP; (S) CMS to NCS, 1994.

ONE IDEA: D. W. Winnicott, *Playing and Reality* (New York: Routledge, 1989), p. 1; (L) LR to D. W. Winnicott, Sep 30, 1955, UFSP; (E) in James Stevenson, *Sometimes, But Not Always: A Novel* (Boston: Little, Brown, 1967); Art Buchwald, introduction, *Best Cartoons of the World II* (New York: Atlas World Press Review, 1976), n.p.; CMS, "Foreword (or Backword)" to Nellor and Molica, *Funny Fizzles*; SKI, (T) pp. 12–13: CMS, from memory, places the reader's letter in 1951–53, but the resulting strip did not appear until May 31, 1961; (one idea: see a variety of interviews from figures throughout CMS's life, from CRB and BB to AL); (P) Feb 22, 1951; (C) JHS quoted in Black; (P) Sep 16, 1965, with CMS holograph inscription on original, courtesy of PVP; (I) CMS to PVP, Dec 20, 1955, courtesy of PVP; (P) Jul 23, 1985, with CMS holograph inscription on original, courtesy of CA; (Q) Mellott, n.p.; (P) Jul 23, 1985; (I) CA, Jun 23, 2004; (C) (Q) Penny Colburn, "You're a Good Man, too, Sparky Schulz," n.d., 1969, Ghirardelli Square Theatre, courtesy of JPK; (I) AL, Jan 5, 2005; (I) JD, May 10, 2005; (Q) Christie Fairchild and Laurie Fialkowski, "Charlie Brown, Meet Your Creator Charles Schulz," *The Jolly Roger* (San Anselmo, CA: Sir Francis Drake High School); Feb 14, 1969, p. 1; (Q) Scobie, p. 81; *CBS&M*, pp. 35–36; Burr Snider, "For the Schultzes [*sic*], Skating isn't Just Peanuts," *San Francisco Examiner*, May 12, 1980; (Q) "Peanuts Creator Cartoonist of Year," *San Antonio News*, n.d., May 1956; "Peanuts Confidential," p. 13; (Q) Exline, p. 16; CFBMS, p. 8; (Q) Mildred Bettinger, "Security Is Being a Successful Cartoonist," *The Valuator*, Spring 1969, p. 23.; (Q) Hendrick, n.p.; *PGC*, p. 25; (V) (Q) *The Mike Douglas Show*, March 7, 1979; (Q) Goodman, n.p.

CHARLIE BROWN: (I) TK, May 3, 2002; (Q) Morrow, 72; (Q) Cynthia Boyd, "Good grief, it's the real Charlie Brown," *St. Paul Pioneer Press*, Apr 17, 1979, p. 5; CFB to CMS, Dec 23, 1977, CMS Studio Archive; CFBMS, p. 1 (N.B. Charlie F. Brown's memoir, *Me and Charlie Brown: A Book of Good Griefs*, written in 1977, was published in 1985, two years after his death (Feb 5, 1983) by a small press in St. Paul: Entheo; (Q) (C) Charles Solomon, "Schulz: His Work Isn't Kids' Stuff," Dec 16, 1983, VI-10; *GG*, 168; Jim Klobuchar, *Eight Miles Without a Pothole: As Close to Heaven as I'm Going to Get* (McGregor, MN: Voyageur Press, 1986), p. 190.

HOME TO MINNESOTA: *GG*, p. 101; (A) 3rd Annual Pikes Peak Winter Festival, Colorado Springs, CO, *Holiday*, Feb 1950, p. 92; (L) Henry

L. Halverson to JHS, CMS, and MLS, MCS, Oct 15, 1951, courtesy of JD; (L) CMS to John Selby, Mar 5, 1952; (I) ASJ, Sep 13, 2001; (I) PVP, Jul 12, 2001; Allan Keller, "Peanuts Isn't Peanuts," *New York World-Telegram* and *Sun Saturday Magazine*, May 5, 1956, p. 5; CMS, *Security Is a Thumb and a Blanket*, n.p.; (I) PS, Jan 27, 2005; Vance Packard, *The Status Seekers* New York: David McKay, 1959), pp. 98–107; ASI; (I) DE and WME, Sep 14, 2002.

## 16. PEANUTS, INC.

E: CS in "Neighbors Honor Barber; 42 Years on the Corner," p. 6.

PENTHOUSE STUDIO: *PJ*, p. 158; "Peanuts Go Far," *The Illustrator*, Summer 1954; CMS interview by Murray Olderman, Mar 27, 1991; (I) JS, Oct 16, 2002; (L) CMS to HG, Apr 7, 1954, UFSP; (L) HG to CMS, Jun 8, 1954.

TAKING OFF: Vance Packard, "How Does Your Income Compare with Others?" *Collier's*, Nov 23, 1956; (L) CMS to HG, Sep 14, 1954; (M) LR, n.d., attached to CMS request, Mar 9, 1955, UFSP; Packard, *The Status Seekers*, pp. 98–107; see *The Saturday Evening Post* photo, captioned in "Carl F. Schulz Makes the 'Post' Via Story of Son Charles," *Master Barber & Beautician*, Feb 1957, p. 14; *Most Walker's Private Scrapbook: Celebrating a Life of Love and Laughter* (Kansas City, MO: Andrews McMeel, 2000), p. 223; (M) unsigned to LR, Jan 26, 1954; (L) CMS to LR, Oct 22, 1953; (L) HG to CMS, Feb 2, 1954; (L) HG to Virginia Evans, Dec 5, 1957 (see also Peanuts Strip Subscriber List, Feb 11, 1957); (M) Dec 5, 1957, and United Feature Syndicate press release, n.d., 1957; (C) *Columbia Daily Spectator*, Nov 13, 1957, n.p., UFSP; (EM) Susan Bishop (*Cornell Daily Sun*) to DTM, Mar 2, 2005 (see also *New York World-Telegram*, Oct 26, 1953, p. 16); (L) Felix R. McKnight to CMS, Aug 9, 1956; (L) University of Southern California Card Stunt Committee to United Feature Syndicate, Oct 28, 1957; (L) Evan H. Turner to JH, Aug 11, 1962; (M) loan from Rhode Island School of Design Museum to JH, Apr 4, 1957; "Child's Garden of Reverses," *Time*, Mar 3, 1958, p. 58; (L) Clare R. Liggett to JH, Dec 12, 1956; (L) June Chatfield to United Feature Syndicate, Oct 10, 1957; (L) Timothy Leary to CMS, Dec 23, 1954; "The Hippies: Philosophy of a Subculture," *Time* (cover story), Jul 7, 1967, p. 23; (L) Timothy Leary to

United Feature Syndicate, Nov 13, 1956; (L) Gene Shalit to LR, May 15, 1957; (P) Feb 1, 1954.

CARTOONISTS: GG, pp. x, 125, 235; (V) (Q) *Comics, The Ninth Art*; PVP, "The 1st Platoon," supplement to *Parade Rest*, May 1989, p. 7; RCH, *The Art of the Funnies*, pp. 202–203; MW, *Backstage at the Strips* (Harrisburg, PA: A&W Visual Library, 1975), pp. 45, 99–100; (I) MW, Jun 5, 2002; MW and BJ, eds., *The National Cartoonists Society Album* (New York: NCS, 1988), p. 205; Stephen Becker, *Comic Art in America* (New York: Simon & Schuster, 1959), pp. 361–362; (S) CMS, "On Cartooning"; (I) BM, Dec 5, 2000; Jennings, p. 26; *Evening Chronicle* (Allentown, PA), Oct 2, 1950, p. 21; (Q) Dorf, pp. 22–23; Keillor, p. 267; (M) HG to CMS, Apr 25, 1956, UFSP; (C) (Q) Hendrick, n.p.; (Q) Hall, "It Scares Me!," p. 17; ASI; (C) (Q) Torri Minton, "Good Grief, Charlie Schulz," *San Francisco Chronicle*, May 9, 1989, n.p.; (I) JFe, Jul 18, 2002; (I) BJ, Jun 7, 2001; (P) Jun 9, 1953; CFBMS, pp. 5, 9, 10–11; (I) GL, Jul 11, 2001; (I) JD, May 8–10, 2005; (I) RN, May 15, 2001; (Q) Digitale, p. 2A.

PEANUTS, INC: GG, pp. 157, 253; (Q) Motenko, p. 5; GGI, p. 43; (L) CMS to HG, Nov 5, 1958, UFSP; (I) SGo, May 31, 2001; HG to CMS, Jul 16, 1956; (L) HG to CMS, Nov 15, 1956; (L) HG to CMS, Mar 16, 1955; (L) HG to CMS, Jun 15, 1955; (M) unsigned to accounting department, Jun 13, 1955; (I) HG to Charlie Brown (Lawrence, KS), Aug 23, 1955; (L) HG to Penrod Dennis, Oct 23, 1956; (L) HG to Doug Keys, May 25, 1956; U.S. Navy to United Feature Syndicate, May 26, 1958; (L) HG to CMS, Nov 10, 1958; (L) CMS to HG, Nov 13, 1956; (L) CMS to a "Miss Crawford," Oct 7, 1954, RGJ Files, courtesy of RGJ; (L) CMS to Walt Kelly, Nov 15, 1954, courtesy of PMcD; LCI; *PJ*, p. 158; (C) "Thanks for the Laughter," *Boston Post*, n.d., May 1956, n.p.; (L) Beatrice A. Harrison to CMS, Jul 11, 1956; (C) Kathlyn Kapanka to the editor, *Detroit Free Press*, n.d., 1956, in "Why Millions of Newspaper Readers Love Peanuts," United Feature Syndicate promotional material, 1956; (L) William L. Anderson to Don Hardenbrook, Dec 13, 1956; (L) HG to Doug Keys, May 25, 1956; see JH to John William Hardy, Jun 21, 1956, and *passim*, UFSP; (L) JH to CMS, Sep 7, 1954; (L) CMS to JH, Aug 27, 1954; (L) JH to CMS, Feb 10, 1955; (L) CMS to HG, Mar 19, 1957; (L) CMS to Elizabeth Swaim, Manuscript Division, Library of Congress (see AP story, Sep 4, 2000, about Swaim donating letter to LOC after her death); CMS identified the strip Hoover had requested in Willmar Thorkelson, "Cartoonist Turns Over Tenth of 'Peanuts' to the Church," *Minneapolis Star*, Mar 18, 1955, p. 29; (L) CMS to JH, Aug 27, 1954; (L) CMS to JH, Sep 7, 1956; Terry Galanoy to CMS, Aug 16, 1956; (L) William F. Brown to JH, Feb 1, 1957; (L) JH to CMS, Feb 10, 1956; C. J. Kellogg to HG, Dec 11, 1956; (L) CMS to JH, Feb 8, 1957; (S) LR quoted by CMS to Beaglefest, Jul 13, 1997 (see also John Schnapp to LR, Apr 29, 1955).

ART INSTRUCTION: (S) CMS, DeYoung Museum; *The Larry King Show*, Apr 28, 1988; *PJ*, pp. 28, 30; (I) DR, Jun 1, 2004, Mar 20, 2001, Sep 27, 2001; (I) GL, Jul 11, 2001; (C) Kenena MacKenzie, "Our Minnesota Presents Bart Bartholomew," n.d., 1941, Charles L. Bartholomew Papers, 1895–1941, MNHS; "Details of Course of Instruction," AII, 1959, State Archives Notebooks, Minnesota Attorney General, MNHS; (I) JS, Oct 16, 2001; (I) HKL, Sep 20, 2002; "Fifty Years of Service," *The Illustrator*, Spring 1948, p. 14; (S) CMS, SBWC, 1989.

MINNEHAHA: *GG*, p. 91; (L) LR to CMS, Mar 1, 1955; (I) PVP, Jul 12, 2001; (I) FPA, Apr 17, 2002; Thorkelson, p. 29; (I) CMS to JH, Apr 11, 1955; Morrow, p. 70; JHS quoted in Black; (V) CMS by JFS, Minneapolis, MN, Aug 10, 1992; (L) RS to DTM, Sep 14, 2002; (L) JHS to ROG and HG, Jun 19, 1954, UFSP; (DIA) Henry L. Halverson, Jan 21, 1956, pp. 128–129, MCSC; Halverson Genealogy, prepared by Ruth E. Halverson, courtesy of JJM; (I) ASJ, Oct 15, 2001; (C) courtesy of JD.

FIRST REUBEN: (Q) Exline, p. 19; *New York Herald Tribune*, Apr 27, 1956; SKI, tape 13, (T) pp. 5–6, 10–11; (L) Harold H. Anderson to CMS, Jul 27, 1956, UFSP; (I) PMcD and KOC, Feb 15, 2002.

## 17. THE CALL OF CALIFORNIA

E: Kevin Starr, "California, A Dream," in Claudia K. Jurman and James J. Rawls, eds., *California: A Place, a People, a Dream* (San Francisco and Oakland: Chronicle Books and Oakland Museum of California, 1986), p. 18.

FORTUNE, FAME, and FUNDAMENTALISM: (V) (Q) "Close-Up on *Peanuts*"; (I) HG to CMS, Apr 12, 1957, and May 9, 1957, UFSP; "Peanuts Confidential," p. 13; (press release) *USS Coral Sea*, May 9, 1956, UFSP; K. L. Wilson, pp. 15, 63; (L) CMS to HG, Mar 19, 1957; Keller, p.

5; SKI, tape 14, (T) p. 5; CMS, *Happiness Is a Warm Puppy* (San Francisco: DP, 1962); K. F. Hall, "It Scares Me!" pp. 17–18; (A) "Meet the Man Behind Charlie Brown," for Ford Falcon, Ford Motor Company, n.d., 1960, UFSP; editorial subheading to Morrow, p. 34; (V) CMS, *The Tonight Show*, Feb 7, 1973; "Child's Garden of Reverses," p. 58; (V) CMS, *Today* show, Feb 18, 1958; (L) HG to CMS, Feb 6, 1958; (Q) M. H. Hall, p. 69; (Q) Steven V. Roberts, "You're a Brave Man, Charlie Brown," *New York Times*, May 26, 1969, p. 20; (C) (Q) Saltiel, n.p.; LCI; (L) HG to CMS, Jun 22, 1955; (L) JH to CMS, Feb 6, 1957; (I) PSch, Dec 5, 2002; (L) PSch to CMS, Nov 30, 1999; " 'Sparky' Touched Friend's Life," *Express-Times* (Easton, PA), Feb 18, 2000, p. C-2; Will Jones, "Artist Makes Good Comic," *Minneapolis Star Tribune*, n.d., Jun 1957, clipped to letter, CMS to HG, Jun 6, 1956 (see also telegram, LR to CMS, Jun 7, 1957); (L) CMS to HG, Jun 6, 1957; *J. Walter Thompson Company News*, Vol. 15, No. 43, Oct 26, 1960; (Q) Chris Ware, "Charles Schulz's Preliminary Drawings," *McSweeney's Quarterly Concern*, No. 13, Spring 2004, p. 68 (see also Isaacs, pp. 15–17); Waugh, p. 344; Fredric Wertham, "The Comics . . . Very Funny!" *Saturday Review of Literature*, May 29, 1948, pp. 28–29; Rasula, pp. 66–67, 75; Fredric Wertham, *The Seduction of the Innocent* (New York: Rinehart, 1954), p. 381; James Newell Emery, "Those Vicious Comics," *Teachers Digest*, Nov 1945, pp. 32–33; (I) JT, Dec 18, 2002; (I) JCT, Dec 18, 2002; JCT, "Sparky's Pastor Remembers," in Liverett, p. 33; Beresford, p. 45; (L) CMS to JH, May 22, 1958; (L) JH to CMS, May 28, 1958; *Gospel Trumpet*, n.d., First Church of God in Minneapolis, courtesy of NOE; Avis Kriebel, Thomas Cockerham, *25th Anniversary, 1951–1976*, pamphlet prepared for the First Church of God in Minneapolis, 1976; "Cartoonist Guest Editor," *Lookout*, Oct 10, 1958, p. 2; *Minneapolis Star*, Mar 18, 1955; K. F. Hall, in Liverett, p. 95; (L) CMS to JF, Dec 31, 1957; ASI.

THE REVEREND GRAHAM: *New York Times*, May 15, 1936, p. 31; *New York Times*, Sep 1, 1957, p. 1; *New York Times*, May 16, 1937, p. 22; *New York Times*, Sep 3, 1957, p. 29; CMS, "Knowing You Are Not Alone," p. 9; (L) HKL to DTM, Sep 20, 2002, Oct 1, 2002.

GROWING LEGEND: (C) Eileen Lockwood, " 'Father' of 'Peanuts' . . . ," *Minneapolis Star*, May 4, 1956, n.p., USFP; (L) Shirley T. Black to CMS, Nov 19, 1963; (N) (U) "Sparky, circa 1998/99," courtesy of JFS; " 'Peanuts' Artist Visits the News," p. 6; Gordon Gould, "It's Good

Ol' Charlie Schulz!" *Chicago Tribune Sunday Magazine*, Oct 6, 1957, p. 18; CMS quoted in Owen and Nancie Spann, *Your Child? I Thought It Was My Child!* (Pasadena, CA: Ward Ritchie Press, 1977), p. 131; (L) JPK to DTM, Jun 17, 2001; SKI, tape 14, (T) pp. 13–14; "The Cartoonist as Human Being: A Conversation with Virgil Partch," *Northwest Review*, Vol. IV, No. 1, Fall-Winter 1960, p. 63; MCS, foreword, *Snoopy's Guide to the Writing Life* (Cincinnati, OH: Writer's Digest Books, 2002), p. 3; Tasha Robinson, "Berkeley Breathed," *The Onion*, Vol. 37, No. 28, Aug 15, 2001; Barrier interview; *CBS&M*, p. 22; LCI; (P) May 30, 1951; (V) (Q) Lee Mendelson, *A Boy Named Charlie Brown*; (Q) Jon Borgzinner, "A Leaf, a Drop, a Cartoon Is Born," *Life*, Mar 17, 1967, p. 74; (I) ASJ, Dec 12, 2001; (L) CMS to JF, Mar 27, 1957; (P) Nov 12, 1965; (P) Nov 15, 1965; (I) JD, May 9, 2005; (I) PS, Apr 17, 2002; (C) "Up at Yale, They're Nuts About Our Peanuts," *New York World-Telegram*, Jan 31, 1958, n.p., UFSP; (P) Nov 16, 1965; *New York Times*, Apr 21, 1964, p. 23; (I) ROG, Sep 25, 2001; (L) CMS to HG, Feb 16, 1960; (P) Nov 17, 1965; (P) Nov 22, 1965; (L) Vincent T. Tajiri to Stuart Hawkins, Oct 3, 1957, UFSP; (I) ER, Jan 9, 2003; JHS quoted in Jonas, p. 81; Jennings, p. 26.

LUCY, JOYCE: (P) Oct 8, 1972; (L) CMS to Gail Rudrick and John Whiting (NCS Living Library), n.d., 1965; (P) Jan 24, 1954; (P) May 13, 1968; (I) MSH, Nov 9, 2005; (I) HKL, Sep 20, 2002, Nov 14, 2002; (I) PVP, Jul 12, 2001; (I) LVP, Jul 12, 2001; (P) Apr 16, 1957; (I) JD, May 9, 2005; (P) Dec 12, 1963; (P) Nov 4, 1958; (P) Mar 27, 1959; JD to MCS, Interview Jan 10, 1980, courtesy of MCS; (P) May 5, 1961; (EM) LVP to DTM, Jul 1, 2002; (Q) Kidd, n.p.; (P) Sep 5, 1953; (I) JST to DTM, Jun 21, 2001; (P) Oct 17, 1962; "The World According to Peanuts," p. 81; (I) CG, Nov 13, 2000; (P) May 3, 1958; (L) CMS to PVP and LVP, Feb 1, 1957, courtesy of PVP and LVP; (I) ERH, Nov 2, 2000; (P) Jul 19, 1956; (I) CRB, May 16, 2001; JHS quoted in Ersland; Barrier interview; SKI (T) p. 56; Thomas Hine, *Populuxe* (New York: MJF Books, 1986), p. 3; Joshua Zeitz, "Boomer Century," *American Heritage*, Oct 2005, p. 36; (I) WME, Nov 13, 2002; (I) GL, Jul 11, 2001; (I) ER, Jan 9, 2003; CMS, "What the Last 20 Years Have Meant to Me"; (L) CMS to PVP and LVP, Feb 1, 1957; (P) Nov 17, 1957; (P) May 30, 1953.

MARRIAGE; LUCY AND CHARLIE BROWN: JHS quoted in Ersland; (L) Henry L. Halverson to JHS, CMS, MSH, MCS, Oct 16, 1951, courtesy of JD; (P) Aug 9, 1956; (I) ASJ, Oct 15, 2001; (L) RPS to ASJ, n.d., 2001, courtesy of ASJ; Thorkelson, p. 29; (L) CMS to HG, Apr 15, 1955, UFSP; (D) HLH, Feb 1, 1955, MCSC; (I) JD, May 10, 2005; (Q) M. H. Hall, p. 21; (I) PVP, Jul 12, 2001; (I) MCS to DTM, Mar 7, 2005.

IT'S ONLY A GAME: (L) HG to CMS, Mar 7, 1957, UFSP; (L) LR to Joseph R. Fawcett, May 8, 1957; (L) LR to CMS, Jun 26, 1957; (M) UFS-CMS Royalty Statement, *It's Only a Game*, Nov 30, 1957, to Dec 28, 1957, courtesy of JS; (I) DB, Sep 10, 2001; (A) (C) *Minneapolis Sunday Tribune*, Nov 10, 1957; GG, p. 236; Ware, p. 60; JS, Oct 16, 2001: $100 per week, not per page, as reported elsewhere; (I) JS, Jul 17, 2001, Jul 31, 2001, Oct 16, 2001, Aug 10, 2004; (L) CMS to JH, Aug 3, 1955; (I) BM, Dec 5, 2000; Matt Groening, foreword, *The Complete Peanuts, 1955–1956* (Seattle, WA: Fantagraphics Books, 2002), p. xii; Jim Sasseville, *It's Only a Game by Charles M. Schulz and Jim Sasseville* (Thousand Oaks, CA: About Comics, 2004), pp. 49, 81, 180–181, 184, 56; (I) DR, Sep 4, 2001; Bill Ryan, "Selections from a Book in Progress or Retrogress," *Avatar*, No. 2, Jun 23–Jul 6, 1967, p. 12.

LEAVING FOR GOOD: (I) JD, May 10, 2005; (EM) JD to DTM, May 18, 2005; (P) Jul 8, 1959; (Q) LeBaron, *PD*, Nov. 23, 1997; Childress, p. 13; Jonas, p. 28; (I) MCS, May 15, 2001; JHS quoted in Ersland; (I) AK, Feb 25, 2002; (I) WME to DTM, Sep 14, 2002; (I) RF, Sep 20, 2002; (I) JT, Dec 18, 2002; (P) Jan 24, 1954; (S) CMS, "On Cartooning"; (I) DE, Sep 14, 2002; Thorkelson, p. 29; K. F. Hall, in Liverett, p. 95; (L) WME to DTM, Nov 13, 2002; CMS *Time* files, Mar 18, 1965; "Comic Strip Artist Buys Sebastopol Home," *PD*, Feb 5, 1958; "For Sale: A Showplace in California's Sonoma County" (San Francisco: Previews, Inc., listing No. 95132), n.d., 1964, UFSP; (C) JHS quoted in Black.

## 18. COFFEE LANE

E: (Q) Morrow, p. 71.

FIRST YEARS: (I) JFS, Sep 7, 2000; (I) MCS, Sep 12, 2000, Feb 1, 2001; K. L. Wilson, p. 14; (EM) MCS to DTM, May 10, 2004; Kirse Granat May, *Golden State, Golden Youth: The California Image in Popular Culture, 1955–1966* (Chapel Hill, NC: University of North Carolina Press, 2002), pp. 9–25; (V) (Q) "Close-Up on *Peanuts*"; (C) *Sonoma West Times &*

*News*, n.d., 1968; (I) MCS to DTM, Feb 1, 2001; LeBaron, *PD*, Nov 23, 1997.

LICENSING *PEANUTS*: (L) Harris Sirinsky, Foote, Cone & Belding, to United Feature Syndicate, Aug 7, 1959, UFSP; Roger Bradfield, *Charles Schulz: Master Cartoonist* (Minneapolis, MN: Art Instruction Schools, 1986), p. 19; (M) United Feature Syndicate, Sep 27, 1960, UFSP; CMS, *Time* files, Mar 16, 1965; GGI, pp. 41–42, 44–45; J. Walter Thompson Co. to United Feature Syndicate, Aug 28, 1961; *J. Walter Thompson Company News*, Vol. 15, No. 43, Oct 26, 1960; (L) CMS to LR, Jan 14, 1960; (I) WL, Jan 28, 2002; (M) J. Walter Thompson Co. re: "Advertisement No. 16145," n.d., 1962; Robert McNamara quoted in *The Fog of War*, an Errol Morris Film, 2003; (L) LR to William P. Steven, Nov 19, 1959; (L) CMS to LR, Jan 14, 1960; (P) Dec 16, 1961; (L) HG to CMS, Sep 24, 1959; RCH, "A Geezer's Century," *The Comics Journal*, No. 230, Feb 2001, p. 111; (L) W. P. Steven to LR, Nov 23, 1959, Nov 7, 1959; (L) LR to W. P. Steven, Nov 20, 1959; (M) LR to JH, Nov 28, 1967; David Chelsea, "Dear Sparky . . ." *The Comics Journal*, No. 200, Dec 1997, p. 54; (L) JFeif to CMS, Dec 20, 1959, UFSP; (P) Dec 17, 1959; (P) Apr 25, 1958; (P) Aug 28, 1956; (P) May 23, 1960; (P) Feb 10, 1959; William Zinsser, "Enough Is a Warm Too Much," *Look*, Feb 21, 1967, p. 11; *Chicago Tribune Sunday Magazine*, Feb 23, 1958, p. 10; Apr 27, 1958, p. 39; May 25, 1958, p. 36; "The Cellini of Chrome," *Time* (cover story), Nov. 4, 1957; (C) anonymous syndicate executive quoted in Ray Shaw, "Comic Strip Figures Move More Into Ads, Get Own TV Shows," *Wall Street Journal*, n.d., 1961, UFSP; T. S. Eliot quoted in Joshua Zeitz, "Boomer Century," *American Heritage*, Oct 2005, p. 39.

BUILDING THE COFFEE GROUNDS: (I) JD, May 8–10, 2005; JHS quoted in Ersland; H. Stuart Hughes, "California—The America to Come," *Commentary*, May 1956, p. 454; (Q) LeBaron, Nov. 23, 1997; (I) CG, Sep 21, 2000; (L) CMS to HG, Dec 16, 1958; "Cartoonist Sued by Contractor," *PD*, Jun 4, 1959; "For Sale: A Showplace in California's Sonoma County"; (L) CMS to LR, Apr 18, 1960; (L) LR to CMS, Apr 22, 1960; (P) Oct 1, 1966; (Q) Jennings, n.p.; (I) AB, Apr 17, 2001; (P) Mar 3, 1963; (I) CFS, Sep 14, 2000; Arms, p. 13; (P) May 5, 1966; Packard, *The Status Seekers*, p. 62; "Good Grief, Curly Hair," *Newsweek*, Mar 6, 1961, pp. 50, 68; "Ingenue Visits 'Peanuts,' " n.p.; (I) BM, Dec 5, 2000;

John Tebbel, "The Not-So Peanuts World of Charles M. Schulz," *Saturday Review*, Apr 12, 1969; Borgzinner, pp. 73, 78B; ASJ quoted in Michael A. Schuman, *People to Know • Charles M. Schulz: Cartoonist and Creator of Peanuts* (Berkeley Heights, NJ: Enslow Publishers, 2002), p. 65; MCS, "In the Valley of the Moon," manuscript (U), CMS Studio Archive; (I) FGS, Dec 6, 2002; Beresford, p. 41; (I) PP, Dec 4, 2000; (I) MSH, Nov 8, 2005; Joint Tenancy Deed, 650 Junipero Serra Blvd., Aug 7, 1964; (I) SB, Apr 19, 2000; (L) CMS to LR, Dec 2, 1960, UFSP; CS holograph inscription in Coffee Lane guest book; CMS in Stearn, pp. 92–93; (I) RS, Sep 14, 2002; PS, Jan 27, 2005.

DETERMINED: Lois Rich-McCoy, *Millionairess: Self-Made Women of America* (New York: Harper & Row, 1978), pp. 77, 81, 88; Genevieve Stuttaford, "Happiness Is 'Determined, International,'" *San Francisco Sunday Examiner and Chronicle*, n.d., 1967, n.p., (A) DP/Brentanos, *New York Times*, Nov 27, 1965, p. 16; (Q) LeBaron, Nov 23, 1997; (Q) Hurd, p. 49; Tebbel, p. 90; Trusty, p. 319; (Q) "On Happiness," *Life*, Dec 14, 1962, n.p.; (Q) David Cay Johnson, "Connie Boucher, 72, a Pioneer in Licensing Cartoon Characters," *New York Times*, Dec. 1995, A-29; (L) DP quoted in Maurice Dolbier, "Contents Notes," *New York Herald Tribune*, Oct 14, 1962, n.p.; (Q) (C) "Happiness Goes On and On," *Life*, n.d., 1964, p. 71; *New York Times Book Review*, Dec 2, 1962–Sep 29, 1963, Oct. 6, 1963–Feb 16, 1964; Jennings, p. 26; (I) LC, May 31, 2001; (A) DP/Washington Mills Co. in *Art Directing*, n.d., 1967, p. 11; (I) ST, Apr 7, 2003; "Peanuts," *New York Times*, Mar 12, 1967; Crossword Puzzle, *New York Times*, Oct 12, 1963, p. 16; (P) Apr 25, 1960; (P) Oct 12, 1960.

CRITICS: (I) LM quoting JHS, Jun 20, 2001; Richard Schickel, "Smaller Peanuts, Bigger Shells," *Book Week*, Dec 27, 1964, p. 9; (L) Schickel to CMS, Mar 13, 1965; (Q) Goodman, n.p.; Zinsser, p. 11; Sir William Hawthorne quoted by May Sarton, Sep 2, 1968, in *Selected Letters, 1955–1995* (New York: W. W. Norton, 2002), p. 187; (Q) Phelan, p. 38; (L) Frank G. Darlington to CMS, Jan 18, 1961; (P) Jun 20, 1964; LCI; (L) Phyllis D. Smith to Lawrence R. Quinn, Oct 11, 1989, Lawrence R. Quinn collection; (I) BMcL, Feb 25, 2003; Borgzinner, p. 73; Barnaby Conrad, "You're a Good Man, Charlie Schulz," *New York Times Sunday Magazine*, sec. VI, p. 33; (Q) Dorf, p. 24.

## 19. GOSPEL

E: CMS in P20, p. 33.

MAKING *A CHARLIE BROWN CHRISTMAS*: (M) CMS *Newsweek* files: Cal Fentress, Feb 14, 1961, p. 3; BM, "Animation Artist," in *TMAT*, p. 61; (Q) Exline, p. 18; LM, "Charles M. Schulz, All-American," *TMAT*, p. 43; (Q) Bob Edwards, *Morning Edition*, National Public Radio, Dec 6, 1995; (Q) P20, p. 91; (S) LM, CMSMRC, n.d., Dec 2005 (see Roger Colton, "The Charles Schulz Museum celebrates the 40th anniversary of 'A Charlie Brown Christmas,' " Jim Hill Media, Jan 23, 2006, http: www.trakwords.net/article); (I) BM, Oct 10, 2002; (Q) Morch, p. 5; (L) CMS to PVP and LVP, Feb 1, 1957, courtesy of LVP; (Q) *TMAT*, pp. 17, 20; (P) Dec 9, 1952; CMS *Time* files, Nov 29, 1965; (P) Dec 18, 1966; (V) BM on LM, Jason Mendelson, *The Making of "A Charlie Brown Christmas,"* A Lee Mendelson Production, 2001.

FAITH REVISED: GGI, p. 21; (Q) (C) Eugene Griessman, "Charles Schulz," *Atlanta Weekly*, Nov. 15, 1981, n.p.; BBC; CMS, "Knowing You Are Not Alone," p. 8; P50, n.p.; John Updike, *Museums and Women* (New York: Alfred A. Knopf, 1972), p. 43; (Q) K. Martin, n.p.; (Q) Mellott, n.p.; (Q) RM&GG, p. 18; (EM) JD, May 18, 2005; Elizabeth Hardwick, *American Fictions* (New York: Modern Library Paperbacks, 1999), p. 116; Ken Michaels, "You're a Good Man, Charlie Schulz," *Houston Post*, Nov 2, 1969, p. 23; (flap copy) Robert L. Short, *The Gospel According to Peanuts* (Louisville, KY: Westminster John Knox Press, 2000); T. Franklin Miller, "Remembering Charles Schulz," in Liverett, p. 30; *Christianity Today*, Vol. 10, No. 5, Dec 3, 1965 (see also Richard N. Ostling to Steve Libby, Nov 22, 1965, CMSMRC); (I) RLS, Jan 5, 2006; (Q) Bettinger, p. 20; (I) BM, Dec 5, 2000; (P) Jan 31, 1957, Dec 3, 1952; Michael Mott, *The Seven Mountains of Thomas Merton* (Boston: Houghton Mifflin, 1984), p. 437; John Updike, "Notes and Comment," *The New Yorker*, Dec 13, 1969, p. 45; (I) ASJ, Oct 15, 2001; (I) EE, Oct 25, 2002; JHS quoted in Ersland; (Q) Jonas, p. 28; (Q) "A Dialogue . . ." p. 50; Alan Haacke, "Amy Schulz skates with Peanuts gang and glides to new life," *Church*, Nov 17, 1979, p. 7.

BROADCAST: P20, p. 91; (I) FS, Oct 23, 2003; David Halberstam, *The Powers That Be* (New York: Alfred A. Knopf, 1979), pp. 152–154; (L)

HG to CMS, Nov 27, 1959, UFSP; Scott McGuire, "The Peanuts Animation and Video Page" (http://web.mit.edu/smcguire/www/peanuts-animation .html); John Allen quoted in P20, p. 91; *TMAT*, p. 32; Neil Compton, "TV Chronicle," *Commentary*, April 1966, p. 83; Michelle Mercer, " 'Charlie Brown Christmas' Keeps Giving," *All Things Considered*, National Public Radio, Dec 22, 2003; (L) Mrs. Benjamin Cubler to CMS, Dec 19, 1966.

DEATH OF CARL: (C) "Second General Vice President Schulz Dies in California," p. 32; GGI, p. 20; Monte Schulz, "Sunday Night After Dinner," CMS Studio Archives (U); CS in *Time* file, Mar 24, 1965; "Carl Schulz Succumbs at Son's Home," *PD*, May 30, 1966, n.p.; *GG*, p. 103; CS, Certificate of Death, State of California, June 3, 1966; (I) CFS, Sep 14, 2000; (I) JD, May 8, 2005; (I) DE and WME, Sep 14, 2002; BN, Sep 12, 2002; *In Memoriam*, CS funeral records, AP; (I) LN, Feb 15, 2001; (Q) (C) *Des Moines Register*, June 2, 1989, n.p.; (V) "Close-Up on Peanuts"; (I) SB, Sep 14, 2000.

## 20. THE DAWNING OF THE AGE OF SNOOPY

E: (P) Mar 2, 1958.

DAY IN THE LIFE; MORNINGS: (Q) *GG*, p. 48; JHS quoted in Ersland; (EM) JD to DTM, Nov 20, 2005; CMS in *The Cartoonist Cookbook* (New York: Hobbs, Dorman & Company, 1966), p. 76; (I) MCS, Feb 1, 2001; (EM) MCS to DTM, May 10, 2004; (Q) Dorf, p. 11; A&E; (Q) *The Larry King Show*, Apr 28, 1988, (Q) Goodman, n.p.; (I) SB, Jan 29, 2001; (I) ASJ, Jan 31, 2001; (I) MSH, Nov 9, 2005; (P) Apr 17, 1974.

PARENTING: (I) RN, May 15, 2001; (I) JD, May 9, 2005; (Q) "A Dialogue . . . ," p. 135; (Q) Arms, p. 13; MCS interview with MSH, Apr 20, 1981; (Q) Jonas, pp. 80, 20; CMS *Time* files, Mar 18, 1965; K. L. Wilson, p. 79; (I) MSH, Nov 9, 2005; (I) ASJ, Oct 15, 2001; (Q) Snider, n.p.; (Q) GG, p. 100; (I) BB, CRB, May 16, 2001; (P) Aug 10, 1953.

MARRIAGE; LUCY AND SCHROEDER: (I) WL, Jun 19, 2001; (I) JD, May 9–10, 2005; (P) Nov 21, 1954; (P) Jul 28, 1968; (P) Jan 12, 1955; (P) Feb 29, 1968; (P) Nov 29, 1971; (P) Feb 18, 1979; (P) Oct 11, 1989; (P) Mar 20, 1969; (V) (Q) Crommie interview; (V) (Q) *It's a Pied Piper, Charlie Brown*, 2000; (P) Oct 2, 1974; (P) Oct 3, 1974; (L) CMS to AA, Dec 5, 1968, AP.

DAY AT THE DRAWING BOARD: (L) CMS to BGS, Jun 23, 1967, courtesy of BGS; (Q) *Youth*, p. 9; (Q) Conrad, p. 33; (Q) Barrier interview; (Q) Phelan, p. 38; (V) (Q) "Close-Up on Peanuts"; (V) (Q) *The Tonight Show*, Feb 7, 1973, ASI; CMS quoted by JFS in introduction to Kidd, n.p.; RLS, "Robert L. Short On 'Peanuts,' " *Christian Herald*, Sep. 1967, p. 14; (Q) Jennings, p. 26; (Q) Hurd, p. 54; (V) (Q) *The Dick Cavett Show*, Sep 2, 1978; *PJ*, p. 179; (M) CMS *Newsweek* files, Bill Flynn, from Sebastopol, Feb 21, 1961; LCI; BBC.

DOROTHY: (I) JD, May 9, 2005; Monte Schulz, "Sunday Night After Dinner"; (I) PS, Jun 20, 2001; (I) SB, Sep 26, 2002; CMS *Time* files, Mar 18, 1965; (DIA) Henry L. Halverson, Jan 21, 1956, p. 147, MCSC; (I) EE, Oct 25, 2002; (Q) Jonas, pp. 80–81; (I) ASJ, Sep 13, 2001 (see also interview with JST, Jun 21, 2001); (P) Aug 6, 1969 (see also Sep 1, 1967).

DAY; CHILDREN: (Q) Steinberg, p. 39; (I) MSH, Nov 8, 2005; (I) MCS, Apr 22, 2004, Feb 1, 2001; (L) LR to CMS, Apr 28, 1958, UFSP; (I) JST, Jun 21, 2001; GG, p. 190; (I) ASJ, Oct 15, 2001; (I) CFS, Sep 14, 2000; (V) (Q) *The Mike Douglas Show*, Mar 7, 1979, *The Dick Cavett Show*, Sep 2, 1978 SKI, and *passim*; (Q) "A Dialogue . . . ," p. 50; (L) Ruth E. Halverson to JJM, Feb 14, 1990, courtesy of JJM.

PRODUCT: (I) SB, Sep 14, 2000; CMS *Time* files, Mar 25, 1965; (Q) Roberts, p. 20; Barrier interview; Bradfield, p. 19; *GG*, p. 158; (Q) Dorf, p. 24; K. Martin, n.p.; Welbourn, p. 10; *Youth*, p. 14; LCI; K. L. Wilson, p. 62; (I) MVG, Jun 10, 2002.

MILQUETOAST: Geoffrey O'Brien, *Dream Time: Chapters from the Sixties* (Washington, DC: Counterpoint, 2002), p. 29; (I) PP, Dec 4, 2000; Rich-McCoy, p. 81; (I) SB, Sep 26, 2002; (P) May 24, 1964; (I) AL, Jan 24, 2002 (see also interview with LC, May 31, 2001); (I) JSlad, Apr 6, 2001; (I) WME, Sep 14, 2002.

DAY; AFTERNOONS; FAME: (L) Al Chop to CMS, Aug 14, 1995; (U) interview/memoir of a fan's visit to CMS at Coffee Lane, n.d., 1963, CMS Studio Archive; *Youth*, p. 13; (Q) Welbourn, p. 10; (Q) Conrad, pp. 32–33; (I) BB, May 16, 2001; K. L. Wilson, p. 63; (L) Brian LaFountain to CMS, n.d., CMS Studio Archive; (EM) David Gonzol to DTM, Aug 6, 2003; (Q) B. McIntosh, p. 8; (all correspondence in response to Lucy and Linus moving, see *PJ*, pp. 174–175); Rachel Gonzales to CMS, Nov 6, 1997, CMS Studio Archive; Virginia Shearer, "Second Thoughts: Charlie's

Sack," *Mill Valley Record*, Jul 11, 1973, n.p. (see also letter, Shearer to CMS, Aug 14, 1973); (L) Lisa J. Clemson to CMS, Aug 4, 1998, CMS Studio Archive; (L) Carrie Buscher to CMS, Aug 27, 1998, CMS Studio Archive; (P) Feb 10, 1968; Gary Fishgall, *Gonna Do Great Things: The Life of Sammy Davis, Jr.* (New York: Simon & Schuster, 2003), p. 157; (I) Kaye Ballard, Sep 30, 2002; (I) BM, Oct 10, 2002; (P) Jun 1, 1961; (P) Nov 4, 1966; (P) Jan 8, 1969; (I) JD, May 11, 2005; (Q) Jennings, p. 26; "For Sale: A Showplace in California's Sonoma County," listing brochure, Previews Incorporated, San Francisco, 1964, holograph inscription CMS, JH, LR, UFSP; (Q) *Youth*, p. 9; (Q) "A Dialogue . . . ," p. 136; (P) Jul 10, 1962; (P) Jun 28, 1967; (P) Nov 12, 1959; (P) Jan 21, 1968; (I) MCS, May 16, 2001; (P) Jan 29, 1967; (I) BM, Dec 5, 2001; (I) JS, Oct 6, 2001, Sep 17, 2002; (I) LVP, Mar 18, 2002; JHS quoted in Ersland; SKI, (T) p. 6; (L) CMS to K. F. Hall, May 21, 1965; (P) Aug 8, 1966; (Q) Roberts, p. 20; LCI; *CBS Newsletter*, Vol. 2, No. 4, Apr 1967, p. 4; Cynthia Robins, "29 Years of Being 8 Years Old," *San Francisco Examiner*, Mar 16, 1978, p. 30; Andy Meisler, "Don't Grow Up," *New Choices for Retirement Living*, June 1995, p. 57; (I) JD, May 9, 2005; (L) CMS to TOH, n.d., 1971, TOHC; Kim Thompson, Mark Evanier, "You're an Expensive Thing to Collect, Charlie Brown!" Oct 14, 2005 (http://www.newsfromme.com/archives/2005_10_14.html#010453); (L) HG to CMS, Jun 20, 1968, UFSP; (L) HG to CMS, Aug 8, 1968; K. F. Hall, "It Scares Me," p. 18; *Life*, Mar 17, 1965, p. 74; *New York Times*, Apr 16, 1967, Sec. VI, p. 33; (P) April 23, 1966; Judith Martin, " 'Peanuts': Basically Civilized," *Washington Post*, Aug 15, 1972, p. B1; Richard Schickel, "Smaller Peanuts, Bigger Shells," *Book Week*, Dec 27, 1964, p. 9; Conrad, p. 33; *Saturday Review*, April 12, 1969, p. 72; K. Martin, n.p.

SNOOPY, TO THE MOON: (P) Nov 19, 1951; Borgzinner, p. 74; Ronald Carey, *The War Above the Trees* (Victoria, BC: Trafford Publishing, 2004), p. 36; Peter Mersky, *F-8 Crusader Units of the Vietnam War* (London: Osprey Publishing, 1998), p. 112 (see also J. M. Syverson, North American Aviation, Inc., Downey, CA., to JH, May 19, 1959, Apr 28, 1960; and William H. Farr, USAF, to CMS, Dec 27, 1959; UFSP); Budge Williams, "Losing Comic Strips Takes a Little Fun Out of His Life," *Online Athens* (Georgia), Jan 22, 2000; *PJ*, pp. 81, 84, 173; (P) Jun 28, 1957; (P) Nov 26, 1955; (C) Scott Long, "Schulz' Endearing Kids Have Book to

Themselves," *Minneapolis Sunday Tribune*, Oct 3, 1954, n.p.; (P) Nov 19, 1958; (Q) Thierry Groensteen, "The Schulz System: Why Peanuts Works," *Nemo: The Classic Comics Library*, No. 31/32, Jan 1992, p. 35; (A) Ford Falcon, Ford Motor Company, in Kidd (paperback edition), n.p.; (P) Mar 29, 1962; (V) (Q) *It's a Pied Piper, Charlie Brown*, 2000; *PGC*, pp. 39, 62; LCI; Hank Ketcham quoted in Dan Taylor, "Dennis' 'Dad' Drops a Line," *PD*, Apr 8, 2001; (P) Jan 9, 1966; *Youth*, p. 7; (Q) *The Larry King Show*, Apr 28, 1988; (I) MCS, Sep 12, 2000; (Q) Conrad, pp. 32–33; 999; BBC; CMS, *Security Is a Thumb and a Blanket*, n.p.; (Q) Michaels, p. 25 (see also Childress, p. 14, and ASI: "I'm not a philosopher"); S. Hynes to DTM, May 29, 2004; (P) May 5, 1968; (P) Dec 25, 1968; (P) Mar 21, 1968; (P) Oct 27, 1969; (P) Jan 8, 1966; (P) Nov 10, 1968; (P) Oct 11, 1967; Jonathan Franzen, "The Comfort Zone: Growing Up with Charlie Brown," *The New Yorker*, Nov 29, 2004, p. 70; P20, pp. 138, 139, 144; (P) Jun 20, 1969; (P) May 5, 1968; MW quoted in Jason Whiton, ed., *Mort Walker: Conversations* (Jackson, MS: University Press of Mississippi, 2005), p. 50; (P) Dec 23, 1968; Jonathan Schell, *The Real War* (New York: Da Capo, 2001), p. 291; (P) Oct 17, 1954; O'Brien, p. 56; "The Hippies: Philosophy of a Subculture," *Time*, July 7, 1967, p. 22; Sally Dryer quoted in *The Making of a Charlie Brown Christmas*, documentary film, a Lee Mendelson production, 2002; David J. Coyle, "Curse You, Red Baron!! Giving the Guardsmen Their Due" (http://members@aol.com/Shake6677DFroyalg.html); GG, p. 248; (liner notes) Robert Schwartz, *Snoopy and His Friends The Royal Guardsmen*, Gernhard Enterprises, Laurie Records, Inc., n.d., 1967; Convair to CMS, June 11, 1959, UFSP; (P) Mar 14, 1969; NASA official quoted in Roberts, p. 20; NASA, *Apollo 10 Mission Report*, Jun 17, 1969, pp. 3–4, 9; Eugene A. Cernan quoted on Walter Cronkite, *CBS News*, 2000; *Il Progresso* (New York), May 23, 1969, p. 1; *San Jose Mercury News* quoted in P20, p. 51; Renata Adler, *Canaries in the Mineshaft* (New York: St. Martin's Press, 2001), p. 232.

## PART FIVE

(P) Aug 13, 1967; (E) T. E. Lawrence (attributed), Robert Bolt, David Lean's *Lawrence of Arabia*, film, 1962.

## 21. A GOOD MAN

E: AVD, Mar 8, 2002.

SPARKY AND JOYCE: (I) BB, May 16, 2001; GGI, p. 40; (Q) Conrad, p. 33; (L) LR to CMS, Mar 5, 1963, May 2, 1963; CMS *Time* files, Mar 15, 1965; (I) JD, May 9–10, 2005; (I) WL, Mar 6, 2001; (I) RA, Nov 14, 2003; (L) D. Porecki to CMS, May 14, 1997; (P) Aug 27, 1971; (EM) JD, May 18, 2005; (I) JST, Jun 21, 2001; (P) Aug 9, 1958; (I) MCS, Oct 5, 2000; (I) JST, Jun 21, 2001; (I) ASJ, Oct 15, 2001; (P) Feb 7, 1968; (I) PS, Jun 7, 2001; (I) MSH, Nov 8–9, 2005; A&E; (P) Sep 17, 1968; (L) JD to DTM, Oct 28, 2000; *PJ*, p. 81; see CMS, second row, center, of Carter V. Carter photograph of Miss Kelly's B-5 class at Gordon School, 1932, AP; (V) (Q) "Close-Up on Peanuts"; (P) Dec 18, 1966; (P) Jan 13, 1962; (Q) RM&GG, p. 6; Groensteen, p. 35; Dwight Whitney, "Charles Schulz's 'Peanuts' Philosophy," *TV Guide*, Oct 28, 1972, p. 36; JD quoted on www.naainakai.com, 2002; (L) CMS to HG, Nov 13, 1956, UFSP; (P) Feb 21, 1954; (I) WL, Jun 19, 2001.

YOU'RE A GOOD MAN, CHARLIE BROWN: CG (synopsis), *YAGMBC*, Tam-Witmark catalog; (L) CG to CMS, Apr 17, 1965, CGS, courtesy of CG (see also letter, LM to CG, Oct 26, 1965, CGS); (L) CG to JH, Apr 29, 1965, CGS; (L) CMS to CG, Dec 6, 1966, CGS; GG, p. 203; A&E; (L) CG to Dick Seff, n.d., 1966 (describes meeting at Sardi's with Arthur Whitelaw), CGS, courtesy of CG; (I) CG, Nov 13, 2000; CG (John Gordon, pseud.), "The Good and the Grief of Charlie Brown," in *YAGMBC* (New York: The Peanuts Company, 1967), n.p.; (I) GP, Apr 20, 2004; Edith Oliver, "The Theatre—Off Broadway: Celebration on St. Marks Place," *The New Yorker*, Mar 18, 1967, pp. 121, 123; P20, p. 94 (Mendelson offers several versions of his opinion of *YAGMCB*, including a contradictory telling in A&E, 1995); Kerr, "Charlie Brown and Combo: Musical Adapted from Comic Strip 'Peanuts,' " *New York Times*, Mar 8, 1967, p. 51; GP, Apr 20 2004: $8 per ticket (see also Jesse McKinley, obituary of CG, *New York Times*, Jul 27, 2002, p. A24; Lawrence R. Quinn Collection, 1968–1995; *PGC*, p. 74; (I) CG, Nov 13, 2000.

JANELL: (S) CMS, De Young Museum; (I) JPK, Jun 25, 2002, Apr 18, 2001; (C) Herb Caen, n.d., courtesy of JPK; *Gospel Trumpet*, n.d., First Church of God, Minneapolis, courtesy of NOE; K. F. Hall in Liverett,

p. 95; (I) GP, Apr 20, 2004; (I) JPK, Jun 9, 2001, Jun 15, 2001, Oct 21, 2001, Jun 6, 2002; (L) JPK to DTM, Jul 27, 2001; (I) CRB, May 16, 2001; (EM) DRF to DTM, Jan 7, 2002; (L) Ruth E. Halverson to JJM, Feb 14, 1990, courtesy of JJM; (P) Jan 6, 1968; (V) (Q) *A Day with Charles Schulz*, Meri Gyves, Forestville School, Sep 1, 1990; (C) JPK quoted in John L. Wasserman, "People Jump When Lucy Says What She Thinks," *San Francisco Chronicle*, Aug 16, 1968, n.p.; (V) CMS, *Time and Again*, MSNBC, Nov. 17, 1997; (I) PS, Jun 20, 2001; JPK quoted in Colburn, n.p.

1968: (L) CMS to PVP, Jan 24, 1968, courtesy of PVP; (I) GP, Apr 20, 2004; (L) CMS to Ethel S. Kennedy, Jul 1, 1968; (L) Ethel S. Kennedy to CMS, Aug 1, 1968, courtesy of Mrs. Robert F. Kennedy; Goulart, p. 27; (Q) *Today* show, Nov 1968; JD quoted in Ersland; JD quoted in Jonas, p. 80.

## 22. ARENA

E: Samuel Taylor Coleridge, "Kubla Khan," *The Oxford Book of English Verse, 1250–1900* (Oxford, UK: Clarendon Press, 1908), p. 651.

CREATION: (C) Jerry Hulse, "Schulz Puts His Cartoon Friends on Ice," *Los Angeles Times*, Mar 15, 1970, n.p.; (C) Don W. Martin, "Bay Area Beat," n.d., 1969, n.p.; ASJ, Oct 15, 2001; "Redwood Empire Ice Arena History," Santa Rosa, CA, 2006 (http://www.snoopyshomeice.com/history.html); (I) JSlad, Apr 6, 2001; SKI, (T) pp. 6, 12; (Q) Mellott, n.p.; "New Empire Ice Arena Is as Swiss as Fondue," *PD*, Apr 13, 1969, p. 4-B; *Welcome to the Redwood Empire Arena*, Santa Rosa, CA, n.d., 1969, p. 1; JST quoted in *PD*, Nov 26, 2000; (I) LSB, May 18, 2001; JHS quoted in Ersland; (Q) Hurd, p. 47; K. L. Wilson, p. 15; (C) JHS quoted in Carolyn Lund, "Meachams to Bring a Little Bit of Switzerland to Santa Rosa," *PD*, Sep 2, 1968, n.p.; Joint Tenancy Grant Deed, Sonoma County, Robert C. Maple and Alice H. Maple to CMS and JHS, Aug 21, 1967, courtesy of ECA.

MEREDITH: (C) JHS quoted in "Don't Miss Ice Arena Opening Tomorrow," *PD*, n.d., 1969, n.p.; (I) JD, May 9–10, 2005; (I) BB, May 16, 2001; (I) MSH, Nov 8–9, 2005; JHS quoted in Ersland; (P) May 13, 1972; (EM) MCS to DTM, May 5, 2004.

CONSTRUCTION: (P) Jan 2, 1969; (P) Jan 31, 1969; (P) Mar 21, 1969; Bill Udell, "You're a Good Man, Charles Schulz," *Skating*, June

1969, p. 7; (I) BB, May 16, 2001; JHS quoted in Ersland; (I) ED, May 9, 2005; (I) JD, May 8, 2005 (see also interview with LSB, Mar 18, 2001); (I) TMT, Fruiht & Tomasi Architects, now TLCD Architecture, Mar 4, 2003; (I) GLeB, Oct 18, 2001; see Guest Book, Coffee Lane, Nov 11, 1960, CMS Studio Archive; (I) JD, May 8–9, 2005; JHS quoted in Lund, n.p.; (I) RN, May 15, 2001; (Q) Hurd, p. 47; (C) (photo caption) *PD*, n.d., 1969; (pamphlet) *"When you've seen one ice arena, you've seen them all!,"* Redwood Empire Ice Arena, Santa Rosa, CA, n.d., 1969, p. 1; (Q) Hurd, p. 47; (P) May 18, 1959.

UNHAPPINESS: (P) Aug 1, 1968; GGI (unpublished passage, disc 2); (I) RLS, Jan 5, 2006; (I) SB, Sep 26, 2002; (C) Dan Hruby, "Ice Warms Schulz' Heart," *San Jose Mercury News*, n.d., 1968, n.p.; (EM) DRF, Jan 7, 2002; (P) Jan 10, 1968; (I) DRF, Jan 30, 2001; (Q) M. H. Hall, p. 19; (I) RLS, Jan 5, 2006; (I) CRB, May 16, 2001; (I) BB, May 16, 2001; (P) Jul 29, 1970; (I) KB, Sep 30, 2002; (P) Jan 22, 1968; (P) Jan 3, 1968; (P) Jan 29, 1968; (I) RA, Nov 14, 2003; (I) WL, Mar 3, 2001; (I) JPK, Apr 18, 2001; (I) JD, May 9–11 2005; ASJ quoted in Schuman, p. 65; CMS *Time* Files, Mar 18, 1965; (I) MCS to DTM, Feb 5, 2001; (I) MSH, Nov 9, 2005; (I) CFS, Nov 14, 2003; (P) Mar 27, 1959; (P) May 23, 1969; (P) Jul 7, 1967; (Q) W. A. McIntosh interview; (Q) Exline, p. 14; (P) Mar 1, 1968.

OPENING: M. Thomas Inge, *Charles M. Schulz: Conversations* (Jackson, MS: University Press of Mississippi, 2000), p. xvi (see also video *Happy 30th Birthday Redwood Empire Ice Arena*, Nov 1999, City of Santa Rosa, Multi-Image/Video Presentations); (I) CRB, May 16, 2001; Beresford, p. 41; JHS quoted in Lund, n.p.; Wallace A. Lagorio, "Ice Arena Is Built in Santa Rosa by Creator of 'Peanuts,' " *Sacramento Bee*, Jun 8, 1969, p. B13; *PD*, Apr 29, 1969; "New Empire Ice Arena Is as Swiss as Fondue," *PD*, Apr 13, 1969, p. 4–B; Hulse, n.p.; Lagorio, p. B13; Martin, "Bay Area Beat"; (C) "Opening of Ice Arena Will Benefit Agency," *PD*, n.d.; Roby Gemmell, "Happiness Is . . . Opening a Magnificent Ice Arena," *PD*, Apr 29, 1969, p. 16 (see also JA, Jan 31, 2002; (C) S. Graves, "While 1,700 Watched Ice Stars Sparkle in New SR Arena," *PD*, Apr 29, 1969, n.p.; (I) JPK, Apr 17, 2001; (I) ECA, Apr 9, 2003; "Olympic Charmer: Peggy Fleming," *Life*, Feb 23, 1968; Jane and Michael Stern, *Sixties People* (New York: Alfred A. Knopf, 1990), p. 125; (I) JSlad, Apr 6, 2001; (P) Jan 8,

1969; (P) Dec 30, 1969; (C) Virginia Payette, "Comments," May 12, 1969; (I) ML, Mar 17, 2003; (I) WL, Oct 10, 2002.

1969: (Q) Christie Fairchild and Laurie Fialkowski, "Charlie Brown, Meet Your Creator Charles Schulz," *The Jolly Roger* (San Anselmo, CA: Sir Francis Drake High School), Feb 14, 1969, p. 1; (P) Feb 8, 1969; (L) Ronald Reagan to CMS, Mar 9, 1970, Dec 6, 1974, Jul 30, 1970; Barbara Walters, *Today* show, Nov 18, 1968; (Q) *The Tonight Show*, Feb 7, 1973; (A) (C) Brentano's in *San Francisco Chronicle*, Jun 20, 1969, n.p.; Inge, *Conversations*, p. xvi; (I) PS, Jun 20, 2001; Michaels, pp. 25, 27; "The 'Combine' Behind Charlie Brown, Etcetera," *San Francisco Chronicle*, Mar 13, 1970, p. 48; *Publishers Weekly*'s 1969 compilation of sales quoted in Russel Nye, *The Unembarrassed Muse: The Popular Arts in America* (New York: Dial Press, 1970), pp. 54–55; JHS, *Snoopy Snoops* (Redwood Empire Ice Arena newsletter), Vol. 2, No. 6, Aug 1970, p. 1; "Supervisors Argue Six Hours on Value of the Ice Arena," *PD*, Feb 17, 1971, p. 2; (Q) Hurd, p. 46; *PD*, Apr 29, 1979, p. 4-C; (I) JD, May 8, 2005; (I) ECA, Feb 1, 2002; CMS, JHS, Letter of Agreement, Oct 14, 1970 (see also RN to James B. Keegan, Wells Fargo Bank, Santa Rosa, Oct 15, 1970); (I) RN, May 15, 2001; (L) CMS to DR, May 8, 1961, courtesy of Marc Ratner; (P) Sep 24, 1971; James B. Keegan to United Feature Syndicate, Dec 20, 1972, UFSP; *Snoopy Snoops*, Vol. 1, No. 2, Apr 1970, p. 3 (see also interview with LSB, May 18, 2001); (P) Feb 8, 1970; (I) RDD, Jun 18, 2001; (I) JSlad, Apr 6, 2001; (P) Jun 3, 1954; (P) Nov 5, 1972; (I) ECA to DTM, Apr 9, 2003; (I) MCS, May 25, 2005; *"When you've seen one ice arena, you've seen them all!"* p. 1; (P) Jan 7, 1969.

TRACEY, PART ONE: (L) Margie Walton to TOH, n.d., 1973, courtesy of TOH; (I) TOH, Jun 25–26, 2001, Jan 8, 2002, Apr 16, 2002 (see also TOH, book proposal, n.d., Jun 2001, courtesy of TOH); CMS on tape recording made at lunch at the Redwood Empire Ice Arena, March 16, 1970, (T) in TOHC; TOH, "Mutual Love of Books and Bookstores," in book proposal; (EM) TOH to DTM, Jul 5, 2001, Apr 6, 2002; Morrow, p. 71; (P) Jun 13, 1971; CMS, black blank book, CMS Studio Archive (see also LCI; (P) Apr 6, 1997; (P) May 20, 1970; (P) Feb 7, 1968; (L) CMS to TOH, n.d., May-June 1970; (P) Jul 8, 1970; (P) Jul 9, 1970; (P) Jul 10, 1970; (P) Jul 13, 1970; (I) MB, Oct 23, 2002 (see also interview with JFS, Oct 21, 2002; (P) Jul 14, 1970; (P) Mar 18, 1970; (P) Jul 11, 1970; (P) Aug

12, 1970; (PC) CMS to TOH, Jul 1970, TOHC; (P) original strip, Jul 16, 1970, TOHC; (P) Nov 15, 1970; (P) Aug 28, 1969; (I) WL, Jun 19, 2001; (I) JD, May 8–10, 2005; (DR) CMS to TOH, n.d., 1970, TOHC.

## 23. DOGHOUSE

E: (Q) Peter Joseph, *Good Times: An Oral History of America in the Nineteen Sixties* (New York: Charterhouse, 1973), p. 285.

TRACEY, PART TWO: (P) Dec 31, 1970; (I) JD, May 9–10, 2005; (I) ECA, Apr 9, 2003; (P) Apr 27, 1958; (DR) CMS to TOH, n.d., 1971 (Snoopy on doghouse: "Rats! I hate it when I don't get any love letters!"), TOHC; DJW; (I) DJW, Jul 9, 2001; (P) Jul 16, 1967; (P) Feb 16, 1971; (L) CMS to TOH, n.d., 1970, TOHC; (P) Mar 8, 1971; (I) TOH, Jan 8, 2002; (P) Sunday page, n.d., c. 1962–1965, not available on UMCSL: reprinted in CMS, *Sunday's Fun Day, Charlie Brown* (New York: Holt, Rinehart & Winston, 1965), n.p.; (I) RDM, Mar 4, 2006; (P) Mar 31, 1976; (C) Ken Martin, "Have It Your Own Way, Charlie Schulz!" n.d., Oct 1971; (Q) M. H. Hall, p. 19; (P) Jun 9, 1952; (C) *Chicago Sun-Times*, n.d., 1980; Rich-McCoy, p. 87; (P) Feb 6, 1958; (I) TOH, Jan 30, 2002, Jun 26, 2001; (P) May 30, 1971; (P) Dec 27, 1971; (P) Mar 7, 1991; (P) Mar 9, 1991; (P) Sep 14, 1971; (L) JF to Craig Cohen, Oct 20, 1971, UFSP; (P) May 12, 1972; (I) BG, Oct 2, 2001; (Q) Mellott, n.p.; Robins, p. 30; (I) WH, Dec 5, 2002; Jaguar Owner's Manual, CMS Studio Archive; (I) MCS, Sep 12, 2000; (I) CFS, Sep 14, 2000; (I) LJ, May 8, 2002; (Q) Waggoner and Wolmuth, p. 86; (I) DJW, Jul 9, 2001 (see also Georgeann Koelin, "Charlie's Angel" *St. Paul Pioneer Press and Dispatch*, Jan 28, 1990, p. 12-E); (P) May 17, 1968; DWJ to Lumiere Productions, Oct 2005; (I) TOH, Jan 8, 2002; (P) Aug 28, 1971.

CHALK HILL ROAD: (I) CSil, Dec 8, 2005 (see also interview with MCS, Dec 9, 2005; (P) Feb 21, 1972; (I) RLS, Jan 5, 2006; (P) Dec 18, 1970; (I) RN, May 15, 2001; (I) WL, Apr 1, 2002; (I) KB, Sep 30, 2002; (I) BM, Dec 5, 2000; (I) JPK, May 6, 2002; (I) ECA, Apr 9, 2003; (I) GLeB, May 18, 2001; (I) KKT, Mar 4, 2003; (I) JST, Jun 21, 2001; (I) ASJ, Oct 15, 2001; (I) EE, Oct 25, 2002.

ALONE AGAIN: (I) ASJ, Oct 15, 2001; (P) May 4, 1951, *The Complete Peanuts, 1950–1952,* Vol. 1, (Seattle, WA: Fantagraphics Books, 2004),

p. 62; (P) Mar 25, 1953; (P) Aug 11, 1954; (P) Jul 3, 1956; (P) Jul 2, 1956; (I) HKL, Oct 1, 2002; (I) HKL, Nov 14, 2002; BBC; (I) GL, Jul 11, 2001; CMS, *I Take My Religion Seriously*, p. 38; (P) May 27, 1966; (P) Jul 5, 1976, May 8, 1984; (I) MCS, Sep 12, 2000, Nov 19, 2000; (I) JFS, Apr 9, 2003; (I) JST, Jun 21, 2001.

## 24. HAPPINESS

E: Leo Tolstoy, *Anna Karenina*, translated by Richard Pevear and Larissa Volokhonsky (New York: Viking Penguin, 2001), p. 28.

JEANNIE: (I) JFS, Oct 20–21, 2001, Oct 23–24, 2002, Sep 13, 2000, Dec 8, 2005; SKI, (T) pp. 8, 25; (S) CMS, Beaglefest, Jul 13, 1977; (L) JFS to DTM, n.d., Nov 2002; (I) JD, May 10, 2005; (V) (Q) Crommie interview (see also interview with JK, Jun 3, 2004); LCI; Jennifer M. Contino, "Never A Blockhead: Jean Schulz on Peanuts" (http://www.comicon.com/cgi-bin/ultimatebb.cgi?ubb=get_topic&f=36&t=002091); (M) JFS, n.d., courtesy of JFS; JFS, reminiscences (U), n.d., courtesy of JFS; (I) JFS, Jun 1, 2001; JFS Journal, n.d., courtesy of JFS; (L) JFS to DTM, Dec 9, 2000; Archer Baxter Forsyth, *Mentations* (Santa Rosa, CA: One Snoopy Place, 1997), pp. 136, 140, 153–154; (L) JFS, "Christmas in April," Aug 1989, courtesy of RDM, PP, and SP; (I) GLeB, Oct 24, 2002, Dec 9, 2005; (I) MOH, Dec 26, 2003; (I) EJC, Mar 28, 2002; JFS, introduction, *Mentations*, n.p.; (I) MCS, May 7, 2004.

JEANNIE & SPARKY: Oct 21, 1972: most likely date (see *PDB*, 1972); (Q) Welbourn, p. 11; (I) JFS, Jan 8, 2003, Dec 9, 2005; (M) JFS, n.d., May 1989, courtesy of JFS; (I) JFS, Oct 21, 2001; JHS-CMS divorce papers, filed Superior Court of California, Sonoma County, Dec 11, 1972; (P) Nov 26, 1972; *PJ*, p. 20; (P) Jul 25, 1974.

DIVORCE: (Editorial) *PD*, Dec 17, 1972; (P) Feb 26, 1973; (I) JD, May 9, 2005; (L) JD to BM, Feb 23, 2000, courtesy of BM; (I) JST, Jun 21, 2001; (I) MCS, Sep 12, 2000; (I) ASJ, Oct 15, 2001; (I) MSH, Nov 8, 2005; (I) RD, Nov 14, 2003: "They went at it with sticks. They were raining blows on each other"; (I) MCS, Dec 8, 2005; Barrier interview; GGI, p. 45; FGS in Liverett, p. 53; (I) FGS, Dec 6, 2002; *GG*, p. 103; (I) JFS, Oct 21, 2002; (I) EJC, Oct 24, 2002; (I) TOH, Jun 26, 2001; (P) May 18, 1972; (M) JFS, n.d.; "In His Place," *People*, Feb 12, 2001, p. 138; "Gentle

Genius," *People*, Feb 28, 2000, p. 57 (see also Waggoner and Wolmuth, p. 86, which gives 1973 as the year CMS met JFS); (I) JFS, Oct 24, 2002, Oct 21, 2001; (I) GLeB, Oct 24, 2002, Dec 9, 2005 (see also DR, Feb 22, 2002); (I) BN, Feb 28, 2002; (I) WME and DE, Sep 14, 2002; (I) RN, May 15, 2001; (I) MCS, May 16, 2005 (and in earlier interviews); (I) ED, May 11, 2005; (I) JST, Jun 21, 2001; (I) MSH, Nov 8, 2005; (I) EJC, Oct 24, 2002; (P) Aug 5, 1973; (I) ASJ, Sep 13, 2001; SKI, (T) p. 14; (Q) Maher, p. 7; (I) TOH, Jun 26, 2001; (P) Jun 10, 1973; JD court papers, filed March 15, 1973, Superior Court of California, County of Sonoma; (L) CMS to DRF and DF, Mar 23, 1973, courtesy of DRF; (I) JFS, Oct 21, 2001; (C) Mrs. Robert B. Maye, Orrville, OH, to *Akron Beacon Journal*, n.d., Mar 1973; (L) CMS, "Here Is Why 'Peanuts' Is Sad," *Akron Beacon Journal*, Mar 16, 1973.

MR. SACK: (P) Jun 12, 1973; (P) Jun 13, 1973; (P) June 14, 1973; (P) Jun 15, 1973; (P) Jun 19, 1973; Pete Alfano, "Charlie Brown Has a Problem," *Newsday*, Jun 24, 1973, n.p.; *PJ*, p. 164; GGI, p. 29; (P) Dec 22, 1976.

POOR, SWEET BABY: (I) JFS, Oct 21, 2001, Dec 7, 2000; (I) EP, Jan 31, 2001; GG, p. 248; (S) CMS, "On Cartooning," NCS; (I) TOH, Jun 26, 2001; (P) Jan 24, 1973; "Gentle Genius," p. 57; the final judgment of dissolution of marriage was entered in Book 119 of Judgments, p. 90, Superior Court of California, Sonoma County, Aug 7, 1973; (I) JD, May 9, 2005; Maher, p. 7.

## PART SIX

E: CMS to K. F. Hall, Jul 8, 1963.

## 25. POOR, SWEET BABY

E: (P) Sunday, April 8, 1973.

BLENDING FAMILIES: Barrier interview; JFS, reminiscences (U); (Q) Nancy Faber, "Good Grief, Charles Schulz! Charlie Brown and 'Peanuts' Are Turning 25," *People*, Sep 29, 1975, p. 15; (EM) JFS, Sep 4, 2005; (P) May 22, 1976; (P) May 21, 1976; (Q) Mellott, n.p.; Margaret O'Connell, "Jeannie Schulz: From Peanuts to Powder Puffs" (http://www.

sequentialtart.com/archive/sept02/jschulz.shtml) (see also Jean Schulz, "The Powder Puff Experience," *This World* section, *San Francisco Sunday Examiner & Chronicle*, Jun 27, 1976, pp. 16–17); (P) Jun 21, 1975; (I) ED, May 8, 2005; JD quoted in Tim Tesconi, *PD*, Feb 27, 1978, p. 1-B. (L) JD to BM, Feb 23, 2000; (I) RDM, Apr 24, 2004; James E. Roper, "Tax ruling backs Schulz's ex-wife," *Editor & Publisher*, Oct 22, 1983, and " 'Peanuts' Cartoonist's ex-wife wins IRS tax dispute," *PD*, Oct 4, 1983, p. 1; (I) ASJ, Oct 15, 2001; (I) KMM, Oct 23, 2002; (Q) Pauline Wessa, "Cartoonist Schulz reveals how artist got hooked on diet of Peanuts," *Citizen-Journal* (Boyne City, MI), Oct 27, 1975, p. 11; (I) JST, Jun 21, 2001; CMS and JFS quoted in Owen and Nancie Spann, pp. 132–133; (I) EJC, Oct 24, 2002, Oct 29, 2002; (I) HBC, Oct 24, 2002; (I) FGS, Dec 6, 2002.

REMARRIAGE: (I) JFS, Mar 27, 2002, Jan 8, 2003, Oct 21, 2001; CMS quoted in Cynthia Gorney, "The *Peanuts* Progenitor," *Washington Post*, Oct 2, 1985, p. D-2; (Q) (M) JFS, n.d., May 1989; (I) WL, Apr 19, 2001; (L) JFS to DTM, n.d., 2003; (L) JFS to DTM, Dec 9, 2000; friends of JFS quoted anonymously in Witt, p. 20; JFS quoted in David Bowman, "A Failure's Guide to Charlie Brown & Peanuts," *Pasatiempo* magazine, *The New Mexican*, Dec 23–29, 2005, p. 43.

LATER LUCY: (P) May 24, 1965; JFS quoted in Bowman, p. 43; (P) Jan 6, 1986; (P) Apr 12, 1992; (I) HBC, Oct 24, 2002; (P) Feb 23, 1980; (P) Jan 1, 1996; (P) Feb 25, 1963; (P) Apr 1, 1973; (P) Apr 2, 1998; (P) Jun 29, 1986; (P) Apr 7, 1968; (P) Jan 18, 1998; (L) JFS to DTM, Dec 9, 2000; (P) Oct 23, 1988; *Youth*, Mar 24, 1968, p. 5; (P) Sep 29, 1968; (P) Nov 16, 1952; (P) Oct 24, 1999.

NICE: (I) BM, Dec 5, 2000; (I) LJ, May 8, 2002; BBC (see, also, "Good Grief!" BBC Radio, Apr 13, 2000); Barrier interview; LCI; (I) MVG, Jun 10, 2002; (I) JFS, Jan 30, 2001, Mar 27, 2002, Oct 21, 2001; (I) DRF, May 17, 2001; (P) Nov 5, 1969; (I) MSH, Nov 8, 2005; LJ quoted in Murray Whyte, "Whole Works? Good Grief!" *Toronto Star*, Apr 25, 2004, n.p.; (I) PP, Dec 4, 2000; (I) WT, Dec 5, 2000; (I) RGJ, May 30, 2002; (I) DR, Nov 4, 2002, Jun 1, 2004; (I) BMcL, Feb 25, 2003; (I) EE, Nov 1, 2002, Oct 20, 2002; (I) RN, May 15, 2001; (I) JH, May 31, 2001; (I) MBC, Jun 4, 2002; LCI; GGI, p. 37; (P) Sep 7, 1974; (P) Sep 3–18, 1974; (P) Sep 18, 1974; (P) Oct 24, 1974; (L) CMS to ASJ, Mar 22, 1982, courtesy of ASJ.

DR. DOOLITTLE: (L) MD to JFS, Feb 25, 2000; (I) MD, Oct 22, 2001.

TRIPS; STRIPS: Waggoner and Wolmuth, p. 82; CA quoted in *Evening Star* (Washington, DC) Feb 5, 1970, p. D-1; JFS quoted in Contino; friends of JFS quoted anonymously in Witt, p. 20; (I) JFS, Oct 21–24, 2002, Apr 16, 2001; (Q) B. McIntosh, p. 8; (Q) Minton, n.p.; (L) CMS to Katherine Crosby in *GG*, p. 45; (P) Jun 16, 1975; (L) Jack Lumner to CMS, Nov 27, 1973; (P) Sep 2, 1997; Bledsoe, p. C-1; *PDB*, 1975 (see also interview with LM, Jun 20, 2001); Lee Mendelson, *Happy Birthday, Charlie Brown* (New York: Random House, 1979), p. 136; (I) MCS, May 10, 2004; *PJ*, p. 100; (I) GD, Mar 22, 2002; (I) MB, Oct 23, 2002; (Q) Meisler, p. 59 (see also email, Ame Van Iden, Wolf Kasteler Public Relations, to DTM, Apr 4, 2003, and letter, Ame Van Iden, Susan Patricola Public Relations Inc., to CMS, n.d., 1994); (I) EJC, Oct 29, 2002.

## 26. PLUSH

E: (P) Feb 23, 1963.

MERCHANT EMPIRE: Mei Fong and Debra Lau, "Earnings from the Crypt," Forbes.com, Feb 28, 2001; (M) MVG, United Media Licensing, Apr 24, 1985, UFSP; United Media, 2002 fact sheet; "The 'Peanuts' Vendor," *USA Today*, Oct 4, 1989, p. D-1; *GG*, p. 160; Waggoner and Wolmuth, p. 82; LCI; Jamie Beckett, "Snoopy Barrage on the Way," *San Francisco Chronicle*, n.d., 1989, attached to United Media Licensing memo, Aug 4, 1989; (Q) Vernon Scott, "Charlie Brown is 25," UPI, Oct 2, 1975, n.p.; United Media "October 1987 Cartoon-Q Recap," Dec 17, 1987 (see also Theodore Roszak, *Bugs*, New York: Doubleday, 1992, p. 11); "Psychiatric Help, 5 Cents"; Schulz/Syndicate Agreement, Jan 23, 1976, p. 3 (see also ECA to Charles H. Cleminshaw, Jan 23, 1976, UFSP); Ron Briley, *Class at Bat, Gender on Deck, and Race in the Hole: A Line-Up of Essays on Twentieth Century American Culture and America's Game* (Jefferson, NC: McFarland & Co, 2003), p. 307; (Q) Sharon Johnson, "The Cartoon Creature as Salesman: Better Than Ever," *New York Times*, Feb 11, 1979, Sec. III, p. 3; Robert Jefferson, "Insurers Look for Awareness," *Inside Print*, Oct 1986, pp. 15, 16; Witt, p. 10; (I) GL, Jul 11, 2001; (P) Apr 26, 1987.

AUTONOMY: (I) PMcD and KOC, Feb 15, 2002; Gorney, p. D-2; (L) Robin D. Smith to CMS, Mar 31, 1998; (Q) Michael Barrier, "Working for Peanuts," *Nation's Business*, Nov 1988, p. 67; (Q) Dorf, p. 23; see Garry Trudeau, introduction, *Comic Relief: Drawings from the Cartoonists Thanksgiving Day Hunger Project* (New York: Henry Holt, 1986); (Q) Masuhiko Hirobuchi, interview (U) n.d., 1990 UFSP; Richard Harrington, "Cartoonists with a Cause," *Washington Post*, Sep 17, 1985, p. C-1; (P) Nov 28, 1985.

FAITH REVISED: (Q) Hirobuchi; (Q) Mellott, n.p.; (P) Sep 19, 1966; (P) Sep 24, 1966; (P) Oct 1, 1966; *PJ*, p. 215; 100 million *Peanuts* readers by 1975: *Scripps-Howard News*, Vol. 41, No. 9, Nov 1985 (total world population of literate people: 2.5 billion); United Media, promotion pamphlet "POW! This year's Peanuts is going to knock your socks off!," n.d., 1990, UFSP; (I) RN, May 15, 2001; (I) EC, May 31, 2001; Henry Mitchell, "Any Day: Charles Schulz's Cartoon Complex," *Washington Post*, Oct. 24, 1979, p. B-1; (Q) Dorf, p. 25; (I) JFS to DTM, Jun 5, 2003; (P) Mar 10, 1977; GGI, p. 42; (I) PSt, Dec 8, 2005; (I) RD, Nov 14, 2003; (P) Apr 9, 1996; (Q) Isaacs, p. 17; (L) Charles H. Cleminshaw to William C. Payette, Oct 15, 1974, UFSP; (P) Mar 14, 1995; GGI, p. 34; (I) RDM, Mar 8, 2002; (I) DM, Jul 9, 2001; *PJ*, p. 179; (I) CG, Dec 5, 2000; Garry Trudeau, " 'I Hate Charlie Brown': An Appreciation," *Washington Post*, Dec 16, 1999, p. A-38.

GARFIELD: Jim Davis, *Garfield at 25: In Dog Years I'd Be Dead* (New York: Ballantine Books, 2002), pp. 19, 62; Davis, *Garfield*, Jun 19, 1978; Davis, *Garfield*, Jun 23, 1978; (C) Dan Aucoin, "That Darn Cat," *Boston Globe*, Jun 9, 2003, n.p.; Davis to Walter Shapiro, *Washington Post*, n.d., 1982, quoted in Chris Suellentrop, "Garfield: Why we hate the Mouse but not the cartoon copycat," *Slate*, June 11, 2004; (I) RDM, Sep 22, 2004, Apr 24, 2002; (M) Jim Gleason to MVG, R. Metz, et al., Jan 23, 1986, UFSP; (C) Davis quoted in Charlotte Sheppherd, "Pen Point," *Ball State University Alumnus Magazine*, Muncie, IN, Mar 2000, n.p., UFSP; (M) "October 1987 Cartoon-Q Recap," United Media, Dec 17, 1987; GGI, pp. 22, 24; (L) ECA to Charles H. Cleminshaw, Dec 6, 1974, UFSP; (I) ECA, Feb 1, 2002; RM&GG, p. 24; Glen Cadigan, "Al Plastino," *The Legion Companion* (Raleigh, NC: TwoMorrows Publishing, 2003), p. 16; (I) SG, Feb 8, 2002; (I) RDM, Mar 8, 2002; United Media reported $84.9 million in revenue in 1998; *Peanuts* netted $51.8 million, or 61 percent of their total revenue that year: George Lauer, " 'Peanuts' empire future unclear," *PD*, Mar 2, 2000; Barrier interview.

CONTRADICTORY: GGI, p. 15; (I) PMcD and KOC, Feb 15, 2002; (I) MSH, Nov 8, 2005; (N) JFS to DTM, Jan 15, 2007; (I) DH, Dec 6, 2000; (I) NN, Apr 11, 2002; (P) Jul 5, 1996; (P) May 13, 1984; (I) RGJ, May 30, 2002; (I) ND, Nov 14, 2003; (see also interview with MMur, Apr 23, 2004, to whom CMS revealed that the strip about being in the back-seat of the car was "about being an only child"; *CBS&M*, p. 10; (P) Aug 6, 1972; (L) Rita Sherman to JFS, Dec 15, 2000, CMS Studio Archive; (I) CB, Oct 18, 2001; (I) TOH, Jun 26, 2001; *PJ*, p. 87.

HOSPITAL: (P) Jul 7, 1999; (P) Jul 13, 1979; (P) Jul 13, 1979; (P) Jul 18, 1979; (P) Jul 19, 1979; (P) Jul 17, 1979; (P) Jul 20, 1979; (P) Jul 24, 1979; (P) Jul 26, 1979; (P) Jul 27, 1979; see CMS to ASJ, Nov 4, 1981, courtesy of ASJ (see also interview with RDM, Mar 8, 2002); (I) MCS, Nov 30, 2004; *PGC*, pp. 114–115; *GG*, p. 229; see CMS to ASJ, Aug 27, 1981; CMS notations, *Snoopy 1981 Date Book*; see *New York Times*, Sep 3, 1981, p. B26; (P) July 22, 1979; LCI; (L) CMS to Lloyd and Millie Neu-mann, Sep 16, 1981, courtesy of LN.

ANGST: JFS to SK, CBS News *60 Minutes*, October 1999, (T) pp. 3, 14, courtesy of SK; (P) Dec 12, 1972; JFS quoted in Bowman, p. 42; Ann Shields, "Happiness Is a Warm Hockey Stick," (U) n.d., 1989, courtesy of AS; (I) JST, Jun 21, 2001; (P) Jul 2, 1968; (I) JFS, Sep 14, 2000.

## 27. STILL LOOKING

E: (P) Mar 29, 1971.

IN THE FOOTHILLS: LCI; SKI, (T) p. 15; (I) EE, Apr 18, 2001; (Q) *Vanity Fair*, Oct 1996, p. 310; (P) Jun 12, 1992; CMS in Stearn, p. 94; CMS, "What the Last 20 Years Have Meant to Me"; (I) JFS, Oct 21, 2002; (I) JD, May 9, 2005.

AGING: (I) GLom, Apr 17, 2001; (Q) Roberts p. 20; *GG*, p. 242; (L) LJ, Nov 15, 2002; (I) CRB and BB, may 16, 2001; (P) Feb 24, 1997; Steinberg, p. 39; (L) LJ to JFS, Feb 14, 2000; (I) LJ, May 8, 2002; (I) WL, Apr 23, 2001; (I) EP, Oct 18, 2001; (I) RW, Oct 23, 2002; (I) RGJ, May 30, 2002; (C) Karen Kresge quoted in Dwight Chapin, "Getting it down cold," *San Francisco Examiner*, Nov 26, 1982, n.p.; (I) KKT, Mar 4, 2003;

(V) KKT, *Happy 30th Birthday Redwood Empire Ice Arena*; (I) LJam, Oct 25, 2002; (L) MSH to JJM, Jan 5, 1990, courtesy JJM; (I) MSH, Nov 9, 2005; (L) CMS to ASJ, Nov 4, 1981; ASJ, "Report" (school paper), n.d., c. 1974, CMS Studio Archive; (I) ASJ, Sep 13, 2001; (I) ASJ, Oct 15, 2001; (P) Feb 15, 1954; (P) Dec 15, 1979; (P) Mar 4, 1986; CMS, "What the Last 20 Years Have Meant to Me"; CMS in Stearn, pp. 94–95; (P) May 4, 1969; (P) June 25, 1978; Amy Wallace, David Wallechinsky, Irving Wallace, "10 Famous Cartoonists Select Their Own Favorite Cartoons," *The Book of Lists #3* (New York: William Morrow, 1983), p. 180; (P) Apr 18, 1971; (I) MCS to DTM, May 23, 2004; (EM) ASJ to DTM, Nov 28, 2001; (Q) Steinberg, p. 39; GG, p. 102; CMS quoted in Digitale, p. 2A; (I) HBC, Oct 24, 2002; (I) JST, Jun 21, 2001; (I) JD, May 9, 2005; SKI, (T) p. 18; LJ, *The Lives Behind the Lines . . . 20 Years of For Better or For Worse* (Kansas City, MO: Andrews McMeel, 1999), pp. 160–161; (V) (Q) *Life & Times: Lynn Johnston*, Canadian Broadcasting Company, 1998; (L) LJ to DTM, May 17, 2002; (DEP) CMS, *Skippy, Inc. v. CPC International Inc.*, p. 17; (P) Nov 23, 1996 (U), courtesy of JFS and EP.

ELDER STATESMAN, ETERNAL BOY: (Q) B. McIntosh, p. 11; CMS, signed, untitled statement about F. Scott Fitzgerald, n.d., CMS Studio Archive; ASI; (Q) K. Martin; Whoopi Goldberg, foreword, *The Complete Peanuts, 1959–1960* (Seattle, WA: Fantagraphics Books, 2006), p. xi; (EM) PG to DTM, Jun 15, 2001; GGI, pp. 11, 33; (Q) *Minneapolis Star Tribune*, Nov 23, 1997, p. E6; (I) JFS, Dec 7, 2000, Oct 17, 2001; (Q) Isaacs, p. 38; (I) JFeif, Jan 24, 2002; (Q) Motenko, p. 5; GG, pp. 195–197, 214, 220, 248; Barrier interview; ASI; Andrew Christie, "Bill Watterson," *Honk!*, No. 2, Jan 1987, pp. 29, 32; Gene Williams, "Watterson: Calvin's other alter ego," *Cleveland Plain Dealer Magazine*, Aug 30, 1987, p. 7; Bill Watterson, *Calvin and Hobbes Sunday Pages, 1985–1995*, preface by Lucy Shelton Caswell (Kansas City, MO: Andrews McMeel, 2001), p. 5; Ivan Brunetti, "Whither Shermy," *Raw, Boiled and Cooked: Comics on the Verge* (Maryland Institute College of Art, 2004), p. 14; Berkeley Breathed quoted in Tasha Robinson, "Berkeley Breathed," *The Onion*, Vol. 37, No. 28, Aug 15, 2001; Bill Watterson, "The Cheapening of the Comics," *The Comics Journal*, No. 137, Sep 1990, pp. 93, 97; Bill Watterson, *The Calvin and Hobbes Tenth Anniversary Book* (Kansas City, MO: Andrews McMeel, 1995), pp. 11, 17; (I) RW, Oct 22, 2002; (I) JFS, Oct 21, 2002; Steinberg, p. 39;

CMS in Stearn, p. 94; *PJ*, p. 22; (P) Feb 23, 1990; (L) JFS, annual holiday greeting, Oct 1995, courtesy of RDM; (L) Fern Wick to CMS, Jun 8, 1997; (EM) LJ to DTM, May 20, 2002; (S) CMS, "On Cartooning," NCS; (I) TE, Jun 21, 2001; (P) May 30, 1998; CMS, holograph notes, CMS Studio Archive (see also Kidd, n.p.); (Q) Meisler, p. 57; (P) May 10, 1997; (Q) B. McIntosh, p. 9; (Q) Dorf, p. 25; (V) (Q) "Comics, the Ninth Art," p40 (New York: Pharos Books, 1990), p. 158; (I) BM, Oct 10, 2002; (I) WT, Oct 10, 2002.

LIGHT ROMANCE: (I) LJ, May 8, 2002; (I) JSlad, Apr 6, 2001; CMS in Stearn, p. 96; (I) RGJ, May 30, 2002; (I) MB, Oct 23, 2002; *GG*, p. xi; (L) Federico Fellini to JFS, Nov 3, 1992, courtesy of JFS; (I) AL, Mar 29, 2001; (N) JFS to DTM, Jan 15, 2007; (V) JFS home videos, 1986–1987, courtesy of JFS; (I) AS, Jul 11, 2003; (P) Sep 14, 1973; see also Whoopi Goldberg, foreword, *The Complete Peanuts, 1959–1960*, p. x; (V) (Q) *The Whoopi Goldberg Show*, Dec 9, 1992; (I) JFS, Oct 21, 2001; (P) Sep 14, 1990; (P) Sep 15, 1990; ASI; (P) Jan 16, 1990; (L) JFS to SP and PP, n.d., Dec 1989, courtesy of SP and PP; (I) KOC, Feb 15, 2002; (P) Mar 6, 1991; (L) CMS to SDR, Aug 5, 1996, courtesy of SDR; (I) SDR, Sep 27, 2001; (P) Mar 1, 1990; (L) Herbert Block to Lynn Johnston, n.d., July 2000, Herbert Block Papers (Lynn Johnston file, Container 38), Manuscript Division, Library of Congress; LJ quoted in *GG*, p. 240; (L) LJ to CMS, n.d., in *GG*, p. 240; Tom Heintjes, "The Lynn Johnston Interview," *Hogan's Alley*, Vol. 1, pp. 48–74, No. 1, Autumn 1994,; (P) Jul 28, 1956; GLeB, *PD*, Nov 23, 1997, n.p.; (L) LJ, Nov 15, 2002; LJ quoted in Murray Whyte, "Whole Works? Good Grief!" *Toronto Star*, April 25, 2004; (L) LJ to JFS, Feb 14, 2000, courtesy of JFS; LCI; (P) Sep 12 and 13, 1967; (P) Apr 25, 1992.

SNOWMEN: CMS to RGJ, taped interview for *GG*; (C) GLeB, *PD*, Oct. 6, 1994, n.p.; (I) BMcL, Feb 25, 2003; (P) Nov 10, 1996; (P) Nov 10, 1996; (P) Dec 12, 1951; (P) Jan 15, 1953; (P) Nov 13, 1952; (P) Jan 4, 1952; (P) Jan 7, 1954; (P) Jan 6, 1955; (P) Feb 22, 1970; (P) Feb 18, 1962; (P) Jan 19, 1962; (P) Feb 18, 1962; (P) Feb 2, 1995; (P) Feb 2, 1995; (P) Nov 20, 1982.

LAST DAILY: (I) JFS, Oct 23, 2002; CMS quoted by JFS to Jocelyn Y. Stewart, "Snoopy's Legal Guardian" *Los Angeles Times*, Mar 8, 2006, p. 1; David Astor, "Conversation Covers the Peanuts Pause," *Editor & Publisher*,

Dec 20, 1997, p. 30; (P) Apr 3, 1983; K. L. Wilson, p. 66; LCI; CFS quoted in Schuman, p. 106; (I) MSH, Nov 9, 2005; (I) BMcL, Feb 25, 2003; (I) EP, Dec 7, 2000; Derrick to Kim Thompson to DTM, Apr 27, 2004: the total is 17,897 strips: 15,391 daily strips and 2,506 Sundays, which takes into account leap years, the fact that Sunday strips did not begun until Jan 1952, and the single vacation Schulz took, from Nov 27, 1997, through Dec 31, 1997; ASI; (P) Jan 29, 1999; GGI, p. 15.

## 28. DAILIES DONE

E: (P) Feb 9, 1960.

COLON CANCER; STROKE: (L) LJ to Herbert Block, Feb 24, 2000, Herbert Block Papers; (I) MS to DTM, Oct 5, 2000; (I) PS, Jun 7, 2001; (DR) CMS, Nov 23, 1999, courtesy of JFS; (I) EJC, Oct 29, 2002; (L) JFS to RDM, Jan 7, 2000, courtesy of RDM; (I) JFS, Jun 1, 2003, Jun 17, 2003; (I) HBC, Oct 24, 2002; *PD*, Dec 3, 1999; (I) SPas, Jul 9, 2003.

RETIREMENT: (L) CMS to readers, et al., Dec 14, 1999, CMS Studio Archive; (I) EE, Apr 18, 2001; (I) SB, Sep 14, 2000; (I) EP, Dec 7, 2000; (Q) Peter Joseph, *Good Times* (New York: Charterhouse, 1973), p. 287; Matt Cooper, "Proust, *Peanuts*, and Snow Days," *Slate*, Jan 3, 2000; (I) JFS, Apr 8, 2003; (V) (Q) Al Roker interview, *Today* show, taped Dec 20, 1999, aired Jan 3, 2000; (I) PB, Apr 15, 2002; (L) LJ to Herbert Block, Jul 22, 2000; (I) LJ, May 8, 2002; (I) CG, Oct 11, 2002.

SECULAR HUMANIST: ASI; GG, p. 137; (C) RGJ quoted in Michael Lollar, "Biographer Draws Schulz Out," n.d., courtesy of DRF; RM&GG, p. 17.

FINAL DAYS, FINAL STRIP: (L) LJ to Herbert Block, Jul 22, 2000; (I) RDM, Apr 24, 2002; (I) AL, Mar 29, 2001; (I) JSh, Jun 2, 2004; (I) GD, Mar 22, 2002; see JFS note attached to *PD* Sunday Comics, Feb 6, 2000, CMS Studio Archive; "Gentle Genius," p. 56; (L) Abraham J. Twerski to JFS, Mar 3, 2000, courtesy of JFS; (I) RA, Nov 14, 2003; (I) MSH to DTM, Nov 9, 2005; (I) JST, Jun 21, 2001; (I) RDM, Apr 24, 2002; (V) MS, Feb 12, 2000, Santa Rosa; (P) Feb 13, 2000.

# INDEX

# BOOKS BY DAVID MICHAELIS

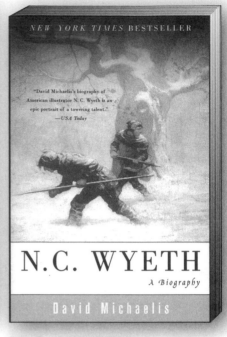

## SCHULZ AND PEANUTS
### A Biography

ISBN 978-0-06-093799-7 (paperback)

"Michaelis leaves us with both a shrewd appreciation of Schulz's minimalist art and a sympathetic understanding of Schulz the man." —*The New York Times*

"A landmark biography.... The most significant work written about one of the century's undisputed pop culture giants."
—*The Los Angeles Times*

## N.C. WYETH
### A Biography

ISBN 978-0-06-008926-9 (paperback)

"An epic portrait of a towering talent...this biography is a rip-roaring read."

—*USA Today*

"Well written, conscientious, and, on the whole, enthralling. Michaelis is a demon researcher and can turn a phrase."

—*The New York Times Book Review*